The 31st
Infantry Regiment

Dave,

Thanks for your help in researching the 4th Battalion's deployment to the Republic of South Viet Nam.

Jim Simms

10.9.18

The 31st Infantry Regiment

A History of "America's Foreign Legion" in Peace and War

BY THE MEMBERS OF THE
31ST INFANTRY REGIMENT ASSOCIATION

Foreword by
General Barry R. McCaffrey

Afterword by
General Stephen J. Townsend

McFarland & Company, Inc., Publishers
Jefferson, North Carolina

LIBRARY OF CONGRESS CATALOGUING-IN-PUBLICATION DATA

Names: 31st Infantry Regiment Association, issuing body.
Title: The 31st Infantry Regiment : a history of
"America's Foreign Legion," in peace and war /
31st Infantry Regiment Association ;
foreword by General Barry R. McCaffrey ;
afterword by General Stephen J. Townsend.
Other titles: History of "America's Foreign Legion," in peace and war
Description: Jefferson, North Carolina : McFarland & Company, Inc.,
Publishers, 2018 | Includes bibliographical references and index.
Identifiers: LCCN 2018015752 | ISBN 9781476669090
(softcover : acid free paper) ∞
Subjects: LCSH: United States. Army. Infantry Regiment,
31st (1916–1957)—History. | United States. Army. Infantry, 31st—History. |
United States. Army. Infantry Regiment, 31st (2005–)—History.
Classification: LCC UA29 31st .A25 2018 | DDC 356/.1130973—dc23
LC record available at https://lccn.loc.gov/2018015752

BRITISH LIBRARY CATALOGUING DATA ARE AVAILABLE

ISBN (print) 978-1-4766-6909-0
ISBN (ebook) 978-1-4766-3276-6

Front cover: Members of the 31st Infantry Regiment in Manila,
Philippines, circa 1930s (United States Army)

Printed in the United States of America

*McFarland & Company, Inc., Publishers
Box 611, Jefferson, North Carolina 28640
www.mcfarlandpub.com*

To The Polar Bears—
the soldiers who served and are serving
in the 31st Infantry Regiment,
in peace and war

Acknowledgments

The family of the late Karl H. Lowe, 31st Infantry Regiment Association Historian for twenty years, has been extremely supportive of the effort to publish *The 31st Infantry Regiment*. Without that crucial support, this book would never have gone to press.

Numerous Polar Bears and their families have over the years shared their personal stories, clippings, photographs and much else to flesh out the continuing story of the Regiment. Rita Springer and Sallie Pierson Holden, for example, were friends together as children of members of the Regiment in the Philippines before World War II and have shared memories and photos. Darrell W. Stark, son of Bataan Death March survivor Darrell Stark, deserves equal acknowledgment.

Support for the history of the Regiment continues. LTC Isaac Rademacher, at this writing the Commanding Officer of 4th Battalion, 31st Infantry, provides significant support in numerous ways; so also CPT (Ret.) Mike Strand, Commander of the 31st Infantry Regiment Association, as well as COL (Ret.) Ron Corson, Senior Director of the Association. Others: CPT Ross Boston, CPT Kevin Lusted, SSG John Flynn, 1SG (Ret.) Ivan Barker, Chaplain (COL, Ret) Bill Burns, SSG (Ret.) Paul Fisk, SFC Jay-R Strawder, CSM (Ret.) and Honorary Sergeant Major of the Regiment Dan Wood, Yabut Kriszha, Jerry Kleiman, Clark Washington; Kaitlyn Crain Enriquez and the other staff members of the Still Pictures Branch at the National Archives; Jim Logue for providing photographs.

LTG (Ret.) Robert L. "Sam" Wetzel, who commanded the 4th Battalion, 31st Infantry in combat in Vietnam and is now the Colonel of the Regiment; BG (Ret.) Hal Nelson; LTC (Ret.) John Wheately; COL (Ret.) Michael Crutcher; Les Hines, Vietnam Historian of the Americal Division Veterans Association; the entire staff of the U.S. Army Heritage and Education Center (Military History Institute Archives) in Carlisle, Pennsylvania, but especially Rich Baker, Tom Buffenbarger, Steve Bye, Rodney Foytik, Mrs. Marlea Leljedal, Shannon Schwaller and Troy Vevasis.

Ms. Sheon Montgomery, Assistant Archivist, Vietnam Archive, Texas Tech University. Jennifer A. Nichols of the U.S. Army Center of Military History and its research staff. LTC (Ret.) Joseph E. "Sepp" Scanlin, curator of the Fort Drum Museum and S2 of 4-31 on its first deployment to Afghanistan.

Bud Shatzer and Tim Nosal, of the American Battle Monuments Commission, and David Cantrell, web wizard.

Table of Contents

Foreword
by General Barry R. McCaffrey

It is an honor for me to write the foreword to this 100th Anniversary history of the famous U.S. Army 31st Infantry Regiment—"America's Foreign Legion." The 31st Regiment Association Historian and veteran Grady Smith, and Mike Strand, veteran and Commander of the 31st Infantry Regiment Association, have put together a gift to the soldiers of the Regiment. As a side note, Mike Strand and I spent many months as fellow patients in the care of Walter Reed Army Medical Center after being wounded in Vietnam.

The U.S. Army infantry force is a tight community. LTG Sam Wetzel, USA (Ret.)— the Honorary Colonel of the 31st Infantry Regiment—is one of the finest combat leaders I have ever known. He had a distinguished record as a 31st Infantry Regiment battalion commander in bloody fighting in Vietnam. He then went on during his long career to be part of the senior Army leadership that rescued our forces and led us to recovery during the disastrous decade that followed our withdrawal from that divisive conflict. I was privileged to serve as one of General Wetzel's 3rd Infantry Division (Mech) battalion commanders in Germany during this rebuilding process. During my career, I served under nine infantry division commanders. General Wetzel was the most effective and respected field soldier, coach, and leader.

The 100-year history of the 31st Infantry Regiment chronicles service through the decades characterized by incredible valor, discipline, bloody losses, sacrifice and distinction. For over a hundred years, the Regiment never came home as an entire unit. Activated on 13 August 1916 in the Philippines, the Regiment then deployed and served with honor in military operations in America's wars throughout the Far East and beyond.

The campaigns were endless. During the Siberian Expedition of 1918–1920, the Regiment earned its famous distinction as the Polar Bears, fighting a complex array of Reds and Whites and criminals on the northern rim of a disintegrating Russian empire. In 1932, the Regiment found itself in China with the Allied intervention during the Shanghai Incident. The Regiment stood guard with British and French Forces in quasi-confrontation with the Imperial Japanese Army and active combat against Chinese patriotic forces.

The Regiment then returned to the Philippines, standing guard in Manila and training the Philippine Army during the '30s and up to the savage surprise Japanese attack on the Philippines following the disaster at Pearl Harbor in the opening hours of World War II. The incredible courage of the 31st Regiment in the protracted defense of Bataan

1

was a legend for the ages—as was the terrible 68-mile death march of 60,000 U.S. and Philippine soldiers following the surrender. Sixteen hundred soldiers of the 31st Infantry Regiment marched into captivity, from which most would never return. They died of starvation, abuse, and were lost at sea while trapped in prisoner-of-war transports sunk by Allied air power. The Colonel of the Regiment buried his Colors before the surrender—and then bravely went to his death at the hands of the Japanese.

Occupation duty for the 31st Infantry in both Korea and Japan followed the Pacific War. The most victorious Army on earth—8 million strong—evaporated in 1945 and bottomed out at 536,000 men. There was no money, no training, and no sense that another conflict against global communist adversaries loomed ahead.

In 1950, the Regiment was thrown suddenly into combat in Korea in a state of disastrous unpreparedness during the Marine-Army landings at Inchon, Korea. The 31st Regiment, like the entire post–World War II Armed Forces, had huge shortfalls in combat equipment, leadership, and manpower. The U.S. was shamefully unprepared to fight. The Regiment's ranks were filled out with untrained KATUSA's from the streets of Seoul (Korean draftees as augmentation to the U.S. Army). Soldiers of the 31st Regiment would pay for this unpreparedness with their lives.

The bloody campaign north into the mountains culminated in the Chinese PLA onslaught during the bitter winter battles on the Yalu and at the Chosin Reservoir. Two battalions of the 31st Regiment and the attached Task Force Faith 1-32nd Infantry were ground up in this nonstop battle by the 80th and 81st PLA divisions. Seven Chinese regiments swarmed the three U.S. battalions in 20-degrees-below-zero weather. The 43-year-old Regimental commander Col. Alan McLean became the second 31st Regimental commander to die in captivity. LTC Don Faith was killed in action and awarded the Medal of Honor. The sacrifice of the Regiment eviscerated the Chinese combat formations and without question helped enable the survival of the brave Marines of 1st Marine Division who were able to break out to the south and the U.S. Navy evacuation at Hungnam.

The 31st Infantry Regiment next took part in the offensive of 1951 and the intense combat of Heartbreak Ridge. My dad, Colonel William J. McCaffrey, took command of the Regimental survivors after the disaster on the Yalu and re-organized and trained them. He then led them in combat from late February 1951 to just before 1 January 1952. The brave Colombian Infantry Battalion was attached. Many experienced veteran World War II company grade officers, to include from the legendary 442nd Infantry, joined the Regiment. The Regiment received all new equipment. The 31st Regiment mission was to hold twenty miles of the General Outpost line during the Chinese Spring Offensive of 1951. The Regiment was then loaned to the 1st Marine Division for the defense of Seoul. Later, under the command of 7th ID CG MG Claude Ferenbaugh, the 31st Infantry took part in the UN Spring Offensive. They suffered 1,000 casualties in the first week. The intense fighting was platoon and company combat against Chinese bunker positions on mountain ridges with pole charges and flame throwers. Dad was decorated twice with the second and third awards of the Silver Star. He also received the second award of his Combat Infantry Badge, first earned fighting in the Italian Theater in World War II.

Combat never stopped for the 31st Infantry Regiment. There were terrible battles at Heartbreak Ridge and in Central Korea during 1952. The bloodiest year for the Regiment was 1953 and the fighting on Pork Chop Hill. The last battle of the war for the soldiers of 31st Regiment was the intense combat in the Chorwon Valley 26–27 July 1953.

The next bloody war for the 31st Infantry Regiment soon loomed in Southeast Asia. Vietnam saw the 4th Battalion 31st Infantry deploying to the huge battles of I and III Corps Tactical Zones for over five years of combat. Under the valiant leadership of LTC Hank Henry in 1969, the battalion saw intense fighting in the Battle of Hiep Duc, for which the unit was recognized with the Presidential Unit Citation. The battalion also saw very protracted fighting in support of the Marines and the Americal Division in I Corps Tactical Zone, winning a total of 5 unit awards for valor.

The 6th Battalion of the 31st Regiment took part in some of the most violent high-intensity battles of the Vietnam War and was honored by winning 7 unit awards for valor. The 6th Battalion 31st soldiers took part in the division-size battle, fighting in the bloody urban combat of the Cholon sector of Saigon during TET '68. Subsequently, the battalion was committed in the terrible cross-border fighting of the "Fish Hook" in Cambodia. The late Colonel Karl Lowe, who did much of the research and writing of this Regimental history, commanded a 31st Infantry Regiment company as an infantry Captain during these battles—earning four Purple Hearts for wounds received in combat.

These were very demanding years for the soldiers of the 31st Infantry Regiment. All Vietnam veterans feel proud of our service—but have deep sorrow for the 59,000 U.S. killed and 303,000 wounded—as well as the 2 million Vietnamese total who died during the long conflict.

The 31st Infantry regiment continues to live on in the combat troops of 4th Battalion 31st Infantry Regiment assigned to the famous 10th Mountain Division at Fort Drum, New York. LTG Steve Townsend commanded the battalion in combat as an LTC. He now serves at this writing as the three-star commander of all Allied combat forces in Iraq and Syria. Like most senior officers and NCO's of his generation, LTG Townsend has lived a life of constant combat deployments during the long years of the Global War on Terror. More than 60,000 U.S. troops have been killed and wounded during this endless struggle to keep the American people safe from domestic terror. General Townsend has written the "Afterword" to this Regimental history, which pays tribute to the soldiers of the Regiment who have served during this longest conflict in American history.

The continuing deployments of the 31st Infantry have taken these brave current-generation soldiers to six major deployments since 9/11. Their courage was recognized by the Valorous Unit Award and the Meritorious Unit Commendation. During their initial 15-month deployment to Iraq, the battalion made over 50 combat air assaults and suffered 26 KIA. The 31st Infantry Regiment soldiers have also seen heavy fighting in Afghanistan. Battalion soldiers have in addition served assignments in Bosnia, Saudi Arabia, Kuwait, Qatar, Uzbekistan, Djibouti, and Ethiopia.

America recognizes the dedication and courage of the 31st Infantry Regiment defending the American people. For over a hundred years, we have seen the faith and commitment of these brave soldiers facing terrible physical privation, exhaustion, and the incredible dangers of close-range infantry combat. It is a lonely battlefield for the infantry soldier. Part of what keeps these soldiers fighting is the knowledge that they are part of a unit tradition and a history of courage. The team stays with you until death. This tradition continues with the men and women of the 31st Infantry Regiment. The ghosts of these earlier soldiers who fought courageously at Vladivostok, and Shanghai, and Bataan, and the Chosin Reservoir, and Hiep Duc, and BP155 in Iraq, all stand guard behind the currently serving soldiers of the 31st Infantry Regiment.

The 31st Infantry Regiment soldiers who served and died for over a hundred years defending America can be remembered in the words of the 300 Spartans at Thermopylae—

"GO TELL THE SPARTANS, PASSERBY,
THAT HERE, OBEDIENT TO THEIR LAWS, WE LIE."

During Operation Desert Storm, General Barry R. McCaffrey (Ret.) commanded the 24th Infantry Division (Mechanized), executing the "left hook" attack which penetrated 370 kilometers into Iraq and resulted in a decisive battle victory in the First Gulf War. He retired as a four-star general after 32 years of service. At that time, he was the most highly decorated general in the Army. After his retirement he was appointed director of the Office of National Drug Control Policy during President Clinton's administration. He is currently a military analyst for NBC and MSNBC.

Preface

COL (Ret.) Karl Lowe, the late regimental Association historian, pursued the history of the 31st Infantry Regiment for more than twenty years. At reunions he would talk to Bataan Death March survivors or to the children of Polar Bears who had deployed as part of the American Expeditionary Force Siberia. Korea, Vietnam and the post–9/11 era were all part of his inquiries. He took notes, obtained copies of photographs and followed up with phone calls and emails across a span of decades.

From the very beginning of his efforts, Karl set before himself the goal of a history of the regiment, one battalion of which he served in during the Vietnam War. Without ever losing sight of the big picture of each of the regiment's conflicts, he still deliberately focused on the experiences of the soldier in the field as he studied battle after battle.

His 2014 illness came as a surprise and he was forced to leave the regimental history project, clearly a labor of love, in a mixed state. The narrative was complete from the regimental activation in 1916 through the point in time when his own unit, the 6th Battalion, 31st Infantry left Vietnam. But the story of the 4th Battalion in Southeast Asia was a work in progress—indeed, it halted literally in mid-sentence. He was not given the time either to record his documentary researches in detail or to begin work on the era of the six deployments of the 4th Battalion, 31st Infantry since 9/11. Karl completed incompletely, and that is our loss.

But his work, unfinished though it was, had too much inherent value as history to let it remain in manuscript form. It cried out for completion and publication. LTC (Ret.) James B. Simms, who had served in the 4th Battalion in Vietnam and was a trained historian, assumed responsibility for completing its history. LTC (Ret.) Grady A. Smith did the same for the 10th Mountain Division era, and particularly for the battalion's six post–9/11 deployments. In addition, Smith did the editing.

Scores of historical photographs in this history materially assist in telling the regiment's story. Dozens come from the National Archives going all the way back to 1918, while many others have been gifted to the Association archives from Polar Bears and their families. The donors of many of the pictures are still known, while the names of others have unfortunately been lost. But over the decades they have all provided those pictures freely, for use by the Association in any way that would contribute to telling the regiment's story. Hopefully they will find that condition well met in *The 31st Infantry Regiment*.

Introduction

Although the 31st Infantry Regiment's century-long history has been told in installments through scattered books and articles, until now it has not been available in one comprehensive work. The present book fills that need, providing in a single source the narrative of the 31st's hundred-year contribution to the nation.

The regiment was activated in the Philippines, in the geographical area known as the Pacific Rim. For more than seventy years it fought every one of its battles within that same area—in Siberia, Shanghai, Korea and Vietnam. Even its post–World War II occupation duty in Japan was performed within that area. Only since 9/11 have its combat missions taken it beyond, to Afghanistan and Iraq in South Central Asia. Although most of its battalions have at one time or another been stationed in the United States, the headquarters of the regiment and its 1st battalion have still never served within the nation's borders—hence the nickname, "America's Foreign Legion."

Over the past century, joint operations with other nations have been the norm. In Siberia, the regiment worked in cooperation with the United Kingdom, Canada, China, Italy and Japan. Shanghai brought the regiment together with the British, French, Japanese, Chinese and White Russians. Jointly executed missions with the Marine Corps began early in the regiment's history as well—the U.S. 4th Marine Regiment was already stationed in the Shanghai international settlement, and the commanding officer of the 31st Infantry reported to the Marine commander when the army unit came ashore. Korea and the post–9/11 deployments echo this pattern, both with other nations and with other U.S. Armed Forces.

The recurring presence of the Japanese should be noted. In their ultimately unsuccessful march toward empire, they had already defeated the Russians in the 1904–1905 Russo-Japanese War, and moved eagerly into Siberia in 1918. Japan had seized Manchuria in 1931, and in the following year they welcomed the Shanghai Incident as an opportunity to expand even deeper into Chinese territory. Then, in the Philippines in 1941–1942, the 31st Infantry met the Japanese again. A nominal ally became an implacable enemy.

The crosscurrents created by opposing forces and factions in Siberia challenged the regiment on its very first deployment: leftist reds, monarchist whites and Cossack warlords. And bandits—Russian, Mongol, Manchu, Korean and Chinese. And as sometimes happens, this past proved to be prologue to the regiment's present. A new swirl and mix of violent forces continues to recur in the aftermath of 9/11. Besides nation states such as Afghanistan, Syria, Iraq and Pakistan, among others, there are also religious, tribal and political groups. These factions cycle in and out of active combat or support it: al-Qaeda, the Taliban, Sunni, Shia, Kurds, ISIS. Such complexity places a heavy responsibility on the entire force, on both the chain of command and the line soldiers. Combat and diplomacy are equally the regiment's stock in trade.

Through it all, the regiment—at this writing represented by a single active duty unit, the 4th Battalion, 31st Infantry of the 10th Mountain Division—has carried out its assigned missions in exemplary fashion. Seven Medals of Honor have been awarded to individual members, and across the decades the unit as a whole has earned six Presidential Unit citations. The burden of the present volume is to record how the Polar Bears accomplished all of this by narrating the century-long history of the 31st Infantry Regiment.

Pro Patria.

All professions can learn from their histories, the profession of arms more than most. The centrality of life and death issues is one reason. Another is that in spite of rapid and persistent introduction of new technologies, some aspects of the profession change much more slowly. The dynamics of human and group behavior in combat is a prime example.

—Karl H. Lowe
Forwarding Letter April 12, 2004
"Military History: a Selected Bibliography"
Institute for Defense Analyses

It is a comfort to know that we can learn from our history.

—Stephen Acai
At the dedication of the North Carolina
Vietnam Veterans Memorial
Raleigh, May 23, 1987

Prologue:
Birth of a Regiment
by Karl H. Lowe

World War I had just started its third year in Europe, and the United States' participation was not far over the horizon when the 31st Infantry Regiment was activated in the Philippines on August 13, 1916.

The 31st never served in the United States as a full regiment, earning it the unofficial nickname "America's Foreign Legion." After infantry regiments were discontinued as tactical organizations in 1957, several of the regiment's successor battle groups and subsequently its successor battalions served in the United States, but its Headquarters and the 1st Battalion have never "been home." At the time of this writing, the regiment's only active unit, the 4th Battalion, serves with the 10th Mountain Division at Fort Drum, New York.

The 31st Infantry Regiment's insignia, a polar bear, commemorates the regiment's earliest combat experience during the Siberian Expedition of 1918–1920. The regimental shield is a sea lion from the Philippine Department's shoulder insignia, commemorating the regiment's birth and long service in the Philippines. Its polar bear crest was approved by the War Department in 1924. The regiment's Latin motto, *Pro Patria*, means "For Country."

Two earlier 31st Infantry Regiments were formed in 1813 and 1866 but were later incorporated into other regiments. Their lineages are carried by the regiments into which they were absorbed and are therefore unrelated to the present 31st Infantry.[1] Today's 31st Infantry Regiment was authorized by the National Defense Act of 1916 and was formed in the Philippines later that year to strengthen the forces protecting U.S. interests in the Philippines following its capture from Spain in 1898.[2] Filipinos, although generally inclined toward friendship, did not seek or accept the occupation of their country

The 31st Infantry Regiment Crest (Association archives).

by another colonial power, prompting a series of guerrilla wars against U.S. forces, the last of which ended in
1911. By 1916, six regiments of infantry and a regiment
of cavalry remained in the islands, concentrated mainly
on Luzon and Mindanao where *Insurrectos* remained
troublesome.

Reaction to the National Defense Act of 1916 was
not as orderly as Congress might have intended. Since
the required manpower for new regiments would take
at least a year to recruit, the Army transferred men and
equipment from existing regiments, diluting them all.
In compliance with the order, the Philippine Department formed the 31st Infantry Regiment's Headquarters,
Machine gun, and Supply Companies and 3rd Battalion
on August 13, 1916, at Fort William McKinley (Rizal,
Luzon), with personnel and equipment from the 8th and
27th Infantry Regiments. The 1st Battalion was formed
at Regan Barracks (Albay, Luzon) from the 2nd Battalion
15th Infantry. The 2nd Battalion was formed at Camp
McGrath (Batangas, Luzon) with personnel and equipment from the 13th Infantry.[3]

As B Company's First Sergeant Joe Dundas put it,
"Men went to bed on the night of July 31 as members of
B Company 15th Infantry Regiment and awoke the next
morning in B Company 31st Infantry Regiment." On its
first consolidated morning report, the regiment totaled
35 officers and 1350 enlisted men.

**The 31st Infantry Regiment Shield
(Association archives).**

The 31st Infantry's senior officers and some NCOs had served in the Spanish-
American War 18 years earlier, gaining insight into expeditionary warfare. Others had
served during the more recent Philippine Insurrection, making the regiment more seasoned than its newness would suggest. Colonel William H. Gordon, the Regimental Commander, and Lieutenant Colonel Frederick H. Sargent, his Deputy, had seen action during
the closing years of the Indian Wars in the American West, had fought against Spain in
1898 and then against insurgents during the Philippine Insurrection. They had seen their
Army transformed from a pitifully small internal security force to a modern expeditionary
Army that would expand to over four million men during the next two years.

In December 1916, the 1st Battalion moved to Camp Eldridge (Los Baños) where it
was joined by the 2nd Battalion in February 1917. During February and March, the regiment underwent its first instruction practice, combat firing, and proficiency tests and
there were frequent inspections to assure companies attained a common standard. In
June, Lieutenant Colonel Sargent, the regiment's deputy commander, was promoted to
succeed Colonel Gordon. To guard against a possible surprise attack by Germany to seize
the Philippines, the 2nd and 3rd Battalions moved to Fort Mills on Corregidor, an island
near the mouth of Manila Bay. They were followed a month later by Headquarters,
Machine gun, and Supply Companies. In August and September, all except the 3rd Battalion returned to Fort McKinley.

After the United States entered World War I in April 1917, few additional troops

Bottomside Barracks and Officer Housing above at Fort Mills, Corregidor, seen from Malinta Hill (Association archives).

were sent to the Philippines, causing the regiment's strength to plunge as experienced men were sent to training camps in the United States to help expand the Army for wartime service. Those left behind feared they would sit out the war in the Philippines while others went to France to win the glory, the medals, and the girls back home. By January 1918, the regiment had dwindled to 55 officers and 865 enlisted men, just enough to fully man one battalion. In February and March of that year, the regiment underwent its second round of record practice, combat firing, and proficiency tests, showing impressive results despite its low strength.

With one of the last contingents of new troops to join the regiment in 1917 was a remarkable 21-year-old who would remain associated with the Army and his regiment to the end of his life at age 100. Alf Thompson joined the Army at Fort Collins, Colorado, in the fall of 1917 and was soon sent to the Philippines. Although disappointed that he was not going to war, Thompson was excited to see a part of the world that he had previously known only in school books. Assigned to the 31st Infantry's Machine gun Company on his arrival in Manila, Thompson demonstrated uncommon attention to detail and was soon appointed Company Clerk, a corporal's position. A year later, following his promotion to sergeant and his return to a machine gun section, Thompson applied for Officer Candidate School (OCS) at the urging of his company commander. In those days, OCS was taken mainly by correspondence, supplemented by local instruction and testing at the candidate's home station. Although Thompson passed every test with ease, publication of orders making him a second lieutenant had not yet arrived when the regiment left the Philippines in 1918.

During the spring of 1918, the regiment's strength grew abruptly. Among the replacements arriving at the Army Pier in Manila was Cesar Pares, a Spaniard by birth, who had been sent to the United States by his wealthy parents to study in New York. Fascinated by stories of the American west, he soon abandoned his studies to work on a ranch in

New Mexico. When he turned 18, he and a friend journeyed to Denver by train to see more of the country. After a wild night on the town, they wandered the streets penniless. On a whim, they walked into the Army recruiting station at Fort Logan and enlisted. Pares thought he would soon be returning to his native Europe to fight the Germans. Instead, he was sent to the Philippines and assigned to the 31st Infantry's Headquarters Company.

But in December 1917, when the 8th and 13th Infantry Regiments departed the Philippines to form part of the 8th Division in California, members of the 31st assumed it was only a matter of time before their regiment received similar orders. The 31st was one of only two U.S. infantry regiments left in the Philippines, the other being the 27th in Manila.

On July 11, 1918, a War Department cable queried the U.S. Philippine Department Commander, Major General Charles Bailey: how many men and how much equipment could he deploy and how soon? In Europe, a German offensive was running out of steam but the war's outcome was still far from clear.

Rumors flew in Manila that another regiment would soon depart for Europe. The 8th and 13th Infantry had already departed to form the nucleus of a new division in California and the 27th Infantry Regiment had begun training for trench warfare. The 31st launched its own intensified training but its objective was less clear. The two battalions at Fort McKinley were unexpectedly assembled for an extended fitness march with full field gear, rations, and full canteens. As the march began, the troops were told training would continue 7 days a week until the war was won. That sounded foolish to men stationed 8000 miles from the war zone. What could training in the Philippines possibly contribute to winning the war in Europe unless the 31st was to be sent there? Without further explanation, long marches, and squad and platoon battle drills continued for weeks on end, strengthening muscles but taking a toll on morale.

The USAT *Sheridan* (Association archives).

Letters home were filled with a mix of frustration, speculation, and eagerness. Troops were growing impatient to "get on with it." Most wanted to play a role in ending the war but trudging all over Luzon in intense tropical heat was not their idea of a path to victory. Amid heavy grousing, bets were made on the regiment's departure date for France. There would be no winner. By late summer, news of events in Siberia had begun to spread, giving some an inkling of where they might be headed. Private Alan Ferguson of B Company, later the 31st Infantry's wrestling champ, wrote his parents on July 27, "There have been lots of rumors lately of one or both regiments going to Siberia, and when the *Sheridan* was held over here and the 27th was making such thorough preparations, it seemed likely that they were going, but most of the excitement died down when the *Sheridan* left without them."

On August 7, 1918, the 27th Infantry departed for Siberia, a place few Americans knew anything about.[4] Two days later, Colonel Frederick Sargent, the 31st Infantry's Commander, received a letter of instruction from Headquarters, Philippine Department ordering him to prepare his regiment (45 officers and 1379 enlisted men) for movement. Like the 27th, its destination was Siberia. The rumors Alan Ferguson had heard became reality.

PART I. INITIAL DEPLOYMENTS
by Karl H. Lowe

1 Siberia, 1918–1920

Major General William S. Graves had just assumed command of the 8th Division at Camp Fremont, California on July 18 when he was summoned to meet Secretary of War Newton D. Baker at the Baltimore Hotel in Kansas City. The coded War Department message gave no reason for the meeting and Graves was not told if he would be returning to California. At their meeting, Secretary Baker conveyed the President's orders that Graves take the 27th and 31st Infantry Regiments from the Philippines to Vladivostok, the principal port and population center in Siberian Russia, as the nucleus of an Expeditionary Force. Most of General Graves' staff and 5,218 fillers would come from the 8th Division. Other units sent included D Company, 53rd Telegraph Battalion; 117th Evacuation Hospital (later redesignated the 117th Hospital Train); 4th Field Hospital; 4th Ambulance Company; a Quartermaster Bakery Company; a Veterinary Detachment; an Engineer Detachment; and an Intelligence Detachment composed of men who spoke Russian, Czech, Japanese, or German. Eventually, General Graves' command would total nearly 9000 men. American civilians would also participate, including volunteer Red Cross and YMCA workers, agricultural advisors, and various humanitarian relief workers. The 285-man Russian Railway Service Corps (American rail workers and railroad managers recruited mainly from the Midwest), which would operate trains on the Trans-Siberian Railroad, was already there after a long, unplanned delay in Japan.

On August 10, the 3rd Battalion, 31st Infantry moved by barge from Corregidor to Manila to prepare for departure. The remainder of the regiment moved from Fort McKinley by barge via the Pasig River. The main body and 115 tons of baggage, ammunition, and regimental property left Manila four days later aboard the USAT *Sherman*. As the *Sherman* departed, the young wife of Private Jesse Ward of M Company was having their first child back home in Texarkana, Arkansas. Ward would first see his son at age 2. Private Joe E. Wood of I Company, ill with influenza, inexplicably jumped overboard and drowned as the *Sherman* passed

American Expeditionary Force Siberia shoulder patch (Association archives).

Engine and coal cars, trans–Siberian Railroad (National Archives).

Corregidor. Fillers from Camp Fremont, California sailed for Vladivostok aboard the USAT *Thomas* and USAT *Logan*. Aboard the latter were several lieutenants who had served long enough in France to earn an inverted gold chevron signifying combat service. An excerpt from *"The Log of the Logan,"* a newsletter published aboard ship, reflects their light-hearted spirit as they headed into the unknown:

> One by one these gallant youths explained and expounded to a gaping and credulous audience of admirers in the first cabin saloon just how we fit [fought] and won the second battle of the Marne. On the first night out, they informed all and sundry among the passengers, sprung from a less valiant race, just how fortunate General Graves was in having this sturdy group of gold stripers ordered to the Far East to tell 'em how it is done. The truthful historian will have to admit that to none of the speakers did it occur that to undertake to teach the Yankee how to fight, anywhere on the planet, is all the same as undertaking to teach a Kentuckian to like whiskey. Be that as it may, the bull brigade performed entertainingly and prodigiously until the second night out, when Major Lay broke up the seminary in a riot with the mild inquiry: "Lieutenant, don't you think the War Department is making an awful mistake in risking you in Siberia? In view of the fact that every officer and enlisted man in the 32nd Division was bumped off but yourself, don't you think the government ought to stuff and mount you, and exhibit you as a curiosity, or at least subsidize a lecture tour for you?"

En route to Vladivostok, each of the transports stopped to refuel in Nagasaki, Japan, giving the 31st a two-day opportunity to tour the city a later generation of Americans would destroy in a thundering atomic blast. After being cooped up in the damp holds of troopships for weeks, many men promptly got drunk, starting brawls the Military Police could scarcely control. Many lost their stripes for disorderly conduct.

Siberia

The situation in Siberia was chaotic. Russia had suffered the heaviest casualties of any participant in the First World War and after three years of poor leadership, mind-

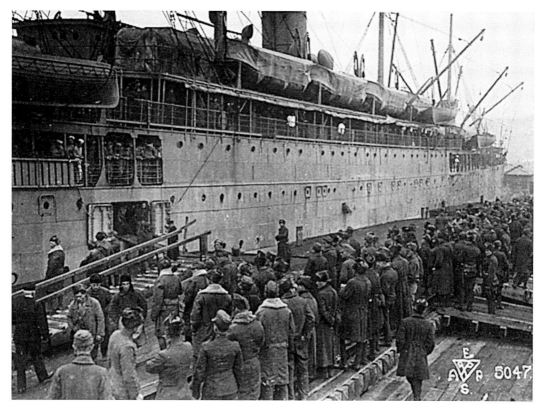

Arrival of ship at American transport docks, Vladivostok, Siberia (National Archives).

numbing hardship, internal discord, and demoralizing defeats, its army had fallen apart. Since the spring of 1917, Russian troops had been shooting or abandoning their officers and simply going home. For most, going home was short-lived because few could survive outside a warring faction in an intensifying civil war. With almost no troops or police left to protect the populace, ill-disciplined armed groups led by monarchists, revolutionaries of the left and right, and Cossack warlords roamed the land, forcibly conscripting new members and looting the countryside to feed, equip, and enrich themselves. Brutality reigned, a habit of heartless blood-letting that still haunts Russia.

Although Russia's revolution had deeper roots, it gained impetus from the political upheavals of 1917. In February of that year, Alexander Kerensky led a revolt that forced the Czar to abdicate. Because German and Austro-Hungarian troops were still deep in Russian territory, Kerensky sought to continue the war, risking the dissolution of his quarrelsome ruling coalition. His ability to continue the war was practically nil with German and Austro-Hungarian troops occupying Russia's most productive lands, the Russian Army rapidly dissolving, and anti-war factions demonstrating in Moscow and St. Petersburg. Seeing an opportunity, Germany enabled safe passage from Switzerland to Russia for 30 Russian revolutionaries led by Nikolai Lenin to seek an alliance of political factions that would take Russia out of the war. By October, Lenin engineered a loose coalition of anti-war parties that unseated Kerensky and vowed to end Russia's participation in the war. After solidifying its grip on power, Lenin's government signed the Treaty of Brest-Litovsk which formally removed Russia from the war and surrendered the non–Russian parts of the Czar's Empire in Europe (Ukraine, Belorussia, Finland, Bessarabia, Estonia, Latvia, and Lithuania) and provinces bordering Turkey.

Although Lenin's Bolsheviks and their left-leaning allies had gained control of the government, their opponents were far from finished, throwing the country into civil war. By the summer of 1918, opposing sides had coalesced into two main factions, leftist "Reds" and Monarchist or Republican "Whites." The Whites remained uncoordinated because their forces were widely dispersed and they could not agree on the form of government they wanted or who would rule if they won. The Reds faced similar problems at first but generally coalesced around the goals of proletarian rule and abolition of property ownership.

With the Russian military's dissolution, supplies sent earlier to aid the country's war effort were left unguarded on the docks and in untended warehouses at Murmansk in European Russia and Vladivostok in Siberia. Vladivostok alone accumulated 725,000 tons, valued at $750,000,000. The Western allies wanted the supplies protected because Siberia was also believed to teem with abandoned German and Austro-Hungarian prisoners of war who had no way to get home and could potentially open a second front against Russia if they acquired sufficient weapons and equipment. That assumption was wrong but in the absence of accurate intelligence, rumors influenced policy decisions. Also in the mix were Czechoslovaks who had been drafted into the Austro-Hungarian Army but had surrendered to the Russians, forming an independent Czech Legion to fight for the Czar. By 1918, their number had swelled to around 70,000, making them a potent, cohesive force in a land where chaos reigned. When the Czar and his family were taken by Red revolutionaries to Yekaterinburg (present day Sverdlovsk) in the Urals, the Czech Legion rushed to free them. They feared Russia's announced departure from the war might doom their homeland's newly acquired independence and therefore wanted the Czar returned to power to resume fighting the Germans.[1] The newly-formed Czechoslovak government pledged to join the war against Germany if the allies would help bring its men home. Lenin demanded that the Czechs disarm before allowing their passage home. The Czechs feared the Russians would then turn them over to Austria-Hungary, which regarded them as traitors. The stand-off sparked hostilities that would continue for two years.

Another reason for allied interest in Siberia was Japan's thinly veiled intent to expand its empire, an aim frustrated by the American-brokered Portsmouth Agreement ending the Russo-Japanese War in 1905. Japan had joined the war against Germany, but only to acquire Germany's Pacific territories. Now taking advantage of a power vacuum in Asiatic Russia, Japanese troops landed there in late 1918, seemingly intent on taking control. President Wilson had requested only 7,000 Japanese to serve as part of an international force assembling at Vladivostok. Japan raised the ante, offering 12,000 troops instead. Its dispatch of troops to Siberia stopped at neither of those numbers. By late December, 74,000 Japanese troops had arrived, dwarfing all the other allied contingents combined. Later, that number might have risen to around 120,000.[2] The Japanese were well-equipped, confident, disciplined, and motivated. Accompanying them were 50,000 Japanese settlers, laborers, and businessmen sent to exploit Siberia's abundant natural resources. Further complicating matters in Siberia were bandits from every corner of northeast Asia—Russian, Mongol, Manchu, Korean, and Chinese, exploiting the absence of effective government control.

When the U.S. 27th Infantry Regiment arrived at Vladivostok, Japanese Lieutenant

Top: Supplies in Warehouse, Vladivostok, Siberia (National Archives). *Bottom:* Officers of A Company, 31st Infantry at mess. New rolling kitchens are being tested, Vladivostok, Siberia 3 December 1918 (National Archives).

General Kikuzu Otani, the International Force's senior officer, dispatched the regiment to Khabarovsk, a major city near the Trans-Siberian Railway's southward bend. He wanted the 27th to relieve Japanese troops fighting Red militia elements there but the Americans would play little role in taking the town. When the Reds fled, the Japanese pursued them all the way to Lake Baikal, taking other cities along the way. For a time, Japan, in a loose alliance with Russian Whites and the Czech Legion, seemed likely to drive the Reds out of every major city east of the Urals but Leon Trotsky, the Bolshevik Commissar for Military Affairs, sent over 600,000 of his best troops to reverse the tide.

That was the situation when the 31st Infantry reached Siberia. Debarking at Vladivostok on August 22, the regiment was cheerfully greeted by the 27th Infantry's Band and cheers from sailors aboard the USS *Brooklyn*, but most of the troops would spend their first night in Siberia in damp, inhospitable warehouses along the waterfront. The regiment departed the next morning to establish a tent camp in Gornastaya Valley, about a mile east of the city. Four companies were then sent north to relieve elements of the 27th Infantry at outposts along the Trans-Siberian Railroad, enabling the 27th to concentrate its strength farther north.[3] Because a tent camp would be inadequate for a long stay, the 31st Infantry's Headquarters, Machine gun Company, and eight rifle companies took control of an abandoned Russian barracks complex in early September. The surrounding hills had been denuded by logging and stripped of underbrush by citizens desperate for firewood, creating a barren moonscape in the midst of Siberia's otherwise densely forested environment.

Before the barracks and outbuildings could be occupied, squatters had to be evicted and the reeking filth they left behind had to be cleaned out. Although the barracks were substantial brick structures, windows were ill-fitting and pot-bellied stoves heated little more than their immediate surroundings. Mattresses were straw-filled, creating a home for bugs of every description and a serious health hazard. They were also a fire hazard, causing one of the Replacement Battalion's barracks to burn down in 1920 when sparks from a coal stove caught a mattress on fire and spread throughout the building before enough unfrozen water could be found. Two members of M Company lost their lives in that tragic blaze. Latrines were outdoors, making every morning a new challenge. Drinking water was drawn by cutting ice blocks from a nearby hilltop quarry, sliding them down the frozen hillside, and hauling them to kitchens to be melted and boiled. When spring came and the quarry thawed, water from nearby streams had to be hauled in by mules. Depending on the time of year, ice, mud, or powdery dust covered the barracks' exterior grounds and fat mosquitoes were constant companions. Despite the irritants, soldiers in Vladivostok soon lived about as comfortably as their counterparts in most barracks back home.

A detachment of roughly platoon size was drawn from the 31st to serve as guards with the 117th Hospital Train. Among them was Private Cesar Pares. Over the coming months, Pares would travel as far west as Irkutsk on the Trans-Siberian Railway, picking up sick and injured American and allied soldiers and scores of desperate civilian refugees. Periodically, bandits blocked the rail line in hopes of extorting food and weapons. They always left disappointed and Pares always found more adventure than he expected.

Pares left the Army in 1921 but missed the excitement and camaraderie. He soon rejoined, becoming an NCO with the 18th Infantry Regiment at Fort Wadsworth, New York. He received a battlefield commission in Italy during World War II and rose to the rank of Major, but reverted to his enlisted rank in 1955 before retiring as a Master Sergeant.

Top: Machine Gun Company of the 31st Infantry Regiment. CPT Allen T. Veatch, mounted, is in the lead. Vladivostok, Siberia, 9 November 1918. *Bottom:* Companies F and G, 31st Infantry Regiment, unloading supplies from American freight cars at Spasskoye, Siberia, 13 November 1918 (both U.S. Army photographs).

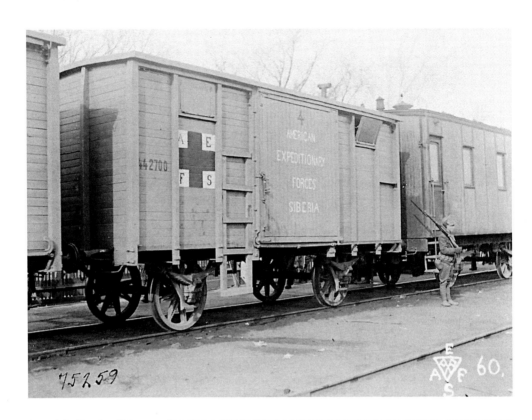

He died at the U.S. Soldiers' and Airmen's Home in Washington, D.C., in December 2000 and is buried in Arlington National Cemetery.

The 31st Infantry's first combat action occurred on August 29, 1918, at Ugolnaya (near Spasskoye) when a patrol came under fire from local partisans. Japan's General Otani ordered the 31st north to Khabarovsk but when General Graves arrived on September 1, he rescinded the order, making it clear that American troops were under American command. He soon issued instructions to relocate units. Companies B and I were sent to Harbin, Manchuria, to guard a spur of the Trans-Siberian Railway in a part of China where no government ruled and where bands of Manchu, Mongolian, Chinese, and Korean bandits known collectively as *Hung Hutze* roamed freely. East of Vladivostok at the Suchan coal mines, Lieutenant Colonel Sylvester Loring assumed command of the allied mine guard, comprised of M Company and detachments of Chinese, British, and Japanese troops. Major Fitzhugh B. Alderdice took F and G Companies to guard the rail yards at Spasskoye and Captain Francis G.

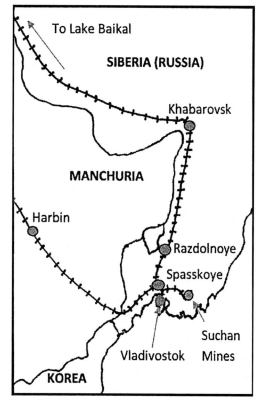

Initial Area of Operations (Association Archives).

Bishop took L Company to Razdolnoye to guard the railway tunnel there. Headquarters, Supply, and Machine gun Companies, along with A, C, D, E, H, and K Companies initially remained at Vladivostok. The rest of 1918 passed without further incident except for the murder of a member of M Company by a drunken Russian officer in Vladivostok.

The 31st grew each month in 1918, swelled steadily by fillers from the 8th Division. Ironically, two of the same regiments (8th and 13th) that formed the 31st Infantry in the Philippines in 1916 were again depleted to bring it to wartime strength. From a complement of 1,562 when it reached Vladivostok, the 31st Infantry grew to 3,589 by the end of 1918. New troops were given a heavy dose of squad tactical training, marksmanship, and forced tactical marches in a replacement battalion before being assigned to their companies. In the first group of reinforcements was Major Sidney C. Graves, son of the American commander. Major Graves had earned the Distinguished Service Cross, Britain's Distinguished Service Order, and the French Croix de Guerre while serving as a captain with the 16th Infantry Regiment in France. He was initially assigned as Executive Officer of the 3rd Battalion, 31st Infantry and later became Assistant Chief of Staff G-3 at Head-

Opposite, top: The first hospital car used to evacuate wounded troops along the line to the base at Vladivostok. This car alone covered 9,000 miles and evacuated over 200 patients. The railhead farthest away from base was 1,100 miles (U.S. Army photograph, taken 4 January 1919).

Bottom: An American hospital train on the Trans-Siberian Railroad (photograph from Association Archives).

31st Infantry on the march from Vladivostok, November 1918 (National Archives).

quarters, AEF Siberia where he would earn a second Distinguished Service Cross for rescuing trapped civilians during an outbreak of fighting in Vladivostok in 1920. Another of the early replacements was Private Forrest Moore of Los Angeles, assigned to H Company in October 1918. In a letter to his mother, Moore describes the barracks and food as good, the locals as friendly, and his comrades in H Company as "men who really know how to soldier." Not everyone shared his view, especially of the barracks and food.

By the end of 1918, the allied force in Siberia included roughly 74,000 Japanese, 70,000 Czechoslovaks, 12,000 Poles, 4000 Romanians, 9,000 Americans, 4,200 Canadians, 4,000 Russian auxiliaries, 2,000 Italians, 2,200 British, and 760 French. Rather than going home to fight Germans, the Czechoslovaks were fighting off a Bolshevik offensive along the Trans-Siberian Railway between Lake Baikal and Yakutsk. Joined by Japanese, Polish, French, and British contingents and a division of Mongolians, they would continue to hold the area against repeated Bolshevik offensives for nearly two years. Around 13,000 Czechoslovaks would die in combat or of disease by the time their contingent reached Vladivostok in 1920.

The first three months of 1919 were extremely cold but Army winter clothing was surprisingly suitable for Siberia's climate. It consisted of a woolen shirt and trousers, a woolen jacket, a three-quarter length sheep-lined overcoat, muskrat cap, muskrat gloves, and heavy four-buckle overshoes. Troops were armed with an M1903 Springfield rifle, an M1918 Browning Automatic Rifle (BAR), or an M1911 .45 caliber pistol, depending on their duties. All of those were still fairly new at the time, representing the state of the art in infantry weapons. Soldiers who fought in Korea 30 years later would still be using the BAR and the trusty .45 caliber pistol would remain in service into the 1990s. The regiment's heaviest weapons were three horse-drawn 37mm field guns with a range of up to 2500 yards. Each was served by a two-man crew.

In the early 1900s, sources of contagious diseases were becoming better understood, but gaps in medical and sanitation knowledge still left soldiers vulnerable to a wide variety of deadly germs. An influenza epidemic swept the world in 1918, killing over twenty million people, including thousands of American soldiers. Twice in the early months of 1919, Headquarters Company was quarantined due to outbreaks of spinal meningitis. Among those stricken was Carl Boling, the regiment's Sergeant Major. Each time a case of influenza occurred in Vladivostok, everyone feared the worst. During the regiment's service in Siberia, 59 of its members would succumb to disease or non-battle injuries.

While towns along the Trans-Siberian railway offered little opportunity for entertainment due to the ever-present danger posed by marauding groups of armed bandits, Vladivostok was bustling, like port cities everywhere. Off-duty life was reasonably pleasant because most locals were friendly to Americans. Nightlife in Vladivostok was a mix of seedy bars, run-down theaters, and brothels near the docks, and upscale hotels and restaurants nearer the city's center. Alf Thompson recalled astonishment at seeing men and women bathing nude together at public bath houses. Men could stroll the streets unarmed but it was best that they stayed together in groups at night in "entertaining" districts. Perhaps just a little more than in most overseas duty stations, the medical staff had its hands full with the consequences of being stationed in a relatively small city with a large international military presence—drunkenness, fights, and venereal disease. Americans generally respected Chinese and Canadian troops, who tended to be disciplined and friendly, but off-duty encounters with most others, especially the British and Japanese, often resulted in fistfights that quickly drew in fellow countrymen and turned into brawls.

The environment fostered an atmosphere in which men who were inclined toward indiscipline or were overtaken by loneliness could easily stray from the fold. During the regiment's two years in Siberia, 50 of its members deserted. Some simply melted into the polyglot international community where they could conceal their identity while others managed to sign on as crewmen on departing commercial cargo ships or whalers. Bill Hartmann recalled that occasionally a man would slip out of the barracks at night without a word to anyone and would never be seen again. Some found a girlfriend to stay with but how they supported themselves and what became of them after the American Army departed is a mystery. A poem by Private Frank Zanfagna of Headquarters Company reveals the depths of some men's loathing for the part of the world into which they had been cast:

> *When the Lord was designing creation, and laying the ocean and land,*
> *With never an hour of relaxation nor a moment to spit on his hands.*
>
> *As anyone will in a hurry, he lets things go by and then,*
> *In all the excitement and worry, he failed to do them over again.*
>
> *So rather than mess up the outfit, he saved every blunder and blob,*
> *And laid them aside in a corner, to use at the end of the job.*

And on the sixth day of his contract, his bonus expired that day,
He bailed out the dregs of creation and shoveled the litter away.

He scraped all the wreckage and tailing and the sewage and scum of the stump,
And he made on the shores of the Arctic, a great international dump.

He rushed the thing through in a hurry and because of the rush he was in,
He dubbed the locality Siberia and Siberia it has always been.

And then feeling glum and sarcastic, because it was Saturday night,
He picked out the dirtiest corner and called it Vladivostok for spite.

It's there they do everything backwards and the mud doesn't dry between rains,
Where money and sawdust is plenty and thievery is thicker than brains.

It's the home of the Jap and the Bohunk,[4] the herring and mud colored crows,
But my strongest impression of Russia got into my head through my nose.

It's the land of infernal odor, and the land of national smells
And the average American soldier would rather be quartered in hell.

But it's back to the states for yours truly, a sadder but wiser young chap.
The Lord played a joke on creation when he dumped Siberia on the map.

Private Herbert G. McDonald, an attached engineer, had similar sentiments. An excerpt from one of his poems follows:

… Siberia, they sent me here, beneath the flag I held so dear.
Tis here that I must do my bit and suffer every day for it.

But as I smell your stinking core, it seems I hate you more and more.
Of every land beneath the skies, you are the one I most despise.

Oh take me anywhere away, from all your odorous decay.
And I will offer up my thanks with every soldier in the ranks.

If I could choose which I would do, go down to hell or live with you,
It wouldn't take me long to tell, for I would answer "give me hell."

Vladivostok also had a more civilized side. There were elegant entertainment establishments at the city's better hotels along Svetlanskaya Street. Some of the younger American officers took weekly Russian language lessons from an attractive young lady who served them tea and played the piano to accompany their singing. She eventually left Vladivostok as the bride of an American lieutenant. Many more of the 31st Infantry's members left Siberia with Russian brides. Sergeant Herman Clay Stone of Columbus, Ohio, was with D Company at Razdolnoye when he met a girl he would take to the Philippines and later to San Francisco where he retired at the Presidio in 1933. When it came time to leave, soldiers had to purchase their wives' passage to Manila, causing some to be left behind due to insufficient funds.

Wherever Americans gather, there will be sports. Siberia was no exception. The 31st Infantry fielded a baseball team that played regularly against a Canadian team on the old Russian military parade ground. History does not record which team had the winning record. Among the Canadians was Raymond Massey, a gunnery officer who would later become famous as a movie actor. His first acting performance was on stage at Vladivostok entertaining American and Canadian troops. Soldiers inclined toward hunting and fishing also had ample opportunities to pursue their sport in the coastal wilderness and swift-running rivers of southern Siberia, but straying too far from one's garrison might invite trouble with Bolsheviks or bandits, as some would soon learn.

Soldiers and even most leaders remained uncertain of their mission, causing occasional disconnects between policies and actions. Some believed their primary responsibility was to help Czechoslovaks fight their way back home. Others assumed they were to round up German and Austrian prisoners of war running loose in Siberia. Most believed they had been sent to fight the Bolsheviks, derisively nicknamed "Bolos." The "brass" had other ideas, fearful that actions favoring either side would stimulate attacks on widely scattered American outposts. When General Graves learned that a soldier had arrested a Russian simply because he was a Bolshevik, he issued the following statement: "Whoever gave you those orders must have made them up himself. The United States is not at war with the Bolsheviki or any other faction in Russia. You have no orders to arrest Bolsheviks or anybody else unless they disturb the peace of the community, attack the people, or the allied soldiers." That order would not last long.

Lieutenant Alf Thompson's diary entries reflect a different viewpoint:

> October 3, 1918: News from the Western Front very encouraging. From the Volga front, not so good. The Tjecks [Czechs] are being driven back by the Bolsheviks. Why can't we get into it? The Russians [white remnants of the empire] are praying for us to help them and Washington holds us here doing routine guard duty while the Japs are fighting through and taking credit, irking the Russians.[5]

> November 1, 1918: News reports still drumming peace but Russia is not improving any and it seems almost certain that reconstruction can only be established through heavy allied military involvement. A failing to come together on the part of Russian generals and governments in Siberia is very noticeable and there are four distinct Russian or Tjeck [Czech] armies in the field, each working separately from the others. However with a good strong allied general staff, unity can be hoped for and then "Goodnight Bolshevike!" No matter if peace does come with Germany, it will not come here for a very long while and so we will doubtless be kept here on duty.[6]

After World War I ended in November 1918, the rationale for keeping American troops in Siberia became even less clear. The mission no longer had anything to do with getting Czechoslovaks back into the war against Germany. While allied governments openly favored Russia's Whites over the Reds, American troops trusted neither because leaders on both sides were corrupt and brutal. As one officer put it, "The peasantry lives in a constant state of mortal fear, never knowing when the blow will descend on them. No crops are raised—nothing. To do so would be merely to take one's life in hand in protecting them from bandits and guerillas."

The White "government" in Siberia was led by Czarist Admiral Alexander V. Kolchak, who proclaimed himself "supreme ruler of Russia," a wishful title under the circumstances. Three autonomous factions nominally operated under his command but he had little influence over any of them. The largest was led by Major General Pavel P. Ivanov-Rinov. Rather than protecting the people in whose name he supposedly acted, Ivanov-Rinov's troops terrorized and plundered without mercy or remorse. Other groups were even worse. Two in particular were led by Cossack Atamans (Chiefs) Grigori Semenov and Ivan Kalmykov. Their followers included Chinese, Mongols, Koreans, Manchu, and Russians. General Graves claimed the main difference between Semenov and Kalmykov was that Kalmykov murdered with his own hands, while Semenov simply ordered others to kill for him.

In March 1919, more replacements arrived, some of whom had fought in France. They were soon to see more action. That month, a distraught schoolteacher came to General Graves' headquarters pleading for protection for her and her brother so they could return home to bury their father, murdered by Ivanov-Rinov's troops. The woman said the Whites came to their village seeking recruits. Finding that all the young men had fled, they took ten old men to the schoolhouse, tortured and killed them, and were guarding the bodies to prevent families from burying them. Graves ordered a detachment, led by an officer, to accompany the pair and investigate the report. The officer subsequently reported:

> I found the floor of the room where these men were held covered with blood and all the walls splashed with blood. The wire and loops of rope that were used to bind the men's wrists were still hanging from the ceiling, covered with blood. I also found that some of these men had been scalded with boiling water and burned with hot irons, heated in a little stove in the room. I visited the spot where the men were shot. Each body had at least three bullets in it, and some had six or more. They were apparently shot in the feet first and then higher in the body.

Outraged, General Graves ordered his men to stop such acts wherever they were encountered. Representatives of Admiral Kolchak's government protested the order to U.S. Ambassador Morris, who in turn instructed General Graves to avoid any interference with Kolchak's troops. Graves refused, saying he was under War Department, not State Department, orders. Secretary of War Newton D. Baker and Army Chief of Staff Peyton C. March supported Graves. General March wrote Graves a letter saying "Keep a stiff upper lip, I am going to stand by you until hell freezes over."

Into Battle

For a time, the Reds avoided provoking Americans. That changed in March 1919, when a Bolshevik ideologue, Yakov Ivanovitch Triapitsyn demanded the withdrawal of all allied soldiers from the Suchan Valley. The five-mile-wide valley's 14 coal mines were the primary source of fuel at the Trans-Siberian Railroad's eastern end. The miners were a polyglot mix of Russians, Koreans, Chinese, and Manchu. Most were openly sympathetic to the Reds while their managers favored the Whites. Koreans, the largest group, had a particular hatred for the Japanese and by extension anyone with whom the Japanese were allied. Japan had invaded their country in 1904 and thereafter ruled it with an oppressive, heavy hand. If Reds gained control of the mines, they would control the railroad and hence, Siberia's economic lifeblood. Something had to be done and the Americans would assume the mission.

In April, the Allies assumed responsibility for the rail line's security and operation. Because that meant safeguarding tracks over which supplies were being sent to forces opposing a Red takeover, Reds logically interpreted the arrangement as pro–Kolchak. Their view was reinforced when on May 21, E Company, 31st Infantry departed Shkotovo to roust an ill-disciplined band of Red partisans from a nearby settlement on the Suchan spur. The three-day operation resulted in several exchanges of fire, but no American casualties. Patrols from Shkotovo became more frequent, involving a mix of rail movements and foot patrols. On May 25, C and D Companies with a platoon from the Regiment's Machine gun Company patrolled around 30 kilometers northwest from Shkotovo while E Company patrolled due north of Shkotovo. None encountered partisans. On June 12 and 13, intelligence-gathering patrols were sent to search for partisan activity between Novo Nezhino and Suchan. On June 16, a larger intelligence patrol sortied from Shkotovo to check out rumored partisan activity southwest of Romanovka. Again, there was no reported contact. Major William N. Joiner, the 1st Battalion's Executive Officer, led C, D, E, and L Companies from Shkotovo to bolster the mine guard. H and K Com-

The Stars and Stripes fly on the flagpole in front of the Allied Mine Detachment Headquarters, with an American sentry posted on the gate, c. 1919 (National Archives photograph).

panies and detachments of the Machine gun and Headquarters Companies were sent to reinforce them. In all, that raised the American contingent in the valley to two battalions, totaling 72 officers and 1860 enlisted men. To prevent the Bolsheviks from taking over the mines and the rail spur, the Americans were spread thin, guarding mines and railway stations.

Among the reinforcements sent into the Suchan Valley was 23-year-old Second Lieutenant Alf Thompson, the regiment's signal platoon leader, who led a mounted patrol along the railway to repair telegraph lines cut by Russian partisans. Alf arrived in Siberia as a sergeant in charge of a machine gun section in August. When he was notified of his commissioning at Vladivostok in October, there were no officers' uniforms available so he had to borrow a lieutenant's rank insignia. He bought his first set of boots (enlisted men wore cloth-wrapped leggings) in Vladivostok only to discover they were made of stiffened, polished, and glued layers of cardboard that came apart on his first march, leaving him shoeless. His feet recovered but he didn't appreciate being referred to as "lieutenant barefoot."

On June 21, 1919, a warm summer day, three enlisted men from H Company, Corporal Harlan S. Daly, Private Harold Bullard, and Private Forrest Moore were captured by a group of Reds while fishing in the shallow Suchan River. They were being marched to Novitskaya by their captors when the partisans came across two more American anglers, Lieutenant Custer Fribley of the Supply Company and Private Eastland W. Reed of H Company. The men were not reported missing until the next morning. A platoon-

The army's standard winter uniform was adaptable to Siberia's climate. Alf Thompson is in the middle in this photograph from the winter of 1918-1919 (Association archives, courtesy Alf Thompson).

size patrol accompanied by Russian auxiliaries learned from villagers where they were taken. Outraged, Colonel Gideon H. Williams, commander of the Allied Mine Guard, dispatched a detachment of the 31st Infantry from Suchan to free them.

Sergeant Herbert L. Reeves of H Company later recalled how the battle for Novitskaya began. His recollections are published in the 1920 Annual Report of the USMA Association of Graduates in which Lieutenant Albert Francis Ward, Class of 1918, is eulogized.

> The organization was marching to the town where the American soldiers were imprisoned, and as we were not really at war with the Bolsheviki, it had been decided to first request the release of the Americans before we took them by force. Lieutenant Ward and his orderly (PFC Dee P. Craig) rode into town bearing a flag of truce. Suddenly, two shots rang out and Lieutenant Ward and his orderly both fell from their horses. The next shots came quick and fast but I managed to get Lieutenant Ward back to cover. He was shot through the head and I knew he was done for. I think he knew it too. As I picked him up, he said, "Don't mind me, look after him. He is hurt worse than I am." He said no more before we could get him to a hospital. But think of what a man he was, sir. His first thought was of the poor kid who was serving him and was already dead when we picked him up.[7]

Furious about their losses to a deceitful foe and intent on recapturing their comrades, H Company pressed the attack, charging from house-to-house with BARs blasting through walls. Private Anastacio D. Montoya, with the lead squad, was hit as the assault began and would later succumb to his wounds. Approaching the town from the opposite direction, a 110-man detachment from M Company led by Lieutenant Gilpin Rumans met stiff resistance as its lead squad tried to cross a wooden fence near the town's edge. The first and third soldiers across, Privates Jesse M. Reed and Charles R. Blake, were shot multiple times (Reed died on the spot and Blake died of his wounds the following morning), forcing the detachment to ground where they remained pinned down by heavy fire. But they were another source of worry for the hard-pressed Reds. Squeezed from two sides, the Reds fled as darkness descended. Sergei Samushenko, the Red leader, was captured during H Company's assault but the American captives on whose behalf the

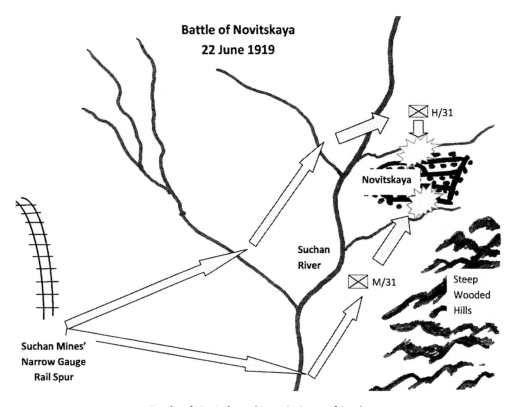

Battle of Novitskaya (Association archives).

assault was launched, had been taken away. Red prisoners reported the men had been taken to the nearby village of Frolovka. Colonel Williams did not pursue, fearing the captives might be executed. The two companies' six-mile return march to Suchan that night was worse than miserable. A heavy downpour began around 10 p.m., drenching the troops and turning their route into a sea of mud. One soldier recalled, "The ambulance could hold no more, so two dead men were placed on our ammo cart. They were tied on, so I held one man's leg to keep up with the *droskie* [Russian for cart] because of the mud." The soaked, exhausted column reached Suchan around 1 a.m. on June 23.

Further west along the Suchan spur, another battle was about to unfold, this one even more devastating. On the evening of June 24, Lieutenant Lawrence D. Butler of A Company reached Romanovka by train with 21 men to reinforce Lieutenant Harry Krieger's 51-man 3rd Platoon of the same company. Butler was to take command of the combined force because Krieger had allegedly soured relations with the locals. Krieger's platoon had pitched their tents in a field at the edge of town. Nearby, a railroad cut formed a steep bluff offering a commanding view of the encampment. Krieger's men outposted the bluff by day but withdrew before dark because the area was known to host large numbers of hostiles and an isolated outpost would stand no chance of returning if attacked. Recognizing the outpost's vulnerability, Butler decided to move the camp the next morning but with darkness near, there was insufficient time to reconnoiter a new site and move before dark. Butler's troops instead pitched their tents alongside the 3rd Platoon's. Passing through Romanovka that night, Lieutenant Colonel Robert L. Eichelberger, the Siberian AEF's G-2 Intelligence Officer reaffirmed Butler's discomfort with

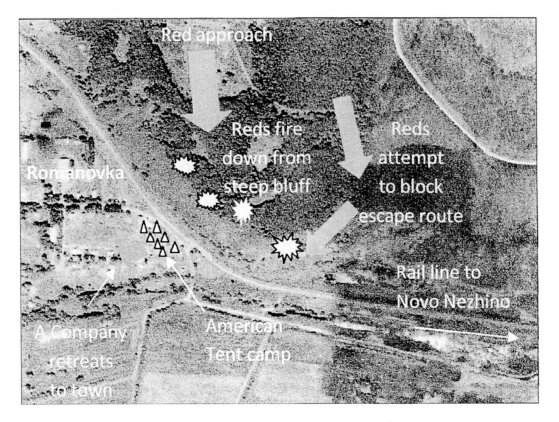

Battle of Romanovka (Association archives).

the situation by admonishing him that his unit was ill-positioned and risked inviting an attack from the adjacent bluff.

The night passed without incident, giving sentries the false impression of another peaceful summer night. Occasionally a dog barked in the village, but there was nothing unusual to observe. Atop the bluff, however, danger approached in the darkness. By dawn, two companies of Reds, led by Sergei Lazo, had positioned themselves among high grass and brush atop the bluff to fire down on the American encampment. Lazo's intent was to wipe out the Americans, seize their weapons and ammunition, and recruit Red sympathizers in the town. Around 5 a.m., the Reds opened fire with deadly effect as early morning light illuminated the somnolent tent camp below. The opening volley hit scores of men in their sleep, along with the lone sentry posted at the camp's south end. He had just completed his guard tour and was about to awaken his platoon sergeant. He lived only long enough to reach the tent. Lieutenant Butler was among those hit as men scrambled out of the tents. Although a bullet tore away part of his lower jaw, he remained in command, directing his men with arm and hand signals to withdraw to a nearby woodpile and then to a cluster of log houses at the edge of town.

To reach the houses, survivors had to cross an open area under heavy fire, suffering more losses. Seeing their duty clearly, PFCs Emmit Lunsford of Claremore, Oklahoma, Roy Jones of Knoxville, Iowa, and George Strakey of Castlegate, Utah, covered their comrades' withdrawal with Browning Automatic Rifles (BARs), firing as fast as they could reload to suppress enemy fire. When others still able reached safety, the trio helped cover each other's withdrawal, joined by covering fire from their grateful comrades in town. All three escaped without injury and continued to fight throughout the long battle that followed. Their selfless action at great personal risk was a major contributor to the detachment's survival. All three were awarded the Distinguished Service Cross (DSC). As the situation grew more desperate, Lieutenant Butler stepped out from his place of cover and swept the main street with a BAR to keep the advancing Reds from entering the town. For his bravery and leadership, he too was awarded the DSC.

Wounded men who could be saved were dragged into houses where they were treated by American medics and local women. A Polish nurse (formerly with the Russian Army) who had befriended one of the American NCOs, Platoon Sergeant Almus E. Beck, repeatedly came under fire as she ran back and forth into the street to help retrieve the wounded and save precious water streaming from a lister bag perforated by bullets. Luckily, she was not hit. She and Almus Beck were married after the battle and she returned to the Philippines with him in 1920. In the cellar of one of the sturdier houses, a stocky Russian woman helped medics tend to the wounded while her three small children looked on. Asked where her husband was, she pointed to the bluff from which the Reds were firing. Also among the partisans were the town's shoe repairman and milk man.

Fearing his battered detachment might be overwhelmed, Lieutenant Butler called for two volunteers to contact E Company at Novo Nezhino, six miles farther down the rail spur. Corporals Valeryan Brodnicki of Chicago and Leo Heinzmann of Los Angeles promptly volunteered and set out at a run through a hail of fire. Although twice wounded, Brodnicki sprinted through intense fire to summon help. Heinzmann followed close on his heels. A short distance from Romanovka, the pair met a train with a 17-man guard detachment from K Company. Heinzmann jumped aboard, ordering the terrified engineer to drive the train to Romanovka. Knowing the train guard detachment would be insufficient to tip the balance, Brodnicki continued alone on foot toward Novo Nezhino. Heinzmann's

The train station at Novo Nezhino, c. 1919 (photograph from Association archives courtesy Alf Thompson).

order to drive the train to Romanovka was countermanded by the train commander, Sergeant Sylvester B. Moore, who later reported his reasoning. The train bearing his 17 men, an unarmed engineer, and Heinzmann would have to pass under the bluff to reach Romanovka and then would have to sprint under fire across open ground to reach the town, just as Butler's detachment had done at great cost. Any thought of trying a flanking move up the bluff would be suicidal against an enemy force estimated to number around 200 men occupying positions from which they could see in every direction. The train returned to Novo Nezhino instead, picking up the bleeding and exhausted Brodnicki en route.

When the train reached Novo Nezhino, Lieutenant Lewis J. Lorimar of E Company put his platoon and a machine gun detachment aboard and sped off for Romanovka after signaling for a hospital train from Kanguaz.[8] The relief force now totaled 77 men, 58 from E Company, 17 from K Company and the two heroes from A Company. Brodnicki, although suffering from his wounds, refused evacuation, returning to Romanovka with the relief force. Although Brodnicki was later recommended for the Medal of Honor, he and Heinzmann both received the DSC for their heroic actions. The appearance of a train bearing heavily armed reinforcements tipped the balance at Romanovka, causing the Bolsheviks to break contact and flee around 8 a.m., although sporadic sniping continued until after the hospital train arrived an hour later. The relief force was shocked by what it found. One of those killed in the tents had been hit 17 times. Lieutenant Sylvian Kendall recalled, "The ground was strewn with blood-soaked bodies of American soldiers. Splintered bones and flesh torn with ghastly holes told plainly that dum-dum bullets had been used. Half of those hit were dead; others were dying or were too injured to rise from the ground. Only a few of those engaged had come through the slaughter without a wound of some kind."

Captain Oscar C. Frundt, the medical officer in charge of the hospital train, quickly brought order to the situation. The injured were taken aboard to have their wounds dressed. Sulfate and morphine were administered to ease their suffering. Those able to eat were given coffee and crackers. When the last of the wounded were aboard, the dead were taken aboard as well. En route to Vladivostok, a blown bridge stopped the train, causing the wounded to be carried in great pain to a freight train waiting on the opposite side. They had to complete the journey to Vladivostok in boxcars, adding to their agony. Several days later, when visited by his men in Vladivostok's military hospital, Lieutenant Butler was found smoking a cigarette. A twisted rag tied over his head and beneath the remains of his jaw took the place of a missing lower lip.

A Company had suffered 19 killed and 25 wounded during the action, most of them hit during the attack on the tent camp early that morning. Many of those shot in their tents were hit repeatedly and either died where they had slept or were shot again as they tried to crawl away. Three succumbed to their wounds that night and two more would die over the next two weeks. A Company's losses were by far the highest of any during the campaign.

Although the Reds retreated, they had drawn American blood and wanted more. While attention focused on Romanovka, a platoon of E Company under Sergeant James Gardner was the only force remaining at Novo Nezhino, guarding its telegraph connection at the railroad station. Worried about the garrison's diminished strength and determined not to allow a repeat of what happened at Romanovka, Gardner's platoon built a log and railroad tie berm around the station to give themselves protection. The precaution paid off. Reds, assuming the platoon would be easy prey, attacked at first light on June 26. Although outnumbered, the Americans held their ground and signaled Lieutenant Lorimar for help. Lorimar hustled his men at Romanovka onto a train and rushed to the rescue but it would take over an hour to reach Novo Nezhino. Meanwhile, several attempts to rush the barricade were repulsed, each leaving more dead and wounded Reds in its wake. When Lorimar's platoon reached Novo Nezhino, the Reds' morale seemed to crumble. The exchange of fire had already diminished to sporadic potshots and it appeared the Reds were abandoning buildings nearest the Americans. At least ten of their dead lay twisted in the street in front of the station. Sensing opportunity, Lorimar ordered an attack. His 58 men sprang over their barricade and charged down the street firing wildly at Reds fleeing in panic. When it was over, 30 Reds had been killed against only one American wounded.

Realizing they had stirred up a hornet's nest, the Red revolutionary headquarters at Frolovka sent an emissary to Suchan. They offered to release their five American captives if the Americans would release several captured partisans, including their leader, Sergei Samuschenko. Colonel Williams initially refused. When a second note arrived with a message from Lieutenant Fribley, the situation began to ease. At least Williams knew the captives were still alive and well. Williams asked Lieutenant Colonel Eichelberger to negotiate an exchange of captives. Eichelberger, who spoke Russian, went alone in the dark to meet with a group of Russians behind their lines. He knew his opponents might decide he was a greater prize than those he was trying to free. After negotiating all night, Eichelberger secured the captives' release, including Lieutenant Fribley's mule, and brought them out with him at dawn. In exchange, Colonel Williams released Samushenko as Eichelberger had promised.

Nearer the Suchan mines, C and D Companies were attacked by a larger force on June 26. Sergeant Ralph Cranford of Franklin, Pennsylvania, acting as a platoon leader, won the DSC for defeating a numerically superior foe without a single loss to his own men. Corporal Arthur Vogel of Heber, California, ran a railway locomotive past a Red-held cliff three times to draw the enemy's fire so they could be identified and destroyed by D Company's supporting machine guns. Vogel repeatedly exposed himself to heavy fire and his Russian assistant was wounded during the action.

Unable to defeat an American unit by direct attack, the Reds embarked on a campaign of disruption. Over the next week, they cut telegraph lines and blew up bridges all along the spur to the Suchan mines from the main trunk of the Trans-Siberian Railway. Without telegraph communications, isolated American detachments under attack would be unable to call for reinforcements and without rail connections, troops would have to move slowly on foot along trails that offered many opportunities for ambush. Worse, the Americans and their allies guarding the mines could no longer be resupplied by train or get their wounded out of the valley. Alarmed at the situation's sudden deterioration, General Graves ordered the garrison commanders at Suchan and Shkotovo to drive the partisans out of the valley. On June 30, the 31st Infantry's strength was 109 officers and 3411 enlisted men. Up to that time, one officer and 28 enlisted men had been killed and one officer and 32 enlisted men had been wounded. Over 200 Bolsheviks had been captured and probably an equal number were killed, based on the number of weapons captured. But comparative tallies of dead and wounded had no meaning. Because the Reds could forcibly recruit anywhere in the region, they had an abundant supply of replacements.

In response to General Graves' order, the counteroffensive's first target was Frolovka where the Reds were believed to have their headquarters. Major Sidney Graves led a detachment consisting of M Company and two machine gun squads, out of the Suchan garrison shortly after midnight on July 2. The men tied down their equipment and moved as quietly as possible to avoid detection by pro–Red locals. They hoped to surprise the Reds at Frolovka and avenge the deaths of their comrades at Romanovka. Soon after Major Graves' detachment left, a stronger second column, led by Colonel Williams, also departed the Suchan garrison. C and D Companies, two machine gun squads, a horse-drawn 37mm field gun, and a Japanese rifle company accompanied Williams. His plan was for the two forces to converge on Frolovka from different directions, maximizing the fire they could collectively bring to bear. All units were to be in pre-designated attack positions before first light. At 5 a.m., Williams initiated the attack from the southwest. On hearing Williams' detachment open fire, Graves attacked from the northwest. Red resistance was surprisingly light and the town was secured by 10 a.m.

But the fight was not over. Reds continued to snipe at the force from a nearby ridge. Lieutenant Fred C. Shepherd of M Company was ordered to take his platoon out to chase the snipers off the ridge. Lieutenant Colonel Eichelberger accompanied him, perhaps hoping to use his Russian language skills to advantage. Now it was the Americans' turn to be surprised. To reach the ridge, Shepherd's platoon had to cross several hundred yards of open ground. As it approached the heavily forested slope, the platoon was met by a sudden, intense outburst of rifle fire. The opening volley seriously wounded Lieutenant Shepherd and one of his men. Seeing the attack falter in the open, Eichelberger

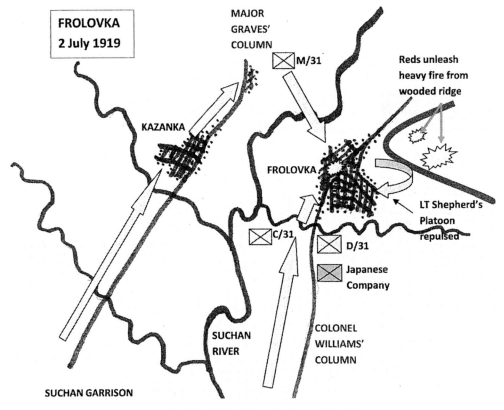

Battle of Frolovka (Association archives).

took command of the center squad, directing them to maintain a steady volume of fire while the other squads pulled back with the wounded to safer ground. Grabbing the wounded soldier's rifle, Eichelberger joined Sergeant Delbert Farrington in covering the remaining squad's withdrawal. Both won the DSC for their actions.

In the early morning hours of July 3, Major Joiner, the 1st Battalion's Executive Officer, led C and D Companies, accompanied by two machine guns and a 37mm assault gun, out of the encampment at Suchan to attack a group of Red partisans at Kazanka. Traveling parallel to the rail line for roughly half the distance and then along a well-traveled path toward the town, Joiner's column made good time, reaching his planned attack position behind a wooded ridge before dawn. A larger column, led by Colonel Williams, left later, intending to converge on Kazanka from the southeast. The plan was for Williams' group to initiate the attack from a wood line near the town. Joiner's group would key on the sound of Williams' guns, attacking near-simultaneously from a slightly greater distance. After traveling just over half the distance to their objective, Williams' group became bogged down in a thick, waist-deep swamp north of Novitskaya. Getting through the swampy tangle with cumbersome 37mm guns and machine guns proved more difficult and time-consuming than anyone expected. Williams sent scouts to find a way around the bog but the guns were mired and would have to be extracted. Bypassing the extensive swamp would add several more hours to the trip because steep gorges flanked the approach.

With no communications between the two columns (field radios did not yet exist), Williams had no way of telling Joiner of the delay. As the locals awoke and began doing their daily business around the town, Joiner feared someone would encounter his men and sound the alarm. He waited nervously, unsure of what to do. At around 8:30 a.m., he decided he could wait no longer and initiated the attack. He began by shelling key buildings with his lone 37mm gun and exploited the resulting confusion with a brisk

Bogged down in a swamp north of Novitskaya (Association archives courtesy Alf Thompson).

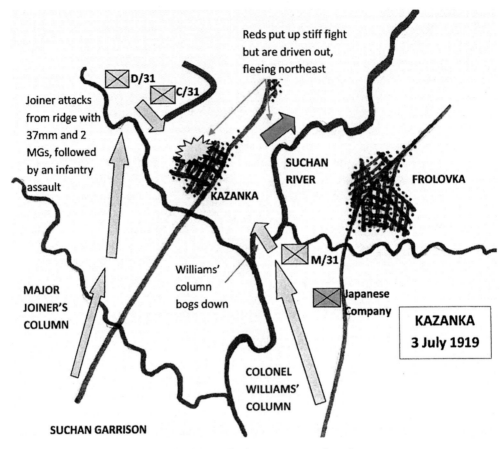

Battle of Kazanka (Association archives).

infantry assault supported by the two machine guns. Because maneuver space was narrow atop the densely wooded ridge, C Company led, with D Company following and then splitting to the right when they reached the open field. Although the partisans were unprepared, they put up a stiff fight, clinging desperately to hasty positions they took up along fences, wood piles, and hedges around the town's edge. Private Peter Bernal of C Company was cut down by a partisan's bullet as his unit maneuvered across an open field between the ridge and town.

Throughout the hour-long battle, C Company's runner, Private John Martens of Anaheim, California, carried orders back and forth between platoons, under constant fire. Tired of being shot at, Martens turned and single-handedly attacked a group of enemy troops firing at him from a patch of scrub, killing one and driving the others away. For his exemplary bravery under fire, he was awarded the DSC. By about 9:30 a.m., the fighting was over. The surviving Reds fled the town, leaving their dead and wounded behind. Major Joiner rested his men while they awaited Colonel Williams' column. Williams arrived near noon, his men exhausted after their arduous hike. In late afternoon, the entire command marched back to Suchan, taking the easiest route available.

Despite Major Joiner's success at Kazanka, things were far from quiet around Suchan. On July 4, the Reds tried and executed a local schoolteacher, a lady who had cooked for the local police, along with an electrician and a telegraph operator. The executions happened practically under the noses of the allied mine guard detachment. The next day, Sergeant James Canney of Dorchester, Massachusetts, was on patrol in the lower Suchan Valley with two other men from D Company when they encountered a 50-man enemy force. Seeing no other alternative, Canney promptly led his patrol in an attack, firing from the hip as they charged. The assault killed one Bolshevik and routed the remainder, who were stunned by Canney's bold attack. Canney earned the DSC for his quick thinking, exemplary leadership, and exceptional personal bravery under fire.

On July 5, Colonel Williams took D and M Companies, a machine gun, a medical detachment, and a Japanese rifle company to pick up supplies at Vladimiro on America Bay, around 25 miles south of Suchan. D Company's PFC Alphia Schurter of Hilltop, Kansas, was seriously wounded along with five others as his company neared the village of Piryatina in the lower valley. Although the firing came from several hundred yards away, D Company immediately went into the attack from the march. Unwilling to be left behind for treatment, Schurter ignored his blood-gushing wound and attacked alongside his comrades, firing steadily and reloading his BAR to suppress enemy fire as he struggled forward.

Seeing Schurter struggling to keep up, his platoon sergeant ordered a medic to stop him and treat his wound. Schurter angrily brushed the man off and had to be physically restrained from continuing so the wound could be treated. Unfortunately, it was too late. Schurter died soon afterward from excessive blood loss. He won the DSC posthumously for exceptional heroism at the cost of his life.

Throughout July, skirmishes continued in the Shkotovo area and partisans destroyed the railroad bridge. After being cut off for three weeks, a battalion of the 31st fought its way down the Suchan Valley to the Sea. Coming under heavy attack at Vladimir Alexandrofskoye on America Bay, Lieutenant Colonel Eichelberger, Lieutenant Winningstad,[9] and several enlisted men commandeered a small boat and headed for Vladivostok, 65 miles away, to get help. En route they were picked up by the cruiser USS *Albany*.

In June and July, Reds destroyed 21 bridges between Shkotovo and Kanguaz and knocked out power houses that ran cars on the narrow gauge mountain railway between Kanguaz and Suchan. In reaction, the 31st Infantry and Russian auxiliary companies intensified patrolling throughout the area. An operations summary for July and August 1919, extracted from that prepared by Major Thomas S. Arms, the last Allied Mine Detachment Commander, is reflected in the table that follows. Refer to the map for the relative locations of the described areas of operation.

Dates	Participating Units	Activity	Results
30 Jun–2 Jul 1919	CPT Crom's column (K/31st Inf, Plt/I/31st Inf, plus Russian auxiliaries)	Combat patrol to Rozdestvenka, Moleny Mys and Petrovka (all south of Novo Nezhino)	Resistance at each village; no U.S. losses
3 Jul 1919	MAJ Joiner's column (D/31st Inf, C/31st Inf, 2 MG, 2 37mm guns); reinforced by COL Williams column (M/31st Inf & Japanese Company)	Combat patrol to Kazanka departed Suchan at 0400, returned 1900	Encountered Red force of 300–500 around 0800; Reds defeated, leaving 30 dead. U.S. losses: 2 WIA in D Co, 1 KIA in C Co
5 Jul 1919	COL Williams column (D/31st Inf, M/31st Inf,	Combat patrol to Peretina (8 mi S of Suchan); pursuit	Dispersed around 50 Reds at Peretino; encountered and

Top: During July 1919, partisans destroyed a bridge in the Shkotovo area. *Bottom*: July and August 1919 Skirmishes (both Association archives).

Dates	Participating Units	Activity	Results
	2 MG, 1 37mm)	to Uruska (14 mi S of Suchan) and Vladimiro-Aleksandrovskoye (20 mi S of Suchan)	engaged around 300 Reds at Uruska; Red casualties unknown; 6 WIA from D/31st Inf
7–14 Jul 1919	CPT Crom's column (K/31st Inf, MG Plt, Russian Company) joins LTC Boykin's	Combat patrol from Tigrovoye (10 mi NW of Suchan) to Brovnichi (8 mi NE of Tigrovoye) and	Strong resistance at Novo Moskva; Red casualties unknown; 1 U.S. officer WIA; 3 Russian auxiliaries WIA, 1 KIA

Dates	Participating Units	Activity	Results
	column (5 Russian Companies, E/31st Inf)	Novo Moskva (20 mi NE of Novo nezhino); Russians returned to Suchan 9 Jul, Americans to Shkotovo via Novo Nezhino 13–14 Jul	
10 Jul 1919 Inf	I/31st Inf, 2 Plts/A/31st	Combat patrol to Lukyanovka (8 mi SE of Novo Nezhino) and Rozdesvenka (5 mi S of Novo Nezhino	Returned to Novo Nezhino around 1900; no resistance, no casualties
15–26 Jul 1919	MAJ Joiner's column (D/31st Inf, H/31st Inf, 2 MG, 2 37mm; joined by C/31st Inf 21 Jul)	Combat patrol from Suchan to Brovnichi (18 mi NW) and nearby villages	H/31st returned to Kangauz 17 Jul; C/31st Inf returned to Kanguaz 23 Jul; all others to Shkotovo 26 Jul; no resistance, no casualties
23–26 Jul 1919	LT Maloy with A/31st Inf	Combat patrol by foot from Shkotovo to cluster of villages 12–20 mi NE	No resistance, no casualties
26 Jul 1919	LT Hellswarth with 3 Plts/C/31st Inf	Combat patrol by rail from Kanguaz to Lukyanovka (8 mi SE of Novo Nezhino)	No resistance, no casualties
28 Jul 1919	CPT Galloway with 3 Plts/D/31st Inf	Combat patrol by rail from Shkotovo to Knevichi (20 mi NE of Vladivostok)	No resistance, no casualties
29 Jul 1919	K/31st Inf	Moved aboard British cruiser HMS *Carlisle* from Shkotovo to Olga Bay, moved by rail to Kanguaz	No resistance, no casualties
30 Jul 1919	CPT Galloway with D/31st Inf	Combat patrol from Shkotovo to Novo Rossiya (20 mi NE)	2 Red KIA; no U.S. casualties
31 Jul 1919	CPT R. L. Herr with D/31st and 60 men from A/31st Inf	Combat patrol from Shkotovo to villages NE of Shkotovo, covering 36 mi in 23 hours through heavy rain	No resistance, no casualties
5–9 Aug 1919	CPT Galloway with D/31st Inf	Combat patrol from Shkotovo to villages 23 mi NE	No resistance, no casualties
6–11 Aug 1919	CPT Scroggs with I/31st Inf, joined by Cossack cavalry	Combat patrol to clusters of villages S of Novo Nezhino, covering 85 mi	No resistance, no casualties; ammunition and weapons found and confiscated
31 Aug 1919	Plt/I/31st Inf with Russian auxiliaries	Combat patrol from Suchan to Nakhoda (on the coast south of Novitskaya) in pursuit of *Hung Hutze* bandits	No resistance, no casualties

The location of Kanguaz is uncertain but is likely the town currently called Fridman, about 10 miles northwest of Suchan, now Partizansk, where the hills of eastern Siberia rise abruptly and the rail spur now winds around steep mountains to reach Suchan. Platoon Sergeant Joe Longuevan described the town as "a mountain terminal where a narrow gauge railroad, through the aid of a cable station, ascends a grade of more than 45 degrees to the peak and then extends to Suchan." The town's topography fits Longuevan's description and there is a cleared area adjacent to the rail line where a military camp might have been. A less likely location might have been the current town of Anisimovka, on the rail line about midway between Novo Nezhino and Suchan. A fairly straight trail crossing the mountains from there leads more directly to Suchan and could conceivably have been the path of a narrow-gauge railway but there are many cross-compartments on its path, making a rail line without tunnels hard to imagine.

After being withdrawn from Harbin (Manchuria) in July, B Company remained in the Suchan area and fought several skirmishes in the lower valley. At the same time, K Company made an expedition against Red partisans at Olga Bay aboard the British cruiser HMS *Carlisle*. The company became impromptu marines. The last skirmish in the Suchan area took place on August 8 when a patrol from H Company, commanded by Captain Owen R. Rhoads, encountered 30 partisans at Litovsk. After a stubborn fight, every Red was killed or captured, without a single loss to the Americans. During the action, Corporal Charles Frankenfeld, caught in the open, came under fire from a hut blocking his squad's path. Rather than seeking cover, he rushed the hut, killing or capturing all of its defenders. His action broke the enemy line at a critical point, exposing the flanks and rear of other positions and allowing enemy troops to be shot down as they tried to relocate or flee. For his bravery, Frankenfeld won the DSC.

With the rail spur destroyed, the movement of coal out of the Suchan mines had been halted for over two months. There was no point in repairing the line because it could be cut anywhere and there were too few troops to protect every mile of track. Keeping allied garrisons in the valley became pointless. The American contingent departed Suchan and other points along the spur on August 19, marching to Nakhoda on America Bay where they boarded the USS *Merritt* for the remainder of the trip to Vladivostok. Causing the allies to abandon the Suchan District was a Pyrrhic victory for the Reds because without an operable rail spur to move coal to the main line, the mines would yield no revenues. Neither did the mines' closure stop allied movements on the Trans-Siberian Railroad. Sources of coal farther north were already making up for the loss of Suchan's output. Moreover, Kolchak's Whites streamed into the valley to exploit the emerging power vacuum. More than 500 Reds had been killed since the fighting began in June and by September the survivors were disinclined to risk another fight.

As the Reds quieted down, Kalmykov and his Cossack Whites, supported by the Japanese, stirred up new trouble. General Graves described the incident:

I had on my desk a report that the Russians on September 2, in the presence of Japanese troops, had arrested an American captain and a corporal at Iman, 250 miles north of Vladivostok, for the reported reason that these men had no passports. As they wore the uniform of the American Army, and as there was no recognized government in Siberia, and further, as no military representative in Siberia was called upon for passports, the reason assigned for the arrest of these men was an insult almost on a par with the arrest.

On the morning of the 7th, I sent Colonel Robinson, my Chief of Staff, to General Rozanov's office and demanded an immediate release of the corporal; the captain having been permitted to leave the day they were arrested. General Rozanov told Colonel Robinson he would investigate and let me know later. This by no means satisfied me, so I directed Colonel Robinson to return and tell General Rozanov it was not a question for him to investigate, and a refusal to order the release of Corporal Spurling would be construed by me as a definite refusal. When General Rozanov got this message, he ordered the corporal released.[10]

Not knowing that General Graves had pressured Rozanov to order Corporal Spurling's release, Major Ed Shamatoulski, Spurling's Battalion Commander, took a detachment of troops by train to Iman. When he arrived, the local Japanese commander informed Shamatoulski that his men would not be permitted to attack the Cossacks and if they did, they would also have to fight the Japanese. Shamatoulski informed the Japanese commander that he intended to rescue Spurling and that Japanese interference would be at their own peril. Major Shamatoulski then ordered his men to disarm three Cossacks who had dug a trench and were preparing to resist. Japanese troops reinforced the Cossacks in the trench, but lost their nerve and stood aside as the Americans dragged the startled Russians from their midst. The prisoners told Shamatoulski that Corporal Spurling had been moved to Khabarovsk. Shamatoulski and his men then departed, taking the three Cossacks along as hostages. General Graves did not learn of Shamatoulski's actions until afterward, but enthusiastically supported them. Major Shamatoulski's moral stand, risking war with an "ally" who outnumbered him eight to one to rescue one of his men, is testimony to the courage and sense of command responsibility prominent in the 31st Infantry at the time.

When Corporal Spurling was released, it was evident that he had been severely beaten. Outraged, General Graves warned Kalmykov that he would be arrested if his troops ever again harassed Americans. Semenov immediately declared his intention of coming to Kalmykov's aid in the event of a fight with Americans. General Graves responded by refusing to turn over rifles the State Department had promised to Admiral Kolchak's "government," knowing they would find their way into the hands of thugs he might have to fight. Graves wrote: "We will be helping to arm the worst criminals in Siberia; we will be neglectful of the interests of the people … and will be helping Japan delay the settlement of conditions in Siberia." Kolchak pleaded that his men badly needed the rifles and that he lacked the resources to control the Cossacks. Finally, on War Department orders, Graves reluctantly turned the weapons over to Kolchak himself.

The Fighting Ends

On October 7, 1919, Colonel Fred W. Bugbee assumed command of the 31st Infantry from Colonel Sargent. Sargent left with a sterling reputation. He was characterized as idealistic, quiet but forceful, energetic, and respected by his regiment. He showed no favoritism or bias, demanding dignity, discipline, and even-handedness from the regiment's leaders, especially the officers. During Colonel Sargent's tenure, several officers were relieved for offenses ranging from incompetence to dereliction of duty. Temporary officers who failed to measure up did not have their commissions renewed when their terms expired and a lieutenant colonel, a West Point graduate, was forced to revert back to his permanent Regular Army grade of captain.[11] The change of command in Vladivostok came just as a new source of trouble arose. On November 16, an insurrection broke out in the city, led by a Czech named Alexander Gaida, who had been commissioned a lieutenant general in Kolchak's "Siberian Army." Fighting raged for two days before the revolt was put down. The 31st Infantry patrolled the city and secured Allied Expeditionary Force Headquarters on Svetanskaya Street. Sergeant George T. Masury of Headquarters Company earned the DSC for rescuing trapped civilians from the besieged Vladivostok railway station. Major Sidney Graves, who had recently been transferred

Left: Colonel Frederick H. Sargent, Commanding Officer, 31st Infantry Regiment, c. 1919 (National Archives). *Right:* Sentries guarding the Trans-Siberian Railroad, 1919 (Association archives).

to the staff of AEF Siberia, earned his second award of the DSC for leading the same action.

On November 22, a train guard detachment was ambushed near Razdolnoye, but the attackers were driven off with no casualties to either side. Four probes were made against C Company in December, but each time the enemy was driven off without inflicting any losses. In the closing days of 1919, around 500 men of Kolchak's infantry mutinied in the Suchan Valley and at Shkotovo, executing 2 of their officers and appropriating stores of weapons and ammunition, which they took with them to the Bolshevik side. A Red victory in Siberia was imminent.

On January 8, 1920, the AEF was ordered withdrawn from Siberia. On receipt of the withdrawal order, the 31st Infantry began its departure from Shkotovo. In bitter cold amid a blowing snowstorm, the evacuation was completed, despite two partisan attacks. Between January 25 and February 3, General Rozonov's Whites were overcome in Amur Province by a combined force of Social Democrats and Bolsheviks, ending White opposition in Siberia. Rioting and looting broke out in Vladivostok in anticipation of the Reds' takeover. A, C, I, and L Companies established police patrols in the city while E and H Companies patrolled outside the city. A Bolshevik government was formed in Vladivostok on January 31. A large parade was held to celebrate the conflict's end and on February 3, American patrols in and around the city were discontinued. On February 6, Admiral Kolchak was apprehended by Czech troops, who turned him over to the Bolsheviks at Yakutsk. He was shot and his body thrown into a nearby river. Over 57,000 surviving Czechoslovak troops withdrew from central Siberia, turning over the trains that had been home for two years to allied authorities at Vladivostok. Over the next several months, they were returned to Europe aboard allied ships. More than 13,000 of their colleagues had perished in Siberia. Japanese troops remained in Siberia until 1922.

On February 15, the 31st Infantry began leaving Siberia. For the next 45 days, the Transports *Crook*, *Dix*, *Great Northern*, and *South Bend* would carry the Polar Bears back to Manila, where their odyssey began. With the last contingent departing was a young Pennsylvanian named William G. Hartman. Eager to participate in the Great War as a pilot, he enlisted in the fall of 1918 at age 16. When he arrived at the Army's east coast port of embarkation at Hoboken, New Jersey, he was put on a train headed west with hundreds of similarly bewildered troops who thought they had enlisted to fight in Europe. They had no idea where the train was going, except that it was headed in the wrong direction. At Fort McDowell (Angel Island, California), the recruits were issued winter uniforms and put aboard a ship headed for Vladivostok, but were not told their destination. Because Hartman was literate and exhibited an aptitude for mechanical things, he was assigned to AEF Headquarters as a radio operator. In late 1919, he was sent to G Company as a replacement and became the company's clerk on its return to Manila. Later assigned to the Presidio of San Francisco, Hartman left the Army in 1922 as a sergeant. When War II came, he was 39. Eager to do his part, he rejoined the Army as a private, serving with the 4th and 16th Armored Divisions in Europe during the final push from Germany into Czechoslovakia. He retired in 1959 as a Master Sergeant, 41 years after his military service began. He died in 1997 at the Soldier's and Airmen's Home in Washington, D.C., and is buried at Arlington National Cemetery.

The 31st Infantry's last contingent left Siberia on April 1, 1920. Lieutenant Sylvian Kindall recalled "We were out of Siberia at last … there was no cheering and little to be said. In the long months past, perhaps something of the dark, brooding Asiatic spirit had crept into our lives." Republican Congresswoman Jeanette Rankin of Montana took a more negative view of the campaign's participants, proposing that the troops be discharged in Siberia and that the U.S. purchase land for them to settle there because their bodies would be too diseased and their morals too corrupted to ever be permitted to come home. They did not go home, at least not as units. The 27th and 31st Infantry Regiments returned to the Philippines and while the 27th departed for Hawaii in 1921, the 31st remained abroad until 1987 when its 1st Battalion was inactivated in Korea.

The regiment had carried out its orders with courage, humanity, and dignity. Sixteen of its members had been awarded the Distinguished Service Cross, 24 were killed in action, 8 died of wounds received in action, and 52 were wounded in action, testifying to the valor of a generation of Americans fighting in a far-off, miserable place to accomplish an unclear mission. It would not be the last time.

In October of 1920, American dead were exhumed and returned to the United States.

2 Return to Manila, 1920–1932

Fort William McKinley, near Manila, became the 31st Infantry Regiment's home on its return from Siberia. When its last contingent returned from Siberia on April 17, 1920, the entire regiment was stationed at the same post for the first time in its history. In commemoration of its service there, the 31st began calling itself the "Polar Bears," a nickname that endured. By then, most of the regiment's members had completed a 2-year tour of overseas duty, enabling them to depart for the United States soon after returning to Manila. Among those departing was Colonel Frederick W. Bugbee (46), the Regimental Commander, who was succeeded by Colonel Ralph H. Van Deman (55) on April 5, 1920.

During the Spanish-American War Van Deman had left his job as an Army surgeon to volunteer for an intelligence development and mapping mission in Cuba, Puerto Rico, and the Philippines. In 1901, he was assigned to the Bureau of Insurgent Records in Manila, where he developed an indigenous counter-intelligence network. He was one of the first nine officers selected to attend the Army War College. In 1907, he became Chief of the General Staff's Mapping Division. He was expelled from China when the Japanese Ambassador protested American mapping of China's rails, roads, and rivers. In 1917, he persuaded the Secretary of War to establish a Military Intelligence Division on the War Department General Staff, earning him fame as the father of modern military intelligence. In 1920, he returned to the Philippines to command the 31st Infantry. In command for 3 years, Van Deman was the longest-serving commander the regiment has had.

Colonel Van Deman's influence was much wider than the scope of his duties in the regiment. Before leaving Washington, he persuaded the Secretary of War that it would be useful for officers stationed in the Philippines and China to travel throughout East Asia and report back to the War Department Intelligence Staff on what they observed. He encouraged selected officers to travel to places of military interest while on leave status or en route home when their overseas tours of duty ended. Before departing, those officers were briefed by Colonel Van Deman on sites they and their wives might find interesting, providing cover for observing things of intelligence value. In Manila, Van Deman persuaded the Governor General to support periodic exchange visits with the British in Singapore and Hong Kong, the Dutch in the East Indies (now Indonesia), and the French in Indochina (now Vietnam, Laos, and Cambodia). Officers with friends in the 15th Infantry Regiment at Tientsin, China, were encouraged to visit them on annual leave and explore some of China in the process. To Van Deman, it was important for promising officers to learn about the region's terrain, population, and military establish-

46

ments. He took his cue from European armies with long histories of sending observers to distant shores, but Van Deman had to be more creative, because although the War Department approved such endeavors, no money came with the approval.

The 31st Infantry's return to Manila was not as pleasant as expected for some. Men who had married Russian women in Siberia had to arrange for their commercial passage to Manila, since the Army had no funds to move dependents from Siberia. The task was especially difficult because there was no passenger service between Vladivostok and Manila, requiring a journey to Japan and a change of shipping companies there. Further complicating matters, troops arriving from Vladivostok were quarantined in Manila's port area for two weeks, unable to search for accommodations for wives who were already en route. When wives finally arrived, men had trouble finding them a decent place to live because others stationed in the area occupied the best private quarters available.

Officers were quartered based on seniority. The regimental commander, executive officer, and battalion commanders were assigned comfortable government-leased quarters on General Luna and Padre Burgos Streets in Intramuros or at Cuartel de España or Fort Santiago inside the old walled city. Most others lived in rented private quarters in Manila's Malate District but some lived in distant Pasay, 15 miles further south, requiring them to commute to Manila by car or bus. All enlisted personnel, regardless of grade, were required to maintain a space in the barracks, but those married to Filipinas kept a second residence in town.

When the 27th Infantry departed for Hawaii in December 1920, the 45th and 57th Philippine Scout Infantry Regiments were formed at Fort McKinley with American officers and Filipino enlisted personnel. To make room for the new units, the 31st Infantry Regiment's Headquarters Company, Band, and 1st Battalion moved to Cuartel de España,

On a break (Association archives).

an old Spanish barracks tucked inside the southwest corner of Intramuros. Service Company moved to nearby Santa Lucia Barracks, a long three-story building adjacent to Santa Lucia Gate near the port. The 2nd and 3rd Battalions moved to Estado Mayor (also known as Cuartel de Infantería), the former Spanish Viceroy's compound along the Pasig River, just outside the walled city's southeast side.

Adding to the move's turbulence, men who had completed their two-year overseas tours were leaving each month. Their replacements took months to form team relationships and acclimatize themselves to conditions in the Philippines. By the spring of 1921, the regiment could finally settle down to a garrison routine. Reveille was at 6:00, breakfast at 6:30 followed by close and extended order drill, which started each day at 8:00. Indoor classes in company day rooms were held from 11:00 to 11:30, followed by dinner at noon. From 1:00 to 4:00 each afternoon, quiet was observed in the barracks, permitting men to sleep since training was considered impractical in the tropical heat. Wool shirts were prescribed for drill because of their absorbent qualities. Battalion parades and inspections were held on Saturday mornings.

Infantrymen caught guard duty every 12 days, serving on a guard force formed from details from every company. Men stationed at Estado Mayor had to march a considerable distance in the afternoon heat to regimental guard mount in Cuartel de España's courtyard. Among the most dreaded guard posts was Headquarters, Philippine Department at Fort Santiago. This detail had a long, hot (or wet, depending on the season) march down General Luna Street, past the Cathedral and Fire Station #4, through the Army Ordnance Depot, to the guard room at the foot of the stairs leading to Topside, the office of the Philippine Department Commander.

As the only all–American infantry regiment in the Philippines, the 31st performed security and ceremonial functions for the Governor General. When a gunfight broke out between members of the Philippine Constabulary and Manila's civil police in 1920, the 31st was called to intercede. The regiment served as General Leonard Wood's honor guard when he became Governor General in 1921 and performed the same function for General Douglas MacArthur when he became Military Advisor to the Philippine Commonwealth in 1935. In 1922, the regiment paraded in honor of Japan's Baron General Tanaka and Britain's Prince of Wales, among others.

View of a sentry box on top of the wall, Manila, Philippines, between 1935 and 1937 (Association archives, courtesy Jim Zimmerman).

Although garrison duty was normally unexciting, there were abundant sources of off-duty recreation. In June 1920, the Philippine Department authorized rest and recreation (R&R) leave to China and Japan for officers and enlisted men of outstanding bearing and appearance. On June 28, the first R&R contingents left for leave at Cheefoo, Chingwangtao, and Tsingtao, China, and Nagasaki, Japan. Second Lieutenants Ralph M. Oder and Edward M. Miner were the first members of the regiment to participate. Troops could also take R&R at Camp John Hay, a rest and recreation (R&R) center in the cool hills of northern Luzon, near Baguio, or obtain passes to numerous other scenic spots in the Philippines.

The 31st also played a role in humanitarian relief operations. In mid–January 1922, four officers and 60 enlisted men of the 2nd and 3rd Battalions erected three tent cities for people left homeless by a fire that ravaged Manila's Tondo district. They erected more than 250 tents in less than 4 hours, earning the regiment a letter of appreciation from Manila's Mayor.[1] Another relief effort, not verified by surviving records, is a dispatch of troops to Japan in 1923. The following, reprinted from the December 1938 *United States Army Recruiting News*, reports:

> When a terrific tidal wave, earthquake, and fire very nearly leveled several Japanese coastal cities and the Japanese government sent out a frantic appeal for relief, the War Department radioed Headquarters of the 31st Infantry to dispatch immediately a picked group of officers and men, with supplies, to Kobe and Yokohama. The radio message was received at the headquarters of the regiment late on a payday night (August 31, 1923) when personnel of the regiment were scattered all over the Manila area. Yet within three hours after the message had been received, every man of the 31st Infantry was back in his barracks. The "round-up" was effected by telephone, by word of mouth, and by motorcycle messengers who raced all over the Manila area. The hundred percent response to the midnight message is typical of the spirit of this regiment of infantry, a spirit which continues to this day.

A powerful earthquake, followed by a tsunami, struck Japan's Kanto Plain on September 1, 1923, resulting in over 100,000 deaths and 1.9 million left homeless. The American Consulate and several others were destroyed and the American, British, and Italian Consuls lost their lives. On September 3, President Coolidge initiated a Red Cross relief drive that collected $12 million. Although some 1930s–era veterans (Pat Ramey, Farrell Lowe, Emmitt Rimmer, and Ernest Cloud) heard about the regiment's participation in the subsequent relief effort from old-timers who were stationed at Manila with them, no surviving records verify the mission.[2] According to these men's recollections, a composite battalion was formed at Estado Mayor under the Deputy Regimental Commander, Lieutenant Colonel Gunstler, and dispatched with relief supplies aboard Navy ships to the Japanese port of Nagasaki. Regardless of U.S. government support, it seems likely that U.S. troops and relief supplies never got beyond Nagasaki because anti-foreign rioting broke out in and around Tokyo, Yokohama, and Kobe in the disaster's wake. Korean and Chinese émigrés were accused of looting and arson, prompting the massacre of thousands by vengeful mobs and in some cases, by Japanese troops and police. Whole sections of the devastated cities were closed to outsiders to conceal the massacres. Under the circumstances, it would have been difficult for any foreign power to conduct humanitarian assistance operations.

In 1923, First Lieutenant Goodwyn took a two-month leave to tour East Asia, a beneficiary of Colonel Van Deman's intelligence development effort. Goodwyn traveled to China, Korea, and Japan on official military orders and on his return to Manila in June, submitted his report to the Commanding General, Philippine Department, retaining an "onion skin" copy for his own files.

Lieutenant Goodwyn traveled from Manila to Shanghai aboard the destroyer USS *Pillsbury*, which was dispatched to explore the mouth of the Yangtze Kiang River for a suitable submarine base (none was found). Arriving 3 months before the great earthquake, *Pillsbury* next paid a port call at Kobe, Japan, where Goodwyn caught a steamer to Yokohama. His subsequent travels took him by train to Tokyo, Nikko, Kamakura, Kyoto, and Shimonoseki before catching another steamer to Fusan (Pusan), Korea. From there, he traveled by train to Keijo (Seoul). Mukden, Peking (Beijing), Hankow, Nanking, Shanghai, Canton, and Hong Kong, gaining an education of immeasurable value to a young officer. Some of his observations, none surprising, are summarized as follows:

1. Japanese troops everywhere seem well-equipped, well-drilled, well-dressed, and disciplined. They are ubiquitous on the streets of all cities visited, including those in Korea. Photography of Japanese military facilities is prohibited but was able to watch Japanese soldiers drill at several locations. Troops are responsive and their training is effective. Japanese rails are efficient and electrification of the country is being advanced by construction of more hydroelectric power plants. Arable land is efficiently cultivated but fertilized with human waste, inviting disease. Japanese seem less hostile toward foreigners since the Naval Limitations Treaty was signed in Washington.

2. Japanese troops in Korea seem to have little to do but are everywhere and clearly resented. Korea is poorly developed and although the Japanese are doing some development, little is exported or imported. The Korean people seem shiftless and indifferent to foreigners.

3. Manchurian troops are paid by the local warlord, Chan Tao Lin, who is friendly to westerners. Troops there are better equipped and drilled here than elsewhere in China. Locals believe Chan Tao Lin is a Japanese puppet and his army is paid by Japan.

4. Troops observed elsewhere in China are dirty, poorly clothed, ill-equipped, and their units are skeletonized by desertion because the government has insufficient funds to pay or equip them. Drills seem ineffectual. Located eight arsenals. Army and police are unable to cope with widespread banditry, causing people weary of insecurity and strife to hunger for change. China's agriculture is less efficient than Japan's and only its largest cities have electricity and sewage. The government does little for its people and there is little unity in Chinese society, with factions unable to find common ground. As in Japan, the rail system linking major cities is well-run and well-maintained but travel beyond the larger cities is primitive since few roads are paved.

The 31st Infantry was assigned to the Philippine Division from October 22, 1921, to June 26, 1931. Throughout that period, division field training exercises were held at Fort McKinley (Rizal), Fort Mills (Corregidor), and Fort Stotsenburg (Angeles). Until 1936, the 31st Infantry's planned wartime station was on the fortress island of Corregidor, dominating the entrance to Manila Bay. Annual field exercises began further north at Lingayen Gulf but always ended at Corregidor. They were usually preceded with a no-notice alert to determine how much of the regiment could be assembled in an emergency and what had to be done to improve alert procedures and reunite stragglers with their units.

In the Field (Association archives).

The experience of one of the regiment's members illustrates a pattern that became routine during the 1930s. On December 18, 1931, Private Ernest Calvin Cloud of Stone County, Missouri, was assigned to G Company at Estado Mayor. Having lied about his age at the recruiting station, he was just 16 years old when he started basic training at Fort McKinley's B Range. Before Cloud had been in the Philippines two months, the Philippine Department curtailed basic training and sent the regiment on War Plan Orange maneuvers.[3] The 31st traveled from Manila to Fort McKinley, the Philippine Division's assembly area, and then up to Lingayen Gulf, an expected landing site if the Japanese were to invade. From Lingayen Gulf, the 31st practiced a series of southward delaying actions past Clark Field and Fort Stotsenburg to the Calumpit Bridge, down the Bataan Peninsula, and across the 2.9 mile North Channel to Corregidor. The exercise was to have been a dress rehearsal for how to fight the war, but ten years later the Japanese got to Lingayen Gulf first. No stockpiles of food, medicine, barrier materials, and ammunition were established along intended delay lines and protected dispersal fields for aircraft did not exist, rendering a coherent defense much more problematic than planners expected.

In 1930 and 1931, a bewildering succession of command changes threw the regiment into 15 months of turmoil. When Colonel James Kimbrough completed his standard 24-month command tour in March 1930, he was succeeded by Colonel Earle W. Tanner (54), who remained in command only 5 months. The reason for Colonel Tanner's unusually short command tour is not recorded. Lieutenant Colonel Edward L. Hooper (51), his deputy, served as interim commander for 4 months while awaiting Tanner's successor, Colonel Gustave A. Wieser (57), who died just one month later in January 1931.

Colonel Wieser's death was a sad blow to the regiment and the Army. He was a well-known, respected advocate of a professional NCO corps who had served as an NCO during the Spanish-American War, where his performance earned him a commission. He later commanded the 3rd Infantry Regiment on the Mexican border, earning him an equally stellar reputation as one of the Army's best trainers. Colonel Wieser's deputy, Lieutenant Colonel George A. Lynch (50), commanded for the next 5 months while awaiting Colonel Lorenzo Gasser's arrival.

As at all overseas garrisons, officers were permitted to bring their families to the Philippines at government expense. Among those to do so was Captain Robert L. Wright, who commanded B Company in Manila after completing the Infantry Officers Advanced Course at Fort Benning. With his wife and two children (Homer and Mary Elizabeth, aged 9 and 11), Wright sailed from New York City on the USAT *Grant*, a former German passenger ship of World War I vintage. Two weeks later, the *Grant* reached the Panama Canal where mules slowly pulled the ship through locks while passengers sweltered in the searing tropical heat. Two weeks thereafter, the ship stopped briefly at San Francisco to refuel and take on supplies before sailing on to Manila via refueling stops at Hawaii and Guam. The entire journey took an agonizing 52 days. In Manila, the Wrights eventually took up residence in the Sequoia Apartments, connected Spanish-style houses with tiled floors, no screens, and mosquito netting over each bed. Mrs. Wright was able to hire a cook, a houseboy, and a housekeeper who came daily. The children went to school from 7 to noon, enabling everyone to get home for lunch and a siesta since studying was impossible in the heat. School lasted only from September to March because of the heat.

On Monday, 1 February 1932, the Wright children came home to find their dad hurriedly packing and rushing back to the Cuartel de España, where his company was stationed. Rumors had been circulating that the Japanese might invade China. That night, the entire 31st Infantry Regiment boarded the USAT *Chaumont* bound for Shanghai.

3 Shanghai, 1932

In Shanghai, events were unfolding that would generate the first of the 31st Infantry's peacekeeping missions. Shanghai was a unique experiment in colonialism. China had given Britain trade rights in the city in 1843, but retained responsibility for protecting foreign residents. Over time, France and the United States joined Britain in the Trade Market. Dissatisfied with Chinese public services and security, the three created a protected International Settlement on July 11, 1854, linking their communities under a common governing body with its own court, defense budget, and full powers of self-government. Later, Russia and Japan joined the arrangement. Chinese citizens could live in the Settlement and take part in its government, but had to pay taxes to the governing body like all other residents.

Shanghai, 1932. The Garden Bridge spans Soochow Creek (foreground) where it flows into the Whangpoo River. The Anglican church spire is at lower right. The building with the cupola across the street is the British Embassy. Shanghai's Bund (the stock exchange) and the German, American and Japanese consulates are to the left of the bridge. (Unless otherwise noted, all photographs in this chapter are from Association archives, courtesy the Klein family. All were taken in 1932).

By 1899, the International Settlement had become roughly 7.5 miles long and 2.3 miles wide and by 1925, its inhabitants included over 40,000 foreigners and around 1.2 million Chinese. Its multinational security force, the 2,000-man Shanghai Volunteer Corps (SVC), included contingents from each nationality constituting the government, including four companies of Americans. The only paid component of the SVC was a White Russian Regiment which served as an adjunct to the Shanghai Municipal Police. Also included in the SVC were Chinese and Japanese companies, an odd combination, given the animosity between their countries. In 1927, the 4th Marine Regiment reinforced the garrison, establishing a close working relationship with the British-led SVC and British Empire troops. The British contingent, which would grow to four regiments during the emergency, was initially a Sikh regiment from India. French troops garrisoned the separately administered French Concession adjacent to the International Settlement. They served under their own national command and France was not represented in the SVC.

In 1931, Japan annexed Manchuria, renamed it *Manchukuo*, and began provoking incidents aimed at creating an excuse to grab more of China. The excuse came in January 1932 when Japanese citizens, including a monk, were slain by vengeful Chinese mobs in Shanghai. Japan provoked the outburst and was prepared to exploit it with a fleet of 30 combatant ships, including an aircraft carrier, anchored along the Whangpoo (Huangpu) River. Disregarding the Shanghai Municipal Council's agreement to compensate victims' families and property owners, Japanese warships shelled the Woosung forts guarding the city's seaward approaches and its carrier launched 40 aircraft to bomb the city on January 28. The next morning, 3000 Japanese Marines came ashore to seize the city's Hongkew business district but initially made little headway, battling a surprisingly resolute, well-trained metropolitan police force and Chinese Nationalist troops.

The Mission

Fearing it might be Japan's next target, China's government fled Nanking (Nanjing), 190 miles to the northwest, to a safer refuge further inland. Approaching Shanghai's western edge, the Chinese Nineteenth Route Army, a 30,000-man force from the Canton area led by warlord Jiang Guangnai, added another complication. Jiang's brutal reputation and his German-trained troops worried Shanghai's city council, prompting them to extend a bribe to keep his troops out of the city. Jiang accepted the bribe but ordered his troops in anyway. Because Jiang despised foreign concessions, his army posed a greater threat to the International Settlement than the Japanese who were partners in the concession. If fighting spilled into the International Settlement, the SVC would likely be overwhelmed, prompting frantic calls for reinforcement. British troops from Hong Kong and Malaya, French troops from Indochina, and American troops from the Philippines were promptly alerted and dispatched. Early on Monday, February 1, 1932, Colonel Lorenzo D. Gasser, Commander of the 31st Infantry Regiment in Manila, received the following order, passed down from Headquarters, Philippine Department:

Washington D.C., Jan 31, 1932
(Rec'd) 8 A. M. February 1. 1932

From the Chief of Staff

To Commanding General
Philippine Department

On request of the American Consul General, Shanghai, to furnish further protection for American lives and property in International Settlement, President directs that the 31st Infantry be dispatched to Shanghai at once. Navy will furnish transportation using *Chaumont* or other craft. Equip troops for indefinite stay and every emergency. Leave animals behind for present. On arrival have Commanding Officer report to senior American Officer ashore for instructions and duty.

MacArthur

Within the hour, officers were assembled at Regimental Headquarters to receive a verbal movement order. The move required transferring the post of Manila, its property, installations, animals, and records to the 45th Infantry (Philippine Scouts). By noon, detachments of Medical, Signal, Quartermaster, Finance, Ordnance, and Chemical Warfare troops were attached to the regiment from other units in Manila. Officers from throughout the Philippine Department were reassigned to the 31st to bring its leadership up to full wartime authorization but few enlisted men were available to flesh out the under-strength line companies. In less than 12 hours, the regiment, which had been in the same barracks for nearly 12 years, made a complete transition from garrison duty in the tropics to preparation for battle under winter conditions in China. That night, the 31st began boarding USAT *Chaumont*, which got underway the next morning.

Aboard ship, COL Gasser assembled his officers to emphasize the mission's international character, stressing the importance of orderliness and discipline. British, French, Chinese, Russian, and Japanese troops of the SVC would observe the 31st closely and draw conclusions about the American Army's quality. The 31st Infantry would not give them reason to doubt the ability and dedication of American soldiers. Aboard ship, cholera inoculations were administered and tropical khaki uniforms were exchanged for winter wool olive drab. Little information was available about the situation unfolding in Shanghai, but a contingency plan was developed to make a forced landing under cover of machine gun and howitzer fire from the *Chaumont*'s decks.

On February 4, debarkation orders were published, directing the issue of two sandwiches per man, filling canteens, and establishing ammunition distribution points aboard ship. The *Chaumont* dropped anchor the next morning near the mouth of the Whangpoo River, awaiting instructions from the senior American officer ashore, the 4th Marine Regiment's Commander. Japanese dive bombers were devastating northeastern Shanghai and a steady exchange of artillery fire could be heard in the distance. Tension ran high as the regiment awaited instructions. Three hours later, the *Chaumont* resumed its journey up the Whangpoo, sailing between Chinese forts and Japanese warships which had been firing at each other only minutes earlier. As though coordinated, all held their fire as the *Chaumont* passed. Neither the Japanese nor Chinese wished to add to their list of enemies—at least not then.

In Shanghai

As the *Chaumont* berthed at the China Merchants dock, unloading parties promptly went to work. F Company debarked to guard supplies that would be stored in the New World Building that night. The remainder of the regiment remained aboard ship, debarking the next morning. The regimental band played at the column's head as F Company marched three miles from the dock to the New World Building at the intersection of Nanking and Tibet Roads. Chinese civilians watched pensively, not knowing what to

expect from the newcomers. Shanghai Municipal Police and British-led Sikh troops guarded every intersection. Explosions echoed in the distance, shaking the ground as Japanese and Chinese guns resumed their thundering exchange along the river.

Headquarters and Machine gun Companies and the 2nd and 3rd Battalions took quarters in the New World Building. The 1st Battalion spent its first night ashore under the Shanghai Race Track's grandstand, moving later to an abandoned library on adjacent Bubbling Well Road. The 31st Infantry and 4th Marine Regiments formed a task force under the latter's commander. On February 7, a sergeant of the 31st Infantry raised an American garrison flag on a makeshift pole. Ceremonies raising the flag each morning and lowering it each evening was an expression of pride and a symbol of solidarity among all Americans in the city.

Chapei District, where the most intense fighting occurred between Chinese and

On February 7, a sergeant of the 31st Infantry raised an American garrison flag on a makeshift pole.

Opposite, top: This photograph of F Company's march down Tibet Road is inscribed, "The yanks come."

Bottom: Sikh troops from Britain's Indian Army. In 1863 the International Settlement was established when the British and American sections united. But unlike Hong Kong, a British Crown Colony, Shanghai remained sovereign Chinese territory. In 1932, foreign armies came to protect the expanded International Settlement.

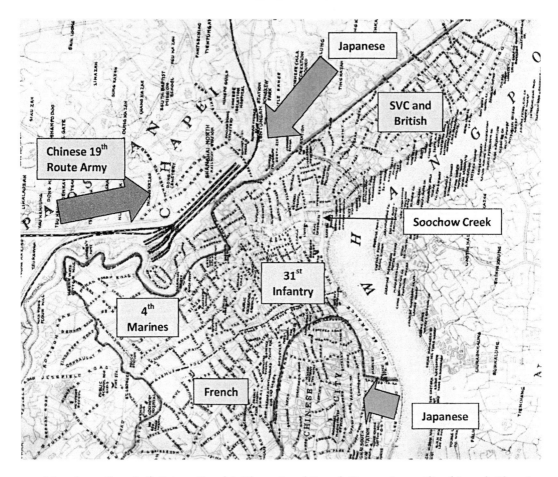

Map shows Shanghai's International Settlement and French Concession outlined in red. Chapei District, where the most intense fighting occurred between Chinese and Japanese troops, is just north of the Settlement boundary around the rail yard.

Japanese troops, is just north of the Settlement boundary around the rail yard. The *Chaumont* docked just south of where Soochow Creek enters the Whangpoo River. The 31st Infantry was billeted adjacent to the oval-shaped Public Recreation Ground in the center of the International Settlement.

The International Settlement's perimeter was ringed with strong concrete blockhouses and steel observation turrets. Each blockhouse had a heavy steel door, telephone connections, firing ports for 2 machine guns and 8 rifles, and a searchlight on a parapet above. Living conditions were hospitable since each blockhouse had its own urinal, electric heater, and folding cots for use between guard shifts. On the outside, blockhouses were fortified with triple layers of sandbags to absorb shrapnel and reduce the risk of penetration by antitank weapons. Only a direct hit by artillery posed a threat. Medics were attached to each company, ensuring prompt treatment of injuries. Hot meals were brought forward by truck and a Salvation Army car made regular rounds with cans of hot coffee to help keep men awake on guard duty.

The regiment's area of responsibility faced the suburb of Chapei, where Chinese troops confronted the Japanese. COL Gasser, his battalion commanders, and members of the regimental staff reconnoitered the perimeter on February 6. Over the next 48 hours, the 2nd Battalion relieved the Royal Scots Fusiliers along Soochow (Suzhou) Creek while the 1st Battalion reinforced the Settlement Police in the southern sector. The 3rd Battalion and Howitzer Platoon remained at the New World Building in reserve. A squad of riflemen manned each outpost in the regiment's sector. Troops marched to their posts in full field gear and with bayonets fixed. Uniform discipline (complete, clean uniform with overcoat and polished footwear) was rigidly enforced to convey a thoroughly professional, intimidating image. Sentries were

Right: Steel observation turret. *Below:* A squad of the 31st Infantry Regiment in Shanghai.

ordered to keep Chinese and Japanese troops, other than members of the SVC, out of the International Settlement. If Chinese troops were driven into the Settlement by pursuing Japanese, they were to be disarmed and turned over to the Settlement Police Force. If mobs tried to storm the perimeter, troops were to shoot only if authorized by an NCO and only to wound, if possible.

On February 10, the 2nd Battalion's sector was extended across Soochow Creek to relieve units of the SVC, which moved farther northeast. The 3rd Battalion assumed responsibility for patrolling south of the creek. Chinese troops occupying positions opposite the 2nd Battalion pointed their weapons at Americans who warily returned the gesture. American troops never knew what to expect from the Chinese, some of whom were overtly friendly while others were sullen and menacing. On February 12, the combatants agreed to a truce. The next day, passes were issued to 50 men of the 31st, permitting them the liberty of the International Settlement.

The cease-fire did not hold. The Japanese reinforced their Marine contingent to 7,000 men and demanded that all Chinese troops withdraw 20 kilometers from the International Settlement's boundaries. In effect, that would mean surrendering all of Shanghai. Fighting intensified in the city's Hongkew District as Chinese reinforcements arrived, prompting Japan to dispatch reinforcements of its own, eventually swelling its force to over 90,000 men. To counter the Japanese buildup, China's German-trained Fifth Army, was sent to the city's northeastern quadrant with two divisions but they arrived without support or their German trainer and advisor, Colonel Georg Wetzell, who absented himself from the fighting.

A public execution. Toward the end of January 1932, the Chinese Nineteenth Route Army, a 30,000-man force from the Canton area led by warlord Jiang Guangnai, added another complication. The reputation of Jiang and his German-trained troops for brutality had plenty of competition from Chinese communists, the Japanese military and Nationalist police.

Outside the Settlement perimeter, barbarity and inhumanity took place on a bewildering scale. To avoid provoking an attack on the International Settlement, Americans and their allies were not permitted to intervene, forcing them to watch helplessly as fellow humans were brutalized. Chinese Communists executed officials of the Nationalist government and other Chinese who were suspected of collaborating or fraternizing with Japanese troops. Nationalist police executed people suspected of aiding the Communists or Japanese. In a field just a few blocks away, Japanese officers wielding Samurai swords beheaded captured Chinese officers, suspected spies, and public officials. Age and gender meant nothing. The Chinese people were victims of every side. Unless they lived in the International Settlement, they had no one to turn to for protection. In consequence, the International Settlement became a magnet for refugees.

On February 16, fighting unexpectedly resumed. Small arms fire rattled in sudden, intense exchanges throughout the day while warplanes struck the city repeatedly. Artillery from both sides thundered in earth-shaking outbursts, indiscriminately killing hundreds of civilians. As night fell, the sky glowed red from city's burning northern districts. Much of the area would be wrecked by bombs, artillery, and fierce house-to-house fighting over the next several days. Hampered by slow, cumbersome, corruption-plagued logistics, Chinese defenses deteriorated steadily under relentless Japanese pressure. On February 18, the 31st Infantry's 3rd Battalion relieved SVC units in the sector north of Soochow Creek where fighting was heaviest. The 1st Battalion assumed responsibility for a sector south of Soochow Creek.

Toward evening on February 20, two armored cars armed with 37mm cannon and machine guns, accompanied by a platoon of Japanese Marines, halted 10 feet from Blockhouse B. Members of the 31st Infantry's Howitzer Platoon and a squad from I Company manned the outpost. Across the intersection, a Chinese machine gun poked from a second story window. The weapon's operator, a friendly sort who exchanged daily greetings with the Americans, was nicknamed "Charlie Chan" by the troops. Charlie operated his gun well and periodically threw German-made "potato masher" grenades at the armored cars, seeking to roll them underneath where there was no armor. After a brisk fight that resulted in no casualties on either side, the Japanese withdrew, leaving Charlie

Here Japanese Marines are in action near Chapei's railroad station.

An intense artillery exchange resulted in hundreds of civilian casualties, and that night the northern part of the city was left in flames.

in firm control of his intersection. During the exchange, Blockhouse B took numerous hits meant for the Japanese. Fragments from Charlie Chan's grenades sprung hundreds of small leaks in the outpost's sandbag face. From then on, the site was known as "windy corner."

On February 22, a civilian emissary for the Chinese Nineteenth Route Army's commander asked the 3rd Battalion, 31st Infantry's Commander, Major Leonard T. Gerow, if any Japanese troops were in his sector. Gerow, who would later became a lieutenant general and command V Corps in Europe during World War II, noticed the man looking nervously at an American work detail wearing blue denim fatigue uniforms, the color worn by Japanese Marines. Until World War II, Army work details wore blue denim fatigue uniforms similar to those worn by the Navy. Gerow soon recognized the problem and banned denims from the perimeter. On February 25, Britain's Argyll and Sutherland Highlanders relieved the 31st Infantry throughout its sector of the perimeter.

On February 29, a Japanese flanking maneuver unhinged Chinese defenses northeast of the city. An unsupported division-scale counterattack failed, spelling imminent defeat for the Chinese. Fighting slackened on March 2, when the supply-starved Chinese Nineteenth Route Army withdrew westward to escape a looming double envelopment by Japanese troops. On March 4, the League of Nations passed a resolution demanding a

Top: A vehicle patrol with an armored car. *Bottom:* Armored cars in the city.

Chinese soldiers are shown manning a bomb-blasted sector north of Soochow Creek.

ceasefire. Two days later, the Chinese unilaterally agreed to cease operations but sporadic skirmishes continued wherever the Japanese pressed too hard against isolated pockets of the Chinese Fifth Army.

On March 7, the USAT *Grant* docked at Shanghai with 159 reinforcements from Manila. All were given a short period of orientation training before being sent to line companies. These were the only reinforcements sent to the regiment during its stay in Shanghai, still leaving the regiment far short of its wartime authorization. All platoons and companies were maintained but were around one-third smaller than they would have been at full strength. On March 8, the 1st Battalion dispersed a mob of Chinese beating Japanese civilians who lived in the settlement. The next day, the Japanese naval landing force Chief of Staff called on the 1st Battalion Commander, Major Robert O. Baldwin, to convey his admiral's appreciation. On March 14, a League of Nations delegation arrived to broker a peace agreement. On March 18, the Woosung forts fell to the Japanese and soon thereafter Shanghai's commercial life began returning to normal, albeit under Japanese control.

Throughout its time on line, the 31st was well organized, equipped, and supplied. The Howitzer Platoon had two 75mm howitzers positioned behind the most dangerous sector. Machine gun companies (D, H, and M) each had 16 .30 caliber water-cooled machine guns and each rifle company had 4 air-cooled .30 calibers that were lighter and easier to handle. All 84 machine guns were kept at blockhouses. If trouble had come, the 31st would have taken a heavy toll. An ammunition supply point was established near each blockhouse and an ammunition reserve was kept at each battalion headquarters. Extra rifle ammunition, grenades, tear gas candles, and magazines for automatic rifles

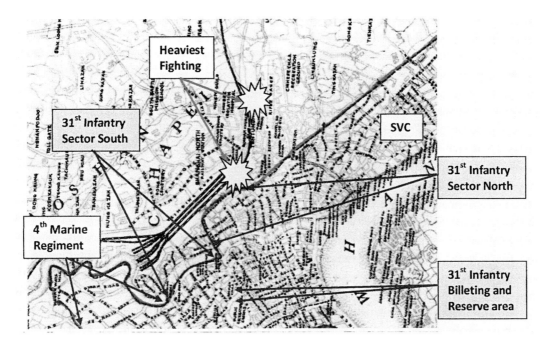

Heaviest Fighting

31st Infantry Sector South

4th Marine Regiment

SVC

31st Infantry Sector North

31st Infantry Billeting and Reserve area

Map shows the 31st Infantry Regiment's sectors relative to the zone of heaviest fighting between the Japanese and Chinese.

were kept in forward positions. That way, positions could be doubled in strength in minutes if an emergency arose. Reinforcement routes were reconnoitered and guides were posted at key points to ensure reinforcements could reach their stations by day or night. Large signboards in Chinese were placed at each post to show Chinese troops permissible points of entry if they were forced to retreat into the International Settlement.

On March 11, the 31st Infantry was relieved by Britain's Argyll and Sutherland Highlanders but a week later, the 2nd Battalion returned to the line, relieving the British. At that point, the entire regimental line was manned by only two companies because the fighting between Japanese and Chinese had mostly ended and refugees were beginning to stream back to Chapei from the Settlement. On March 25, the 3rd Battalion relieved the 2nd Battalion and on April 1, the 31st Infantry handed off its sector on both sides of Soochow Creek to the British East Lancashire Regiment. At that point, the 31st Infantry became the Settlement's general reserve, concentrating on training and internal security patrols.

The winter of 1932 was cold and wet, aiding the spread of disease in the International Settlement's refugee-crowded streets. Sanitation and food storage were constant problems because rats greatly outnumbered humans. Two members of the 31st, whose names are now lost to history, died of influenza during their tour of duty and were buried in Shanghai. Consul General Edwin S. Cunningham and Colonel Lorenzo Gasser led the burial procession. Although under fire on numerous occasions when Chinese and Japanese troops fired wildly at each other around the settlement's perimeter, no member of the regiment was ever hit. The only American to die in combat was Robert Short, an Army Reserve Lieutenant working for Boeing Aviation. He was delivering an experimental fighter plane to the Chinese at Nanking when Japanese planes began bombing Shanghai.

Some sectors of the city were reduced to rubble by the fighting.

He took off on his own to intercede. On February 22, he attacked a flight of Japanese naval aircraft bombing a Chinese railway station. He shot down one bomber before going down in flames himself.[1] He was given a hero's funeral by the Chinese.

Although street fighting, artillery duels, and bombing raids had ended by late March, the peace that followed was uneasy. More than 20,000 Chinese civilians and 4000 Chinese troops had perished. Japan suffered 3000 killed but had clearly prevailed, a reality formalized by the Shanghai Ceasefire Agreement on May 5. The fighting had revealed China's military weakness and emboldened the Japanese to initiate another spasm of aggression in 1937 that would ultimately cost millions of lives and bring humiliation and utter devastation to its own homeland.

Settling In

As the crisis in Shanghai faded, the 31st Infantry settled down to a routine of garrison life. Training on individual soldier skills, squad and platoon battle drill, weapons maintenance, and even rifle and pistol marksmanship practice at military ranges around the city predominated. Unlike Manila where the duty day ended at noon due to the heat, the duty day in cooler Shanghai typically consumed all daylight hours. Sports competitions with the 4th Marines and British regiments punctuated the boredom. When the duty day ended, soldiers could receive a pass to leave the barracks and wander at their leisure around the International Settlement but were required to travel armed and in pairs. "Tea Houses" with cheap Chinese beer and attractive "hostesses" beckoned as they do in various forms around every military garrison worldwide. Unlike the constant international brawling that occurred at Vladivostok a generation earlier, troops of every national contingent were generally well-behaved, perhaps mindful of the importance of making a positive impression on others, especially the Japanese.

With peace restored, several of the 31st Infantry's officers requested and received permission to have their families join them from Manila. Among them was Captain Robert Wright, B Company's Commanding Officer. He and several other officers rented suites for their families at the comfortable Cathay Mansions Hotel near the regiment's barracks. Mrs. Wright and the children traveled to Shanghai by commercial ocean liner with a stop en route at Hong Kong. At Shanghai, the Wright children were enrolled at the American Mission School, to which they were taken by rickshaw daily. While danger abounded outside the International Settlement, people of every nationality could be confident of their safety inside its boundaries. Criminal activity certainly existed, but with so many armed soldiers and police moving about, serious offenses tended to be less common than in a typical American or European city of similar size. The Settlement's orderly main streets were more like those in contemporary Singapore than other Asian cities of the era.

With the children at school and the men on duty, the ladies shopped together on the International Settlement's famed market streets. Jade, silver, and copper jewelry or housewares could be bought from skilled artisans at a fraction of their value. One silversmith in particular seemed a craftsman of rare talent. His artful designs inspired the wives of the regiment's surgeons, Mrs. William F. Sappington and Mrs. Charles M. Rylander, to suggest presenting silver cups to companies with the lowest venereal disease rates. VD was a serious matter in the 1930s since soldiers could be hospitalized for a month or more, during which they received no pay and for which they owed the Army additional time on their enlistments to make up for lost service. If an officer became infected with any strain of VD, he was required to resign. Regimental surgeons conducted monthly inspections to make sure no one was concealing an infection. To reduce the risks, several companies bought exclusive rights to brothels that agreed to serve no other customers. The regiment's surgeons made weekly inspections of the establishments to make sure they maintained proper health and sanitation standards. What would have been illegal in the Philippines, a U.S. territory, seemed a virtue in Shanghai.

The Shanghai Bowl

The silver cup idea soon grew to grander proportions. Inspired by the impressive ceremonial silver of British regiments in the Shanghai garrison, the officers' wives decided it would be nice to commemorate the regiment's service in Shanghai with a silver punch bowl and cups to be used at "*Despididas* and *Bienvenidas*" (hail and farewell) celebrations at Manila's Army-Navy Club when they returned. It was soon decided that each officer would buy one cup engraved with his name and each would pay a share of the punch bowl's cost. The regiment's 66 officers collected $1,600 for the set but the ladies heavily influenced its design. A ceremony called "the passing of the cups" was devised before the silver set was even completed.

The solid silver Shanghai bowl is 18 inches in diameter and 10 inches deep. It was originally displayed on an inch-thick triangular teakwood base, 12 inches per side, bearing

The Shanghai Bowl (Association archive).

three silver plaques on which were inscribed the purchasers' names. The teakwood base did not survive World War II but the Shanghai Bowl and the tradition it spawned live on. The purchasers formally deeded the bowl and the original cups to the regiment to keep the regiment's service in Shanghai forever fresh in the memory of those to come. And so it has. The only restriction established by the purchasers is that "the original 66 cups representing the 66 officers on duty with the US Army Troops in Shanghai would be all that would ever be with the punch bowl." That restriction was lifted by the regimental commander when the bowl and cups were returned to the regiment's custody in Korea in 1946.

When the regiment set sail for Manila aboard the USAT *Republic* in June 1932, its machine guns were wrapped in oriental rugs. Embroidered tablecloths and sets of fine china dishes were set aside for troop dining halls and every family carried back a treasure trove of fine goods. Fortunately, the Philippine government gave the regiment "freedom of the port," so no customs checks were made. The famous Shanghai Bowl that today graces regimental headquarters at Fort Drum, New York, followed the regiment to Manila in July 1932, becoming a treasured centerpiece of the regiment's traditions and a reflection of the bond between the regiment and its families and the bond across time existing among officers of the regiment.

Return to Manila

In June, when the 31st Infantry received orders to return to Manila, the event prompted a round of comradely farewells. The first of those was a presentation ceremony on June 28 at the Marine Corps Officers' Club. There, Lieutenant Colonel Frank A. Barker, the 4th Marine Regiment's interim commander, presented an enlarged Marine Corps insignia to Colonel Gasser for display at the 31st Infantry's headquarters in Manila. An article in the August 27, 1932, edition of the *Army and Navy Journal* describes the event:

> Colonel Barker spoke of the fine spirit of cooperation which had existed between the Marines and the Regulars and the pleasure afforded the Marines by their close contact with a Regular regiment and expressed a desire that the two Services could more often serve together. He offered the gift on behalf of his Marines in Shanghai as a symbol of the deep appreciation and respect which the Marines felt for the 31st Infantry and as a reminder of the common mission which so closely bound the two Services together under the most trying conditions in Shanghai.

Colonel Gasser's response in accepting the gift was equally appreciative of the Marines' brotherly spirit and of the pleasant associations resulting from their shared service in Shanghai. The following evening, the Marines hosted a U.S.–only farewell reception for the 31st Infantry's officers and wives at the Columbia Country Club. Both commanders' wish that their regiments could serve together once more was granted a decade later when Japan invaded the Philippines, but it was not an experience either would have wanted. Like the base on which the Shanghai Bowl was once displayed, the Marine Corps' gift to the regiment did not survive World War II. Its fate is unknown but the headquarters building in which it was displayed at Manila's Cuartel de España was burned by the Japanese as American troops approached to recapture the city in 1945.

Not to be outdone by the United States Marine Corps, the British Army also hosted farewells for the 31st Infantry. On the morning of June 28, a review was held in the regiment's honor on the International Settlement's parade ground with all British Regiments and the British-led Shanghai Volunteer Corps participating. In his farewell address to the regiment, Brigadier George Fleming, Commander of the British garrison, spoke highly of the regiment's professionalism, esprit, and comradeship as the regiment stood shoulder-to-shoulder with his troops to protect the International Settlement. That evening, the officers of the British Brigade hosted a reception at the French Club in the 31st Infantry's honor. On display around the room were trophies earned or captured by the regiments over their several hundred years of existence, including a silver statue of Arthur Wellesley, Duke of Wellington, who had commanded one of the garrison's regiments 136 years earlier. The display reaffirmed for officers of the 31st the wisdom of listening to their ladies when they suggested buying a regimental punch bowl and cups. As Brigadier Fleming escorted Colonel Gasser to the door at the end of the evening, the British band played "The Star Spangled Banner" and "God Save the King."

Most touching of the ceremonies marking the 31st Infantry's departure was its final parade to the docks. On July 1, the regiment's garrison flag was lowered for the last time at 6 p.m. as a bugler sounded "Retreat." Assembled on the parade field in front of its vacated billets, the regiment stood aligned by order of march. Colonel Gasser expressed pride in the regiment's professional bearing and deportment, noting that the eyes of the world would still be watching as they departed. On his command, the regiment began its march down Nanking Road. The Marine Band led, followed by the 31st Infantry's commander and staff, the 31st Infantry Band, Headquarters Company, Service Company, 2nd, 3rd, and 1st Battalions. A detachment of 5 armored cars from the SVC and a mounted Municipal Police escort preceded the column to clear traffic. A Guard of Honor composed of the 4th Marines; 1st Battalion, East Lancashire Regiment; 1st Battalion, Wiltshire Regiment; and 1st Battalion, Lincolnshire Regiment rendered a farewell "present arms" near

The Stars and Stripes and the Regimental colors, on parade in Shanghai.

the junction of Nanking Road and the Bund. There, a British military band replaced the Marine Band at the column's head. As the 31st neared the wharf, the SVC's White Russian Regiment rendered the final salute. While the 31st boarded the USAT *Republic* for its return to Manila, the British and Marine bands played popular tunes. As the last troops began ascending the gangplank, the band played the "Star Spangled Banner" with a large crowd of well-wishers standing reverently at attention.

Returning to the Philippines on July 28, PFC Ernest Calvin Cloud was among the last 36 men to arrive at Manila. They were a rear detachment left to transfer ammunition and property to the 4th Marine Regiment and ensure the regiment's billets were left clean and ready for new occupants. Since February, Cloud's home station, Estado Mayor, had been "guarded" by Philippine Scouts. Before departing for Shanghai, the 31st stored their locked foot lockers in locked company supply rooms, but on returning, they found all the locks were gone and many of their belongings had been "liberated." Ernest didn't care about the khaki uniforms he lost, but he was mad as hell about losing a 2-strand chain bracelet given him by a Stone County, Missouri, girl who later became his wife.

Ernest returned to the United States in 1934 and was discharged at Fort McDowell (Angel Island, California) on 27 July. He was shocked to learn that no one back home had ever heard of the Shanghai Expedition and most people didn't care. When Ernest participated in full uniform in a Labor Day celebration at Crane, Missouri, he expected people would honor veterans. What he got instead was jeers from a group of Civilian Conservation Corps jerks, driving their girls around in a new, olive drab 1935 Chevy pickup with USA in blocked white letters on the hood. Not much has changed in that respect. It was not much different for most men returning home in 1945, 1953, 1971, or today. Soldiers are heroes and the apple of every girl's eye when a war starts, but instant outcasts when a war ends or goes badly. It has been the same for soldiers of every country, win or lose, since the dawn of time. We do what we must and get on with our lives, quietly feeling sorry for the unfortunates who never felt the comradeship of a soldier's life and who will never experience the excitement of being whisked from boyhood to manhood to the tune of bullets passing by or through.

4 Manila Again, 1932–1941

On its return from Shanghai in 1932, the 31st Infantry resumed its accustomed training schedule. Once each year, the regiment went to Fort McKinley's B Range, just outside Manila, for firing practice and small unit training. Separately, it also conducted a two-week annual field exercise at its wartime defense area. A previous defense plan would have concentrated the regiment at Fort Mills on Corregidor but after the regiment's return from China, it alternately exercised near expected landing areas on Luzon. One was south of Manila near Batangas and Los Baños and the other was to the north between Fort Stotsenburg and the Lingayen Gulf. Most training, however, was held in and around the regiment's garrison in Manila. Classes on soldier skills were held during morning hours in the shade of walls or palm and mimosa trees around Manila's walled city to fend off the heat. The duty day ended at 1 p.m. due to the heat. Training was conducted in the barracks during much of the rainy season. Once a month, rain or shine, companies independently conducted a 15-mile forced march with full field pack. The march proceeded down Dewey Boulevard, past the Army-Navy Club, and past the partially submerged hulks of Spanish ships in Manila Bay that had been sunk by Admiral Dewey's fleet in 1898.

Unfortunately, training took a back seat to supporting the garrison. Rifle companies had an average assigned strength of 2 officers and 70 enlisted men instead of their wartime authorization of 6 officers and 178 enlisted men. When cooks, clerks, supply personnel, orderlies,

Philippine Department Shoulder Patch (Association archive).

72

Delta Company, 31st Infantry, on the march in route step, Manila, Philippines, 1932. The 4th Battalion, 31st Infantry traces its lineage to D Company (Association archives, courtesy Beverly J. Schallert).

guard details, and personnel on leave, pass, sick call, unauthorized absence, hospitalization, or confinement were subtracted from a company's field strength, most could muster only around 20 men for training. Headquarters, Service, and Machine gun Companies were larger, but they too were below authorized strength and also had to share in garrison support details. The result precluded even squad or platoon training until the regiment went to the field because leaders could not plan on any unit mustering even half its strength on any given day. Even during regimental maneuvers, some members of every company would remain in Manila due to the various diversions cited above.

Because the duty day ended at 1 p.m., much of a soldier's time was spent off-post. For the athletically inclined, the regiment had baseball, basketball, swimming, track and field, and boxing teams that competed with teams from other units. Taking the annual Philippine Department trophy for these competitions was a particular source of unit pride. Weekly boxing matches were held at Jose Rizal Stadium, drawing huge crowds and heavy betting. Downtown Manila provided the usual array of soldier hangouts, including Tom's Dixie Kitchen, the Poodle Dog, the Oriental Bar, and Cumming's Café, along with myriad others of lesser renown. Prostitution, brawling, loan sharking, and gambling caused the same disciplinary problems in Manila as at any garrison town worldwide, keeping MPs and the staff at Sternberg Army Hospital busy. Officers' off-duty relaxation tended to center around the municipal golf course in the dry moat around Manila's old walled city and the tennis courts and bars at the Army-Navy Club. For those interested in seeing more than Manila, there were boat cruises to the Sulu Archipelago and Mindanao, or bus trips to Lake Taal, Laguna de Bay, Lamon Bay, and other scenic destinations. Nestled on a mountainside cooled by breezes from the South China Sea was Camp John Hay, near Baguio, a particular favorite destination for rest and recreation leave and religious retreats. The Philippine people were friendly, attractive girls were abundant, and the cost of everything was far below stateside prices.

Vice President John Nance Garner visited the Philippines in November 1935 for the inauguration of Manuel L. Quezon as President of the Philippines. While there he visited the 31st Infantry Regiment. The picture shows him shaking hands with CPT Albert Pierson, as Garner's aide, LTC Oliver S. Wood, makes the introduction. By World War II Pierson was a general, and served as Assistant Division Commander of the 11th Airborne Division in New Guinea and the Philippines (Association archives, courtesy Sallie Pierson Holden).

Soldiers seeking to advance their education could attend the University of the Philippines, which offered courses like those at land grant colleges back home. Farrell D. Lowe was among those who took advantage of the opportunity. Drawn into the Army by the Great Depression, Farrell was one of the first replacements to join F Company after its return from Shanghai. A bright, ambitious young man with a year of college in the U.S., he soon became F Company's clerk. By the time he departed the Philippines in 1937, he had nearly finished his college education. He also played intramural sports and assisted the Regimental Chaplain on holidays. Among athletic adventures was being persuaded by Floyd Barnhart, the 31st Infantry's Heavyweight Champion boxer, to enter regimental tryouts as a flyweight contender. When no other contenders appeared, Farrell became the 31st Infantry's Flyweight Champion without ever taking a punch.

Farrell remembers the regiment's NCOs as true professionals, dedicated to the Service and to each other. When one of the first sergeants was about to retire in 1935 as a technical sergeant (E-6), Sergeant Major James B. Screen voluntarily took a one-grade reduction for a month so a lower-ranking friend could retire as a master sergeant. At the time, sergeant major was a duty position normally held by a master sergeant E-7 (3 chevrons and 3 rockers), then the highest enlisted grade. When Screen's friend retired at the end of the month, Screen got his rank back and lost no pay. His friend got the honor, although without additional pay, of retiring as a master sergeant, a grade honoring his performance as a dedicated leader of soldiers.

Inspired by such men, Farrell took the Military Academy entry examination, competing with four other applicants for the Philippine Department's two allocations. The other four applicants were sons of West Point graduates stationed in Manila. When the results were announced, Farrell finished second of the five and was scheduled to depart on the next ship for the U.S. A day later, he was unexpectedly summoned to take another physical exam. Being a healthy farm boy who had already been found fit, he didn't worry. To his shock, the exam revealed a "previously undiscovered" hearing defect that disqualified him from the Military Academy. He had no hearing defect but there was no appeal. Applicant number three received the appointment. Disappointed, Farrell decided to nevertheless make the best of his situation.

Sergeant Major Screen smelled a rat. He told First Sergeant Keeney to have Farrell apply for a clerk position at Philippine Department Headquarters but he would have to transfer to Service Company to get the job. On Keeney's advice, Farrell accepted. He would work in the Philippine Department's Message Center, the portal through which all military communications in and out of the Philippines flowed, keeping him exceptionally well informed. His new office was one door down the hall from a major on General MacArthur's staff named Dwight D. Eisenhower, a future President of the United States. Ike too took a liking to him. In the summer of 1935, Farrell was unexpectedly promoted to Corporal. When he discovered he could apply for a Reserve commission, he eagerly did so. His application was accepted but to qualify, he would first have to be approved by a board of officers who would judge him on his knowledge of the Manual for Courts Martial and ability to command troops in close and extended order drill. This time, however, there would be no phony physical exam.

Farrell easily passed the military knowledge test but had never drilled troops. First Sergeant Keeney, believing Farrell had gotten a raw deal on West Point, had Farrell notify the Post Adjutant that he was designating F Company as his demonstration unit. Keeney assembled F Company, explained what was at stake, and put the company through its paces. On the appointed day, Sergeant Major Screen (himself a Reserve captain) had bleachers erected at the reviewing site in front of the old walled city opposite Jose Rizal Park, one of the most stirring vistas in Manila. He ensured that supportive spectators from the garrison would attend and arranged for the regimental band to be "coincidentally" practicing there at the same time. When the reviewing officers arrived, Farrell played the company commander's role but First Sergeant Keeney issued most of the drill commands. The band played appropriate music, flags fluttered in the breeze, F Company performed flawlessly, and the spectators cheered and applauded. The reviewers' vote was five to one in Farrell's favor. Soon after, he received orders and an ID card making him a Reserve second lieutenant. He was still, however, a Corporal in the Regular Army. Actually serving as an officer would have to await the Army's expansion. That came in 1939 and Farrell was among the first volunteers for commissioned service. He served in Europe during World War II, and retired as a Lieutenant Colonel in 1954. At the time of this writing he was 98, the 31st Infantry's oldest living veteran.

In contrast to the regiment's uncomfortable return from Siberia in 1920, a replacement's arrival in the Philippines was greeted by the Philippine Department band and a welcoming committee composed of sponsors and their families and personnel who would depart several days later on the same ship. Among those arriving during the interwar period was Second Lieutenant Arthur G. Christensen, a 1936 ROTC graduate of North Dakota Agricultural College. On his arrival at Pier 7, he was met by his company commander, First Lieutenant Henry C. Britt, who was also his sponsor. Before even seeing his new quarters, he was driven to Ah Wong's, a Chinese tailor shop operated as a Post Exchange concession. Ah Wong fitted all new arrivals for khaki tropical work uniforms and a silk-lined white mess uniform to be ready in time for the *Bienvenida-Despedida* (hail and farewell) scheduled two days later to give Ah Wong time to work his magic with silk and cotton. Tailored khaki work uniforms cost P15 ($7.50) with rank insignia embroidered on at no extra charge and white mess uniforms cost P25 ($12.50).

Lieutenant Christensen was then driven to the Army-Navy Club to meet officers he would serve with and take a furnished room as his residence. Room service was provided as part of his rental fee. The Army-Navy Club included a restaurant, several bars, a reading room, bowling alley, swimming pool, and tennis courts, a stark contrast to Spartan officer's accommodations at garrisons back home. Christensen's only previous duty station was Fort Abraham Lincoln, North Dakota which had barely changed since George

Change of Command, 31st Infantry Regiment, February 1936. The passing of the command is symbolized as COL S.T. Mackall presents the new commander, COL C.S. Hamilton, his newly engraved cup. The Shanghai Bowl sits on the table behind them in front of the Colors. Each departing officer on the left will present his newly arrived counterpart on the right with an engraved cup. The Regimental toast at that time: "Unity and Loyalty" (Association archives, courtesy Beverly J. Schallert).

Armstrong Custer left there in 1876 for his final rendezvous with destiny at Little Big Horn.

Christensen's married counterparts among the new arrivals were housed with their sponsor's family until they could find their own rental. Because quarters were small, such gracious sponsorship arrangements ensured that new arrivals quickly found quarters of their own. If an officer brought a car with him (enlisted personnel could not ship a car at government expense), he turned its papers over to the Quartermaster, who would have it picked up at the dock, taken through Philippine customs, and delivered to his quarters with a full tank of gas.

Receptions were less regal for enlisted personnel. A leased civilian bus took them from Pier 7 to regimental headquarters at Cuartel de España for in-processing. There, an NCO from each company marched the new arrivals to their barracks or took them by truck if they were to be stationed at Estado Mayor (2nd and 3rd Battalions) or Santa Lucia Barracks (Service Company). In the companies, informal sponsorship was arranged by squad members eager to show off their "old timer's" knowledge of the post and city. Each battalion was housed in a quartel, four company-size barracks enclosing an open assembly area. Each barracks had an orderly room (company headquarters), day room (recreation hall), mess hall (dining room and kitchen), arms room, supply room, and latrine on the ground floor. The ground floor was screened, but the second floor where troops slept was not because mosquitoes don't fly that high. Just in case, beds were covered with mosquito netting. To take advantage of evening breezes, the second floor was open to a covered porch that ran around the entire building. Men contributed a dollar or two from their monthly pay to hire servants who performed kitchen detail, shined shoes, made beds, and kept the barracks clean, relieving soldiers of the most distasteful aspects of barracks living. The contrast to life in garrisons in the United States made Manila one of the Army's most sought-after duty stations.

The Army's interwar strength in the Philippines fluctuated from a low of around 10,000 in 1932 to around 26,000 in 1939, 12,000 of them in Philippine Scout units with American officers and Filipino enlisted personnel serving in the U.S. Army. If war came, they would fight alongside 6000 Philippine Constabulary (lightly armed police), a 20,000-man Philippine National Army formed in January 1936, and a Philippine Army Reserve of 4800 officers and 104,000 enlisted men in 10 ill-trained, ill-equipped divisions.

Infantry regiments were reorganized in 1939 with a headquarters company, service company, company-size medical detachment, antitank company (replacing the old howitzer platoon), 9 rifle companies, and 3 heavy weapons companies which replaced the former machine gun company and 3 of the original 12 rifle companies. Antitank Company was authorized eight 37mm truck-drawn guns and the heavy weapons companies were each authorized two 81mm mortars, two .50 caliber machine guns, and sixteen water-cooled .30 caliber machine guns. Each of the rifle companies included a weapons platoon with four air-cooled .30 caliber machine guns and two 60mm mortars. At least that was the way it was on paper. Actual availability of heavy weapons lagged behind that authorization by two years or more.

In 1940, the 31st Infantry traded its M-1903 Springfield rifles for Garand M-1s. Some old timers who claimed they could "shoot the wings off a gnat" at 750 yards with the Springfield did not like the new Garand with its more modest 550 yard accuracy, but its durability in mud and rain and 8-round clip eventually overcame complaints. Many other things also changed that year. The Selective Service Act instituted a peacetime draft and

Congress approved calling the National Guard into Federal Service. The combination enabled the Army to expand rapidly from its 1939 strength of around 243,000 to 1.2 million.

In October 1940, second lieutenants with more than a year of service were promoted to temporary first lieutenant and first lieutenants were promoted to temporary captain. Most were promoted without additional pay since the law provided that first lieutenants with fewer than three years' service would continue to receive second lieutenants' pay and captains with fewer than seven years' service would continue to draw first lieutenants' pay. In January 1941 captains with more than seventeen years' service were promoted to temporary major. Older officers who had commanded companies for years suddenly became surplus to the regiment's authorization. They became "instructors" with the Philippine Army, moved to the Philippine Department Staff, or were returned to the states, leaving companies of the 31st Infantry commanded by much younger officers.

Unlike some units in the U.S., those in the Philippines did not have to train with wooden mock-ups, but most new weapons the regiment was authorized did not arrive until 1941. Even then, the results were not always helpful. One company requesting replacements for inoperative .30 caliber machine guns received Navy Marlin guns wrapped in cosmoline-coated newspapers dated 1918. To overcome ammunition shortages, Antitank Company became particularly creative, inserting a sleeve with a .22 caliber rifle barrel in its 37mm antitank guns for training. They may have been the first unit in the Army to develop and train with sub-caliber devices. Communications equipment

National and Regimental Flags. Manila, 1932 (Association archives).

was similarly sparse. There were backpack SCR-195 radios in every battalion headquarters but batteries died fast in the tropics and were hard to get. Companies were issued "walkie-talkies" that had a planning range of two miles, but their signal was too weak to penetrate foliage. As a result, wire and runners were as much in use in 1941 as they had been in 1918. There were few trucks in the regiment, requiring 6 civilian bus lines to move troops to distant field maneuvers.

Antitank Company received its guns in April 1941. They included four 37mm wheeled guns and four old British "one-pounders." Starting with a cadre of one captain, two lieutenants, and 25 enlisted men, the company was reinforced by 60 additional enlisted men in June. Organized in two platoons of four gun squads each, the company had an authorized strength of 180 officers and men, a strength it never reached. Eight Dodge weapons carriers towed the guns and carried the crews. A command car, a supply truck, and a kitchen truck rounded out the company's transportation.

As the tocsin of war sounded ever louder across the seas, all personnel scheduled to return to the U.S. had their tours extended indefinitely in March 1941. The families of officers and NCOs were ordered to return to the States. By July, most were gone. Close friends, First Sergeant Arthur C. Houghtby (C Company), Technical Sergeant John B. Fry (Service Company) and Sergeant Abie Abraham (C Company), went together to bid the departing families farewell. Abraham's wife, whose American father came to the Philippines in 1898 and married a Filipina, knew no other home and would remain in Manila throughout the war with her two daughters. Before Mary Houghtby took her long walk up the gangplank onto the USAT *Washington*, Arthur gave her a long last kiss, wiped her tears, and said "Honey, don't worry, the Japs won't dare attack the Philippines as long as us Americans are here." As the *Washington* pulled away, the band played "Till We Meet Again." Houghtby murmured, "My God, I'm going to miss her." They would not meet again. Barely a year after Mary's departure, Arthur died as a Prisoner of War at Camp O'Donnell, on May 20, 1942.

In April 1941, the USAT *Republic* and the *President Pierce* docked at Pier 7 in Manila. Aboard were over 3,000 men, 700 of whom joined the 31st Infantry, the first real growth the regiment experienced since it returned from Shanghai in 1932. Rifle companies received 40 additional men each, while the three weapons companies, Headquarters Company, and Service Company received a slightly larger number. Most of the new men arrived untrained from the Pacific Transfer Point at Fort McDowell, California. They were sent to Fort McKinley's B Range for two months of basic training under the regiment's own NCOs, a task that consumed most of the cadre's time until late June. During basic training, troops lived in tents lined up in neat rows on open ground. Training consisted mainly of close order drill, marksmanship, weapons maintenance, field sanitation, organization of a defensive position, squad assault tactics, and seemingly endless forced marches in the sweltering heat.

Arriving aboard the *Republic* was a pair of recruits whose friendship got them both through tough times, but fate would take one of them before the war ended. Dale L. Snyder from L'Anse, Michigan, and Joseph Q. Johnson from Memphis, Tennessee, became friends at the Army's Pacific Transit Depot at Fort McDowell, California. Tall for his age, Johnson was a 14-year-old kid when he enlisted, prompting Snyder to take the youngster under his wing. When they arrived in Manila, both were assigned to D Company, the 1st Battalion's heavy weapons company. They were assigned together to the 1st Platoon, manning a water-cooled .30 caliber machine gun—affectionately called a "pig in a blanket."

The men of Headquarters Company stand inspection with their equipment (Association archives, courtesy Beverly Schallert).

During basic training at Fort McKinley they shared the same tent, and when other recruits and instructors ribbed Johnson about his age, Snyder stepped in and told them "Enough is enough, just let the kid do his job." Snyder became Johnson's mentor, teaching him how to cope with life in a hell-raising Army. The two went on pass together whenever they had the money and enjoyed mingling with Filipinos, a happy, friendly people who seemed to genuinely like Americans. They tended to stay away from the most popular GI hangouts because there was always plenty of trouble wherever large groups of GIs gathered. Johnson remembers most of the older men in his company as "boozers, brawlers, and whore chasers who moved from one overseas assignment to another, but they were soldiers first and foremost and most were damn good ones." They were a spit and polish outfit.

Also among the replacements arriving on the SS *President Pierce* was Private Ward Redshaw, who stood 6'7" and wore size 15 shoes. Ward left his widowed mother's home in western Canada and joined the U.S. Army at Seattle in April 1941. His recruiter promised he could apply for duty with the Philippine Department's Photo Detachment but to get the job he would have to enlist for the 31st Infantry in Manila. Arriving at Fort McDowell for his shots, uniforms, and passage to Manila, he was delayed because the supply sergeant couldn't find any size 15 shoes in the Army supply system. In desperation, the supply officer gave Ward $6.50 to buy an appropriate pair of civilian shoes. Ward bought a nice pair of Florsheim wingtips that he thought would look sharp with his crisp new khaki uniform. Although the startled supply officer fussed and fumed when he saw what Ward bought with the Army's money, he sent him to the Philippines, wingtips and all. When his ship stopped in Hawaii for a layover, a captain offered to make him an MP (they needed *big* MPs in Hawaii). Ward politely declined. Later, he wished he had taken the offer. In Manila, Ward was assigned to G Company. Seeing his wingtips, the supply sergeant took him to Fort McKinley to get two pairs of proper Army shoes made. A month later, the recruiter's promise became reality. Ward was reassigned to the Philippine Department's Photo Detachment but when the Philippines went on alert in October, Ward was sent back to G Company.

In August 1941, the USAT *Washington* reached Manila with the last contingent of replacements to reach the Philippines before the war. After waiting over an hour for clearance from port authorities, the *Washington* docked at Pier 7. Among those disembarking was Chaplain Robert Preston Taylor, a reserve lieutenant in the Army Air Corps who had taken a one-year leave of absence from his church in Texas to minister to Air Corps members in the Philippines. No condition of his employment contract would be honored and he would never return to his church. He was instead assigned as the 31st Infantry's Chaplain. So much for the Army's promises—even God stands no chance against bureaucrats. As a bus took him and a group of fellow officers down Dewey Boulevard from the port, Taylor gazed in wonder at the walled gardens surrounding the old city, alive with rose-purple rhododendrons, scarlet hibiscus, and huge China roses. The bells of Santo Domingo Cathedral pealed and traffic came to a near standstill as his bus competed with pony carts, taxis, cars, trucks, and an occasional military vehicle. No one seemed in a hurry. Taylor survived the war and remained in uniform afterward, transferring to the Air Force when that Service was formed. In 1962, President Kennedy appointed him Air Force Chief of Chaplains and promoted him to major general. He died in Arizona in 1995.

Private Joe Johnson was finding it easier than expected to gain respect. Among those who saw potential in him was D Company's departing bugler. Eager to learn the instrument, "the kid" practiced diligently in a shed near the bandstand until he developed the necessary callous on his lip. He was soon recognized as the best bugler in the regiment. As a reward, early each morning he was sent with the guard detail to General MacArthur's headquarters where he blew "General's Call" each morning as MacArthur arrived. MacArthur's headquarters was at 1 Calle Victoria near Cuartel De España. Although retired from the Army in 1937 after serving as military advisor to the Philippine Commonwealth, he remained in the Philippines in that capacity in the employ of the Commonwealth government. He was recalled to active duty in July 1941 to head what became U.S. Army Forces Far East (USAFFE). As his reputation for earnestness grew, Joe "the kid" Johnson's circle of friends grew steadily, including men from all over the country. In addition to Dale Snyder, Johnson's mentor, there was Raymond Rico from California, Wayne Seiling from Kansas, Earl Petrimeaux from Minnesota, Norris Cathey from Arkansas, and Dewey Smithwick from North Carolina. Sadly, all would die before the war ended. "The kid" would survive to eventually tell their families what happened to them and where they were buried. His survivor's guilt would last a lifetime.

On July 22, 1941, Japan occupied French Indochina, acquiring bases that dominated the South China Sea west of the Philippines. To the north, Japanese-held Formosa (now

The 31st Infantry Regiment passing in review (Association archives, courtesy Beverly J. Schallert).

Taiwan) was only 65 miles from the northernmost island of the Philippines. In the Central Pacific, Japan violated its League of Nations mandate and fortified the Marianas and Carolines, former German colonies that had been placed under Japanese "protection" after World War I. They became menacing air bases astride U.S. sea lanes between Hawaii and the Philippines. Japan made it clear that the Dutch East Indies (now Indonesia) were targeted for takeover just as French Indochina had been. It was only a matter of time before war with the United States and Great Britain would follow.

Against that unsettled backdrop, the 31st Infantry Regiment celebrated its 25th Anniversary Organization Day on August 13, 1941. It would be the regiment's last celebration for four bitter years.

The weather was bright and sunny when General MacArthur took the regiment's salute as it paraded proudly down Dewey Boulevard. The parade was accompanied by military displays at Wallace Field. Private William J. Garleb, a recruit in H Company, remembers that day as one of the happiest of his life. His squad demonstrated setting up, loading, firing, and displacing its .30 caliber machine gun with crisp precision. It was what he had practiced repeatedly at Fort McKinley during basic training and now he was having his graduation exercise to the applause of an appreciative crowd. Later, there was a barbeque at nearby Harrison Park. In the evening, there were boxing matches at Jose Rizal Stadium. An extract of the address given by Colonel Albert M. Jones, the regimental commander, on that occasion follows:

Fellow members of the 31st Infantry:

Today, August 13th, we commemorate the Silver Anniversary of our regiment's organization. Due to unsettled world conditions, the Army of the United States is now engaged in intensively preparing to meet any emergency. Our regiment occupies a key strategic position in this far eastern possession. It is ready for prompt expeditionary employment. It is a reservoir of trained troop leaders. It is prepared to take its position in the defense of the Philippines.... During the past 6 months, our ranks have been greatly increased by the absorption of the highest type of young American manhood. In the face of a threatening international situation, these patriotic young men volunteered for service in this exposed outpost. We have subjected them to intensive training under trying tropical conditions. The soldier of today, more than ever, must spend his time learning the things that make a man efficient in combat, that make him act intelligently in an emergency and that toughen him physically to withstand the rigors of modern warfare. In no other arm must so much trust be placed in the individual soldier as in the Infantry.

Since I assumed command of the regiment, it has more than doubled in strength. Its armament, transportation, and equipment have been tremendously increased and modernized. Its officers and NCOs have worked ceaselessly and tirelessly to train these young men in the fundamentals of soldiering…. We know not what lies ahead. We must be fully prepared. We must not spare ourselves. I have absolute faith in the ability of our regiment to accomplish all of its many and varied missions. The honor and glory of the 31st Infantry established by our predecessors must and will be upheld by us.

On that day, there were still four men in the 31st Infantry who had served with the regiment in Siberia 21 years before. They included First Sergeant Beresford O. Seale (Headquarters, 2d Battalion), Staff Sergeant Sam Dietz (Service Company), Staff Sergeant John P. Flynn (L Company), and PFC John Labasewski (A Company). Thirty-eight others had served with other units during World War I. First Sergeant Emmanuel Hamburger (Antitank Company) served with "Black Jack" Pershing in Mexico in 1916 and in France with the 1st Division during World War I. By the time World War II came four months later, Sam Dietz had departed the regiment. Emmanuel Hamburger was still Antitank Company's first sergeant. He would survive the war. Beresford Seale would become E Company's First Sergeant, earning the Silver Star trying to rally his company at Layac Junction. In captivity under the Japanese, he worked as a plumber in Manila's Bilibid Prison where he died of disease and starvation. John Flynn received a battlefield commission after the battle of Abucay Hacienda in January 1942. He had already become the most decorated man in the regiment, earning the Distinguished Service Cross, the Silver Star, and two Purple Hearts. He died in captivity in 1944 when the "hell ship" taking him to Japan was sunk by the U.S. Navy. John Labasewski, the regiment's oldest private, died on the same ship.

In the summer of 1941, the tempo of training picked up. Beginning in late summer, the regiment conducted a 3-day exercise per month to toughen the men for the rigors of combat and familiarize them with their intended wartime operating area. At the time, the 31st Infantry was responsible for defending Batangas, Tayabas, and Lamon Bays south of Manila. On September 1, the Philippine Army began mobilizing. On that date, the 31st Infantry Regiment was reassigned from the Philippine Department to the Philippine Division which had since 1931 included only Philippine Scout units. The transfer order was not posted and therefore went unnoticed to men of the regiment who continued to wear the blue and white seahorse patch of the Philippine Department, rather than the red and gold Carabao (water buffalo) patch of the Philippine Division. Still short of its wartime authorization, the 31st was required to send officers and NCOs to help mobilize and train new Philippine Army units. More than half of the regiment's officers and an average of 10 NCOs per company were soon sent to hastily built posts all over the Philippines to train and help lead the Philippine Army and form two corps staffs. Their loss would be sorely felt in the months ahead, but without them it is doubtful that the ten Philippine Army reserve divisions could have fought as well as they did. Although Filipinos came in for considerable criticism from their American comrades for fleeing under pressure, few remember that two battalions in every Filipino regiment had not even received basic training when the war started and most Filipino soldiers had never even seen a rifle before being inducted. Recruited from isolated tribes that spoke at least 40 distinctly different languages, many units could not understand the Tagalog language of their officers, who were mainly from Luzon's major cities. Despite that and the fact that most Filipinos were armed with old Springfield M-1903 rifles and had few heavy weapons, they constituted Bataan's main line of defense for nearly four months and suffered over 80 percent of the campaign's battle casualties.

On October 25, the 31st Infantry boarded leased civilian busses at Fort McKinley's B range and traveled nearly 100 miles to establish coastal defenses north of Subic Bay.

On reaching their destination, the troops were dropped off and the buses returned to Manila. Philippine fishermen alerted the men that a Japanese ship was offshore warning fishermen away. The Filipinos thought the ship might have been laying mines near the U.S. naval base at Subic Bay. The information was duly passed through channels to MacArthur's intelligence staff in Manila, but no response was noted. On completing its training, the 31st marched 30 miles a day back to Fort McKinley in the unrelenting tropical heat. Private Garleb noticed that his squad leader, Corporal George Eckhardt, Jr., did not flop on the ground and rest at halts as most others did. He remained standing and kept his pack on, but never seemed to get tired. Garleb followed his example and found that it worked. He also learned from some of the "old hands" to put a pebble under his tongue to keep from getting too thirsty.

There were always moments of

Philippine Division Shoulder Patch (Association archives).

A portion of the entire 31st Infantry Regiment in formation, in front of the barracks on Corregidor, Philippine Islands, 1932 (Association archives, courtesy Beverly J. Schallert).

MG Grant, the Philippine Department Commander, reviewing the 1st Battalion, 31st Infantry (Association archives).

comic relief amid the regiment's preparations for war. Private Harold O. "Red" Dyer was one of the new men in the 31st and a real character, according to fellow members of F Company. Dyer, a 6'2" Texan, got the nickname "Red" because of his reddish pink complexion and reddish blonde hair. After taking all the ribbing he could stand, Dyer persuaded the company barber to dye his hair and his fuzzy wisp of a mustache coal black. No one recognized him when he walked out of the barbershop. At recall formation, his secret vanished when he took his place in the ranks. His buddies howled with laughter, disrupting the formation, but First Sergeant George Shirk was not amused. Dyer's moustache-in-the-making quickly came off but it took months for his hair to return to its natural color. First Sergeant Shirk (Modena, Pennsylvania) died at the hands of his Japanese captors on January 19, 1944, while on a labor detail at Clark Field. Private Dyer (Galveston, Texas) was wounded during the battle for Abucay Hacienda in January 1942 and died in captivity at Cabanatuan POW Camp on July 21, 1942.

In November 1941, unusually heavy Japanese troop movements throughout East Asia and the Western Pacific alarmed U.S. intelligence. On November 27, USAFFE was placed on war alert. On that day, the SS *Henderson* delivered the regiment's long-awaited 60mm and 81mm mortars. PFC Paul Kerchum of D Company was sent by his first sergeant with a Dodge 4x4 truck, a signed requisition, and a four-man detail to pick up the weapons. At Service Company's arms room, Kerchum was issued the mortars, but no ammunition. When he asked where to draw the ammunition, the master sergeant issuing the weapons responded in frustration "There ain't any, soldier." Kerchum made the mistake of asking why. His response was a fiery blast. "Look son, the ammunition is due to

In 1936 Company H, 31st Infantry Regiment won the Edwin Howard Clark Trophy for being the best machine gun company in the entire United States Army. The win meant that the trophy would leave the continental United States for the first time in its history. The trophy was named for CPT Edwin H. Clark, who served in World War I in a machine gun unit (Association archives).

arrive with a convoy from the states in about two weeks. It's not up to you or me to judge the decisions of the brass, so pick up your mortars, be thankful for what you got, and haul your smart ass out of here!"[1] Ten days later, Japan attacked Hawaii, slamming the door shut on shipping lanes to the Philippines. When war came, 81mm mortars would have to make do with mostly old, unreliable 75mm Stokes mortar ammunition left over from World War I and the 60s would be useless because their ammunition never arrived.

Despite a series of war alerts in late November, life in the Philippines changed little. Captain Arthur Christensen and some of his friends went to Camp John Hay for Thanksgiving. In Manila, Japanese residents remained free to move about as they pleased, sometimes provoking the ire of American soldiers who had come to view them as enemies after seeing or hearing about Japanese atrocities in China.

On December 6, the movie *Sergeant York*, starring Gary Cooper in the title role, was playing in Manila. The Metropolitan Theater near Estado Mayor was jammed beyond capacity with Filipinos and Americans vying for seats to see a shy World War I hero from Pall Mall, Tennessee, single-handedly destroy a company of Germans. For a few more days at least, war was still only a movie in Manila.

Paul Kerchum was at a bar with some of his buddies when two Japanese civilians made an offensive gesture as they departed. Kerchum tore after them, saw them jump into a cab, and lit into them through an open back window. When the door opened, Kerchum and one of the Japanese spilled into the street and were still flailing away at each other when the MPs arrived. When the matter was brought to the attention of Lieutenant Lloyd Murphy, Kerchum's company commander, he decided to press charges, referring Kerchum for trial by Special Court Martial. His trial date was set for December 7, 1941, a day that lives in infamy for other reasons. Kerchum was informed by the Staff Judge Advocate's office on December 15 that the charges were dropped. Japanese bombs were falling on Manila at the time.

PART II. WORLD WAR II
by Karl H. Lowe

5 Enemy Attacks in the Philippines, 1941–1942

On the evening of December 7, 1941, a loud party was underway at the Manila Hotel's Fiesta Pavilion. Major General Lewis Brereton, commander of Army Air Forces in the Far East was attending a party thrown by the 27th Bomb Group, recently arrived from the U.S. ahead of their planes. The party, marked by raucous laughter, off-key singing, tinkling glass, and squealing girls would continue into the wee hours of the morning. Observing from the Hotel's Bamboo Bar under a cascade of scarlet bougainvillea, First Lieutenant Dwight Hunkins of H Company remarked to his friends, "I hope they can fly better than they can sing."[1] His friends were Lieutenants George Williams, an infantry officer recently reassigned to the Philippine Army, Joe McClellan, an Army aviator and descendant of General George McClellan of Civil War fame, Bill Tooley, a Signal Corps officer with the 31st Infantry's Headquarters Company, and Ralph Emerson Hibbs, the 31st Infantry Regiment's 2nd Battalion Surgeon. None of them knew it yet but they would be at war the next morning and when it was over only one of them would still be alive.[2]

Word of Pearl Harbor Arrives

Ralph Hibbs awoke in the early hours of December 8 to the steady ringing of a telephone in General Brereton's suite across the garden.[3] Through open windows, Hibbs heard Brereton's gruff, irritated voice, "Hello? Those sons of bitches! You've got to be kidding!" After another flurry of curses, Brereton slammed down the receiver. Soon other phones rang, subdued voices filled the courtyard, followed by hurried footsteps, doors slamming, and cars zooming off through the otherwise quiet city. Unconcerned, Hibbs went back to sleep. He didn't know this would be the last night he would spend in a bed for more than three years. At 6:30, as Hibbs drove his old Chevy through the suburb of Pasay to his battalion's bivouac site near Nichols Field, a vendor flashed the Manila morning paper at him: "HAWAII BOMBED—WAR!" As he entered the bivouac area, men were already digging foxholes. Major Lloyd C. Moffitt, the 2nd Battalion Commander, informed Hibbs that he was now a captain. "As of this morning, all company grade officers are promoted one grade." First Sergeant Joe Wilson suggested that despite his high grade, Hibbs should start digging a foxhole "because the Nips are scheduled to arrive any minute."

At about the same time, Sergeant Mike Gilewitch, D Company's Supply Sergeant, opened his supply room and by habit turned on the radio he inherited with the job.

Hangar and planes damaged and set afire by Japanese bombers at Pearl Harbor (National Archives).

Expecting to hear music, he was surprised to hear "The Japanese have bombed Pearl Harbor and other American military bases in Hawaii." Gilewitch rushed through the orderly room to Captain Chris Heffernan's office, brushing off First Sergeant Evlyn Dempsey's "What the hell do you think you're doing."[4] "Captain, we're at war with Japan! Come to the supply room, they're on the radio telling about it now." In a flash, everyone dashed to the supply room to hear about the attack. Heffernan turned down the volume and called regimental headquarters. The group watched the captain's expression change to bewilderment as he received his orders. "Headquarters says to proceed as usual."

When the captain and first sergeant departed, Gilewitch called headquarters again, explaining that the company had sixteen .30 caliber machine guns whose ammunition had to be loaded into 250-round fabric belts with one slow, hand cranked machine. The duty officer replied, "Your commanding officer has his orders. No ammo will be opened! An inspection team will be by to ensure those orders are not violated. If any boxes are opened, the commanding officer and supply sergeant will be court martialed." Gilewitch was stunned by such blind stupidity, but he persisted. Headquarters finally relented and authorized the issue of pistols and seven rounds of .45 caliber ammunition, but machine gun ammunition was to remain locked up. A few minutes later, the supply room phone rang. It was the lieutenant from regimental headquarters again, directing the issue of gas masks. To make sure it was done, the signature list was to be delivered to headquarters. Gilewitch grumbled to himself "We're gonna have more trouble with our own headquarters than with the Japanese." His thoughts were prophetic.

Around 9 a.m., First Sergeant Arthur Houghtby dispatched PFC Andy Nickerson[5] with C Company's 1934 Dodge truck to pick up the company's supply sergeant, Abie Abraham, at his quarters in Manila. Screeching to a halt in front of Abraham's house, Nickerson shouted "Mrs. Abraham, is your husband home?" "He's behind the house

U.S. aircraft destroyed as a result of the Japanese bombing on Pearl Harbor, December 7, 1941. Attempt at salvage after machine gun attack (National Archives).

fixing the fence to keep the dogs out. What's up Andy?" "The Japs bombed Pearl Harbor, all hell broke loose, and the captain wants everyone back at the barracks." Throwing his uniform and boots into the truck, Abraham jumped aboard, still dirty and sweaty from his yard work. As Nickerson and Abraham drove toward the Cuartel de España, Dewey Boulevard was already crowded with people fleeing Manila in buses, trucks, *carromatas* (two wheeled carriages), and *calesas* (pony carts).

The 2nd and 3rd Battalions from nearby Estado Mayor, flush with hundreds of green replacements, were on their annual range firing exercise at Fort McKinley's B Range when three waves of Japanese planes attacked adjacent Nichols Field around 9:30 a.m. on December 9.[6] A stray bomb landed in the 2nd Battalion's bivouac area but no one was hurt. On the airfield, however, there was great devastation. Buildings and wrecked planes billowed thick black smoke and flames into the air. One bomb struck next to the Pan Am Communications Center, killing its civilian operator. Around 11 a.m., units in bivouac were directed to move into dispersed company assembly areas under the cover of trees. Company commanders were ordered to reconnoiter positions for defense against possible Japanese airborne landings.

The First Casualty in the Philippines

What the men at B Range did not know is that the 31st Infantry had already suffered its first casualty. Sergeant Cecil Brand and Private James Morgan of E Company were on detail at Camp John Hay, 120 miles north of Manila, when the first wave of bombers hit. Sergeant Brand was killed instantly when a bomb hit the officer's club where he was taking inventory. He was the first American soldier killed in action in the Philippines.

The 2nd Battalion's field headquarters was situated on a slight knoll only 500 yards from the end of the Nichols Field runway, offering a grandstand view of the morning's events. Preparing for a second wave of Japanese bombers, Private Bill Garleb worked feverishly to set up his Browning .30 caliber machine gun on an antiaircraft tripod. He remarked to his squad leader, Sergeant George Eckhardt, "How crazy is it for Japan to attack America?" Japanese planes returned around 11:30 a.m. The 2nd and 3rd Battalions watched them twist and dive in a swirling aerial dogfight against American P-40s. Stray rounds and spent shells from the dogfight landed among the troops below, precipitating panic in the ranks. Men scattered to find whatever cover they could, leaving machine guns sitting harmlessly atop antiaircraft mounts. Private Bill Garleb jumped into a ravine and burrowed into what seemed to be an animal's lair, covering his head with his hands and trying to shut out the sounds of war erupting around him.

When the raid ended, sheepish men emerged to the angry barking of NCOs. During their baptism of fire, few had demonstrated the coolness and discipline they would need in combat. Near sunset, a spotter plane came in low over Nichols Field. This time there would be no timidity. Nearly every weapon in the 2nd and 3rd Battalions blazed away at the plane. Unfortunately, aircraft recognition had not been part of the new recruits' training. The plane was American. When the pilot bailed out, troops continued firing, ignoring his frantic waving and yelling. Slugs ripped through the helpless man's body and parachute. Commanders' and NCOs' "cease firing" orders were ignored and in one case, an officer had to drag a wild-eyed machine gunner away from his gun. The pilot was shot through his left lung and landed limply, but he was alive and angry, screaming, "You shot me in the air, you shot me on the way down, you sons-of-bitches!" He was still spewing obscenities as an ambulance took him off to the aid station.

The series of raids caught most U.S. planes on the ground, destroying most B-17 bombers at Clark Field and practically wiping out the P-35 and P-40 squadrons based at Clark, Nichols, and Iba Fields. From then on, there would be almost no air support for Luzon's defenders. Although 20 airmen had been killed and over a hundred wounded on Nichols Field, when quiet returned, men resumed the work they had been doing before the raids. A group of carpenters returned from their places of shelter to resume building a new barracks block at the wrecked airfield. Soon they were hammering away as if nothing had happened.

As Japanese planes flew low over Manila after bombing Nichols Field, nearly every man in the 1st Battalion fired at them with his pistol, still the only weapon with ammunition in the battalion. It was a futile gesture of defiance and a sad omen of things to come. With planes still passing overhead, every bugler in the 1st Battalion sounded the call to arms, a call few had ever heard. In company supply rooms, phones rang and instructions were finally given by regimental headquarters to issue all ammunition. Accountability and responsibility suddenly ceased. First sergeants at the Cuartel called formations, ordering the men to be back on the parade ground in full khaki field uniform

U.S. aircraft destroyed as a result of the Japanese bombing on Pearl Harbor, December 7, 1941. A heap of demolished planes and wrecked hangar (National Archives).

with weapon, gas mask, and weapons cleaning equipment in ten minutes. The companies were ready, but it would take the rest of the day and all night to get machine gun ammunition belted. There was no ammunition for the new 60mm mortars, a condition that would not change during the intense combat to come. Although they still had no belted ammunition, the 1st Battalion's machine gunners hoisted heavy wooden antiaircraft tripods atop the walls of Intramuros to gain better firing positions against low-flying aircraft.

Near noon, the 1st Battalion marched out of the Cuartel de España to the "sunken gardens," a dry moat surrounding the walled citadel. Riflemen dug in along the moat's rim while machine gunners mounted their guns atop the city's walls. By nightfall on December 9, two 250-round belts of ammunition per machine gun were issued but only eight extra belts were available to replenish them if they had to be fired. There were no more cloth belts available but without them the guns would quickly become useless. As the regiment waited for further instructions, First Sergeant Houghtby began laughing. "What's so damned funny?" asked his puzzled commander, Captain Richard Carnahan. "Oh, I was just thinking how we heard all Japs had bad eyes from eating rice and many of 'em are cross-eyed and can't shoot straight." Carnahan grumbled, "It'd be a helluva note if one of 'em aims at you and hits me!"[7]

The 31st Infantry remained in the Manila area as a security force while things deteriorated rapidly in other parts of Luzon. On December 10, Nichols Field was bombed and strafed again and Cavite Naval Base was also bombed, although most of the U.S. Asiatic Fleet had already departed for Australia. Two submarines still at the dock were sunk and over 200 torpedoes stacked on adjacent docks went up like Fourth of July fireworks. That day, 4000 Japanese troops landed on Northern Luzon and began moving inland against light resistance from ill-equipped Philippine Army units that had only recently been formed. The U.S. Army's Philippine Division, with the 31st (U.S.), 45th (PS)[8] and 57th (PS) Infantry Regiments, was kept in reserve around Manila while the weaker Philippine Army was being thrashed. The 4th Marine Regiment, only recently arrived from Shanghai, was also kept in reserve, guarding naval installations that were being systematically destroyed by Japanese bombers. The 26th Cavalry (PS) and three Philippine Scout field artillery battalions (23rd, 24th, and 88th) from Ft. Stotsenburg fanned out across central Luzon to cover the Philippine Army's steady retreat.

Opening Moves

At 2 a.m. on December 12, the 31st Infantry, less the 1st Battalion, boarded trucks, civilian buses, and taxicabs and headed north from Fort McKinley to a destination still unknown to the troops. The column reached San Fernando, Pampanga Province, at dawn and continued moving. Three flights of Japanese fighters passed overhead, but showed no interest in the convoys below. Even when traffic jammed at the Calumpit Bridge, Japanese planes seemed uninterested. The column's only anti-aircraft protection was provided by BARs and air-cooled .30 caliber machine guns poked through holes cut in the roofs of buses. Around 1 p.m. on December 13, the regiment's lead element was dropped off near kilometer post 137.3 on the Pilar-Bagac Road which crosses the center of the Bataan Peninsula. The next morning, the 3rd Battalion marched westward, taking up positions about 3 miles east of the barrio of Bagac to guard against possible Japanese landings on Bagac Bay.

Colonel Charles L. Steel, the 31st Infantry's commander, became ill and was taken to the field hospital at Limay on December 14, leaving his executive officer, Lieutenant Colonel Irvin E. Doane, in command. (The regiment's chain of command at the time is shown in Appendix 2.) Under Doane, the 2nd and 3rd Battalions began intensive training and conditioning. Anticipating possible contingencies, Doane also pushed out patrols to give his men better knowledge of the terrain. One patrol went all the way to the Bamban River, about 20 miles north of Fort Stotsenburg in central Luzon to select a delay line. Their effort was in vain. The only delay would be whatever resistance the 26th Cavalry, the artillery, and a few Philippine Army divisions could muster as they drew back toward Bataan.

Emboldened by the success of their initial landings, the Japanese landed 43,000 more men at Lingayen Gulf on December 22. In five days, the Japanese reached Fort Stotsenburg in Central Luzon, pushing steadily closer to Manila. To the south of Manila, Japanese troops landed at Legaspi, and although fewer in number, were also making steady progress. Cavite Naval Base and Sangley Point Naval Air Station were bombed repeatedly from Japanese bases on Formosa, sending columns of smoke high over Manila Bay while frustrated Marines and sailors watched helplessly, unable to strike back.

On Christmas Eve, at Philippine President Manuel Quezon's urging, General Douglas

The 31st Infantry Regiment on maneuvers, fall 1941 (Association archives, courtesy Thompson collection).

MacArthur declared Manila an open city. Quezon sought to spare the civilian population from Japanese bombing by vacating bases in the city so that there would no longer be military targets there. Under the Laws of War, an open city is not to be attacked. An emergency police force that included the 31st Infantry's B Company remained in Manila, augmenting the 12th and 808th MP Companies, Philippine Constabulary units, and the city's police force. The units manned check points at bridges and key buildings around the city against sabotage and espionage. Manila had a sizable number of Japanese civilian residents whose loyalty to Japan was openly expressed and clearly understood. For most of the soldiers, however, security duty was sheer boredom, broken only by flirting with Filipinas passing by.

After spending nearly three weeks in the Luneta area along Manila Bay fruitlessly guarding against Japanese paratroop landings that never came, the rest of the 1st Battalion boarded barges before daylight on Christmas morning. They were taken to Corregidor, an island dominating Manila Bay's entrance. Once ashore, the 1st Battalion marched up a long hill to the parade ground in front of "Topside," the world's longest barracks. In peacetime, Topside housed three coast artillery regiments and an antiaircraft regiment, but now it was nearly empty since most gunners were at their battle stations, which included Forts Drum and Hughes on smaller islands near the mouth of Manila Bay. Only a few coast artillery personnel and a battalion of Marines, recently arrived from Subic Bay, occupied the huge building.

At dusk on Christmas Eve, the 31st Infantry, less the 1st Battalion, reached a position just north of Abucay Hacienda. There they began developing what became the Main Line of Resistance (MLR). For the next four days, the 31st labored around the clock, stringing barbed wire, digging positions, stringing communications wire, setting night aiming stakes for automatic weapons, pacing distances to likely points of enemy attack, and registering artillery and mortar concentrations. To the regiment's right was a series of fish ponds separated by narrow dikes and extending about a kilometer to the east to Manila Bay. The line extended inland about two kilometers west of the barrio of Matabang where excellent cover and good fields of fire existed on flat ground.

Manila was bombed twice on Christmas Day. The bombings continued for several days, signaling Japanese contempt for the Laws of War. On December 28, Colonel Steel returned to the regiment, looking much older than his 50 years, according to one of his former officers. After completing the position at Matabang, the 31st moved north to establish a delay line near Layac where the main road from Central Luzon enters the Bataan Peninsula. After digging and laying wire for two days, the 2nd and 3rd Battalions marched westward toward the town of Olongapo on Subic Bay. Their mission was to hold the nearby Zig Zag Pass against a possible Japanese landing. The 3rd Battalion was located about 600 yards east of the pass in reserve. The 2nd Battalion occupied positions recently abandoned by the 4th Marines at the point where Route 7 reaches its highest point at Zig Zag Pass and begins descending to Subic Bay. Below, G Company outposted the beaches around Subic Bay. With only 128 men and no artillery support, trying to outpost nearly 40 miles of beach was unimaginable. Subic Bay Naval Base had been abandoned and was partially destroyed by the Navy and Japanese bombers, but some of its facilities remained usable. As many as possible were blown up by the 2nd Battalion. On New Year's Eve, the 2nd and 3rd Battalions were ordered to withdraw to the Bataan Peninsula.

The withdrawal along Route 7 was uneventful until the 3rd Battalion reached the village of Dinalupihan, where the road takes a sharp southward turn toward Layac. Diving out of the clouds, Japanese planes suddenly struck the column. The attack was particularly surprising because the Japanese had ignored the more congested route entering Bataan from San Fernando. Corporals Jack Cape of K Company and Jack Wood of M Company were wounded as bombs fell randomly among troops scattering to find shelter. Miraculously, they were the day's only casualties. During the raid, Lieutenant Roy Zoberbier seemed to be everywhere at once, getting M Company's machine guns into action against the planes as the 3rd Battalion headed for the Culo River, marking Bataan's northern edge.[9] For his coolness under fire, Zoberbier earned the Silver Star.

By the time Captain John Pray's G Company, the rear guard, was finally ordered to withdraw to Bataan, the main withdrawal route had become too dangerous, so the men made their way into Bataan on jungle trails leading south from Highway 7. Because dense underbrush and steep ravines would make the trip difficult, they were ordered to keep only their weapons, ammunition, canteens, and a small back pack. Private Ward Redshaw wanted to keep his extra pair of size 15 boots because they were impossible to find in the Philippines. His platoon sergeant, Staff Sergeant Thomas Fortune, told him to throw them away. Reluctantly he did. That eventually got him out of combat. After a month of fighting in the jungle, Redshaw's only pair of boots became worn out. When Colonel Steel saw that he had only shreds on his feet and found that he could not get new boots, he ordered Redshaw transferred to a Signal unit in southern Bataan. Fate sometimes works in mysterious ways.

Air Attack on Corregidor

A few days before the 3rd Battalion was bombed at Dinalupihan, the 1st Battalion experienced its baptism of fire on Corregidor. While bombing Cavite and Sangley Point Naval Stations across the Bay, Japanese planes had always gone out of their way to avoid flying over Corregidor, perhaps believing that American anti-aircraft units were better equipped than they really were. Suddenly on December 29, wave after wave of Japanese planes struck the island. The 1st Battalion had not prepared foxholes because they were told by men stationed on the island that Topside Barracks was bombproof. They soon learned otherwise. Sergeant Mike Gilewitch did not trust the bombproof story and headed for a wooded area as sirens wailed all over the island. He ran from place to place in the woods, seeking shelter from machine gun bullets that were spattering all around him. As he dove for a shallow depression, a bomb blast tossed him into the air like a limp rag doll and deposited him on his back about ten feet away. Although conscious, he could not move. Eventually he was able to move his jaw and eyes, then his fingers and toes, and finally his arms and legs, but his head felt like it was stuffed with cotton. He couldn't hear and thought the raid was over until he

The standing figure, left, CPT Ray B. Stroud, was commanding officer of M Company, 3rd Battalion. He is at the CP of 31st Infantry Regiment during maneuvers, September 23, 1941. He survived the battles, the Bataan Death March and almost three years in the Cabanatuan POW camp, only to die when the unmarked hell ship he was on, the *Arisan Maru*, was sunk by a U.S. submarine (Association archives, courtesy Thompson collection).

noticed dust being kicked up by bullets striking the ground near him. As he rolled toward a concrete culvert, a bomb landed in his intended refuge, sending shards of metal and chunks of concrete flying past him and causing him to shake uncontrollably.

The first sound Gilewitch heard when his hearing returned was the groaning of Private John Lajewski, whose right leg was severely mangled by a bomb blast. Gilewitch put a tourniquet above the wound and used his first aid kit to cover as much of the wound as possible, but it was too extensive. Gilewitch ran through the bombing and strafing to the barracks where there were medical supplies. After grabbing a case of bandages and first aid packets, he grabbed a folded cot on his way out. After thoroughly bandaging Lajewski's leg, Gilewitch and his armorer carried him through the woods on the cot, twisting and turning through underbrush and between trees for what seemed an eternity while bombs and bullets continued to strike the island. On reaching the barracks, Gilewitch turned Lajewski over to a medic and ran back outside. Something strange had happened. Before he heard Lajewski groaning, Gilewitch was shaking so badly with fright that he could barely function and his eyes watered constantly. Once he realized he had to help someone else, fear left him and did not return throughout the raid.

Corporal Wayne Lewis of D Company was on Corregidor's landing dock when the raid began. He quickly learned not to lay flat on the concrete. When a bomb struck, the concussion caused his head to bounce like a ball, raising huge bruises and almost knocking him unconscious. As the first wave of bombers passed, Lewis rose groggily and staggered toward shore to find a more protected spot. Before he could get off the long pier, the second wave of bombers struck. Again, Lewis dropped to the dock to avoid being strafed. This time, he raised his body slightly off the dock with his arms to cushion the shock. That didn't work either, because the dock bucked upward when a bomb struck, beating Lewis in the face and bloodying his nose. Bomb fragments, pieces of spent anti-aircraft shells, and chunks of concrete spattered against nearby rocks. From the shore, chunks of rock and parts of trees were sent flying onto the dock and into the water. To Lewis, it seemed that sooner or later something lethal was bound to strike the place where he lay.

On the heights and surrounding smaller islands, the 60th and 200th Antiaircraft Regiments blazed away at the Japanese in a losing battle. Their fire was reinforced by Army and Marine machine gunners sending up as much lead as possible. Seeing an unmanned .50 caliber machine gun sandbagged for aerial firing, Mike Gilewitch jumped into the revetment and started to aim the weapon when a big Marine jumped in beside him. He ordered Gilewitch out, yelling, "this is a Marine gun and no one fires it but a Marine." Gilewitch argued that no one was firing it and together, they might be able to bring down a Japanese plane. The glowering Marine stuck his .45 caliber pistol in Gilewitch's face and said "Out!" Gilewitch left in disgust. The Marine remained with the gun, guarding it jealously, but he never attempted to fire it. "More stupidity," grumbled Gilewitch "At this rate, we'll defeat ourselves without any help from the Japanese." After nearly three thundering hours, the Japanese made their last strafing run and headed north.

Curiosity brought Gilewitch back to Topside Barracks after the raid ended. Some bombs had gone through the roof and detonated on the third floor, ripping out walls and exposing steel beams in the floor, but none reached any farther down. On the ground floor at one end of the barracks, Marines were lying all over the place. All appeared to be asleep and unharmed. Gilewitch didn't realize what he was seeing until he heard a medic murmuring "done for" as he checked one of the men for signs of life. They had all been killed by concussion. Returning to the wooded area where he and others from his company had sought refuge, Gilewitch saw a few men lying on the ground in varying states of agony. Private Vernon Sutton, with a bloody, mangled arm, was crying frantically for a medic.[10] Corporal Earl Petrimeaux, whose legs were both shattered at the thighs, yelled at Sutton to shut up. "Look at me, I wish I only had your troubles." Petrimeaux lost both legs and died the next day. The only other 31st Infantry member killed in the raid was Private George S. Gensel of D Company, who was hit in the stomach by a large bomb fragment. Mike Gilewitch was also among the wounded, but didn't know it until his armorer noticed his right elbow was bleeding and badly bruised. A bomb fragment had struck him.

D Company suffered the most casualties. In addition to the two dead and three wounded already mentioned, Sergeant Cyril M. Provaznik was hit in the forehead by a spent machine gun bullet but survived. Bomb fragments wounded privates Leo Boles and Elijah Millsap. Others wounded in the raid included Privates Charles W. Gardner of

1st Battalion Headquarters, Sherman E. Crookshank and Russell L. Villars of A Company, and Sergeant James B. Cabral of C Company. Private Villars was awarded the Silver Star for engaging Japanese planes from an exposed position with his BAR until a bomb blast disabled him. His right leg was amputated at the aid station on Corregidor.[11] Others were temporarily dazed by concussion, but remained on duty. That afternoon, the 1st Battalion filed back down the steep hill to the dock where they boarded barges for Bataan.

Disaster at Layac

Bataan was chosen as a defensive position because of its dominance, along with the nearby island of Corregidor, over the entrance to Manila Bay. As long as American troops controlled Bataan and Corregidor, the Japanese would be unable to use Manila's harbor, or so it was thought. The peninsula is 30 miles long and about 25 miles across at its widest point. A spine of mountains bisects it, with an east-west valley cutting across the peninsula's middle between clusters of mountains. On the north are Mt. Santa Rosa (3,052 feet) and Mt. Natib (4,222 feet), connected by saddle ridges to each other and to Mt. Silanganan (3620 feet). Across a broad valley to the south are the twin peaks of Mt. Bataan and Mt. Samat (each over 4,500 feet). Numerous steep ravines and fast-running streams form spines running down from the mountains, segmenting the peninsula into compartments covered with dense tropical forest.

In 1942, a single paved road ran down the peninsula's east side from the farming village of Layac in the north to the small customs port of Mariveles in the south. A road running along the South China Sea on the west was only a fair-weather gravel track. An east-west connector runs between the two north-south roads, traversing the mid-peninsula valley between the towns of Pilar and Bagac. Numerous trails follow spines running off the mountains.

General MacArthur divided Bataan into two sectors. On the east where the terrain was most favorable to the attacker was II Corps, under Major General George Parker. On the more easily defended west was I Corps, under Major General Jonathan M. Wainwright. I and II Corps were ad hoc organizations not authorized by the War Department. Their numerals duplicated those of corps already existing in the U.S.

By January 5, the regiment was reunited. The Band, B Company, and the Medical Detachment had reached Bataan on December 28, the first elements of the regiment to arrive.[12] They left Manila as Japanese troops entered from the south. Japanese planes struck repeatedly along the route, but no one was hit. As the convoy reached the railhead at San Fernando, much of the surrounding area was in flames but they made it safely to Bataan. With them they brought a bus packed solid with food taken from an abandoned government warehouse in Manila. On the night of January 30, the rest of the 1st Battalion reached Bataan by barge from Corregidor. On January 4, the 2nd and 3rd Battalions crossed the Culo River and took up positions just west of the barrio of Culis. Behind them, the 14th Engineer Battalion (Philippine Scouts) blew up the road transiting the narrow Zig-Zag Pass.

Commanders made a reconnaissance while the reunited regiment bivouacked for the night. At dawn on January 5, work began on the new position, a westward extension of the forward security line the regiment had begun a week earlier near Layac. With the 1st Battalion on the right and 2nd on the left, the regiment occupied a front of about 1500 yards. Sergeant Earl Walk of H Company positioned his platoon's .50 caliber machine gun beside a trail entering the regiment's left flank. His 81mm mortar was placed about 150 yards farther back. He remembered the red clay earth being so hard that picks barely chipped the surface. Several men poured out their canteens or urinated to soften the clay—to no avail.

The 3rd Battalion was in reserve, digging in behind a ridge 1,000 yards to the southwest. Behind the 31st Infantry, dug in on higher ridges, were the 23rd and 88th Field Artillery Battalions, Philippine Scout units equipped with twelve 75mm field guns each. On the regiment's right, occupying positions the 31st had prepared earlier, was the Philippine Army's 71st Division, a poorly equipped unit that had received little training. The boundary between the 31st Infantry and the Filipinos was the main road leading south into the Bataan Peninsula. Although roads make an easily identifiable boundary, they should be assigned to and defended by only one unit since the enemy is certain to use the approach and should not be given a seam to exploit. The blunder would prove costly.

The evening meal on January 5 was only half the normal ration, a harbinger of worse to come. Pursuant to another bad decision by senior officers, 65,000 rounds of .30 caliber ammunition were dumped on the ground behind the forward rifle companies' positions. Several company commanders objected vehemently, arguing that they had no vehicles and could not carry that much ammunition if a withdrawal became necessary. They were overruled. At least one position was almost guaranteed to fold. B Company, the first to arrive, held the critical right of the line adjacent to the main road leading into Bataan. The company occupied a flat, open area with few trees or shrubs. A shallow, swampy stream bisected the sector, causing the unit to bend in an arc that could cause troops to fire on each other if attacked in the center. There was no barbed wire available to canalize or slow an attack. Soldiers are no fools and no one believed this was a serious defensive position. Consequently, foxholes were dug haphazardly and machine guns were positioned in the open as if on the range. The atmosphere was one of just waiting for the order to move to a more defensible site.

The transfer of most of B Company's best officers and NCOs to the Philippine Army in December had sapped its leadership, making a bad situation worse. Even less excusable, no senior officer of the regiment inspected the line. All day long, farm carts passed in front of B Company unchallenged on their way to Layac. That evening, two Filipinos came into the company area carrying a washtub of ice and San Miguel beer that they sold for a peso a bottle. Those who had the money guzzled the cool brew to fend off the oppressive heat. The 31st Infantry spent its last day of relative peace in a relaxed mood. Japanese troops that had mauled the Philippine Army all across Luzon were near but they would be no match for real American troops—or would they?

Around midnight, the 26th Cavalry's lead unit came through the line and began filing into positions on the 31st Infantry's left. The hardy Philippine Scouts had fought a constant delaying action for two weeks and were thoroughly exhausted, but they came through in good order and began digging in as soon as they reached their positions. Most would get no sleep that night or the next. At around 1 a.m. on January 6, as the last Scout unit crossed the bridge at Layac, the 14th Engineers blew up the Culo River Bridge with a thundering blast, closing the main route into Bataan. The battle for the rest of Luzon was over but the battle for Bataan would soon begin.

A native hut near Nichols Field, demolished by a direct hit in the air raid of December 9, 1941 (U.S. Army photograph).

Mortars and Artillery Open the Battle

Around 10 a.m. on January 6, Japanese troops could be clearly seen moving across open fields toward the Culo River. They were quickly taken under fire by the 75mm Howitzers of nearby Philippine Scout and Philippine Army field artillery battalions. The barrage went unanswered for about 30 minutes, leaving pack animals, Japanese soldiers, and artillery caissons strewn along Highway 7 and scattered across adjacent cane fields. Japanese guns went into hasty firing positions but were quickly suppressed by accurate counterbattery fire. Around 11 a.m. Japanese artillery withdrew beyond the range of the 75mm guns and unleashed a counterfire barrage, smashing one battery after another of Philippine Army and Scout artillery, plainly visible on the heights. Japanese 105mm and 150mm guns outranged the defenders and were supported by aerial observers who flew unchallenged over the battlefield. Artillery prime movers were in assembly areas near Abucay and could not be called forward to move the guns out of harm's way because Japanese aerial observers could bring in accurate fire on the only road available. Still, most gunners stayed at their posts under fire for nearly three hours, losing heavily. Private John Lally, an 18-year-old medic with G Company, characterized the 23rd Field Artillery's stand as "the bravest thing I ever saw." The few surviving guns had to be pushed to the rear along steep jungle trails. By 2 p.m., all Scout and Philippine Army artillery had been smashed or driven out of position.

With opposing artillery suppressed, Japanese artillery shifted its attention to the Philippine 71st Division holding the right of the line. The initial barrage threw up a large dust cloud in a plowed cane field in front of the Filipinos, giving Japanese infantrymen concealment as they moved up to the Culo River. The barrage then advanced onto the Filipinos' positions. The continuous geysers of dust and the loud, earth-shaking "carrump" of impacting shells was unnerving to even those not directly affected. When the barrage was lifted, there was an exchange of gunfire for about ten minutes as Japanese infantry engaged Filipinos still holding the line.

Next, the barrage shifted to the 31st Infantry, engulfing the 2nd Battalion in a deafening roar of concussive explosions for about five minutes. On the left flank, Sergeant Earl Walk's machine gunners hunkered down in shallow foxholes, wishing they had dug deeper into the hard clay earth and praying to be spared. All Walk could see was choking clouds of brown dust amid the steady thunderclaps of bursting shells. Private Bill Garleb, seemed to disappear when a round burst near the edge of his foxhole. To his amazement, the explosion sent all the blast and fragmentation upward from the hard soil, leaving Garleb unhurt but temporarily deaf. It was the first time the men had experienced incoming artillery and it was more than some could bear. PFC James Spencer, a 1st Battalion medic, raised his head just long enough to see two panic-stricken soldiers abandon their foxholes and dash toward the rear. Captain Richard Carnahan of C Company, waving a pistol, intercepted them, forcing them back to their positions. Captain John Pray of G Company remembered seeing a red bird singing its heart out only five feet from his foxhole as shells crashed all around. It could have flown away, but chose to stay and watch this bizarre display of human madness. If the bird could stand it, so could Pray. He slithered out of his foxhole and crawled along the line to steady his men and check for casualties. Three times his men reported him killed as he disappeared in convulsive clouds of smoke and debris when shells burst near him. Each time, when the dust cleared, Pray crawled on unhurt.

6 Jungle Warfare

The barrage soon lifted, but the worst was yet to come. No artillery had yet hit B Company's sector, but Japanese infantry suddenly appeared in a cane field on its exposed right flank. Private Harold Garrett recalled that "it seemed that whole field got up and moved." As the firing began, one soldier recalled "It seemed like a bunch of bees hit our position," but not a single man was hit. Corporal Milton Alexander raked the field with his .30 caliber machine gun while two others nearby opened up with BARs. For a moment, the Japanese seemed to falter under the sudden outburst of automatic fire, but their advance soon drifted southward along B Company's right flank. Amid the steady crackle of rifle and machine gun fire, Lieutenant Murphy ordered one of his platoons to move around the stream in the company's center to reinforce the right flank. They were in the open as Japanese mortars opened up and although no rounds landed near them, they fled in panic toward Philippine Scout artillery positions on higher ground about 800 yards to the rear. Their panic precipitated a full-scale rout as the entire company, including the command post, abruptly abandoned its positions and fled.

Corporal Paul Kerchum, sweating heavily and running clumsily with his machine gun over his shoulder, had gone about 100 yards with his squad leader, Sergeant Donald Bridges, who was carrying the gun's tripod and several belts of ammunition.[1] Kerchum shouted, "What the hell's going on, Don? We ain't supposed to be doing this." Seeing that the Japanese were not pursuing them, the two men dropped behind cover, completely out of breath.[2] There was no one on their left or right, but there were plenty of B Company men scrambling up the slope behind them. Most ended their retreat when they reached Philippine Scout artillery positions, but at least one man kept going all the way to Limay, about 15 miles down the peninsula.[3] Ashamed of their behavior, most hoped for a chance to make amends that day, but it was too late for their commander. For his company's lack of discipline under fire, Lieutenant Lloyd C. Murphy was relieved of command and was replaced by Captain John W. Thompson.[4]

Small Arms Join the Fight

In contrast, C Company stubbornly held its positions as Japanese infantry closed in with bayonets fixed. Private George Uzelac shook with fright until he began ripping into the packed Japanese ranks with his BAR. The weapon's loud metallic stuttering sound had a calming influence on him. Lieutenant Colonel Ed Bowes, the 1st Battalion's Commander, ordered his reserve, Captain Cecil Welchko's A Company, to counterattack to regain control of B Company's abandoned sector.[5] The unsupported attack didn't get very far before it faltered under a brief flurry of machine gun, rifle, and mortar fire. Not a single man was hit, but A Company would go no further.

Desperate to retake B Company's lost positions, Colonel Steel committed Lieutenant Colonel Jasper Brady's 3d Battalion to the fight. At the time, the 3d Battalion was in good defensive positions and could perhaps have salvaged the situation from where it stood. I Company was dug in on the forward slope of the first ridge south of the Culo River Bridge and had a commanding view of the main road and B Company's sector to its front. On its left, L Company was dug in among scrub brush just forward of a drainage ditch and had a recently plowed cane field to its front, providing excellent cover and clear fields of fire. Behind I Company, K Company was dug in on the ridge's reverse slope and could also cover the main road passing just east of its positions. Nevertheless, Colonel Steel was determined to reoccupy B Company's untenable sector in the valley below. Shortly after 4 p.m., acting on Steel's orders, Lieutenant Colonel Brady directed Captains Ray Stroud (I Company) and Donald Thompson (L Company) to move forward and reoccupy B Company's abandoned positions.[6] Captain Tom Bell's M Company would support the attack with his heavy and light machine guns and 81mm mortars. Unfortunately, Japanese aerial observers spotted the 3d Battalion forming to attack and trouble was not far behind.

In the distance, Private Grant Workman heard a salvo of four guns, followed by another and another. In seconds, rounds began crashing into I Company, sending bushes, chunks of clay, stinging clouds of dust, and hot shell splinters flying in all directions. One man after another went down. Staff Sergeant John Juvan (Milwaukee) and Private James Clement (Cincinnati) were killed outright and Privates Raymond E. Campbell, John McCann, and William Roberts were seriously wounded.[7] Like B Company, I Company broke and fled to the rear. Unable to locate Captain Stroud in the melee, Lieutenant Charles Baker tried to rally the company. He and Private Woodrow Griffith earned the Silver Star that day for trying to do what others could not.[8] Captain Stroud was relieved of command for abandoning his company during the bombardment, although his command post was cut off from the rest of the company by artillery fire. Nevertheless, he was replaced by Captain Richard Roshe.[9]

In contrast, Company L, with Staff Sergeant Otto Jensen's heavy weapons platoon of M Company attached and accompanied by the 3d Battalion's executive officer, Major James J. O'Donovan, displayed aggressiveness and confidence, advancing by bounds from the bivouac area. First Sergeant William McNulty led the point squad, moving about 100 yards ahead of the company's main body. Despite several encounters with probing Japanese troops, McNulty's point element suffered only one casualty throughout the advance.[10] For his aggressiveness, personal bravery, and exemplary leadership in spearheading L Company's attack, First Sergeant McNulty earned the Distinguished Service Cross. Enduring almost constant shelling from Japanese mortars and artillery, L Company dashed forward 30 or 40 paces at a time, hitting the ground as shells slammed in around them, then rushing forward again before the dust settled. McNulty never allowed his men to falter, setting the pace by personal example. Private Wilburn Snyder, an 18-year-old, recalled "There wasn't any doubt in our minds that we could whip the Japs." Corporal Paul Kerchum, one of the men who had halted just behind B Company's positions, was surprised to see Captain Thompson waving his men forward with a .45 caliber pistol. Advancing on L Company's right, M Company's machine gunners, led by Lieutenant

Ernest Fountain, also moved forward by bounds to keep pouring a steady volume of fire across the north-south highway. Japanese troops attempting to cross the highway into B Company's former position were scattered, retreating to a mango grove several hundred yards to the north.

On reaching a wooded hill about 400 yards to the rear of B Company's former position, L Company encountered the commander of the Philippine Army's 3d Battalion 72d Infantry Regiment, who requested support on his left flank, where B Company had abandoned its positions. The officer said his troops were still holding their position and sent a runner to escort Staff Sergeant John P. Flynn of the 3d Battalion Headquarters and PFC Manuel R. Rogers of L Company to his left flank company to see the situation for themselves. Moving cautiously into the valley and across the highway via a drainage ditch, the group reached the command post of L Company, 72d Infantry. The Filipinos were indeed still holding their sector but their situation was tenuous since the whole 72d Regiment had only a single machine gun left. The group's arrival attracted enemy fire from a mango grove about 150 yards away. Sergeant Flynn sent Rogers back to inform Major O'Donovan of the situation and then moved alone across the highway to B Company's former position, finding it empty. As he moved along the abandoned line, he was fired on by an enemy patrol moving through a cane field about 400 yards away. About a half hour later, Rogers and PFC Grady Gentry, sent forward to serve as runners, joined him. Now under steady fire, Flynn sent Rogers back to tell O'Donovan that B Company's sector was empty, leaving a 500-yard gap in the line. A few minutes later, Rogers returned, unable to get through the artillery barrage still landing behind them. Undaunted, PFC Gentry asked to give it a try and was soon off. Three times that day Gentry braved increasingly heavy small arms, mortar, and artillery fire to convey messages back and forth between Flynn and O'Donovan. For his courage under fire, he was awarded the Silver Star.

Late in the afternoon, Captain Coral M. Talbot's K Company came abreast of L Company and was dispatched by Major O'Donovan to establish contact with whoever held the 1st Battalion's right flank. L Company continued covering the road from its hillside position. Accompanied by Lieutenant Fountain and Lieutenant Zoberbier's platoon of M Company, K Company occupied B Company's abandoned position near dusk. Shortly after dark, one of its patrols linked up with A Company, about 300 yards to the west. The remainder of M Company moved up to provide support, arriving shortly after dark. Major O'Donovan ordered K Company to shift to the right to reinforce the Filipinos and moved L Company up on their left. As K Company settled into its new positions east of the highway, patrols guided by green-lensed flashlights could be seen moving out of the mango grove from which Flynn and Rogers had taken fire earlier in the day. Captain Talbot ordered Lieutenant Zoberbier's machine gun platoon to open fire. The Japanese did not move around any more that night.

Stopped on the right, the Japanese shifted their attention to the left where the 26th Cavalry held the foothills of Bataan's formidable mountain spine. Despite heavy shelling that seemed to intensify around 8 p.m., the line held, but the situation was bad. All supporting artillery was out of action, the Philippine Army's 71st Division was a battered fragment that could not hope to hold its line, the 31st Infantry Regiment had lost two companies, even if only temporarily, and a squadron of the 26th Cavalry had suffered heavy losses during the evening's bombardment. To the rear, II Corps' ammunition dump had been bombed, setting the adjacent town afire and blocking the main road with rubble. Colonel Steel recommended withdrawing that night to avoid being targeted by Japanese

A building burns after being hit during a Japanese air raid in Barrio Parañaque, Philippines, December 13, 1941 (U.S. Army photograph).

planes the next day. Although some men may still have felt confident of victory, Steel did not. Major General Parker agreed and ordered the withdrawal.

Giving up the Layac Line was fateful because it opened the door to Bataan. From the foothills of Mount Natib in the center, Japanese troops would gain positional advantage over American and Filipino troops trying to hold lower ground to the east and west. Moreover, steep jungle trails up and over the mountain offered the Japanese a corridor into II Corps' rear. American and Filipino artillery, forced to displace from the mountain's forward slopes, faced a formidable task in finding new firing positions that could support a new line. Everything depended on establishing and holding a strong position in the center. Unfortunately, that task would fall to one of the weakest units in the line—the Philippine Army's 51st Division.

At 10 p.m., the 26th Cavalry and 31st Infantry received a warning order to move back three miles and board trucks and buses that would be waiting on the main road. Because the trail behind the 26th Cavalry and 31st Infantry ran east-west, both regiments had to withdraw parallel to the front, a particularly perilous operation at night while enemy patrols probed for weak spots in the line. Although a bright half-moon and clear skies helped the troops stay on course, the natural illumination also helped Japanese reconnaissance patrols see what was happening. At midnight, the Philippine 71st Division departed and K Company fanned out to cover its sector. Kitchen and supply vehicles that had been lined up on the main road also departed at midnight. On the east-west trail, guides were posted at intervals to keep the withdrawal on course. Companies E and K of the 31st would cover the regiment's withdrawal.

A motorized battalion of the 26th Cavalry pulled out with the main body of the 31st Infantry around 1:30 a.m. on January 7. The roar and gradually fading noises of vehicle engines no doubt alerted the Japanese that a major withdrawal was underway. K Company, covering the right of the line, came out without incident behind the main body. The withdrawal went surprisingly well until Captain Robert S. Sauer's E Company, the last unit on line, began withdrawing. Knowing the entire sector was being vacated, the Japanese attacked, moving quickly around E Company's open flanks. Finding its withdrawal route under Japanese control and under attack from all sides, the company came apart, breaking into small groups to fight a running retreat into the jungle. Hearing the steady rattle of gunfire from E Company's area, Captain Eugene Conrad's F Company turned around to attack a Japanese unit that had reached the east-west trail. Conrad's unexpected initiative took some pressure off of E Company, but it would be days before E Company's last stragglers found their way through the jungle to rejoin the regiment. Miraculously, only four men had been killed and two were missing and presumed dead.[11] Captain Sauer's and First Sergeant Beresford Seale's extraordinary efforts to bring their men out alive that night earned them both the Silver Star. The regiment had now lost a third of its rifle companies at Layac. All would soon be recovered, but the damage was done. Having gained the Layac line without much of a fight, the Japanese came to have little respect for the best America could muster. They would show their lack of respect four months later on a trek that became known as the Death March.

Counterattack at Abucay

Around 7:30 a.m. on January 7, the 31st Infantry reached kilometer post 139 near the barrio of Pandan on the main north-south highway. The regiment dug in from Manila Bay to a point about 1000 yards west of the highway. The men worked feverishly to create a position that would not be penetrated. They were determined that there would be no repeat of the shameful experience they had just endured at Layac. To their left, the Air Corps Regiment was also digging in, but not very well. The 31st was tapped to send experienced officers and NCOs to show them how—a drain on the regiment's thin leadership. By January 15, the Pandan position was well prepared, completely wired in, and expertly camouflaged. The regiment could take justifiable pride in its accomplishment, but it would not have the opportunity to defend the position. That night, the regiment was ordered to move to a new assembly area 20 km to the rear at a former Philippine Army training camp west of Balanga. The move was completed by eight the next morning. There, the regiment had a hot meal that would be its last for three days.

After two days of fighting at Layac, eight days of hard physical labor building defensive positions at Pandan on half rations, and a 20-kilometer forced march from Balanga at night without rest, men simply dropped to the ground and slept, oblivious to their surroundings. Balanga had been bombed the day before and was still burning, but the troops paid little attention. Around noon on January 16, the weary regiment was alerted to move again. The Philippine Army's 51st Division had disintegrated and the 31st was ordered to restore a wide gap that had been cut into the line near Abucay Hacienda. Fifteen minutes later, the regiment was back on the road with the 2d Battalion leading. Marching 16 kilometers with only two 10-minute rest stops, the 31st reached its jump-off position around 7 p.m. Filipino troops of the 51st Division were still straggling to the rear, shouting "Japs coming." Behind them, they left their division command post surrounded by the enemy. By 1 a.m. on January 17, the 31st Infantry's lead elements had advanced to within 700 yards of Abucay Hacienda, a small farming settlement marked by its prominent Spanish-built church.

Because the terrain in the 2d Battalion's zone was overgrown with dense vegetation and segmented by ravines and ridges, soldiers became separated from their comrades. In one such incident, Privates Michael J. Campbell, Albert L. Taylor, and George L. Bullock of G Company found themselves isolated when their platoon fell back under enemy mortar and small arms fire.[12] Joining a five-man patrol from an adjacent company, the group advanced deeper into enemy territory, only to be stopped by a sudden outburst of fire that wounded five members of the patrol. Japanese troops advanced on their exposed position, moving in short rushes preceded by grenade attacks. Tenaciously clinging to his position for two hours, Private Campbell and his comrades picked off at least twelve of the enemy trying to overrun them. Campbell withdrew only after the wounded reached safety and after receiving a direct order from his commanding officer to withdraw. For his tenacity in the face of overwhelming odds, Private Campbell was awarded the Silver Star.

After bringing its companies into alignment, the 3d Battalion's advance resumed with I Company on the left, K in the center, and L on the right. Shortly afterward, I Company began taking small arms and mortar fire and was halted to enable the 1st Battalion to come abreast on its left. Because of the regiment's unfamiliarity with the area, it was decided to halt the attack until daylight. The men had not eaten since 4 a.m. on January 16, intensifying the weakening effect of half rations.

At 8:15 a.m. on January 17, the 1st and 2d Battalions advanced in parallel columns flanking Trail 12. To overcome its disgrace at Layac, Colonel Steel gave B Company the honor of leading the 1st Battalion's advance. The men had shown little faith in Lieutenant Murphy, their previous commander, but considered Captain John Thompson a professional worthy of their confidence. The advance went well despite sporadic small arms fire. Most of the Japanese fire came from snipers in trees overlooking the trails. On his own initiative, Corporal Charles Ball moved up to the head of B Company's column, repeatedly stitching the treetops with his BAR to shoot snipers out of their perches. Ball was an Indian from Montana's Fort Belknap Reservation, where he learned to track and hunt from his father and uncles. The experience gave him a keen eye for anything unusual in his surroundings. Although Japanese snipers expertly tucked sprigs of vegetation into their belts, leggings, and hats to hide their positions, their camouflage wilted quickly in the tropical heat, exposing them to Ball's sharp eyes. His BAR also gave him a range advantage over Japanese snipers' .25 caliber Arisaka rifles, making the outcome of every outburst of fire on B Company's path a certainty. Ball and his boyhood friend, Private Joe Longknife of K Company, became legends for their uncanny ability to spot and shoot snipers out of trees.

The 51st Division's isolated command post was rescued around 10 a.m. Just beyond, the 1st Battalion ran into stiff resistance as it emerged from an acacia grove. Machine gun fire was so heavy it cut a nearby cane field about knee high. Fortunately, the ground sloped away to the rear, causing the Japanese to fire high. On the skyline across the cane field stood the church spire of Abucay Hacienda, the battalion's objective. For what seemed an eternity, B Company lay pinned down by machine gun fire, but eventually there arose problems greater than the Japanese. Corporal Paul Kerchum lay atop a colony of red ants. When they bit him in unmentionable places, he jumped up as if shocked by a cattle prod, hollering "let's get the hell out of here," dashing blindly toward the Japanese. Taken by surprise, Kerchum's entire platoon jumped up and followed his example, charging across the field, shouting and firing wildly. Startled by the Americans suddenly charging at them, the Japanese retreated in disorder down a steep slope. Following in hot pursuit, B Company's Weapons Platoon drifted steadily to the left, stopping on a steep slope overlooking the Balantay River. The rest of the company eventually formed around it, but it didn't take long for another Japanese unit to begin probing the position its comrades had just lost. Private Ronald T. Wangberg, the company's only Jewish member, spotted a squad-size patrol moving across an open glade in the valley below. He picked them off one by one as they ran back and forth trying to find cover.

B Company was now in a very exposed position, awaiting the arrival of other companies to take up positions on its flank. Captain Thompson decided he would need help to hold the position if the Japanese realized how vulnerable his company was. Communications between units relied entirely on messengers, there was no artillery in range, and II Corps had already denied a request for tank support due to concerns about Japanese aerial observation. That left only mortars. With all 30 rounds of their 81mm ammunition exhausted, D Company gunners fired World War I–era 75mm Stokes mortar ammunition from their larger 81mm tubes, causing the rounds to wobble erratically in flight. Perhaps three of every ten detonated. Several detonated in the dry cane field, setting it afire. As the wind blew the flames and acrid smoke back in B Company's direction, Captain Thompson yelled "cease fire, cease fire," but it was too late. Several 75mm rounds landed among his men, catching them in the open as they tried to escape.

After withdrawing, B Company established new positions farther to the rear, but the Japanese were not far behind. Repeated attacks failed to break B Company's new line, but snipers managed to infiltrate behind them. Corporal Paul Kerchum was checking the line after a spate of firing when he tapped the helmet of Private Jim Broadrick who was standing in a narrow foxhole, seemingly asleep. Kerchum hadn't gone much farther when someone yelled, "Better get down corporal, they just got Broadrick." The day's fight had been bloody, costing B Company five dead and seven wounded, one of whom later died of his wounds. The company had regained its pride, but at a high cost.[13]

The 1st Battalion's other companies fared little better. Advancing into an open field in front of A Company, Lieutenant Charles Litkowski, Corporal Robert H. Dickson, and Private Leonard Prusak were cut down by a burst of machine gun fire. Litkowski and Prusak were hit in the head and killed instantly, but Dickson was still alive, although barely and not for long. Private John Cierciersky, a medic, tried to help him, but was killed by the same machine gun. Perhaps five others in A Company were wounded that day as Americans and Japanese blazed away at each other across open ground.[14] C Company's only casualty of the day was Sergeant Edgar Congdon, killed by a burst of machine gun fire. D Company, supporting the rifle companies with machine gun and mortar fire, suffered almost as many casualties as the companies they supported.[15]

Throughout the fight, the 1st Battalion drifted ever farther to the left, opening a gap between itself and the 2d Battalion. K Company was sent from the 3d Battalion to plug the gap between the 1st and 2d Battalions. The Philippine Scout 45th Infantry, starting 6,000 yards farther south, came abreast of the 31st Infantry in late afternoon, forming a combined assault force of 13 rifle companies and 4 machine gun companies, backed by 5 more rifle companies and 2 machine gun companies in reserve. Sergeant Earl Walk recalls that H Company moved up the main highway toward Abucay on 1934 Dodge weapons carriers until they were stopped by mortar fire. Private Clarence Carrico was hit in the chest by a mortar fragment and was evacuated to the field hospital at Limay.[16] Captain Dwight T. Hunkins ordered the vehicles hidden in a wooded area and the company proceeded on foot for about 1,000 yards, reaching a well-prepared position abandoned earlier by Filipino troops. Several Filipino stragglers were incorporated into the company as ammunition bearers. Sergeant Earl Walk had his platoon set up its 2 mortars and its .50 caliber machine gun where they could best cover a sugar cane field in front of the position. Japanese small arms fire whizzed and snapped all around. When Walk fired 20 rounds at the enemy-held woodline with his two mortars, the sector became quiet for a while.

That day, four American P-40 Warhawks, operating from a concealed strip cut into the jungle near Mariveles Point on Bataan, conducted surprise raids against Japanese planes operating over the front lines. Unfortunately, they came too late to prevent another Japanese bombing raid. Corporal William Easler and Private Robert E. Ragan were relaxing in a foxhole in the shade of a huge tree. Without warning, a bomb crashed through the tree's branches, landing directly in the foxhole and blowing its occupants to eternity. Others were luckier. Sergeant Walk heard a dull thud, followed by a muffled explosion. He was bowled over backward by concussion as the ground rose to form a huge mound about ten feet in front of him. A bomb had burrowed deep into the earth before exploding. Several days later, a Japanese mortar round landed next to one of H Company's machine gun positions, setting off a hand grenade Corporal Franklin O. Warr was carrying in his gas mask container. Warr died of his extensive wounds.

At 4 p.m. on January 19, the 2d and 3d Battalions of the 31st Infantry and 1st and 2d Battalions of the 45th Infantry renewed their advance but by 7 p.m., units had become separated in the dense jungle growth. The 2d Battalion, 31st Infantry, advancing with F, G, and E Companies abreast, had to cross a steep ravine to reach its objective. They were supported by a few rounds of artillery from the Philippine 41st Division, but had no other protective fire as they entered the gap. The men climbed hand over hand down slippery vines, crossed a knee-deep creek, and ascended the opposite slope in the same manner. As they climbed, they could hear Japanese leaders shouting commands above them. In the tangled underbrush, men became separated from their units and confusion reigned.

On the ridge, the 2d Battalion hit what turned out to be the main body of an enemy regiment moving in the opposite direction. In the ensuing action, Private Elmer C. Duffy was hit by a burst of machine gun fire while walking point for F Company. He was probably already dead but no one could be sure. Disregarding his own safety, PFC Elmer P. Buehrig dashed forward to aid Duffy and was hit in the face by a burst from the same gun. For his selfless sacrifice, Buehrig was posthumously awarded the Distinguished Service Cross. Private "Red" Dyer charged into the field firing his BAR from the waist. Hit in the arm and chest as he charged out alone, Dyer continued firing until he collapsed. Miraculously, he was still alive and was later transported to a field hospital where he recovered from his wounds.[17] Seven others from F Company were wounded before sundown.[18] When a Japanese machine gun halted E Company's advance, PFC James H. Cody and Private Albert F. Tresch[19] volunteered to silence it. Crawling forward with BARs and hand grenades, the duo not only destroyed the Japanese machine gun and killed its crew, but they also put a second Japanese gun out of action. Their deed earned them both the Silver Star.

Some of the regiment's hand grenades turned out to be unmarked practice grenades and few of the others detonated, costing men their lives. PFC Ron Wangberg responded to a Japanese machine gun's fire on B Company by crawling forward in the darkness and throwing grenades at the gun. His first grenade exploded, but missed. Wangberg crawled still closer and threw another grenade, this time a dud. The Japanese gun crew heard him moving toward them and killed him with a sustained burst of fire. For his valiant effort, Wangberg was posthumously awarded the Distinguished Service Cross. Private Dale L. Snyder, a machine gunner with D Company, joined another man in volunteering to attack the same Japanese gun. Crossing 100 yards of open cane field under constant fire, he and his partner reached a point where they could engage the enemy gun with grenades. Miraculously, Dale Snyder succeeded where Wangberg had died trying. The gun was destroyed. For his bravery, Snyder received the Silver Star. When word of the bad grenades reached the company supply sergeants, Sergeant Mike Gilewitch found that some had only a little powder in them and others had none at all.

Major O'Donovan, the 2d Battalion's Executive Officer, reached G Company in the ravine late in the afternoon. He ordered, "Attack at once," but saying it was easier than doing it. Before nightfall, two of the company's platoons had scaled a dry waterfall and reached the top. The remaining platoon did not reach the top until after dark. As it arrived, it engaged a group of Japanese, but both sides became disoriented in the dark tangle of jungle vegetation. His own men accidentally killed Corporal Stanley P. Nogacek as he returned from a reconnaissance.

The combination of guns, fear, and darkness were to prove tragic again. Uncertain of F Company's progress in front of him, Lieutenant Robert Magee placed an attached machine gun platoon from H Company at ten foot intervals along a trail and warned his men to be on the lookout for infiltrators. He sent Corporal Hugh Piper ahead to find F Company. Long after dark, the machine gun platoon's point man heard a slight rustling noise on the trail. He jumped up and began firing wildly at a ghostly figure trying to move stealthily in his direction. Hit by the sentry's first burst, Corporal Piper screamed weakly, "Don't shoot, don't shoot!" It was too late. Piper fell dead, hit six times.

As the platoon gathered to see what had happened, Japanese 47mm knee mortars opened up from a short distance away. One shell, luckily a dud, hit the rim of Private Bill Garleb's helmet, slamming his face into the dirt and breaking his glasses. Lieutenant Magee ordered his men to pull back, holding each other's pistol belts as they followed the trail down a precipitous ravine. Magee and Staff Sergeant Williams led, followed by the sobbing soldier who had killed Piper, then Private Garleb, Private Charles A. Henderson, and the rest of the platoon.[20] As Japanese artillery opened up on the platoon's former position, Garleb realized Henderson was no longer behind him. Reaching a stream, the four men in front were unable to find the path up the opposite bank in the darkness and hid under a ledge to await daylight as the crescendo of fire intensified.

It soon became apparent that they were caught between opposing lines as American mortars and 75mm field guns, and Japanese artillery fired round after round into and across the ravine. The soldier who had killed Piper lost control of his bladder and sobbed,

"We're going to be killed. Please God, don't let us die." Japanese assault troops had entered the ravine and were heading their way, although it was uncertain whether they had been seen. Magee put his cocked pistol against the whimpering man's forehead and whispered, "Shut your mouth. Another word and I'll blow your damned head off." Fortunately, they remained undetected as Japanese troops stumbled back into the ravine after their attack failed. With the first rays of dawn, the four found the path up the friendly side of the ravine and scrambled to safety. Major Lloyd C. Moffitt, the 2d Battalion's Commander, greeted them, "We thought you were dead." They were soon reunited with the rest of their platoon who had made it safely across the ravine ahead of the Japanese during the night.

On January 20, the 31st and 45th Infantry Regiments renewed their attacks, but the effort was impossible to synchronize in the thick jungle terrain. Companies and sometimes platoons fought alone along narrow jungle trails and across the deep ravines segmenting the battlefield. As the 3d Battalion moved forward, M Company fired 80 rounds of its precious 81mm mortar ammunition to keep the Japanese pinned down while I and L Companies advanced across a cane field. Unfortunately, it was too little to keep the Japanese pinned down long enough for the entire battalion to get across the field.

Private Burton Ellis, a medic with I Company, was hit in both legs by a burst of machine gun fire. Corporal Marchel D. Easley tried to rescue him, but was cut down by a burst from the same gun that got Ellis. Easley was dead and no one could reach Ellis, an agonizing situation for a unit whose medics risked so much to help wounded infantrymen. After dark, a Filipino doctor and his helper came out to rescue Ellis, guided by a lantern. Ellis survived because his tight leggings kept him from bleeding to death. Moving far to the left, L Company attacked the grove from which Easley and Ellis had been shot. To scout the way, Sergeant Clifford Clegg led a patrol around the edge of the field through thicker vegetation. Spotting a four-man Japanese patrol, Clegg's squad ambushed the group, killing or wounding them all. Cautiously, Clegg and his men moved away, fearful of attracting a larger group of Japanese. As time went by and the patrol did not return, Staff Sergeants John Flynn and William W. White went out to investigate. They found Clegg's squad crouched no more than 50 yards from a group of about 70 Japanese sitting in a clearing, talking and apparently ignorant of danger. There were several Japanese posted in trees, but they seemed oblivious to their duties, talking with their comrades below.

While Private Peter Chamote kept watch, Clegg brought the rest of the company forward, moving them quietly into positions where they could engage the Japanese.[21] Some were unable to see through the thick grass and underbrush that concealed their presence, but were instructed to fire in the direction of the Japanese voices. Such conditions generally cause inexperienced soldiers to fire high, probably wasting much of the available firepower and dissipating its shock effect. On order, the entire company opened fire, scattering the Japanese who quickly responded with heavy fire of their own. Seven Americans were hit in the ensuing melee. Private John Lally, one of the company's medics, carried several men to safety under fire despite being painfully wounded himself. For repeated heroism that day, Lally was awarded the Distinguished Service Cross. Later, as he was helping to evacuate the wounded to the Regimental Aid Station, a mortar shell blew him into the air, blinding him from the concussion. Although still partially blind and not fully recovered from his wounds, Lally returned from the hospital several weeks later and faithfully continued his duties.

As L Company withdrew from the ambush site, Captain Thompson called for mortar fire, but there was none to send. Captain John Pray of G Company came to L Company's position in a nearby ravine and offered his help. His company had attacked the same position several days earlier and knew the terrain well. Reinforced by G Company, Captain Thompson sent a message to battalion asking for permission to attack, but no response came. At dusk, I Company was ordered to attack but made little headway in the face of intense machine gun and mortar fire. Around 9 p.m., a detail from Battalion Headquarters brought up canned rations and all companies were withdrawn to the back side of a protective ridge to eat in relative safety.

All night long, Japanese voices could be heard infiltrating between the 31st and 45th Infantry Regiments. The same was true on the 45th Infantry's left flank. The uncoordinated attacks launched on January 17 through 20 had opened gaps between adjacent regiments and the Japanese were quick to exploit them. On the morning of January 20, the 3d Battalion dug in on the forward slope of a long ridge with I Company on the right and L Company on the left. That afternoon, K Company attacked over the same ground I Company had covered the day before. After taking several casualties on its intended path, K Company drifted to the left and ended up on the 1st Battalion's right flank. As Japanese troops infiltrated between the 31st and 45th Infantry, the 1st Battalion wheeled to the left to face a threat mounting on its flank. K Company, occupying a major trail intersection west of Abucay Hacienda, became the pivotal hinge between the 1st and 3d Battalions. On the right, the Japanese attempted to cross a small, bare hill about 300 yards from L Company. A machine gun section under Sergeant Harry Neff kept the hill swept clean each time the Japanese appeared. Lieutenant Armentrout, the attached artillery forward observer, guessed the area behind the hill might be an assembly area and called for fire. Screams and groans could be heard between the whistling and crumping of 75mm shells, confirming Armentrout's suspicions. Shortly afterward, Private Julius Stewart scattered several groups of survivors, dropping several with his BAR as they tried to cross the Hacienda Road into the barrio.[22]

On the evening of January 20, the weary troops were ordered to dig in. Japanese snipers had infiltrated behind the 31st and 45th Infantry and an entire Japanese division was moving across the Balantay River. The main blow fell against the 31st Infantry's 1st Battalion at 10 a.m. on January 21. As the battalion gave ground under steady pressure, the gap began to widen between the 31st and 45th Infantry. Japanese troops poured into the breach and infiltrated behind the 1st Battalion. After dark, the 1st Battalion began withdrawing, company by company, down a narrow jungle trail traversing a winding, steep-sided ravine behind and parallel to the regiment's line. Once the 1st Battalion passed behind it, the 3d Battalion began withdrawing, leaving K Company in place to cover its departure. Soon after L Company withdrew, around 11:30 p.m., Japanese troops cut the trail to K Company's east, causing Captain Talbot to organize a hasty horseshoe-shaped defensive position around the trail junction.

Knowing his company was in danger of becoming surrounded, Talbot selected a third of his men to form a detachment left in contact under Lieutenant James I. Mallette. The men were posted to cover trails entering the company's perimeter and received orders to intensify their fire to make it appear the full company was still in place, giving their comrades a chance to make it to safety down the ravine to their rear. When Captain Talbot ordered that the wounded be evacuated with the first platoon to depart, PFC Richard F. Gomes, a BAR gunner wounded in the hip and both legs, refused evacuation,

1LT Coral M. Talbot (later CPT), center, on maneuvers, October 10, 1941. Eight weeks later the Japanese landed. He would make it through the Defense of the Philippines and the Bataan Death March, but die in Cabanatuan POW camp of cerebral malaria (Association archives, courtesy the Thompson collection).

arguing that he would only slow down his comrades trying to escape down the steep jungle trail.[23] As the main body departed under increasingly heavy fire, PFC Gomes told a fellow squad member, Private Clifford H. Mygrant, to collect all the BAR ammunition he could and place it near Gomes' position. Superior numbers of Japanese troops had crawled dangerously close to K Company's thinly held line and would likely overrun it unless sustained firepower could be delivered to hold them back long enough for the remaining detachment to escape. The company's only remaining mortar had no ammunition left and the regiment's supporting artillery battalion had already displaced out of range. Moreover, the detachment had no radio to call for or adjust fire.

The situation grew increasingly desperate as the number of men left to hold the company's sector shrank. Knowing he was sacrificing his life, PFC Gomes volunteered to stay behind alone to cover the detachment's withdrawal. With the Japanese closing in, Lieutenant Mallette and Private Mygrant stayed with him as long as they could but could not persuade Gomes to allow them to help him reach safety. From his position of advantage overlooking the four-way trail junction, Gomes kept up a steady rate of fire, traversing his automatic weapon to keep fire on each trail as the last of his comrades departed. Given his wounds, such exertions must have been excruciatingly painful. Captain Ralph E. Hibbs, the 3d Battalion's Surgeon, heard a lone gun still firing up on the ridge as he loaded the last of the wounded survivors into a makeshift ambulance in the valley below.

Without PFC Gomes' selfless act of courage and self-sacrifice, it is doubtful that any of his comrades in the last detachment could have escaped. Soon after Lieutenant Mallette and Private Mygrant departed Gomes' position, a sustained burst of fire from Gomes' weapon was answered by exploding hand grenades and intense rifle and machine gun fire as Japanese troops swarmed over K Company's former position. PFC Richard Felix Gomes, the only son of a Portuguese immigrant family from the Azores, had sacrificed his life.

The next day, Sergeant Morris F. Lewis, K Company's Mess Sergeant, heard Captain Talbot telling Colonel Steel and Lieutenant Colonel Brady that Gomes should receive the Medal of Honor. On the roster Lieutenant Colonel Brady and Major Marshall Hurt compiled during their captivity at Cabanatuan, is an annotation next to Gomes' name, "M.H. recommended. After being wounded, and withdrawal of company ordered, told Mygrant to leave him and he would cover withdrawal of Co. Killed a few moments later while firing his AR rapidly." Today, no one knows if Gomes' Medal of Honor recommendation ever left Lieutenant General MacArthur's Headquarters on Corregidor where it would have had to be forwarded by submarine to the U.S. for approval. Gomes was, however, awarded the Distinguished Service Cross posthumously in February 1942, perhaps pending approval of the higher award. Local commanders could authorize award of the DSC, but only the President could approve the Medal of Honor.

Private Patrick Davie, now the only survivor of the K Company detachment left in contact, testified to Gomes' heroic deed in writing. Clifford Mygrant, hit in the legs during the action, died in captivity. Lieutenant Colonel Jasper Brady and Major Marshall Hurt also died in captivity, as did all of K Company's leaders above the grade of sergeant. Morris Lewis is still living, but was in the rear at the time of the action and has no personal knowledge of the event other than the conversation he overheard between Captain Talbot and his seniors. There is little doubt that Gomes' conscious self-sacrifice was sufficient to earn him the Medal of Honor and it might have been awarded if the 31st Infantry's records had been preserved. Unfortunately, most were destroyed before the surrender, leaving Gomes' Medal of Honor recommendation in limbo.

There were many other acts of heroism that day as individuals shunned danger to accomplish a difficult mission under the worst of conditions. Private Walter J. Cox, a medic with I Company, earned the Silver Star for dashing across a fire-swept trail to come to the rescue of several L Company men who had been hit. He pulled one man to safety and was hit himself while rescuing a second. Lieutenant Dean K. Wood of I Company received the Silver Star for exposing his position and drawing Japanese fire while Cox performed his rescue. When Cox went down, Wood dashed across the trail, firing as he charged. He was hit while helping Cox get the second man to safety. His Silver Star was subsequently upgraded to a Distinguished Service Cross. Two other 3d Battalion medics, PFC Edward J. Golkas and Private William O. Mann, were killed that day trying to help wounded comrades. Mann, wounded during his first foray to rescue a wounded man, was killed during a second rescue attempt, earning him the Distinguished Service Cross posthumously.

At night, Japanese snipers infiltrated through gaps in the line and climbed trees to await their quarry. Shortly after daybreak on January 23, a sniper's bullet found its victim in C Company. Corporal Charles Peterson lay sprawled in the dirt, quivering, with blood oozing from his temple. In a moment he was still. "Oh God, he's dead, my buddy's dead," sobbed PFC Andy Nickerson as he stood staring at Peterson's lifeless face. "Someone get

Nickerson back in his hole," yelled Sergeant Abraham, the company supply sergeant. Staff Sergeant Gerald Farnham quickly complied, knocking Nickerson for a loop, just as another shot rang out. No one was hit this time. Lieutenant Ralph Simmons ordered Private John Novak to find the shooter. The fire could only have come from a cluster of three mango trees, so the hunt was easy. When Simmons' patrol opened fire, the sniper fell quickly, dangling from a rope holding him to the tree. Men kept shooting long after he was dead but Nickerson wasn't satisfied and asked Simmons to allow him to blow the man's head off. Private Walter Southard, disgusted at the request, shouted, "What the hell's the matter with you, you getting' bloodthirsty?" "Go to hell, go straight to hell!" sobbed the grieving trooper as he took aim at the dead sniper.[24]

Japanese bombers soon returned, seriously wounding Corporal Charles Adams and killing Private Jose Campos. When the planes departed, "photo Joe," a reconnaissance plane, watched for signs of another target. C Company lay pinned down all day long for fear they would bring on another air or artillery attack. In the heat the bodies of the dead gave off a foul odor from which there was no escape. To this day, C Company's survivors refer to the position as "Dead Man's Hill."

Around noon, Captain John Pray of G Company became impatient for news of what was happening. As part of the 2d Battalion, he was supposed to exploit any success gained by the 3d Battalion's attack, but he did not know the 3d Battalion's plan or where it was. He decided to act on his own initiative. Over the next five hours, he managed to move his company, now down to 55 men, around the mangrove cluster where I and L Companies had been held up. Suddenly, the company was engulfed in a steady stream of rifle and machine gun fire. Two men were killed and eight were wounded. G Company was now little more than a platoon.

By nightfall, the 31st and 45th Infantry Regiments had pulled back almost to the line from which they began their counterattack five days earlier. The troops were exhausted. They had received little food or water, suffered heavy casualties, and got little sleep because Japanese infantry tended to be active at night and Japanese bombers and artillery were active by day. Against that backdrop, a Japanese infantry regiment struggled up Mount Natib in the center of the line and wearily descended down the mountain's back side into the rear of the II Corps' line. It was hard for the Americans and Filipinos to recognize, but the Japanese were also running out of steam.

7 Surrender

On January 24, the 31st Infantry was ordered to withdraw, covering the rest of II Corps as it abandoned the main line of resistance. One rifle company and one machine gun platoon per battalion were left behind to screen the main body's withdrawal. A provisional tank group consisting of two National Guard tank battalions and a battalion of 75mm self-propelled howitzers assisted them.[1] As the covering force began withdrawing at midnight on January 25, the Japanese attacked, shouting "Samurai." The infantry fought a stout delaying action before falling in behind a waiting screen of tanks and self-propelled howitzers that remained undetected by the enemy. When the infantry was safely behind them, the tanks and howitzers opened fire at close range, firing straight down trails densely packed with Japanese troops. The engagement threw the Japanese into a chaotic retreat, leaving hundreds dead or dying on the trails behind them.

At about 1:30 a.m. on January 25, the 31st Infantry's last elements to withdraw reached the barrio of Wawa on Manila Bay. Men quickly fell into an exhausted sleep. At 4 a.m. they were awakened for their first hot meal in two days—still half rations. There would be no more sleep that day because the regiment was again designated the covering force for II Corps. All of II Corps except the 31st Infantry had withdrawn to the Pandan Line. Fortunately, the Japanese were so exhausted and depleted that they could not pursue the dispirited units that came off the Abucay Line. By evening it became clear that a covering force was no longer needed and the 31st was ordered to withdraw to a bivouac area two kilometers west of Limay. At 3 a.m. on January 26, the 1st Battalion was ordered to occupy a sector on the new line.

From January 28 to February 1, the regiment got a sorely needed rest. The time was spent cleaning equipment and searching for food since rations supplied by the Army were insufficient to keep men functioning in the tropical heat. The entire Bataan Force was starting to feel the effects of gradual starvation, having been on half rations since the end of December 1941. Moreover, medicine was running out and Bataan's tropical jungle, with its plethora of diseases and unsanitary living conditions, was taking its toll. Malaria and dysentery became particularly rampant.

On February 1, the regiment was ordered north to an assembly area on the San Vicente River. The motor move was completed around 1 a.m. on February 2. On February 5, amid a sporadic enemy barrage, a howitzer shell hit the 3d Battalion Command Post, wounding Captains Donald G. Thompson of L Company and Richard Roshe of I Company. At dusk on February 5, the regiment moved by truck to assembly areas on the Alangan and Lamao Rivers. The 1st and 2d Battalions were posted just over a mile west of the main highway's crossing of the Alangan River. The Regimental Headquarters and 3d

Battalion were located about a mile and a half west of Lamao, near II Corps Headquarters. The regiment would stay in those positions until April 3. On March 1, Colonel Charles L. Steel moved up to become chief of Staff of II Corps. Lieutenant Colonel Jasper E. Brady replaced him as commander of the 31st Infantry. Major Marshall Hurt, who had been the Regimental Adjutant, replaced Brady as 3d Battalion Commander. On March 27, Lieutenant Colonel Cyril Q. Marron took command of the 2d Battalion, replacing Major Lloyd C. Moffit, who remained with the battalion as Marron's executive officer.

In early March, replacements were sent to the 31st Infantry from the Army Air Corps' 7th Chemical Company, and from the Philippine Department's 808th MP Company and Quartermaster Section. What the better-fed replacements found shocked them. Veteran infantrymen of the 31st were emaciated, covered with jungle sores, and most were sick with serious diseases. Their khaki uniforms had become little more than filthy sweat-soaked rags. Rations had declined to eight ounces of rice and one can of fish per day. To make matters worse, moist rice quickly became moldy in the tropical heat, adding to the rampant diarrhea in the camps. All carabao (water buffalo) on Bataan had already been butchered and eaten, as had the Quartermaster's pack mules, the 26th Cavalry Regiment's horses, and General Wainwright's horse. Men constantly foraged for edible roots and herbs, snails, snakes, monkeys, bananas, wild pigs, and stray chickens, but with over 70,000 American and Filipino soldiers on Bataan, the jungle was nearly picked clean of edible material. Although there were eleven cases of C-rations on each company's mess truck, they were reserved for "emergency" use only and it was a court martial offense to open them without authorization from Philippine Department Headquarters. Everyone grew weaker by the day and by April, the 31st Infantry Regiment mustered less than a full strength battalion of men able to walk unassisted. How bad would it have to get before someone in authority decided to declare the situation an emergency?

Mount Samat, the Last Battle

On April 1, 1942, the Japanese resumed their attack, practically destroying the Philippine Army's 41st Division. Filipino units that had fought bravely in January now simply evaporated under a thundering artillery barrage that lasted for several hours. Bunkers, foxholes, and the men who occupied them were churned and plowed under as the earth erupted again and again in geysers of dirt, steel shards, splintered trees, and broken bodies. Barbed wire that had been salvaged from the abandoned Abucay line at great effort and risk was blasted into shreds, opening wide corridors for waiting Japanese infantry. Any remaining communications wire was cut repeatedly by the barrage, leaving commanders unsure of who, if anyone, remained for them to command. Several thousand stragglers, including intact battalions, fled to adjacent sectors, creating a confused mess with no one quite sure of who was in charge. Bombers and fighters struck anything that moved, making it impossible for reinforcements to move forward. At 6 the next evening, the 31st Infantry was put on alert.

At 4 a.m. on Good Friday, April 3, 1942, the skeletal 31st Infantry began moving toward the breach, nearing the San Vicente River around five that evening with the 1st Battalion in the lead. Thunder and lightning boiled out of a darkening sky, signaling the possibility of a storm, but the coming storm would not be of nature's making. Corporals Irvin Hicks and Paul Kerchum of B Company recall that there was no briefing on the situation, only an order to move up. Those too sick or malnourished to fight were simply left behind, as were most heavy weapons. There were few men strong enough to carry a water-cooled machine gun and most mortars were out of ammunition anyway, so some rifle companies went forward with only rifles and BARs. Hicks and Kerchum were exceptions. They and their squads were still in fairly good shape due to repeated midnight raids on the Quartermaster food storage area, not far from their bivouac site. Many others had done the same, even though getting caught was a punishable offense. Starvation was a greater punishment, so the risk seemed well worth taking. On the evening of April 5, companies received a hot meal in a clearing south of the San Vicente River. They were also issued C-rations and cigarettes, the first they had in months. "We got three cans of dry and three cans of wet rations," recalls Private Tillman J. Rutledge. "We were so hungry some of us sat down and ate all six cans." Around 4 p.m., Colonel Brady assembled his company commanders and asked Captain Taylor, the regimental chaplain, to lead them in prayer.

Pouring through areas abandoned by units of the Philippine Army, Japanese troops gained the lower slopes of Mount Samat. The 31st Infantry would have to counterattack to throw them back and B Company would lead the attack. The order to attack drove some men to desperation. Here and there throughout the bivouac area, M-1 rifles and .45 caliber pistols barked as weakened men shot off toes or parts of other limbs to avoid having to go into battle. Private Romie C. Gregory, struggling to carry his machine gun, felt his morale sink. "It seemed like the whole Filipino Army was going the other way." As B Company advanced cautiously up a ridge, Lieutenant "Hootch" Sutphin, always in the lead, shot two Japanese snipers out of the trees with his M-1.[2] Japanese mortars opened up, wounding Sergeants Donald Bridges and George Wood. Captain Thompson ordered Kerchum and Hicks to set up their machine gun and spray the jungle ahead of the company, but they saw no enemy troops. After firing intermittently for about ten minutes, the company pulled back as word came that there were no friendly troops on the 31st Infantry's left or right. Private John Armellino, a veteran of two years each in Panama and the Philippines, recalls the horrible stench of death and the haunting sight of gauze bandages hanging from branches in streamers when his company found what had been a Philippine Army division's casualty collecting station.

Between midnight on April 5 and 1 a.m. on April 6, the 2d and 3d Battalions passed through the 1st Battalion and almost immediately G Company, leading the column, ran into a fight. Privates Guy H. Prichard, Jr., and James G. Deaton, G Company's point men, were hit by machine gun fire. Prichard, a quiet 20-year-old from Rensville, Pennsylvania, was killed instantly, and Deaton, a tall blond kid from Denver, was hit in the stomach and lay unable to move. Private Wil Sweeney dropped with his .30 caliber machine gun into the center of the trail and began firing steady bursts, just as he had been taught on Fort McKinley's B Range. Privates George Bullock and Albert Taylor crawled up on his left and right with BARs. "Sweeney would fire a burst, then I would fire a burst, and then Bullock would fire," recalled Taylor. "It was 30 minutes before we fought our way far enough to get Pritchard and Deaton out." Deaton died on the way to the Battalion Aid Station. Captain Denton Rees, a dentist assigned to the Regimental Aid Station, recalled "Our casualties were severe and it was difficult to evacuate them, but we managed with the help of the walking wounded."

The 2d Battalion continued its advance, although more slowly and cautiously. In the dark, men stumbled repeatedly into enemy units, fired at their muzzle flashes, threw unreliable hand grenades, and continued moving forward in a fatalistic assault. Nearby, intense firing erupted in the sector of the Philippine Army's 21st Division, signaling the beginning of the end for that unit. Outflanking the enemy after several hours of maneuvering at great cost, G Company finally drove the Japanese up a steep ridge, securing what was intended to be the regiment's line of departure. Although the 31st Infantry, with the remnant of a battalion of tanks attached, had been scheduled to attack at daybreak, conditions had now changed. F Company started to advance at 5:30 a.m., but the tanks did not show up and the scheduled 80-gun artillery barrage did not happen. Shortly after F Company started moving, they walked into an ambush. "The Fourth of July broke loose," recalled Tillman Rutledge. "They let us by and then tried to separate us from the main body." As their buddies were hit, men would rifle through their packs in search of cans of rations. Simultaneously, the Japanese hit the tail of the 2d Battalion's column, adding to the confusion.

The 2d Battalion was not alone in its troubles. The 1st Battalion, left to guard a trail junction behind the 2d Battalion, also came under attack. Private Armellino and another man had just reached their designated listening post about 100 yards in front of A Company when the Japanese attack began. Rifle, machine gun, and mortar fire and excited American and Japanese voices reverberated under the jungle canopy in a continuous cacophony for what seemed like an hour. When the enemy withdrew, Armellino and his buddy cautiously returned to their company only to find precious breakfast scattered all over the ground. Milk cans formerly filled with drinking water were riddled with bullet holes. Staff Sergeant Thomas Lupton, the company's mess sergeant, was being loaded onto a makeshift stretcher. One of his legs was blown off and he was near death from loss of blood. He died on the way to the hospital.

Near dawn on April 6, surviving officers reported that the 21st Division had been enveloped during the night and had scattered while escaping the trap. The 31st Infantry Regiment's Antitank Company, attached to the 21st Division, was caught up in the retreat. There was no one left holding the sector. Lieutenant Colonel Brady ordered his men to halt, knowing they lacked the strength to hold an entire division sector even if they were successful in reaching the line. There would be no time to react to Brady's order. The 2d Battalion, still in front, spotted what appeared to be a Japanese regiment moving toward them from Mount Samat. The Americans opened up with mortars and the Japanese responded in kind. Captain Ralph Hibbs, the 2d Battalion's surgeon, was blown into the air, but landed without a scratch. Another man nearby was hit in the trachea, almost severing it. Hibbs, still dazed and temporarily deaf, applied a pressure bandage to keep the blood from flowing into the man's lungs.

Although General Clifford Bluemel, the western sector commander, denied Colonel Brady's request to shift to a defensive posture, Brady ordered the 1st and 2d Battalions to dig in on the most defensible terrain available, sent patrols out to establish contact with remnants of the Philippine Army's 51st Division, and moved the 3d Battalion into a reserve position. To assist the 1st Battalion in securing some steep hills in its assigned sector, a battery of four 75mm guns was assigned the mission of laying down suppressive fire on the objective. The 1st Battalion advanced on line as the battery opened fire. Japanese artillery responded, reducing the battery to three guns, then two, and finally the last gun was silenced. A Company's left flank platoon advanced with only 15 men but 6 fell to mortar and artillery fire before they reached the crest of the ridge. At the top, they occupied former Filipino positions. Swollen, stinking corpses littered the area, making the men wish they were just about anywhere else. Japanese small arms fire soon thinned the platoon to seven men, but they managed to hold on.

Around 2 p.m., Colonel Brady sent his reserve companies, K and L, forward to help the 2d Battalion hold its line. The 2d Battalion was taking the brunt of the Japanese 4th Division's main attack. Captain Don Thompson of L Company was just receiving his orders to move forward when a Japanese shell landed nearby, peppering him with shrapnel and tree splinters and causing him to go deaf. He was evacuated to a field hospital. At 3 p.m., the 31st was ordered to withdraw to the San Vicente River, moving overland since all trails were in Japanese hands. K and L Companies covered the withdrawal. Men too weak to struggle with heavy weapons through the thick, tangled jungle simply took them apart and threw the parts into the jungle. One machine gun squad, despairing of ever getting out alive, set up their gun and fired for over an hour until a series of explosions signaled the end of their war.

As A Company's left flank platoon withdrew, it did so individually. The first man dashed down the bullet-swept slope safely. The second had a head wound and froze. When someone slapped him, he threw down his weapon and ran toward the Japanese and was killed. The others made their way to a covered position at the foot of the hill. C Company rallied nearby as desperate men shouted to each other over the chaotic din of explosions and gunfire. A barbed wire fence blocked the 1st Battalion's withdrawal until Lieutenants Alfred Lee and Charles Hodgins[3] held down a section of the fence, firing their pistols at the enemy to keep them away as men scrambled over the wire. Planes attacked the struggling mass with cannon fire while Japanese troops fired down on them from the heights they had just abandoned. Although few of those hit were killed, men dropped everything and ran in wild panic, hoping to find a spot that could shelter them from the hellish storm of fire. The 1st Battalion ceased to exist as a fighting unit.

Remnants of the 31st Infantry's Antitank Company, totaling three 37mm antitank guns, were positioned to cover the Pilar-Bagac Road. As six Japanese tanks appeared, two of the 37mm guns fired over 40 rounds, mortally wounding the Japanese 7th Tank Regiment's commander, Colonel Sonoda, and disabling two of his tanks. The remaining tanks spotted the two antitank guns and knocked them both out. While the third gun was being re-positioned to join the fight, it came under intense artillery fire, causing First Sergeant Emanuel Hamburger and the gun's five crewmen to take cover in a dugout. Before taking cover, Hamburger ordered one of the men to remove the weapon's breech block. Seeing what appeared to be a platoon of Japanese approaching, Hamburger and two of the drivers fired at them through slits in the log embrasure. During a lull in the firing, three of the crewmen scurried out of the dugout and escaped. A fourth, Private Homer J. Hernandez of Overton, Texas, also got out but was shot and bayoneted. As Hamburger and the others tried to follow, they were met by a spray of bullets, forcing them back inside. Private James Mines urged Hamburger to surrender. Hamburger tied his handkerchief to a stick and handed it to Mines who refused it. "Oh no, you're the Sergeant, you go first." At the age of 45, a veteran of the Mexican Expedition against Pancho Villa in 1916, combat with the 1st Division during World War I, nine years of service in China, and eight in the Philippines, Hamburger went into captivity.[4]

Taking up a new position along the San Vicente River, what was left of the 31st sent patrols out to its flanks to establish contact with neighboring units. Major Addison W. Dunham, who had recently become the 1st Battalion Commander, was receiving a report from one of the patrols when three rounds of artillery came roaring in, making a sound like a freight train according to Corporal Joe Keys. Major Dunham (Cambridge, Nebraska), Corporal Charles Ball (Browning, Montana), and Privates Clyde L. Wasson (Bell, California) and Carl E. Gladwetz (home town unknown) were killed instantly. Charles Ball had been B Company's hero ever since he began picking snipers out of trees on the way to Abucay Hacienda in January, but an exploding artillery shell makes no distinctions. Now, half a world away from the Indian Reservation he proudly called home, Charles Ball lay dead. Joe Keys had part of his left arm blown off and Paul Kerchum took a large fragment in his right calf. The number of able-bodied men remaining in B Company had just declined by a third. Everyone who still could ran across the slope to take shelter from the barrage.

At 6 a.m. on April 7, Japanese artillery and infantry struck what remained of the Philippine Army's 51st Division on a trail adjacent to the 31st Infantry. Weakened by disease, hunger, and battle losses, the Filipinos could hold on no longer. Surviving Filipino soldiers melted into the jungle to save themselves. Soon the 31st was also under attack. Around 9 a.m., the regiment was ordered to withdraw to an assembly area near Lamao. The withdrawal route traversed extremely rough and heavily vegetated terrain, causing units to become separated and men to become isolated groups of stragglers. They did not know it, but the entire II Corps line had evaporated. Philippine Army, Philippine Scout, and American troops became intermingled in the general retreat. When the 31st Infantry's remnants reached the Alangan River, there were somewhere between 200 and 300 effectives left. Other regiments of the U.S. Philippine Division were in a similar condition.

The Surrender

By the evening of April 8, the situation was clearly hopeless. Senior officers were told that General King would surrender the Bataan Force the next morning. At 7 a.m. the next day, radio operators listening to General King's command frequency heard "DITCH, DITCH, DITCH," the coded signal to surrender. Although exhausted and dispirited, the 31st did not surrender of its own accord. Rather than issuing the order to surrender, officers told their men of the situation and advised them that the time had come for them to decide for themselves what to do. Some of the stronger officers, including Major Peter Calyer, the 31st's Operations Officer, led a group into the Mariveles Mountains to become guerrillas. When word of the impending surrender reached H Company, Sergeant Walk had one 81mm mortar round left. He set the mortar to fire at maximum range, fired the 6 lb. projectile at an unseen foe, had his men disassemble the sights and tripod, and scattered pieces of the weapon into the jungle as they marched down the trail toward an unknown fate. One of the regiment's last casualties on Bataan was Major Lloyd C. Moffit, killed by a shrapnel wound to the head in an air attack less than an hour before the surrender. The plucky little major had been relieved of command in March after accidentally shooting himself in the foot while briefing his officers with a drawn pistol, but gamely stayed with the 2d Battalion as its Executive Officer to the very end.

Opposite, top: **In a captured Japanese photograph, U.S. soldiers and sailors surrendering to the Japanese forces at Corregidor, Philippine Islands (National Archives).**
  Bottom: **The Bataan Death March. Those who could not walk were carried by comrades in makeshift slings (National Archives).**

砲爆撃に全く機能を失ったコレヒドール島、ザヤリー砲台
コレヒドールの地下要塞から出て来た敵、みな手をあげて

At the time of the surrender, the 31st Infantry's headquarters was collocated with the headquarters of II Corps and the Philippine Division on Signal Hill, a promontory of Mount Bataan known as "Little Baguio" for its cool breezes and breathtaking view.[5] Lieutenant Colonel Jasper Brady told his headquarters security element to bury the regiment's most cherished possessions to keep them from falling into Japanese hands. Major General Maxson S. Lough, Colonel Harrison Browne and several officers who had been transferred from the 31st to corps staffs or other units before the war were present at the time.

At around 8 a.m., Staff Sergeant Joseph Crea (Headquarters Company), Corporal Robert Scruby (F Company), and Staff Sergeant James H. Steed (H Company), wrapped the regimental colors, national colors, a regimental photo album, and several other items of historical value in waxed canvas. The items were placed in a field safe that was buried face down to a depth of four feet on the east side of the gravel trail from Signal Hill. Leaves were spread over the site to make it appear undisturbed.[6] Near that time, Corporal Lou Read (Antitank Company) recalls seeing Master Sergeant Stefan Widerynski (Service

American and Filipino prisoners, captured at Corregidor, arrive at Bilibid prison by foot and truck as Japanese look on (National Archives).

Opposite, top: Bataan Death March (National Archives).

Bottom: Japanese combat photograph of Death March soldiers. The three Americans in the foreground are officers, hands tied with commo wire. The middle officer is a nurse. A Japanese soldier has hung a sack around the neck of the nearest American, turning him into a pack animal. Note that the Filipino soldiers in the background have been allowed to keep their fatigue hats, but the Americans are bare-headed (National Archives).

Company), Sergeant Steed, and Captain Herbert H. Eichlin (L Company) burying foot-lockers containing pistols, Philippine pesos, and the regiment's records nearby.[7]

With ammunition, rations, and supplies practically exhausted and most of his best units destroyed, Major General Edward P. King surrendered the Luzon Force on the morning of April 9. Most of the campaign's survivors were herded into columns and marched 68 miles north to Camp O'Donnell. More died of exhaustion, disease, and random execution by their captors. Their trek, marked by the extreme brutality of their Japanese guards, became known as the Bataan Death March.

Not all of the 31st's survivors surrendered. Some managed to link up with bands of their comrades or Filipino guerrillas to continue hindering the Japanese in any way they could. Those too weak to run or just plain unlucky were summarily executed if captured later. Since Corregidor had not yet fallen, others escaped to the island by barge or anything that would float. Among them were Joe "the kid" Johnson and Dale Snyder, best friends since they met at Fort McDowell, California, on the way to the Philippines over a year earlier. Johnson ran into Snyder around dusk on the day of the surrender. Both still had their weapons and the Japanese had not yet reached their location near the village of Cabcaben, near the tip of the Bataan Peninsula. After searching the beach in vain for anything that would float, they saw a Navy launch headed for Corregidor. Yelling at the top of their lungs, they plunged into the water and swam faster than they ever thought they could. The launch slowed nearly to a stop but was so overloaded it looked as if it might capsize if one of them tried to come aboard. Rather than leave them behind, some-

one threw them a line and they were towed nearly five miles to Corregidor. The trip was dark and frightening, particularly with the Japanese closing the door behind them and sharks infesting the waters they traveled. On Corregidor they were fed a canteen cup of cracked wheat and condensed milk, given a rifle and some clean clothes, and attached to the 4th Marines for beach defense duty.

The Marines treated escapees from Bataan like heroes, but the escape was only temporary. Within days, Japanese artillery began pounding the island, turning it into a mass of dust, debris, and splinters. Troops spent their days in Malinta Tunnel and nights manning beach defenses. Finally, on the night of May 5, the expected amphibious assault came. Japanese troops landed on the side of the island opposite Johnson and Snyder's position. At dawn, a Marine captain jumped into the shell hole where a squad of soldiers and Marines had established a fighting position. He said the Japanese were between them and the tunnel and things looked bad. Around 1 p.m.

Execution by beheading (National Archives).

Top: During the siege of Corregidor, Philippine Islands, the Finance Office, U.S. Army, Manila, shared lateral Number 12 of Malinta Tunnel with the Signal Corps. Members of the Finance Office staff in the foreground appear grim. March/April 1942 (National Archives). *Bottom:* Military grave marker, Manila American Cemetery (American Battle Monuments Commission).

Japanese and American voices called out across the island saying the garrison had been surrendered by General Wainwright at noon. With nowhere left to run, men yielded to the inevitable and shuffled under guard into the 92d Coast Artillery Regiment's abandoned motor park, nicknamed "the garage." Men were selected to perform funeral detail, first roping Japanese bodies into a pile and setting them afire and then doing the same with dead Americans. They were eventually herded onto barges, taken to Manila, and paraded through the city streets to Bilibid Prison. Several days later, they were loaded onto cattle cars and taken to Cabanatuan, a camp housing over 5,000 Americans. Unlike the men captured on Bataan, those captured on Corregidor were spared the Death March, but that did not assure their survival.[8]

Another group that had escaped to Corregidor was led by Captain Earl Short, the 31st Infantry's former Headquarters Commandant. The night before the surrender, Short took Sergeants Howard J. Linn and Thomas Proulx, with the Shanghai Bowl and 99 cups, by barge to Corregidor. There, they hoped to get the treasure out by submarine. For a month, the isolated island endured nearly constant aerial bombing and artillery bombardment. Finally, with the garrison's collapse imminent, Short decided he could no longer leave the regiment's proudest treasure at risk. At around 11 p.m. on May 2, Short's detail buried the bowl and cups on the west side of Malinta Hill just above the Bottomside Bakery. There it would remain for four years—a mute testimony to the Polar Bear Regiment's determination to keep its traditions alive.

8 Captivity

After being surrendered as part of the Bataan Defense Force on April 9, 1942, the 31st Infantry Regiment played no further role as a unit during World War II. The regiment lived on, however, in the spirit of those who endured 42 months of captivity under exceptionally brutal conditions in the Philippines, Formosa, Manchuria, and Japan, and in the actions of those who continued to evade or resist the Japanese as members of scattered guerrilla bands in the mountains and jungles of the Philippines. Although much has been written about both aspects of the era, it would be inaccurate to characterize individual actions after Bataan's surrender as actions of the 31st Infantry Regiment. Instead, this chapter is devoted primarily to honoring those known to have died in captivity. Their number, far exceeding the regiment's battle casualties, speaks volumes about their circumstances.

Practically all members of the 31st Infantry entered captivity malnourished and sick.

One of the POWs walks past some of the dwelling places of the prisoners. January 1945 (U.S. Army photograph, National Archives).

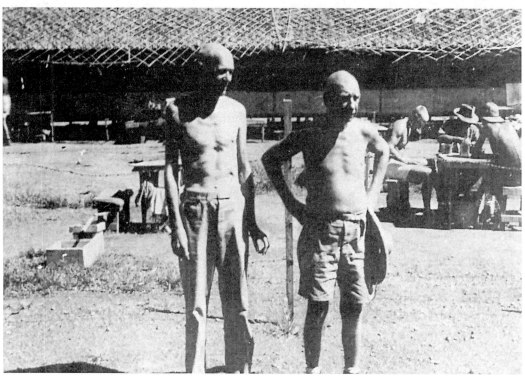

Because General MacArthur first decided to defend Luzon at Lingayen Gulf and several beaches south of Manila, his staff had not pre-stocked supplies of food, fuel, and medicine on the Bataan Peninsula or developed the bastion for a protracted defense. In consequence, American and Filipino troops who fought there went on half rations in early January and their portions became ever smaller and less nourishing through April. Most medicines ran out by early February, leaving soldiers to cope with the combined weakening effects of gradual starvation and diseases ranging from malaria and diphtheria to dysentery and vitamin deficiency diseases. Thus, those who fought at Bataan went into captivity seriously weakened. Their captors did all they could to worsen their condition.

The Death March

Those who trusted Japanese pledges of decent treatment if they accepted surrender were immediately disabused of that hope. The Bataan garrison's survivors, over 60,000

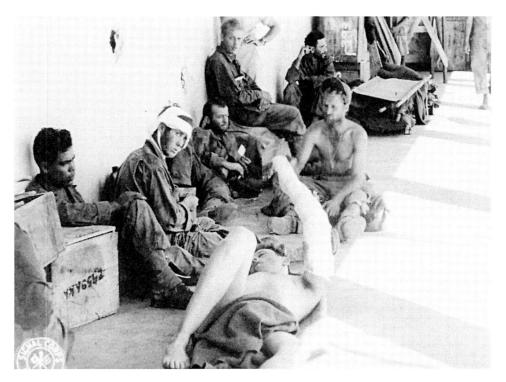

On the porch of an emergency hospital, these released American POWs, liberated by U.S. Rangers from the Cabanatuan prison camp, wait for transfer to a base hospital. January 1945 (U.S. Army photograph, National Archives).

Opposite, top: An unidentified GI chops wood for the kitchen (in the background) run by SGT Grossman. It was called Major Fitch's kitchen. A Japanese guard was 20 feet behind the camera in this 1943 photograph (National Archives).
  Bottom: MAJ Paul R. Wing (left), formerly executive officer of MG Spencer B. Akin, discusses camp conditions with LTC John Ball, Field Artillery officer. January 1945 (U.S. Army photograph, National Archives).

men, were marched 68 miles under a blazing sun, denied potable water and relief stops, and subjected to extreme brutality and summary executions by scornful, sadistic Japanese guards. About 1,600 of that number were members of the 31st Infantry, most of whom survived the march. Filipino civilians who tried to give them food or water along the way were bayoneted or beheaded.

Once at Camp O'Donnell, thousands of men from hundreds of units were crammed into a former Philippine Army training center. Sanitation facilities were sparse and quickly overwhelmed. There was no medicine and what passed for food was seriously deficient in caloric content. Brutality and summary executions at the hands of Japanese guards continued unabated. The number of men who died in captivity in May 1942 exceeded the number who died in combat and it would still be several years before the survivors would be liberated.

The Camps

Those captured at Corregidor did not experience the Death March. They were generally better fed and healthier since the island was better provisioned and its defenders did not have to live in malarial jungles. A week or so after the island surrendered on May 6, 1942, they were taken by barge to Manila and marched through the city's streets to

A group of American soldiers marching to an evacuation hospital after their liberation from the Cabanatuan prison camp by the 6th Ranger Battalion, January 1945 (U.S. Army photograph, National Archives).

Bilibid, a pre-war high security prison. After being screened, most prisoners were taken by train from Bilibid to Cabanatuan in central Luzon.

Around the same time, most of those captured at Bataan and held initially at Camp O'Donnell were moved to Cabanatuan. Some suspected of having information of value to the Japanese were held at Bilibid. Other men were sent there later from various labor details or were too ill to be moved. Men who were particularly resistant to the Japanese at Bilibid or were captured in underground organizations were taken to the old Spanish dungeons under Fort Santiago. No known survivors emerged. Others were sent to prison work camps on the islands of Mindanao and Palawan or were taken to work details at places like Nichols Field to extend the runway. There, the sadistic brutality of Japanese guards was unsurpassed as a number of prisoners were beaten to death for sport. At Palawan, the Japanese guard force slaughtered the prisoners when it became clear that they could not be removed before American troops landed on the island.

The Hell Ships

In 1944, when Japan recognized that American forces would soon land on Luzon and Mindanao, the two largest islands of the Philippines, they crammed thousands of men, including most surviving officers, into the unventilated holds of unmarked "hell

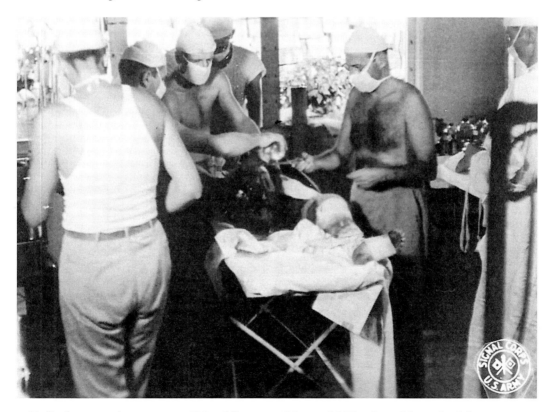

Medical personnel operate on a U.S. soldier, one of the 511 POWs released from the Cabanatuan prison camp by the 6th Ranger Battalion in January 1945 (U.S. Army photograph, National Archives).

ships." Those too weak or too sick to be of value as slave labor in Japanese mines and construction projects were left behind to die at Cabanatuan and other camps. On the hell ships, hundreds of men had only a single bucket among them for sanitation and had nowhere to lie down or escape the suffocating heat and stench. Many died standing.

Three of the hell ships carrying members of the 31st Infantry, the *Shinyo Maru*, *Arisan Maru* and *Oryoku Maru*, were sunk by the U.S. Navy, sending men who had endured three years of starvation, illness, and maltreatment to watery graves. The *Shinyo Maru* departed Mindanao on September 3, 1944, with 750 American POWs. It was torpedoed by the USS *Paddle* four days later, killing 668 of the Americans aboard. The *Arisan Maru* departed Manila on October 10, 1944, with 1,800 American POWs. It was torpedoed by the USS *Snook*, killing 1,795 of the Americans aboard. The *Oryoku Maru* departed Manila on December 13, 1944, with 1,800 American POWs aboard. It was sunk two days later near Subic Bay by American carrier planes. Angry Japanese guards shot men trying to escape from the sinking ship's hold and shot still more as they struggled in the water. Those who made it to shore were recaptured and taken to Japan aboard two other hell ships departing the Philippines on December 27 and January 2. Of the 1,800 who started the hellish journey on December 13 with the *Oryoku Maru* 1,426, died.

One arm gone, this unidentified internee at the Cabanatuan POW camp walks through an American evacuation hospital shortly after Rangers freed over 500 Japanese-held prisoners, in January 1945 (U.S. Army photograph, National Archives).

Slave Labor Camps

For prisoners who made it to Formosa, Manchuria, and Japan, conditions were sometimes better and sometimes not. The unaccustomed cold weather added to men's misery, costing many weakened men their lives. At other places, mine cave-ins and other forms of industrial accidents took more lives. Some were subjected to secret biological warfare experiments in Manchuria and others were killed by the American atomic bombings of Japanese cities where they were performing slave labor.

Internment

Jean George was 22 when she was invited to a dance at the High Commissioner's mansion in Manila and met Lieutenant Walter E. O'Brien, Jr., of the 31st Infantry. They fell in love at first sight and were engaged in November 1941. Unfortunately, their time together was cut all too short by the outbreak of war only a month later.

Jean was born and educated in Manila. Her father, an Australian, was Secretary-Treasurer of the American Oxygen and Acetylene Company there. When the war broke out, Walter O'Brien went to Bataan with the 31st Infantry while Jean stayed with her family in Manila. Her older sister, Marian, was already married and gave birth to a son during a Japanese air raid. Marian, her husband, and their baby were interned at Santo Tomas University in Manila in January 1942.

Not far away on the Bataan Peninsula, after enduring four months of combat, starvation, and illness, Walter O'Brien and most other survivors of the 31st Infantry were surrendered with the rest of the Luzon Force on April 9, 1942. Most endured the Death March and suffered further brutal treatment at Camp O'Donnell and Cabanatuan or Bilibid POW Camps. The Japanese initially left Jean's family alone in hopes that her father might keep supplying the Japanese oxygen and acetylene. Very little was actually delivered. Valves were constantly being left open or "lost." By June 1942, the Japanese became fed up and sent Jean's family into internment with hundreds of other civilians.

At Santo Tomas Internment Camp (unaffectionately known as STIC U by its inmates), Jean served on the vegetable detail. She washed them, cut them into servings, loaded them into gallon-size wicker baskets, and carried them to the kitchen with the help of another internee, Howard Stark. Howard fell in love with her and proposed that they marry after the war, but she rejected him, explaining that she was engaged to Walter O'Brien. On September 7, 1944, Walter was one of 751 POWs crammed into the hold of a Japanese cargo ship, the *Shinyo Maru*, headed for Japan. The unmarked ship was torpedoed by the USS *Paddle*, killing 688 of those aboard, including Walter.

On February 3, 1945, the U.S. 44th Tank Battalion led elements of the 1st Cavalry and 37th Infantry Divisions onto the grounds of Santo Tomas, liberating the internees. The Japanese promptly shelled the camp, seriously wounding two of Jean's friends, Veda Trembley and Rita Johnson, before they could get out of harm's way. Jean narrowly missed the same fate or worse, leaving the same building just before the shell hit. Luckily, Jean's whole family survived and eventually moved to Bremerton and Vancouver, Washington. When Jean reached Seattle aboard the USNS *Eberle*, Walter O'Brien's family met her at the dock to tell her of his death.

A year later, Howard Stark came back into Jean's life and they married. Over the

Pat L. Parker (left), of Calvin, Oklahoma, and James H. Cowan, from Fullerton, California, are shown talking over their experiences while resting in an advance American hospital after being rescued from a Japanese prison camp near Cabanatuan, Luzon. These two men are the sole survivors of a group of 600 men who were forced to work until they either died from maltreatment or were killed on the dreaded Nichols Field near Manila. 15 February 1945 (U.S. Army photograph, National Archives).

next five years, Jean had 3 children, became a U.S. citizen, and went to work in Puget Sound Naval Shipyard. Howard died in 1972, but Jean never remarried. On the third Thursday of each month, she attended meetings of the Kitsap Chapter of American Ex-POWs and was a life member of the 31st Infantry Regiment Association in honor of her first true love, Walter O'Brien. She died in 2002.

The Cabanatuan Roster

By the time liberation came, more than a thousand members of the 31st Infantry Regiment had perished. Among the dead were most of the regiment's officers and senior NCOs. While at Cabanatuan POW Camp, Lieutenant Colonel Jasper Brady and Major Marshall Hurt covertly compiled a roster of those who had served with the regiment during the war. It covers the period December 8, 1941, through October 10, 1944, when Brady and Hurt were taken from Cabanatuan to be transported to Japan. It lists names, ranks, service numbers, hometowns, combat wounds, decorations earned, next of kin, and pending awards and disciplinary action. For those who died in combat or captivity before Brady and Hurt were taken to their deaths aboard the *Arisan Maru*, the circumstance and place of burial is annotated. Given the conditions under which the roster was prepared, it is remarkably legible and thorough. There are, however, some inevitable gaps, such as the hometowns or next of kin of men who died before the roster was begun. Because the roster was compiled from the memories of leaders incarcerated at Cabanatuan, some spellings of names may also be inaccurate.

The night before Brady and Hurt were to leave Cabanatuan, they hid the roster under one of the barracks buildings. Brady left instructions with several men left behind that the information must get back into U.S. hands. Brady annotated the roster, "825 known dead as POWs by late 1944," and signed his name and service number on the front inside cover. The roster was recovered by the 6th Ranger Battalion during Cabanatuan's liberation and was eventually given to Anne Brady, Jasper Brady's widow. With the aid of survivors, she further annotated the roster to indicate the deaths of 330 others who died aboard hell ships or in Japanese work camps.

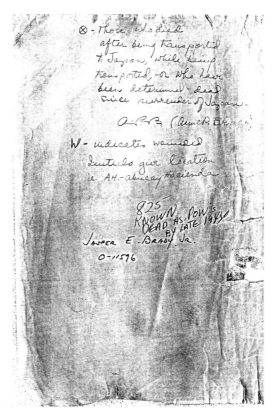

The inside front cover of the Cabanatuan Roster. The first handwriting is LTC Brady's widow's: she explains that the circled X indicates "Those who died after being transported to Japan, while being transported, or who have been determined dead since surrender of Japan. A.P.B. (Anne P. Brady) W—indicates wounded. Initials give location, i.e., A.H.— Abucay Hacienda." Then in his last written communication as Commanding Officer of the Regiment, LTC Brady writes: "825 known dead as POWs by late 1944. Jasper E. Brady, Jr. O-11596" (Association archives).

9 Occupation Duty: Korea and Japan, 1946–1950

Korea

A little-known chapter in the 31st Infantry Regiment's history is its part in the occupation of Korea after World War II. From 1910 to 1945, Korea, then known by its Japanese name, Chosen, was a province of Japan. During World War II, Koreans were drafted into the Japanese Army, forming the bulk of the labor service units that built airfields and fortifications across Japan's far-flung Pacific empire. When the war ended, the Soviets entered Korea and disarmed Japanese forces north of the 38th Parallel, while the U.S. XXIV Corps (6th, 7th, and 40th Infantry Divisions) disarmed Japanese troops in the country's southern half. The 7th Division, headquartered at Seoul, occupied the northernmost portion of the U.S. sector.

The 184th Infantry Regiment, a California National Guard unit, served with the 7th Division since 1943 and went to Korea with the division in September 1945. When the California National Guard was reconstituted in 1946, the 184th's colors were returned to its pre-war headquarters at Sacramento.[1] General Douglas MacArthur, then commanding all U.S. forces in the Far East, brought the 31st Infantry back to the active rolls to take the 184th Infantry's place on January 19, 1946. In a ceremony marking the occasion, Brigadier General Leroy Seward passed the 31st Infantry's colors to Colonel Lee Wallace, the regiment's first postwar commander. General MacArthur flew in for the occasion from Tokyo to show his respect for the regiment. Men of the 184th woke up the next morning as members of the 31st.

The regimental colors passed between the old and new commanders at the reactivation ceremony are a story of their own. Because the 31st's colors were still buried on Mount Bataan in the Philippines at the time, no official colors were available for the reactivation ceremony. The regimental commander asked Staff Sergeant Charles Bartlett to have temporary colors made in Seoul for the occasion. Copied from a photo, they were all the regiment had until official Colors were received in 1948.

Present at the reactivation were Sergeant Johnnie E. Potts and Staff Sergeant Joseph M. Wolfe, who fought at Bataan and rejoined the 31st when it was reactivated.[2] A photo in the 7th Division's album shows a squad of Bataan vets, including Potts and Wolfe, standing in front of the regimental formation during the reactivation. Wolfe was perhaps

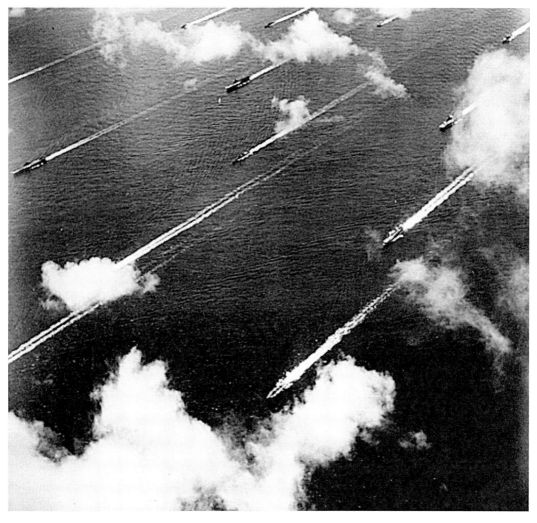

Ships of 3rd Fleet steam into Tokyo Bay, Japan, for the occupation (U.S. Navy photograph, National Archives).

the best machine gunner in an outfit blessed with many. Another was John A. Lynch, who would later become the 31st Infantry's Sergeant Major. When 75mm recoilless rifles were issued in 1947, they arrived without manuals. Joe Wolfe disassembled the weapon, identified its parts and their function, and reassembled it. He explained that while in POW camps in the Philippines, members of the 31st spent their time exchanging ideas on how they could have improved their weapons. The Army later adopted several of their ideas, including spotting rifles on antitank weapons and .30 cal. sub-caliber training devices for antitank weapons.

In celebration of the 31st Infantry's first post-war Organization Day, General of the Army Douglas MacArthur paid tribute to his former Guard of Honor with the following congratulatory message issued on August 4, 1946:

There is no unit in the American Army which has served with greater distinction both in peace and in war, than the 31st Infantry. Never stationed within our continental limits, as the advanced element

General of the Army Douglas MacArthur, Supreme Commander for the Allied Powers, inspects the Honor Guard of the 31st Infantry Regiment, which had been under his command in 1941 in the Philippine Islands. This was his initial visit to Korea. COL Ralph E. Leighton of Sacramento, California, is on the General's right. 15 August 1948 (U.S. Army photograph).

in our Pacific defense, the Regiment has always performed its assigned mission with marked gallantry and commendable precision. At Bataan, it achieved its greatest glory as its lines held firm time and time again against the assault of overwhelmingly superior forces. As it now faces a future of continued service in our country's cause, its regimental colors fly under a halo of tradition, of honor, duty and sacrifice, which will be an inspiration for American Armies for all time to come.

Another distinguished officer who sent greetings for the occasion was Lieutenant General Robert L. Eichelberger, who had won the Distinguished Service Cross in combat with the 31st in Siberia. He was a lieutenant colonel serving as S-2 of the AEF in 1918 and rose to command the Eighth Army during World War II.

Officers and men of the 31st Infantry regiment:

My association with the 31st Infantry Regiment extends back 27 years. I feel highly honored that I have been remembered and asked to send you a message on this first organization day after the end of World War II. When I learned some time ago that this proud old regiment was reactivated in Korea as part of the 7th Infantry Division, I was highly gratified. Furthermore, it seemed significant that the 31st should be re-created in Korea to continue its long career of service overseas.

I first knew the regiment in Eastern Siberia in 1919 when I accompanied it during its military operations in the Suchan District. An American force of 10,000 built around the 31st and 27th Infantry Regiments had been sent to Vladivostok with the mission of restoring the railroads and bringing economic relief to revolution-torn Siberia. Our mission involved maintaining strict neutrality in the midst of a madhouse of intrigue, double-dealing, burning, torture, and ambushing. Bolsheviki, White Russian, Japanese, Chinese, British, French, Czechs, and Poles were among the many factions present in Siberia at the time. It was inevitable that, upon occasion, our troops saw action. American columns were ambushed. Small groups were surprised and captured while on peaceful missions—and we retaliated. I was personally involved in most of the incidents. In bearing the brunt of the fighting, the 31st conducted itself nobly. Since those early days of my career, the regiment has always been near to my heart. As a combatant on the spot, I can assure you that you have reason to be proud of the record of the 31st in Siberia.

I need but mention the proudest and saddest chapter of the history of the 31st. The gallant and aggressive manner in which it acted as the backbone of our forces defending Bataan Peninsula will remain recorded in our military history forever. I hope that, on this organization day, you present members of the regiment will look deeply into the history of the 31st and gain from its past achievements the inspiration and the unit spirit that will be necessary to make the future of the regiment as glorious as has been its past.

I thank you.

/s/Robert L. Eichelberger

Lieutenant General Commanding the Eighth United States Army

Reproduced: Hq 31st Inf, APO 7

15 August 1946

Among the most unusual career patterns of any Polar Bear of that era is that of PFC Nick Loundagin, who served with G Company at Chunchon. His memories of Korea focus on hills that only went up and showers that rarely worked. Nick left the Army in 1947 and got a Navy appointment as supply officer of the USNS *Simon B. Buckner*, transferring to the USNS *Fred C. Ainsworth* just in time to take the 31st back to Inchon in 1950. Nick later helped evacuate the regiment from Hungnam. Weary of life at sea, Nick got his pilot's license on the GI Bill after the war and later flew tons of explosives and hundreds of infantrymen to Vietnam, perhaps including men who would become members of the 31st Infantry's 4th and 6th Battalions.

As old-timers accumulated enough points to go home, the 31st received two groups of replacements in 1946 to keep it operational, but by the end of 1947, it was down to just over 800 men. Most of the 31st Infantry was based in Seoul, but the 2nd Battalion was at Chunchon in eastern Korea. In Seoul, the 31st Infantry was based alongside the 32nd Infantry at a former Japanese Army post that had once been a university campus. Companies rotated from Seoul and Chunchon to three observation posts (OPs) along the 38th Parallel, extending from the Taebek Mountains eastward to the Sea of Japan. The 32nd did the same from the western side of the Taebek Range, extending to the Yellow Sea. Duty on the OPs was rough. Chow was usually lousy and cold, mail was usually late, and the Quonset huts were cold in the winter and hot in the summer. Just across the 38th Parallel were at least five Russian divisions, several of them manned by Koreans who joined the Red Army to liberate their country from the Japanese in 1945. Russians, scanning their sector with binoculars and probably sniper scopes, outposted and patrolled the border just as our men did.

There was an atmosphere of constant tension along the border and occasionally shots were exchanged. Periodic loudspeaker propaganda directed at U.S. outposts warned that the Soviets would soon wipe out the Americans. Incidents were more common in the 32nd Infantry's sector because the city of Kaesong and the Ongjin Peninsula were tempting targets due to their isolation from the rest of South Korea. In July 1946, Soviet fighters chased a U.S. liaison plane away from the border and later that month Soviet troops fired at a U.S. patrol that strayed into North Korea. In August 1947, three soldiers checking communications wire strayed across the border and were held by the Soviets for nearly 2 weeks. A month later, a U.S. patrol was ambushed near the border, but suffered no casualties.

A GI's life in Korea was primitive initially, but gradually improved, thanks largely to the ingenuity and resourcefulness of Army engineers. Because there had been no fighting in South Korea during the war, former Japanese barracks and support facilities remained intact. From the outside, the compounds resembled German Kasernes, after which they were modeled in the 1930s. On the inside, things were different. Japan did not have indoor plumbing before the occupation and it took U.S. engineers over a year to develop a satisfactory plumbing and sewage system.

Recreation facilities were developed to relieve the boredom of the border patrol mission. At Seoul, the 7th Infantry Division Enlisted Men's Service Club, staffed by USO ladies, provided a well-stocked library, game rooms, and a bar. Occasional shows, put on by tour groups from the United States, Australia, or the Philippines, were the highlight of the club's activities. A smaller Service Club was built for the 2nd Battalion at Chunchon. The 7th Division football team, the "Ramblers" played the 6th Division and teams from divisions based in Japan (1st Cavalry, 11th Airborne, 24th and 25th Infantry) at Hourglass Field in Seoul. Boxing, basketball, baseball, and marksmanship tournaments were also popular. Bataan Theater was built especially for the 31st Infantry's entertainment. Hourglass Beach recreation area was built on a scenic east coast bay for soldiers on leave. One form of recreation had its hazards. Venereal diseases were rampant in Asia and syphilis was a particular problem. Troops who contracted the disease were sent to a special treatment and recuperation facility where stern lectures on safety precautions and grim films showing the consequences of unsafe pleasure were mandatory. In September 1948, a train bringing troops back from the recovery center derailed. Several "Polar Bears" were among the 36 men killed.

American families lived just an hour's drive from the tense border with North Korea. Husbands and fathers in the 31st knew they might have to fight a delaying action long enough to give their families time to reach evacuation sites at Kimpo airfield and the port of Inchon. Among the dependent family members living in Seoul was Dulce Bartlett and her three daughters. Her husband, Staff Sergeant Charles Bartlett of the Regimental S-1 Section, was the man who had a temporary set of regimental colors made by a Seoul tailor. Dulce and her children lived at Camp Sobengo, adjacent to the 7th Division headquarters complex. The complex included an all-grades dependent school, a theater, a library, a small PX/commissary, and precious little else American. The 377th Station Hospital and the Service Club were downtown. Few Americans had cars in Korea because there were few improved roads and no gas stations, so most travel was done by tram or train. Telephone service was "Douglas Switch" operated by the 7th Signal Battalion.

American food was mainly of the canned and boxed variety and the supply was uneven, ebbing and flowing with the arrival of resupply ships from the U.S. There were few cattle in Korea and hence no milk or ice cream. Powdered milk was a staple of children's diets. Although fish was abundant, the absence of a beef industry in Korea made it necessary to ship frozen beef and lamb from Australia and New Zealand. Vegetables from the Korean economy had to be boiled thoroughly since TB was still rampant, aggravated by the oriental practice of fertilizing with "night soil." A quartermaster bakery provided bread, doughnuts, and cake to mess halls and the local commissary. Stoves were coal or wood fired since the electrical system was not strong enough to power electric ranges. Worse, all electricity was generated in the Russian sector and they often turned it off, leaving Dulce and her family to play pinochle by candlelight or Coleman lantern.

The entrance to the 31st Infantry Regiment's cantonment area, Seoul, 1946 (Association archives).

Drinking water was delivered to quarters twice a day by tanker truck, but families had to leave their empty Jerry cans on the curb. There were also compensations. The Bartletts had a houseboy and two housemaids who helped with the cleaning and household chores. Most important, the tour brought the Bartletts and many families like them a treasury of memories of hardships overcome and fellowship to be cherished as long as they live.

As the Army shrank from over 8 million men in 1945 to only 536,000 the next year, all units suffered shortages. The 31st Infantry's strength declined progressively to under a third of its wartime authorization. 3d Battalion was reduced to zero strength in 1947 and the other battalions were subsequently reduced to two rifle companies each. By 1948, the remaining companies were reduced to 2 platoons each. That left the 31st badly undermanned for its border surveillance mission. The regiment manned 3 OPs along the 38th Parallel and patrolled between them on foot and by jeep. There was little time for tactical training, since guard duty and patrolling consumed most of the regiment's available manpower every day. Despite the shortages, annual regimental maneuvers were held, but there was never enough time to prepare for them.

North of the 38th parallel, Stalin formed a communist government in 1948. Almost immediately, North Korea's Army, the *Inmun Gun*, was formed from ethnic Korean members of the Soviet and Chinese Communist Armies, relieving Soviet troops on the border. While relations with the Soviets had been tense, the North Koreans were overtly aggressive. Sniping against U.S. patrols, "accidental" shelling of OPs and convoys by mortars and antitank rockets, and antiaircraft fire directed against U.S. spotter planes heightened tension on the Peninsula. On July 14, 1948, a routine relief of one of the 32nd Infantry's outposts was underway just south of Kaesong when a group of Koreans dressed in civilian clothes pulled out weapons and grenades, killing Private Charles Labita of Brooklyn. Labita has the dubious distinction of being the first American soldier killed in action in Korea, nearly two years before the outbreak of the Korean War.

As the Soviets departed, U.S. forces were withdrawn in increments. The 7th Division was the first unit to leave. In December 1948, the 31st Infantry happily departed Korea for a quieter tour of duty in Japan. When the regiment passed through Inchon on its way to Japan, the sign over the port's entry ramp said "Through these portals pass the best damn soldiers in the world." When the regiment returned to Inchon in September 1950 under less pleasant circumstances, the sign was still there, knocked slightly ajar by U.S. naval gunfire. Left in place to cover the approaches to Seoul, the 32nd Infantry Regiment, 48th Field Artillery Battalion, and 7th Reconnaissance Company formed the 5th Regimental Combat Team. A month later, on January 10, 1949, the 6th Infantry Division was inactivated at Pusan. The 5th Regimental Combat Team departed for Schofield Barracks, Hawaii on June 29, formally ending the U.S. occupation of South Korea, leaving only a 500 man Military Assistance and Advisory Group to help equip and train South Korea's Army. They would have only one more year of peace.

Occupation of Japan

During their first month in Japan, members of the Polar Bear regiment constantly packed, unpacked, and repacked duffle bags as they shuttled ever farther north. They first moved from Camp Drake near Tokyo to Camp Haugen near the northern end of Honshu. Finally, while the 1st Battalion remained on Honshu to help reconstitute the 32nd Infantry, the rest of the 31st moved further north to Camp Crawford on Hokkaido, replacing a regiment of the 11th Airborne Division.[3] When the 31st reached Camp Crawford, it numbered only 70 officers and 1800 enlisted men.[4]

To Hokkaido's north and northeast are Sakhalin and the Kurile Islands. Northern Sakhalin had long been Russian but the island's southern half had belonged to Japan. A four-power agreement near the end of World War II gave the Soviet Union the remainder of Sakhalin and the Kuriles but denied it the right to occupy Hokkaido, frustrating Josef Stalin's grander aims. Occupation of Hokkaido, one of Japan's home islands, would have given the Soviets an opportunity to establish a puppet government there and convert the island to a springboard for threatening Honshu, Japan's main island. In the winter, Russian troops could be seen patrolling the shores of nearby islands whose Japanese population was evicted when the Soviets took charge.

The 7th Infantry Division's other regiments, the 17th and 32nd, were based on Honshu. The separation accentuated a psychological distance between the 31st, which had not yet served with the 7th Division in combat, and its sister regiments which had served with the division through four campaigns of World War II. The 31st therefore had the same "bastard" relationship with the 7th Division that it had with the Philippine Division before World War II. Moreover, the regiment's polar bear insignia seemed particularly fitting for a unit stationed in Japan's cold north. Some called Hokkaido "the rock," like Alcatraz, a place to get sent if a soldier screwed up elsewhere.

The main installation for American forces in the Sapporo area, where the 31st Infantry settled, was Camp Crawford. It had brick single-story platoon barracks for about 4,500 troops, officer and NCO clubs, a large Service club for junior enlisted men, a field house (gym), chapel, theater, PX, commissary, quartermaster laundry, quartermaster bakery, steam plant, bowling lanes, and a large family housing area with an all-grades school. The Army hospital was in downtown Sapporo. Mount Eniwa, an extinct volcano, loomed over the post and the adjacent village of Makomanai. To the north and west were miles of steep, forested hills inhabited by more black bears than people. Because Hokkaido was sparsely populated, training land was more plentiful than on Japan's other islands. The most popular bivouac site for field maneuvers was a scenic mountain meadow over-looking Sapporo, Hokkaido's largest city. The site was used by Japanese farmers for grazing sheep and therefore had its unpleasant side as well. Eighteen miles deeper in the mountains was Shimamatsu Training Area, near the village of Eniwa. Firing ranges for heavy weapons were 25 miles away at Chitose. Japan's raid on Pearl Harbor was planned at Building 5 on Chitose airfield. Winds from Siberia bring Hokkaido its first snowfall in early November and snow generally stays on the ground until late May. In mid-winter, snow depth averages 5 feet and drifts may exceed 15 feet.

Ainu Indians, akin to the Aleuts and Eskimos of North America, inhabit parts of Hokkaido. Hot springs dot the island, which has seven active volcanoes. Jozankei and Noboribetsu were particularly popular recreation sites for GIs because bathing at indoor hot springs was strictly in the nude and there were no separate facilities for men and women. The same was true of public toilets, a shock to most Americans. Sapporo had a university, as well as a thriving red light district and bars aplenty to transform a GI's pay into a hangover or worse. MP patrols kept order downtown since Japan's police had no jurisdiction over Americans during the occupation era.

Arriving in Japan at the beginning of winter in 1948, the 7th Division established a Ski Cadre Instructors' School at Nagano to train selected members on cold weather operations.[5] Graduates returned to their units to provide

Downtown Sapporo, September 1949. The unit in the foreground is the Heavy Mortar Company, the Honor Company for that month. Notice the number of Japanese lining both sides of the street (Association archives).

instruction on winter cross-country movements and outdoor survival. Initial training was hampered by equipment shortages, but in February 1949, all rifle companies of the 2nd Battalion conducted snowshoe marches near Camp Crawford.[6] In March, both battalions conducted overnight bivouacs during which troops honed land navigation skills while officers conducted a tactical exercise without troops, walking the layout of a defensive position.[7]

In April, inspectors from the IX Corps G-3 Section tested every enlisted man in the regiment, using the Army's newly-standardized Mobilization Training Plan. The results demonstrated a near-universal challenge facing commanders throughout the post-war Army. Soldiers generally did well at hands-on proficiency tests but scored poorly on the exam's written portion. According to the regiment's annual history, the disparity could be "directly attributed to the fact that the average grade completed in school by the men of the regiment was 8.23 years."[8] In response, the 7th Division's first training memorandum published in Japan mandated a minimum of four hours' instruction each week during the duty day for any soldier unable to read and write at fifth grade level.[9]

By the end of April, the Regimental S-3, Lieutenant Colonel Ralph E. Leighton, announced that "The 31st Infantry Regiment, during the last month has passed the boundary marker. No longer is it a group of individuals wearing as part of their uniforms the crest of a regiment. It is a team. The change has been slow in coming; now that it is here, we are prepared and are ready for any tactical mission that may come."[10] It was an exaggeration but marked the regiment's entry into a new phase of training. The Polar Bears began weapons proficiency training in April with snow still on the ground.

The regiment received 800 new soldiers as it began its new training phase. Around 500 were first-term enlisted men, transferred from the 1st Cavalry Division.[11] As with most such mass transfers, the sending unit rarely sends its best, giving Camp Crawford a reputation as a place to send cast-offs. The other 300 were new recruits who had just completed eight weeks of basic training in the United States. Rather than further diffuse his scarce cadre of NCOs to provide the new men advanced individual training, Colonel John D. Miller, the 31st's new commander, established two provisional training companies. Although contravening 7th Division guidance, putting the new men in separate units made the best use of limited trainers while still allowing the bulk of the regiment to progress in its training.[12] It also fostered a sense of unity and cohesion among the new men.

Sergeants are supposed to teach soldiers how to shoot but the 31st Infantry had a shortage of capable NCOs. In response, battalions conducted preliminary marksmanship instruction in large groups using lectures and demonstrations, poor substitutes for hands-on training under experienced sergeants. Range firing began in late May, using .22 caliber rifles, a cost-saving measure, to reinforce the four fundamentals of marksmanship prior to firing military rifles. New soldiers in the two training companies fired the M1 rifle, .45 caliber pistol, and the Browning automatic rifle for familiarization, and conducted record firing with carbines.[13]

Major General William F. Dean, commanding general of the 7th Infantry Division during and since the move from Korea to Japan, recognized that the NCO shortage posed a potentially crippling problem for the division's reconstitution.[14] In Training Memo #1 he urged subordinates to foster and develop junior leaders. "There is a singular opportunity for all ranks to display and exercise sound progressive leadership, not only in the accomplishment of the occupational mission, but in the training mission as well. The outstanding leader will be exemplified by the well trained squad, platoon, company and battalion for which he is responsible."[15]

While acting as the regimental commander, Lieutenant Colonel Marion W. Schewe established the Regimental Leadership School at Camp Crawford in February 1949. All but three of the first 34 candidates completed the course.[16] But expectations that the new school's output would resolve the regiment's NCO shortfall proved illusory. The program of instruction soon shifted from general leadership instruction to squad leader duties and responsibilities. The school began accepting fewer candidates, hoping for better results by concentrating only on those who demonstrated leadership potential. Over 25 percent of enrollees were relieved from the fourth class because they were unable to perform as squad leaders.[17]

Graduating fewer men from the Leadership School slowed progress in the regiment's overall training program. The scarcity of trained NCOs and the diversion of the best NCOs to serve as cadre for the Leadership School forced commanders to acknowledge that in many cases sergeants conducting unit training "did not have the least idea of what they were supposed to do as squad leaders, or that they knew any tactics at all."[18] Battalions implemented their own squad leader training programs to augment instruction at the Leadership School, but success was minimal.

NCO leadership was sapped by other demands as well. Many NCOs were diverted from leadership positions to fill garrison roles not addressed by Army manpower authorizations. Forcing units to keep diverted NCOs on their rolls further inhibited the attainment of combat readiness. Worse, NCOs with the highest aptitude scores were skimmed off at every level, sending the least capable down to infantry battalions. The situation became so bad that Lieutenant General Almond felt compelled to intervene. Noting that "the subordinate commands are extremely short of individuals with high mental qualifications and overburdened with those possessing the lowest potential," he prohibited GHQ's staff sections from screening projected replacements and directed that they accept personnel without prior consideration of GCT score or civilian skill.[19]

In June 1949, the provisional basic training companies were broken up and their members were distributed throughout the 2nd and 3rd Battalions. At that point, a new challenge arose. Men who had rotated with the regiment from Korea were completing their tours and began to rotate home.[20] As a result, graduates of the regiment's Leadership School began departing in numbers sufficient to threaten the regiment's training program. The situation was mitigated only slightly by reducing rifle squads from twelve men to nine, making sergeants' jobs easier.[21]

In August 1949, rifle squads practiced combat firing at Shimamatsu. Both battalions established bivouacs there under field conditions. Problems identified by evaluators included poor control of movement, ignorance of how to use terrain effectively during movement, and leaders' failure to inform soldiers of the situation and their mission. A series of company-size alerts trained company and battalion commanders on their roles in the Eighth Army's plan for the defense of Japan. The regimental S-3 expressed satisfaction with the companies' ability to execute their missions once they arrived at a designated location, but found the coordination of transportation a concern.[22] By the end of August, all rifle squads had passed their combat firing tests—a minor miracle given the shortage of available NCOs.

The Polar Bears stood down for three days to celebrate their first Organization Day since 1941. Colonel Miller designated "America's Foreign Legion" as the official theme of

MG John B. Coulter, Commanding General of the 7th Infantry Division, and COL Eustis L. Poland, CO of the 31st Infantry Regiment, attach World War II Battle Streamers to the Regimental Colors on Army Day, April 6, 1948 (Association archives).

the 33rd anniversary celebration, emphasizing that the Polar Bears were the only regulars never to have served in the United States. He sought to further enhance unit pride by erroneously claiming the title, "First American Unit in Tokyo," as a result of the regiment's humanitarian deployment to that city from Manila following the 1923 earthquake (the earthquake was actually in Nagasaki). He further highlighted the 31st Infantry Regiment's possession of the only "peacetime" award ever presented up to that time—the "Yangtze" campaign streamer affixed to the regiment's colors for service in Shanghai in 1932.[23]

Colonel Miller authorized the establishment of an "Honor Company" plaque, to be awarded monthly "to the company with the best record for the month, based on the lowest number of Courts-Martial, Venereal Disease, and Delinquency Reports, plus the best showing in parades and inspections."[24] For the Polar Bears, such measures were timely and appropriate. Incidents of indiscipline had risen sharply in June and July. The number of soldiers reported AWOL during that period rose from 74 to 96. Similarly, soldiers tried by Summary Courts-Martial (typically conducted at the company level) rose from 21 to 34, and Special Courts-Martial (for serious or violent crimes) doubled from 5 to 10. Finally, the number of soldiers who contracted a venereal disease increased 63 percent to 30 confirmed cases in July.[25]

Although the division summary for July contains no analysis of the sudden increase, two contributing factors can be assumed. First, the sudden influx of first-term enlistees as replacements, typically still teenagers with money in their pockets and away from home for the first time. Second, the shortage of NCOs meant that many of these young men lacked the supervision to keep them in line on and off duty. Soldiers had little exposure to military justice in Basic Training so they encountered military regulations and military justice only after having committed a punishable offense at their first duty station.

Athletic competitions provided an outlet for pent-up energies. The 31st Infantry Regiment did particularly well in identifying soldiers with sports experience or athletic potential and motivating them to perform. As a result, Polar Bear teams won seven of eight regimental-level competitions conducted by the 7th Infantry Division in 1949.[26] In Small Arms Competition, Lieutenant Colonel Bolland, the 2nd Battalion commander, won individual first place for both M1 rifle and M1911A1 pistol competitions.[27] In the 7th Division there was no policy of excusing team members from training in order to practice their sports. All athletic activities—including competitions—were conducted after the conclusion of the duty day.[28]

Given the requirement to complete battalion-level certification by the end of the year and the certainty that winter weather would hamper training, the IX Corps G-3 accelerated the testing schedule for all units. All maneuver training unit tests were to be completed by December 3.[29] Colonel Miller ordered battalions to maximize their time in the field to avoid wasting time moving to and from training areas and firing ranges.[30] Combat units discontinued their occupation duties in August, allowing commanders to focus solely on combat training.[31] In the infantry regiments, the increased OPTEMPO delivered not just better training—no distractions or breaks meant that soldiers retained instruction better—but also improved morale and discipline. As Major Lester K. Olson, the regimental S-3, noted in his training summary for September, "with an increased workload, the men of the regiment have maintained themselves with an even higher morale and 'esprit-de-corps.'"[32]

The intensified training period began with the Army's five-event Physical Fitness Test. Battalions then moved to local training areas to conduct platoon-level training and testing. Rifle platoons were measured against the standards of Army Field Forces Training Test 7-2. This graded exercise required platoons to attack a prepared defensive position. Specific performance measures included the platoon leader's field order, movement of the platoon to the assault position, emplacement of supporting fires, conduct of the assault, and consolidation and reorganization of the platoon on seizure of the enemy position. Of eighteen rifle platoons in the 31st Infantry at the time, four failed the test. Fire discipline among both assault and support elements, level of detail and specificity of squad leaders' orders, and knowledge and use of terrain to conceal movement were the most often-cited reasons for failure. After a week of additional training, the four weak platoons were retested and earned a passing score.[33]

Other testing included day and night evaluations of the Intelligence and Reconnaissance Platoon, and machine gun and 81mm mortar tests for the battalions' heavy weapons companies. Personnel turbulence began to seriously affect training proficiency. Much of the benefit of training conducted between May and September was lost due to rotations. Moreover, the accelerated training and testing schedule forced Colonel Miller to shut down the Regimental Leadership School and return the cadre to their platoons and companies. Few replacements received in the Far East up to October 1949 received more than eight weeks of basic training. The regiment forecast that by the end of 1949, training would have to return to basic unit training to accommodate the large number of replacements.[34] The regiment's monthly summaries showed that leader proficiency did not improve enough to permit platoon, company, and battalion-level training until late 1949.

In keeping with General MacArthur's desire to build combined arms experience at every level, September concluded with a combined arms live fire exercise (CALFEX) conducted jointly by the 31st Infantry Regiment and the 31st Field Artillery Battalion. This firepower demonstration served two purposes. First, it gave replacements a clearer impression of the firepower available to an infantry regiment. Second, it helped both units prepare for battalion-level testing. In addition to the CALFEX, the 31st FAB fired two live immediate suppression missions in support of company-level maneuvers. In all, the 31st FAB fired over 800 rounds of standard 155mm high explosive ammunition during September's training.[35]

While the regiment supported its battalions' tests, Colonel Miller also trained his headquarters and support elements. When his battalions conducted a week-long bivouac at Shimamatsu, the regiment's Headquarters, Medical, and Service Companies also deployed to support them. This first field deployment of the entire regiment quickly revealed some potentially crippling basic equipment shortages. Without sufficient lister bags for potable water storage, the regiment was forced to transport five-gallon cans to and from Camp Crawford daily. Given the conditions of roads in rural Japan in 1949, this significantly increased the maintenance requirements for the regiment's truck fleet and consumed fuel that the regiment could ill afford. The Regimental S-4, Captain Theodore S. Staiger, reported that the 1948 Table of Organization & Equipment didn't provide enough tents even for the reduced strength of the regiment. Commanders were forced to choose between protecting the health of their soldiers or the serviceability of their equipment and supplies.

By the end of September, no replacement boots in the most common sizes could be found anywhere in the division, and the two pair of fatigues issued to each soldier proved insufficient to provide clean and dry uniforms at the end of the training day. These shortfalls were partially remedied by the end of October with the issue of an additional fatigue uniform to each soldier, but boot repair and replacement remained a problem well into the opening weeks of the Korean War.[36]

In early October 1949, Colonel F.M. Harris and a detachment of officers and senior NCOs from the Office of the Commander of Army Field Forces (OCAFF) inspected training throughout the 7th Infantry Division. OCAFF's reports provide insight into the progress of training around the Army and the general attitude toward training among the Army's senior leaders. Interspersed with comments on units' tactical skills is what soldiers call "chicken shit." For example, inspectors who visited the 31st Infantry faulted it for "a general lack of smartness on the part of individuals" and "laxness in saluting during off-duty hours." On the whole, however, the regiment earned high marks for its training and administration and received an overall rating of "very satisfactory."[37]

The 2nd Battalion was in the middle of practicing attack problems for upcoming tests when the inspectors arrived at Shimamatsu. Commenting on a battalion-level approach march movement to contact, inspectors found the problem well-planned and satisfactorily executed. The next day, F Company conducted a live-fire attack supported by a battery of 105mm howitzers from the 57th Field Artillery Battalion, an exercise the inspectors termed "excellent" in its planning and execution. Of particular note, inspectors praised the company commander and battalion staff for their conduct of a post-exercise critique. Significantly, deficiencies noted during execution resulted primarily from leadership failures at company and platoon level (e.g., unclear company order, disoriented platoon leaders) and not from errors by NCOs. Other elements of the regiment also earned high marks. The I&R Platoon's training on patrolling and observation post procedures was "well prepared and effectively presented" and the Medical Company's training on field expedient first aid rated "excellent" for being both "interesting and effective."[38] No unit in the regiment earned less than a "satisfactory" rating.

Both battalions executed Reinforced Battalion Combat Firing Tests in November 1949, supported by the 57th Field Artillery Battalion. To add realism, F-80 "Shooting Stars" from the 49th Fighter Wing flew close-air support sorties for each battalion. Having earned a "very satisfactory" rating from the IX Corps evaluators, 3rd Battalion returned to Camp Crawford where it conducted an emergency deployment readiness exercise. Alerted on November 21, the battalion moved by rail to Chitose's abandoned airfield. There, the battalion established a defensive perimeter to defend against a notional attack by Soviet paratroops. The 2nd Battalion, having failed its graded exercise, conducted a seven-day review of all training from squad to battalion level. Returning to Shimamatsu on November 30, the IX Corps staff certified the battalion as combat ready. Despite Siberian weather, Heavy Mortar Company passed its training test on December 15, and all replacements that had arrived since the late summer fired their weapons for record in deep snow the week before Christmas.[39]

Severe weather kept the troops indoors for the remainder of 1949. The 31st Infantry concentrated on cold weather training and movement with skis and snowshoes in the first three weeks of 1950, while the regimental staff conducted a command post exercise. Captain Richard J. Hertel of E Company experimented with a unique piece of improvised equipment—the "Gunboggon." Hoping to improve the cross-country mobility of crew-served weapons in heavy snow, Captain Hertel had plywood sleds built, to which crews attached .30 caliber machine guns. The experiment exceeded expectations because the regimental S-3 recommended "Gunboggon's use by 57mm and 75mm recoilless rifle crews as well."[40]

The Polar Bears interrupted training to welcome a new commander in February. Colonel Richard P. Ovenshine became the regiment's third commander in eleven months. Ovenshine had experience on division staffs during World War II and briefly commanded the 165th Infantry Regiment during the initial occupation of Japan.[41] He concurrently became Camp Crawford's commander. Headquarters, 7th Infantry Division moved to Sendai on northern Honshu. Departure of division headquarters and its supporting signal, replacement, and reconnaissance companies relieved crowded conditions at Camp Crawford. For the remainder of the month, training centered on winter skills, culminating in a regimental ski and snowshoe competition. The event combined land navigation, marksmanship, and first aid with winter survival and cross-country movement. In addition, the regiment conducted a two-week refresher course for platoon sergeants, emphasizing leadership principles and how to best impart instruction on tactical tasks.[42]

In March 1950, warmer weather allowed the resumption of squad and crew-level training. Light machine gun and 60mm and 81mm mortar sections deployed to firing ranges near Camp Crawford for ten days of live-fire practice and qualification while 57mm anti-tank crews conducted familiarization firing with antiquated 2.36 inch rocket launchers.

Two other significant events occurred in March. First, cadre from the Eighth Army Air Transportability School traveled to Hokkaido to train the regiment in air movement. Regimental and battalion staff officers attended a 17-hour planner's course to acquaint them with the basics of load planning, while enlisted soldiers and company grade officers attended a 12-hour basic proficiency course in loading and securing cargo. The second event was a two-week squad leader refresher course, patterned after the previous month's platoon sergeant training. Again taught by the Regimental Leadership School's cadre, the focus remained on the principles of leadership, effective instruction, and the duties and responsibilities of squad leaders in a tactical setting.[43]

Near the end of March, the entire 31st Infantry Regimental Combat Team (RCT) moved to Shimamatsu for an RCT Firing Exercise. The event was graded by Eighth Army umpires. Included in the RCT were the 57th Field Artillery Battalion (105mm towed howitzers), a battery of the 31st Field Artillery Battalion (155mm towed howitzers), and a company each from the 13th Engineer Battalion, 7th Medical Battalion, and 77th Tank Battalion. This was the first time the entire RCT had trained together. The senior observer concluded that the 31st RCT needed to devote more attention to training as a team, not as a grouping of individual units. He rated the RCT's performance as unsatisfactory.[44]

Reacting to that disappointing showing, Colonel Ovenshine directed that units review all subjects trained since the previous summer, beginning with basic individual tasks and progressing through all levels of collective training to include battalion maneuvers. Two RCT-level command post exercises were conducted with leaders and staff from all subordinate and supporting units to eliminate command and control problems experienced in March. When soldiers from the rifle companies were not engaged in collective training, they were constructing and using an improved rifle marksmanship range. Unlike existing static ranges, the new range employed life-size targets at unknown distances. Instead of lying prone in the open, firers on the new range had to acquire and engage targets from behind cover. The range received the division commander's praise for its combat realism.[45]

In April, the 31st Infantry Regiment lost over 200 experienced officers, NCOs and soldiers while receiving fewer than 30 replacements. The loss could not have come at a worse time, amid preparations for the RCT exercise retest. The regiment was also forced to suspend training for two days in mid-month to receive 56 Japanese soldiers who were being repatriated from Soviet Siberia. The mission irritated the regiment's leadership, who were earnestly preparing for the retest.[46] Despite the manpower losses and unwanted distraction, the 31st RCT earned "very satisfactory" ratings on its retest. The Division G-3 observer recorded that this exercise "showed a vast improvement over the March test, proving the results of five weeks of intensive combat team training which the 31st had undergone prior to this retest."[47]

The battalion commanders offered differing views of the obstacles they faced. Lieutenant Colonel Robert R. Summers, commanding the 2nd Battalion, focused on personnel problems. In priority, he listed a shortage of officers, a shortage of competent NCOs, and constant turnover of enlisted personnel as the chief impediments to achieving and maintaining a high state of readiness. Summers lacked one of his two authorized majors and five captains. Five of his nine rifle platoons and the battalion intelligence section had no officer. Lieutenant Colonel William R. Reilly, commanding the 3rd Battalion, attributed his battalion's shortcomings to resource shortfalls. Limited field training opportunities during the harsh winter, a shortage of winter gear for soldiers, the absence of 57mm recoilless rifles, and the advanced age of his crew-served weapons ranked as his most significant obstacles. Reilly also lacked his second field grade officer, but had more lieutenants and captains than the 2nd Battalion.

Both officers reported an almost complete lack of anti-tank capability. Like every other regiment in Japan, the 31st Infantry had 2.36-inch rocket launchers instead of 75mm and 57mm recoilless rifles. The 2nd Battalion had two recoilless rifles but they arrived without sights or mounts. Anti-tank teams had not yet received the more powerful 3.5-inch rocket launcher then in limited production. Both battalions reported every authorized vehicle as mission-capable, although they still lacked four quarter-ton trucks (jeeps).

By the summer of 1950, the 31st Infantry Regiment was no longer the loose aggregation of individuals shipped from Korea to Japan eighteen months earlier. It had developed a sense of pride and cohesion, and markedly improved the combat readiness of its individual soldiers, platoons, companies, and battalions. Unfortunately, the 31st, like the other regiments of the 7th Infantry Division, had to give up many of its trained soldiers, NCOs, and officers to fill the first three divisions to deploy to combat in Korea. When its own turn came, the 31st Infantry had to be hastily rebuilt with a mixture of new recruits and recalled reservists, augmented by over 1,800 Koreans with little or no military experience in their own or anyone else's army.

The history of the 31st Infantry Regiment in occupation-era Japan is a sad testimony to the negligence of the nation's civilian leadership. Blaming Japan-like divisions' unreadiness for combat in Korea on an "occupation mentality" glossed over the harsh realities commanders faced in trying to train their units to meet even the most minimal standards of combat readiness. It soon became evident that the 2nd and 3rd Infantry Divisions sent from the United States were no more combat ready than those that had been stationed in Japan. It is important that historians understand and convey the root causes of Task Force Smith's defeat at Osan and the subsequent rout and near destruction of several American divisions. It is a testament to the dedication and ability of officers like Colonel Richard P. Ovenshine that hastily rebuilt regiments were able to carry out the UN Counteroffensive of September 1950 and survive the subsequent campaign.

PART III. KOREA
by Karl H. Lowe

10 Inchon, 1950

When North Korean troops invaded the Republic of Korea on June 25, 1950, the 31st Infantry Regiment, stationed at Camp Crawford, Japan, had only two battalions due to a general manpower shortage that affected nearly all regiments in Japan.[1] Because the 7th Infantry Division, the 31st Infantry Regiment's parent, was stationed closest to the Soviet Union, it was to continue occupying and protecting Japan while the other three divisions deployed to Korea. In keeping with that plan, its three infantry regiments, the 17th, 31st, and 32nd, were stripped to help fill the three divisions that deployed to Korea in July. Replacements from the U.S. arrived slowly because the Army only had ten active divisions, all understrength.[2]

In Korea, the situation quickly grew desperate. Better-trained, better-armed, and better-motivated North Koreans inflicted heavy losses on the first American units to arrive from Japan.[3] World War II–era 2.36-inch antitank rockets bounced harmlessly off of Soviet-supplied T-34 tanks and there were too few troops to keep the North Koreans from streaming around the 24th Infantry Division, the first to arrive, precipitating a series of panicky retreats southward. The 25th Infantry and 1st Cavalry Divisions fared little better, barely clinging to the southeastern corner of Korea by the end of July.

In Japan, the depleted 7th Division soon began receiving replacements, a combination of green recruits from the U.S. and more seasoned men drawn from troop units all over the United States. The 12th Armored Infantry Battalion from Ft. Hood, Texas, for example, deployed almost en masse in mid–July from Fairfield-Suisun Airfield (later Travis Air Force Base) near San Francisco, but its troops deployed in platoon-size packets to Japan. On arrival, they were sent as individual replacements to different regiments and dispersed further among needy companies, losing the cohesion and tactical proficiency they had cultivated for a year or more at Fort Hood. In the U.S., battalions of the 2nd Armored, 3rd Infantry, and 11th Airborne Divisions were drawn down to skeletons and some were completely zeroed out.[4]

In August 1950, 340 replacements were arriving in Japan and Korea by air each day, not enough to replace the losses early deploying units had suffered. By August 5, 7,858 men had been killed or seriously wounded and only 7,711 replacements had arrived in the Far East. The 2nd Infantry Division from Fort Lewis, Washington, the 1st Marine Brigade from Camp Pendleton, California, the 5th Regimental Combat Team from Schofield Barracks, Hawaii, and the partially-formed 29th Infantry Regiment from Okinawa were sent to plug gaps in the steadily shrinking perimeter protecting Korea's southernmost port, Pusan. Although the 7th Division was closer to Korea than any of those units, it was not as combat-ready.

After being scattered all over Japan to secure the vacated garrisons of divisions that had deployed to Korea, the 7th Division was assembled for pre-deployment training at Camp Fuji, a dusty firing range near the town of Gotemba in the shadow of Japan's famed Mount Fuji. The division had only 574 officers and 8,200 enlisted men, barely half of its authorized strength. Before deploying to combat, it would have to form units missing from its authorized structure. To help fill the void, 8,307 Koreans were gathered off the streets of South Korean towns, packed aboard ships, and shipped to Japan to join the 7th Division. They were called Korean Augmentation to the U.S. Army (KATUSA). Of the total, the 31st Infantry received 1,857 Koreans, roughly half the regiment's strength. While the numbers must have looked good to planners in Tokyo and Washington, the practical impact was more negative than positive. Most KATUSAs spoke no English, making cooperation difficult at best. They received almost no military training, firing only five rounds from their newly issued Springfield M-1 rifles in Japan, and they had great difficulty adjusting to American food and field sanitation standards. GIs in rifle squads were paired with KATUSA counterparts while heavy weapons elements made their KATUSAs ammunition bearers. Seeing a disaster in the making, Colonel Richard P. Ovenshine, the regimental commander, planned a full program of training for his polyglot outfit, but he would not get the time.

On September 3, Typhoon Kezia roared across southern Japan with winds up to 110 miles an hour, wrecking the port city of Kobe where the 1st Marine Division was staging. The typhoon also wrought havoc at Camp Fuji, scattering squad tents all over the landscape. Warned of the storm's approach, most men fled to the more substantial private dwellings and public buildings of Gotemba and other nearby villages. In most cases, they were graciously welcomed by Japanese families, but the mix of muddy GI boots and tatami rice mat floors was most unwelcome. In Japan, people take off their footwear before entering a residence. Accompanying heavy rains turned Camp Fuji into a sea of mud, putting an end to the idea of serious training. Three days later, the 7th Division received orders to move by road and train to the port of Yokohama. The last serial reached the port on September 7 and was quickly herded onto a waiting ship. Hundreds of the regiment's newest replacements had not even been assigned to companies yet.

Typical of the latest arrivals was 19-year-old Private Don Monterosso. Don enlisted in March 1950 and took basic training at Camp Roberts, California—away from Michigan for the first time in his life and desperately homesick. Basic and advanced individual training was 16 weeks of dismounted drill, physical conditioning, military courtesy, and "don't worry about all that combat stuff, you'll get that in your permanent unit." What later saved Don's life, though, was the 70 hours he spent firing a Garand M-1 rifle at targets ranging out to 550 yards. When the Korean War began, Don was en route to Fort Sam Houston, Texas, but he didn't get to stay very long. In early September, he left McChord Field, near Tacoma, Washington on a Dakota C-47 transport to Haneda Air Base near Tokyo, stopping in Alaska en route. At the Far East Command's Transfer Point at Camp Zama, he was assigned to the 7th Division. The next day he was given a set of the division's "hourglass" shoulder patches and herded onto a train to Yokohama. There, he was promptly hustled aboard the attack transport *Simon B. Buckner* with hundreds of similarly bewildered newcomers.

Despite the rush, the division's troopships would stay at anchor in the harbor for another three days while tanks, trucks, howitzers, communication vans, and heavy engineer equipment were loaded onto cargo ships and Navy LSTs. The 7th Division's ships departed Yokohama on the morning of September 10, joining the 1st Marine Division and other units of the hastily formed X Corps at a rendezvous point off the Japanese island of Kyushu. The convoy included 261 ships from seven countries. Many of the cargo ships' crewmen were former members of the Imperial Japanese Navy who had been fighting Americans just five years earlier. At sea, men became violently ill, overworking sanitation facilities and turning overcrowded troop compartments into slimy, stinking hell holes. Don Monterosso curled up under his poncho in a gun bucket[5] on the deck, preferring the rain and salt spray to the stench below.

Inchon

Unit commanders opened Top Secret orders once the ships were underway, informing them that Inchon was their destination. The 1st Marine Division would go ashore on September 15. The 7th Infantry Division would follow, landing just south of the port. On September 15, Don Monterosso was assigned to A Company, but he didn't know anyone in the unit and couldn't understand his KATUSA partner. After a rough journey in the typhoon's wake, ships dropped anchor ten miles from Inchon on September 16. Outside the harbor, the battleship USS *Missouri*, five cruisers, and six destroyers were pounding enemy positions deeper inland.

Troops of the 31st Infantry Regiment land at Inchon Harbor aboard LSTs (U.S. Army photograph, National Archives).

The day before, the 5th Marine Regiment took Wolmi-do, an island dominating Inchon's narrow shipping channel. Ships could not enter the tidal harbor without getting stuck and there were no landing craft to take the 7th Division ashore since they were still in use by the Marines. Tides at Inchon can fall as much as 32 feet in 12 hours, leaving only mud flats in their wake. The only time troops could land was a two-hour period before high tide and a similar period after high tide. On September 18, the 32nd Infantry became the first of the 7th Division's regiments to go ashore, establishing blocking positions astride Seoul's southern approaches. Finally, on September 19, landing craft came alongside the 31st Infantry's transports and began taking troops ashore.

The next morning, the 31st Infantry, less its 3rd Battalion, established hasty defensive positions south of Seoul. Its mission was to stop North Koreans from getting into Seoul from the south. The 3rd Battalion remained in reserve near Inchon. As any unit tends to be when it first enters combat, the 31st was jittery. Many men went ashore not knowing a single person in their unit. Mixing green, jittery troops with lethal weapons often leads to fatal accidents. Private Paul H. Nielson of K Company became one of the regiment's first fatalities in Korea when he failed to heed a sentry's warning and was shot by one of his comrades. On the morning of September 21, the 7th Reconnaissance Company and 73rd Tank Battalion led the advance to Suwon Airfield, with two battalions of the 31st Infantry close behind them. After several minor skirmishes along the route, the force reached the airfield late that afternoon.

On to Osan

With its 8,000 foot concrete runway, Suwon airfield was a critical prize, necessary for both aerial resupply and fighter operations, but there were still enemy troops in the area and more were arriving. Intelligence reported that enemy forces, including tanks, were gathering on high ground south of Suwon.

Just after dark on September 21 and again after midnight on September 22, two platoons of North Korean tanks attempted to storm the airfield. They lost four tanks of their own and destroyed one American tank. On the morning of September 23, the 1st Battalion entered the city of Suwon. In and around the town, the task force captured 240 North Koreans, most of whom discarded their weapons and surrendered without a fight. All looked tired and hungry, having marched for days to escape the Eighth Army's counteroffensive.

Advancing on a parallel axis on the opposite side of the Suwon-Osan highway was the 2nd Battalion. Near the village of Pyongjam-ni, the battalion's lead unit, Captain Charles Howard's G Company, encountered heavy small arms, machine gun, mortar, and tank fire. While G Company took whatever cover could be found, the rest of the 2nd Battalion, reinforced by A Company, conducted a wide envelopment around the town to take a hill blocking the way to Osan.

Sergeant Charles A. Lonsford, then a platoon sergeant (2nd Platoon A Company), recalls that his company's objective was a ridge two kilometers south of the line of departure. Against light resistance, his company quickly gained its objective and aggressively pursued fleeing North Koreans, soon outdistancing the rest of the regiment. After being ordered twice to stop, the company halted on its objective and waited for the 2nd Battalion to catch up. An aerial observer reported four enemy tanks astride the battalion's path.

During the extended halt, Lonsford dozed off and awoke amid a tank battle. Two North Korean T-34 tanks were knocked out by the 73rd Tank Battalion less than 200 yards from where he slept.

PFC Glenn Justice, a 57mm Recoilless Rifle gunner in G Company, was moving across a wide, foul-smelling rice paddy when the shooting began. As the outgoing fire intensified, his head started aching, his ears became stopped up, his throat went dry, and his heart was pounding. He was in combat for the first time, experiencing an unsettling mixture of fear and exhilaration. North Korean mortar fire "walked" along the adjacent road where tanks were stopping to fire on North Korean positions. Lieutenant William G. Fuss and Master Sergeant Kenneth J. Whalen of G Company's 4th Platoon had just climbed aboard one of the tanks to get a better view of the enemy positions when a mortar round struck the turret, killing both men instantly. In all, five men in G Company were killed and seven were wounded as small arms and mortar fire hammered the area.

Although it seemed like an eternity to men trying to find protection where there was none, American artillery eventually suppressed the mortars and pounded the hillside blocking G Company's advance. As artillery fire shifted to the hill's backside, G Company began moving up the forward slope, firing as they went. Frightened North Koreans soon began abandoning their foxholes to flee over the top but few made it. When a North

Defending a ridgeline (U.S. Army photograph, National Archives).

Korean fell to the bark of his carbine, Glenn Justice felt sick, realizing he had just shot a human being. Nearby, KATUSAs were blatantly firing into the air. Few would shoot fellow Koreans because friends and relatives had been forcibly conscripted by the North Koreans as they rolled across South Korea. When the fighting ended, 67 enemy soldiers lay dead in front of the ridge, 38 more were killed on the back side, and 7 frightened POWs squatted amid the carnage.

Late that afternoon, one of the 2nd Battalion's patrols encountered a force equipped with at least two heavy machine guns and a mortar. They seemed determined to break through to the north. Late into the night, firefights erupted throughout the area as patrols from both sides probed each other's positions. Enemy mortar fire hit inside the 2nd Battalion's perimeter after dark and a brief tank attack was repulsed by the 73rd Tank Battalion. As illumination flares died out, the area remained lit by the flaming hulks of five enemy tanks.

On September 25, the 2nd Battalion, with A Company, 73rd Tank Battalion attached, continued its advance toward Osan while the 1st Battalion sent patrols onto high ground south and east of Suwon. One patrol sighted three truckloads of enemy troops that had by-passed the 2nd Battalion. Late that morning, the 57th Field Artillery's aerial observer spotted approximately 500 enemy troops and two tanks just 1,000 yards from the 2nd Battalion's CP. As the fighting intensified, Colonel Ovenshine approved a request to pull the 2nd Battalion back due to the heavy volume of fire it was taking. The 57th and 92nd Field Artillery Battalions blasted the area, dispersing the enemy force. Nearly 100 enemy soldiers surrendered before dark. The prisoners revealed they were members of the 105th Tank Brigade, totaling around 3,000 troops.

Around noon, the Regimental Tank Company and a supply column arrived from Inchon. As if to greet them, the North Koreans fired four 75mm recoilless rifle rounds into the Suwon Airfield perimeter. The rounds landed near the regimental CP, but caused no casualties. PFC Boyce McCreary, a 19-year-old supply truck driver in the 31st Infantry's Headquarters Company recalls that his truck, laden with ammunition, was shot up in an ambush en route to the airfield. Seven of his eight tires were punctured and there were bullet holes all over the truck's cab and cargo bed but he was not hit and the ammunition did not ignite. God smiled on him that day and every day thereafter was a precious gift.

PFCs James R. Brawner and Irwin Katter of the regiment's Heavy Mortar Company were manning an outpost on the airfield perimeter when their platoon sergeant told them to check the adjacent village to make sure no civilians remained there. An airstrike was scheduled to hit the village and he wanted to avoid killing civilians. The pair had just reached the edge of the village when a pair of U.S. Air Force F-80 "Shooting Stars" dove to attack, firing just over their heads. As the planes made repeated strafing passes, Brawner and Katter crawled along a ditch all the way back to the perimeter. They did not want to be seen by a fast-flying fighter pilot who might mistake them for North Koreans.

Three tanks from the 1st Cavalry Division's 70th Tank Battalion carrying a platoon from L Company of the 7th Cavalry Regiment met the 31st Infantry's 2nd Battalion near Osan on the morning of September 26. There was no radio communication between the 31st's rifle companies and the approaching cavalrymen, so the meeting was a surprise to those at the tip of both spears. Until then, only North Korean tanks had approached from the south. The linkup could have ended in tragedy as tankers, antitank gunners, and artillerymen all zeroed in on the approaching column. A lone 57mm recoilless rifle round struck the lead tank, but did not explode. Fortunately, the tankers knew they were nearing "friendly" lines and did not respond. Someone with experience at Fort Hood recognized the tanks as American and passed the word not to shoot. Just in the nick of time! The meeting linked the Pusan perimeter's defenders with the Inchon invasion force.

Near daybreak on September 27, the 2nd Battalion attacked Hill 113 against stiff resistance on the southern and eastern slopes. The North Koreans were expertly camouflaged and made extensive use of snipers to impede the advance. Rudy Reyes of F Company's 1st Platoon, recalls that his platoon leader, Lieutenant Don C. Engh of Del Norte, California led his platoon's wild charge over the top of the ridge. Engh was killed by a grenade or mortar round just as he reached the other side. By nightfall, the 2nd Battalion controlled the hill's southwest face, but the enemy still held the reverse slope. Companies K and L relieved Companies E and F during the night.

At noon the next day, an air strike and heavy mortar and artillery concentrations hammered enemy positions in preparation for the final assault by A, G, K, and L Companies of the 31st Infantry and A Company, 73rd Tank Battalion. Enemy resistance had already melted away, however, leaving 14 destroyed tanks, 6 antitank guns, several mortars, large numbers of small arms, and nearly 300 enemy dead littering the battlefield.

Men of the 31st Infantry Regiment move cautiously through high grass as they flush out snipers (U.S. Army photograph, National Archives).

SGT William C. MacCullock (Albuquerque, New Mexico), Company G, 31st Infantry Regiment, is being evacuated after being wounded in action (U.S. Army photograph, National Archives).

The week's toll for the 31st Infantry and attached units was 25 dead and 75 wounded. Typical of the division's recent fillers, Don Monterosso was away from the United States for the first time in his life, traveled by plane for the first time, went to sea for the first time, and was shot at for the first time—and he was barely 19.

On October 1, the 31st mopped up isolated resistance between Suwon and Osan and conducted motorized patrols along the 40-mile corridor between the towns to keep the road open. At noon, the 1st Cavalry Division assumed responsibility for Osan, extending its area of influence to the east and west against scattered light resistance. Truck convoys carrying jubilant units of the 7th and 8th ROK (Republic of Korea) Infantry Divisions streamed through on their way to Seoul. On October 2, the U.S. 5th Cavalry Regiment assumed responsibility for the 31st Infantry's sector. With enemy resistance nearly ended, Colonel Ovenshine initiated the training program he had been unable to conduct in Japan. Naval aviation and the 57th Field Artillery Battalion supported a series of battalion live fire assault exercises. A particular objective of the training was fostering mutual confidence, cohesion, and teamwork among the regiment's American and Korean members.

On the morning of October 4, an L-19 Piper Cub named the "Blue Goose" landed at Suwon. Painted on its fuselage was X Corps' blue and white shoulder patch. Major General Ned Almond, X Corps' commander, had come to watch the regiment's training. In a foul mood, he was quick to find fault with the way the training was being conducted. Almond felt Colonel Ovenshine was too old to command in combat and was displeased by what he considered sluggish performance during the attack to take Osan. The next day, the 17th Infantry Regiment's Heavy Mortar Company fired on one of its own battalions during a similar training exercise, killing 5 men and wounding 55 others. All aircraft available to X Corps were diverted to evacuate casualties and bring in doctors and plasma. Someone's head would roll, but not the one most people expected.[6] In a move few understood, Almond sacked Colonel Ovenshine, replacing him with Colonel Allan D. MacLean, formerly G-3 of the Eighth Army.

Back to Sea

Before dawn on October 5, the 31st Infantry's motor column departed Suwon for the port of Pusan, a journey of over 350 miles—36 hours if all went well. Unfortunately, there were not enough trucks in the whole corps to move the entire 7th Division, so drivers would have to make multiple trips. Radio contact was lost shortly after the column got underway and because of the 17th Infantry's mortar incident, no aircraft were available to monitor the convoy's progress and report the locations of disabled vehicles. Traversing battle damaged roads through areas where North Korean troops still lurked, drivers were cautioned not to stop for any reason. There would be no way to call for help if they got ambushed. By 8 a.m., the convoy extended 55 miles from lead to trail. With most radios not working, convoy discipline broke down from the start. Some convoy segments stopped in towns along the route for the night. The next morning, convoy segment commanders were ordered to stop the trucks at a rail crossing near Taejon to transfer their passengers to trains for the remainder of the trip to Pusan.

Things soon got worse. An ammunition train blew up in a tunnel near Andong, blocking the rail line to Pusan. Around the same time, a 32nd Infantry convoy segment was ambushed, wounding 11 men and holding up the rest of the convoy for over two hours. Over the next several days more convoy segments were ambushed, further delaying the division's closure. The segment reached Pusan on October 11. That day, the ROK 3rd and Capitol Divisions took Wonsan, North Korea. There was no longer a need for X Corps to make an amphibious landing there. It looked like the 7th Division's role in the war might soon end. Rumors spread that the division would be boarding ships to return to Japan. On October 16, the 7th Division embarked at Pusan aboard the attack transports *Mason M. Patrick, Fred C. Ainsworth,* and *William F. Mitchell* and several LSTs. Aboard ship, they were issued winter parkas and other assorted winter gear. Dreams of an early return to Japan abruptly vanished.

On October 20, the seaward approaches to Wonsan were still heavily mined, making it impossible to get transports or LSTs ashore. Further north, ROK I Corps entered the cities of Hungnam and Hamhung against light resistance. North Korean troops were fleeing without much of a fight while ROK troops pursued them tenaciously, dashing up Korea's northeastern panhandle toward the Chinese and Russian borders. Finally on October 24, after eight agonizing days at anchor, the 7th Division received sailing orders. The division would land at the fishing village of Iwon, almost midway up the panhandle between Hungnam and the Russian border.

On October 27, the first snow fell in North Korea and the temperature fell below freezing. The ROK 26th Infantry Regiment, tasked to secure the northern approaches to the Hamhung-Hungnam area, encountered enemy troops as they entered the mountains.

They were surprised when the enemy failed to withdraw as they had in every previous engagement in North Korea. Instead, the fight got so intense that the ROKs backed off, but not before taking a dozen or so prisoners. They were members of the Chinese Peoples' Liberation Army (PLA).

On October 29, a turbulent sea tossed huge waves onto the shore at Iwon, washing away sand ramps used to unload trucks and other heavy cargo. The 17th Infantry was already ashore, but the 31st would have to stay at sea until November 4 and the 32nd Infantry could not land until November 9. On October 31, the 17th Infantry (less one battalion) and the 49th Field Artillery Battalion made a 120-mile motor march along a one-lane dirt road to the inland town of Pungsan to relieve a regiment of the ROK Capitol Division. Just after 5:00 a.m. the next morning, they were hit with a mortar barrage, followed closely by a ground attack that reached the artillery positions. The attackers were North Koreans, their determination perhaps bolstered by the presence of tens of thousands of Chinese troops somewhere behind them. The war was about to get a lot tougher.

11 North Korea, 1950

Into the Mountains

On November 1, the Chinese People's Liberation Army attacked and nearly destroyed the ROK 15th Infantry and U.S. 8th Cavalry Regiments near Unsan, in the foothills of North Korea's Taebaek Mountains. For the next week, the Eighth Army was attacked repeatedly and began pulling its most advanced units back toward the Chongchon River to avoid another disaster, but more attacks were coming. Seeking to flank the Chinese, General MacArthur ordered X Corps to attack to the northwest and link up with the Eighth Army. Such a feat would severely stretch the corps' three divisions. The 3rd Infantry Division, recently arrived at Wonsan, was moving up the coastal road and rail line to Hungnam. The 1st Marine Division had reached the Changjin (Chosin) Reservoir north of Hungnam and the 7th Infantry Division reached the Pujon (Fusen) Reservoir farther east, trying to keep contact with the ROK I Corps, which was racing northeastward along the North Korean panhandle toward Chongjin.

8th Army-X Corps intended attack routes (map from Association archives).

As the last elements of the 31st Infantry landed at Iwon on November 8, the regiment began moving north through rugged mountains east of the Pujon Reservoir. Its mission was to advance to the Yalu River, establishing contact with the 5th Marine Regiment on the left and the 17th Infantry Regiment on the right. The initial advance encountered only scattered resistance from enemy troops who fired from a safe distance and quickly melted away. The situation seemed so quiet that Major Clifton Z. Couch, the 3rd Battalion's Executive Officer, and Captain Herbert L. Bryant, Commanding the 3rd Battalion's Headquarters Company, went into the hills together to hunt Siberian tigers. On the morning of November 21, the 17th Infantry reached Hyesanjin on the Yalu River, bordering the Chinese province of Manchuria. A reinforced platoon of the 32nd Infantry Regiment (Task Force Kingston) and an ROK regiment reached the river at points farther east.[1]

On Thanksgiving Day (November 23), the 31st Infantry was scattered across northeastern Korea. Advancing along tracks that could scarcely be called roads, the Regimental Headquarters and 3rd Battalion were in the mountains near the northeast end of the Pujon (Fusen) Reservoir.[2] The 1st Battalion was near the reservoir's southeast end near Pungsan and the 2nd Battalion was protecting the 7th Division's Command Post near Pukchong. Units did their best to get a hot turkey meal with all the trimmings to the troops, but road conditions made that impossible for most. Whatever arrived was cold and got even colder when food was exposed to temperatures below zero.

Thanksgiving was not quiet for men in the rifle companies. Most were on patrol, looking for an elusive enemy. Wherever they went, local civilians reported hundreds of Chinese troops ahead of them. North of Pungsan, a pitiful column of refugees was spotted trudging south along a winding mountain road. Here and there, gunfire crackled across barren ridges as two patrols made contact with a larger Chinese force ambling slowly down a road just a few hundred yards behind the refugees. The outnumbered patrols inflicted some losses, but soon withdrew to Pungsan. The refugees struggled to safety among the retreating GIs and KATUSAs.

At Pungsan, a distraught old woman pleaded with the Americans through an ROK liaison officer to bomb her village. She cried repeatedly "kill everyone in it." Confused, the officer asked why she was so eager to kill her own people. She said any who are left alive have no life worth living. Chinese troops came during the previous night, took over their homes, took all the young girls, and told the men to leave. When villagers refused, the Chinese took all the men and boys out and shot them. Everyone else fled. The Chinese apparently considered Mao's "swim in the sea of the people" doctrine valid only in their own country.

On November 24, Colonel McLean received orders to take his regiment, less the 1st Battalion (most of which would remain at Pungsan), to relieve the 5th Marine Regiment east of the Changjin (Chosin) Reservoir. The 1st Battalion 32nd Infantry, led by Lieutenant Colonel Don Carlos Faith, was the nearest of the 7th Infantry Division's battalions to the Marines. It was therefore attached to the 31st RCT in place of the 1-31st and began moving north on November 25 to relieve the Marines east of the reservoir. The 57th Field Artillery Battalion (less C Battery), D Battery 15th Antiaircraft Automatic Weapons Battalion, and C Company 13th Engineer Battalion were also attached to the 31st Infantry to form the 31st Regimental Combat Team (31st RCT).

To reach the Changjin Reservoir, the 31st had to backtrack to the coast, traveling 140 miles to go only 25 as the crow flies because a steep mountain range without roads stood between the reservoirs. The regiment's motor convoy departed Pungsan around daybreak on November 26. The 31st RCT's 319 vehicles had almost no off-route capability in Korea's steep, icy mountains. American units, reliant on trucks to move supplies, heavy weapons, and casualties, were tied to narrow, poorly maintained roads that wound tortuously through icy valleys. Most bridges on those roads were single-lane structures spanning deep ravines. If blown, there was usually no by-pass. The risk of being ambushed at a blown bridge or a narrow defile was a constant companion to the long, slow-moving convoys snaking their way through the mountains.

In contrast, Chinese units traveled with what their soldiers could carry, supplemented by horses and forced civilian labor, allowing them almost unrestricted freedom to maneuver between and behind the Americans. The opportunities were not lost on Chinese generals, accustomed to that way of fighting. But

Aid Station. Medics work on a wounded soldier (U.S. Army photograph, National Archives).

senior American commanders had a different frame of reference. Believing they would be able to detect Chinese logistical preparations for an attack across the Yalu, they saw nothing and therefore assumed there was no buildup underway. The Chinese too would learn lessons. They could not live off the land in sparsely populated, frozen North Korea as they had in their own country.

Underestimating the enemy and the difficulty of the terrain was not limited to X Corps. The 2nd Infantry Division, operating west of the Taebaek Mountains near Kunuri, would suffer the highest losses of any division at any time in the war while trying to cover the Eighth Army's retreat to Pyongyang. In war, mastery of the terrain is central to success and in this war, the Chinese used terrain like chess champions, isolating UN units wherever an opportunity appeared.

The 7th Marine Regiment had reached Yudam-ni, just west of the Changjin Reservoir, on November 23, while the 1st Marine Regiment established defensive positions at the critical road junction of Hagaru-ri, at the southern tip of the reservoir and at Koto-ri, on the main supply route to the coast. On the morning of November 25, the 5th Marine Regiment, which had been advancing up the reservoir's east side, began pulling back around the reservoir's southern end to join the 7th Marine Regiment at Yudam-ni. On November 27, the 7th Marine Regiment attempted an attack to the northwest but was stopped cold by Chinese troops controlling the surrounding hills.

Although unknown at the time, the 5th Marine Regiment's westward shift would save the 1st Marine Division from destruction. If the 5th and 7th Marines had remained split with the reservoir between them, each would have borne the weight of two Chinese divisions. Concentrated instead near Yudam-ni and supported by 36 105mm howitzers, their five infantry battalions had sufficient strength to maintain a more coherent line and would retain sufficient strength to come out intact. Behind them, the 1st Marine Regiment, subsequently reinforced by the Army's 2nd Battalion 31st Infantry and other smaller units, held the escape route open. On the reservoir's east side where the 5th Marines had been, two Army infantry battalions and two field artillery batteries (totaling 8 105mm howitzers) of the 31st RCT began arriving on the afternoon of November 27. They would be too thinly stretched to hold off the two Chinese divisions (80th and 81st) waiting to pounce.

As the last elements of the 5th Marines passed through Hagaru-ri on their way to Yudam-ni, the 31st RCT's 3rd Battalion began moving north on a narrow, slippery dirt road paralleling the Changjin Reservoir's east side. By then, the 1st Battalion, 32nd Infantry had already moved further north, relieving the 3rd Battalion 5th Marine Regiment on high ground overlooking the reservoir's mid-point on November 26. The 31st Infantry Regiment's Forward Command Post (CP) tucked itself in behind the 1st Battalion, 32nd Infantry atop a ridge. Its forward location offered a good vantage point for overseeing the attack Colonel MacLean planned to launch the next day. Faithful to the last orders he received, he intended to attack toward the northwest as soon as his 2nd Battalion reached the Reservoir. Just behind him was the Regimental Heavy Mortar Company (less one platoon), positioned to support the attack's intended kick-off the next morning.

The area was quiet when the 3rd Battalion 31st Infantry and the two field artillery batteries[3] reached the Pungnyu-ri inlet in late afternoon of November 27. Lieutenant Colonel Reilly ordered K Company to move along the ridge overlooking the inlet from the east, while L Company continued along the road adjacent to the Reservoir. I Company would follow K Company. But the infantrymen of the 3rd Battalion were in no condition to continue moving. They had walked for 2 days and a night and most were so exhausted they fell asleep next to the road while the company commanders met with Reilly. Seeing his men's condition, Reilly cancelled his order a half hour later and directed his companies to stop for the night. They would take up positions enabling them to continue in the morning according to the plan Reilly had directed earlier.

About a mile to their south, the 57th Field Artillery Battalion's CP and D Battery, 15th Antiaircraft Artillery Battalion stopped for the night. Because darkness and falling temperatures would make the roads harder to traverse, the task force stopped for the night. I and K Companies and most of M (Heavy Weapons) Company occupied a long ridge overlooking the inlet while L Company occupied positions on lower ground near a bridge leading north from the inlet. They had just completed a bone-chilling 140-mile journey through the mountains in open trucks. The last 11 miles from Hagaru-ri to the inlet were the worst. The temperature fell quickly as a brisk Siberian wind swept in from the reservoir. The rifle companies dismounted at the inlet, ambled around clumsily to regain their circulation, and then trudged wearily up the ridge to dig into rocky, frozen ground at dusk. Soon after arriving, L Company sent out a patrol of 18 men to the northeast. The patrol crested a hill overlooking the inlet and returned before nightfall, reporting "not a Chink in sight." They could not have gone far in the short time they were out.

As the main body was settling in at the inlet, the 31st Infantry's Tank Company, Headquarters Company, and Service Company were just reaching the ruins of the former village of Hudong-ni, about 3 miles south of the inlet. With night approaching, they stopped and formed a hasty perimeter. The 57th FA Battalion's Service Battery stopped for the night a half mile further south at Sasu-ri. The last element on the road that day was the 31st Infantry's Medical Company, which passed through Hudong-ni near midnight in a column of jeeps, ambulances, and trucks. At the time, the 2nd Battalion was still securing the 7th Division's Rear CP at Pukchong, about two day's motor march from the inlet. Inexplicably, its battalion commander was just receiving orders to join the RCT east of the Chosin Reservoir.

Saga of the Intelligence and Reconnaissance Platoon

Big battles unfold from small ones, the results of which shape the outcome in ways often overlooked in official histories. East of the Chosin Reservoir, the opening shots were fired around 6 p.m. on November 27, 1950, by a regiment of the Chinese 80th Division as it encountered a patrol from the 31st Infantry's Intelligence and Reconnaissance (I&R) Platoon. The Chinese were trying to reach the reservoir but their encounter with the little I&R Platoon would cost their lead regiment time and perhaps a third of its strength. When its attack reached the 3-31st Infantry's main line early the next morning, it lacked the strength to sustain the attack all the way to the reservoir, sparing the 31st RCT and the 1st Marine Division a catastrophe. The 80th would never recover from this initial encounter and would bleed itself nearly dry in the four days and five nights that followed.

Earlier that afternoon, the I&R Platoon had been escorting the 31st RCT's Headquarters when that segment of the motor column reached an abandoned schoolhouse at Hudong-ni. Brigadier General Henry I. Hodes, the 7th Infantry Division's Assistant Commander, was there and expressed concern about the time it took to move from east of the Fusen Reservoir, where the rest of the 7th Infantry Division was, to the Chosin Reservoir where the 31st RCT was just arriving.[4] Although the reservoirs were only about 25 air miles apart, there were no identifiable roads between them, causing the 31st RCT to travel 140 miles, much of it along icy single-lane roads through the mountains. Looking for a way to better connect the division's elements, Hodes directed First Lieutenant Richard B. Coke, leader of the 31st Infantry's Intelligence and Reconnaissance Platoon, to search for a route connecting the reservoirs. His order proved fateful for the platoon.

Although only recently reassigned from I Company, Lieutenant Coke, a tall ex-paratrooper from Texas, led a seasoned and cohesive platoon whose four senior NCOs had all served in the platoon since before the 31st Infantry moved to Japan from Korea in 1948. They had patrolled the 38th parallel separating North and South Korea and on several occasions came under fire from Russian and North Korean troops on the other side. Platoon Sergeant Paul T. Embry was beloved and respected by his men, as were his three squad leaders, Sergeants First Class John Q. Adams (1st Squad), Richard G Cooper (2nd Squad), and Willis S. "Sam" Muncy (3rd Squad). The platoon numbered 43 men, including 17 Korean Augmentees to the U.S. Army (KATUSA). They traveled in eleven vehicles and their main armament included six .50 caliber heavy machine guns, three .30 caliber light machine guns, and two 60mm light mortars.

With about three hours of daylight left, Lieutenant Coke took the platoon north through the 3rd Battalion's positions, following a trail beside a narrow gauge rail line along the Pungyuri-gang, a tributary feeding the Changjin reservoir from the northeast. About two miles past the 31st Infantry's combat outpost line, Coke dropped off Sergeant Muncy's squad and continued moving northeast with the rest of the platoon. The lead element was to contact Muncy every 30 minutes by radio, providing a potential source of quick reinforcement and a radio relay to the nearby Heavy Mortar Company in an emergency. No calls ever came.

Around 4 p.m., the platoon's main body halted at a cluster of four or five Korean huts located on defensible ground above the main trail. Since darkness would come in less than an hour, Coke decided to halt and dig in for the night. Platoon Sergeant Embrey and the squad leaders sited positions about 50 yards apart overlooking a railroad cut to the north. Digging in was easier said than done since the ground was frozen and entrenching tools became brittle and broke in such extreme temperatures. Although men worked with picks and shovels from their vehicles' pioneer equipment, they dared not break a sweat since there was no way to dry out and hypothermia would strike when cold combined with moisture.

Around 6 p.m., a jeep from regimental headquarters pulled into the platoon's perimeter to deliver mail. The platoon was not hard to find since there was only one road leading in its direction but why anyone should risk his neck to deliver mail so far from the RCT's main body, particularly alone and in the dark, is a mystery. As the driver stepped from his vehicle, he was killed by a burst of fire from beyond the perimeter. Suddenly the night came alive with the sound of bugles, shouts, and beating on metal pans. Small arms fire laced the perimeter as enemy soldiers set off trip flares near the railroad cut. Chinese troops were running through the cut five abreast in a continuous column.

Sergeants Adams and Cooper directed their men to hold their fire until they could clearly see their targets. They did not have long to wait. As the platoon's six heavy and light machine guns chattered to life almost in unison, Adams ran to the platoon's command post (CP) but found neither Lieutenant Coke nor Master Sergeant Embry there. Emerging from the CP, Adams spotted them about 50 yards south of the perimeter, heading back toward the platoon. They had gone on a short reconnaissance by themselves and would soon be cut off. Master Sergeant Embry was killed before he could reach the perimeter and Lieutenant Coke was wounded and captured.

Although the platoon took a fearful toll, piling up several hundred Chinese in the railroad cut alone, they could not stop the swarm of enemy troops coming at them. One by one, positions fell silent as Chinese troops fanned out to the flanks and moved in for the kill. Corporal Donald Trudeau, who had joined the platoon in Japan in 1949, was among its steadiest members, blazing away with his Browning Automatic Rifle until the barrel glowed red. Adams remembers Trudeau as "The finest BAR man I had ever seen. He knew his job and never shirked his duty, no matter how high the risk."[5] When Trudeau's weapon fell silent, Adams headed back to the CP with his radio operator to call for help. Minutes later, the door was thrown open by someone shouting "GI, GI!" A grenade rolled in, followed by an explosion that slammed Adams into a corner and brought part of the roof and wall down on him. He lay stunned for several minutes, covered with debris and unable to hear. His radio operator lay dead nearby.

Outside, Sergeant Cooper saw Adams and his radio operator enter the CP and witnessed the explosion that followed. Presuming both were dead, he was stunned to see Adams emerge from the debris covered in dust with his flak jacket still smoking and a dazed look on his face. Survivors of positions that had fallen silent converged around the CP, putting up a fight resembling Custer's last stand. Sergeant Cooper grabbed a 60mm mortar from a jeep and held it against the jeep's wheel while Adams slammed several rounds down the tube in rapid succession. Fired at a near-direct angle, the first few rounds hadn't even armed when they whistled through the enemy ranks, sowing confusion. Elevating the tube to near maximum angle, Cooper and Adams hoped to produce a protective barrier of fire around the dwindling number of survivors around them. Explosions followed in quick succession just 30 yards away, blowing dirt, fragmentation, blood, and bone back in their direction but nothing seemed to work. The Chinese just kept coming, no matter how many of them were killed or wounded. Some in the last wave had only grenades while others had no weapons at all. The latter picked up weapons and ammunition from dead comrades and continued the assault.

Groups of Chinese soon streamed through the CP area. Adams felt the blow of a rifle butt glancing off his forehead, cascading down to his nose to his jaw where it knocked out several teeth. With his adrenalin pumping, he somehow managed to kill the offender with a bayonet but it was now clear that the platoon was overrun. Taking advantage of the confusion, Adams ducked into the shadows and cautiously worked his way up the tallest hill in sight. Along the perimeter, he witnessed squads of Chinese rounding up surviving GIs and KATUSAs and shooting several who were unable to walk. He could see thousands of enemy troops being herded back into ranks beyond the platoon's position and hurrying off to the southwest along the same route the platoon had followed from the reservoir. There was no way to warn Sam Muncy or the regiment.

Several miles further back, Sam Muncy's 3rd Squad soon saw the Chinese coming their way. They reached Muncy's position near midnight and attacked from the march. As before, they came on in a long column initially and began fanning out to the flanks when the 3rd Squad opened fire. Occupying a less defensible position with an exposed left flank, the 3rd Squad hastily mounted up, inflicting as much damage as it could before retreating to the RCT's perimeter. One squad with just three machine guns could not hope to stop a regiment.

When daylight came on November 28, Sergeant Adams could see his platoon's former positions from his concealed perch amid scrub vegetation atop a nearby hill. Chinese troops were still combing the area for anything of value, military or otherwise. The area between the railroad cut and the platoon's perimeter was littered with clumps of Chinese dead. At the cut, the dead looked to be four or five deep and five or more across for a distance of about 50 yards. Wherever there had been an automatic weapons position along the platoon's perimeter, there were more stacks of enemy dead. Making his way around the back side of the hill, he saw six men huddled in a clearing. Moving closer for a better look, he recognized them as members of his platoon. They were Sergeant First Class Dick Cooper, Corporal Jim Arie, CPL Ananias Janvrin, PFC George Peachy, and two KATUSAs. Arie was the only one among them who was not wounded. Janvrin would soon die of his wounds. During his escape the night before, Cooper had come across Master Sergeant Embrey's body, confirming that he died trying to return to the platoon.

For the next six days, the small band of survivors moved as stealthily as possible through areas controlled by the Chinese. They reached Marine lines at Hagaru-ri just in time for the withdrawal to Hungnam. Sam Muncy's squad was fed into the line on November 28 to replace losses suffered by K Company earlier that morning when the same regiment that had overrun the I&R Platoon struck the 3rd Battalion's perimeter. All of Muncy's men survived but several had close calls during the desperate withdrawal to

Aid station heavily sandbagged to defend against indirect enemy fire as wounded are unloaded.
Note the empty ammo cases used for dismounting vehicles in wet weather (U.S. Army photograph,
National Archives).

Hagaru-ri. Corporal John Weinreich (3rd Squad) was captured during the withdrawal
but escaped by hiding among the dead. He made his way alone to the Marine perimeter
at Hagaru-ri.

Sergeants Cooper and Muncy were evacuated by air from Hagaru-ri and recovered
from their wounds at a hospital in Japan. Both returned to the I&R Platoon after its
reconstitution in South Korea and served until September 1951. Both eventually retired
from the Army as senior NCOs and are still living as of this writing. John Quincy Adams
also returned to the I&R Platoon after recovering from his wounds. He was promoted
to Master Sergeant in 1951 and became the acting Platoon Leader. He became First Sergeant of Headquarters Company before being wounded a third time and was evacuated
to Japan and then the U.S. in 1952. He died in January 2005. Master Sergeant Paul T.
Embrey's body was never recovered and probably remains buried near where he died in
North Korea. First Lieutenant Richard B. Coke, Jr., died in captivity at POW Camp 1. His
body was returned as part of Operation Glory in September 1954. He is buried at Fort
Sam Houston National Cemetery in San Antonio, Texas.

12 The Chosin Reservoir

George Rasula was a captain serving as Assistant S-3 of the 31st Infantry Regiment at Hudong-ni. His overview of the action summarizes the events to follow.

During operations east of the Chosin reservoir, the main battle was fought by units in a perimeter located on the south side of an inlet formed by the Pungnyuri-gang, a river that flows into the reservoir from the northeast. On 27–28 November the 1st Battalion, 32nd Infantry had been located about four kilometers north of the inlet. It withdrew in the early morning hours of 29 November to join the 3rd Battalion, 31st Infantry in the main perimeter. Here the battle continued into the morning of 1 December. The breakout began at noon and became a moving battle as the enemy followed the breakout column until it faced the main Chinese blocking position on Hill 1221. The column was eventually destroyed a few kilometers south of the hill. The 31st Regimental Combat Team, with only two infantry battalions and part of an artillery battalion, had faced the assaults of two CCF divisions backed up by one regiment of a third division, all part of the Chinese commander's main effort to capture Hagaru-ri before the arrival of two Marine regiments withdrawing from Yudam-ni on the reservoir's west side.

Chinese Marshal Peng Teh-huai's plan was to first destroy the U.S. 1st Marine Division in the Chosin Reservoir area. He would exploit the resulting gap by throwing up to four armies, totaling fifteen divisions, against the Hamhung-Hungnam area to cut off and destroy the U.S. 7th Infantry Division and ROK I Corps in North Korea's eastern panhandle. When the plan was being developed, the U.S. 5th Marine Regiment was still on the reservoir's east side, the U.S. 7th Marine Regiment was still moving toward Yudam-ni on the reservoir's west side, and the U.S. 1st Marine Regiment was establishing widely separated strong points along the main supply route between Hagaru-ri at the south end of the reservoir and Koto-ri, about 14 miles further south.

Peng's plan was to commit his 20th Army (58th, 59th, 60th, and 89th Divisions) against the 7th Marines west of the reservoir and his 27th Army (79th, 80th, 81st, and 90th Divisions) against the 5th Marines east of the reservoir. The 42nd Army (124th, 125th, and 126th Divisions), would hit key points along the 1st Marine Division's supply route between Hamhung, near the coast, and Hagaru-ri at the south end of the Chosin Reservoir. The latter would close the door to Marines trying to escape from both sides of the reservoir. The 26th Army (76th, 77th, 78th, and 88th Divisions) would remain in reserve to exploit the success of the others.[1] Unknown to Peng at the time, the 5th Marines would shift to the west, reinforcing the 7th Marine Regiment at Yudam-ni the day his attack was to begin. The Marines would be replaced on the reservoir's east side by the Army's 31st RCT, but by nightfall on November 27 only two of the 31st RCT's infantry battalions had arrived. Consequently, the critical area around Hill 1221 and approaches to it from the northeast were not occupied.

One regiment of the Chinese 80th Division struck the 1st Battalion, 32nd Infantry from the north. Another struck from the northeast, slicing through I and K Companies of the 3rd Battalion, 31st Infantry to overrun the Battalion Command Post and A Battery, 57th Field Artillery. The third passed around Hill 1456, which overlooks the inlet's east side, striking the 57th Field Artillery Battalion's Command Post and D Battery, 15th Anti-aircraft Artillery Battalion. A regiment of the 81st Division occupied Hill 1221, right where the 31st Infantry's Medical Company had to negotiate a hairpin turn en route to the inlet.

Just after midnight, the Medical Company's convoy came under intense fire from Hill 1221 and was all but wiped out. Captain Harvey Galloway, the Regimental Surgeon, was among the survivors to reach the inlet that night. He had a bullet in his brain but was still coherent, reporting he knew exactly where the bullet was lodged. Captain Hank Wamble, the Medical Company Executive Officer also reached the perimeter, but had been shot in the chest and was barely able to breathe. Sometime before daylight, SFC George Chastain, who had escaped in the opposite direction, stumbled into the Tank Company's perimeter alone and dazed. After his driver was killed and his jeep was disabled in the ambush, he crawled all the way back to Hudong-ni in a ditch. The ambush meant Chinese troops had occupied terrain dominating the road between Hudong-ni and the inlet. The door was suddenly slammed shut behind the RCT's main body, and it would not reopen.

In the rifle companies arrayed north and east of the inlet, men arrived at their designated positions about an hour before dark and quickly became exhausted trying to dig foxholes in the frozen earth. Water turned to ice in their canteens, offering no relief when parched throats signaled the need to replace fluids lost to perspiration. Few expected the Chinese to attack under such conditions. At dusk, NCO's barked, "half on watch." The bitter cold, plummeting to -20°F, numbed mind and body. Numerous sentries, seeking refuge from the biting Siberian wind, "stood" their watch in sleeping bags—a sure recipe for dozing off. With 50 feet or more between foxholes, there were easily exploitable gaps all along the bald, uneven ridge. If even a single foxhole was overrun, it could open a gap large enough to run a company through. Because the ground was uneven, few men could support each other's positions, particularly in the dark.

Few officers or NCOs checked the line since the frozen snow was crunchy and the sound of a man thrashing and slipping around on it was a sure give-away on a night when only the wind's eerie whistle and an occasional muffled cough broke the silence. On snow-covered ground revealing no clear demarcation line, there was also the risk of straying outside the perimeter in the dark and getting shot by one's own sentries. Neither is an excuse for leaders not doing what they must, but it happened often in units operating under such conditions all over Korea, just as it had in Europe during World War II.

Attacks on the 31st RCT were like those that also hit the Marines at Yudam-ni that night. Small teams of Chinese scouts crawled stealthily across the frozen snow, trying to identify gaps they could exploit. Once they found them, they led assault formations forward to the nearest covered and concealed position to await the attack signal. Around 2:00 a.m., the noise of bugles and yak horns, followed by the crunching sound of thousands of feet running up snow-crusted ravines alerted men on the perimeter. To some who had been sleeping, reality did not set in until it was almost too late. The shooting had barely begun before the first wave of Chinese began setting off trip flares perhaps a hundred yards from the forward line. The Chinese chanted in grunting tones as they struggled uphill in ragged formations. Sergeant Bill G. Rowland of I Company described the attack: "They came in from our rear and from both sides. The third wave had machine guns to cover the assault troops of the first and second waves. When they came in it was hard to keep them out of our holes." PFC Lewis Shannon of I Company's 3rd Platoon recalled: "They came running in mass, spread only a few yards apart, yelling and screaming, 'GI surrender,' making noise with bugles and whistles, and running over their own dead and wounded until they were killed."

Muzzle flashes blinked in the darkness on both sides, slapping bullets into the frozen snow and bodies at random. Urgent cries for medics were lost among the deafening roar of an increasingly intense firefight. Gloved hands were obstacles when trying to replace the ammunition clip in an M-1 rifle. The clip, holding eight rounds of .30 caliber ammunition, is inserted into the top of the rifle's chamber with a man's thumb, hoping he can be quick enough to get it out of the way of the bolt slamming forward when the clip is seated, an awkward thing to do even in a warm place in broad daylight. Shaking from cold and fear in the dark, performing that act often cost men too much time when there was none to spare. Stomach-knotting panic sets in when an enemy soldier is about to shoot as you clumsily fumble with an empty weapon in a narrow two-man foxhole with a wounded or dead buddy slumped against you. That was the last thing some riflemen in I and K Companies would experience in their much-too-short lives.

Incrementally, the 31st RCT's 57mm and 75mm recoilless rifles, 81mm and 107mm mortars, and 105mm howitzers added their weight to the rattle of rifle and automatic weapons fire from the line companies. The momentum of the Chinese assault quickly made any form of indirect fire impractical. Urged on by blaring bugles, shepherd's horns, and whistles, Chinese troops surged through the forward companies in waves. Some exchanged fire at close range with GIs and KATUSAs or threw grenades into their foxholes, but most just streamed around them, heading for the reservoir without firing a shot or slowing down. About 20 yards behind the first wave came another and yet another behind that. Hundreds of Chinese went down, but the weight of their numbers, concentrated where they could minimize the distance they would have to travel over open ground to breach the thin American line, proved overwhelming.

Some Chinese units undoubtedly melted away under the intense fire, but so did parts of I and K Companies. One by one, foxholes fell silent. Their inhabitants were either dead, too badly wounded to continue fighting, or too alone and terrified to risk exposing themselves. M Company's 75mm recoilless rifles and .50 caliber machine guns, attached to I and K Companies, suffered the same fate as the companies they supported and were temporarily lost during the long night. PFC Milton Margan's recollection typifies a situation unfolding all along the ridge: "Sergeant Tony Mandino was killed in a fox hole with me. PFC Gordon Lee, the mail clerk, and PFC Dominik Cataldo were in the same hole. Lee was wounded but somehow made it home, but I never saw Cataldo again."[2]

In places, survivors slipped out of their holes and ran down the back side of the ridge alongside the Chinese, hoping they would not be recognized by the enemy or shot down by their own troops as they approached American units nearer the inlet. Among them were PFC Ed Reeves and his KATUSA partner, Bak Ho Yah of K Company's 3rd Platoon. Foxholes on both sides of them on higher ground were overrun by the enemy, leaving Reeves and Bak exposed on three sides. Recognizing the futility of staying in place, they rolled out of the back of their foxhole and ran toward the reservoir. Bursts of American automatic weapons fire laced the fields around them as they ran, forcing them to take cover several times, while trying to stay at least a few yards away from clusters of fast-moving Chinese. After what seemed an eternity of playing cat and mouse with the enemy and periodically taking cover from long sweeping arcs of American machine gun fire, they came close enough to one of the many "rings of fire" to recognize American voices over the din. Their shouts of "GIs comin' in" were met by "hold your fire GIs are coming in." They had reached Captain Earle H. Jordan Jr.'s M Company CP, but trouble was still all around them. Jordan's men were locked in a struggle for survival as waves of Chinese charged down the slope to their front and both flanks. Many had already passed M Company and were attacking the artillery positions in the valley below.

When he learned his 3rd Platoon had been overrun, Captain Robert J. Kitz, K Company's Commander, pulled his CP out of the attack's path. He reached A Battery's positions in the valley just ahead of the Chinese. Others in K Company who saw their CP leaving joined the retreat. Much of K Company's line quickly unraveled, leaving I Company alone on the ridge. When Captain Harold L. Hodge, commanding A Battery, 57th FA, was informed that the infantry was pulling out in front of him, he ordered his howitzers leveled at the ridge to hit the Chinese with direct fire. Because artillery rounds were exploding among K and M Companies' survivors, his fire had to be lifted and his cannoneers instantly became infantrymen. The left side of the 3rd Battalion's line had collapsed. On the right, Captain Auburn "Pop" Marr's I Company was also penetrated but most of his line held on all night. His company journal reported only two men killed that night, but there were substantial numbers of wounded.

M Company's CP and the 81mm Mortar Platoon were arrayed around an adobe and thatch farm house situated in a shallow wash behind I Company. Although most men in that position were killed or wounded during the night, often in hand-to-hand combat, the position held. PFC Ed Reeves and KATUSA Bak Ho Yah, who joined the defenders after pulling out of K Company's line, were posted along a fence when two large caliber shells slammed into it in quick succession, showering the defenders with splinters, shards of hot steel, and clods of flying dirt. They were probably 105mm shells fired by Captain Hodge's A Battery 57th Artillery. Reeves and Bak saved their lives by running to where the first round hit. They dropped to the ground just in time to see a third round strike right where they had been lying. Men in the forward areas were in as much danger from the fire of American units situated nearer the reservoir as from the Chinese swarming around them. Reeves recalls Captain James W. Conner, the 3rd Battalion's Chaplain, walking calmly through it all, talking to the position's defenders and giving each man a swig of whiskey. Since all water was frozen, whiskey was the only liquid available.

Farther back, clusters of Chinese picked their way across 500 yards of open ground to reach A Battery. Knowing they were among their enemy, the Chinese threw grenades or shot at everything that moved, and some that didn't. Americans, on the other hand, could not as easily distinguish friend from foe among the shadowy figures running through their area. The problem was aggravated by the fact that most Americans could not distinguish between Chinese voices and those of their own KATUSAs. Ray Vallowe of the 57th Artillery recalls: "In South Korea we had been told about North Koreans infiltrating our lines wearing American uniforms obtained from captured or killed American soldiers. Just having KATUSA's in our area wearing our uniforms made us jittery." Several tents and vehicles were set ablaze in the intense exchange of fire, illuminating their immediate vicinity and the furtive movements of men from both sides struggling to avoid being shot. In a scene from hell, shadows shot at shadows.

Near the inlet bridge behind K Company's former line, everyone in the 3rd Battalion's CP was either killed or wounded, including Lieutenant Colonel William R. Reilly, the Battalion Commander. The CP was in a sturdy mud house, surrounded by a courtyard. Enemy troops arrived too quickly for the position to be evacuated, so the men inside were caught up in the fight. Wounded by a machine gun round that passed through his right leg and another that took off several toes, Colonel Reilly sat propped against an interior wall and fired his pistol at enemy soldiers trying to crawl through a window on the opposite side of the room. Captain Melville E. Adams, the S-4, and Major Clifton Z. Couch, the Battalion Executive Officer, were both shot in the chest defending the open doorway. Lieutenant Johnson, the Air Force Liaison Officer, was killed when a mortar round detonated on the roof above him. Lieutenant James A. Anderson, the Assistant Fire Support Coordinator, complained of having trouble getting his pistol out of his holster. When the flash of an explosion outside momentarily illuminated the darkened room, Reilly realized why. Anderson's right arm had been blown off by the mortar round that killed Lieutenant Johnson. Anderson, probably in shock, did not seem to know his arm was missing. Reilly took Anderson's pistol out of his holster and put it in his left hand, but to little purpose. The young officer quietly bled to death where he sat. Around 3:00 a.m., a Chinese concussion grenade sailed through the window, wounding Reilly again and knocking him unconscious.

Outside the CP, tucked into shadowed corners of the surrounding courtyard, were members of the 3rd Battalion's Headquarters Company, including the Company Headquarters and a squad from the Pioneer and Ammunition Platoon. Their original position, located in a mud hut nearer the bridge, was in danger of becoming isolated early in the battle, causing the group to retreat to the courtyard around the Battalion CP, which they thought had been abandoned. They fought from there most of the night, several times at close quarters when Chinese troops flooded into the courtyard. Neither they nor the men inside knew the other group of Americans was there.

Just 20 feet across the courtyard in a mud hut housing part of the 3rd Battalion's Communications Platoon, a similar drama was unfolding. There, a bullet passed through the wall, hitting PFC John Hale in the back and perforating one of his lungs as he sat at the switchboard. The 3rd Battalion's Communications Chief, Staff Sergeant Harry Cutting, took over the switchboard while PFC Don Mayville made Hale as comfortable as he could. Shortly afterward, two men brought in a badly wounded KATUSA, laying him on a pile of straw opposite the switchboard. He lay moaning *Etai, Etai,* Japanese for "it hurts" and died during the night. Staff Sergeant Max Maynard, the battalion's Radio Section Chief, rushed into the hut asking for a rifle because his had been hit while exchanging fire with the Chinese outside. He took PFC Mayville's carbine and went back outside to rejoin the fray. He was killed soon afterward. Near the outdoor latrine, PFC Joseph M. Harper was hit in the chest and lay unattended, laboring for air while the firefight raged all around him. When Don Mayville went there in the morning, he found Harper laying on his back with his eyes still open and a ghastly expression on his frozen face. Years later, Mayville would still shudder at the memory of his dead friend's staring green eyes.

In A Battery's area, several Chinese soldiers stopped to look for food and to warm themselves at a fire barrel. They became easy targets in the firelight and were quickly shot down by Captain Hodge and several others. At the nearby 3rd Battalion Aid Station, a medic was killed while treating a critically wounded man in a blackout tent. When A Battery was overrun, survivors of K Company and A Battery made their way back to B

Battery, which was positioned nearer the reservoir and oriented north to support the 1st Battalion, 32nd Infantry.

No one knew or cared which units they fought among. Most were only interested in finding shelter from the outbursts of fire lashing back and forth around the inlet. At daylight, many Chinese were still there, but it was obvious from their diminished fire that they were nearly out of ammunition. Knowing they could not retreat the way they had come without being gunned down, they stayed put and fought with whatever weapons and ammunition they could find. Lieutenant Hank Traywick, the 3rd Battalion Motor Officer, gathered any men he could to retake the Battalion CP. Captain Robert McClay, the 3rd Battalion Adjutant, gathered still more men to reach M Company's battered CP. Others, led by Captain Kitz and Captain Hodge, retook A Battery's positions. A cook who had hidden under a trailer throughout the night reported seeing the Chinese leading away an American and 12 Koreans just before dawn. About 30 Chinese were captured during the various counterattacks launched after daylight.

Half a mile farther south, another fight broke out near dawn at the 57th FA Battalion's CP. There was no infantry at the site, but D Battery, 15th AAA, with its four twin 40mm "Dusters" and four quad .50 caliber machine guns, all mounted on half-tracks, offered ample protection. Lieutenant Colonel Ray O. Embree was awakened by the sound of mortar fire dropping around his CP. As he rushed to his radio to find out what was happening, a burst of automatic weapons fire hit him in both legs. With his bones broken, he dropped to his knees like a sack of flour. He was out of the fight before he could even enter it.

From the hill overlooking the site, another column of enemy soldiers was hurrying down to the valley to join the fight. The snowy hillside made running figures stand out as in daylight. Captain James R. McClymont, commanding D Battery, ordered his twin 40mm guns to engage the fast-moving column. The enemy unit practically evaporated in a long, crackling burst of explosions. Around the same time, enemy troops overran D Battery's 1st Platoon. With a small group of antiaircraft and field artillery support personnel and fire support from his 2nd Platoon, Captain McClymont retook the position. Among the dead at the 1st Platoon's overrun CP was Major Max Morris, the 57th FA Battalion's Executive Officer.

The first night's fighting had taken a severe toll on leaders. All four of the most senior officers in the two battalions at the inlet were dead or seriously wounded. The Artillery XO, Major Morris, was dead and the Infantry XO, Major Couch, would not regain consciousness. Command of neither battalion passed immediately to the surviving senior officers, Major Harvey H. Storms, the 3rd Battalion's S-3, and Major Robert J. Tolly, the 57th FA's S-3. Their battalion commanders were seriously wounded but were still giving orders from the aid station the next day. The 3rd Battalion Surgeon was dead and over a third of the regiment's 170 medical personnel were killed or wounded when the Medical Company convoy was ambushed at Hill 1221. Radios critical to maintaining internal cohesion and coordinating external support had also been destroyed.

Because the 3rd Battalion switchboard had been damaged during the fighting, PFC Mayville went outside at daybreak to string wire to the CP across the courtyard. He was shocked to find so many bodies lying all around his hut. Among the perimeter's still living defenders were PFCs Bernie Schwartz and Tommy Melbourne of the Pioneer and Ammunition Platoon, two of Mayville's best friends from basic training. As Mayville looked up, he saw Colonel Riley sitting against the outside wall of the CP, silently watching his every move: "He looked so helpless and that was upsetting to me because I wondered who was running the show."

After daybreak, the 57th FA Battalion's Command Post and D Battery 15th AAA moved hurriedly to the inlet to join the main body. They left their dead behind, along with a destroyed half-track. The artillery repositioned to avoid offering the same target as the night before, but the Chinese were watching from the hills, paying particular attention to the heavy weapons' dispositions. By late afternoon, K Company regained its original positions atop the ridgeline, aided by air strikes and reinforcements from L Company. The wounded were collected at a makeshift aid station in one of the mess tents at the inlet.

That afternoon, Master Sergeant John Watlington, a recalled reservist from Tennessee who served as the 3rd Battalion's Operations Sergeant, came into the communications shack to ask if there was a medic around. From a considerable distance away, a burst of automatic weapons fire stitched through the hut's thin back wall, killing Watlington as he stood in the doorway. Daylight had not brought safety anywhere in the perimeter.

Farther north, another consolidation was taking place. Colonel MacLean's forward CP, with about 60 vehicles, moved into the 1st Battalion, 32nd Infantry's perimeter about 4 miles north of the inlet. McLean had no idea of how bad the situation was at the inlet, did not know where his 2nd Battalion or Tank Company was, did not know that his Medical Company had been ambushed, and did not know that his Intelligence and Reconnaissance Platoon had been sent by General Hodes on a scouting mission from which it would never return. That morning, Lieutenant Colonel Richard R. Reidy's 2nd Battalion began moving by open rail car from Pukchong to Hamhung. The battalion's trucks followed by road, reaching Hamhung late that night. They were still 72 miles from the RCT's main perimeter at the Pungyuri inlet, a full day's motor march on an icy, single track road along which ambush sites were being established by the Chinese 42nd Army. At Hamhung, Reidy was instructed by Colonel Frank Millburn, X Corps' G-3, that he should move by road and rail to Majong-dong the next morning and that X Corps trucks would take his troops the rest of the way to the reservoir. Unaware of the delay, Colonel MacLean expected to hear that the 2nd Battalion had reached the inlet during the night. Operating in a communication void would prove fatal.

From Hudong-ni, the Tank Company, accompanied by General Hodes, attempted to break through to the inlet early on November 28. SFC George Chastain accompanied them to point out positions from which the Chinese had ambushed his company the night before. When they reached the hairpin curve, Chastain asked Captain Drake to stop his jeep. Standing beside the road with General Hodes and Captain Drake, he was pointing at a path up the side of Hill 1221 when a bullet drilled through his head, killing him instantly and spraying the officers with his blood. Hodes and Drake scurried back to safety behind their vehicles.

As the two lead tanks approached Medical Company vehicles blocking the road, a Chinese soldier armed with an American 3.5-inch rocket launcher hit the lead tank, knocking it out. The second tank was also hit and slid off the road when it tried to bypass the knocked out lead tank. Both were abandoned by their crews who barely escaped with their lives as Chinese troops swarmed over the site. Two more tanks tried to negotiate the narrow, icy path up Hill 1221 but one slipped over a steep embankment and the other threw a track. Two more became stuck as they tried to parallel the road along a marshy stream. Chinese troops swarmed over them, trying to open their grill doors to throw hand grenades into their engine compartments. Tanks farther back dusted the Chinese off with machine gun fire. Both of the bogged tanks managed to extricate themselves and withdraw to Hudong-ni. After another unsuccessful try in the early afternoon, Captain Drake called off the attack and pulled what remained of his company back to Hudong-ni. He would need infantry and air support to breach the enemy roadblock, and he had neither.

Before nightfall on November 28, the Chinese resumed their attack, striking almost exactly where they had the night before. Again, the porous infantry line was penetrated, even though they had been reinforced by two rifle platoons and most heavy weapons of Captain William W. Etchemendy's L Company. Chinese troops again got as far as the artillery positions. Unlike the night before, however, the rifle companies stood their ground, even when penetrated. For a time, a large group of Chinese halted at K Company's overrun mess tent to enjoy what would be the last meal for most. They were caught in a devastating crossfire after regrouping near the bridge spanning the inlet. The 57th Field Artillery, reinforced by the 15th AAA's twin 40mm Dusters and Quad .50s, took a horrendous toll on their tormentors.

There was an ominous new development in the fight. One body of enemy troops approached from the south near dawn, taking control of the road and rail line between the reservoir and the perimeter. They were probably from the same unit that ambushed the Medical Company the night before. Unlike the light brown quilted uniforms and white covers of the troops who attacked from the north and northeast, these troops wore a heavy brown-green uniform, were armed with large numbers of American .45 caliber Thompson submachine guns, and had plenty of ammunition. The attacks from the northeast were no less intense, but some enemy soldiers on that end of the line were seen armed with only hand grenades, indicating a probable shortage of ammunition. Strangely, the two attacks were uncoordinated since they neither started nor ended at the same time. There was ample evidence that the 31st RCT was being attacked by two Chinese divisions, but no one was putting the story together yet, leaving Colonel MacLean and his superiors with an incomplete picture of what the 31st RCT was up against.

More than forty years later, when China opened its Korean War archives to American scholars, it was revealed that all six regiments of the 80th and 81st Divisions, reinforced by a regiment of the 90th Division farther east, attacked the 31st RCT over a four-day period and that most of those regiments were destroyed in the process. It is a remarkable testament to the determination and courage of desperate men that two half–American, half–KATUSA infantry battalions, supported by only 8 howitzers and 8 antiaircraft weapons were able to hold off 21 Chinese infantry battalions for 4 days and 5 nights. After fighting at the Chosin Reservoir, neither the 80th nor 81st Divisions ever returned to combat. Because they had suffered so many casualties, including the majority of their officers, both were used to replace losses in other divisions.[3]

The 1st Battalion, 32nd Infantry, still four miles north of the inlet, was having troubles of its own. Like the 3rd Battalion, 31st Infantry at the inlet, its perimeter was hard pressed to hold against steady pressure from the Chinese. Complicating matters, the weather was getting worse. Snow began falling sometime after midnight and visibility was gradually deteriorating. Men from the Regimental CP, including Sergeant Major John A. Lynch, Jr., filled empty foxholes among the depleted rifle squads. Lynch was a former machine gunner who had served with the regiment since its reactivation at Seoul in 1946.

Around 2:00 a.m. on November 29, Colonel MacLean directed Lieutenant Colonel Faith to pull his battalion back to the inlet before daybreak if possible. Faith set the departure time for 4:30 a.m., but some men didn't get the word until they heard vehicles starting and idling their engines in unison, a sure sign the battalion was leaving. Sergeant Major Lynch sent PFC Laverne Tate, the S-1's driver with whom he shared a foxhole, to see who was in the adjacent foxhole on the left while Lynch checked the one on the right. Both were empty and there was no one in the foxholes beyond those either. The company had departed without telling its fillers. Lynch and Tate scurried down the hill just in time to join the rear of the departing column.

There is a curious footnote to this story. In the final stages of fighting east of the reservoir, Sergeant Major Lynch was wounded and taken, unconscious, to Marine lines at Hagaru-ri and from there by air to an Army hospital at Hungnam. When he awoke, the National Colors were wrapped around his chest. Someone had apparently removed them from their packing container where the S-1 truck was unloaded, taking them to the inlet during the initial withdrawal, and wrapping them around Lynch when he was evacuated. Neither Major Robbins, PFC Tate, nor Sergeant Major Lynch know when, who, or how.

When the warning order for the withdrawal was issued, Major Hugh W. Robbins, the Regimental Adjutant, gathered anyone he could find to help unload headquarters trucks to make room for the wounded. In the S-1 truck were the National and Regimental Colors, still on their disassembled staffs and packed in the wooden olive drab boxes in which they had traveled from Japan several months before. In the dark, soldiers unloading the trucks, mostly KATUSAs, had no opportunity to sort through what they were discarding. Their instructions were simply to empty the trucks to make room for the wounded and that is what they did. The boxed Colors likely went into a discard pile with field desks, typewriters, numerous boxes of records, and all the other trappings of a personnel and administration shop. Someone suggested burning the abandoned equipment, but that idea was squelched to avoid making the convoy an illuminated target. Moreover, Lieutenant Colonel Faith directed that any vehicles that could not be operated would be disabled, but not destroyed since it was the regiment's intention to return to the area within 24 hours. It is now clear that Chinese troops found the regimental colors in their packing container and took them back to China with them because they are now displayed in the People's Army Museum in Beijing.

Colonel MacLean seemingly still planned to attack northward as soon as the 2nd Battalion arrived at the inlet. He probably assumed the battalion had already arrived, but he had no radio contact with either the 2nd or 3rd Battalions. At the time, the 2nd Battalion was loaded aboard trucks at Majong-dong, as ordered by X Corps G-3, but was ordered off the road to make way for a convoy laden with ammunition for the Marines at Koto-ri. Given the congestion on a single lane road, X Corps issued new orders. The battalion would proceed north the next morning, November 30. For the 31st RCT, it would be much too late. The battalion could have made a huge difference in helping the Tank Company break through the ambush site at Hill 1221 and it would have provided a denser line at the inlet, perhaps enabling the regiment to hold the Chinese at bay on November 27 and 28, but while X Corps fumbled its instructions, the RCT's fate was being sealed.

Just north of the inlet, Colonel Faith's convoy encountered a log roadblock, covered by enemy automatic weapons fire. While Faith and a group of men he collected from vehicles near the head of the column removed the obstacle, he ordered a dismounted platoon and a recoilless rifle section to outflank the enemy from higher ground. Perhaps seeing what was happening, the enemy fled across the frozen inlet toward what was presumed to be American lines. The roadblock was removed and the convoy's lead element rolled into what had been the 3rd Battalion's perimeter at around 9:00 a.m. At the time, the inlet's defenders were still heavily engaged, trying to eject the Chinese from their midst. Men in Faith's flanking rifle company who reached the crest of Hill 1324 overlooking the inlet had a panoramic view of what was taking place. In the valley, they could see two large columns of Chinese troops still advancing on the inlet from the south and knots of enemy troops still fighting their way down from the eastern ridges. It was obvious that the inlet had nearly been overrun during the night because numerous tents and vehicles were either on fire or destroyed and hundreds of bodies from both sides littered the ground, particularly around the 3rd Battalion's CP and A Battery's positions.

One person who did not make it into the perimeter that day was Colonel Allan Duart MacLean, the 31st Infantry Regiment's Commander. He was 43 years old at the time, nine years older than the regiment he commanded. When the vehicle column encountered the roadblock near the Pungnyu-ri Bridge, the command group split into two parts. One went forward with Lieutenant Colonel Faith to clear the roadblock and the other remained atop a slight rise with Colonel MacLean. Although there was some incoming fire, most assumed it was probably spent rounds from fighting that was still raging in and around the inlet. Captain Erwin B. Bigger, Commanding D Company, 32nd Infantry, was standing with MacLean looking across the flat inlet. In the dim distance, they could see a long column of troops approaching on foot from the south. There were flashes of firing from the head of the column and fire from the inlet was obviously hitting the approaching troops. MacLean exclaimed, "Those are all my boys, they'll cut each other to pieces." He no doubt assumed the oncoming column was the long-awaited 2nd Battalion running headlong into the 3rd Battalion. It was not, but it would have been hard to tell across a mile of hazy battlefield. MacLean then gave Bigger a verbal order for Lieutenant Colonel Faith that detailed where he wanted Faith's battalion on the perimeter and where he was to meet MacLean.

Eager to take charge of the situation and stop what he assumed was a fratricidal engagement between two of his battalions, MacLean ran across the frozen inlet alone, crossing a small, brush-covered island before proceeding to the south bank. Bigger, Faith, and several others saw him fall several times as he crossed the final stretch of ice. Bigger was too far away to help and looked on in horror to see Chinese soldiers rising to shoot at MacLean from the south bank. The Colonel nevertheless rose each time he fell and staggered on. Bigger saw Chinese soldiers come out onto the ice to grab MacLean and drag him to the south bank where they quickly took him away. A search was mounted by Faith after his battalion entered the perimeter but it was too late. The Chinese had departed and MacLean was being marched away in a column of POWs. A soldier released from captivity at the war's end reported what happened. MacLean was still able to walk but grew steadily weaker each day of the trek and had to be helped by other POWs. On the night of December 3, he died and was buried in a ditch beside the road. He was the second commander of the 31st Infantry to die in captivity, following Jasper Brady's death on a Japanese hell ship by only six years.

13 Task Force Faith

When Major Hugh Robbins, the Regimental Adjutant, reached the inlet, he was shocked by the number of casualties and the scale of destruction. At the 3rd Battalion's battered CP, he found Lieutenant Colonel Reilly in good spirits, but physically incapacitated. Captain Melville Adams, the S-4, was dying of his wounds. Lieutenant Paul Dill, M Company's Executive Officer, was dying, and so was Captain Hank Wamble, the Medical Company Commander. All around the CP were the bodies of dead GIs and Chinese, all mixed together where they had fallen. After conferring briefly with Reilly and learning that he was the senior surviving officer, Lieutenant Colonel Faith assumed command of the 31st RCT. He spent the rest of the morning locating the remains of the 3rd Battalion and organizing a perimeter. The 3rd Battalion, 31st Infantry under Major Harvey Storms remained on the east ridge. Faith's own 1st Battalion 32nd Infantry, under Major Crosby Miller, filled in around the 3rd Battalion's flanks. The heavy mortars, howitzers, and anti-aircraft guns were arrayed in the center. Major Bob Tolly commanded the artillery, but only four of his howitzers remained operable.

Major Hugh Robbins, acting as the Task Force S-4, supervised the redistribution of supplies to units around the perimeter. Around 3:00 p.m., an air drop by C-119s provided emergency supplies, but the results were not satisfying. Some landed outside the perimeter and were lost to the Chinese. In one case, a parachute failed to open, sending its cargo hurtling down like a meteor, killing a KATUSA. Missing was ammunition for the 40mm Dusters, a particularly effective weapon that was running perilously low. It landed instead at Hudong-ni where the tank company destroyed it because it had no 40mm weapons.

That afternoon, Brigadier General Hodes came into the inlet perimeter by helicopter to see for himself what was happening. PFC Ed Reeves, who had found refuge at the Battalion CP the night his company was overrun, remembers hearing Lieutenant Colonel Reilly arguing with Hodes, who had just ordered him and Lieutenant Colonel Embree loaded aboard his helicopter for evacuation to Hagaru-ri. Reilly said he couldn't abandon his men and claimed unrealistically that his wounds wouldn't keep him from doing anything he needed to do. Hodes knew that neither battalion commander could function effectively since neither could even stand up, much less walk. He gave Reilly and Embree no choice, ordering some of the able-bodied men near the CP to put them on the helicopter without further delay.

Meanwhile, Captain Drake was trying again to fight his Tank Company past the hairpin turn at Hill 1221 to break through to the RCT's main body at the inlet. He took 12 tanks, a mortar, and a scratch force of less than a company, assembled from Headquarters and Service Companies and a platoon from the 13th Engineer Battalion. Again, the tanks were unable to get traction on the slippery mountainside and the troops on foot came under such heavy fire that they could make no headway. About 20 were killed or wounded. A single Marine Corsair flew a strike mission in support of the assault, but because there was no direct communication between the pilot and the troops on the ground, he fired at Americans as much as Chinese. In frustration, Chaplain Martin C. Hoehn, accompanying the assault force, grabbed a Thompson sub-machine gun and fired magazine after magazine, each time asking God for forgiveness.

Because high mountains blocked line-of-sight radio transmissions, there was no communication between the RCT's main body at the inlet and the elements at Hudong-ni, only four miles away. A coordinated assault by the tank-infantry force from Hudong-ni and the troops at the inlet might have stood a chance, but by itself the Hudong-ni force had too few infantrymen to overcome Chinese dominance on the hills above the hairpin.

Just before midnight on November 29, the Chinese renewed their attack on the inlet, striking the sector held by A and B Companies of the 32nd Infantry. The attack was repulsed with heavy losses after about an hour. The Chinese later made a second try, striking A Company 32nd Infantry where the road entered the perimeter from the south. Preceded by a mortar attack, the Chinese overran a platoon that included a heavy machine gun and a 75mm recoilless rifle. The latter was destroyed by mortar fire, killing its crew. After a sharp firefight, the Chinese overran the .50 caliber machine gun position, capturing its crew and several others before withdrawing. Throughout the night Chinese raiding parties penetrated gaps in the perimeter, intent on knocking out the 15th AAA's quad .50 caliber and 40mm guns that had proven so devastating.

In the 3rd Battalion CP, PFC Don Mayville had been sitting for hours on a floor that had a fire under it while he operated an SCR 608 Radio. He could only communicate with the 57th Field Artillery Battalion. Weary from three nights with little sleep, he got permission from Lieutenant Jules "Rocky" Rybolt, the Battalion Communications Officer, to lie down on the lower floor in front of the fire to catch a few minutes rest. Just as Mayville lay down, a burst of fire passed through the CP's outer wall, hitting Rybolt in the forehead. He called out to his friend, Lieutenant Bob Boyer, standing about 10 feet away on the other side of the room, "Bob, I'm hit," and slumped to the floor.

On November 30, several more airdrops delivered sorely needed ammunition and other supplies. Major General David G. Barr, Commanding General of the 7th Infantry Division, landed at the inlet by helicopter that morning. On meeting with Lieutenant Colonel Faith, Barr learned for the first time that Colonel MacLean had been captured. What conversation passed between Faith and Barr is unknown. Barr was in no position to give Faith any orders, because X Corps had transferred operational control of all troops from Koto-ri north to Major General Oliver P. Smith, Commander of the 1st Marine Division. Lieutenant General Almond, the Corps Commander, had ordered Smith to assemble all units from both sides of the reservoir at Hagaru-ri and fight their way back to the Hungnam area where the entire corps would concentrate.

Reinforcements Stopped

Fifteen miles to the south near Koto-ri, another drama was unfolding. Captain Charles Peckham's B Company, which was to temporarily replace E Company in the 2nd

Battalion, arrived ahead of the battalion and was attached to Task Force Drysdale, commanded by Lieutenant Douglas B. Drysdale of the British Royal Marines.[1] The task force, numbering about 900 men and including a Marine Tank Company, was ordered to move 11 miles north to reinforce the 3rd Battalion 1st Marines at Hagaru-ri and clear Chinese roadblocks along the route. The temperature was minus 32 degrees. About halfway to its destination, the task force was ambushed from hills flanking both sides of the road. B Company took the full force of the ambush and was chopped to pieces.

A Chinese .50 caliber machine gun, firing from a hillside around 1,000 yards away pinned down B Company's center platoon and was hitting some of the men on the ground who could find no protection. Ordered by Lieutenant Bill Meanor to knock out the gun with his 57mm recoilless rifle, Corporal James Vickers and his assistant gunner would have to expose themselves to intense enemy fire from commanding heights on both sides of the road. To reduce their risks, the team moved after each time they fired. After firing two rounds, Vickers' assistant gunner was killed. Vickers had been wounded twice, once by shrapnel and another by a burst from a Chinese submachine gun. Down to his last round, a white phosphorous shell, Vickers rose, took careful aim despite the bullets spattering all around him, and fired again. This time he struck his target. Many men would live to see another sunrise due to his heroic determination.

Shortly after the ambush began, a mortar round detonated between Corporal Thomas Batts, his platoon leader and another of his comrades. Batts was knocked unconscious and the others were killed. When he awoke, he found his BAR lying across his lap. An intense battle was raging all around him and he quickly joined in. Someone handed him a grenade and as soon as he threw it, a Chinese soldier fired two rounds into his hand. Unable to use his BAR any longer, he gave it to a friend and told him to get out any way he could. The man was killed. Batts took a pistol and crawled into a mortar crater to protect himself. He was wounded four more times during the night, but killed 18 Chinese soldiers as they passed or approached his lonely position. When morning came, the Chinese demanded that the task force's survivors surrender or be killed.

Lieutenant Alfred J. Anderson gathered as many survivors as he could and formed a perimeter along a river bank to fight off groups of Chinese closing in from all sides. The Chinese surged down the hillsides in waves and they died the same way. Lieutenant George Snippen later recalled there were so many Chinese bodies in front of the perimeter that the ground was no longer visible. Twice the Chinese penetrated the perimeter, but their admission fee was death. Armed with only a .45 caliber pistol, Anderson several times deflected enemy weapons with one arm and shot their owners at point blank range. His example stirred his battered group to perform superhuman feats to avoid being overrun. At 6:00 the next morning, Anderson led his contingent, 19 of them seriously wounded, into the Marine perimeter at Koto-ri.

Sixty-five of B Company's men were taken prisoner by the Chinese during the night. Technical Sergeant Frank Kaiser, Corporal John McReady, and Private Elliot Sortillo were among those captured. Sortillo was only 16 at the time and would spend his 17th, 18th, and 19th birthdays as an involuntary guest of the Chinese. McReady escaped the next morning, but was soon recaptured and spent the next 33 months as a POW. "I watched most of those guys get captured but I couldn't do anything to help them because I was out of ammo," recalls Vickers. But Vickers had done all he could earlier. For their actions in the battle, Corporals Batts and Vickers were belatedly awarded the Silver Star in separate ceremonies 52 years later.

Unaware of what was happening farther north, the 2nd Battalion departed Majong-dong by truck convoy at 6:45 a.m. on November 30. About a mile into the narrow Fun-chilin Pass, they were struck by an ambush. Four vehicles were knocked out in the ensuing firefight, but infantrymen dismounted farther back and counterattacked to keep the Chinese away. It soon became apparent, however, that Chinese troops were streaming around their flanks, obliging the advance to stop. Recognizing that the Chinese controlled all the high ground around him, Lieutenant Colonel Reidy called for air strikes to pin the Chinese down long enough for his men to get a toe-hold on the high ground. One came in late afternoon, but did little good. The Chinese still held all the high cards. Frustrated and aware that it would be dark soon, Reidy ordered his men to dig in and establish an all-around defense. They were still three miles short of Koto-ri.

At 5:30 p.m., an officer from the corps staff arrived with a message from Lieutenant General Almond. It ordered Reidy to advance at once to join the remainder of the RCT at the inlet. Dutifully, Reidy issued the movement order at 7:15, specifying 9:00 p.m. as departure time. By the time company commanders could assure that all of their men had been collected and vehicles that could not be restarted were pushed off the road and their cargo transferred, the movement began two and a half hours late. Confusion reigned in F Company when a booby trap blew up at a roadblock on a bridge, precipitating a near rout. Snow had begun falling and visibility was getting progressively worse. Around 1:30 a.m. on December 1, the Chinese struck again, splitting the column. Part of the battalion continued to Koto-ri that night, but more than half of the force stayed in place until morning, not wanting to risk another ambush in the dark. The 2nd Battalion made it no further than Koto-ri, reinforcing the Marines and taking charge of soldiers from other Army units that could get no further north.

Withdrawal from the Inlet

While the 2nd Battalion was stalled, things were growing steadily more desperate at the inlet. By then, there were over 600 wounded in the perimeter and practically no way to get them out except by truck past the gauntlet at Hill 1221 to Hudong-ni and on to Hagaru-ri. Unknown to Lieutenant Colonel Faith or anyone else at the inlet, there was no longer an American presence at Hudong-ni. The Tank Company, Headquarters Company, Service Company, and Service Battery 57th Field Artillery, totaling 345 men and 16 tanks, had been ordered by General Hodes to pull back to Marine lines at Hagaru-ri on the afternoon of November 30. Although Hodes was acting under orders from Major General Barr, Barr no longer had authority over the 31st RCT since all units north of Koto-ri, including Army units, had been placed under Marine command.

At around 8:00 on the night of November 30, the Chinese unleashed a 45-minute mortar barrage against the inlet while assault parties crawled close to the line. Attacks struck repeatedly all along the line, building to an intensity exceeding that of earlier nights, but they were not well coordinated, giving the heavy weapons in the perimeter's center an opportunity to concentrate on one attack at a time. K and L Companies of the 31st absorbed the hardest blows and again lost heavily but they held on stubbornly most of the night. PFC Stanley E. Anderson of L Company distinguished himself by turning back one of the attacks almost single-handedly with his 3.5 inch rocket launcher, firing it repeatedly at any cluster of Chinese he could see. Around 3:00 a.m. on December 1, the line was penetrated. Faith sent a platoon-size counterattack force to retake the knob dominating the northeast portion of the perimeter, but to no avail.

When daylight came, the Chinese held the position they had gained during the night. From the highest point on the ridge, they placed increasingly accurate mortar fire on heavy weapons in the inlet. After conferring with his subordinate commanders, Lieutenant Colonel Faith, ordered preparations for a breakout. No one had much faith in being able to hold the perimeter another night. The 1st Battalion, 32nd Infantry would lead, followed by the 57th Field Artillery with the 15th AAA and the heavy mortars attached. All heavy weapons except the AAA were ordered to expend their remaining ammunition and then destroy their tubes and fight as infantry. The wounded would be loaded onto trucks in the center of the column. The 3rd Battalion 31st Infantry would bring up the rear. Everything left behind was to be destroyed.

By 11 a.m. on December 1, the convoy was loaded and ready to

A photograph of Capt. Don C. Faith Jr., during World War II, wearing his 82nd Airborne patch. By the end of the war, he was a lieutenant colonel and had earned two Bronze Stars. Eventually he would get the Medal of Honor for his actions in Korea, where he was killed in action (courtesy Defense POW/MIA Accounting Agency).

move, but it would have to await air cover to make the move. Chinese troops had been watching and began moving down from the hills to take up positions along the only available withdrawal route. Others lobbed mortar shells into the perimeter, killing and wounding more men. Major Hugh Robbins was among them, hit in the arm and legs by fragmentation and knocked from his feet by the blast. Sergeant Major Lynch dragged him to a slit trench, bandaged his wounds, and loaded him onto a truck. The RCT's senior leadership was eroding more by the hour. Just before 1 p.m., Marine F4U Corsairs arrived overhead from the USS *Leyte*. Captain Stamford, the Marine Air Liaison Officer, directed them to make a dummy run to identify American marker panels at the head of the column. That accomplished, the Corsairs came around to engage. At the head of the column, Chinese troops attacked, closing to within 50 yards of the convoy's lead element. As the lead Corsair approached over the convoy, it prematurely released its napalm tank, hitting Americans and Chinese alike. Peering out between slats in a truck carrying the wounded, Hugh Robbins watched in horror as he saw Master Sergeant David B. Smith, the Regiment's Assistant Sergeant Major, enveloped in flames. Witnesses recall that five GIs and a KATUSA were killed outright and another eight or nine GIs were badly burned and loaded onto trucks. Still others continued walking and fighting despite severe burns. For the rest of the day, Corsairs returned in flights of four to six aircraft, strafing and bombing enemy positions all along the escape route.

When the column started moving again, infantrymen from the 3rd Battalion streamed past the trucks to help push the Chinese out of the way, but in so doing, they were abandoning the rear of the column. The few officers who remained unwounded had no radios to control subordinate units and therefore controlled only those men within the sound of their voices. Amid the constant banging and chattering of weapons, punctuated by exploding grenades and volleys of mortar fire, no one's voice carried very far. Unit integrity evaporated as men took any cover they could find, returned fire, and followed whoever seemed to be leading. Corporal Milton Margan recalls that he, Captain Auburn "Pop" Marr, and PFC Thomas J. Morris were at the tail of the column coming out of the inlet. Morris was firing a .30 caliber machine gun from the hip as they withdrew. He was captured when the Chinese pinned down and surrounded the trio. Captain Marr was killed by the Chinese as he attempted to surrender. Master Sergeant Ivan H. Long of the 3rd Battalion's S-2 Section was captured along with two other men as they attempted in vain to fight off a Chinese company attacking the rear of the truck column. The rear guard had evaporated.

After departing the inlet, what remained of the RCT focused on protecting the long column of trucks laden with wounded to Hagaru-ri, just a few more miles down the road. As trucks became disabled, the wounded were unloaded onto the road under fire and helped or dragged into ditches or behind whatever cover could be found. The most seriously wounded were loaded onto other trucks, swelling the number of men on each truck to the point that some died from the additional trauma. Disabled trucks were pushed off to the side to allow others to pass. Somehow the convoy struggled on, but its pace was dreadfully slow, causing ever more casualties.

As the head of the column reached a blown bridge just short of Hill 1221, the trucks had to negotiate a swampy by-pass. Major Hugh Robbins recalls:

> We came to a bridge which had been destroyed and our motor column turned off the road and into a wide riverbed to by-pass the obstacle. Great mounds of frozen earth covered with tough grass carpeted the riverbed over which we now bounced. For about 100 yards we bounced and crashed up and down over those hummocks with the wounded screaming in anguish as they were jostled and slammed into one another on the truck bed. I luckily still had on my steel helmet and thus was able to protect my head from banging against the front and sides of the truck bed which might have knocked me out otherwise. At that, I had a bruised head for days afterwards. Eventually, a half-track pulled Robbins' truck back onto the roadway and it continued south, but more trouble lay ahead. At the hairpin turn where the Medical Company had been ambushed four days earlier, the Chinese occupied positions that had been dug by the 5th Marines when they occupied the area until November 27. From there, they controlled the pass.

As trucks slowed, Chinese troops on the hills concentrated on killing drivers. Bullets whacked, slapped, and pinged from all directions as the trucks were hit repeatedly, killing some of the wounded inside and wounding others again and again. Some of the less seriously wounded or men who had taken refuge in nearby ditches risked all to take the wheel of trucks whose drivers were killed or too badly wounded to continue driving. On both flanks of the convoy, counterattacks were mounted under the most adverse conditions, but several succeeded in clearing segments of the roadway. Near the first saddle in the road, Major Harvey Storms, acting as the 3rd Battalion's commander, was severely wounded and loaded onto a truck with the other wounded. He perished on the truck. At nearly the same time, Major Crosby Miller, acting commander of the 1st Battalion 32nd Infantry, was also wounded near the head of the column. By that time, the senior man still walking in each of the infantry battalions was probably a captain who did not know everyone above him had been killed or too badly wounded to command. With nearly all radios knocked out of action, some officers and NCOS led by example to try to overcome impossible odds while others assumed someone more senior would come along and tell them what to do. The latter would wait in vain because the chain of command was steadily being eroded by bullets. Lieutenant Colonel Faith was the only field grade officer still unwounded, but not for long.

With the convoy stalled, Lieutenant Colonel Faith tried desperately to organize a counterattack to clear the steep slopes dominating the road. Here and there, attacks of platoon and company strength got off to weak starts and most of the early efforts resulted in all or most of the participants being killed or wounded. Major Robbins, recognizing that the convoy might be stuck for good, decided that he would rather die fighting than wait for the Chinese to come down the hill and finish him off. He struggled out of the mass of other wounded men around him in the truck, slid painfully to the ground, and began collecting able-bodied soldiers, many of them walking wounded like himself, to attack Chinese positions overlooking the road. After fighting through a line of Chinese-held foxholes, most made it to the crest of Hill 1221, firing wildly and throwing all the hand grenades they had left as they struggled up the steep slope. Others were doing the same thing. Captain Robert Kitz, commanding K Company, gathered around 210 men who had taken cover along the road. At first, he had trouble getting men to move out of sheltered locations near the trucks, but with the help of other officers and NCOs from a variety of units, he managed to get people on their feet and moving uphill. Most were low on ammunition and many were wounded men who had struggled out of the trucks under intense fire, but they picked up weapons and ammunition from the dead and went up the hill anyway. Darkness was approaching when the group fought its way through the line of Chinese foxholes and bunkers dominating the road. Rather than fanning out to the right to overrun the remaining Chinese from the flank or rear, the men continued to struggle up the steep hill, responsive only to the instinct to survive. Once the exhausted climbers reached the top and saw the hopelessness of the convoy's situation below, they kept going, headed south toward safety. Past the crest of Hill 1221, they struggled down to the rail line, following it south until they encountered more opposition, and then crossed a frozen section of the reservoir, with the Chinese close behind. They reached Marine lines at Hagaru-ri around midnight.

Although Kitz's attack had punched a hole in the Chinese gauntlet, the hole was only a sliver in a much wider line. All around the slope, Chinese troops continued to pour rifle and automatic weapons fire onto the stalled convoy, killing or again wounding many of the previously wounded men in the trucks. Men too weak to move moaned or screamed for help, but help was in short supply. The able bodied men who had been escorting the convoy were falling victim to the same fire, adding hundreds more to the number of dead and wounded. Recognizing the situation's urgency, Captain Earle H. Jordan, Jr., commanding M Company, formed another ad hoc group to attack up the fire-swept slope. Jordan, already wounded during the first night's action at the inlet, had kept what remained of his company in its position through four days and nights of hell until the breakout. With Lieutenants John E. Gray, his 81mm Mortar Platoon Leader, and

Robert G. Schmitt, his Heavy Machine Gun Platoon Leader, he assembled a group of about 30 men to form up for the attack. They had only rifles, carbines, and hand grenades left, but they would try. Schmitt's arm was in a sling from an earlier shoulder wound and Gray, like Jordan, had also been wounded during earlier fighting. The group attacked the north slope of Hill 1221, not far from where Kitz's group had attacked, and fought its way through the Chinese. Lieutenant Schmitt and perhaps 20 others were killed or lay too badly wounded to continue. Lieutenant Gray was wounded a second time, but remained in action, despite injuries to one hand and both legs. About 10 men, including Jordan and Gray, made it to the top, exhausted and with no ammunition left. Unwilling to abandon the wounded, Jordan led the men down the reverse slope of the hill toward a log roadblock near the head of the vehicle column. Shouting like banshees, they ran, limped, and stumbled back through the Chinese line from behind, taking some small arms fire, but suffering no more casualties. Back on the road, they gathered others to help them move the log roadblock aside. Captain Jordan and Lieutenant Gray would later receive the Distinguished Service Cross for their actions.

At dusk, most of Hill 1221 had been cleared by the various counterattacks and Navy/Marine air strikes launched late that afternoon. There still remained one stubborn strongpoint. The Chinese remained dug in near the nose of the hairpin turn where the 31st Infantry's Medical Company had been ambushed on the night of November 27 and where the Regimental Tank Company had tried unsuccessfully to break through to the inlet on November 28 and 29. With the help of several other officers from his battalion, Colonel Faith gathered a group of about 300 men and managed to get a final counterattack moving, attempting to get around the position to take it from behind. Corporal George Pryor of the 3rd Battalion's Communications Platoon kicked, screamed, and cajoled men to join him in attacking the roadblock. He succeeded, leading a bulldog-like assault that quickly lost sight of Faith's attack struggling up adjacent furrows. Pryor was shot in the leg but struggled on. Shortly after the assault began, Don Carlos Faith was knocked off his feet by a hand grenade. He did not get back up, prompting some to presume him dead. A grenade fragment had entered his chest above the heart, but he was still breathing. Lieutenant Fields E. Shelton of the 31st Infantry's Heavy Mortar Company was with Faith when he was hit and was wounded by the same grenade blast. He tried to get Faith back down to the road, but was too weak to carry him. He wrapped him up as well as possible and went back down to the road for help. Several soldiers carried him back to the road and laid him across the hood of his jeep. Because the jeep could not get around larger vehicles blocking the road, he was transferred into the cab of a truck at the head of the column.

Once Captain Jordan and his men removed the log roadblock and Faith's counterattack cleared the adjacent high ground, the convoy resumed moving. Here and there, groups of able-bodied men and walking wounded helped the more seriously wounded along the road or the railroad running parallel to the reservoir's eastern shore. Many got no further because there were still numerous pockets of Chinese troops all over the area. Descending from the saddle on Hill 1221 near dark, the convoy snaked its way slowly down icy roads. By this time, none of the quad.50 caliber machine guns or 40mm "Dusters" remained in action. Any fire support would have to come from the dwindling number of infantrymen moving along the sides of the road in front of the trucks. Exhausted and nearly out of ammunition, they would be of little help. Just after passing the abandoned village of Twiggae, the convoy encountered a blown bridge which slowed everything to a crawl as the trucks negotiated a difficult detour. Again the Chinese peppered the trucks with small arms fire, adding to the misery the wounded were already enduring. Every time the column stopped, several trucks stalled out and could not be restarted. The wounded from those trucks had to be loaded onto other vehicles, adding to the pain and suffering of all. Disabled vehicles were pushed off the road with great difficulty by men whose wounds reopened under the strain. The number of wounded men aboard each vehicle nearly doubled to 40 or 50 by the time the convoy passed Twiggae. Colonel Faith and the lead truck's other occupants were killed in a final ambush that stopped the convoy's remnant just short of Hudong-ri. Faith was posthumously awarded the Medal of Honor for his aggressive leadership in attempting the breakout. Of the task force's original complement of nearly 3,300 men, only 385 of those who reached Marine lines at Hagaru-ri from the inlet were unwounded. Not one vehicle or piece of heavy equipment made it through.

After dark, PFC Lewis D. Shannon of K Company helped an officer (probably Captain Swenty of the 1st Battalion, 32nd Infantry) round up as many able-bodied men as possible, including about 40 walking wounded, to make a break for safety. Many were too badly wounded to operate a weapon. The captain, a KATUSA, PFC Shannon, and

LTC Faith was declared Killed in Action, Remains not Recovered. In 2004, a joint U.S.–North Korean team surveyed the area where Faith and other Americans were last seen, and many intermingled remains were recovered. Over the years, the slow process of positive identification was conducted by the Joint POW/MIA Accounting Command and the Armed Forces DNA Identification Laboratory. Tests positively identified LTC Faith, and included comparison with his brother's DNA. Sixty-three years after the battle, soldiers of the Caisson Platoon, 3d U.S. Infantry Regiment (The Old Guard), transport the remains of LTC Faith to his final resting place in Arlington National Cemetery, Apr. 17, 2013, Section 4, Gravesite 3016-RH (U.S. Army Photograph by Sgt. Jose A. Torres, Jr.).

an unknown American GI walked point, driving off any Chinese who came too close. Encountering a strongpoint that was too large to overcome, the group left the road under fire and continued moving south along the railroad tracks. The brightness of a full moon reflecting off the snow stands out in the memories of those trying desperately to get away. Corporal William J. Smith of I Company recalls, "The moon was so bright you could only move when the moon went behind the clouds, or else the Chinese would fire at you. You had to be perfectly still. If you moved, chances are you got hit or killed." By the time Shannon's group reached Hagaru-ri, their number had swollen to roughly 100 men, more than double the number they started with. The actions of the group's small point element saved many men who otherwise would have perished along the road.

For the men left on the vehicles at the final ambush site, the ordeal was far from over. Some crawled off of the trucks and dropped to the roadway. A few of those were able to make it onto the ice and crawl or stumble to safety at Hagaru-ri, about two miles away. Others, too weak to go any further, lay on the roadbed or in nearby ditches and were shot by the Chinese the next morning. Still others, too weak to get off of the trucks met a worse fate. When the Chinese arrived, an officer who spoke excellent English ordered all the trucks evacuated. Because most of the men remaining on the trucks were too badly wounded to move, few could comply with his instructions. PFC Ed Reeves of K Company was among the men left on the trucks. For two days, Chinese came and went through the convoy, first removing all stretchers and dumping the wounded in heaps on the cold metal floor of the trucks. On the ridge, more Chinese appeared, ready to ambush whoever came to rescue the wounded. They were bait. When it became obvious no help was coming, the Chinese decided to end the game.

On December 3, a flurry of shots rang out from the head of the column and smoke began to rise above the convoy. The Chinese were shooting everyone on the road and under the trucks. Those too badly injured to move were left aboard the trucks and set afire with whatever gasoline the Chinese could drain from the vehicles' gas tanks. On trucks with empty gas tanks, an executioner came aboard with a rifle and shot every man between the eyes. Men resigned to their fate waited quietly for the death shot to end their misery. Reeves recalls being hit, but the shot only grazed his scalp, leaving him a bloody mess, but still alive. The next morning, Chinese troops began pulling dead GIs and KATUSAs into piles on the road. They unzipped sleeping bags in which the wounded had traveled, searched the bodies, and unceremoniously flung lifeless corpses onto piles. When they searched him, they found Reeves alive and beat him senseless with rifle butts before throwing him onto the pile of corpses. When they left, he began a daylong ordeal, crawling all the way to Hagaru-ri across the ice. His story, *Beautiful Feet and Real Peace*, is an epic of human endurance and determination to survive. Sergeant First Class Sam Muncy, shot in the ankle, was also aboard one of the trucks. Before the Chinese arrived, Muncy climbed out and lay in a ditch. He still agonizingly recalls the screams of comrades who perished in the inferno as the trucks were set on fire. Feigning death until dark, he managed to crawl out across the frozen reservoir where he was helped to Marine lines.

On December 2, 1950, elements of the 31st Infantry Regiment were scattered across five locations, the extremes separated by 140 miles:

- The 3rd Battalion, Heavy Mortar Company (less 1st Platoon), Tank Company, part of Headquarters Company, and part of Medical Company, were east of the Chosin Reservoir under 1st Marine Division control.

- The 2nd Battalion (less F Company), part of Headquarters Company, part of Medical Company, Service Company, Heavy Mortar Company's 1st Platoon, and B Company reinforced by elements of D Company were at Koto-ri attached to the 1st Marine Division.
- The 1st Battalion (less B Company) was under 7th Infantry Division control at Untaek.
- E Company was providing security for the 7th Infantry Division Command Post at Pungsan.
- Elements of the Regimental Staff and Service Company's Headquarters were at Hungnam-up to coordinate command, supply and administration. Lieutenant Colonel Deshon, the Regimental Executive Officer, assumed command of the elements under 7th Infantry Division control.

Stragglers arrived at Hagaru-ri from the reservoir's east side in clusters of varying numbers over the next several days. Most suffered from exposure and only 385 were neither wounded nor badly frostbitten. They joined several hundred others who had withdrawn from Hudong-ni on November 30. Anyone able to fight was sent directly into the perimeter to join one of the composite Army battalions being formed to thicken the Marine perimeter. They formed six ad hoc rifle companies of about 90 men each, including KATUSAs. They had no crew-served weapons. Troops were armed with pistols, M-1 Rifles, Carbines, and a few BARs. The Regimental Tank Company was attached to the 1st Marine Tank Battalion. This ad hoc organization, totaling around 600 men, defended its assigned sector at Hagaru-ri against constant attacks for the next five days. Its orders from the 1st Marine Division were to be prepared to attack south to Koto-ri 24 hours after Marine Units from Yudam-ni reached Hagaru-ri.

Attempting to maintain unit integrity, commanders re-formed the 1st Battalion 32nd Infantry and 3rd Battalion 31st Infantry, but exceptions had to be made to keep the companies reasonably balanced. The reconstituted RCT's rough composition was:

1st Battalion, commanded by Major Jones, S-3 of the 1st Battalion 32nd Infantry, with:

A Company, commanded by 1st Lieutenant Smith (XO, A Co 32nd Inf) and composed of men from Headquarters and A Companies of the 1st Battalion 32nd Infantry and Headquarters Battery of the 57th Field Artillery Battalion;

B Company, commanded by Captain Thacker (S-1, 57th FA Bn) and composed of men from B Company 32nd Infantry, the 31st Infantry's Antitank/Mine Platoon, and C Company 13th Engineer Battalion;

C Company, commanded by Captain Dowell (1st Bn 32nd Inf) and composed of men from C Company 32nd Infantry and Heavy Mortar Company 31st Infantry.

3rd Battalion, commanded by Major Carl Witte (S-2, 31st Inf), with:

I Company, commanded by Captain George Rasula (Asst S-3, 31st Inf) and composed of men from I Company 31st Infantry and Service Battery 57th Field Artillery Battalion;

K Company, commanded by Captain Robert Kitz (CO, K Company 31st Inf) and composed of men from K, M, and Headquarters Companies 31st Infantry;

L Company, commanded by 1st Lieutenant Robert Boyer and composed of men from L Company 31st Infantry and a platoon from the 7th Signal Company. Lieutenant Boyer was killed on December 5 during an attack on the Hagaru-ri perimeter.

C-47 transport planes were taking the most seriously wounded out of Hagaru-ri's air strip as quickly as possible. Units could not keep track of who was being evacuated because they remained under constant attack on the perimeter and because the wounded entered the Marine perimeter at various places for the next five days and did not go through their own units. Tanks were sent to try and reach stalled vehicles but could not make it. They did bring back a few more groups of wounded stragglers.

When news of the scope of the disaster at Chosin reached X Corps Headquarters at Hungnam, new orders were soon to follow. On December 3, Operations Order Number 28, Headquarters 7th Infantry Division, directed the 31st Regimental Combat Team to assemble in the Hamhung Area. Operations Order Number 29, Headquarters 7th Infantry Division, issued the following day, directed the 31st Infantry to reorganize and form the division reserve in the vicinity of Hamhung. In response, the 1st Battalion was ordered to move via truck to vicinity of Pukchong. Headquarters and Service elements moved by motor and rail from Hungnam up to Hamhung. The 1st Battalion departed Untaek at 4:20 p.m. on December 4 and reached Pukchong at 11:45 the next morning. There, they were ordered to proceed immediately to Hamhung. At the time, the 2nd Battalion was still bottled up at Koto-ri and the 3rd Battalion's survivors were under constant attack holding a section of the Marine perimeter at Hagaru-ri. It would be another week before all surviving elements of 31st Infantry could be reunited at Hamhung.

On December 7, All Army troops at Hagaru-ri, except those in the 31st Infantry's Tank Company, were reorganized to form a single provisional battalion of four companies. The Tank Company was attached to the 5th Marine Regiment, while the Provisional Battalion was attached to the 7th Marine Regiment. It was assigned responsibility for protecting the regiment's left flank in its attack to Koto-ri. After breaking through Chinese lines around Hagaru-ri, two companies composed mostly of men from the 31st Infantry were sent out to screen farther east, securing high ground out to 1000 yards from the road. That afternoon, a strong enemy roadblock was encountered about 4 miles south of Hagaru-ri. Two composite companies, composed mostly of men from the 32nd Infantry and 57th Field Artillery, overran the enemy positions. That night, the security screen was pulled back to within 100 yards of the road to avoid becoming cut off from the main body of the 7th Marine Regiment advancing along the road. The Chinese attacked the column twice during the night of December 7–8, destroying the trucks carrying the Provisional Battalion's CP. Both attacks were repulsed, but with substantial losses to the Provisional Battalion. All members of the CP had been killed or wounded.

The Provisional Battalion reached the Marine perimeter at Koto-ri at 6:30 a.m. on December 8. Over half of their number had fought for 4 days and 5 nights at the Chosin perimeter, escaped across the ice to Hagaru-ri under harrowing conditions, helped the Marines withstand another 5 days and nights of attacks at Hagaru-ri, and then fought their way out to Koto-ri. There they were welcomed by the 2nd Battalion 31st Infantry, which had warming tents set up inside the perimeter. Bone weary, men of the Provisional Battalion found the warmest spots available and were soon asleep. Their slumber was not to last very long, however. At 3:30 p.m. they were ordered to attack two hills northwest of Koto-ri and to hold the road open against enemy attacks. Considerable reorganization was required because of the number of casualties sustained between Hagaru-ri and Koto-ri. Only two companies could be assembled from the survivors. Both objectives were secured against light opposition. The Provisional Battalion held the hills until rear elements of 1st Marine Division's column halted.

At 7 a.m. on December 9, the attack resumed. The 31st Infantry's first two objectives overlooking the Funchilin Pass were quickly secured against light opposition but an intense snowstorm began during the attack and the temperature dropped 10 degrees, reaching 20 degrees below zero. At 10 a.m., the unit dug in on hills overlooking the evacuation route and remained there until the morning of December 10. At 7 a.m. on December 10, the attack continued, linking up with reconnaissance elements of the U.S. 3rd Infantry Division near Chinhung-ni. There, the men loaded aboard trucks and continued south to Hamhung. where the convoy arrived just before noon the next day. There, the Provisional Battalion was dissolved and its survivors were reunited with their parent regiments. The 3rd Battalion 31st Infantry had only 1 officer and 47 enlisted men and around 40 KATUSAs left.

Official casualty figures for the 31st Infantry Regiment show that 496 Americans were killed in action or died after being captured in North Korea between November 8 and December 12, 1950. No accounting exists for KATUSAs. who constituted roughly half the regiment's strength. Estimates of the number of American and KATUSA soldiers killed or missing at or near the Chosin Reservoir between November 27 and December 2, 1950, range between 1,200 and 1,500. Most were likely buried near where they fell. Although many died in and around the two battalion perimeters, many more were killed along the road and railroad as the column moved south and others died on the slopes of Hill 1221 trying to overcome the ambush. Several hundred died in and near the destroyed trucks, a convoy that stretched over four kilometers. More than twice that

With glowing lights, two trucks with replacements for the 31st Infantry Regiment move up to the front lines through Yumok Chong (U.S. Army photograph, National Archives).

number were wounded or suffered frostbite so severe that they had to be evacuated to Japan or the United States.

On December 15, the 31st Infantry's remnant departed Hungnam by sea, arriving at Pusan four days later. Behind them, engineers rigged the docks and important buildings with tons of explosives. Forlorn North Korean refugees crowded into the dock area to get aboard the departing American ships. Many were Christians, desperate to get away from the advancing Chinese. Although more than 100,000 were evacuated, thousands probably perished when engineers set off the charges as the last landing craft departed on Christmas Eve.

On December 26, the regiment moved 80 miles north of Pusan to Yongchon, where it rested, refitted, and received replacements. Since B Company, part of the 2nd Battalion, and nearly all of the 3rd Battalion had been destroyed in North Korea, men from the strongest companies were transferred to the battered remnants of others, evening the distribution of combat experience as replacements were absorbed.

The Chinese were not resting and refitting. They were simply absorbing whatever manpower could be scraped together in Manchuria to pursue retreating UN forces deep into South Korea. As Seoul and other major South Korean cities fell one after another, there were again doubts at high levels that the UN Command could establish and hold a coherent line with units that had been decimated in North Korea. Rumors flew that Allied forces would soon be evacuated to Japan. Two factors intervened to prevent that disaster from happening. First, the Chinese were nearing the end of their logistical tether and their best combat units had taken serious losses in driving the UN out of North Korea. The North Koreans were little help since their Army, the *Inmun Gun*, had all but evaporated by the end of November and was being rebuilt almost from scratch by forcibly recruiting men and boys everywhere possible, including POW Camps. Second, the U.S. Army proved to be much more resilient and determined than its critics were willing to admit. Infused with new blood, units that had been all but wiped out a month before suddenly became vengeance-bent tigers, eager to erase the stain of defeat they had suffered in North Korea.

14 Back to the Offensive: 1951

The UN Command's situation after the withdrawal from North Korea was desperate. The 2nd, 7th, and 25th Infantry Divisions, 1st Cavalry Division, and 1st Marine Division had each lost roughly the equivalent of a regiment while fighting their way out of North Korea's frozen highlands. The newly-arrived Turkish Brigade suffered losses that would cripple most units but the Turks bravely stayed in the fight. Few infantry regiments that fought their way back across the 38th parallel could muster more than two thirds of their original strength. Trucks, half-tracks, howitzers, and discarded personal equipment littered the main withdrawal routes.

Adding more gloom to the situation, Lieutenant General Walton Walker, Commander of the Eighth Army, was killed in a jeep accident as 1950 came to a close. A characteristically bitter Korean winter froze the ground to the consistency of rock, making it almost impossible to dig in and establish a line behind which the UN command could regain its strength. Taking full advantage of the situation, Chinese forces swept through abandoned Pyongyang and continued to push southward. They soon swept across the Han and took Seoul on January 4, 1951. Regardless of their condition, there was no time for depleted units on either side to rest and refit.

The 31st Infantry Regiment moved north from Pusan by truck on the day Seoul fell to the Chinese, arriving just behind the center of the UN line near Chechon. Weary infantrymen and engineers established defensive positions in depth along the road and rail lines between Tanyang and Chechon to protect X Corps supply lines. On January 27, the 7th Division attempted a counterattack to help straighten the UN line, but heavy rains and muddy roads made progress nearly impossible. It was becoming apparent, though, that the Chinese were also nearing the end of their tether. UN aircraft hammered Chinese and North Korean supply routes daily and UN troops were proving much more resilient than anyone could have predicted.

Back on the Attack

On January 29, the 31st Infantry moved onto a series of long ridges and hills defining the 7th Division's main line of resistance (MLR) astride the Tanyang Pass. They would not have to wait long for their return to action. The following night the Chinese attacked in a series of three waves, each spaced about 300 yards apart. As Chinese bugles blared

195

Tanks of the 31st Heavy Tank company, 31st Infantry Regiment, fire on enemy positions near Mundung-Ni, 27 October 1951 (U.S. Army photograph, National Archives).

to signal the attack, their mortars and heavier guns began to shell the ridgeline. American searchlights behind the line aimed their beams at low-hanging clouds to provide reflected illumination for the infantrymen up front. Illuminated by the sudden light, the first wave of Chinese, about ten rows deep, came under fire from every American weapon in range. Rifles and carbines, BARs, machine guns, recoilless rifles, mortars, and artillery created a deafening orchestra of noise and flying metal that turned the valley into a slaughterhouse. The first wave quickly turned into a pile of mangled bodies whose few survivors shielded themselves with the bodies of dead comrades. The second wave stopped several hundred yards away, dropped to prone, sitting, and kneeling positions, and concentrated their fire against troops of the 2nd Battalion holding the lowest part of the ridge. Stationary in the open, the Chinese had no chance against massed American firepower and they too added their bodies to the harvest of death. The third wave came through the barrage at a dead run, moving through the first and second waves as quickly as they could. Some got to within 20 yards of the American line to throw hand grenades, but were mown down. None penetrated the line.

It was over in just under an hour. Afterward the night was eerily quiet. If there were wounded Chinese in front of the American positions, they made no sound and either crawled back to their own line or died silently where they lay in the damp, cold night. The next morning, Koreans came out of nearby villages to carry the dead to burial grounds. G Company counted 330 bodies being carried away. A nearby company of the

Opposite, top: **Men of the 31st prepare to give covering fire to the assault squad during an attack on Hill 710 (Association archives).**

Bottom: **PFC Donald L. Dewees (Laramie, Wyoming), 31st Heavy Tank Company, 31st Infantry Regiment, 7th Infantry Division, wounded by enemy mortar fire while on patrol near Mundung-Ni, Korea, receives aid from a medic, 27 October 1951 (U.S. Army photograph, National Archives).**

17th Infantry Regiment counted 387 Chinese dead in front of their positions, and so it went all along the line. Someone dubbed the place "Massacre Valley."

In China, families would in time grieve for sons whose bodies now rested in Korean soil, learning of their fate only when they failed to return home at the war's end or when a crippled brother or friend came home early with the news. To governments on both sides, numbers of casualties were faceless abstractions, mere indicators of how well or how poorly their generals waged campaigns. There were many millions of similarly "faceless" young men in China to take their places, and so the fighting continued, no matter how many times there would be a "Massacre Valley."

On January 31, 1951, the 187th Airborne Regimental Combat Team and the 6th ROK Division relieved the U.S. 7th Division in the Tanyang area. Because hell was being unleashed against the ROK 8th Division around Wonju, the 187th was abruptly shifted westward to plug the gap, leaving the 6th ROK Division to hold the sector alone, a fact soon discovered by the Chinese. Because ROK troops were not as well armed and trained as those of other UN armies, the Chinese would regularly pile on wherever they found a ROK division occupying a critical point in the line. Because the Tanyang Pass was a natural corridor to the south, the Chinese wanted it badly. The 6th ROK Division was driven off the MLR in disarray, opening a wide gap in the line. The 31st Infantry went right back into action, encountering stubborn resistance from Chinese troops who were unwilling to yield ground that had cost them dearly a few days before. Good weather and clear skies enabled the Air Force to dominate the fight, clearing the path for GIs by strafing, bombing, and napalming Chinese troops who had neither air cover nor anti-aircraft support.

In mid–February, the 7th Division resumed the offensive, supporting the ROK 5th Division's attack to retake Hongchon as part of Operation Roundup. To accomplish its part of the mission, the 31st Infantry had to cross a wide valley in full view of the Chinese. Artillery, air strikes, heavy mortars, and a platoon of tanks focused their attention on a steep hill dominating the enemy line, but to no avail. The Chinese responded with machine guns, mortars, and artillery of their own, forcing GIs to take cover among the rocks and whatever folds in the ground they could find. G Company was sent up the hill again as another round of artillery and napalm struck the Chinese dominating the upper slope. The attack went forward with fixed bayonets while artillery and mortars blasted the hill. As American infantrymen reached the enemy trenches, the fighting continued at close quarters, often with bayonets and rifle butts when weapons couldn't be reloaded fast enough to engage Chinese who would suddenly appear from behind wrecked bunkers and collapsed sections of trench. When platoon sergeants took the report from squad leaders to determine their losses, miraculously only one man had been killed and two wounded.

Thereafter the 7th Division took up positions supporting the ROK 3d and 5th Divisions in the Chechon and Tanyang areas and secured the pass between Chechon and Wonju to prepare for further offensive operations. When Operation Killer, a general UN counteroffensive, began on February 21, the 7th Division struck repeatedly along the Wonju-Kangnung Road, driving the Chinese all the way back to the Soyang River in central Korea by March 21. Patrols chased guerrillas out of rear areas while engineers rebuilt bridges and roads that had been washed away by heavy spring rains. There was now a general counteroffensive underway and every private understood the tide of war had turned again. The 7th Division relieved the 1st Marine Division in the Hongchon-Inje

Polar Bears under heavy fire on Hill 364 near T'omok-Kol, May 1951. Medic CPL Leonard Wolper tends the wounds of PVT Roger M. Silvernail. Note that Silvernail's boots extend into the crater of an enemy mortar round, and that his rifle and that of the man just above him on the hill have fixed bayonets, anticipating hand-to-hand combat (U.S. Army photograph by CPL Richard Sarater, National Archives).

area on April 4 and began its attack as part of Operation Rugged the next morning. Five days later, the division was across the 38th Parallel again, capturing the town of Yangge on April 16.

When a Chinese counterattack collapsed the ROK 5th Division, the 7th Division held off a series of Chinese counterattacks against its exposed flank in the Inje-Hamyang-ni area between April 23 and 27. On May 1, the 7th Infantry Division was transferred to IX Corps control, taking up positions along Line No-Name just south of the Hongchon River. The UN counteroffensive resumed on May 20, recapturing Chunchon and Hwa-chon by the end of the month. Several thousand demoralized, half-starved Chinese troops surrendered to the division. It was becoming evident that the Chinese had outrun their supply lines.

Hell Hill

On June 4, the 31st Infantry Regiment penetrated Chinese lines near the Hwachon Reservoir and took the heights overlooking the town of Kumhwa at the Iron Triangle's

Above: Men of Companies E and F, 2nd Battalion, 31st Infantry Regiment, raise the American flag after they have taken their objective, Hill 300, near Hwachon, 31 May 1951. *Left:* SGT Cliff L. Tate (Rogersville, Alabama) 31st Infantry Regiment, 7th Infantry Division and a Korean interpreter interrogate a Chinese prisoner at Hwachon, Korea. SGT Tate is asking for information about a buddy captured by the prisoner's unit near the Chosin Reservoir in December. Photograph taken 16 June 1951 (both U.S. Army photographs, National Archives).

apex before its attack was halted. The regiment's attack started quietly enough, but soon ran into a buzz saw. I Company's action is illustrative. At 3 p.m. on June 5, I Company, initially in reserve near the village of Hwachon-Myon, was ordered to take the largest hill (later dubbed "Hell Hill") overlooking the reservoir. Artillery pounded the crest while riflemen trudged up the long, steep slope. Sergeant Charles Bielecki, a squad leader with the 2nd Platoon, recalls that midway up the hill, someone gave the order to fix bayonets. Soon afterward, artillery fire was lifted and his Commanding Officer, Lieutenant Richard Smock, shouted, "commence firing." Until then, no one had fired on the company and there was no enemy visible to shoot at. Bielecki muttered to himself, "looks like this is going to be a cake walk." It wasn't.

As I Company approached the Chinese trenches, automatic weapons fire erupted all along the hill's crest. Lieutenant Smock was one of the first men hit. He and his runner were both hit in the head and killed instantly. Lieutenant Blair J. Willard immediately took command and the attack continued. Knowing a retreat down the long open hillside would be suicidal, Willard summoned a

Right: Secretary of Defense George C. Marshall tours the front lines. GEN Matthew B. Ridgeway, CINCUNC, and LTG James A. Van Fleet, CG of the 8th U.S. Army, are in the rear of the vehicle, 8 June 1951 (U.S. Army photograph, National Archives). *Below:* Soldiers of the 31st Infantry Regiment examine a captured Japanese 105 mm howitzer near Hwachon, Korea, 15 June 1951 (U.S. Army photograph).

A stretcher bearer comes to the aid of a wounded man of Company E, 2nd Battalion, 31st Infantry, who was hit while advancing on an enemy-held hill near Hwachon, 31 May 1951 (U.S. Army photograph, National Archives).

reserve of strength, leading a charge that overran the enemy trench line with bayonets and rifle butts. As the company moved across open ground toward a second line of trenches, one of Sergeant Bielecki's men warned him of a Chinese soldier on his left, previously hidden from view. He turned and fired, hitting the man several times at close range.

Moments later, the trench came alive. Grenades flew over the parapets by the dozens, followed closely by a blaze of automatic weapons fire. Fortunately, most of the grenades were duds, but automatic weapons fire took its toll. During the dash to the enemy's trenches, the 2nd Platoon's 2nd Squad somehow got out in front of the rest of the company. They soon found themselves surrounded by Chinese troops who hit them with everything they had at close range. Eight men went in and seven quickly went down. Among them was the squad leader, Corporal James C. Toth, a reservist from Atwood, Kansas. A bullet struck him in the forehead as he shouted to PFC Don Monterosso to pull back. Toth's facial expression changed to surprise and he stopped shouting in mid-sentence and crumpled to the ground. Moments later, Monterosso was tossed into the air like a limp rag doll when a grenade exploded at his feet. When he landed, his helmet and rifle were gone and he had no idea which direction to run, but luckily he made the right decision and his mangled legs somehow cooperated.

Seeing a ragged-looking figure coming across the hill toward him, Bielecki raised his rifle to shoot. A terrified voice shouted, "Don't shoot, it's me, Monterosso, please don't shoot." Monterosso was a mess and it was a wonder he was even able to stand, much less run. Both legs were ripped open and bleeding profusely and his trousers were a shredded mass of rags. Medics helped him to safety and began patching him up. He spent the night at the battalion aid station. After a painful evacuation by ambulance over barely passable roads to the 8076th MASH (Swedish), Monterosso was moved by air to Osaka Army Hospital in Japan. After three operations and six weeks in the hospital, he was back on the line in Korea. He soldiered on with I Company until his tour in Korea ended in October 1951. When he departed, he was one of the few men remaining who had gone ashore at Inchon just over a year earlier.

Throughout his life, Don Monterrosso's legs still hurt when winter's icy chill swept across the lakes of his native Michigan. When he died, he had been confined to a wheel chair for two years. Memories of Korea lingered like his wounds, inspiring him to write poetry that commemorated the lives of his fallen comrades. Don's own words in a letter he wrote to the author in 1997 sum it up best:

> I remember all that happened to me in my 14 months and 20 days in the Far East. I also remember faces, but few names. There were so many I never got to know, many of them younger than my 19 years. The faces whose names I will never forget are Corporal Toth, Lieutenant Wilson, Higa, Jaime, Peoples, Captain Joy, Merchant, Bielecki, Jamerino, and Jordan. I am 64 now and a semi-invalid, but in my mind I am forever that 19-year-old infantryman, humping the hills and mountains of Korea with a pack on my back and a rifle in my hand. I came home 44 years ago, but a part of me will always be in Korea. Some nights I still fight the battles, climb the hills, hunch over the fires, wonder how I made it home, and shed tears for those who didn't.

About an hour after the fighting began on "Hell Hill," a company of ROK troops wearing yellow scarves arrived behind I Company to lend their support. Before they ever reached the first trench line, the Chinese sent up four red flares, their signal for a counterattack. As bugles began blowing in the distance, the ROKs ran right back down the hill without firing a shot.

The Chinese counterattack failed to reckon with the fury of I Company's First Sergeant, Benjamin F. Wilson. Born at Vashon, Washington in 1922, he enlisted in the Army in the summer of 1940 and was stationed at Schofield Barracks, Hawaii when the Japanese attacked Pearl Harbor. He went to OCS in 1942 and was commissioned in the Infantry, but when the war was over, he resigned his commission and went home. His departure was only temporary. The Army suited him infinitely better than Washington's lumber mills and he was back in uniform nine months later. Because the Army was thinning its officer ranks and had no room for an experienced lieutenant, he enlisted as a private. He rose quickly through the ranks to become I Company's First Sergeant by the summer of 1951. As a First Sergeant, he could stay well to the rear if he wished, tending to requisitions for rations and ammunition, submitting daily strength reports, and handling the plethora of administrative details that keep a rifle company functioning. He of course did all of that, but he was also a born fighter who couldn't stay out of the action when his troops were in the thick of it.

His Medal of Honor citation reads:

> On June 5, 1951, Company I was committed to attack and secure commanding terrain stubbornly defended by a numerically superior hostile force emplaced in well-fortified positions. When the spearheading element was pinned down by withering hostile fire, Master Sergeant Wilson dashed forward and, firing his rifle and throwing grenades, neutralized the position and killed 4 enemy soldiers. After the assault platoon moved up, occupied the position, and established a base of fire, Wilson led a bayonet attack that reduced the objective and killed 27 more enemy soldiers. While friendly forces were consolidating the newly won gain, the enemy launched a counterattack and Wilson, realizing the imminent threat of being overrun, made a determined lone-man charge, killing 7 and wounding

2 of the enemy, and routing the remainder in disorder. After the position was organized, he led an assault, carrying to within approximately 15 yards of the final objective when enemy fire halted the advance. He ordered the platoon to withdraw and although painfully wounded in this action, remained to provide covering fire. During an ensuing counterattack, the commanding officer and 1st Platoon Leader became casualties. Unhesitatingly, Wilson charged the enemy ranks and fought valiantly, killing 3 enemy soldiers with his rifle before it was wrested from his hands. He then annihilated 4 others with his entrenching tool. His courageous action enabled his comrades to reorganize and effect an orderly withdrawal. While directing evacuation of the wounded, he suffered a second wound, but elected to remain on the position until assured that all of his men had reached safety.

Sergeant Francis Monfette, a squad leader from Decatur, Georgia, was badly wounded during the final assault and was lying exposed in the open, forward of the trench line when the Chinese counterattacked. A medic tried to dash to his aid and was cut down in the attempt. Another managed to crawl out to him and drag him to safety. He had been hit sixteen times but clung feebly to life until the next morning. For over an hour the fighting swirled around the barren hilltop with the combatants hopelessly intermixed, often fighting at ranges of fifteen to twenty feet and sometimes fighting hand to hand with whatever they could swing or throw when they ran out of ammunition. Charles Bielecki recalls feeling someone push him abruptly from behind. When he turned to see who it was, he found a Chinese soldier's bloody arm and shoulder on the ground behind him, but there was no owner in sight. An artillery or mortar round must have torn the man's arm off and propelled it across the hilltop.

The fight took down a high percentage of leaders. Around the same time Lieutenant Smock was hit, Lieutenant Tally J. "Bugs" Sheppard, I Company's 1st Platoon Leader, was killed by automatic weapons fire. Sheppard was popular with his men and his loss was sorely felt. He was a small town boy from Lucas County, Ohio, near Toledo, who helped his family run a general merchandise store. He talked endlessly about going back there when his tour of duty ended. Like thirteen other members of the 3d Battalion, his future ended on a hot, barren hillside in central Korea that day. Platoon Sergeant Bill Rowland kept his 2nd Platoon together, keeping his men from bunching up, shifting the fires of key weapons, directing the redistribution of ammunition, directing the evacuation of casualties, and the myriad of other things an experienced infantry NCO does instinctively in combat. He was a rock on whom all could rely.

The rock of rocks, First Sergeant Ben Wilson, was being carried down the hill on a stretcher as the battle neared its climax. When his stretcher bearers set him down to rest, Wilson, in obvious pain, arose from the stretcher and trudged back up the hill without a word. No one could tell him he did not belong there. Everyone understood that he would rather stay with his company than suffer the indignity of being carried to an aid station.

With the Chinese appearing on the hill in staggering numbers, it became apparent to Lieutenant Willard that his unit might soon be cut off and destroyed if it continued to cling to "Hell Hill's" summit. He called in mortar and artillery fire and as it became effective, he gave the order to pull back, adding, "I don't want anybody turning and running." Some did turn and run, but most dutifully backed down the hill, firing up at the Chinese as they poured over I Company's former positions. Incoming artillery kept the Chinese down long enough for the company to escape and dig in on a nearby ridgeline as evening fell.

I Company again attacked "Hell Hill" on June 6. Just one day after the exploit that earned him the Medal of Honor, First Sergeant Ben Wilson killed 33 more Chinese soldiers with his rifle, bayonet, and hand grenades in a similar one-man assault. In the process, he reopened the wounds he suffered the day before and was finally evacuated to a hospital. He was again recommended for the Medal of Honor, but Army policy prohibited any man from being awarded more than one. Wilson received the Distinguished Service Cross instead and was commissioned when he returned to the States. He retired from the Army as a major in 1960 and died in Hawaii in 1988.

One day after Ben Wilson's second one-man war, on June 7, 1951, PFC Jack G. Hanson of F Company earned the Medal of Honor at nearby Pachi-dong. Jack was born on 18 September 1930 at Escatawpa, Mississippi, and entered the Army at Galveston, Texas, in the fall of 1950 as the Korean War was in its opening months. He was assigned to F Company, 2nd Battalion 31st Infantry, 7th Infantry Division on his arrival in Korea in the spring of 1951. His Medal of Honor citation reads:

> PFC Hanson, a machine gunner with the 1st Platoon, Company F, distinguished himself by conspicuous gallantry and intrepidity above and beyond the call of duty. F Company, in defensive positions on two strategic hills separated by a wide saddle, was relentlessly attacked at approximately 0300 hours, the brunt of the attack striking the divide within range of PFC Hanson's machine gun. In the initial phase of the action, 4 riflemen were wounded and evacuated and the numerically superior enemy, advancing under cover of darkness, infiltrated and posed an imminent threat to the company command post and 1st platoon. When his platoon received orders to move to a more secure position, PFC Hanson voluntarily remained behind to provide protective fire for the withdrawal. During the withdrawal, PFC Hanson's assistant gunner and 3 riflemen were wounded and crawled to safety, leaving Hanson manning a lone-man defense. After the 1st Platoon reorganized, it counterattacked and restored control of its original positions at 0530 hours. PFC Hanson's body was found lying in front of his emplacement, his machine gun ammunition expended, his pistol lying empty in his right hand, a machete with blood on the blade in his left hand, and 22 enemy dead around his position. PFC Hanson's consummate valor, inspirational conduct, and willing self-sacrifice enabled his company to contain the enemy and regain the commanding ground, reflecting lasting glory on himself and the noble traditions of the military service.

Many members of F Company owe Jack Hanson their lives—although dead for 48 years, he lives on in their memory and in the memory of his grateful and proud regiment.

American artillery's preponderance and continuing, determined infantry attacks convinced the badly depleted Chinese that they could no longer hold the Hwachon corridor. As a chilly summer rain reduced visibility and turned the heights overlooking the reservoir into a muddy, blood-soaked version of hell, the Chinese fought a weak rear guard action and quietly slipped away during the morning of June 10. In six days of intense close quarters fighting, 47 Polar Bear soldiers had paid for that desolate string of hills with their lives. As he dug in on "Hell Hill," Sergeant Charles Bielecki suddenly realized that of the 12 men who had been in his squad when they went up to the Chosin Reservoir seven months earlier, he was the only one left. In fact, he was one of fewer than 20 men left in the whole company who had been at Chosin. But where Chosin had been an excruciating debacle that hastened the UN's departure from North Korea, Hwachon was an undeniable victory. American and allied units that had been on the ropes just a few months before had pushed the Chinese back out of South Korea and posed a renewed threat to North Korea. No unit could have been prouder of its role in the reversal of that tide than the men of the Polar Bear Regiment.

On June 23, the 7th Division was pulled off line to serve as IX Corps' reserve. In that role, it occupied and upgraded Line Kansas, a fallback position for the corps. Because its regiments had little time since returning from North Korea to mold its old-timers and

Top: Men of Company E, 2nd Battalion, 31st Infantry, advance up an enemy held hill near Hwachon, 31 May 1951 (U.S. Army photograph, National Archives). *Bottom:* CPT Joseph B. Conmy (Pleasantville, New York) and CPT Richard Mitchell (Santa Ana, California) inspect a vehicle recaptured from the Chinese Communists at Hwachon, Korea after their unit, the 31st Infantry Regiment, lost it at the Chosin Reservoir the previous December. Note the unit identification on the bumper; 16 June 1951 (U.S. Army photograph).

replacements into real teams, the division wisely used its time in reserve to conduct unit and individual proficiency training.

Peace Talks but No Peace

The UN summer counteroffensive of 1951 seemed to have had a profound effect on China's assessment of its armies' prospects. Its most experienced units, veterans of the decades-long Chinese Civil War, had nearly evaporated in seven months of constant hard fighting. The winter of 1950–51 sent several division equivalents of China's ill-clad peasant soldiers to the grave from frostbite and hypothermia. Somehow the Chinese managed to continue replacing their losses, but they could not adequately feed or supply them. The sustained onslaught of UN forces all across the peninsula created the real possibility that the Chinese Army could soon be crushed in Central Korea, no matter how many men China rushed across the Yalu. UN forces were simply moving too fast for the Chinese to establish tenable new positions. Worse, the UN had complete control of the air, seriously hindering movement of supplies and replacements on North Korea's ruined roads and rails. Consultations with Stalin made it clear that China could expect little help from the Soviet Union if its defense of North Korea collapsed. It was time to start talking peace while China still held half of the peninsula.

After armistice talks began on July 10, 1951, the battle line in central Korea changed only a few miles in either direction throughout the war's remainder. Each side tried to improve its positions by capturing or vigorously defending key terrain but the days of

COL W.J. McCaffrey, Commanding Officer of 31st Infantry Regiment, congratulates SFC Maurice Melancony, 3rd Battalion, 31st Infantry Regiment, after awarding him the Silver Star during ceremonies held north of Hwachon (U.S. Army photograph, National Archives).

MG Claude B. Ferenbaugh (left), CG of the 7th Infantry Division, congratulates COL William J. McCaffrey CO, 31st Infantry Regiment, 7th Infantry Division, after awarding him the 2nd Oak Leaf Cluster to the Silver Star during ceremonies near Yanggu, Korea, 27 October 1951 (U.S. Army photograph, National Archives).

deep offensives to the north or south were over. No one predicted at the time that the war would drag on for another two years. The talks were made possible by two factors: the UN decided it was no longer worth the human cost of going north again and China had badly overextended its Army and needed time to refit and dig in.

The UN Command, rather than collapsing after its rout from North Korea, had become stronger. More nations were sending troops to Korea while American and ROK divisions that had nearly been destroyed in late 1950, were hitting back surprisingly hard. Taking full advantage of their superior firepower and mobile logistics, UN forces were driving the Chinese and their North Korean partners steadily back up the peninsula and could easily have made another run for Pyongyang and Wonsan if things continued the way they were going in 1951's first six months. If those two cities had been recaptured, North Korea could not have remained a viable nation. It would have been cramped in the mountains north of the Chong'chon River with insufficient agriculture to feed itself, no east-west transportation routes to tie it together, and little more than the demolished cities of Hungnam and Hamhung to support heavy industry. China's leaders had made it evident that they were willing to pay practically any price to keep democracy away from their doorstep. Neither the UN nor the Truman Administration was willing to pay the blood tax for capturing and holding an additional third of that miserable peninsula or pushing all the way to the Yalu again. Thus, young men on both sides bled and died while old men argued over arcane details on flat maps.

After nearly two months in reserve, the 7th Division returned to the front line on August 7, 1951. It took two days to relieve the 24th Infantry Division due to conditions that could charitably be called daunting. Fall rains had again turned central Korea's highlands to mud. Streams winding their way swiftly down mountain valleys brought flooding everywhere. Bridges were washed out and the constant rain, mixed with morning mists,

Opposite, top: His Eminence Francis Cardinal Spellman celebrates Christmas Mass at the CP of the 31st Infantry Regiment, Heartbreak Ridge, Korea 25 December 1951.

Bottom: Taking their Christmas meal at the CP of the 31st Infantry Regiment, Heartbreak Ridge are (L to R) MG W.B. Palmer, CG of 10th U.S. Corps; His Eminence Francis Cardinal Spellman; COL Noel M. Cox, CO of 31st Infantry Regiment, who later would be wounded in action; GEN James A. Van Fleet, CG of 8th U.S. Army; and MG Lyman L. Lemnitzer, CG of 7th Infantry Division, 25 December 1951 (both U.S. Army photographs, National Archives).

made it difficult to operate. On August 26, the division conducted a series of limited objective attacks to establish patrol bases in front of Line Wyoming. The attacks were also intended to break up a Chinese buildup along the Pukhan River. To gain information, the division's probing attacks established new outposts from which constant patrols could gather new information on enemy dispositions. The Chinese did not sit back and take the attacks lightly. They responded with probing attacks of their own to try to regain hills they lost.

On September 21, Operation Cleaver, a fast-moving tank-infantry raid, was launched against the eastern end of the Iron Triangle. The offensive positioned the UN Command for another big push up the center if ordered to do so. On October 5, the 7th Division went back into reserve. On October 23, the division went back on line, rejoining X Corps to relieve the 2nd Infantry Division northeast of the Hwachon Reservoir. Along Line Minnesota, the division concentrated on improving its positions, building bunkers and communications trenches to protect against a renewed Chinese offensive. The give and take along the line took its toll a few men at a time. Patrols went out, sometimes getting ambushed and sometimes ambushing Chinese patrols or raiding their bunkers. The Chinese did the same, probing constantly for weak spots and periodically sending out larger units in attempts to breach the UN line.

15 Central Korea, 1952

The Year Dawns

During January 1952, the 31st Infantry held the left half of the Division sector. The Columbian Battalion joined the regiment near the end of the month. Patrol actions continued until February 5, when the regiment went into reserve. On February 23, the 7th Division was relieved on line by the 25th Division and returned to IX Corps control near Taegong-ni. Regimental and battalion exercises were conducted until March 17 when the 31st Infantry was detached to X Corps to perform a rear area security role.

On February 1, 1952, an F Company attack on an enemy bunker complex was repulsed, leaving three wounded men stranded under heavy enemy fire. First Lieutenant Isidro G. Urbano of Lane, California, G Company's Executive Officer, organized a litter team to rescue the wounded soldiers. Despite enemy mortar fire, he led his team to the bunker's vicinity to rescue the wounded. As the team was treating the first casualty, they heard a faint call for help from another. Under protective fire from his team, Lieutenant Urbano rushed to the wounded man, administered first aid, and carried him to protective cover. Disregarding enemy fire, he rushed back to the bunker to retrieve the third man, a rifleman who had been killed but no one could be sure at the time. For his heroism, Lieutenant Urbano was awarded the Bronze Star for Valor. The award in no way matched the esteem in which he was held by his troops who revere him still. He was killed in action on September 18, 1952, while commanding G Company.

In trenches and bunkers all along the mountainous ridges and peaks of Central Korea, soldiers on both sides stood watch in the bitter cold. The Chinese wore rubber-soled canvas sneakers wrapped in rags to insulate them against the frozen ground. Americans generally wore several pairs of wool socks under leather combat boots, often stuffed inside rubber galoshes or "shoepacs" that caused men's feet to sweat. Chinese soldiers wore lightweight quilted cotton jackets and trousers with wrapped leggings to keep body heat from escaping. Americans wore heavy wool shirts and trousers over cotton underwear or long-johns, often wearing a cotton field jacket and parka and white camouflage cover over the whole mess. Both sides wore pile caps with turned-up bills and long ear flaps that tied under the chin. Over that, an American soldier was supposed to wear a steel helmet and helmet liner. It would be hard to say that either side stayed warm, but it was certain that American uniforms were not as well designed to give a soldier freedom of motion.

Patrols were sent by both sides into the intervening valleys to discover each other's weaknesses, learn what the other side was up to, and sometimes to ambush opposing

31st Heavy Tank Company on the move (U.S. Army photograph, National Archives).

patrols. To many Americans on the line, there was little sense to what they were told to do. The front remained generally static, so why should a soldier risk his life going out on a patrol to capture a Chinese soldier who had no more clue about what was going on than he did? Why expend lives trying to take hills that were in the shadow of higher hills still held by the Chinese? Why cling to bald, isolated fingers of ridges that had no economic or military value? Why not just booby trap and mine the more isolated outposts and call in artillery when someone intruded and set off a trip flare, mine, or booby trap? The Chinese seemed adept at tunneling into rock, weathering the artillery and air strikes, and coming back to well camouflaged bunkers when American infantry got too close. But sometimes their tunnels caved in from the concussion, trapping hundreds in the earth's dark womb. In contrast, Americans tended to build on the surface and only tunnel occasionally on the backside of hills. Atop the ridges were sandbag bunkers built with heavy timbers. Visible to the naked eye, they were artillery magnets in a tree-barren landscape. Bunkers were connected by World War I–like communications trenches, complete with parapets, duckboard flooring, and timber-reinforced sides. When enemy artillery came in, sandbag bunkers often collapsed, crushing or suffocating people inside. The walls of trenches collapsed and duckboard flooring added more splinters to the flying debris. There were no safe havens on the line for either side.

Interior of a Battalion Aid Station, March 30, 1953 (U.S. Army Signal Corps Photograph, National Archives).

On the bunker line it was clear to every man in the grade of captain and below that higher headquarters had too little to do in this static "no win" war. They appeared to plan for the sake of planning and most of their plans and directives seemed to cost lives and limbs without yielding any real advantage. When the "brass" came to "visit" with their inevitable bevvy of well-dressed, clean-looking straphangers, many seemed to pay more attention to how tidy soldiers, trenches, and bunkers looked than how well cared for the troops were, how tactically effective their dispositions and defense plans were, or what could be done to improve the tactical situation. There was seemingly a stateside-like preoccupation with administration, positive statistics, professional briefings, nice-looking vehicles, and showy command posts. If that was the sense of priority conveyed by furrowed brows or offhand comments during the rare visits of army, corps, or division commanders, it quickly flowed down the command chain and nearly everyone eventually complied, even if they hated it and had other ideas about what was important.

Not all visitors to the line were senior officers. In early February, Bill Mauldin, the cartoonist who sketched "Willie and Joe" cartoons during World War II, visited I Company. He was doing a series of articles and sketches for *Collier's* magazine and needed the down-to-earth feeling of an infantryman. The men rigged up an extra bunk for him

Rocket team of the 2nd Rocket Team, Artillery Battery, 40th Infantry Division, loads rocket launchers at their post in the 31st Infantry Regiment, 7th Infantry Division area as they prepare for action against the Chinese Communist Forces near Kumwha, 7 May 1952 (U.S. Army photograph).

in a squad bunker and he ate Army chow out of the same mess kits as the troops he lived with. He spent his first day with I Company watching artillery, mortars, and recoilless rifles pound suspected enemy positions on the opposite side of the valley. His experiences appeared in the 26 April 1952 edition of *Collier's*. While Mauldin's letter to "Willie" is humorous fiction, the events he described are real and so are the characters. They included Lieutenant Murry Kleinfeld (a new officer in I Company), Sergeant Steve Heardman (squad leader), Corporal Rex Munson (radio operator), PFC Donald Queen (rifleman), and PFC Frank Silva (BAR man).

Captain George Casey commanded I Company at the time of Mauldin's visit. Casey later rose to the grade of Major General and was killed in Vietnam while commanding the 1st Cavalry Division. Lieutenant Lee H. Miller, I Company's 2nd Platoon Leader, was responsible for hosting Mauldin's visit. Miller left the Army after the war and wrote a book about his experiences but never published it. Captivated by the manuscript his mother gave him after his father's death, Miller's son Keith published the book, *Korea's Sleeping Ghosts*, in memory of his father and those who served with him.

The regiment returned to 7th Division control on April 23, just in time to relieve the 2nd Infantry Division in the Kumhwa area. As the Chinese became more aggressive with mortar and artillery attacks, bunker lines were reinforced and camouflaged. Patrols became steadily more dangerous as both sides attempted to lure each other into traps.

On July 2, 1952, a C Company patrol was ambushed as it was returning to friendly lines. In the initial outburst of fire, the patrol leader and seven others were wounded and PFC Robert D. Hanna was killed. Lieutenant Anthony F. Silveira volunteered to lead a relief force to rescue the patrol. Acting as point man, he led his men to the scene of the ambush and in the face of continuing fire, began locating and recovering the wounded. After ensuring that all had been recovered and their wounds were treated, he led a rear

Chaplain (CPT) Kenny Lynch conducts services north of Hwachon, Korea, for men of Company B, 31st Regimental Combat Team, 7th Infantry Division (U.S. Army photograph, National Archives).

guard action while the wounded were helped to safety. For his actions, he received the Bronze Star for Valor.

The 31st Infantry remained on line until September 24, when the 32nd Infantry relieved it. In October, action picked up all along the line as the Chinese established strong outposts to protect their main line and the UN Command conducted a series of probing actions to seek weak spots in the thickened Chinese line. If it made no sense to make another try to go north in October 1951, it made even less sense to try it a year later after the Chinese had been given the gift of time to reinforce, resupply and dig in deep.

Triangle Hill

The 31st Infantry launched Operation Showdown on October 14, 1952, to seize Triangle Ill (Hill 598) and a set of twin peaks nicknamed Jane Russell Hill near Kumhwa. In preparation for the attack, Lieutenant Urbano of G Company was killed while leading a patrol up the "bowling alley" toward Triangle Hill. Lieutenant Charles Shields, who commanded a smoke generator detachment supporting the 2nd Battalion at the time, remembers Urbano as a great guy loved by the men he led. Urbano's patrol set the stage for the most violent and costly fight since the regiment returned from North Korea nearly two years earlier.

First Lieutenant Edward R. Schowalter of Company A earned the Medal of Honor during fierce fighting at Triangle Hill on October 14. Ed was a native of New Orleans, graduated from Virginia Military Institute, and joined the 31st Infantry in Korea in 1952. His Medal of Honor citation says best what happened:

First Lieutenant Schowalter, commanding Company A, distinguished himself by conspicuous gallantry and indomitable courage above and beyond the call of duty in action against the enemy. Committed to attack and occupy a key approach to his battalion's objective, the 1st platoon of his company came under vicious small arms, grenade, and mortar fire within 50 yards of the enemy held strongpoint, halting the advance and inflicting several casualties. The 2nd Platoon moved up in support, and although wounded, Lieutenant Schowalter spearheaded the assault. Nearing the objective he was severely wounded by a grenade but, refusing medical aid, he led his men into the trenches and began routing the enemy from their bunkers with grenades. Suddenly a burst of fire from a hidden cove off the trench wounded him again. Although suffering from his wounds, he refused to relinquish command and continued directing and encouraging his company until the objective was secured.

Later, Ed served twice in Vietnam and eventually retired as a colonel.

A day after Ed Schowalter's heroic action, PFC Ralph E. Pomeroy of Company E also earned the Medal of Honor. Pomeroy was born on March 26, 1930, at Quinwood,

Medics work on a wounded soldier (U.S. Army photograph, National Archives).

West Virginia, where he entered the Army in the spring of 1951. He was assigned to the 31st Infantry on his arrival in Korea in the fall of 1951. His Medal of Honor citation reads:

PFC Pomeroy, a machine gunner with Company E, distinguished himself by conspicuous gallantry and indomitable courage above and beyond the call of duty in action against the enemy. While his comrades were consolidating on a key terrain feature, he manned a machine gun at the end of a communication trench on the forward slope to protect the platoon's flank and prevent a surprise attack. When the enemy attacked through a ravine leading directly to his firing position, he immediately opened fire on the advancing troops, inflicting a heavy toll and blunting the assault. At this juncture the enemy directed intense concentrations of mortar fire on his position in an attempt to neutralize his gun. Despite withering fire and bursting shells, he maintained his heroic stand and poured crippling fire into the ranks of the hostile force until a mortar burst severely wounded him and rendered his gun mount inoperable. Quickly removing the hot, heavy weapon, he cradled it in his arms and, moving forward with grim determination, raked the attacking forces with a hail of fire. Although wounded a second time, he pursued his relentless course until his ammunition was expended and then, using the machine gun as a club, he courageously closed with the enemy in hand-to-hand combat until he was mortally wounded.

Medal of Honor winner Ralph E. Pomeroy. A member of E Company, 31st Infantry Regiment, 7th Infantry Division, he was from Quinwood, West Virginia. When he earned his posthumous award, he was 22 years old (Wikimedia Commons).

The 7th Division cycled battalions forward as the Chinese launched a series of determined counterattacks to retake the hills. Triangle Hill was lost and the bodies of the men who died there were not recovered. Sergeant First Class Richard E. Fordyce of C Company may have been the last American on Triangle Hill by the evening of October 14. He occupied the hill's crest with three other men, all wounded, and was unaware of the withdrawal order given earlier that evening. His little group came off the hill around midnight because they were out of ammunition and American artillery was targeting their area. There were still a lot of American bodies on the hill at the time and the artillery bombardment was so severe that some bodies were probably completely destroyed. He was certain that the Chinese did not take any prisoners that day.

On November 14, the 7th Division was relieved by the 25th Division and went into Eighth Army reserve at Kapyong. After a period of extensive training, the division returned to the line on December 27 1952, relieving the 2nd Infantry Division in the Chorwon Valley. The 31st Infantry Regiment held the right half of the division line.

16 The Bloodiest Year: 1953

Another Year of War Dawns

On January 25, 1953, Company E, supported by air strikes and artillery, raided T-Bone Hill, but was repelled. The 17th Infantry relieved the regiment on line the next day. On February 27, the 31st Infantry returned to the line, relieving the 32nd Infantry. The Chinese launched a series of five attacks against the 7th Division line, driving the Colombian Battalion off of Old Baldy on March 23. For the next two days, the 31st Infantry counterattacked, but could not regain the position. Sergeant Buddy G. Jenkins of A Company was on adjacent Westview OP the night the Chinese took Old Baldy. His company was being replaced by the Colombians when the attack came. Amid total confusion, A Company managed to regroup and counterattack against a Chinese unit heading toward Pork Chop Hill.

Chinese attacks resumed on April 16, trying for three days to throw the 31st Infantry off of Pork Chop Hill, a place immortalized in a movie of the same name starring Gregory Peck as Lieutenant Joe Clemons. Clemons earned the Distinguished Service Cross in that action, leading the men of K Company to Herculean exertions in see-saw fighting to retake lost portions of the hill. The hill was originally defended by E Company, commanded by First Lieutenant Thomas V. Harrold. When the Chinese overran sections of the position, they were driven out in fighting at close quarters. Rifle butts, entrenching tools, and even bare hands came into play as men struggling to stay alive fought each other to the death. Companies K and L were thrown into the fight to regain control of lost portions of E Company's trench line. What follows is a paraphrased version of S.L.A. Marshall's account of K Company's role in the operation. Marshall was at the time an Operations Analyst for the Eighth Army.

Regiment knew little of what had occurred on Pork Chop Hill. They and 2nd Battalion only knew that E Company's trench line had been overrun. What little information they had came from Lieutenant Harrold who had been unable to leave his bunker. Regiment recognized that the Chinese on the hill might soon be reinforced through the valley. K Company, less its detached weapons platoon, numbered 135 men commanded by Lieutenant Joseph G. Clemons, Jr. The men had spent a quiet night in a reserve position behind Hill 347. They had a late meal and a few hours' sleep. At 0330, Clemons was ordered to move the company to an attack position behind Hill 200, just south of Pork Chop. The trucks were already on their way but K Company was ready when the convoy arrived. The men were loaded down with ammunition. Each rifleman had a full clip loaded, all ammo pouches full, and carried an extra bandolier. Each rifleman also carried

A view of Old Baldy as seen from an outpost of Companies D and L of the 31st Infantry Regiment, 7th Infantry Division following the signing of the armistice agreement between UNC Forces and Communist Forces fighting in Korea, 27 July 1953 (U.S. Army photograph, National Archives).

three or more grenades. The six BARs in each platoon had twelve magazines per weapon. Each light machine gun crew carried five boxes of ammo. As recommended by Lieutenant Harrold, each platoon brought a flamethrower and a 3.5-inch rocket launcher.

When Company K unloaded from the trucks behind Hill 200, Lieutenant Colonel John N. Davis, the 3d Battalion Commander, was waiting with instructions. He suggested that Lieutenant Clemons attack Pork Chop's rear slope with two platoons abreast and one in reserve. The situation on the summit was not briefed to Clemons because Davis did not know what was up there. Clemons was left with the impression that the Chinese held the hill and his own men could fire without constraint. While K Company assaulted the rear, two platoons of L Company would attack up a ridge on Pork Chop's right side. This risked a cross-fire at the point where the converging forces would be in greatest danger from the Chinese.

American variable time fused artillery fire was blasting the top of the hill. Davis told Clemons, "Tell me when you're ready to go and I'll have it lifted." Clemons got his platoon leaders together and said, "Hit the hill hard and get to the top as fast as you can go. Success depends on speed. We must close before daylight." They moved out with 2nd Platoon on the right, 1st on the left, and 3d in reserve. The lead platoons walked in column for 400 yards down the road to the assault line at the foot of Pork Chop. From there, it was only 170 yards to the nearest fighting bunkers but the trek uphill was very steep, the slope was rocky and cratered, and it was the darkest hour of the night.

By the time the 2nd Platoon reached the lower side of the five-layered concertina wire that circled the hill, SFC Walter Kuzmick felt that the too-brisk start had been a mistake. His legs felt like rubber. His men, panting hard, tugged at rocks and shrubs to assist them up the slope. The more heavily burdened men straggled, separating the heavier weapons from the riflemen they were intended to support. Despite his sense of foreboding, Kuzmick yelled, "Keep going! Make it snappy!" The men in front found gaps in the wire barricade cut by shellfire. They slipped through, following Kuzmick onto the hill. In the dark he didn't notice that the heavy weapons carriers had quit moving, dropped their burdens, and lay down next to the wire. For the next hour, he would be too busy to notice their absence.

Enemy artillery and mortars responded to the attack but dropped harmlessly into the valley, nearly 100 yards behind the line of departure. Because the barbed wire confronting the 1st Platoon was still intact, men lay across the bands, allowing others to use them as a bridge. Though the company completed the climb without incident so far, it had taken them 29 minutes to travel the 170 yards from the assault line to the top. Chinese artillery hit them immediately when they topped the rise. They fired for 10 minutes, then lifted for 10 minutes, a routine they continued throughout the fight.

The first man to enter the bunker line, Corporal William H. Bridges, saw two Chinese rise from among the rocks and fire directly down at 1st Platoon with submachine guns. He yelled a warning and dove into the trench. The burst cut down five men behind him. Private Rudolph Gordon reached the trench at almost the same moment. Turning left, the two men headed for the second bunker down the line. Three grenades came at them from behind its far wall. They all fell short. Gordon and Bridges grenaded back. Protected by the bunker, the Chinese grenadiers made poor targets, exposing their heads and shoulders just long enough to heave a grenade.

As more 1st Platoon men reached the trench, two squads tried to form up on either side of the first bunker, though in the narrow trench they were vulnerable. To protect the platoon, Corporal Arsenio Correa jumped onto the parapet with his light machine gun and fired two boxes of ammo at the bunker door, only 25 yards away. Enemy grenadiers focused their attention on him, but he was safely beyond their range. Taking advantage of the diversion, SFC Lewis J. Hankey, Corporal Wilfred Volk, and Private Pak Song crawled

1LT McCall, Company M, 31st Infantry Regiment, 7th Infantry Division, brings in enemy prisoners captured during the battle for Pork Chop Hill, Korea, 17 April 1953 (U.S. Army photograph, National Archives).

along the parapet to within 5 yards of the bunker. From there, they threw ten grenades over the wall and the Chinese answered with their own. The attack silenced the Chinese, but in the exchange, Pak was hit in the head by the same explosion that shattered Hankey's leg. Volk treated them where they fell and then helped them to safety behind the bunker while he rejoined the fight.

Kuzmick's men encountered their first fire as they neared the chow bunker, some yards downhill from the main trench. Fortunately, the fire was high and did no harm. On reaching the main trench, Kuzmick kept his squads moving abreast, intending to mop up the ditch while securing the ground on both sides as he swept toward the former E Company Command Post. He took the precaution because it was still dark and he worried that if he moved his troops in column in the trench the Chinese might come in behind them and cut them off.

On the outer wing, Sergeant Rollin Johnson's squad became strung out as some men sought cover to escape the fire sweeping across the slope. Lieutenant Robert S. Cook accompanied Johnson to help control the maneuver toward the CP. Walking along the rampart with Private Edgar P. Bordelon, he got some distance ahead. At the first bunker, he encountered one of E Company's KATUSAs who had survived the night by hugging the sandbag revetment. The three advanced another 15 yards to a point where Cook could see the CP bunker's door. He saw no activity. Bordelon fired a few rounds at it with his carbine. A voice from inside pleaded, "Hold your fire! We're GIs." Wanting to see more, Cook did not instantly warn the skirmishers behind him that there might be GIs in the bunkers ahead.

Meanwhile, Sergeant Norbert Huffman's squad was still struggling up the hill. The slope was an obstacle course of rock outcroppings and shell craters. Here and there were smoke-blackened tree stumps that looked like sitting men in the half-light. Kuzmick tried to regulate the advance of his center with the flankers, but it was impossible. Huffman got to within 12 yards of the rear of the CP bunker without ever seeing it. There was a prone Chinese with a light machine gun on the bunker roof. Huffman was still crawling forward when a cluster of five or six grenades, thrown from the far side of the bunker, landed on and around him. One blew off his right hand and fragments penetrated his skull, neck, and chest. As he lay wounded, the machine gunner fired a quick burst at him.

Cook had just jumped to the rampart, waving his arms toward Kuzmick's men and yelling, "Come on! Keep moving! We've got it made!" He still said nothing of the Americans in the CP. Near the bunker where Cook had found the KATUSA, a Chinese crawling along the rampart heaved a grenade. Another came from behind the CP. The two grenades exploded simultaneously between Cook and the KATUSA, shattering one of Cook's legs and hitting the Korean in the stomach and groin. Before anyone could fire, five Chinese jumped from behind the bunker and into the trench, disappearing among the debris. Private Thomas M. Dugan stopped to put a tourniquet on Huffman's stump. Seeing that he was unconscious and bleeding from numerous wounds, Dugan carried him back to the chow bunker where he could be treated by medics and evacuated to safety.

The men measured up to some tough standards. Although exhausted from their ascent up the slope, they had pressed on through an artillery barrage, advancing without hesitation to overrun a succession of enemy-held positions. Although nothing in their training could prepare them for what they encountered, they responded like professionals. No one had told them that they would get within 20 feet of the enemy and still not see him.

Kuzmick dashed toward the CP bunker door, intending to grenade it. Just as he neared the door, Lieutenant Attridge of E Company looked out. His head was bandaged and his arm was cocked to throw a grenade. The sight of Attridge stopped Kuzmick cold. Clemons, right on his heels, was so astonished he just gaped. They had not been told about the many E Company wounded in the CP bunker. They thought E Company had been wiped out and they would find no live friends on the hill. Before a word was spoken, three rounds of artillery landed among them. Their source was never determined. Because the Chinese fire had lifted a few minutes before, the men concluded they were "shorts" from their own supporting batteries. One round exploded in the bunker door, giving Attridge his second head wound. The others fell about 25 yards behind Kuzmick, wounding three of his Koreans.

Until then the flankers had kept pressing despite their weariness. But the impression that their own guns had fired on them had a greater impact on their morale than the wounding of Cook and Huffman. Shock stopped their momentum at the worst possible moment. Kuzmick's men lay inert, bewildered and listless. For several minutes no one made an attempt to do anything. The flank as a whole never got going again. "In war, a resolute soul can bind the excited minds of many men in a kind of bloody mesmerism. But one small accident can in a twinkling, snap that chain of force."[1]

> Private Samuel K. Maxwell went alone into the CP bunker. There were five wounded men inside, one missing a leg. Attridge was still conscious. Lieutenant Harrold told Maxwell to return to the fight. He would look after his own men. The sun was edging over the horizon, bathing the scene in daylight's first rays. Private George Atkins, from the 2nd Platoon's rear guard, brought news to Clemons. From a high knob, he had looked westward and had seen many Chinese moving toward the hill from the direction of Princeton OP. Clemons called on the radio. "Would the artillery plaster Princeton OP and drop a curtain of fire in the valley between Pork Chop and Hasakkol to choke off reinforcement? The answer was yes, but the requested fire never came."[2]

A few of Kuzmick's men started moving down the trench. Before they could pass the CP bunker, they were stopped by automatic weapons fire coming from downhill on their right. The fire was from L Company, attacking up the ridge. Kuzmick's men tried to signal L Company to shut it off, but the fire was too intense to allow anyone to stand exposed. It subsided only after the Chinese bled L Company into silence. At this point, K Company lost all group initiative. Any energy that remained was channeled into personal effort. The attack carried on only where resolute individuals engaged in widely separated and almost unrelated actions.

Clemons faced a dilemma. The harder he pressed the right forward, the greater his disorganization. Supply remained unassured, his channels of communication to the outside were narrowing, and his heavy weapons carriers were shirking the fight. He did not have enough able-bodied men to take the hill by storm, but had too many to plead fatal weakness. Those who continued fighting were dangerously dispersed. To withdraw them and regroup would yield hard-won ground to the enemy. It was time to get his house in order, but answers weren't coming very readily. With his Executive Officer, Lieutenant Tsugi Ohashi, he went back to the chow bunker to consider his next move.

On the right of Pork Chop, Sergeant Johnson, joined by Sergeant Robert E. Hoffman, continued to move straight down the trench. They soon reached a bunker where two men from E Company's 3d Platoon had survived the night by playing possum. At dawn three Chinese had discovered them and began to grenade their hiding place. Having snatched a few hours' sleep, the men decided to fight back, although between them they had only one helmet and a dirty carbine that wouldn't fire automatic. They took 15-minute turns at the fire post, one man operating as a sniper while the other stayed down. Their initiative was just enough to keep the Chinese from rushing them.

One of the men motioned to Hoffman and Johnson to move on down the trench to take the Chinese from the flank while he held their attention from the front. By then, several other men had reached the spot. Before Johnson could start his move, seven artillery rounds exploded along the embankment. One silenced the Chinese, but another landed among the Americans. Corporal Robert Rosserelli was an arm's length from Johnson when the first round struck. The explosion sat him down hard on his buttocks and the shock was so violent that he just sat there stunned, certain that his behind had been blown away. Because the trench was partly covered and filled with debris, he temporarily lost sight of Johnson.

Then he heard Johnson say calmly, "Well I'll be damned, I'm wounded." As Johnson stood up, the shoulder of his field jacket was already blood-soaked. Despite what must have been a very painful wound, he called out in a booming voice, "Hoffman, it's time for you to take over." For the next 20 minutes Hoffman could hear him belaboring stragglers farther down the trench. "Damn you, get up there and help Hoffman."

Almost coincidentally, the first flamethrower reached Lieutenant Clemons as Johnson disappeared across the slope. Its operator, PFC William W. Sykes, was given a squad to run interference for him as he advanced toward a bunker 50 yards away on the left side of the hill. Approximately a dozen Chinese were nesting there, some inside and others behind sandbag revetments. The squad moved forward cautiously, spread over both embankments. As they came within throwing distance of the bunker, a shower of grenades landed among them, wounding every member of the squad. The Chinese had quit the bunker, regrouped on higher ground, and grenaded the squad from the flank. Not seeing how it had happened, Sykes continued right down the trench with his flamethrower and flamed the bunker's doorway for a full 30 seconds. As the doorframe caught fire, a grenade landed in the trench, shooting fragments into Sykes' buttocks. He couldn't make his legs move. PFC James Freley helped him from the hill, surprised that Sykes had made his run, gotten hit, and retired without uttering a sound.

Clemons made a rough guess that he had lost at least half of his men. Most had been knocked out by hand grenades or artillery. Apart from the worrisome noise of the enemy's burp guns, they had done little damage. Clemons worried that his men were about out of ammunition, though fanned out as they were, he could only guess. He decided that it was time to bring his reserve platoon into the fight.

Two enemy-occupied bunkers, on opposite sides of the trench and 40 feet apart, had stalled the advance on the right side of the hill. Burp gun fire laced the ditch, the gunners operating from behind bunker walls, grenadiers covering the embankments. Sergeant Hoffman looked at his watch. It was 0745. The company had been on the hill approximately two hours. Its attack had not yet carried more than 200 yards. It was clear to Hoffman that the company was already beyond the point of exhaustion. Some riflemen were dragging their weapons as if too spent to carry them. Others sat in the trench staring vacantly. When NCOs tried to direct them, their words were slurred, as if uttered by sleepwalkers.

But the job was not yet half done. The Chinese still held two-thirds of the trench line, including all of the covered parts of the trench. The artillery had made it easier for the remnants of the two sides to hold their positions. The collapse of a great part of the trench made any sighting along it impossible. Bunker doorframes had broken under the weight of artillery hitting sandbagged roofs. Timbers that had supported the near end of the covered trench were splintered and fallen, closing the trench to observation and giving cover to its defenders. From within the ruins, grenades were hurled at the Americans in surprising numbers, and incessant burp gun fire on both sides of the hill kept them pinned to defilades churned up by the night's shelling.

Feeling that his men were stretched to the breaking point, Clemons saw no choice but to mark time while waiting for help. He was no longer in touch with the outside. The artillery had cut his field telephone wire and his five radios had been knocked out one-by-one. Three of the operators had been hit and evacuated. From the chow bunker, where the wounded were taken back to Hill 200, a half-track was shuttling out the worst cases. Its predecessor had been hit by a mortar round that killed the driver and further wounded two passengers. From Hill 200, casualties were moved onward by litter jeep and helicopter.

L Company, which had fought its way up the right side of the hill, was about to bolster K Company's ranks, but not much. It had started up the ridge with two platoons, totaling 62 men under the command of Lieutenant Forrest J. Crittenden. When Critten-

Medics of the 31st Infantry Regiment, 7th Infantry division unload wounded troops from an M-39 personnel carrier at a forward aid station in Korea. The men were wounded during the fight for Pork Chop Hill, 17 April 1953 (U.S. Army photograph, National Archives).

den was wounded, Lieutenant Homer F. Bechtel promptly took command, but was soon struck down by an enemy hand grenade. When Lieutenant Arthur A. Marshall brought the survivors to join K Company, only 12 remained and they were reduced to 10 by a burst of machine gun fire before they reached the trench.

As the fight slackened around 0800, men on both sides left the trench to seek better positions on the slopes. The smell of death below was overpowering in places. Above, shell holes and large rocks offered a measure of safety. This scrambling brought the two sides closer together, but there was no upsurge in fighting. Both sides were spent. Exhausted, out of water and short of ammunition, men conserved whatever energy and firepower they had left. The weather was cool and clear, one of the season's better days.

At 0814, two squads from G Company 17th Infantry arrived to reinforce K Company. Until then, Clemons did not know that any part of that regiment was anywhere near. As Clemons sent the squads to reinforce the hill's left side, a voice from behind him inquired, "Could you tell me the situation?" Clemons turned to see his brother-in-law, Lieutenant Walter B. Russell, who he thought was still in the States. He shouted in amazement, "What the hell are you doing here?"

Russell, commanding G Company of the 17th, explained that his orders were to assist K and L Companies in mopping up on the hill and then to get back down as soon as possible. Clemons suddenly realized the gulf of comprehension separating his command from higher headquarters. He had only 35 men left from K Company, 10 from L Company and 12 frightened and lightly wounded survivors of E Company who had been rescued from various bunkers. Lieutenant Harrold had already left the hill with the more seriously wounded survivors. Clemons knew the force he had left was incapable of further offensive action and doubted that it could defend very long either.

Suddenly, Chinese artillery and mortars again swept across the slope, joined by an intense barrage of automatic weapons fire. The Chinese had also been reinforced and were getting ready for another push. Lieutenant Marshall with L Company's 10 men and Lieutenant Ess, with the two squads from G Company of the 17th Infantry, took over the left sector. Lieutenant Russell brought the rest of G Company up on the right. Clemons and Ohashi regrouped K Company to hold the center. Throughout the day, the fight continued and the casualties continued to mount.

By late afternoon, only 25 men remained unwounded in K and L Companies together. With Ohashi and Kuzmick, Clemons positioned the survivors in a tight group around the highest point they held on the hill. He then returned to his CP with a runner and a radio they had salvaged and called Lieutenant Colonel Davis at around 1640. He reported, "We have about 20 men left. There is no fight left in this company. If we can't be relieved, we should be withdrawn." Brigadier General Arthur Trudeau, the Assistant Division Commander, was with Davis when the call came in. He would have to come up with reinforcements quickly and get them up the hill before nightfall. He did, relieving the depleted remnant of K Company just after dark. Pork Chop continued to be held, preventing the Chinese from breaking through anywhere along the 7th Division's line despite 15,000 rounds of artillery and repeated assaults.

In May 1953, the 31st Infantry held the left of the 7th Division line, releasing the Colombian Battalion to division control. Constant patrols kept the line active. In June, Outposts Dale and Pork Chop came under renewed enemy pressure, but managed to hold. The Chinese were trying to capture positions that would give them observation vantage points dominating the critical Chorwon Valley. The valley was crucial to both

Aerial view of the Aid Station of the 3rd Battalion, 31st Infantry Regiment, 7th Infantry Division, March 30, 1953 (U.S. Army Signal Corps Photograph National Archives).

sides. For the Chinese and North Koreans, it represented a possible UN invasion corridor opening the way to Wonsan and Pyongyang. For the UN, it represented a Chinese invasion corridor pointed southwest that could isolate Seoul. Neither side could afford to yield high ground since the peace talks at Panmunjom would likely end soon.

From June 10 to June 18, the fight for positional advantage centered on a shell-blasted outpost named Harry. Harry was just another bunker and trench complex atop a barren 1,200-foot hill among the many in central Korea, but its importance was greatly disproportionate to the hill's size. Harry controlled access to the strategic Hang San-ni Valley's northern entrance. If Harry had been lost, the peace process might have changed at Panmunjom because its capture would have given the Chinese a salient pointed toward Seoul, unhinging the UN line. To prevent that from happening, the 31st Infantry Regiment rotated one or two companies to OP Harry each night in a "hold at all costs" mission. To provide some perspective, 1,200 feet is twice the height of the Washington Monument, a healthy trek for the riflemen who slogged up and down the steep slope in the darkness to avoid letting the Chinese know when companies were being rotated.

Harry was only 350 yards from Chinese positions atop higher ground on a series of ridges called Star Hill. The Greek Battalion that had held the outpost before being relieved by the 31st called Harry "The Death Place" because it was regularly blasted by Chinese mortars and artillery whose observers could see every move made by GIs in the OP. Cap-

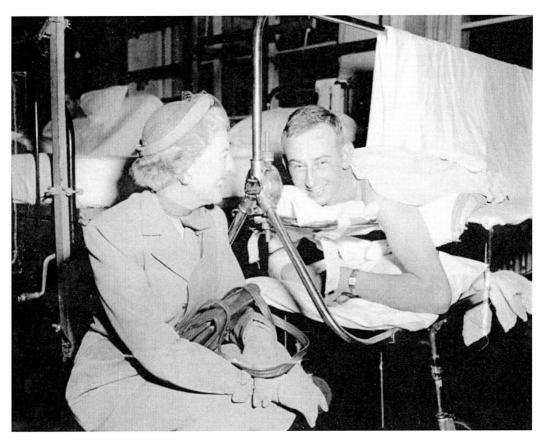

PVT Sylvester Opbroek of C Company, 31st Infantry Regiment, is visited by Mrs. Mark W. Clark, wife of the general, May 12 1953. Opbroek lost a leg from this wound, but went on to graduate from the University of Southern California, becoming a Certified Public Accountant (Association archives).

tain John Holdorf, Commander of E company at the time, remembers Harry as "a barren, scorched, and forbidding looking place that had death written all over it."

On July 6, the Chinese came across the valley again in a coordinated attack against Pork Chop Hill. They penetrated the position repeatedly in five days of bitter fighting, but the 31st held on. By the fifth day of fighting, both sides held portions of the hill and neither could dislodge the other. On July 10, all UN forces were ordered to withdraw from the position, ceding to the Chinese the most bitterly contested piece of real estate in central Korea.

The last action of the war for the Polar Bears came on 26–27 July 1953 at Observation Points (OPs) Westview and Dale overlooking the Chorwon Valley. The OPs were held respectively by K and I Companies of the 31st Infantry. Westview is a low, bald knob connected to Old Baldy by a saddle ridge.[3] It was only large enough to accommodate a platoon but the Chinese were determined to take it. They came charging up the hill three nights before the ceasefire, lugging huge boxes of ammo and rations, giving every indication that they intended to take the hill and keep it. Pouring wave after wave up the hill, they took half of the hill, but L Company counterattacked, driving them back down the trench line in close quarters combat with grenades, small arms, and occasionally rifle

butts. When their grip on the last section of trench was broken, the survivors scurried across the barren 200-yard long saddle back to the safety of Chinese lines on Old Baldy. There, they were chopped to pieces by artillery. For the next two nights, they probed Westview again and again, losing more men in the process. On Monday night, the defenders, some of whom had hardly slept for four days, felt sure the Chinese would come again to try to retrieve the bodies of their dead. At 9:45 p.m., the order came to cease all firing. A minute later, an outguard warned, "They're coming, the Chinks are coming down." No one fired. Weapons that would have been used without hesitation any night before were silent. There was no shouting, no jubilation, only a few muttered prayers and handshakes between men who had seen too many others carried from the battlefield. Suddenly there was peace.

Opposite, top: Moving day, following the signing of the Armistice, July 1953 (U.S. Army photograph, National Archives).

Bottom, left: Members of Company D and Company L, 31st Infantry Regiment, 7th Infantry Division, prepare to move out of their bunkers following the signing of the armistice agreement between UNC Forces and Communist Forces, 27 July 1953 (U.S. Army photograph, National Archives).

Bottom, right: (L to R) CPL Caspar Molinaro and CPL John Baron (both of Gary, Indiana), Company K, 31st Infantry Regiment, 7th Infantry Division, write letters home following the signing of the armistice agreement between UNC Forces and Communist Forces in Korea, 31 July 1953 (U.S. Army photograph, National Archives).

17 The Cold War in Korea: 1953–1987

The Korean War was ended in July 1953 by an armistice, not a peace treaty. In effect, hostilities have continued in Korea ever since, although sporadically and on a smaller scale. The 31st Infantry Regiment remained with the 7th Infantry Division, guarding Seoul's northern approaches. Unlike all other U.S. infantry regiments, it had never served in the continental United States, continuing to earn its nickname, "America's Foreign Legion." Those who served along the DMZ after the armistice were every bit as much in combat as their brothers who fought in Vietnam or who are fighting today in Iraq and Afghanistan. They and their KATUSA and ROK comrades did their duty "on the fence" with the expectation that they might encounter North Korean infiltrators who would try to kill anyone in their path.[1] A soldier "on the Z" never knew what to expect. Most days and nights were uneventful but violence could flare at any time and often did, costing 90 Americans and 300 ROK soldiers their lives since the armistice. GIs received little recognition for their service and any awards or combat pay they earned seemed to be given grudgingly. This is the story of just one regiment's part in that too easily forgotten war.

In 1956, the Army was drastically reduced in size, straining its ability to meet worldwide commitments. Tactical nuclear weapons and a matching deterrence strategy were seen by the Eisenhower Administration as a way to reduce manpower requirements and costs. The Davy Crockett nuclear recoilless rifle; 203mm and 280mm nuclear artillery; and a host of nuclear rockets and missiles ushered in the Army's restructuring for tactical nuclear warfare. The three-regiment structure adopted only 17 years earlier was abandoned in favor of forming five smaller battle groups in all infantry and airborne divisions. These "Pentomic" divisions were intended to operate as isolated "hedgehogs" capable of all-around defense in a nuclear war.

On July 31, 1957, the 31st Infantry Regiment was reorganized at Camp Casey as the 1st Battle Group, 31st Infantry, remaining under the 7th Infantry Division.[2] The Pentomic concept was implemented without testing and did not last long but it ended the role of infantry regiments as tactical formations. Regimental lineages were preserved through the Combat Arms Regimental System (CARS), a lingering source of confusion. Companies of the old regiment bestowed their lineages and honors to successor battle groups. For example, A Company of the old regiment passed its lineage to the 1st Battle Group, B Company to the 2nd Battle Group, C Company to the 3rd Battle Group, and so on. The Pentomic structure had numerous other shortcomings and drawbacks, prompting its abandonment after only five years.[3]

Between 1962 and 1964, battle groups were replaced by brigades, restoring the division's triangular structure. Brigades were initially austere headquarters intended only to orchestrate the operations of a varied number and mix of maneuver battalions. Over time, they evolved into fixed structures. In July 1963, the 31st Infantry's 1st and 2nd Battalions were formed from the 1st Battle Group at Camp Casey as part of the 7th Division's 3rd Brigade. The two new battalions took their lineages from A and B Companies of the old regiment, rather than from the original 1st and 2nd Battalions. That unpopular practice endures, to the frustration of every generation since.

While lineages were passed from the old regiment to successor battle groups and battalions, the Shanghai Bowl and other regimental memorabilia could not be shared by all new battalions of the 31st Infantry.[4] New army regulations decreed that the lowest numbered or lettered successor element of each regiment *stationed in the continental United States* would become custodian of regimental memorabilia. Despite the regulation, the 1st Battle Group and then the 1st Battalion retained custody although they were never stationed in the U.S. As battalions were later moved around or inactivated, much of the regiment's memorabilia was lost or stolen.

Today, there is precious little memorabilia remaining except the Shanghai Bowl and cups and items donated to the 4th Battalion Museum by the regiment's faithful veterans.

Life in Postwar Korea

Living conditions after the Korean War were even more Spartan than they had been after World War II. Combat units initially lived in tent camps arrayed in depth behind the line of hills and ridges where the war ended. Don Williams recalls that in 1955, the troop train from Pusan halted near Tongduchon in front of a massive pile of wrecked vehicles salvaged from nearby battlefields. Troop units at Camp Casey were still housed in tents until 1956.[5] The area in and around the camp remained dangerous, since mines still littered the old battlefield on which the post was being built. Don Williams, then a PFC with the 31st Infantry's Service Company, recalls hearing an explosion in 1955 and learning later that an officer had stepped on an old land mine inside the camp. Nearby villages were off limits and the only recreation on post was a movie theater in one of the few Quonset huts on the base. Soldiers who kept out of trouble could earn a week's R&R in Japan, a country still primitive by U.S. standards at the time, but a paradise compared to Korea.

Korea was divided by a demilitarized zone (DMZ) extending 151 miles across its waist. The zone is 2.5 miles wide on either side of the Military Demarcation Line (MDL), a six-foot wide barbed wire corridor. Until the late 1950s, there was no fence along the MDL, making it easy for North Koreans to slip across. Soldiers stationed anywhere north of Seoul slept with loaded weapons near them. U.S. and Republic of Korea (ROK) troops patrolled the DMZ daily but the MDL was routinely penetrated by North Korean infiltrators. The "Z," as GIs called it, is not a pretty place. "It is a landscape of nightmare," wrote William Holinger, "this wasteland of a demilitarized zone: artillery craters, barbed wire, minefields, graveyards, the skeletons of villages and the remains of rice paddies. The earth has been shelled, mined, overgrown, booby-trapped, burned and abandoned to grow wild yet another time."[6]

Guard posts dotting hilltops along the DMZ were small forts consisting of a circular trench, interspersed with log and sandbag fighting bunkers. An observation post dominated the center atop the highest ground. Around the perimeter were multiple strands of concertina wire, augmented with trip flares and mines. Each outpost was manned by at least 10 infantrymen around the clock. Radio relay sites situated on hilltops between outposts were augmented by scouts, cooks, supply clerks, and medics. Rats and sanitation problems were their constant companions. Miserable living conditions, particularly in the winter, made a soldier's time "on the fence" extremely unpopular. The 31st Infantry's first post-armistice casualty occurred on July 29, 1953, when Corporal William Bell, a squad leader in I Company, was killed when a rusty white phosphorous

Right: Korea, 1955. Polar Bear Don Williams poses in front of a hill from which the camp took harassing fire (Association archives). *Below:* Winter quarters for Polar Bears. Korea, 1955–56 (Association archives).

grenade went off in his hand while clearing the site of former OP Dale. He had earned the Bronze Star for his part in the fighting to regain the outpost from the Chinese just a month before.[7]

In camps, squad tents were "heated" by kerosene stoves and the metal Quonset huts and Butler buildings erected later on were heated by field stoves. Regardless of the type of structure, there was never enough warmth to influence the temperature more than a few feet from the heat source. Most troops slept on cots until the 1960s because there were few bunks available. For more than half of every year, most men slept fully dressed, less boots, curled up on cots in "arctic" sleeping bags covered with GI blankets and poncho liners. Getting warm was beyond anyone's expectation. Along the border fence, soldiers in stationary positions alternated sleeping in two-hour shifts but many a night was sleepless due to bone-chilling weather or enemy activity. Gunfire was random and common, sometimes initiated by North Koreans and sometimes by scared soldiers who heard a sound in the dark. A soldier scanning his sector with an infrared scope, or later a starlight scope, would often detect an enemy scope staring right back. Foot patrols were particularly dangerous because in the early years there was a risk of losing orientation in the dark and straying into North Korea. Worse still, patrols risked being ambushed by North Koreans hiding along the trail.

Squad-size patrols operated around the clock to deter or detect infiltration. Stationary watch posts staked out known or suspected infiltration routes to intercept enemy agents. Men were dropped off in pairs to occupy foxholes just before dark and remained there until daylight regardless of weather. The atmosphere was always spooky since the enemy was never far away and was seldom seen before he opened fire. "Things are sensed or heard before they are seen along the fence," wrote William Holinger. "You can see nothing, only the mist, and the voices have no source, they are the cries of ghost soldiers raining down from an unseen sky." In the event the barrier system was breached, mobile reserves were kept ready. Each battalion had gun jeeps and troop carriers with ammunition uploaded and gas topped off, ready to roll.

In 1955–56, corrugated steel Quonset huts were erected to replace tents. Service clubs, post exchanges, and administrative offices were housed in larger Quonset huts since few camps had permanent buildings. Baseball diamonds and football fields were later established on the larger camps and command-sponsored teams were formed to build esprit de corps and offer an outlet for troops' pent-up energy. Smaller camps nearer the DMZ had no recreation facilities. They, like their predecessors of 1945–48, were just places of temporary lodging for troops who patrolled the fence and the mobile reaction forces that backed them up.

Off-post recreation opportunities were few. Korea had been devastated by a three-year war that shattered its cities and towns, wrecked its transportation network, and left its people impoverished. Larceny, prostitution, and black marketeering probably generated more revenue than Korea's government raised in taxes. Theft was elevated to an art form by hundreds of "slickie boys" inhabiting the vicinity of every military camp. A slickie boy could steal a radio and leave the music behind by taking an expensive radio from a barracks window sill and substituting a cheap transistor, tuned to the same station and volume. Fences were no obstacle, leaving both personal and military property at constant risk of theft. Trucks that stopped at intersections or railroad crossings would be stripped of whatever they carried in the short interval they remained stationary. The proceeds found their way into black market stalls in every major city, buoying the economy.

As near any military installation, establishments eager to take a soldier's pay sprang up in profusion. Laundries, tailor shops, shoeshine stands, souvenir shops, and the like were prominent but they did not necessarily harvest the most cash. Bored and lonely soldiers, many of them away from home for the first time in their lives, were easy prey to cheap liquor and the charms of "tea hostesses" who provided affection for a fee in the back rooms of bars or nearby "hotels." Affection was often accompanied by infection, prompting Provost Marshals to place offending establishments off limits. Commanders, chaplains, MPs, and medical personnel had their hands full trying to keep the problem under control. Coming down with a case of venereal disease would not only cause debilitating physical agony, but might also result in being docked a month's pay and a one-grade reduction or worse.

By 1955, the U.S. Army in Korea had been reduced from its wartime high of six divisions to only two. Among them was the 7th Infantry Division, the only one that had served in Korea during the occupation (1946–48), returned for the war, and remained after the armistice.[8] For a time, service in Korea became more like service in other overseas areas, except that camps remained temporary installations and no dependents were allowed in the country. Training routines were like those in the U.S. Annual weapons qualification took place at small arms ranges cut into hillsides at or near most large camps. Larger-caliber live fire and maneuvers took place at larger training areas like the infamous "Nightmare Range" established on land made barren by battles fought on Seoul's approaches during the war.

The "Second Korean Conflict"

Most U.S. allies left South Korea by 1957 and the Chinese left North Korea in 1958. Called a "police action" or "conflict" by U.S. politicians, the three-year Korean War had cost more than 33,000 Americans their lives. In contrast, eight Americans died in sporadic incidents along the DMZ over the next thirteen years. In 1966, the scale and tempo of incidents along the DMZ rose dramatically. The impetus came from Vietnam. In 1965, the ROK sent its best division, the Capitol Division, and a Marine Brigade to fight alongside U.S. forces in Vietnam.[9] In September 1966, the ROK 9th "White Horse" Division followed.[10] In that year, the two U.S. infantry divisions in Korea (2nd and 7th) dropped well below authorized manpower and materiel readiness dipped severely as priority for everything shifted to Vietnam. Sensing an opportunity, Kim Il Sung, North Korea's dictator, escalated tensions. Perhaps Kim was prodded to mount "a fraternal effort" to force the ROK to recall its forces from Vietnam but Kim was an opportunist, always probing for an opportunity to topple the ROK government or cause the U.S. to withdraw from Korea. Curiously, despite his intensification of hostilities, he never initiated the mobilization steps necessary for a full-scale invasion of the ROK. He no doubt remembered how close his regime had come to extinction in 1950.

A month after the ROK sent its 9th Division to Vietnam, Kim signaled his intent in a speech to the Korean Worker's Party Convention on October 5, 1966:

> In the present situation, the US imperialists should be dealt blows and their forces dispersed to the maximum in Asia and Europe, Africa and Latin America. They should be bound hand and foot everywhere they are. All the socialist countries should oppose the aggression of U.S. imperialism in Vietnam and render every possible support to the people of Vietnam. As the DRV (Democratic

Republic of Vietnam) is being attacked by the U.S. imperialists, the socialist countries should fight more sharply against them.[11]

In concert, the Chinese withdrew their delegate from the Military Armistice Commission at Panmunjon in 1966 and did not return until 1971.

Within weeks after Kim's speech, larger North Korean combat patrols began probing the DMZ. Booby traps were set out along familiar U.S. and ROK patrol routes, mines were placed on trails patrolled by jeeps and armored personnel carriers, and mortar and antitank fire sometimes accompanied the probes, either as distractions or in direct support of an attack. On November 2, 1966, U.S. President Lyndon Johnson was staying at Walker Hill Resort near Seoul after talks with ROK President Park Chung Hee. Early that morning, North Koreans ambushed an eight-man patrol of the U.S. 1st Battalion 23rd Infantry, killing seven of its members and seriously wounding the sole survivor. The ambush, timed to embarrass both Presidents, signaled the opening of a second Korean conflict that would continue for the next three years.

In that opening attack, PFC David L. Bibee, a 17-year-old, was the only survivor. Wounded by shrapnel in 48 places in his leg and shoulder, he survived by playing dead. In a vain effort to save his fellow patrol members, Private Ernest D. Reynolds launched a one-man counter-attack against the North Koreans, sacrificing his life in the process. Recommended posthumously for the Medal of Honor, the Kansas City, Missouri, native had been in Korea less than three weeks. The attackers were from a unit trained for guerrilla operations in the South. Fanatical, dedicated communists, they would commit suicide with a grenade rather than face capture.[12]

Interior of bivouac tent, Korea, 1955–56 (Association archives).

For the next three years, attacks along the DMZ, amphibious landings by commandos, sabotage, and guerrilla raids would become the norm. Artillery was used by ROK troops in April 1967 to repel an incursion by more than 100 men. By June of that year, infiltrations had reached deeper into the country. A barracks housing troops of the U.S. 2nd Infantry Division at Camp Howze was dynamited and four South Korean police and a civilian were killed in a battle with North Koreans near Taegu. In response, U.S. Army Special Forces teams from Okinawa were sent into the mountains of south central Korea to hunt down infiltrators. Units of the 7th Infantry Division conducted air assaults and ground patrols from Camps Casey and Kaiser. Despite intensified U.S. and ROK counter-infiltration operations, two South Korean trains were derailed in September, one carrying U.S. military supplies. In October, North Korean artillery fired more than 50 rounds at an ROK Army camp, the first time North Korean artillery had fired across the DMZ since 1953.[13]

At the time, two U.S. brigade headquarters and five maneuver battalions, including four from the 2nd Infantry Division and one from the 7th Infantry Division, were based north of the Imjin River, manning an 18.5-mile sector. The rest of the 151-mile DMZ was manned by the ROK Army. A rotation system was inaugurated in October 1967, alternating all infantry battalions to "the Z," as it was known in soldier parlance.

Between May 1967 and January 1968, there were more than 300 attacks in the U.S. sector, killing 15 U.S. soldiers and wounding 65.[14] Because U.S. troops were routinely in combat there, the Commander-in-Chief of U.S. Pacific Command requested that the area between the DMZ and the Imjin River be designated a hostile fire zone. The Secretary of Defense approved the request. His approval note stated: "The men serving along the demilitarized zone are no longer involved in Cold War operations. They are in every sense of the word involved in combat where vehicles are blown up by mines, patrols are ambushed, and psychological operations are conducted on a continuing basis…."[15] Hostile fire pay, $65 a month, became effective on April 1, 1968. Receiving it required at least six days a month north of the Imjin River. Formerly, only the month in which a GI was wounded was counted. Every U.S. Service member who served anywhere in Korea, including offshore and over its airspace, between October 1, 1966, and June 30, 1974, received the Armed Forces Expeditionary Medal.[16]

Soldiers in Korea nevertheless felt ignored amid their country's preoccupation with Vietnam. William Holinger, Operations Officer (S-3) of the 1st Battalion, 31st Infantry in 1968–69, expressed that frustration in his novel, *The Fence Walker*. "If we're killed on a patrol or a guard post, crushed in a jeep accident, or shot by a nervous GI on the fence, no one will ever write about us in the Times or erect a monument or read a Gettysburg Address over our graves. There's too much going on elsewhere; what we're doing is trivial in comparison. We'll never be part of the national memory." Soldiers worried most about a prohibition against flying helicopters into the DMZ. "If someone gets wounded, it would take us four or five hours to get him out (by foot trail and road) and by that time he might be dead," said one officer.[17]

In 1967, a barrier defense system was erected. It consisted of a line of obstacles— tanglefoot and anti-personnel mines; a 10-foot-high chain link fence with triple concertina wire on top and six-foot steel pickets driven into the ground; and a line of towers and foxholes interconnected by landline and radio. Holinger wrote: "My God, I thought, how can such a thing be beautiful? Its rusted chain links caught the light from the morning sky and the light turned it red, and it became a soaring red curtain rising and falling, following the contour of the hills." U.S. troops reinforced their sector, manned guard posts in the middle of no-man's land north of the barrier, and conducted aggressive patrols and stakeouts. Rome plows cleared vegetation along roads leading to guard posts. Defoliants were also used to eliminate hiding places for North Koreans attempting to infiltrate or attack U.S. units.[18]

On August 10, 1967, work details from the 2nd and 3rd Platoons of B Company 2nd Battalion 31st Infantry were working with the 13th Engineer Battalion to repair a section of fence and clear vegetation that might conceal North Korean infiltration. Near noon, a light rain began and the details departed the work site aboard two trucks headed back to their home base for lunch. Four men on each truck were armed with M-14 rifles while the rest were unarmed.[19] As the lead truck down-shifted about half-way up a steep hill, North Korean infiltrators jumped out of the underbrush and lobbed grenades onto the truck's hood and open bed. At least eight grenades landed on or near the truck. One of the first landed on the right side of the hood near the windshield, killing the 3rd Platoon Sergeant, SFC Phillip Boudreaux, and seriously wounding the driver. With its driver disabled, the truck rolled back down the muddy slope and jack-knifed, overturning the water trailer it was towing. Other North Koreans opened fire with automatic weapons, including a heavy machine gun. PFC Donald J. Czaplicki was killed by a grenade that

Headquarters, 1st Brigade and Headquarters 2nd Battalion, 31st Infantry Regiment, Camp Kaiser, 1963 (U.S. Army photograph, National Archives).

landed in the crowded truck bed and PFC Jerry D. Skaggs was killed by automatic weapons fire.

Sergeant Edwin H. Parpart, Jr., one of the squad leaders present, mistakenly thought the vehicle had hit a land mine. He recalls:

> We cut wood for several hours and were heading back to Camp Casey when we hit a land mine with a deuce and a half. Killed instantly was an E-7 who was less than a year from retiring. Another man took a .50 caliber round in the head. After I helped get the guys off the truck the lieutenant in charge sent me up the hill to the O.P. to call for backup. While crawling up the hill, I could hear this zinging sound all around me. At the debriefing the next day, I was told this was .50 caliber fire that the guys could see bouncing around in the brush and off the rocks and kicking up sand. I was so damned scared I didn't even know I was being shot at.

Second Lieutenant David Beach, the only officer present, reported that after the grenade attack, other North Koreans, some no more than 50 yards away, began firing at the truck with submachine guns. A heavier gun firing from the North Korean side of the border supported the attack. About half of the 25 to 30 men crammed into the lead truck were able to get out and find cover while the rest did the best they could to lay flat in the truck bed during the entire 30 minutes it took for the reaction force to arrive.

The second truck, a terrain feature behind, stopped at the sound of the initial explosions and did not enter the ambush zone. After about 15 minutes, it continued to the crest of the intervening hill where the ambush site came into view. There, unarmed troops dismounted and took cover while those who were armed fired at the infiltrators. Outgunned, they had little effect but they did divert attention from the men in the lead truck at a critical time, perhaps saving them from being overrun. Lieutenant Beach reported, "We're pretty sure we hit one. A dozen men saw one infiltrator fall and be picked up. We may have wounded a couple more." In the ambush area, the reaction force found three North Korean fatigue caps, submachine gun magazines, cartridge belts, and spent cartridges. The attackers fled across the border to safety.

Ronnie Hebert, with the 2-31st Infantry's Scout Platoon at nearby Camp Matta that day, recalls, "Our five gun jeeps went off to the zone as fast as they could go. The driver and copilot with M14s, and the machine gunner standing up hanging on to the M60."[20] The primary reaction force, traveling aboard M-113 Armored Personnel Carriers, was a platoon of the 1-38th Infantry, an adjacent 2nd Infantry Division unit. The ambush was the first known to have taken place in broad daylight.

Nearly coincident with the Tet Offensive in Vietnam in 1968, 31 North Koreans infiltrated through the U.S. sector of the DMZ to attack the ROK Presidential Palace in Seoul, known as the Blue House. Their mission was to assassinate President Park Chung Hee. They came within a few blocks of the palace before being stopped by ROK troops and police. Twenty-eight of the infiltrators were killed, one was captured, and two escaped. The captured infiltrator said the U.S. Embassy was also one of their targets.[21] Shortly after the Blue House raid, the North Koreans seized the USS *Pueblo* in international waters near Wonsan. Its 83-man crew was captured after a brief fight in which one U.S. sailor was killed.[22] Things were definitely getting hotter.

The North Koreans were masters of propaganda. Loudspeakers blared in English or Korean throughout the night along the DMZ. Music played and a sultry woman's voice told soldiers she could make life more pleasant for them in the north. After the *Pueblo*'s capture, Commander Lloyd Bucher's voice was broadcast to further humiliate the United States. Showing that there were captured Americans in North Korea and that no apparent

By SPEC. 4
TOM GRAHAM
S&S Korea Bureau

SEOUL—Three American soldiers were killed and 16 Americans and one Korean were wounded w h e n their t r u c k was ambushed by North Koreans late Thursday morning 300 yards south of the Demilitarized Z o n e in South Korea.

An estimated force of 17 North Koreans first attacked the truck with grenades

Sgt. David Bunnell, squad leader from Bravo Company, 2d Bn., 31st Inf., 7th Inf. Div., crouches with rifle ready to provide cover as other soldiers remove wrecked truck from ambush site in Korea. Bunnell was on a truck behind the one which was hit near the DMZ. (S&S Photo by SP5 Jim Konschuh)

Front page of the Korean edition of the *Stars & Stripes*, Aug. 12, 1967. When their vehicle was ambushed while on patrol, three 31st Infantry Regiment soldiers were killed: SFC Phillip Boudreaux, PFC Donald J. Czaplicki and PFC Jerry D. Skaggs, all of B Company, 2nd Battalion. The photograph caption reports that the foreground soldier, SGT David Bunnell, a squad leader from Bravo Company, is ready to provide covering fire as the ambushed vehicle is evacuated. Bunnell was in the vehicle right behind the truck that was hit. The following April, a fourth Polar Bear was killed in action: PFC Robert R. Bisbee, from the same company and battalion (Association archives).

effort was being made to free them was meant to convey a sense of hopelessness to those manning "the Z." Other speakers would rail about U.S. and ROK weakness and North Korea's superior strength. Perhaps the only people who really believed those broadcasts were U.S. military intelligence analysts who were seeing an Army of 1.2 million men in the north, generously armed by the Soviets and Chinese while U.S. readiness lagged. North Korea's weaknesses seemed invisible to the intelligence community but much of North Korea's "strength" was and is illusory. The NKPA is plagued with poor to nonexistent maintenance on mostly obsolete equipment, low fuel supplies, a lack of spare parts, poor and infrequent unit training, sparse rations, and a host of other problems whose impact is harder to see.

Throughout 1968, firefights became routine all along the DMZ. Around 700 actions were recorded. Not all casualties resulted from hostile fire. In March 1968, a KATUSA

Korea, 1955. Three Polar Bears of the Service Company at Camp Casey (Association archives).

assigned to 2-31st Infantry's Combat Support Company was seriously wounded when he stepped on a land mine left over from the Korean War.[23] He had been on guard duty along the fence at night and went out to get firewood. The next morning, the 13th Engineers were sent in to check the site. To their surprise, they found an extensive minefield consisting of American antitank and anti-personnel mines. They spent nearly the whole day blowing up ordnance probably emplaced by their predecessors a generation earlier.

The largest battle of the three-year surge was fought by B Company 2-31st Infantry on April 21, 1968. It was the second time the company had seen action and it would again lose one of its own. PFC Robert R. Bisbee (Marblehead, Massachusetts) of the 2nd Platoon was killed and three other members of his squad were wounded before a reaction force arrived by armored personnel carrier to render assistance.[24] The wounded included Sergeant Ed Parpart, who had also been in the August 10, 1967, ambush. The firefight raged for over two hours as a company of North Koreans tried to kill the Americans. Five North Koreans were killed and their bodies were recovered afterward. One of the bodies, shot three times in the chest, was that of an officer, perhaps explaining why the North Koreans fought for so long. Perhaps unsure of whether he was dead or alive, they might have been trying to retrieve him to keep any information he might have had from falling into American hands.

Sergeant Parpart recalls an event that seemingly foretold the ambush:

Two or three days before the incident I had run a patrol with personnel from the unit that was to relieve us. When the patrol began, we had taken over from a 2nd Division unit and had the area from the left flank of the battalion AO to B Company's Observation Post. After we passed OP Hendricks we stumbled on a North Korean patrol and clearing party. We heard them hacking bushes and talking before we saw them. As we passed them, our KATUSA told us that they wanted him to shoot us and take the radio and join them. On returning from patrol, we were debriefed and told of the NK party. We could tell they were clearing fields of fire and all units should be aware that something was about to happen. I never knew what happened to that info and why it never got passed on.[25]

The April 21 patrol began as an orientation, with an experienced patrol leader, Sergeant Parpart, teaching a new squad leader, Sergeant Steve Grace, the ropes. Grace had been in Korea only 6 days at the time. Both squads had only five men. The ambush began just after 4:00 p.m. on an otherwise pleasant Sunday. Specialist Thomas E. White, one of the participants, recalled the incident for the 7th Division newspaper: "Sergeant Parpart told everyone to halt while he climbed the slope. He said, 'White, give me the field glasses,' and went half way up before he was hit by enemy fire from the top of the hill."

Parpart called out, "Ambush! Ambush! Get down, I've been hit." He later recalled from his hospital bed, "I decided to move up to a vantage point overlooking the entire area. From the top of the hill we would have been able to observe the entire area and still remain relatively well hidden and protected. I was almost to the top when a North Korean jumped out of the underbrush and fired two rounds from an AK-47." After he was hit, Parpart ran down the hill and fell after stepping into a hole. He called out to the other squad leader and another man for help.

One of them, who did not want his name disclosed, recalled,

Sarge and I made it to where Parpart was and pulled him down under cover. He was bleeding pretty badly from wounds in his arm and leg so I used my fatigue shirt and T-shirt to patch him up as best I could. We all thought we got the ones who had fired down on us from the hill because the firing had died down but then they opened up on us from the rear. Supporting fire came from across the MDL, from behind a rice dike, a North Korean guard post, and the wood line on our side of the zone. Sarge said follow me and we took off, leaving Parpart alone so we could protect the flank. The advancing enemy numbered around twenty on that side of the hill.

Tom White recalls that the opening shots sounded like a cap gun. Once men saw puffs of dust being kicked up around them, reality set in. Everyone took cover except Private Bisbee. White continues, "I started climbing up the hill and that was the last I saw of Bisbee. I couldn't go very far because the North Koreans were throwing grenades down at us. I got far enough to see one patrol member wrapping his fatigue shirt around Sergeant Parpart's leg and his T-shirt around his arm. Someone yelled at the radio man to get some help."

A GI yelled, "I'm going to go get one of them." He began weaving in and out of the bushes, working his way around the hill to get to the enemy's flank. Meanwhile, a KATUSA at the bottom of the hill, Corporal Ha, fired at three North Koreans running across a field. One fell but got back up. Corporal Ha fired again and the North Korean dropped heavily and never moved again. Specialist White recalls: "We started firing at the enemy on our right flank as two men moved around the hill to a small knoll."

Sergeant Parpart adds: "When the two took off from the position where they had dragged me, grenades started coming in from the top of the hill. One hit on either side of me. It was like being the warm-up catcher in a baseball game, but this time it was grenades all up and down the line." The two men who had just left Parpart moved down the hill to protect the right flank but were pinned down by automatic weapons fire. Parpart directed Private Robert R. Bisbee to get to higher ground to spot enemy positions. Sergeant Grace, pinned down behind a berm, recalled: "All I did was stick my rifle above the berm and fire in the direction he called. He kept calling out directions—left, right, up, down. The guy below me blasted one of the enemy as he got up from behind a dike in the field. A warning from Bisbee that grenades were coming in on my position sent me over the top. It was a good thing because the grenades landed where I had been. Instead of being killed, I was just wounded by flying shrapnel."

The soldier with him continues:

> I can remember the Sarge going over the top and then the explosions. I looked up and got the sign from Bisbee that he was OK so I didn't worry too much. Then Bisbee pointed out six or seven coming toward my position. What they did then, I'll never forget. They took cover and then sent one man to stand in the field to act as a dummy. He just stood there waiting to be shot. Well, Bisbee drew up and shot him but that was just what the North Koreans were waiting for because when he did they killed him. He fell down off the cliff and at first I thought he was only badly wounded. When I got to him, he was already dead. It was right after Bisbee got hit that I got one through the stomach.

The other sergeant saw Bisbee fall seven or eight feet to the ground below. Although wounded himself, he crawled over to his wounded comrade and, remembering what he had learned in first aid classes, brought up his knees to relieve some of the pressure that comes with a stomach wound. He could hear the North Koreans coming his way, laughing and talking. They knew Bisbee was dead and the other two men were wounded and they were coming to finish them off. Suddenly, armored personnel carriers from the reaction force, the 1-23rd Infantry, rumbled in and moved on line with the two pinned-down squads. The North Koreans continued to fight for a while but were no match for the tracks' heavier firepower. Several more were shot down before they could reach safety.

On April 27, a patrol led by Sergeant Isaacs from B Company's 3rd Platoon was ambushed near the same area. A lone North Korean jumped out of a hole and shot the point man, who was new to the company. He also shot a PFC named Taylor and a KATUSA Private named Lim. Lim died but the others lived.[26]

Between November 1967 and April 1968, antiwar protests and the highest casualty rate of the war in Vietnam heightened American political anxiety. U.S.–ROK relations became strained by the sudden upturn in North Korean activity. President Park raised the possibility of withdrawing his troops from Vietnam unless the United States took firmer measures to counter North Korean infiltration. Park also wanted to retaliate against the North, while the United States, already hard-pressed in Vietnam, wished to avoid precipitating a second war.[27] Meanwhile, North Korean attacks increased along the DMZ and a 120-man commando team landed on South Korea's east coast. All the infiltrators were eventually killed or captured, but only after the loss of many civilian lives. During 1968 alone, 1,245 North Korean agents were arrested in the South. On October 3, 1968, an outpost manned by the 1st Battalion 31st Infantry spotted a North Korean trying to get back through the wire headed north. He never made it.[28]

To assuage President Park's anxiety, thousands of replacements headed for Vietnam were diverted to Korea in the first few months of 1968. Concurrently, a tour extension was implemented for members of the two U.S. divisions in Korea. Although junior enlisted strength neared full authorizations, officer and noncommissioned officer (NCO) levels remained critically low. Commanders sent promising young specialists and corporals to division NCO academies and quickly advanced soldiers who demonstrated leadership potential. Both divisions began a massive training program in light infantry tactics. "Imjin Scouts" training instructed soldiers on operations peculiar to Korea. To earn an Imjin Scout patch, soldiers had to participate in 25 patrols in the DMZ. It was not uncommon for infantrymen to participate in 50 or more during a year's tour of duty. The Combat Infantry Badge (CIB) was authorized for eligible soldiers along the DMZ but because its award was so restrictive, the 7th Infantry Division created a similar badge with a bayonet and the division insignia in a wreath.[29]

These actions, coupled with aggressive patrolling and air-land-sea surveillance, made a difference. Hostile actions declined from more than 700 in 1968, to just over 100 in 1969. The crew of the USS *Pueblo* was released by the North Koreans just before Christmas 1968. Though the number of events declined, the North Koreans were not done. In April 1969, a North Korean MiG fighter shot down a U.S. Navy EC-121 intelligence aircraft, killing its 31-man crew. A U.S. Army helicopter was downed in August when it strayed across the DMZ. U.S. reaction was swift. President Nixon ordered a naval task force of 23 warships into the Sea of Japan off the Korean coast.[30]

On August 17, 1969, PFC George Grant of the 1-31st Infantry was killed in an ambush while working with the 13th Engineers to clear brush from a suspected infiltration trail.[31] Grant was hit in the chest by automatic weapons fire and died before help could arrive. The last GIs killed in the brush fire war died on October 18, 1969. Four men from another unit of the 7th Infantry Division were killed in a daylight ambush along the DMZ. Their jeep was flying a white truce flag. Each man was shot through the head. The attack ended quickly and the ambushers slipped away before a reaction force could reach the site.

As 1969 came to a close, provocative incidents by the North Koreans decreased as quickly as they had started three years before. Between 1966 and 1969, North Korean attacks along the DMZ killed 44 Americans and wounded 111.[32] During the same period, 326 ROKs were killed and 600 wounded, while the North Koreans lost 715 killed and an unknown number of wounded. When those killed before and after the three-year escalation are included, the number of Americans killed in Korea since the war's end total 90, more than the combined total of those killed in action in the Dominican Republic (1965), Grenada (1983), Panama (1989–90), and Somalia (1993).

In 1971, the U.S. presence along the DMZ shrank to just one battalion of the 7th Infantry Division. It was stationed at Camp Greaves, located just across the Imjin River on the western corridor. From Camp Greaves, one company at a time rotated to Camp Liberty Bell, a tent camp from which units manned Guard Posts Collier and Oullette, patrolled a five-mile section of the fence, and manned the guard post at Freedom Bridge. ROK units took over the rest of the sector. As ROK forces returned from Vietnam, the U.S. 7th Infantry Division was withdrawn after serving 23 years in Korea. Its withdrawal resulted from Congressional demands for a "peace dividend" after the costly eight-year war in Vietnam. With only 13 divisions left in the Army, the strategic reserve in the U.S. had grown too thin to continue keeping two divisions in Korea.

The division's final review in Seoul took place on April 1, 1971. With it, both battalions of the 31st Infantry were also inactivated. For the first time in 21 years, there were no elements of the 31st Infantry left in Korea.

The Last Years, 1971–1987

The 1st Battalion 31st Infantry was reactivated on June 17, 1971, and was assigned to the 2nd Infantry Division. The battalion was mechanized and remained at Camp Greaves

Korea, 1955–56. SSG Shelby (right), with Robert Whitman (left), Harold Williams (front) and Keith Bennett (rear) (Association archives).

from 1972 to 1976 when it returned to Camp Casey. By the mid–1970s companies in Korea were barely at 50 percent strength and rifle squads generally numbered only six men. During the infamous tree-cutting incident in 1976, the 1st Battalion sent a company-sized mechanized reaction force from Camp Casey to the Imjin. If the North Koreans had attacked, the "Bearcats" would have been the covering force for units withdrawing across the Imjin.

During most of the 31st Infantry Regiment's tour in Korea since 1953, Camp Casey, near Tongduchon, was its home, including its successor battle group and both successor battalions. It is the largest of the U.S. camps established after the Korean War and grew from a muddy tent camp to a modern installation with permanent barracks, paved roads, support facilities, and an airfield. In 1987, the 1st Battalion 31st Infantry ended its tour in Korea and was inactivated. It served there a total of 39 years, longer than any other U.S. unit. It remains "America's Foreign Legion," the only U.S. Army infantry battalion that never served in the United States.

PART IV. VIETNAM AND CAMBODIA
A. The 4th Battalion
by James B. Simms

18 Fort Devens, Deployment, Initial Operations

The 4th Battalion, 31st Infantry, was activated as a part of the 196th Light Infantry Brigade (LIB) at Fort Devens, Massachusetts, on September 10, 1965. Other components of the brigade were the 2-1st Infantry, 3-21st Infantry, F Troop 17th Cavalry, 3-82nd Artillery, 8th Support Battalion, 175th Engineer Company, 587th Signal Company, and the Brigade Headquarters Company.[1] The 196th LIB, called the "Chargers," commanded by Colonel Francis S. Conaty, Jr., was the first of four light infantry brigades formed to reconstitute the Army's strategic reserve after deployments to Vietnam began. The other brigades were the 11th LIB at Schofield Barracks, HI, 198th LIB at Fort Hood, Texas, and 199th LIB at Fort Benning, Georgia.[2] Fort Devens, near the town of Ayer, was just a little over 10,200 acres on which generations of soldiers had trained since 1917. Fort Devens was not large enough to train a modern infantry brigade equipped with weapons that reached well beyond the post's boundaries.

Cadre for the 4-31st Infantry began arriving in early September 1965, and the soldiers arrived from reception stations at Fort Dix, New Jersey, and Fort Knox, Kentucky, in mid–October. Lieutenant Colonel Hugh J. Lynch accepted the battalion's colors at the activation ceremony on November 20, 1965.[3]

1966 Begins

After basic training at Fort Devens, the battalion began advanced individual training in January 1966. Because of space limitations at their home station, the battalion moved to Camp Edwards, Cape Cod, Massachusetts on January 29 for heavy weapons range firing and squad tactics. Although the Cape is an idyllic vacation spot in the summer, the weather is miserable in January and is worse in February.[4]

Returning to Fort Devens in a snow storm in mid–February, the battalion next conducted a twenty-one mile road march to Leominster State Forest. In addition to the physical conditioning role, the training was intended to teach counterinsurgency tactics. With nine inches of snow on the ground, this was agony from start to finish. Whether any learning about counterinsurgency took place was doubtful. Ed Boss remembers that Company A's bivouac site was atop a frigid, windswept mountain. Of course chow was served down in the valley, about an hour round trip through the snow. Soldiers had to make their way down the mountain and back up each time meals were served.

Polar Bears firing on the Camp Edwards rifle range (Association archives).

Riot control training at Camp Drum, New York (Association archives).

Real insurgents would have had a field day with ambushes and booby traps between the chow line and the bivouac site.[5]

On March 31, the battalion moved to Camp Drum (now Fort Drum and home of the 4-31st Infantry since 1996), on a 107,000 acre reservation near Watertown, New York, that offered sufficient land for brigade-level training maneuvers. After Exercise REDCON READY in early May, the brigade's infantrymen were awarded the coveted blue shoulder cord signifying that they were fully trained infantrymen.[6] On May 15th, Colonel Conaty received instructions for the brigade's deployment to the Dominican Republic. However, the brigade received a change in mission to deploy to the Republic of (South) Vietnam in early June.[7] The soldiers prepared for overseas movement, packed, performed maintenance on their equipment, and were given block leave June 16–30.[8]

Deployment

The 196th LIB left Boston on July 15 aboard the troopships USNS *William O. Darby* and USNS *Alexander M. Patch* and sailed through the Panama Canal. They stopped at Long Beach, California, to refuel and replenish rations en route to South Vietnam. In an effort to maintain discipline and a sharp edge, troops were kept busy with physical training, sanitation details, and classes on jungle warfare, survival, weaponry, and tactics. Taking training seriously aboard rolling troopships amid the smells of diesel fuel and sea sickness was more than a challenge.[9]

After a gut-wrenching month at sea, the brigade disembarked at Vung Tau, South

En route by sea to a classified operational area in Southeast Asia (Association archives).

Vietnam, on August 15. The 4-31st Infantry's advance party, led by Lieutenant Colonel Lynch, had arrived by air on August 6 and met the soldiers at the docks. Air Force C-123s airlifted the unit the remaining distance to Tay Ninh, their new home. In the shadow of a dormant volcano called Nui Ba Den (Black Virgin Mountain), Tay Ninh, with a 1966 population of around 200,000, was an important market town and Buddhist religious center surrounded by rubber and tea plantations, along with rice fields. The Cambodian border was only twenty kilometers to the north. Saigon was ninety kilometers to the southeast. The Viet Cong (VC) frequently ambushed convoys and mined the roads. The 196th LIB's arrival at Tay Ninh was accompanied by an unwelcome surprise. General Westmoreland, Commander U.S. Military Assistance Command Vietnam, placed the 196th LIB under the U.S. 25th Infantry Division's control and reassigned an Assistant Division Commander, Brigadier General Edward H. de Saussure, Jr., as the commander. General Westmoreland's policy was to have Brigadier Generals command separate brigades. Colonel Conaty became the Brigade Deputy Commander until another brigade command position was available.[10]

The arrival at Tay Ninh will live forever in the memory of all who endured it. The temperature was 124°F, and the battalion's bivouac area was three kilometers from the airfield, a hike everyone had to make with duffle bag, weapons, and full field gear. There were no facilities of any kind at the battalion's new home, so they lived in tents. Because they arrived during monsoon season, vehicular traffic was impossible around the muddy bivouac site. Consequently, all equipment, supplies, food, and water had to be hauled by hand.[11]

Battalion bivouac area, Tay Ninh. Photo 175th Engineer Company (Association archives).

Operation Athol

The 196th LIB conducted Operation Athol (September 8–13), the 4-31st Infantry's first combat mission.[12] The battalion, with Battery C 3-82nd Artillery attached, supported the Army of Vietnam (ARVN) units at Dau Tieng. The battalion was airlifted by C-123s to Dau Tieng and established a defensive position to reinforce ARVN units and protect Battery C. The Battalion also conducted three search and destroy operations in portions of the Michelin Rubber Plantation. No significant contact was made with the enemy.[13]

Operation Attleboro

The brigade's Operation Attleboro consisted of two phases. The first ran from September 14 to 26, and the second spanned October 18 to November 25.[14] Like several other 196th LIB operations that followed, Operation Attleboro was named after a town near Fort Devens.

On September 18, 4-31st Infantry flew in the rain from Tay Ninh to establish a forward operating base north of Dau Tieng. The battalion lost its first soldier, Specialist

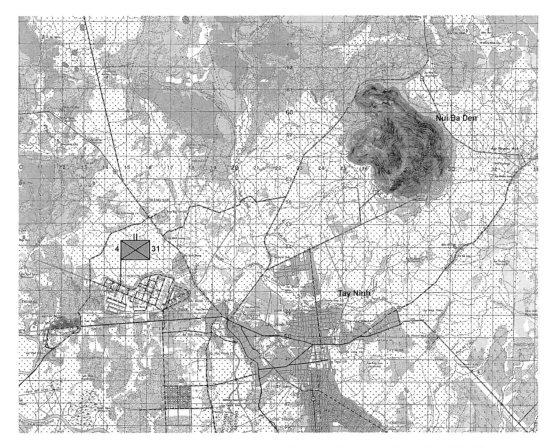

Tay Ninh, 6231-4 [map]. 1:50000. L7014 Series. 29th Engr. Bn. U.S. Army, November 1970. Vietnam Archive Map Collection, The Vietnam Archive, Texas Tech University. Used by permission.

Four Vincent F. Murphy (Grosse Pointe, Michigan), on September 18. Just after midnight on September 19, sniper fire erupted in Company C's sector, followed soon after by a mortar attack on the battalion command post (CP). Captain John M. Harrington (Durham, North Carolina), the Battalion S-4, and his radio operator, Specialist Four Manzie Glover, Jr. (Elizabeth, New Jersey), were killed and sixteen wounded. The following morning, the battalion marched a few kilometers farther north to secure an area where the 175th Engineer Company had cleared the jungle for another forward operating base. Rain continued throughout the day, turning the area into a muddy quagmire. As daylight faded, small arms and mortar fire struck several locations around and within the perimeter, wounding another man. Over the next several days, Company C and then Company B engaged in a series of stiff firefights with the VC.[15] On September 24, Private First Class Robert C. Hauser (Fair Lawn, New Jersey) was killed by friendly fire. On September 25, the battalion returned to Tay Ninh for a stand-down.

The battalion returned to the field on October 6th and continued search and destroy operations in a new area until October 16.[16] On October 7th, Company C found a series of tunnels. Soon after, Company B found a huge rice cache and a large array of farm implements in a nearby area where no civilians lived. With the rain beating on steel helmets, ponchos, and weapons, soldiers searched along trails that showed signs of recent heavy use. Company A was the first to make contact, engaging in a brief firefight that resulted in two men being wounded. No enemy was found, but blood trails, several discarded weapons, and a bundle of documents were discovered. Two days later, Company D found another rice cache and Company A engaged a VC patrol, losing two men wounded and killing three of the enemy.[17] On October 11, the Company C commander, First Lieutenant Franklin S. Pearce, and two of his men were wounded and evacuated. First Lieutenant Pearce, a well-respected commander, lost one of his legs in this action. Firefights erupted throughout the night, and in some cases the enemy got close enough to throw grenades into the perimeter. Companies A, C, and D each found blood trails the next morning, but no bodies or weapons. The following day, air strikes were called in on suspected enemy locations before the battalion was flown back to Tay Ninh.[18]

On October 18, the battalion flew back to Dau Tieng to guard the base. Martha Raye, an actress who had made her debut before World War II, visited Dau Tieng as part of a United Service Organizations (USO) tour. Lieutenant Colonel Lynch declared her an honorary Polar Bear and presented her a set of regimental crests.[19] That night, Company B killed one enemy soldier, and the following morning, found a VC hospital complex with twenty-seven structures above and below ground stocked with medical supplies and clothing plus more than twelve tons of rice, salt, canned milk, and peanuts. That same day, 2-1st Infantry ran into the southern edge of what was later discovered to be the 9th VC Division's base camp near the Saigon River. On October 26 and 27, Companies A and B engaged in firefights that killed nine VC and captured four. There were no U.S. losses.[20] Signs of enemy presence were everywhere, including sampans, construction materials, tunnels, and documents. With the element of surprise gone, the brigade reassembled at Dau Tieng and prepared to attack in force. At that critical juncture on November 1st, Colonel Conaty was reassigned to command the 1st Brigade 25th Infantry Division.[21]

On November 1, the concept and size of Operation Attleboro changed from two battalions to a brigade operation.[22] Brigadier General de Saussure's plan for the enlarged operation was confusing, and its ad hoc execution made matters worse. Also

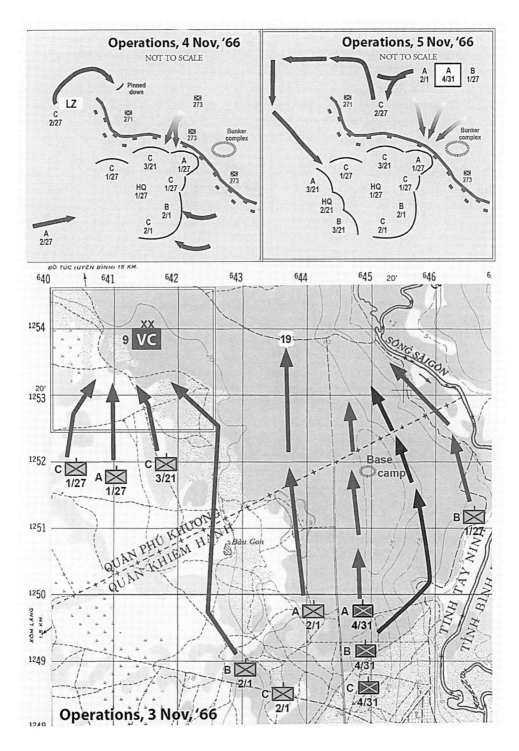

Operation Attleboro, November 3–5th (diagram shows the locations and axis of advance for the individual rifle companies of the 2-1st, 3-21st, 1-27th, 2-27th, and 4-31st Infantry during the196th LIB Phase of the Operation. Map based on diagram developed by *Vietnam Magazine*.

on November 1, because 3-21st Infantry was performing a static security mission and not under the Brigade's operational control, the 25th Infantry Division's 1-27th Infantry came under the operational control (OPCON) of the 196th LIB. However, the 1-27th Infantry was not initially employed as a battalion. Its Company B advanced along the river on the brigade's right flank, while its Company C air assaulted into an isolated landing zone (LZ) on the brigade's extreme left. As Company C 1-27th Infantry landed, it was immediately engaged, suffering six wounded and six killed on the LZ. Included was its commander, who soon died of his wounds. Dust Off helicopters were driven off repeatedly by heavy fire.[23] Between those two companies were the 2-1st and 4-31st Infantry, each with two companies abreast, advancing on parallel axes through the jungle. The companies could not see or support each other in the dense jungle, dooming their advance to be a blind foray into dangerous territory. At 1148 hours, Company B 2-1st Infantry was engaged by VC using small arms and claymores. At 1206 hours, it was determined that Company B 1-27th Infantry was in heavy contact with a reinforced VC company.

Seeking to salvage the situation, the 1-27th Infantry Commander, Major Guy S. "Sandy" Meloy, landed nearby and called for his Company A, then in reserve at Dau Tieng. Major Meloy and every member of his command group were wounded soon after landing, but most stayed in the fight. The 2-27th Infantry was committed as a reaction force to reinforce the 1-27th Infantry. By 1800 hours on November 4, the 196th LIB controlled three infantry battalions and three separate rifle companies in the battle and had one rifle company on standby at Dau Tieng. On November 5, the 1st and 2nd-27th Infantry continued to attack the fortified enemy position, and Companies A and B 3-21st Infantry were committed to secure an LZ site to extract the 1st and 2-27th Infantry.

Brigadier General de Saussure also reacted, but failed to tell Major Meloy what he was doing. To Meloy's surprise, Company C 3-21st Infantry was lifted in from Tay Ninh to join him. He did not know they were coming until the helicopters landed and the company commander reported in on Meloy's command net. Companies B and C, 2-1st Infantry were lifted in the next morning to reinforce Meloy's growing command, but he was again surprised when they arrived because no one had told him they were coming. Later that afternoon, Company C and the battalion command group of 2-27th Infantry, from Meloy's sister battalion, reported they were inbound from Dau Tieng. Misunderstanding where they were to land, they landed two kilometers northwest of Meloy's perimeter and immediately came under fire. The battalion and company commanders were both killed, leaving a lieutenant to hold the isolated company together.[24]

Company A 2-27th Infantry was the next company to arrive. It was sent immediately through what appeared to be a gap in the enemy's line, to reinforce Company C 2-27th and assist its move back to Meloy's expanding perimeter. Two members of Company A 2-27th Infantry, Captain Robert F. Foley and Private First Class John F. Baker, Jr., earned the Medal of Honor (MOH) during their company's failed attempt to break through to Company C 2-27th. On the morning of November 5, Company B 1-27th Infantry linked up with Company A 2-1st Infantry and Company A 4-31st Infantry, forming an ad hoc battalion task force (TF). It circled north of the enemy base area to fight its way through to Company C 2-27th Infantry. When they reached Major Meloy's perimeter late that afternoon, he had ten rifle companies from five battalions under his command.[25]

The 196th LIB became OPCON to the 1st Infantry Division on November 5th and attached to the Division on November 6.[26]

General Westmoreland flew in to talk with the battalion on November 9 and shortly after he departed the VC mortared the site, wounding six men. Meanwhile, Brigadier General de Saussure ordered Lieutenant Colonel Lynch to attack with his other three rifle companies against an enemy force entrenched in concrete emplacements along the east-west road defining the VC base area's southern edge. Because the companies would have to cross an open field swept by at least a dozen machine guns, Lieutenant Colonel Lynch declined the order and was promptly relieved of command on November 10.[27] But Brigadier General de Saussure did not press the order, and the battalion did not move. On November 11, Lieutenant Colonel James P. Coley (El Dorado, AR) assumed command of the battalion in the field near Suoi Da.[28] On November 11, the 196th LIB was released from attachment (less the 2-1st Infantry) to the 1st Infantry Division and airlifted to Tay Ninh base camp on November 12.[29]

The brigade was saved from disaster by Major Meloy, the courage and initiative of individual rifle company commanders, and the discipline of the soldiers involved. Major Meloy was awarded the Distinguished Service Cross (DSC) for his actions.[30]

Brigadier General de Saussure was reassigned on November 13, and Brigadier General Richard T. Knowles assumed command of the 196th LIB on November 14.[31]

During the period November 12–18, the 4-31st Infantry conducted highway security (Roadrunner missions) and search and destroy operations in vicinity of Nui Ba Den. On November 13, Company C's 3rd Platoon was ambushed on patrol near Nui Ba Den, losing two killed and three wounded. Intense enemy fire initially prevented the platoon from recovering the bodies of the two dead soldiers, but they struggled to regain the ground on which their comrades lay and succeeded. The wounded were evacuated by helicopter, under fire, but the company had to carry out the bodies of Privates First Class Michael J. Macarell (Hasbrouck Heights, New Jersey) and Edward J. Piantkowski (Chicago, Illinois) under fire. Air strikes were called in to help extricate the company. On November 14th, Private First Class Nelson F. Pulsifer, Jr. (Lakeside, California) was killed while on patrol near Nui Ba Den. Before the fighting ended, more than 1,100 members of the 9th VC Division were killed. On November 17, the 4-31st Infantry returned to Tay Ninh.[32]

The battle had not gone well for the "Chargers." The fight cost the lives of sixty Americans and another 159 wounded.

Despite confusing directions from Brigade Headquarters, however, the rifle companies performed well.

Tay Ninh Province was reasonably quiet for a time after Operation Attleboro, but there were reports of a renewed buildup along the Cambodian border. To head off an expected enemy offensive against Tay Ninh, the 196th LIB conducted a series of operations intended to draw the enemy into a fight.

Operation Fitchburg

Operation Fitchburg (November 25, 1966–April 8, 1967) was conducted in twenty-five phases. The operation was the northern wing, the anvil, of a hammer and anvil operation.[33]

The 4-31st Infantry participated in nine of the phases. Phase I (November 25–29) saw the battalion providing route security for Highway 26. Phase III (December 1–6) and Phase IV (December 7–14) entailed conducting search and destroy operations vicinity of Nui Ba Den Mountain. On December 1, Specialist Four Kenneth Rhodes (Greenville,

Troops of Company C, 4th Battalion, 31st Infantry, search an evacuated village 15 kilometers southeast of Chu Lai for VC and equipment (U.S. Army photograph).

SC) was killed while setting a booby trap. Phase X (December 22–26) involved relieving TF Staley, and the battalion again assumed the security mission along Highway 26. On Christmas Day, the battalion served dinner to around one hundred Vietnamese children. On December 26, the VC showed their displeasure by mortaring and ambushing Company A, killing Specialist Four Ronald D. Evans (Cincinnati, Ohio) and Private First Class Plummer Williams (Forrest City, AR) with mortar fire. Three days later, Company B was ambushed. Private First Class Robert F. Rathbun (Mansfield, Ohio) was killed in the opening burst of fire, and four others were wounded. Phase XI (December 26–30) involved conducting search and destroy operations in conjunction with one Regional Force (RF)/Popular Force (PF) company in a portion of Area of Operation (AO) Blue.[34]

During Phase XIV (January 7–25), the battalion conducted route security on Highway 26 in AO Blue secured the rock quarry vicinity of Nui Ba Den. On January 20, Staff Sergeant James N. Byers (Westminster, Maryland) of Company B was killed by sniper fire outside a patrol base. During Phase XV (January 26–February 1), Company C again provided security in AO Blue for rock quarry security in the vicinity of Nui Ba Den. Phase XIX (February 17–20) entailed conducting battalion-sized search and destroy operations on Nui Ba Den. Company A, with a Brigade Long Range Reconnaissance Patrol (LRRP) team, searched a tunnel entrance that resulted in the capture of detailed sketches of the tunnel complexes within the mountain and other documents, as well as numerous supplies. Phase XXII (March 5–9) saw the battalion assume security on Highway 26 when it replaced the 3/4 Cavalry in AO Blue. Company A relieved 3-21st Infantry at the rock quarry. Company A 2-34th Armor was attached at 1200 hours on March 5th and secured the eastern portion of Highways 25 and 239. On March 6, the battalion CP received seventy rounds of 75mm recoilless rifle (RR) fire with negative casualties.[35]

19 4th Battalion in Vietnam, 1967

Operation Cedar Falls

Operation Cedar Falls (January 8–26) was intended to prevent enemy exfiltration from the Thanh Dien Forestry Reserve and Iron Triangle areas and to deny Viet Cong/North Vietnam Army (VC/NVA) forces the use of the Saigon River in the sector. The 4-31st Infantry was not part of the 196th LIB task organization for this operation.[1]

Operation Gadsden

Operation Gadsden (February 1–21st) was a search and destroy operation. The 25th Infantry Division directed the 196th LIB to attack in zone to find, fix, and destroy VC/NVA forces and installations and to block infiltration routes across the Cambodian border before the Tet Nguyen Dan (TET) truce period. The operation began with a reconnaissance (recon) in force by the battalion. Near dusk on February 4, after the battalion established its perimeter, Company C sent out a five-man patrol to screen the front of the company's own perimeter and drop off a two-man night listening post. The patrol ran into a large VC force going to attack the battalion position. Specialist Four Richard A. Wood (Dumont, New Jersey) was killed in the ensuing firefight, and the other four patrol members were wounded. The firefight continued for a short period until artillery fire caused the VC to break contact. The battalion had fourteen additional soldiers wounded during the firefight.[2] The next day, Company A encountered the same enemy force. For the next two weeks, 4-31st Infantry's mission in the operation was limited to securing a bridge site (Company A), and providing security for an artillery battery (Company B) and the brigade CP (Company C). On February 13, Company A found five pounds of documents. At 1240 hours on February 15, the battalion was extracted from the field and returned to base camp in Tay Ninh.[3]

Operation Junction City

Operation Junction City (February 22–May 16) was initiated by II Field Force Vietnam in the western portion of War Zone C near the Cambodian border, where intelligence

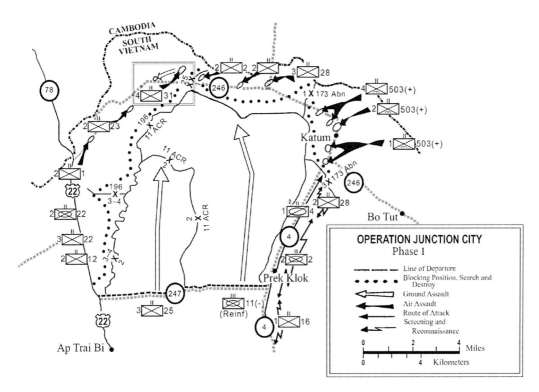

Operation Junction City, Phase I. Diagram of deployment of forces for Phase I based on a diagram developed by the U.S. Army Center of Military History.

located the VC's main political and military headquarters, the Central Office for South Vietnam. This was the largest military offensive conducted in the Vietnam War. The operation was conducted in three phases: Phase I (February 22–March 14), Phase II (March 15–April 16) and Phase III (April 17–May 16). The operation included the 2d Brigade 25th Infantry Division, 3rd Brigade 4th Infantry Division, 173rd Airborne Brigade, 196th LIB, 1st Brigade 9th Infantry Division, 11th Armored Cavalry Regiment, and an ARVN Marine Brigade consisting of the 1st and 5th Marine battalions.[4]

Preparation for Junction City began on February 21 when the 196th LIB, operating with the 3rd Brigade 4th Infantry Division, conducted airmobile assaults from the town of Suoi Da to interdict enemy troop movements east of the Cambodian border. The 4-31st Infantry operated in the northwest side of the operational area. Assaulting into a new LZ every three to four days was risky business, but it limited enemy freedom of action along the Cambodian border.[5]

On February 23, Company A spotted and fired on three enemy soldiers. The enemy escaped but they had been guarding a large way station consisting of 180 bunkers, thirty-two spider holes, and six huts in an enclosed clearing. All bunkers, spider holes, and huts were destroyed. It made no sense to stay, however, since the enemy now knew Company A's location and could easily cut them off in the jungle during the night. By nightfall, Company A was back at Suoi Da.[6]

Also on February 23rd, Company B, commanded by Captain James G. Leckey, checked a previously unsearched area. They were engaged by a large enemy force in a V-shaped bunker complex. As the company's lead platoon approached large log and earth bunkers, they came under fire from several directions at once.[7] The company lost Sergeant James A. Masten (Columbia, New Jersey), Specialists Four John L. Bylon (Chicago, Illinois), a medic assigned to Headquarters Company, and Martin M. Mugavin (Cincinnati, Ohio), a scout dog handler from the 48th Scout Dog Platoon, 196th LIB.

At 0815 hours on February 24, Company B resumed its search just a short distance from where it had encountered the enemy the day before, where they found a large, active base camp. Captain Leckey moved the company into blocking positions and called in air strikes and artillery that continued for most of the day. Under the covering fire of artillery and air strikes, the platoon recovered its dead and wounded as they withdrew to safer ground.[8]

On February 26, Company A found and destroyed thirteen pallets of enemy supplies. Soon afterward, sniper fire began dogging the company as they continued their search. Company C, operating nearby, joined forces with Company A to help flush out the snipers. Three men were wounded, and Staff Sergeant Felicisimo A. Hugo (Wahiawa, Hawaii), of Company A, was killed by automatic weapons fire as the two forces probed each other in the humid, gloomy forest.[9]

On February 28, Companies A and C were attacked by snipers and automatic weapons fire. Company A was engaged by at least a platoon-sized force in bunkers well concealed amid the dense jungle foliage. Artillery fire was brought in to allow Company A to pull back from the contact area and evacuate its wounded. Company A lost Privates First Class Richard L. Boltz (Ridgefield Park, New Jersey) and David C. Holden (Jamaica Plain, Massachusetts) to small arms fire and had three men wounded. Sergeant Wilson J. Isenhart was awarded the DSC for his actions during the attack. His DSC citation describes his actions in detail.

Sergeant Wilson J. Isenhart's DSC citation:
The President of the United States of America, authorized by Act of Congress, July 9, 1918 (amended by act of July 25, 1963), takes pleasure in presenting the Distinguished Service Cross to Sergeant Wilson J. Isenhart, United States Army for extraordinary heroism in connection with military operations involving conflict with an armed hostile force in the Republic of Vietnam, while serving with Company A, 4th Battalion, 31st Infantry, 196th Infantry Brigade. Sergeant Isenhart distinguished himself by exceptionally valorous actions on 28 February 1967 while serving as fire team leader during a search and destroy mission in hostile territory. When an observation post near his unit received intense fire on three sides from a Viet Cong force, Sergeant Isenhart picked up a machine gun and single-handedly charged into Viet Cong as they were closing in on the two men in the post. Unknown to him, the insurgents were backed up by additional men 25 meters to their rear. Heedless of the intense fire, he forced his way toward the wounded men until pinned down by fire so intense that reinforcements behind him were unable to continue their advance. He renewed his assault until his ammunition ran out. When his reinforcements caught up with him and suppressed the insurgents momentarily, Sergeant Isenhart took those few seconds to run to the two wounded men, grabbed one of their weapons and for the second time, single-handedly assaulted the numerically superior Viet Cong. After repulsing the insurgents, he took command of the men with him and set up a defensive perimeter around the observation point. His fearless attacks drove off a greater force than his own and saved the lives of the two men at the post. Sergeant Isenhart's extraordinary heroism and devotion to duty were in keeping with the highest traditions of the military service and reflect great credit upon himself, his unit, and the United States Army.[10]

That afternoon, Company C, operating just east of Company A, discovered a bicycle repair shop in the jungle. The NVA used bicycles to transport supplies down the Ho Chi Minh trail from North Vietnam. An enemy platoon watched and waited for the opportunity to strike as Company C continued its search of the area. The company lost Privates

First Class Johnnie F. Barchak, Jr., (San Antonio, Texas), Jimmy L. Langston (Hartford, CT), Michael L. Myers (Detroit, Michigan) and John T. Wetzel (Buchanan, Michigan) and six wounded as the company continued to attack. Thirteen enemy soldiers were found dead in the forest.[11]

While the rifle companies patrolled the jungle, the battalion's Civil Affairs Section, aided by Vietnamese interpreters and members of the Battalion Aid Station, conducted a vigorous civic action program. Medics treated 725 Vietnamese civilians for various ailments in Tay Ninh and in the nearby village of Ap Cao Xa. Their actions yielded a significant increase in villagers willing to report enemy activity in the area. Moreover, in the areas north and east of Suoi Da where the infantry was operating, there were no longer any civilians. Where villages once existed, clashes between the VC and Americans had made the surrounding areas unsafe, leaving the locals no choice but to flee to the safety of Tay Ninh to seek a new livelihood.[12]

The first two weeks of March brought no further contact with the enemy, but there were signs of their presence. Here and there, troops found unoccupied bunkers, spider holes, occasional fresh graves, and shattered weapons that were the result of the previous month's fighting. The most important discoveries were four newly dug mortar pits and recent truck tire tracks found by Company A, perhaps indicating the enemy was being resupplied.[13] On March 8, Specialist Four George E. Hulse III (Newburgh, New York) from Company A was killed by an accidental M-16 discharge while on the bunker line duty at 196th LIB's Tay Ninh base camp.[14]

Phase II lasted from March 15 to April 15. On March 15, 4-31st Infantry secured Prek Klok and conducted search and destroy operations.[15] The battalion found signs of the enemy daily: foxholes with bloody uniforms, mortar positions, truck tracks, and some weapons, and it engaged the enemy with night ambushes. On March 20, Company D sprang an ambush on a four-man patrol, killing one VC. A search after daybreak revealed blood trails, indicating that additional VC had also been wounded in the ambush. On March 26, Company A discovered a dead VC and seventeen burial trenches arrayed in rows. Because there had been little action so far, the VC were seemingly preparing themselves for the worst. On April 1, Captain Robert N. Bailey's Company A found a cache of 3,200 pounds of polished rice. The company destroyed the cache. The battalion destroyed two enemy base camps on April 5 and 6, but there was no further contact with the enemy.[16] On April 8, the 196th LIB withdrew from Operation Junction City and returned to Tay Ninh to begin preparation for Operation Oregon.[17]

North to I Corps—Task Force Oregon

Operation Oregon

Operation Oregon was slated for April 8 through the 30th. This operation moved units from the III Corps Tactical Zone (CTZ), in II Field Force Vietnam's AO, to Chu Lai in I CTZ of the III Marine Amphibious Force (MAF)'s AO by air and sealift. The 196th LIB was airlifted to Chu Lai on April 9 and placed OPCON to III MAF.[18] In addition, the following units were transferred to I CTZ to form TF Oregon: 2/11th Armored Cavalry Regiment, Company C 2-34th Armor, 2-11th Artillery (155mm howitzer towed), 71st Assault Helicopter Company, 178th Assault Helicopter Company, and Company C

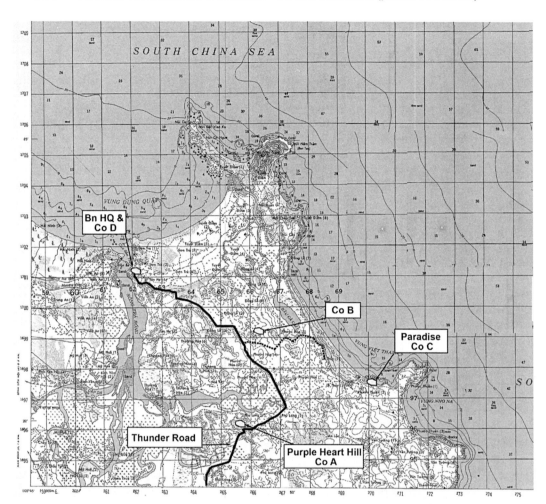

Binh Son, 6739-1. 1:50000. L7014 Series. Army Map Service, December 1965. Vietnam Archive Map Collection, The Vietnam Archive, Texas Tech University. Used by permission.

25th Medical Battalion. Out-of-country resources of 353 C-130 aircraft and U.S. Navy Landing Ship Tanks (LST) were required to move 3,452 men, 973 vehicles, and eight million pounds of cargo. On April 13, the 196th LIB main body arrived in Chu Lai.[19] The brigade became the first U.S. Army ground combat unit in I CTZ, the northernmost of South Vietnam's four military regions.[20] Until that time, the only American ground combat units in I CTZ were U.S. Marines. There had also been six U.S. Army Special Forces detachments along the Cambodian and Laotian borders and advisory teams with the ARVN 1st and 2nd Divisions and the ARVN I Corps.[21]

Later in the month, 3rd Brigade 25th Infantry Division and 1st Brigade 101st Airborne Division joined the 196th LIB in TF Oregon. TF Oregon became operational on April 20, 1967.[22] TF Oregon was formed to allow the U.S. Marines to better protect the port of Da Nang and patrol the Demilitarized Zone (DMZ) separating North and South Vietnam. Two weeks later, Brigadier General Knowles was promoted and took command of TF Oregon. On May 20th, Brigadier General Frank H. Linnell assumed command of the 196th LIB.[23]

Chu Lai was not named for any local geographic feature, but rather it derives from the Mandarin Chinese characters of Lieutenant General Victor H. Krulak's last name. Lieutenant General Krulak, Commander Fleet Marine Force Pacific, selected the site and its name in 1964 while on an inspection tour of possible future airfield locations for the U.S. Marines in Vietnam.[24]

The 4-31st Infantry's new AO from April to November 1967 was in the northeast portion of the Binh Son District, southeast of the Chu Lai airstrip. The AO was bordered on the west by the Tra Bong River, on the east and north by the South China Sea, and on the south by the Republic of Korea (ROK) 2nd Marine Battalion boundary. The battalion headquarters and Company D defensive position was located east of the ferry crossing at the northern end of the Tra Bong River. Company A was located southwest of Phu Long 1 (at what the company called "Purple Heart Hill," because they had twenty-three wounded in twenty-four days at the location). Brigadier General Linnell noted that, in sixty days, more than sixty men had been killed or wounded by mines or booby traps in the area. The grim saying was, "a foot a day in Company A."[25] Company B was located east of the road junction on the main northwest-southeast road, named "Thunder Road" by the battalion, and the road leading east to the coast. Company C's position was located on the South China Sea, named "Paradise" by some in the battalion. While in this AO, the battalion concentrated on saturation patrolling and multiple, recurring small

A USMC AMTRAC of the 5th Marine Division carries members of the 196th Light Infantry Brigade, 15 kilometers southeast of Chu Lai, in a combined effort to search a village for VC and supplies as part of TF Oregon, 27 April 1967 (U.S. Army photograph, National Archives).

Members of Company C, 4th Battalion, 31st Infantry, part of TF Oregon, guard VC suspects taken during a sweep through a small fishing village (U.S. Army photograph, National Archives).

unit search-and-destroy operations. Artillery support was provided by Battery C 3-82nd Artillery located at Chu Lai. On occasion, two 105mm howitzers were deployed forward at Company C's position to provide extended artillery support to the south. Company commanders developed intelligence in their AOs and submitted recommended night and day patrol routes to the battalion S-3 daily. These patrol routes were reviewed by the battalion S-2/S-3 shop, and that day's night patrol routes and next day's patrol routes were flown out daily to the company positions.[26]

On April 21, a patrol from Company D lost four soldiers while conducting a routine search to interdict enemy resupply on the Tra Bong River near the village of Binh Giang in Binh Son District. Specialist Four Thomas A. Mangino (Alliance, Ohio), Privates First Class Paul A. Hasenbeck (Freeburg, Missouri), David M. Winters (Delhi, California) and Daniel Nidds (West Islip, New York) of Battery C 3-82nd Artillery, were last seen in the second of two sampans patrolling on the Tra Bong River, and they were listed as missing in action until they were declared dead between 1974 and 1997.[27]

Between May and July the 196th LIB experienced a "rotational hump," because the brigade was approaching the end of one year in country. The brigade lost 66 percent of its total strength, including 58 percent of its enlisted strength, and fifteen of the eighteen key officers during the period. Officer losses included the brigade commander and all

Captured VC are loaded aboard a USMC AMTRAC for evacuation during a sweep of TF Oregon (U.S. Army photograph, National Archives).

three battalion commanders. Brigadier General Linnell established a special training program for the incoming replacements and told battalion commanders to abandon their productive small-unit operations for safer, company-sized operations until units gained combat experience.[28]

The evening of April 30, two jeeps were ambushed while taking resupply and mail from the battalion's forward base to Company B. The ambush was small, consisting of only five VC armed with automatic rifles, but the element of surprise magnified their strength. The lead jeep sped through the ambush, but the second careened off the road. The driver, Specialist Bruce H. Scragg (Marmet, West Virginia), was killed when the enemy found him pinned in the vehicle, unable to resist.

On May 1, Company B came under sniper fire. When the company responded with an outpouring of rifle, machine gun and grenade launcher fire, the enemy escalated the engagement by firing five 57mm RR rounds into the perimeter. Helicopter gunships arrived at 1500 hours, spraying the enemy positions with rockets and miniguns, causing the VC to back off. Company B lost Staff Sergeant Bobby E. Hunt (Chuckey, Tennessee) during the engagement, and Specialists Four Michael J. Hilburger (Cheektowaga, New York) and Charles E. Miller (Piketon, Ohio) were lost to a booby trap. That evening, Company A spotted a flotilla of ten sampans, one of them mounting a 57mm RR on its deck. A hot exchange of fire soon followed, with artillery bracketing the enemy vessels and smothering them in a thundering rain of 105mm rounds. No survivors were found.[29]

On the morning of May 3, an unknown size enemy force probed the battalion's support base, hitting the mess tent with a sustained burst of automatic weapons fire during breakfast. Artillery was called in on a group of six VC spotted about 400 meters from the perimeter. Moments later, a call came into the battalion tactical operations center reporting that Company D encountered an ambush on a nearby road-clearing operation. Private First Class James R. Dowdy (Granite City, Illinois) was killed, and another soldier was wounded in the opening burst of fire. Company D returned fire killing two of the ambushers and capturing two U.S. M-1 carbines and miscellaneous web gear.[30] On May 5, Specialist Four John J. Thomas (Philadelphia, Pennsylvania) was killed in a meeting engagement, and Staff Sergeant Gregory W. Woods (Pittsburgh, Pennsylvania) was killed while disarming a mine.[31]

On May 11, 1967, Lieutenant Colonel Charles R. Smith, Jr. (San Francisco, California) assumed command of the battalion from Lieutenant Colonel Coley.[32]

When the battalion replaced the U.S. 7th Marine Regiment in the northeast portion of the Binh Son District, it assumed responsibility for Combined Action Platoon (CAP) operations with locally recruited Vietnamese PF. The concept placed a reinforced American rifle squad or platoon, with a PF platoon or RF company to protect a village where the VC had been active. In the early morning hours of May 23, the village of Van Tuong 1, one of five villages constituting the hamlet of Van Tuong, came under attack. Six days earlier, the 2nd Platoon of Company C 4-31st Infantry had arrived to help protect a newly appointed village chief. Captain Mike Ruane, Company C commander, had conceived the idea of using CAP missions in his AO, and he assigned First Lieutenant James L. Williams and his platoon a CAP mission.[33]

A twenty-four hour truce was declared on May 22 in observance of Buddha's birthday. At 0345 hours on May 23, 2nd Platoon Company C was attacked by an estimated two VC companies while in the village of Van Tuong 1, where 114 civilians were treated by a Medical Civil Action Program (MEDCAP) during the day. The platoon had five soldiers killed: Privates First Class Charlie M. Gilmer (Christiansburg, Virginia), Joseph D. King (Carrboro, North Carolina), Donald A. Skinner (Lavallette, New Jersey), Carl R. Stovall (Fort Pierce, Florida), and John T. Trivette (Winston-Salem, North Carolina), and fifteen wounded. A National Policeman was also killed by the VC, and the village chief was killed by friendly fire. The enemy lost seventeen confirmed killed.[34] The same day Company A lost Sergeant Robert D. Thompson (Wymer, West Virginia) to a booby trap.

Specialist Four Richard A. Green was awarded the DSC for his actions on 23 May. His DSC citation describes his actions in detail.

Specialist Fourth Richard A. Green's DSC citation:
The President of the United States takes pleasure in presenting the Distinguished Service Cross to Richard A. Green, United States Army, who distinguished himself by extraordinary heroism on 23 May 1967 while serving as radio operator of an infantry platoon with Company C, 4th Battalion, 31st Infantry, 196th Light Infantry Brigade in the Republic of Vietnam. While on a village pacification mission at An Loc a numerically superior Viet Cong force launched a savage attack on his camp early in the morning, but Specialist Green ignored the intense barrage of machine gun, recoilless rifle and grenade fire and dashed across open ground to a nearby machine gun position. He was seriously wounded by an enemy grenade but refused aid and fought furiously against the determined onslaught. He saw that the withering Viet Cong fire was preventing his comrades from reaching the radio and immediately moved into the open under a hail of bullets to call for air strikes and rein-

forcements. Completely disregarding his own safety, he remained in the open to direct gunships and ordnance on the advancing attackers. With bullets and shrapnel flying all around him he stood up in the midst of the savage firefight to guide the strafing runs using a burning hut as a reference point. He exposed himself to the Viet Cong weapons time after time to inform his commander of the rapidly changing situation and bring air strikes closer to his line. He repeatedly refused to take cover and stayed on the radio until the insurgents were defeated and withdrew after suffering heavy casualties. His fearless actions in the face of grave danger contributed greatly to the successful defense of the village and the rout of the Viet Cong. Specialist Four Green's extraordinary heroism and devotion to duty were in keeping with the highest tradition of the military service and reflect great credit up himself, his unit, and the United States Army.[35]

On May 26, a patrol from Company C stopped four sampans loitering near the shore on the Song Tra Bong River. The eldest fisherman said he "stays on his boat because there are many grey-uniformed soldiers (referring to NVA soldiers) in his village, making him afraid to go home." Four days later, Company A was fired on during a recon in force and killed two VC guerrillas in the ensuing exchange.[36]

During the first eight days of June, the battalion conducted joint operations with the ROK 2nd Marine Battalion. Contact with the enemy occurred daily. On June 3, Company C lost Private First Class Luther Robinson (Beaver, Ohio) in a meeting engagement when he triggered a hand grenade booby trap. Most engagements were brief firefights with small, elusive groups of VC. Mines and booby traps, however, took their toll. Pressure-detonated 105mm howitzer shells were cleverly concealed in or beside roads on which the battalion's resupply convoys traveled. During June, the battalion conducted extensive CAP in the village of Tam Ky, with medical treatment provided to an average of seventy-five persons daily.[37]

Company C lost Specialist Four Robert J. Nicklow (Garrett, Pennsylvania) on July 11 to a booby trap, on July 16, Privates First Class Charles E. Merriman (Knoxville, Tennessee) and Reynaldo S. Torres (Uvalde, Texas), and on July 21 Specialist Four Dennis J. Wahl (Alliance, Ohio) when his jeep hit a mine. On August 9, Private First Class Harvey E. Wynn (Donalsonville, Georgia), from Headquarters Company, was wounded near Binh Son and later died in the hospital. Company A lost Specialist Four Lonnie O. Hill (Atoka, Tennessee) on August 29 to sniper fire during an ambush, and Specialist Four Ralph M. Knight (Attalla, Alabama) was killed on the 30th in an ambush near Phu Long 1 village. The VC appeared to be more interested in evasion than making contact. In August, a VC rice cache was discovered, and 2,850 pounds of rice were given to the people of Son Tra 2 as another act of friendship to people of the area.[38]

The battalion conducted a population relocation operation, resettling villagers of Tuyet Diem to Son Tra I in Binh Giang village. The villagers volunteered to be relocated to escape VC control. The operation began on August 21 and was suspended on August 25 because of the Vietnamese elections. The relocation continued on September 9 and was completed on September 13. The battalion relocated 4,092 villagers, many whom were fishermen and were able to continue their trade at the new location.[39] In early September, the battalion shifted its concentration from road clearing to searching for underground enemy bunker systems, which resulted in less enemy harassment and fewer American casualties.[40] On September 15, the point men of 1st Platoon Company A were engaged with VC small arms and M-79 rounds, killing Specialist Four Ray Collins (Chicago, Illinois) and Private First Class Franklin D. Willett (Herford, Arizona).[41]

On October 2, Company D found a tunnel complex containing one ton of rice near Phu Long Hamlet 3. The tunnel complex was destroyed and the rice evacuated.[42]

Troops of Company C, 4th Battalion 31st Infantry search an evacuated village 15 kilometers south-east of Chu Lai for VC and equipment (U.S. Army photograph, National Archives).

Operations Wheeler and Wallowa

On September 11, Operation Wheeler was begun by the 1st Brigade 101st Airborne Division moving against the 2nd NVA Division northwest of Chu Lai. On October 4, the 3rd Brigade 1st Cavalry Division (Airmobile) joined TF Oregon and began Operation Wallowa.[43]

On October 26, formal Americal Division activation ceremonies were held at Chu Lai. Concurrent with the formal ceremonies, the 196th LIB became assigned to the Americal Division. TF Oregon was inactivated when the Division Headquarters Company was activated on September 25.[44] On October 31, Colonel Louis Gelling assumed command of the 196th LIB. When the brigade was assigned to the division, the authorized rank of the brigade commander was returned to a colonel.[45]

During early November, the battalion continued to operate on the northeastern portion of the Binh Son District. On November 10, Company D lost Private First Class Johnny W. McCain (Ore City, Texas) in a meeting engagement.

Operation Wheeler/Wallowa

Operation Wheeler/Wallowa covered November 11, 1967, through November 11, 1968. On November 11, Operations Wheeler and Wallowa were merged to facilitate better

LZ West as seen from the air (photograph by Jim Logue. Used by permission).

command and control.[46] On November 15, the 196th LIB moved north from Chu Lai into the Que Son Valley to relieve the 1st Brigade of the 101st Airmobile Division and to begin operations there and in the Hiep Duc Valley. The 196th LIB was designated TF Longerbeam, named for Major James L. Longerbeam (Winchester, Pennsylvania), the 4-31st Infantry S-3, who had been wounded earlier. The 196th LIB headquarters moved to Hill 35, just north of Tam Ky, to join in the operation.[47] During the move north, Lieutenant Colonel Jack D. Thomas assumed command of the battalion from Lieutenant Colonel Smith.[48]

The 4-31st Infantry battalion headquarters was established on LZ West (Hill 445), named Nui Liet Kiem (Mountain of Leeches).[49] LZ West became the battalion's base of operations, except for short periods during 1968. LZ West was located about thirty kilometers west of the Brigade Headquarters on LZ Baldy. In May 1971, the battalion moved west of Da Nang.

1967 Battle for Hiep Duc

During Phase I of Operation Wheeler/Wallowa, the battalion was involved in the heaviest fighting since their arrival in Vietnam. The operation's objective was to dislodge the 2nd NVA Division from the Que Son Valley. The 2nd NVA Division Headquarters was reported to be located northwest of LZ West, and the 3rd NVA Regimental Headquarters was located northeast of LZ West. On November 16, Private Lewis L. Sloan (East Point, Georgia) of Company D died in the hospital as result of a grenade attack on a company observation post (OP).[50]

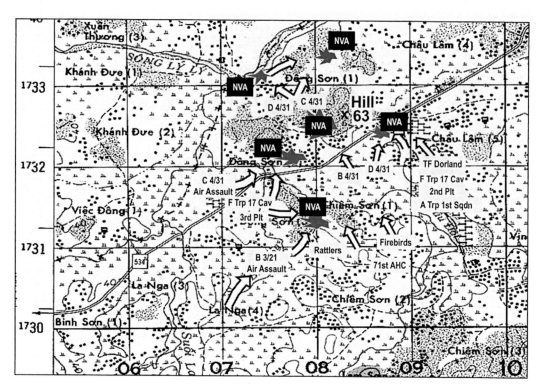

Thanksgiving Day Battle, Hill 63. Map shows locations of Task Force Dorland units and enemy locations during the Thanksgiving Day Battle on November 23, 1967. Tam Ky, 6640-2[map]. 1:50000. L7014 Series. U.S. Army Topographic Command, September 1974. Vietnam Archive Map Collection, The Vietnam Archive, Texas Tech University. Used by permission.

Phase II began with setting up blocking positions in the vicinity of Dong Son Hamlet, eleven kilometers northwest of LZ West in the Que Son Valley.[51]

The fight at Hill 63, which became known as "The Thanksgiving Day Battle," took place from November 23 to November 25.[52] This was the first instance of several years of battles between the 4-31st Infantry and the 2nd NVA Division in the Que Son/Hiep Duc Valleys. The 4-31st Infantry formed an armored-infantry TF named TF Dorland, commanded by Major Gil Dorland, the battalion S-3. The TF consisted of Company B 3-21st Infantry, F Troop 17th Cavalry, A Troop 1/1 Cavalry, Battery B 3-82nd Artillery and Battery C 3-16th Artillery, 155mm howitzers.[53] TF Dorland surprised the enemy, and the battle rapidly expanded. Company B, commanded by Captain James Bierschmidt, and Company D 4-31st Infantry, commanded by Captain Daniel L. Mellon (Fairbanks, Alaska), moved to Hill 63, between Dong Son 1 and Dong Son 2, the reported location of the 3rd NVA Regiment. Company D was attacked from well-camouflaged fortified positions on Hill 63 at a distance of ten meters and was not able to maneuver into good fighting positions. On November 23, Company D lost Corporals Kenneth S. Adams (Santa Barbara, California), Philip F. Adams (Croton Falls, New York), and Rodney E. Loatman (Newark, New Jersey), as well as Private First Class Robert D. Waddell (Batavia, Ohio), and had thirty wounded. Armored Personnel Carriers from F Troop 17th Cavalry joined the battle and were engaged by 57mm RR fire. Company B, A Troop 1/1 Cavalry, and F Troop 17th Cavalry assaulted their objective about 500 meters west of Hill 63. The attack was supported by airstrikes. Company B 3-21st Infantry reinforced the battalion in the afternoon. Major Gilbert Dorland was wounded during this engagement and was awarded the DSC for his control and leadership of the operation.[54]

His DSC citation describes his actions in detail.

Major Gilbert N. Dorland's DSC citation:

Major (Infantry) Gilbert Noyes Dorland, United States Army, for extraordinary heroism in connection with military operations involving conflict with an armed hostile force in the Republic of Vietnam, while serving with Headquarters and Headquarters Company, 4th Battalion, 31st Infantry, 196th Infantry Brigade (Light) (Separate). Major Dorland distinguished himself by exceptionally valorous actions on 23 November 1967 while serving as commander of a two-company task force on a combat operation near Dong Son. While moving toward a suspected enemy location, the infantry elements suddenly received intense hostile automatic weapons and small arms fire. Major Dorland immediately maneuvered his mechanized element in front of the beleaguered infantry troops and directed lethal machine gun fire on the North Vietnamese positions. The armored personnel carrier in which he was riding received a direct hit from an enemy anti-tank weapon. The round killed the track commander and threw Major Dorland to the ground. He was run over and severely wounded by the vehicle as it backed into a defilade position. Although in great pain, he refused to be evacuated and accepted first aid as he continued to direct the deployment of his troops. Braving an increasingly savage hail of bullets and rocket fire, Major Dorland gallantly moved throughout the battlefield to adjust friendly artillery and air strikes and commit reinforcements to critical locations. His fearless and inspiring leadership in close combat with a determined enemy force was responsible for an overwhelming victory. Major Dorland's extraordinary heroism and devotion to duty were in keeping with the highest traditions of the military service and reflect great credit up himself, his unit, and the United State Army.[55]

On November 24, Company D was hit hard again. TF Dorland attacked Dong Son Hamlet on November 25 at 0100 hours. After several hours of fierce combat, the TF entered the hamlet and defeated the enemy on the nearby hill. During the month, the NVA lost 106 soldiers confirmed killed.[56]

Throughout December, intelligence reports indicated that the 2nd NVA Division had 6,500 soldiers north of LZ West and was expected to attack and destroy "an American Brigade." On December 20, Lieutenant Colonel Frederick R. Cully assumed command of the battalion from Lieutenant Colonel Thomas.[57]

The battalion observed a cease-fire from 24 1800 to 25 1800 hours December 1967.[58]

20 4th Battalion in Vietnam, 1968

On January 2, 1968, intelligence reports indicated that enemy forces, including the 21st Regiment, the 40th, 60th and 90th Battalions and 1st Main Force Regiment of the 2nd NVA Division, with strength of approximately 1,500 men, were in the battalion AO. Company D made the first contact with the NVA two kilometers northwest of LZ West. The LZ was attacked at 0240 hours with grenades, probing actions, and mortars.[1] At 0400 hours on January 3, Company D came under heavy attack and was supported by air strikes. Company C, commanded by Captain Joseph Stringham, was deployed and linked up with Company D, commanded by Captain James F. Richards. Company D lost Specialist Four Jack W. McKinnon (Santa Cruz, California) and had seven wounded.[2]

On January 4, Company C 2-1st Infantry and Company A 3-21st Infantry were placed OPCON to the 4-31st Infantry.[3]

On January 4 at 0125 hours, Company D was attacked by the surrounding NVA force with a barrage of automatic weapons and rocket-propelled grenades (RPGs) from two sides and Captain Richards was seriously wounded by grenades, losing an eye. By 0250 hours, Company D had four men killed: Private First Class Billy G. Jent (Vinita, Oklahoma), Privates James D. Osenbaugh (Hutchinson, Kansas), Walter J. Peters (Indio, California), and Robert W. Sorensen (Minneapolis, Minnesota) and fourteen wounded. The heavy enemy fire restricted Company C's attempt to link up with Company D.[4]

At the same time, LZ West was under enemy attack by rockets, mortars, and grenades for three hours. Three men from Headquarters Company were wounded. Later in the day, Captain Richards was evacuated, and Captain Dan Mellon, the Battalion S-2, assumed command of Company D. A search of the perimeter revealed fifteen dead NVA, enemy documents, AK-47 rifles, rocket launchers, and communication equipment.[5]

On January 5 at 0500 hours, the enemy resumed their attack on LZ West with small arms fire and grenades. At 0900 hours, Lieutenant Colonel Cully left LZ West in the command and control (C&C) helicopter to visit the companies positioned in the Que Son Valley. The helicopter was hit by heavy automatic weapons fire and forced to return to LZ West. Later, a resupply helicopter was shot down in the valley. The battalion rescued the helicopter crew, and they were flown out of the area without incident.[6]

During the day of January 5, the two OPCON companies had scattered contact and experienced enemy radio jamming. A gunship was shot up by automatic weapons fire, but landed safely northwest of the battle area.

Company C 2-1st Infantry was ambushed in heavy contact at 1900 hours. At about 0010 hours, Company A 4-31st Infantry linked up with Company C 2-1st Infantry while the battle was ongoing.[7]

At 0500 hours on January 6 when the battle ended, Company C 2-1st Infantry had eighteen killed, including three platoon leaders, plus fifty-four wounded, many of them seriously. Battery A 3-82nd Artillery also lost a forward observer (FO) and his radio telephone operator (RTO) who were attached to Company C. Company C 2-1st Infantry was replaced by Company B 2-1st Infantry.[8]

At first light on January 6, Major Patrick Brady, 54th Medical Detachment, 67th Medical Group, flew his first medevac mission of the day through heavy fog into Companies A and C. About 0900 hours he flew the last of three medevac missions into the companies. The helicopters on the first two missions were damaged and he had to use a replacement helicopter each time. For his actions he was awarded the Medal of Honor.[9]

The TF searched for the enemy on January 7. The enemy mortared and attacked U.S. units that night.[10] On January 8, Company B 4-31st Infantry lost Second Lieutenant Anthony R. Watkins (Ardmore, Oklahoma) and Private First Class Howard M. Bissen (Stacyville, Iowa) in a meeting engagement. Company B, commanded by Captain Bill Speer (Ottawa, Kansas), fought a three-day battle against a large enemy force of 300 to 400 who were armed with old U.S. M-1 30-06 sniper rifles in addition to the typical AK 47s and AK 50s.[11] At dawn on January 9, Company A found sixteen NVA killed after their heavy attack the night before. Also on January 9, Company A lost Private Sisto B. Bojorquez (Eloy, Arizona). In addition, LZ West received heavy mortar fire during the night. The battalion remained in contact through January 27, when the TET Truce began.[12]

On February 3, the 4-31st Infantry was airlifted from LZ West to LZ Baldy and, at 1100 hours, was placed OPCON to the 3rd Brigade 4th Infantry Division to initiate operations between

Photograph shows MG Patrick H. Brady in 1989. Early on the morning of January 6, 1968, MAJ Brady flew three medevac missions to bring out wounded soldiers of the 4th Battalion 31st Infantry Task Force. In each of the first two missions, his Huey was shot up so badly he had to use a different copter for the next medevac. The result of those medevacs of Task Force soldiers was the Medal of Honor (Wikimedia Commons).

Highway 1 and Route 535. Moving the 4-31st Infantry to LZ Baldy enabled the Americal Division to deploy the 3rd Brigade and two of its battalions into the area of Hoi An. The 4-31st Infantry conducted security sweeps along Highway 1 and Route 535 and provided security for LZ Baldy.[13]

The 4-31st Infantry was awarded the Valorous Unit Award for action in the Que Son and Hiep Duc Districts from November 15, 1967, to February 3, 1968.

> 4th Battalion's Valorous Unit Award Citation:
> The 4th Battalion, 31st Infantry, 196th Light Infantry Brigade, Americal Division distinguished itself by extraordinary heroism while engaged in military operations during the period 15 November 1967 to 3 February 1968 in the Que Son and Hiep Duc Districts of the Republic of Vietnam. Initially participating in Operation Wheeler/Wallowa in the Que Son District, the battalion's personnel demonstrated exemplary courage and relentless determination in conducting highly successful search, destroy and interdiction missions. On 22 November 1967, they were committed to an assault upon a large North Vietnamese army force in the vicinity of the Dong Son hamlet. Because of the voluminous fire power and aggressiveness of the unit's members during three consecutive days of fierce fighting, the enemy was forced to break contact and the battle was held as an overwhelming victory of the fighting men of the 4th Battalion, 31st Infantry, 196th Light Infantry Brigade, Americal Division. Subsequently operating in the Hiep Duc District, the battalion's members served as the security force for Fire Support Base West. On the morning of 3 January 1968, a large communist force launched an intensive attack upon the base and pressed on for nine days and nights with violent mortar, rocket and rocket propelled grenade assaults in an attempt to break through the defense. Exhibiting unparalleled bravery and perseverance, the security elements repulsed every enemy attack while the maneuver elements simultaneously engaged and defeated regimental-sized units of the North Vietnamese Army in the Hiep Duc Valley....[14]

The battalion lost Private First Class Mark A. Kolvek (Gary, Indiana) of Company D on February 8 when engaged by automatic weapons fire, and Company B lost Sergeant Joseph P. Bowling (Wichita, Kansas) and Privates First Class Gerald A. Huczek (Roseville, Michigan) and Craig G. Knobloch (East Lansing, Michigan) on February 11 near Liberty Bridge on Go Noi Island.

On February 12, the battalion was airlifted to LZ Polar Bear and began conducting combat operations in vicinity of the LZ.[15] On February 12, Company C lost Private First Class Richard D. Vick (Bemidji, Minnesota) to a booby-trapped 60mm mortar round. On February 13, the company received heavy automatic weapons fire, wounding several men and killing Private First Class Kellynn V. Snow (Salt Lake City, Utah). On the 14th, Specialist Four Charles M. Burke (Mandeville, Louisiana) was killed by a land mine. Also on February 14, Company D suffered three wounded by a VC land mine. On February 19, Company C hit two booby traps (M-26 grenades), wounding an additional five men.[16] The battalion remained OPCON to the 3rd Brigade until February 27.[17]

During the first two weeks of March there was no significant enemy action. On March 4, Specialist Five Everett J. Valandingham (Dallas, Texas), a battalion medic, was killed by mortar fire on LZ Polar Bear. On March 15, Sergeant Leroy W. Katterhenry (Columbus, Ohio) and Private First Class Raymond C. Guest (Redding, California) of Company C were killed in a fire fight southeast of Que Son. On March 19, the battalion built and moved its base of operations to LZ Ryder. Company D made contact on March 23, having one man wounded. On March 26, Company B located a VC aid station. The local populace reported that the VC had left the area five days before. Company B destroyed the empty medical facility. Also on March 26, Company D discovered a vacated VC base camp.[18]

In late March, Company A built and occupied LZ Sooner. At about the same time, the 196th LIB Headquarters moved from LZ Baldy to "Charger Hill" west of Tam Ky.[19]

At the end of March, the battalion became part of TF Delta operating west of LZ Sooner. The operation's objective was to cut enemy supply routes and to locate and destroy enemy staging areas.[20]

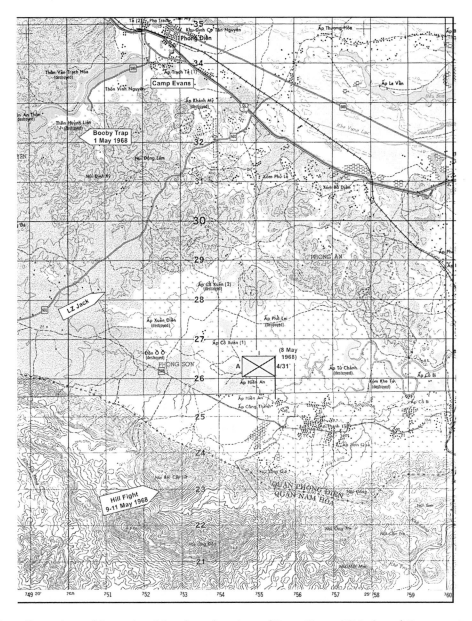

Camp Evans Area of Operation. Map shows locations of Camp Evans, LZ Jack, and Company A on May 8, 1968; and the fight to link up with Company B and 1st Cavalry Division LRRP 1 Zulu on May 9–11. Information courtesy John Mansfield, based on Ap Lai Bang, 6441-1. 1:50000. L7014 Series. Army Map Service, December 1966. Also based on Hai Lang (Thon Dien Sanh), 6442-2. 1:50000. L7014 Series. Army Map Service, March 1974. Both maps are from the Vietnam Archive Map Collection, The Vietnam Archive, Texas Tech University. Used by permission.

In April, Companies B and D formed TF Bravo. TF Bravo's mission was to locate enemy base camps in vicinity of LZ Sooner. Company B discovered a battalion-size base camp and hospital on a jungle peak near LZ Sooner on April 4. The enemy vacated the area just ahead of Company B's arrival, abandoning a weapons cache of five .51 caliber machine guns and over 300 rifles. There was no trace of enemy personnel.[21] On April 11, TF Bravo was ambushed by a dug-in VC main force company. Company B lost Specialist Four Keith N. Atchley (Woodland, Virginia) and Private First Class Larry D. Hatcher (Martinsville, Virginia) during a meeting engagement. The company was prepared for the ambush and destroyed the ambush attempt, killing a lot of NVA and VC soldiers. The Company chased the remainder of the enemy force to a fortified village on a river northwest of Hiep Duc. Two soldiers and Captain Speer were wounded. Captain Speer's wounds cost him an arm.[22] On April 15, Specialist Five James T. McMaster (Rosiclare, Illinois), a medic assigned to Headquarters Company, was killed by small arms fire.[23]

Operation Delaware

Operation Delaware (April 19–May 17) was an airmobile raid into the enemy stronghold of the A Shau Valley. The goal was to exploit the enemy defeat in Operation Pegasus. The objective of Pegasus was the relief of Khe Sanh combat base by the 1st Cavalry Division (Airmobile). The secondary purpose was to prevent another attack on Hue.[24] On April 15, the battalion was alerted to move north to Camp Evans. Between April 17 and 23, the 196th LIB moved north to support the Provisional Corps Vietnam (PCV) in the Hue-Phu Bai area.[25] Units of the 196th LIB were not sent into the A Shau Valley. Instead they were the reserve forces for the operation.[26] The battalion was airlifted by C-123 transports from LZ Baldy to Camp Evans and placed OPCON to the 1st Cavalry Division (Airmobile). In late April, LZ West was dismantled. The 1st Cavalry was moving into the A Shau Valley and the battalion was tasked to secure Camp Evans and the surrounding AO. Camp Evans was located twenty-four kilometers northwest of Hue, just west of Highway One. The battalion conducted security sweeps of roads and lost three wounded to booby traps. On April 24, Company B lost Privates First Class George B. Ayers (Wilkes-Barre, Pennsylvania) and Wilbur F. Mattox (Gainesville, Georgia) to enemy fire. On April 27, Company B lost Specialist Four Martin W. Guard (Santa Ana, California) in an enemy engagement.[27]

On May 1, Company A's 1st Platoon hit a large booby trap southwest of Camp Evans, wounding several and killing five soldiers: First Lieutenant Howard R. Crothers (New Martinsville, West Virginia), who had been with the company only a few days, Privates First Class Thomas K. Lyons (Philadelphia, Pennsylvania), Michael J. Massey (Columbus, Georgia), William P. Townsend Jr. (Reseda, California), and Private Eusebio Solis (San Jose, California).[28]

On May 6, Company A was ordered to dismantle LZ Jack, a company-sized LZ, located about five kilometers southwest of Camp Evans. Captain A. J. Holborn assumed command of Company A on LZ Jack, replacing Captain Byers.[29] The company finished dismantling LZ Jack on May 8.[30]

On May 8, 2nd Platoon Company B was rushed to assist a 1st Cavalry Division LRRP team, 1 Zulu, that was in heavy contact southwest of Camp Evans. The 2nd Platoon received heavy enemy fire while attempting a linkup with the LRRP team. The platoon lost Privates First Class Jimmy R. Brown (Cleburne, Texas), Terrence A. Kandler (Torrance, California), Jimmy R. Wheless (San Angelo, Texas), a rifleman assigned to Headquarters Company, and Russell W. Jarick (Los Angeles, California), a medic also assigned to Headquarters Company, and twelve wounded. At 2000 hours, Company A was ordered to move overland and link up with 2nd Platoon. Company A moved west until 2400 hours, when it established a night defensive position (NDP) and awaited helicopters for an early morning combat assault into an LZ close to the 2nd Platoon position.[31]

On May 9, Company A linked up with 2nd Platoon. It took Company A until the morning of May 11 to take the top of the hill where 2nd Platoon Company B and the LRRP team had fought. Lieutenant John Mansfield describes the combat as "fighting up-close and personal with hand grenades and as much suppressive fire as could be brought to bear on the enemy positions."[32] Seventy-nine fighting positions and spider holes were found on the hill. The three bodies of the LRRP team were recovered.[33] On May 12, Company A was airlifted to a location close to LZ Jack and spent the day rearming and refitting. The company had eighteen wounded and evacuated in the three-day engagement and another nine wounded, who were treated and returned to duty.[34] On May 13, the 196th

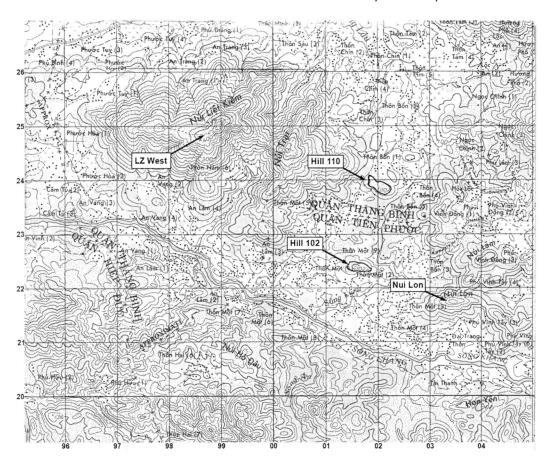

Battle of Nui Lon. Map shows locations of LZ West, Hills 102, 110, and Nui Lon where fighting spanned May 15 through 19. Hiep Duc, 6640-3. 1:50000. L7014 Series. Army Map Service, December 1965. Vietnam Archive Map Collection, The Vietnam Archive, Texas Tech University. Used by permission.

LIB moved by C-123s from the PCV to LZ Baldy.[35] The battalion was rocketed while on the Camp Evans airstrip before departing the northern AO.[36] The redeployment ended the battalion's participation in Operation Delaware.[37] On May 14, the battalion was airlifted by helicopter back from LZ Baldy to LZ West. The battalion began rebuilding LZ West upon arrival.[38] The battalion rear headquarters remained at LZ Baldy during the battalion's deployment to PCV.

On May 15, Companies A and D, operating as TF Alpha, came under heavy mortar fire, and a medical evacuation (MEDEVAC) helicopter received heavy .51 caliber fire while extracting wounded. This action began ten days of fierce fighting southeast of LZ West in the vicinity of Hills 102, 110, and Nui Lon. Company A lost Private Charles A. Cope (St. Louis, Missouri) in a mortar attack. The next day, Specialist Four Richard L. Moss (Tampa, Florida), a medic assigned to Headquarters Company, attached to Company A, died as result of fragmentation wounds.

On May 18, Company A conducted a night assault on Nui Lon. As the company neared its objective it received heavy fire from an adjacent ridgeline. At daybreak, the company was unable to maneuver because of heavy .30 and .51 caliber machine gun fire. The NVA also attacked Company A with mortar and RR fire and "jammed" the company command radio frequency. Company A lost Specialist Four Timothy J. Rizzardini (Ridgecrest, California) and Private First Class Harold D. Peppers (Chicago, Illinois) in the action.[39] Late that afternoon, Company A fired an artillery screen then withdrew to linkup with Company D at their NDP near the village of Vinh Dong (1), approximately one and a half kilometers northwest of Nui Lon. Early on May 19, Company D moved to the top of Nui Lon, where they discovered a bell-shaped bunker complex and several enemy weapons. Company A was then airlifted from their night laager to LZ West.[40]

There was little contact with the enemy over the next several days. On May 24, Company C suffered several casualties from heavy mortar fire. A jet fighter was shot down 8 kilometers east of the company. The pilot was picked up by a helicopter gunship. A second fighter was shot down a few minutes later; the pilot ejected, but his parachute failed to open.[41]

After midnight on May 25, LZ West came under 122mm rocket attack. The Quad 50 bunker took a direct hit, wounding four soldiers. After dawn, Company C found the enemy's rocket launcher position with fourteen empty 122mm rocket canisters. Company C lost four soldiers to enemy fire: Sergeants Steve Gomez (Miami, Florida) and Ronald C. McEuen (Garden Grove, California), Specialist Four Eugene G. O'Connell (Edgewater, New Jersey), and Private First Class Dennis L. Stiglitz (Stephenson, Michigan). Company D lost Private First Class Dennis L. Mack (Detroit, Michigan) the same day in action near Tien Phuoc. Later in the day, a resupply helicopter was shot down, but the crew was rescued. On May 26, Company D found and recovered the body of the second fighter pilot. Company B found and destroyed 124 B-40 rockets. On May 27, Company C discovered another deserted base camp.[42]

The rest of May was spent searching the battle area; a few NVA were spotted, and a great deal of NVA equipment was discovered. June was a quiet month compared to the previous two months, although Company A had heavy enemy contact the night of June 10–11. They were supported by artillery fire and flare ships. The next morning, numerous blood trails were found outside the NDP, but only one Czech assault rifle was found.[43] On June 18, Company D lost Specialist Four Nathaniel Wade (Augusta, Georgia) to friendly fire.

Operation Pocahontas Forest

The objective of Operation Pocahontas Forest (July 6–August 4) was to find, fix and destroy enemy forces in Hiep Duc and Phuoc Chau Valley, known as "Antenna Valley." The Valley got its name because radio operators were required to use a long whip antenna to communicate with LZ West when operating in the valley. TF Cooksey was formed for the operation and included the 4-31st Infantry, 4-3rd Infantry, 4-21st Infantry, 5-46th Infantry, and a company from the 26th Engineers. Two U.S. Marine battalions and the 2nd, 3rd and 5th ARVN Regiments also took part in the operation.[44]

Enemy action increased in July. The battalion rotated companies between LZs Mellon, Richards, Gimlet, O'Conner, and Polar Bear II. Companies A and B found fifteen graves and a deserted VC hospital near LZ O'Conner.[45]

On July 3, Company A lost Private First Class John D. Cox, Jr. (Tucson, Arizona) and Company B lost Private First Class Joseph H. Houtz (Springfield, Missouri) in attacks on their NDPs. Company D was ambushed on July 6, resulting in five wounded, and Private First Class Arthur Harmon (Laurel, Mississippi) was killed in an attack on the NDP. On July 9, Company C lost Private First Class Charles F. Harger, Jr. (Headrick, Oklahoma) in a mortar attack. On July 14, the Company uncovered an enemy cache containing

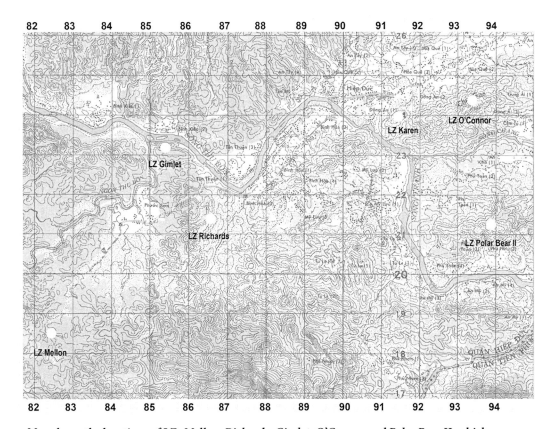

Map shows the locations of LZs Mellon, Richards, Gimlet, O'Conner and Polar Bear II, which were occupied by rotating rifle companies during July through early September 1968. Hiep Duc, 6640-3. 1:50000. L7014 Series. Army Map Service, December 1965. Vietnam Archive Map Collection, The Vietnam Archive, Texas Tech University. Used by permission.

twenty-one bicycles, an AK-47 rifle, tear gas, and a gas mask. Company D discovered a company-sized enemy feeding station base camp near LZ Gimlet.[46] On July 20, Company C lost Specialist Four Willis J. Billeaud, Jr. (Broussard, Louisiana) on LZ Mellon.

Lieutenant Colonel Robert L. "Sam" Wetzel assumed command from Lieutenant Colonel Cully on July 23 on a hilltop near the deserted village of Hiep Duc.[47]

One day in August, General Creighton Abrams, Commander U.S. Military Assistance Command Vietnam, visited Company C on LZ Mellon. First Lieutenant Ed Henry, Company C Commander, accompanied General Abrams on his tour of the firebase.[48] That night, Company C received eighteen incoming grenades and seven mortar rounds, resulting in three wounded.

First Lieutenant John Garrett took over the Recon Platoon shortly after Lieutenant Colonel Wetzel took command. First Lieutenant Garrett trained the platoon for twenty-eight days in night patrolling techniques. The platoon patrolled mainly at night and slept during the day. "The Recon Platoon became famous for capturing many men and weapons at night."[49]

During August contact with the enemy was light. The battalion continued rotating between the same LZs as in July. On August 23, the NVA attacked the south side of LZ West. On August 26, Private First Class Fernando A. Rivera Jr. (New York, New York) was killed during an enemy probe of the NDP. During August, the battalion's AO was sprayed with Agent Orange.[50]

In early September, Typhoon BETH struck Chu Lai with winds in excess of fifty knots. Most air traffic in the American Division AO was grounded during the typhoon. Company C found a large NVA base camp on September 9.[51] The twenty-five hut base camp contained thirty-one SKS-44 rifles, five AK-47 rifles, seven B-40 rocket rounds, nine portable flame throwers, 200 NVA gas masks, 100 pounds of explosives, 400 rounds of 7.62mm pistol ammunition, a five-gallon can filled with RPGs, plus numerous documents and clothing items. Also included were chemical beakers, and eight large tanks (later identified as a component of the Soviet TPO-50M flamethrower), and an assortment of other items. This was the first known Russian TPO-50M flamethrower discovered in South Vietnam.[52]

Operation Golden Fleece

Operation Golden Fleece was conducted by the 196th LIB in conjunction with ARVN forces during the 1968 rice harvest season. Beginning in September, the battalion linked up with elements of the 2-1st Infantry and moved north into Antenna Valley to begin the Operation. Elements of the 196th LIB provided security for Vietnamese farmers harvesting rice. The 196th LIB helped harvest and place under Government of Vietnam (GVN) control more than one million pounds of rice in the Que Son Valley.[53] Subsequently Operation Golden Fleece was conducted yearly.[54]

Company A finished dismantling LZ Mellon on September 17.[55] On October 12, Company C found a large hooch near LZ West and a frame structure erected in 1966 that contained a VC flag, a detailed diagram of LZ West, and a chart showing ARVN and U.S. killed in action. Company C destroyed the complex. VC/NVA activity increased throughout the month around LZ West. Company C had a squad called "Zappers," led by Sergeant Ernan C. Gutierrez. They were a fearless but crazy bunch. If they discovered a hut and believed it to be occupied, they would run yelling toward the hut. The enemy would be too surprised to react. Many VC and NVA soldiers were captured or killed and many weapons collected by the Zappers.[56] Numerous VC rice caches, some totaling over 5,000 pounds, were uncovered. On October 30, Company B found a VC base camp that included a cave complex containing twenty-five 82mm mortar rounds, 6,000 pounds of rice, and a quantity of TNT.[57]

November 9, Companies B and D evacuated 13,500 pounds of rice. On November 13, Company C evacuated 92,000 pounds of rice.[58]

November began with several celebrities visiting LZ West. The Chicago Cubs' Ernie Banks and Baltimore Orioles pitcher Pete Reichert spent the day talking to soldiers. A few days later, Martha Raye made her second visit to the battalion and talked to soldiers in their positions on LZ West.[59]

Battle of Nui Chom Mountain, November 17–23, 1968

The major event of November was an operation on the rugged Nui Chom ridgeline located several kilometers northwest of LZ West. Nui Chom was a formidable obstacle. Triple canopy jungle covered steep and rocky slopes that rose to a height of 944 meters. The ground was slippery and wet from the November monsoons.[60]

On November 17 at 1000 hours, Company D, commanded by Captain Sidney Ordway (Anaheim, California), made contact with the enemy at the base of Nui Chom. Moving up the mountain they found ever increasing enemy emplacements. At 1345 hours, the company encountered a large base camp with a stream flowing through the middle, sleeping positions, and spider holes everywhere.[61]

1st Platoon leader, First Lieutenant John Dolan (Garden City, New York), described the initial contact. The 1st Platoon was walking point along the base of Nui Chom. The experienced men in the platoon felt in their guts that they were in a bad place. Lieutenant Dolan stopped the company and sent out two teams to do a flank recon. When they returned, he took a fire team (Specialists Four Jack Walker (Nacogdoches, Texas), Billy Joe Gillespie (Oklahoma City, Oklahoma), and Lopez on a deep flank recon up toward the Nui Chom ridgeline. They discovered a well-worn trail cut into the ground, wide enough for wheeled carts. They smelled smoke and came to another trail leading directly up the mountain. Soon they saw several armed, well-equipped men in NVA uniforms. The fire team was then engaged by the NVA. Lieutenant Dolan and his group returned fire, hitting some of the enemy. The enemy scattered and left behind two AKs and a radio. The retreating enemy left a blood trail up the mountain. Lieutenant Dolan radioed his platoon and the company commander. It was obvious that the fire team had found an outpost of a large NVA force. The company command group linked up with the 1st Platoon fire team at the site of the NVA outpost. Lieutenant Dolan left his RTO at the trail junction below the site of the initial contact with orders to guide his platoon and the rest of the company to his location farther up the mountain. The fire team lost the blood trail but continued up the trail. One of the fire team noticed a dozen or more strands of communication wire, a likely sign of a large enemy headquarters, alongside the trail going up the mountain. Further up the mountain the trail and the communications wire divided. The two groups split up, and soon both groups were engaged with the enemy.[62]

Captain Ordway was wounded in the forehead and subsequently blinded for life.

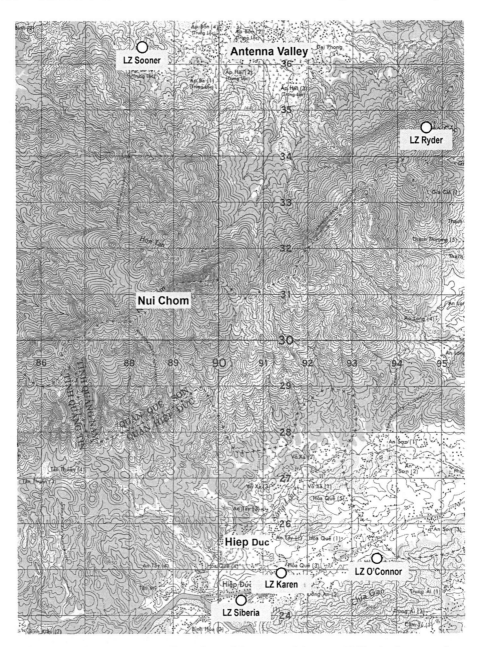

Map shows Nui Chom Mountain, LZs Ryder and Sooner, and Antenna Valley in the general area of Hiep Duc. Hiep Duc, 6640-3. 1:50000. L7014 Series. Army Map Service, December 1965. Vietnam Archive Map Collection, The Vietnam Archive, Texas Tech University. Used by permission.

Field First Sergeant John Neely was also severely wounded. Specialist Four Hubert "Butch" Harris, the battalion RTO for the company, contacted Lieutenant Colonel Wetzel, who was in his C&C helicopter. Specialist Harris informed Lieutenant Colonel Wetzel that the company, including the CP, was in heavy contact and that the company commander and First Sergeant were wounded. Lieutenant Dolan's tcam was further up the mountain and heavily engaged. Upon moving forward, Company D's other two platoons received intense automatic weapons fire. Lieutenant Colonel Wetzel provided guidance to Specialist Harris on how to deploy the company's rifle platoons.[63] Lieutenant James B. Gray, the 2nd Platoon leader, and senior officer in Company D, took command of the company. Gunships of F Troop 8th Cavalry arrived with a Dust Off helicopter to extract Captain Ordway. The first evacuation helicopter received several hits and was forced to return to base. Finally, at 1627 hours, Captain Ordway was extracted by use of a rescue hoist through the trees. Field First Sergeant Neely remained in the field until the next morning. At 1700 hours Company A, commanded by Captain William "Billy" Braswell (Henderson, North Carolina), engaged the enemy about 1,000 meters southwest of Company D's location.[64]

The battle plan was to attack the NVA up the three ridges of Nui Chom Mountain. Company A moved into position on the left of Company D and began moving up the mountain. Company C, now commanded by First Lieutenant Dickie Dixon (North Liberty, Indiana), was to be airlifted to Company D's position and move up the center ridge of the mountain, keeping to the right of Company A. Company B, commanded by Captain White, was to be airlifted from LZ West to LZ Karen, and then airlifted to the base of Nui Chom and attack up the right ridge to the right of Company C. Lieutenant Colonel Wetzel asked Colonel Fritz Kroesen, the 196th LIB Commander, for a company of the 2-1st Infantry from LZ Ross to be attached to the 4-31st Infantry. Lieutenant Colonel Wetzel wanted the 2-1st Infantry company to be able to attack Nui Chu from the right flank along the top of the mountain. Contrary to U.S. Army artillery doctrine, Lieutenant Colonel Wetzel split Battery C 3-82nd Artillery (105mm howitzers) into two sections. Three howitzers were airlifted to LZ Karen to provide extended range of artillery support for the operation, and two howitzers remained on LZ West. The battleship *New Jersey* (BB-62) also provided supporting fire during the operation.[65]

On November 18, both Companies A and D received sporadic fire as they attempted to move up the ridge. Company D had two soldiers wounded, and they were evacuated. There were four air strikes to support the companies, which resulted in large secondary explosions.[66]

On November 19, Company A moved cautiously up the ridge to the point of contact of the day before. They found thirteen dead NVA soldiers; one was believed to be an enemy battalion commander. Documents found on his body indicated that he commanded 360 soldiers.[67] Company A continued to advance, and at 0940 hours, they received heavy AK-47 and .30 caliber machine gun fire from their front. The Company suffered four wounded from sniper fire. The ridgeline was laced with communication wire. Captured enemy documents indicated that the 4-31st Infantry was fighting the 21st Regiment of the 2nd NVA Division. At 1130 hours, LRRP team Tennessee, operating in the battalion AO, was engaged in a firefight. At 1228 hours the team was extracted while under small arms fire.[68]

Company C moved from LZ Karen to the base of the mountain and replaced Company D to the right (northwest) of Company A, at a higher point of the ridge, in an attempt to cut off the enemy's escape route. Company D was airlifted to LZ West. Company B was airlifted from LZ West to LZ Karen and then airlifted to the base of the mountain and moved up the right ridge, to the right of Company C.[69]

Company C observed several evading NVA and discovered a large NVA hospital. A captured NVA nurse said over fifty wounded NVA personnel had been treated at the hospital since the battle began. The battalion needed an LZ on Nui Chom to evacuate wounded and bring in supplies. There was a shelf-like area on the side of the mountain in Company C's location that looked suitable for an LZ if some of the trees were cut down. Lieutenant Colonel Wetzel had two chainsaws put in his C&C helicopter, and he lowered them down one at a time to Company C while the helicopter pilot, Warrant Officer Mike Riley, amazingly hovered with the nose of the helicopter against the top of a tree stump. Company C cut an LZ on the side of the mountain using the chain saws and C4 explosives.[70]

On November 20, all three companies were moving up Nui Chom and all three were in heavy contact. F Troop 17th Cavalry arrived and became OPCON to the battalion.[71] Seven air strikes were called in to the front of the advancing companies. At 0730 hours, Company A spotted an NVA OP and a complex of fortified bunkers. The NVA opened up with small arms fire and machine gun fire killing the point man, Specialist Four Danny Hudson (Chadron, NE), and wounding four men. Company A attacked twice and was forced to pull back each time to allow air strikes against the enemy. In the second attack, six more Company A soldiers were wounded. During the same action Specialist Four William "Doc" Stafford, the 2nd Platoon medic, heard the call for a medic and ran up the hill to a knoll where he spotted the man down about ten or fifteen feet ahead. Enemy fire was heavy, so Doc started to crawl toward the wounded soldier. As Specialist Four Stafford started to get up to go to the wounded man, Private First Class Crescenz said he would provide covering fire on the enemy bunker that was shooting at Specialist Four Stafford. Private First Class Crescenz was shot; Doc checked for vital signs and realized Crescenz (Philadelphia, Pennsylvania) was dead. Private First Class Michael J. Crescenz was awarded the Medal of Honor, and promoted posthumously. His Medal of Honor citation describes his actions in detail.[72] It states,

Medal of Honor winner CPL Michael J. Crescenz. He is the only Vietnam-era winner of the award from the Philadelphia area. The Philadelphia VA Medical Center was renamed the "Corporal Michael J. Crescenz Department of Veterans Affairs Medical Center" in his honor on May 2, 2015 (Wikimedia Commons).

Corporal Michael J. Crescenz, United States Army, distinguished himself by conspicuous gallantry and intrepidity in action on 20 November 1968 while serving as a rifleman with Company A, 4th Battalion, 31st Infantry, 196th Infantry Brigade, Americal Division in the Hiep Duc Valley area of the Republic of Vietnam. On this morning his unit engaged a large, well-entrenched force of the North Vietnamese Army whose initial burst of fire pinned down the lead squad and killed the two point men, halting the advance of Company A. Immediately, Corporal Crescenz left the relative safety of his own position, seized a nearby machine gun and, with complete disregard for his safety, charged 100 meters up a slope toward the enemy's bunkers which he effectively silenced, killing the two occupants of each. Undaunted by the withering machine gun fire around him, Corporal Crescenz courageously moved forward toward a third bunker which he also succeeded in silencing, killing two more of the enemy and momentarily clearing the route of advance for his comrades. Suddenly, intense machine gun fire erupted from an unseen, camouflaged bunker. Realizing the danger to his fellow soldiers, Corporal Crescenz disregarded the barrage of hostile fire directed at him and daringly advanced toward the position. Assaulting with his machine gun, Corporal Crescenz was within 5 meters of the bunker when he was mortally wounded by the fire from the enemy machine gun. As a direct result of his heroic actions, his company was able to maneuver freely with minimal danger and to complete its mission, defeating the enemy. Corporal Crescenz's conspicuous gallantry and extraordinary heroism at the cost of his own life are in the highest traditions of the military service and reflect great credit on him, his unit and the United States Army.[73]

First Lieutenant Kevin Burke volunteered to lead fifteen men to rescue several wounded and dead soldiers. A seriously wounded soldier survived as a result of Lieutenant Burke's action, but Lieutenant Burke (Anita, Iowa) was killed.[74] Lieutenant Kevin Burke was awarded a Distinguished Service Cross, posthumously. His DSC citation describes his actions in detail:

For extraordinary heroism in connection with military operations involving conflict with an armed hostile force in the Republic of Vietnam, while serving with Company A, 4th Battalion 31st Infantry, 196th Infantry Brigade, Americal Division. First Lieutenant Burke distinguished himself by exceptionally valorous actions on 20 November 1968 as a platoon leader on a combat sweep operation near the village of Tan My in Quang Tin Province. During a battle with a large force of North Vietnamese regulars, Lieutenant Burke volunteered to lead fifteen men to rescue several wounded and dead comrades who lay at the base of a hill. Throwing hand grenades and firing his rifle, he came within twenty meters of the hostile positions as he worked his way down the hill. After reaching the casualties, he supervised their evacuation and remained behind to provide covering fire, killing at least five of the communists. When his men had escaped Lieutenant Burke attempted to rescue a seriously injured man who lay next to an enemy bunker. Braving North Vietnamese machine gun fire, he charged the fortification and while returning fire with his rifle, was mortally wounded by the hostile fusillade. First Lieutenant Burk's extraordinary heroism and devotion to duty, at the cost of his life, were in keeping with the highest traditions of the military service and reflect great credit upon himself, his unit, and the United States Army.[75]

Company A burned up four machine gun barrels in the fierce fighting. Company B moved up the eastern slope of Nui Chom to the east of Companies A and C. There they found a deserted base camp with about fifteen bunkers. Captain Braswell requested B-52 airstrikes on the top of Nui Chom.

At dawn on November 21, the battle continued with the three-pronged attack up Nui Chom Mountain. At 0745 hours, Company C received fire from a well-camouflaged NVA bunker that had been destroyed the previous day by an air strike and completely rebuilt overnight.[76] All three companies came in heavy contact when they reached the perimeter bunkers. While Company A was advancing in their area, they were hit with machine gun fire that caught them by surprise. Squad leader Sergeant James Larrick and the point man were wounded. Sergeant Larrick was hit five times and crawled into one of the enemy bunkers his squad had knocked out a short time before. Sergeant Larrick told his squad members not to try to reach him after they had failed on several attempts.[77] On the 21st, Lieutenant Dolan, of Company D, took command of Company A, replacing Captain Braswell, who had less than a week until he was scheduled to rotate back to the United States.

On November 22 at 1051 hours, Company A returned to the area of heavy fighting of the day before and found Sergeant Larrick conscious in the NVA bunker. During the night, NVA soldiers had searched Larrick's pockets thinking he was dead. He hadn't had food or water for a day and a half. Parasites were credited with saving his life, as they stopped the spread of infection.[78] Lieutenant Colonel Wetzel was on the ground with Company A, coordinating air strikes. Colonel Kroesen flew into the LZ on the side of Nui Chom because he wanted to visit the soldiers on the mountain. At one point, Colonel Kroesen went forward to Company A's perimeter to meet with soldiers.[79]

Companies A and C worked closely together as they attacked up the mountain. They encountered enemy bunkers made from logs, and .30 caliber machine guns which continued to slow their advance. Company A tried again to take the bunkers to their front, but again they were blocked. Rain started and it was getting dark, so the company pulled back down the ridge to establish an NDP. Company B also met strong resistance on the ridgeline. As darkness fell, the NVA still held Nui Chom. All during the night, like most nights during the week, batteries of 105 mm, 155 mm, and 8 inch howitzers pounded the peak of Nui Chom. Through November 21, twenty-nine air strikes were directed against NVA positions on Nui Chom.[80]

On November 23, at 0910 hours, Company C 1-46th Infantry was airlifted from LZ Baldy to LZ West and placed OPCON of 4-31st Infantry. Their arrival enabled the battalion to move Company D to Chu Lai for stand down and to get their feet in shape. That morning, Companies B and C along with F Troop 17th Cavalry, remained in contact with the enemy. Company B lost Specialist Four Thomas G. Dickerson (Thomaston, Georgia) and Corporal Harold L. Glover (Silver City, North Carolina) due to enemy action.[81]

At 0940 hours, Company B encountered several bunkers and knocked them out, killing six NVA and capturing two NVA, two .30 caliber machine guns, and three AK-47s. Captain White was wounded in the shoulder during the battle.[82]

The three companies advanced into the NVA base camp while pushing back two companies of NVA. Company C captured a large well-supplied hospital, plus an NVA doctor and two female nurses trying to escape north. When interrogated, the doctor stated he received orders to leave everything behind and move north; he had treated more than sixty wounded NVA during the last week and was resupplied every five days. He also stated that there were two U.S. Special Forces Sergeant First Class prisoners of war (POWs) in the base camp. The POWs were moved out of the base camp and shipped north the day that Company D ran into the bunker complex at the foot of the mountain.[83]

Company A found a battalion-sized base camp on November 23. The CP was in an underground bunker that measured fifty feet by fifty feet. Numerous documents were found, as well as a telephone switchboard and generator. Communications wire connected each of the more than 200 bunkers on the mountain.[84]

The enemy left behind sixty-six confirmed dead. Among the captured equipment were three .30 caliber machine guns, four CHICOM RPD light machine guns, twenty-five AK-47 rifles, two 82mm mortars, ten B-40 rockets, 550 rounds of .51 caliber ammunition, and four small ammunition caches. More than forty fresh graves were discovered.[85] By the afternoon of November 23, the battalion controlled Nui Chom Mountain.[86]

The battalion continued to search the ridge for the next week. The Battalion lost five killed and thirty-three wounded in the battle.[87] B-52 airstrikes were called in on suspected NVA escape routes to the north and west of Nui Chom during the closing days of November.[88]

At 1000 hours on November 24, the American Division approved Lieutenant Colonel Wetzel's request of a boundary extension into Antenna Valley, located in the U.S. 1st Marine Division's AO.[89] Company D 2-1st Infantry became OPCON to the battalion. During the next three weeks the battalion's rifle companies were rotated in and out of Chu Lai for stand down. The battalion continued to work the areas and search for NVA on the sides of Nui Chom Mountain leading into Antenna Valley.[90] On Thanksgiving Day, the battalion Mess Hall, on LZ West, prepared a traditional Thanksgiving meal for all the companies in the battalion.[91]

December 1 found the battalion's three rifle companies continuing to fight on Nui Chom. At 1130 hours, Company D was ambushed by an unknown size NVA force that resulted in three wounded being evacuated to Da Nang and Specialist Four Raymond Alaniz (Wichita Falls, Texas) killed.[92]

On December 3, the battalion began operations in Antenna Valley, northeast of Nui Chom Mountain. At 1618 hours, Company C engaged four NVA, killing three and capturing one POW, who was sent to LZ Baldy. At 2110 hours, F Troop 17th Cavalry engaged two sampans, sinking one. The Recon Platoon surprised four NVA, killing three and wounding one, who was evacuated as a POW the next day; documents and a .45 caliber pistol were evacuated to LZ West.[93] On December 4 at 2225 hours, Company A observed lights and called in an artillery fire mission. There were secondary explosions, and the lights went out.[94] On December 5 at 0655 hours, Company B was airlifted from Chu Lai to LZ West. At 0715 hours, Company C 1-46th Infantry was airlifted from LZ West to LZ Baldy; at 0825 hours 3rd Platoon F Troop 17th Cavalry was airlifted to LZ Baldy. This ended these units' support to the 4-31st Infantry. Company C engaged the NVA on three occasions during the day, resulting in six NVA killed and the capture of three weapons and documents that were evacuated to LZ West.[95]

On December 6, there were numerous exchanges of small arms fire with the enemy, resulting in no friendly casualties and unknown enemy casualties. On December 7 at 1145 hours, Company A made heavy contact that lasted until 1545 hours. Company A was supported by gunships, artillery, and air strikes. The company lost Private First Class Karl P. Dency (Chicago, Illinois), who was killed the day he arrived in the field, and Specialist Four Benjamin L. Hoopengarner (Fraser, Michigan) in a meeting engagement. Company A remained in heavy contact on December 8, engaging the NVA in several fire fights. The company had two wounded, and Private First Class Michael Bach (Cincinnati, Ohio) was killed while his platoon was maneuvering on line. Company A broke contact late in the day. Company C engaged and killed one NVA and one VC. The next day, the battalion continued operations in Antenna Valley with only minor and inconsequential contact.[96]

On December 10, Company A was airlifted to LZ West and replaced by Company B in Antenna Valley. Companies C and D continued to experience light contact with the enemy, and one Company D soldier was wounded and evacuated. No enemy or weapons were found after these engagements.[97]

On December 12, Company C, commanded by Captain John Long (New Bloomfield, Pennsylvania), was conducting a sweep along the north side of the valley when the left flank platoon came under fire from NVA concealed in spider holes. The three platoons used fire and movement to take the enemy position. Specialist Four Donald Johnson (Alma, Georgia) was seriously wounded, and Lieutenant Colonel Wetzel landed in the C&C helicopter, put him on board and flew him directly to Da Nang, saving his life. Company B also made contact with the enemy several times during the day. At 1035 hours, Company D 2-1st Infantry was released from 4-31st Infantry control and airlifted from LZ Sooner to LZ Ross.[98]

On December 13, at 0910 hours, Company B came under heavy automatic weapons fire that resulted in no casualties. Company B was again engaged at 1300 hours, again with no casualties. In both cases, artillery was fired at the suspected enemy positions with unknown results. December 14 saw continued light contact in Antenna Valley.[99]

On December 15, beginning at 0835 hours, Company D was airlifted from LZ Sooner to LZ West and replaced by Company A, which moved into Antenna Valley. Contact with the enemy increased, resulting in twenty VC/NVA killed and no friendly casualties. At 1000 hours, a company of ARVN Mike Special Forces (MSF-14) moved from LZ Baldy to LZ West and became OPCON to the battalion. Throughout the day, Companies A and B were in distant contact with the NVA, engaging them with artillery. The C&C helicopter also engaged and killed eight NVA. On December 16, 3rd Platoon F-17th Cavalry was again placed OPCON to the battalion. From December 16 through the 19th, units, including 3rd Platoon F Troop 17th Cavalry and MSF-14, continued to have light contact in the Antenna Valley, resulting in fifteen VC/NVA killed and some weapons being captured.[100]

On December 20, Company B was in heavy contact with the NVA resulting in three wounded; Specialist Four Raphael J. Frost (Hunter, North Dakota) was killed in the firefight. At 1410 hours, Company C 2-1st Infantry became OPCON to the battalion. At 1925 hours, radar from LZ Sooner picked up movement all around Company B's NDP. Artillery defensive fires were called in with unknown results. There were no friendly casualties. On December 21, Company B was replaced by D Company, which was airlifted from LZ West. During the day, elements from F Troop 17th Cavalry, Companies A, D, and the Recon Platoon engaged the enemy, resulting in six enemy personnel killed.[101]

From December 22 to the end of the year, the battalion continued combat operations in Antenna Valley. During this period, the rifle companies had numerous small engagements. MSF-14 suffered two killed and fourteen wounded when engaged by sniper and mortar fire on December 24. The battalion observed the Christmas cease fire from 24 1900 hours to 25 1645 hours, December.[102] The battalion provided religious services and traditional Christmas food to the companies during the ceasefire. Most of the MSF-14 soldiers got sick eating the turkey meal with all the trimmings, because they were not used to American food.[103] On December 28, F Troop 17th Cavalry found a small arms cache, and the C&C helicopter destroyed six sampans. At 0835 hours on December 29, the MSF-14 company was airlifted to LZ Baldy and then onward to Da Nang and released from OPCON to the battalion.[104] The battalion TF continued search operations in Antenna Valley until the end of the year.[105]

21 4th Battalion in Vietnam, 1969

Operation Fayette Canyon

Operation Fayette Canyon lasted from December 15, 1968, to February 28, 1969. The 196th LIB initiated Operation Fayette Canyon to accelerate combat operations to the north and northeast of Antenna Valley and Nui Mat Ring Mountains to find, fix, and destroy the 1st VC Main Force Regiment of the 2nd NVA Division. The operation was a companion operation to the U.S. Marines' Operation, Taylor Common.[1]

The New Year found the battalion supporting Operation Fayette Canyon and continuing to search for the NVA in Antenna Valley.[2] On January 2, the battalion conducted a major sweep of the valley. Company C moved off LZ Ryder at 0200 hours with three platoons and was engaged by snipers that developed into intense automatic weapons and 60mm mortar fire. Captain Long and his FO Lieutenant Wray on LZ Ryder called in artillery that resulted in a first round hit which silenced the enemy mortar and produced two secondary explosions.[3] Company C then attacked the machine gun positions. The enemy machine gun jammed, enabling the company to kill the NVA crew. The machine gun was a 7.62mm heavy Russian anti-aircraft type with a swivel mount and aerial sight. An AK-47 and SKS rifle were also captured. It was determined that Specialist Four Charles D. Groh (New York, New York) was missing after the operation. Company D was closest to where Specialist Four Groh was lost so it was given the mission to locate him. Company C was airlifted back to LZ Ryder. Second Lieutenant Jerry Josey (Bishopville, South Carolina) joined Company C on December 31.[4]

The same day, Company D, commanded by Captain Whittecar (Salina, Kansas), observed a group of NVA with extensive camouflage crawling along a rice paddy dike not far from Company C's location. Company D engaged the enemy and moved into the area to investigate. They found one AK-47 rifle and numerous blood trails leading to heavy foliage. Company D directed an air strike on the suspected enemy position. The company checked out the area of the airstrike and found a damaged tunnel complex with three dead NVA.[5]

On January 3, Company D located Specialist Four Groh's body; he had been killed by a sniper.[6] His body was evacuated to LZ West on the C&C helicopter.[7] At 1110 hours, a platoon from Company A engaged a group of VC, killing eight and wounding two, who were both medevaced as POWs. One of the dead was determined to be a NVA lieutenant who was acting as a tax collector and was carrying a large amount of money. Three other enemy soldiers, including a doctor, were captured. The POWs, two carbines, one AK-47, two CHICOM grenades, medical supplies, documents, and money were evacuated to LZ West in the C&C helicopter.[8] By the end of the day Companies A, B, and D began operating in and around Hiep Duc. Company C remained OPCON to 2-1st Infantry, operating out of LZ Ryder.[9]

There was little enemy activity during January 4 through the 7th.[10] Weather on January 8 in the morning was bad, and the Brigade put a hold on all operations until close air support was possible. At 0900 hours, the battalion was given permission to resume combat operations.[11] On January 9, Company C was released from OPCON to 2-1st Infantry and returned to battalion control from operations in Antenna Valley.[12] This ended the battalion's participation in Operation Fayette Canyon.

On January 10, Companies A and C made a combat assault into the area of LZ Polar Bear II in UH-1 and CH-47 helicopters. Late in the day, Lieutenant Colonel Robert Longino (Atlanta, Georgia) assumed command from Lieutenant Colonel Wetzel in a brief ceremony in the Memorial Chapel on LZ West.[13]

In the middle of January, the battalion encountered several booby traps. As Company A was moving out of a wood line near the base of LZ West, several enemy soldiers jumped up and ran across an open area in front of the point element in an attempt to have the company follow. The Kit Carson Scout, called "Tom" by Company A, who was with the company command group, became very agitated. Lieutenant Dolan stopped the company and brought Tom forward. Tom found three separate booby-trapped 82mm mortar rounds in the tall grass just in front of the halted company. Lieutenant Dolan believes Tom either set the booby traps or was with the enemy soldiers when they set them because he knew right where to look for them.[14] Two days later Company D found twenty booby traps consisting of punji sticks and "swinging door" devices (a spear attached to a bent sapling which swings forward quickly when the device is tripped, impaling the victim on a sharp point of the spear).[15]

On January 29, a platoon of Company A, commanded by First Lieutenant Eddie Zuleger (Avondale, Arizona), discovered twenty VC enjoying a wine party. The platoon killed one VC and captured fourteen.[16]

During February 1969, the American Division was reorganized into the Reorganization Objective Army Divisions (ROAD) Concept, and the designation of "Light Infantry Brigade" was discontinued. However, the 196th Infantry Brigade retained several units that were authorized in the light infantry brigade structure but not authorized in the infantry brigade.[17]

February began a new era for the battalion. After five years, the GVN wanted to reestablish the Hiep Duc District, and bring a major change to the Hiep Duc and Que Son Valleys. In fall of 1965 about 5,000 civilians left Hiep Duc District and moved near Tam Ky because of fierce NVA attacks and terrorism. On February 1, PF Platoon 115 was airlifted from Tam Ky to LZ Karen with a Vietnamese Psychological Operations (PSYOPS) broadcasting team. The broadcast team accompanied D Company on operations in the Hiep Duc Valley. The Vietnamese forces' efforts brought immediate results, as impressive numbers of Chieu Hois surrendered at LZ Karen. On February 5, thirty-three VC came to LZ Karen to surrender. In addition, Sergeant Ken Herrmann (Buffalo, New York), of the battalion civil affairs section, also broadcast programs directed at local VC. Sergeant Herrmann called known VC by their names and asked them to cooperate with GVN and

Hiep Duc Village, as seen from LZ Siberia (photograph by Jim Logue. Used by permission).

U.S. forces working in the area. Ten VC defectors admitted that they had been prompted to surrender because of Sergeant Herrmann's nightly battalion broadcasts.[18]

On February 12, Company A, commanded by Captain Stanley Yates (Jonesboro, Tennessee), discovered an enemy hospital complex. The next day, the company discovered a VC prison camp in the same area west of LZ West. Company B, commanded by Captain James Condon, disrupted a VC election in Hiep Duc Valley by killing an NVA officer who was coordinating the election for local VC.[19]

Operation Frederick Hill

Operation Frederick Hill ran from March 18, 1969, to March 1, 1971, and was conducted by the 196th Infantry Brigade with the 1/1 Cavalry, in conjunction with the ARVN 5th Regiment.[20]

On March 19, Company C was securing LZ West when it came under a fierce NVA ground attack. NVA soldiers penetrated the bunker line on the northwest side of LZ West, destroying one bunker and seriously wounding one soldier. Some of the enemy got close to the artillery gun pits on the west end of LZ West. The enemy was repulsed by hand-to-hand combat on the bunker line and in the area of the artillery pits. Accurate defensive fire from the battalion's 81mm, 4.2mm mortars sections, the Quad 50 of LZ West and defensive artillery fire support from LZs Center and Ross ended the night attack on LZ West.[21]

On March 22, Company A lost Sergeant David C. Vallance (Hamilton, Montana) and Specialist Four Clarence H. Boolin (Overland Park, Kansas). Headquarters Company lost Specialists Four Richard W. Goden (Baltimore, Maryland), George F. Reynolds, Jr. (Oneonta, New York) and Leonardo Rios-Velazquez, Jr. (Rio Piedras, Puerto Rico), who all died in the crash of a CH-47 on LZ West.

In late April and early May, the battalion assisted in re-establishing the village of Hiep Duc. Company D initiated construction of LZ Siberia. On May 12, Headquarters Company lost Specialist Five Thomas M. Barr (Anchorage, Alaska) and Specialist Four Wendell A. Weston (Warren, Vermont) during a sniper attack on LZ Baldy.[22] On May 28, Company B lost Private Dennis L. Babcock (Mauston, Wisconsin) to sniper fire near Hiep Duc.

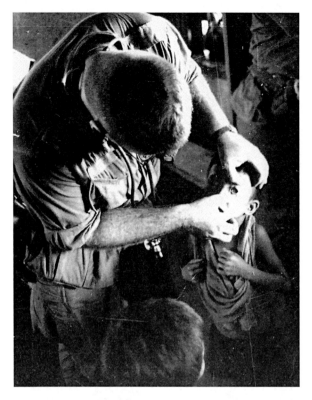

In June, the battalion was again in contact with the 2nd NVA Division. On June 4, Company A lost Privates First Class Max De Sully, Jr. (Portland, Oregon) and Andrew S. Rahilly (New York, New York) in a meeting engagement near Hiep Duc. On June 17, Company B lost Specialist Four Hiris W. Blevins (Little Rock, Arkansas) on LZ Siberia. On June 23, Company B lost Privates First Class Dewey M. Eubanks (Durham, North Carolina), and Theodore M. Hatle (Sisseton, South Dakota), and Recon Platoon lost Private First Class Anson T. Geronzin, Jr. (Clinton, Iowa) in a meeting engagement near Tien Phuoc. On June 24, Company A lost Private First Class Rogers S. Gordon (Middleville, Michigan) during a mortar attack on LZ West, on the 27th Private First Class Steve O. Strasshofer (Parma, Ohio), and on the 28th Private First Class Herbert Logsdon, Jr. (Clarksville, Indiana) in combat operations near Tien Phuoc. During July, the Battalion had two companies committed to a screening mission north of its normal Tactical Area of Responsibility (TAOR).[23] On July 2, Privates First Class Eldon G. Crumley (Lincoln, NE) of Company A and Michael P. Klotz (Hudson, New York), a medic assigned from Headquarters Company, were killed by a command-detonated 105mm round near Tien Phuoc.

On July 4, Lieutenant Colonel

Top: CPT Mohring, the surgeon of the 4th Battalion, 31st Infantry, examines a Vietnamese child during a MEDCAP operation in the village Le Thuy, 4 May 1967. *Bottom:* Chaplain Donald Wilson (Roanoke, Virginia), 4th Battalion, 31st Liaison Team, 196th Brigade, Americal Division, plays marbles with village children, 11 January 1970 (both U.S. Army photographs, National Archives).

Cecil M. "Hank" Henry (Rome, Georgia) assumed command from Lieutenant Colonel Longino in a ceremony on LZ West.[24]

On July 21, Company A lost Sergeant Richard F. Wilder (Baytown, Texas) to sniper fire in an NDP, and on the 25th, Specialist Four Richard K. Larson (Santa Ana, California) was wounded by a booby trap; he later died in the hospital. On July 28, Company B lost Privates First Class Andrew J. Kiniry (Coatesville, Pennsylvania) and Curtis D. Smith (Bessemer City, North Carolina) during a meeting engagement; on the 29th, Corporal Daniel A. Bolduc (Lennoxville, Quebec, Canada) was killed by a mine in an NDP. On August 10, Company D lost Private First Class Thomas D. Snyder (Johnson City, Tennessee) during a fire fight west of Que Son.[25]

On August 11, elements of the 31st Regiment of the 2nd NVA Division attacked LZ West. Subsequent to the attack, the 31st NVA Regiment, after suffering fifty-one killed and an unknown number wounded, was thought to be operating in the vicinity of Hill 441, north across the valley from LZ West, with an estimated strength of 800 to 900 men. This information was obtained from four POWs captured during the attack on LZ West.[26] On August 12, Headquarters Company's Specialist Four William B. Scott (Jacksonville, North Carolina) was wounded in a mortar attack on LZ West; he later died in the hospital. Also on August 12, the out-of-sector screening mission to the north of the TAOR was completed. Between August 12 and 17, the battalion was primarily focused on policing the battlefield around LZ West following the sapper attack on August 11 and 12.[27]

On August 17 at 1655 hours, D Company came under heavy fire and killed three VC/NVA soldiers. Contact was broken, and Company D prepared to receive resupply. The resupply helicopter took heavy fire, wounding both pilots. The pilots managed to fly to and land at LZ Center, and both pilots were medevaced. At 1900 hours, Company D again made contact with the enemy. At 1930 hours, Company D broke contact and moved their NDP.[28] As a result of these engagements, Company D lost Sergeant William P. Gooding (Edison, New Jersey); Specialists Four Frederick Mezzatesta (Whitesboro, New York) and a medic assigned to Headquarters Company, Kim M. Diliberto (Massapequa, New York); Privates First Class James R. Hurst (Jacksonville, Florida), an artilleryman assigned to Battery C 3-82nd Artillery; Matthew Peterson (Florence, South Carolina); Clifford Seals (Eufaula, Oklahoma); and Jay D. Webster, Jr. (Lititz, Pennsylvania). Five men were wounded. (Note: The battalion duty logs state one soldier killed and one missing in action on August 17 and four soldiers killed and one missing in action on August 18. Some of these soldiers listed on the Vietnam Wall as killed on August 17 were killed on August 18.) The unit that engaged Company D was later determined to be the 31st NVA Regiment.[29]

On August 18, at 1335 hours, while searching for a rice cache northeast of Hiep Duc, Company B, commanded by Captain William H. Gayler (Mineral Wells, Texas), made contact with what later proved to be elements of the 1st Main Force NVA Regiment, 2nd NVA Division.[30] The 1969 Battle for Hiep Duc began with the above two meeting engagements.[31]

1969 Battle for Hiep Duc

The Battalion's primary mission was securing the resettlement District of Hiep Duc from encroachment by VC/NVA forces.[32]

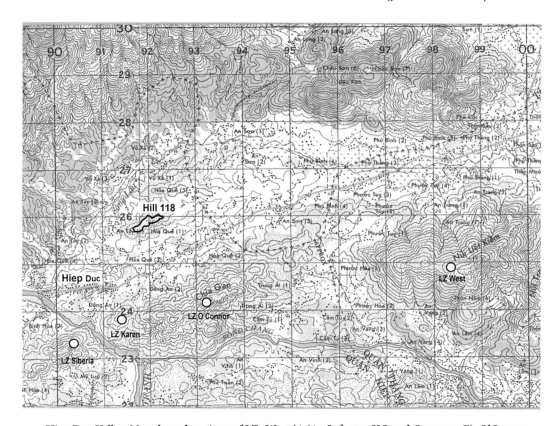

Hiep Duc Valley. Map shows locations of LZs West (4-31st Infantry HQ and Company E), O'Connor, Karen (Hiep Duc District HQ), and Siberia, as well as Hiep Duc Village and Hill 118 (named "Million Dollar Hill" because of the loss of helicopters to enemy fire during a 1967 battle). Hill 118 was the 4-31st TF Forward CP during the August 1969 Battle. Hiep Duc, 6640-3. 1:50000. L7014 Series. Army Map Service, December 1965. Vietnam Archive Map Collection, The Vietnam Archive, Texas Tech University. Used by permission.

The 1969 Battle for Hiep Duc took place from 170001 August to 032400 September. The battalion task organization included Companies A through E 4-31st Infantry, Company A 2-1st Infantry (OPCON 27 August–3 September), Company B 2-1st Infantry (OPCON 20 August–2 September), Company C 2-1st Infantry (OPCON 18–21 August), Company B 1-46th Infantry (OPCON 19–27 August), Company D 1-46th Infantry (OPCON 24–27 August), Battery C 3-82nd Artillery (105mm—Direct Support), and Battery C (-) 3-16th Artillery (155mm—General Support Reinforcing).[33]

On August 18, at 1335 hours, Company B 4-31st Infantry made contact and came under heavy small arms, mortar and RPG fire suffering six wounded. At 1430 hours, Company B began taking heavy enemy fire from the north, southwest and east. Attack helicopters from the 71st Aviation Company supporting Company B, received .51 caliber machine gun fire. Company B remained in contact. Airstrikes and medevacs were requested. At 1840 hours, an air strike began; the supporting jets received heavy small arms fire, but none were hit. At 1930 hours, a medevac was attempted with helicopter gunship support but failed because the medevac helicopter took numerous hits and was forced to abort the mission. At 2035 hours, another medevac was attempted. This one was successful, and eight wounded were extracted. Company B killed nine NVA and captured one AK-47 and one AK-50.[34] Company B lost Specialist Fours Gerald A. Henry (Landis, Arkansas), Thomas L. Stradtman (St. Cloud, Minnesota), Paul W. Vanderboom, Jr. (Fond Du Lac, Wisconsin), Privates First Class Robert A. Fox, (Beardstown, Illinois), Gary W. Harvey (Seattle, Washington), Edwin C. Hockenberry (East Waterford, Pennsylvania), David Lewis (Cleves, Ohio), Vincent T. Masciale (Jacksonville, Florida), one Kit Carson Scout, and twenty wounded. (Note: some of these men are listed as being assigned to other than Company B on the Vietnam Memorial Wall. While these men may have been assigned to the company listed on the Wall they fought and died with Company B.)

At 1140 hours, Company C was airlifted in CH-47s from a field pickup zone to LZ Siberia where they drew extra ammunition and supplies. They were issued orders, and then the Company CP, 1st and 3rd Platoons were airlifted from LZ Siberia to the soccer field next to Hiep Duc in UH-1 aircraft. 2nd Platoon continued to secure LZ Siberia. Company C moved from the soccer field LZ to the top of Hill 118 (known as "million dollar hill") and established a defensive perimeter.[35]

In the late afternoon, Company C was given the order to linkup with and extract Company B. At 2015 hours, 3rd Platoon plus a squad from 1st Platoon Company C, led by First Lieutenant Jim Simms (Clarendon Hills, Illinois), linked up with Company B. Both units moved to an NDP on Hill 118, closing on the NDP at 0305 hours, August 19.[36] The bodies of those killed from Company B were evacuated only part of the way to Hill 118 because 3rd Platoon Company C and Company B made contact with NVA on the way to Hill 118. SPOOKY, a Douglas AC-47 gunship—nick-named "Puff the Magic Dragon"—remained on station throughout the night to support the battalion.[37]

At 1210 hours, August 18, Company D 4-31st Infantry made contact with an estimated company size enemy force near Thon Mot on the Chang River south of LZ West. Artillery and gunship support were brought to bear against the enemy. During the afternoon, the company continued to maneuver against the enemy, but at 1535 hours it was forced to pull back and regroup with seventeen wounded, and one missing in action. At 1735 hours, all wounded were evacuated and contact was temporarily broken. At 1925 hours, the company began receiving mortar fire that was followed by a ground attack from all directions, with the main attack coming from the east. This attack was repelled, but Staff Sergeant Robert K. Spillner (Waipahu, Hawaii) was killed and three men were wounded. SHADOW, an AC-119G gunship, was requested and was on station all night in support of the company. Company D recorded a total of fifty-two NVA killed in this action.

Company C 2-1st Infantry, commanded by Captain Rudolph Yap, arrived at LZ West at 1000 hours and was given the mission to relieve Company D 4-31st Infantry on August 19.

At 1200 hours, the Recon Platoon, commanded by First Lieutenant Robert L. Williams, (Watsonville, California) made contact with the enemy, resulting in four friendly personnel wounded. Contact was broken at 1400 hours, and the Recon Platoon closed on LZ West at 1600 hours. Recon Platoon accounted for five NVA killed.[38]

On August 19, Company D 4-31st Infantry remained in their NDP to provide supporting fire for Company C 2-1st Infantry and the insertion of 3-21st Infantry to the east of Company D's NDP. At 0715 hours artillery fired defensive missions in support of the company because it was receiving heavy small arms and automatic weapons fire from the east and northeast. Mortars and artillery were fired on the area, and enemy small arms fire ceased. Company D 4-31st Infantry evacuated five wounded and the bodies of those missing in action on August 17 and 18.[39] Company C 2-1st Infantry linked up with Company D at 1200 hours. No enemy contact was made during the afternoon, and the two companies set up an NDP.[40] At 2240 hours movement was heard on all sides of their perimeter and at 2255 hours both companies received heavy automatic weapons fire and RPG rounds from the east, south and west, resulting in fourteen wounded. SHADOW was requested and arrived on station at 2310 hours. At 0140 hours, Dust Off extracted ten wounded.[41]

On the morning of August 19, Company B 4-31st Infantry was airlifted to LZ Siberia and replaced 2nd Platoon Company C securing the LZ. Second Platoon Company C was airlifted from LZ Siberia to Hill 118. A section of 81mm mortars from Company E, commanded by Second Lieutenant Charles Allen (Fairfield, Connecticut), displaced from LZ Siberia to Hill 118 to provide organic indirect fire support for the battalion maneuver units. At 1300 hours, Company B 1-46th Infantry, commanded by Captain Alva R. King, became OPCON to 4-31st Infantry after they closed on LZ Karen. Company B 1-46th Infantry linked up with Company C 4-31st Infantry and further coordinated for a combined attack.[42] Company B 2-1st Infantry also became OPCON to 4-31st Infantry and was airlifted to LZ Karen; there they prepared to link up with Company B 1-46th Infantry and Company C 4-31st Infantry on August 21.[43]

An AO extension was granted to the U.S. 2-7th Marines, who began moving to the north of Hiep Duc in an effort to trap the enemy between the Marines and the 31st Infantry TF.[44]

On August 20, Major Roger Lee (Colorado Springs, Colorado), the battalion S-3, established a forward CP on Hill 118.[45] Company B 2-1st Infantry became OPCON to 4-31st Infantry. That morning, Company C 4-31st Infantry and Company B 1-46th Infantry left their combined NDP and began moving east. The 3rd Platoon Company C had the mission of recovering Company B 4-31st Infantry's ten dead that were left in a stream bed when Company B and 3rd Platoon began receiving small arms fire while moving through enemy controlled terrain the night of August 18. The 3rd Platoon secured the ten bodies and was moving toward Hill 118 when the 1st Platoon and the command group made contact with the enemy.[46]

The 1st Platoon Company C, accompanied by Captain Thomas L. Murphy (Savannah, Georgia) and the company command group, received small arms fire at 1020 hours, resulting in four wounded. The platoon and company command group continued to receive small arms fire from the south, east and west and were pinned down, unable to maneuver. COBRA gunships from F Troop 8th Cavalry arrived on station in support of Company C and received small arms fire. It was reported that the enemy was on all sides of the 1st Platoon and the command group and were closing in on the perimeter. At 1510 hours Captain Murphy and five other soldiers were wounded.[47]

One of those wounded was Private First Class Rocky Bleier (Appleton, Wisconsin). He arrived in Company C in early June 1969 and served as an M-79 grenadier in 1st Platoon. He had played football at Notre Dame for four years and was the team captain for the 1967 season. In January 1968, he was drafted in the sixteenth round by the Pittsburgh Steelers. In November 1968, he was drafted into the U.S. Army. When he was medevaced late that night, it was thought he would not be able to play football or walk again. He played for the Steelers in the 1974 season and his tenacity helped the Steelers win the 1975, 1976, 1979 and 1980 Super Bowls. He was one of the few National Football League players who served in Vietnam.[48]

COBRA gunships from F Troop 8th Cavalry provided fire support throughout the day to the surrounded 1st Platoon and command group. At 1520 hours the enemy fire ceased but enemy units remained in the vicinity of the defensive position. At 1545 hours, COBRA gunships received intense ground fire while supporting Company C. At 1645 hours, Company C received incoming mortar fire, resulting in numerous wounded. In the early afternoon 3rd Platoon was given a change in mission, ordered to leave the ten bodies, and directed to link up with the 1st Platoon and command group which occurred at 1835 hours. Company C (-) pulled back to regroup and effected a link up with Company B 1-46th Infantry on Hill 118. While en route to the NDP, a medevac extracted fourteen wounded, including Captain Murphy.[49] Company C suffered four killed: Specialist Four Jerry W. Hill (Vinita, Oklahoma), Privates First Class Frederico V. Dela-Cruz (Agana, Guam), Jimmy L. Jones (Kingsport, Tennessee), James E. Ruttan (Watertown, New York), two missing in action, and twenty-one wounded on August 20. Enemy casualties were unknown.

On August 21, at 0510 hours, a trip flare went off on the perimeter of Company D, and the enemy was engaged with mortars and small arms fire. At 0625, the enemy fired RPGs at Company D, but the rockets fell short of the perimeter. At 0630 hours, Company C 2-1st Infantry killed one NVA and captured one AK-47. At 0655 hours, Company C 2-1st Infantry reported two more NVA killed and one AK-47, two full magazines, and six Chicom grenades captured. At 0700 hours, F Troop 8th Cavalry COBRA gunships came on station and received small arms fire. At 0800 hours, Company D 4-31st Infantry broke contact and was airlifted to LZ West. Company A 4-31st Infantry, commanded by Captain James G. Mantell (Columbus, Georgia), was inserted into Company D's previous location.[50]

At 0845 hours, Company B 2-1st Infantry successfully linked up with Company C 4-31st Infantry. At 0900 and 1055 hours, LZ West received five incoming 122mm rockets, but they caused no damage. Captain John R. Thomas assumed command of Company C 4-31st Infantry during the day.

At 1600 hours, Company A 4-31st Infantry and Company C 2-1st Infantry became OPCON to the 3-21st Infantry and the 3-21st Infantry assumed control of the battle with the 31st NVA Regiment on the southeast side of LZ West. Company B 1-46th Infantry and Company C 4-31st Infantry secured their objectives, resulting in 103 NVA killed. Company B 1-46th Infantry, Company B 2-1st Infantry, and Company C 4-31st Infantry set up a combined NDP on Hill 118. The 3-7th Marines continued to move west into the Que Son Valley and came under heavy automatic and small arms fire.[51]

On August 22, Lieutenant Colonel Henry switched places with Major Lee at the battalion forward CP on Hill 118.[52] At 0615 hours, Company B 2-1st Infantry, Company C 4-31st Infantry and Company B 1-46th Infantry began their attack under the cover of artillery fire. No contact was made as the companies swept through their area until Company B 2-1st Infantry received mortar and small arms fire at 1230 hours. Gunships and artillery were requested. Company B 2-1st Infantry suffered twelve wounded and one missing in action. At 1325 hours, a Dust Off was effected, and contact was broken. In the morning, Company A 4-31st Infantry and Company C 2-1st Infantry moved toward Hill 102, with 2nd Platoon Company A on point, and ran into an ambush. First Lieutenant Stephen D. Moore (Fair Oaks, California), Corporal William J. Zeltner (Philadelphia, Pennsylvania), Privates First Class Daniel H. Love (Watkins Glen, New York), Darrell D. Taylor (Vicksburg, Michigan), and Clarke K. Vickrey (Conroe, Texas), a medic assigned to Headquarters Company, were killed and four others wounded south of Que Son.[53] All companies closed on their NDP at 1700 to prepare adequate defenses.[54]

Intelligence reports from Hiep Duc indicated an impending sapper attack on LZ Siberia, so artillery was fired on the reported enemy grid coordinates. Four secondary explosions were reported. Monitored enemy radio transmission indicated that a large amount of supplies were being shipped from the north to support two regimental-size units in the area.[55]

On August 23 at 0640 hours, a TF with Company B 1-46th Infantry in the lead, followed by Company C 4-31st Infantry and Company B 2-1st Infantry, departed Hill 118, moving northeast. At 0715 hours, the 81mm mortars from Company E 4-31st Infantry on Hill 118 received about thirty incoming 82mm mortar rounds, resulting in four minor wounded (three from 3rd Platoon Company C 4-31st Infantry), and the 81mm mortars returned fire using the grid coordinates picked up by the counter-mortar radar on LZ West. Hill 118 continued to receive sporadic incoming mortar fire throughout the day. At 1010 hours, the 2-7th Marines were located in a blocking position east of Hill 118. At 1400 hours, Company B 1-46th Infantry made contact with an estimated NVA platoon. Company B received heavy small arms fire, automatic weapons fire, and RR fire, resulting in two wounded. A medevac took out the wounded at 1525 hours. The Company recorded eleven NVA killed during this engagement. At 1600 hours, Hill 118 came under enemy mortar fire. F Troop 8th Cavalry COBRA gunships spotted the possible mortar location and engaged it with unknown results. At 2020 hours, LZ West received six rounds of 82mm RR resulting in one wounded. The location of the 82mm RR was observed, and 155mm howitzers and 4.2-inch mortars on LZ West returned fire; the enemy fire then ceased.[56]

On August 24, all elements of 4-31st TF moved from their NDPs to the northeast to find and destroy the enemy. No contact was made unit 1215 hours, when Company B 2-1st Infantry engaged a force of twenty NVA, resulting in two NVA killed and an AK-47 being captured. At 1300 hours, the company received incoming mortar rounds but sustained no casualties. The 2-7th Marines continued to provide blocking and security for the TF. At 1300 hours, Company C 4-31st Infantry recovered Company B's ten bodies and carried them to Hill 118. The bodies were evacuated to Graves Registration at LZ Baldy.[57] At 1500 hours, Company B 2-1st Infantry received small arms and mortar fire resulting in eight wounded and one killed. Mortars on Hill 118 fired in support of Company B, and the enemy fire ceased. At 1750 hours, Company B engaged and killed two NVA and captured two AK-47s. At 1600 hours, Company D 1-46th Infantry, OPCON to the 4-31st TF, was airlifted to LZ Karen. At 1810 hours, a 71st Aviation Company Huey, on a resupply mission to an element of the TF, had a mechanical failure and went down. An element from Company D 4-31st Infantry was immediately airlifted to the crash site and secured the helicopter. The helicopter was later extracted by a CH-47. The helicopter crew suffered no injuries or fatalities.[58]

On August 25 at 1000 and 1025 hours, Company B 2-1st Infantry came under small arms and mortar fire, and 81mm mortars on Hill 118 returned fire. At 1030 hours, Company B 1-46th Infantry began receiving enemy fire as it maneuvered to the east to assist Company B 2-1st Infantry. Company B 1-46th Infantry reported six soldiers wounded and twelve NVA killed. At 1115 hours, Company B 1-46th Infantry was still receiving mortar fire, and artillery was fired on the suspected enemy locations. At 1245 hours, Company B began receiving small arms fire as the enemy attempted to surround the company. The enemy was halted by artillery and mortar fire. At 1215 hours, Company B 4-31st Infantry was airlifted from LZ Siberia to Hill 118 and began moving forward to become part of the TF. 1-46th Infantry took responsibility for the defense of LZ Siberia and close-in defense of Hiep Duc village. At 1500 hours, Company C 4-31st Infantry received small arms sniper fire. Also at 1500 hours, Company B 1-46th Infantry received sniper fire, resulting in four wounded. As the elements advanced, numerous bunkers, trenches, and spider holes were discovered, indicating that it would be a slow process to root out the enemy. At 1530 hours, Company D 1-46th Infantry made heavy contact while moving east, resulting in six wounded. A medevac was conducted, and Company D attempted to continue to move.

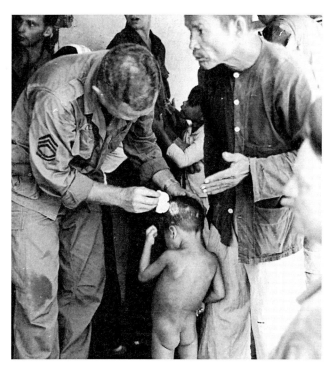

SFC Childers, Company C, 4th Battalion, 31st Infantry, applies an ointment to the head of a Vietnamese child during a MEDCAP operation (U.S. Army photograph, National Archives).

The company was immediately engaged by heavy small arms and mortar fire, resulting in fourteen more wounded. The company pulled back to regroup and secure an LZ for a medevac, which was successfully completed a short time later. Between 1600–1800 hours, friendly 81mm mortar crews received fire from the west end of Hill 118. At 1920 hours, Company D 1-46th Infantry engaged and killed one NVA. A summary of the day's action showed that Company B 2-1st Infantry had killed twenty-five NVA, captured three AK-47s, enemy documents, and one AK-50 and had destroyed twenty bunkers that were six by six feet and had overhead cover. The company suffered seventeen wounded. Company B 1-46th Infantry reported thirty NVA killed, two U.S. M-16s, one SKS, two AK-47s, one AK-50 captured, and seventeen bunkers destroyed. Company B suffered twelve wounded. Company D 1-46th Infantry reported nineteen NVA killed and five bunkers destroyed. They suffered twenty wounded. Total for the day was seventy-four NVA killed, ten weapons captured, and forty-two bunkers destroyed. Contact was broken at 1755 hours, and all companies moved to their NDPs.[59]

On August 26, Company B 4-31st Infantry secured its objective and linked up with the U.S. Marines. Company B made no contact until 1310 hours, when they received incoming mortar rounds, killing Sergeant Norman R. Hetzel (Mahwah, New Jersey) and wounding four. Company B 1-46th Infantry followed Company B 4-31st Infantry to their objective and established an LZ to receive resupply and to evacuate casualties. Company B 2-1st Infantry made contact at 1110 hours when a sniper wounded one man. The company secured their objective without any further enemy resistance. Company C 4-31st

A soldier of Company C, 4th Battalion, 31st Infantry, hands out candy to an eager group of children during a MEDCAP mission (U.S. Army photograph, National Archives).

Infantry attacked to secure their objective. At 0950 hours, Company C was stopped by heavy M-79, small arms, and mortar fire; mortars and artillery were fired in response, and the enemy ceased firing. Company C secured its objective and received sniper fire resulting in two killed and two wounded. At 1150 hours Company C again ran into sniper fire, resulting in three more killed. Those killed were Sergeant First Class Marshall E. Robertson (Portsmouth, Virginia), an acting platoon leader who returned to the field instead of going on Rest and Recuperation out of country, Sergeant Merlin J. Craig (Alexandria, Louisiana), Specialists Four Dennis J. Cannito (West New York, New York), William G. Howell (Gastonia, North Carolina), and Private First Class Donald E. Nelson (Wayne, Michigan). Company D also lost Private First Class Russell A. Taylor (Elkins, West Virginia) in a meeting engagement. All elements closed on their NDPs at 1900 hours and established night defenses.[60]

On August 27 at 0700 hours, Company C 4-31st Infantry was airlifted from the field to LZ West. Companies A and D 4-31st Infantry were airlifted to the field. Company A 2-1st Infantry became OPCON to the 4-31st Infantry, was airlifted to LZ West, and prepared to move to the Que Son Valley the next day. Company B 1-46th Infantry moved to Hill 118. Companies B and D 1-46th Infantry were released from OPCON of 4-31st Infantry and returned to control of 1-46th Infantry for close-in security of Hiep Duc. The 2-7th Marines captured a large amount of personal equipment and three weapons. Company A 2-1st Infantry became OPCON to the 4-31st Infantry and was airlifted to LZ West and prepared to deploy into the valley on August 28. All companies conducted detailed search operations, with negative enemy contact. Company D 1-7th Marines learned from POWs that the 2nd NVA Division was the enemy in contact in the Hiep Duc battle. The Marines reported two NVA killed and two weapons captured.[61]

On August 28, Company A 4-31st Infantry moved to its assigned objective with no enemy contact, found one dead NVA, and destroyed a number of bunkers. Company B 4-31st Infantry moved to its assigned objectives and lost Privates First Class James A. Doughty (Chelmsford, Massachusetts), Robert Gonzales (San Jose, California), Charles E. Jackson (East Chicago, Indiana), Thomas P. McKerns (Mahanoy City, Pennsylvania), and Charlie Simmons, Jr. (Atlanta, Georgia) while attacking a bunker complex. Company B found two dead American soldiers and one M-16 rifle. The recovered missing in action were believed to be members of Company C 4-31st Infantry. At 0840 hours, Company C received sniper fire, resulting in one wounded. At 0930 hours, Company B found one PRC 25, five M-16s, and one M-60 believed to belong to Company D 1-46th Infantry. At 1240 hours, Company B received heavy machine gun fire, resulting in three wounded. The company destroyed a machine gun position, resulting in five NVA killed. The same day, the Marines reported the capture of two 12.7mm anti-aircraft guns.[62]

On August 29 at 0030 hours, a trip flare went off on the perimeter of the Company B 2-1st Infantry NDP, and two NVA were observed carrying what appeared to be mortar rounds and grenades. The enemy was engaged with small arms fire, and during a search in the morning, twenty 60mm mortars rounds were found. At 1920 hours, Company B recovered the body of a U.S. soldier missing in action. Company A 4-31st Infantry linked up with a Marine tank and infantry team. At 1430 hours, Company B 4-31st Infantry discovered the body of one U.S. soldier missing in action. The company also found four reinforced bunkers, numerous spider holes, a 60mm mortar base plate, two NVA packs, one carbine, and seventeen 60mm mortar rounds in the area. Company B 4-31st Infantry moved to the Hiep Duc control fire zone (CFZ) in preparation to be released OPCON to the 1-46th Infantry and to secure LZ Siberia on August 30. At 1500 hours, the Marines discovered seven Vietnamese civilians apparently assassinated by the NVA. Also in the area were large bunkers with overhead cover connected by tunnels capable of housing 100 men. The Marines destroyed the entire complex. At 2200 hours, all elements of the company closed on their NDPs.[63]

On August 30, Company A 4-31st Infantry moved northeast from its NDP, and at 0830 hours, they destroyed seven large bunkers. At 1010 hours, they engaged and killed one VC in a spider hole. All company elements conducted detailed search and destroy operations in designated areas, resulting in numerous bunkers being destroyed, with negative contact.[64]

On August 31, at 0730 hours, Company A 4-31st Infantry discovered six fresh graves, and at 0800 hours, the company found one Vietnamese female who had gunshot wounds. She was evacuated to LZ West for questioning, and three small children were also evacuated to LZ West. Company A 2-1st Infantry found and destroyed enemy structures, while Company D found and destroyed three bunkers and one booby-trap and engaged two VC, with negative results. Company B 2-1st Infantry moved an element to Hill 118 to secure the forward position mortars. At 1900 hours, the mortar section spotted and killed one VC approaching their perimeter.[65]

Initially, the method of reinforcing the battalion was to attach rifle companies to the battalion. At the high point of this battle, the battalion controlled seven rifle companies and had four separate missions. The missions were to protect Hiep Duc, secure LZs

West and Siberia, engage and defeat the enemy forces southeast of LZ West, and engage and defeat the enemy northeast of Hiep Duc. The 196th Infantry Brigade quickly brought two additional control headquarters into the AO to improve the command and control problem.[66]

The 1969 Battle for Hiep Duc achieved "a stunning tactical and psychological victory by protecting the Hiep Duc District and destroying two-thirds of the fighting units of the 2nd NVA Division," which lost more than 1,112 killed in the battle.[67]

The 4-31st Infantry was awarded the Presidential Unit Citation (Army) for Actions during the Battle of Hiep Duc from August 11 to August 31, 1969.

4th Battalion 31st Infantry's Presidential Unit Citation (Army) Citation

The 4th Battalion, 31st Infantry distinguished itself by extraordinary heroism in military operations against hostile enemy forces in Quang Tin Province, Republic of Vietnam, 11 through 31 August 1969. During this period the enemy initiated its autumn campaign with the deployment of two well-trained and equipped regiments near the junction of the Hiep Duc and Song Chang Valleys, with the mission of destroying the newly established Vietnamese Government District at Hiep Duc. The 4th Battalion, 31st Infantry was the first unit of the 196th Infantry Brigade to make contact with the enemy. Throughout the fierce 21-day battle that ensued the battalion bore the brunt of the fighting, inflicting severe losses on enemy personnel and equipment. The battalion's decisive defeat of the major elements of the 1st Viet Cong Regiment and the 3d North Vietnamese Army Regiment contributed significantly to the preservation of Hiep Duc District and resulted in the destruction of the 2d North Vietnamese Army Division. The fighting spirit, valiant perseverance, and extraordinary heroism displayed during this period reflect great credit upon the men of the 4th Battalion, 31st Infantry, the 196th Infantry Brigade and the Americal Division. Their bravery and determination are in keeping with the highest traditions of the United States Army and the Armed Forces of the United States.[68]

On September 1, Company A 4-31st destroyed fifteen bunkers and discovered four graves—containing four NVA killed—and an AK-47. Later they found the body of one U.S. soldier missing in action, believed to be from Company C 4-31st Infantry. The company engaged ten NVA, killing four and wounding two, who were evacuated as POWs by Dust Off. Company A 2-1st Infantry observed eight NVA and called for artillery, resulting in three NVA killed and one hut destroyed. There was no further activity in the day.[69]

On September 2, the 1-46th Infantry was released from the responsibility of securing Hiep Duc CFZ and LZ Siberia. Their battalion's forward CP departed the 4-31st Infantry's AO. Company B 4-31st Infantry was released from OPCON to the 1-46th Infantry and returned to the control of the 4-31st Infantry. The company assumed security of LZ Siberia. Company B 2-1st Infantry was released from OPCON to the 4-31st Infantry and was airlifted to LZ Baldy. On September 3rd, Company A 2-1st Infantry was released from OPCON to the 4-31st Infantry. There was no enemy contact on September 2 and 3.[70]

Enemy activity then decreased significantly. That was largely attributed to the death of Ho Chi Minh, for whom the VC/NVA proclaimed a three-day truce from September 8 to 11. Enemy activity increased after September 11, with attacks by indirect fire against U.S. installations, with LZ Siberia and Hiep Duc CFZ being primary targets. On September 11, LZ Siberia was attacked by the GK-35 Sapper/Recon Battalion 2nd NVA Division. The attack was preceded by small arms and RPG/RR fire.[71] The main attack came from the west against bunkers one, two, and three, with bunker two destroyed by an RPG. LZ Siberia also received sporadic small arms fire from the north. In the initial attack, the enemy wounded seven and Company B lost Privates First Class Alfredo E. Aviles (New York, New York), Gilberto Bustamante (Tampa, Florida), and Woodrow J. Ewald, Jr.

(International Falls, Minnesota), and Sergeant First Class Alfredo Pacolba (Honolulu, Hawaii).[72] SPOOKY arrived on station at 0300 hours; it received fire from .30 and .51 caliber machine guns while providing fire support. At 1000 hours, LZ Siberia received twelve incoming 60mm mortar rounds, wounding four additional soldiers. A search of the area around LZ Siberia discovered seven AK-50s, five AK-57s, eight RPG-1s, one RPG-7, one flamethrower, one pistol, twenty RPG rounds, seven Bangalore torpedoes, 189 Chicom hand grenades, one field phone, and one shaped charge, as well as thirty-one dead NVA. Recon Platoon lost Private First Class Kenneth W. Fields (Fort Pierce, Florida) in a mortar attack on LZ Karen. Also on September 11, the 60th Battalion, 1st NVA Main Force Regiment, and other unidentified units initiated a ground attack against the Hiep Duc CFZ. The ARVN 2-5th Infantry and elements of the 4-31st Infantry reinforced GVN units. As a result of aggressive actions by the combined forces, the Hiep Duc CFZ was cleared of enemy forces on September 13.[73]

After the attack on LZ Siberia on September 11, the battalion was in daily contact with the enemy. LZs West and Siberia received almost daily 82mm mortar fire and RR fire, resulting in numerous soldiers being wounded.

Late in the afternoon on September 12, the point element of the 1st Platoon Company D was ambushed by a large NVA force while in route to the company NDP. Only the platoon leader, non-commissioned officers, and platoon RTOs made it through the ambush to the company NDP and reported that Private First Class James S. Brister (Fairview, Ohio) had been killed. It was determined that fourteen men from the platoon were missing. There was no way to communicate with the missing soldiers because they did not have a radio. Lieutenant Colonel Henry obtained a helicopter equipped with loud speakers and personally flew over the area of the ambush urging any missing soldiers to hide in place, and wait until morning for reinforcements. At first light the next morning, 3rd Platoon located the fourteen missing soldiers, who had consolidated into one group. Private First Class Brister's body was recovered on September 15th.

Company E lost Sergeant Donald W. Churchwell (Birmingham, Alabama) on the 14th in a mortar attack on LZ Siberia. On September 16, Company D lost Private First Class Charlie H. Mitchell (Jolo, West Virginia) in a mortar attack on the company NDP. Company A lost Private First Class Arthur Lewis (Ashland, Virginia), a medic assigned to Headquarters Company, on the 18th from a hand grenade attack on an NDP, and Specialist Four Nels V. Rosenlund II (Arcata, California) on the 21st in a meeting engagement.[74] The battalion rotated rifle companies, the Recon Platoon, and mortar sections to Chu Lai for three-day stand down periods between September 22 and October 1.[75]

From the end of September through mid–December the battalion had light contact with the enemy. The monsoon season began in early October, with heavy downpours during the first half and scattered showers during the remainder of the month, resulting in limited combat operations. A sharp decline in enemy activity occurred, which continued through the end of February.[76] Company B lost Private First Class Roosevelt Wallace (Guyton, Georgia) on October 7 to enemy mortar fire on LZ Siberia. In December, the rifle companies conducted platoon search and clear operations in their assigned AOs.[77] On December 2, Company B lost Private First Class Marvin H. Sanders (Fortuna, Missouri) due to a malfunctioning 81mm mortar round that fell short and hit his bunker on LZ West.

On December 27, Lieutenant Colonel Kenneth L. Skaer (Spokane, Washington) assumed command from Lieutenant Colonel Henry on LZ West.[78]

22 4th Battalion in Vietnam, 1970–1971

During the period of January through the end of March there were numerous contacts with one or two enemy at a time, and enemy contact became moderate to heavy by the end of March.[1] The battalion made more contact with the enemy because of the many sweeps and reconnaissance in force operations conducted in the Battalion AO. Company B lost Sergeant Marion Croom, Jr. (Washington, D.C.) in action on January 15. The company located a 300-bed enemy hospital on January 22. Company D lost Private First Class Warner P. Hughie (Newnan, Georgia), killed by a booby trap near Hiep Duc on March 12, and Staff Sergeant Charles E. Hann (Northfield, Ohio) on March 24 during an enemy meeting engagement. On April 22, Sergeant Keith A. Lochner (Marion, Indiana), from Company A, was killed by a booby-trapped hand grenade near Hiep Duc.

1970 Battle for Hiep Duc

The enemy hid and rested until April 30, when they attacked Hiep Duc, the Vietnamese District Headquarters at LZ Karen, as well as LZ Siberia and LZ West. LZ Siberia was the first to be attacked. The following men were killed in the action: Specialist Four Daniel Flores (San Diego, California), from Company D, Privates First Class Donald Barrett (Dalton, Georgia) and Frank M. Valentine (Litchfield, Ohio), both medics from Headquarters Company, and Private First Class Glen L. Knoblock (Lolita, Texas), from Company E. The enemy employed forces equivalent to two regiments plus support elements of the 2nd NVA Division. LZ West received six separate attacks, beginning at 0535 hours and ending at 2150 hours. A total of twelve 82mm mortar rounds were fired by the enemy. Some 82mm mortars contained Chlorobenzylidene-Malononitrile, a riot control gas (CS) agent.[2] The rifle companies moved to contact, and the Recon Platoon was the first element to engage the enemy. The platoon found ten NVA killed by air strikes earlier in the day. A PF outpost was overrun, and the enemy established a .51 caliber anti-aircraft position. The outpost was recaptured later in the day. By the end of the day, Company C 2-1st Infantry and Company A 3-21st Infantry were attached to the 4-31st Infantry.[3]

On May 1, the enemy opened an offensive in Hiep Duc with a ground attack against Company C 4-31st Infantry. During the day, the enemy attacked Company D 4-31st Infantry, resulting in fourteen wounded, and they attacked Company A 3-21st Infantry, resulting in nineteen wounded.[4] By the end of the day, all organic and attached rifle com-

Left: Troops of Company C, 4th Battalion, 31st Infantry, 196th Infantry Brigade, cautiously proceed during a raid on a VC sampan factory near Chu Lai, 3 December 1970. *Right:* An M-60 machine gunner from Company C, 4th Battalion, 31st Infantry, checks out the area during a raid on a VC sampan factory near Chu Lai, 3 December 1970 (both U.S. Army photographs, National Archives).

panies, except Company B on LZ West, were in contact.[5] On May 2, the enemy attacked Company A 2-1st Infantry—resulting in nine wounded—Recon Platoon, 4-31st Infantry—resulting in four wounded—and Company D 4-31st Infantry—resulting in six wounded.[6] Company B suffered three killed: First Lieutenant John P. Becker (Kenosha, Wisconsin), Sergeant First Class Andrew J. Taylor (Milwaukee, Wisconsin), and Private First Class Curtis Gaither (St. Louis, Missouri), in a fire fight near Hiep Duc. On May 3rd, LZ Siberia received five separate attacks, totaling thirteen 82mm mortar rounds and three unknown types of RR rounds. On May 4, LZ West received a total of fourteen 82mm mortar rounds, and LZ Siberia received ten 82mm rounds and five unknown types RR rounds.[7] On May 5, Sergeant Duane A. Peterson (Isanti, Minnesota) was killed. On May 7, LZ Siberia received enemy mortar fire, resulting in C Battery 3-82nd Artillery losing two killed and twelve wounded. Specialist Four Jack S. Grouf (East Northport, New York), assigned to Headquarters Company 4-31st Infantry, was also killed. By May 12, Hiep Duc was secure by day, and except for the extreme western hamlets, the area was secure at night. On May 14, Company A 3-21st Infantry and Company C 2-1st Infantry were reassigned to their parent battalions. They were replaced by attachment of the 1/1 Cavalry. Their armor capability greatly assisted in mop-up operations. The LZs in the 4-31st Infantry AO continued to receive enemy indirect fire. On May 20, LZ Siberia received nine 82mm mortar rounds, eight containing CS. On May 21, the LZ received fifteen 82mm mortar rounds and seven unknown type rounds. However, the rifle companies were in very light contact during the same period.[8] Company A lost Sergeant Donald G. Kuzilla (Detroit, Michigan), on May 14, and Sergeant William D. Menscer (Statesville, North Carolina), on May 16, due to enemy fire into NDPs.

SP4 Jerry Gehrmann, from Company C, 4th Battalion, 31st Infantry, working with Doan Lanh, a Kit Carson Scout, checks over some papers found during a raid on a VC sampan factory near Chu Lai, 3 December 1970 (U.S. Army photograph, National Archives).

On May 23, Companies C 4-31st Infantry and D 1-46th Infantry were attached to the 1/1 Cavalry. The 3-21st Infantry conducted search and clear operations in the eastern half of Hiep Duc Valley, and the 1/1 Cavalry conducted operations on roads along the northern edge of the valley. Contact picked up again on May 24 through May 29. On May 25, Specialist Four Jeffery J. Benjamin (Keenesburg, Colorado), from Company C, was killed, and on May 29, Sergeant Bruce R. Neeson (Kalamazoo, Michigan), from Company B, was killed in an NDP by RPG fire. The results of the 2nd NVA Division's May offensive were disastrous for the enemy, with over 700 confirmed enemy dead. One villager said he saw thirty to forty wounded going through his village every night. One enemy soldier reported that his regiment lost 700 killed.[9]

The first week in June there was a substantial increase in enemy activity, with LZs Siberia and West being the focal point of attacks.[10] Between June 3 and June 13, LZ Siberia received daily mortar attacks totaling 219 82mm and twenty-five 60mm mortar rounds and three 75mm RR rounds. On June 3, Sergeant Roderick K. Tolbert (Fairfield, Alabama), from Headquarters Company, and Specialist Four Richard L. Kester (Angola, New York), from Company E, were killed on LZ Siberia during a mortar attack. On June 4, Company A had nine wounded by enemy mortar and grenade attacks.[11] In early June, the battalion formed two TFs: TF Delta consisting of Companies A and D, commanded by Captain Dave Tanis (Fayetteville, North Carolina), and TF Bravo consisting of Companies B and C, commanded by Major Erikson. On June 6, while TF Delta was conducting a sweep of their AO, it came under heavy small arms, automatic weapons, and 60mm mortar fire. Company A lost Sergeant First Class Everette B. Caldwell (San Diego, California), Specialist Four Dennis N. Hogenboom (Schoharie, New York), and Private First Class Mark E. Klever (Milwaukee, Wisconsin). Approximately ten mortar rounds landed on the Company D CP, resulting in SGT Lawrence D. Burgess (Ottawa, Kansas), the Company RTO

SGT Stephan Moses (Cynthiana, Kentucky) and SGT Ronnie Hutchins (Fort Smith, Arkansas), both members of 4th Battalion, 31st Infantry, 196th Light Infantry Brigade, display a communist flag which they captured during a search-and-destroy mission, 21 June 1970 (U.S. Army photograph, National Archives).

being killed and Captain Tanis and another soldier being wounded. Captain Tanis lost the lower portion of both his legs as result of the action.[12]

On June 7, Staff Sergeant Robert C. Murray (New York, New York) was killed. He was posthumously awarded the Medal of Honor for his actions near Hiep Duc.

Staff Sergeant Murray's Medal of Honor citation:

Staff Sergeant Robert C. Murray, United States Army, who distinguished himself while serving as a squad leader with Company B near the village of Hiep Duc, Republic of Vietnam on June 7, 1970. Sergeant Murray's squad was searching for an enemy mortar that had been threatening friendly positions when a member of the squad tripped an enemy grenade rigged as a booby trap. Realizing that he had activated the enemy booby trap, the soldier shouted for everybody to take cover. Instantly assessing the danger to the men of his squad Sergeant Murray unhesitatingly and with complete disregard for his own safety, threw himself on the grenade absorbing the full and fatal impact of the explosion. By his gallant actions and self-sacrifice, he prevented the death or injury of the other members of his squad. SSG Murray's extraordinary courage and gallantry, at the cost of his life above and beyond the call of duty, are in keeping with the highest traditions of the military service and reflect great credit on him, his unit, and the United States Army.[13]

On June 11, LZ West received thirty-nine 82mm mortar rounds, some containing CS.[14]

On June 14, Lieutenant Colonel Thomas A. Breen assumed command from Lieutenant Colonel Skaer on LZ West.[15]

On June 18, LZ Prep was opened in the South Central part of the battalion AO by the Recon Platoon. The western part of the area was searched and cleared during July. The battalion combined with the civil defense force (CDG) and worked around Hau Duc to the Southeast of LZ West.[16]

Members of Company C, 4th Battalion, 31st Infantry, inspect material found during a raid on a VC sampan factory near Chu Lai, 3 December 1970 (U.S. Army photograph, National Archives).

Beginning in the third week in June, enemy activity almost ceased in the Hiep Duc area, indicating the withdrawal of enemy forces.[17] The low level of activity continued through the end of July. The number of enemy-initiated events decreased.[18]

On July 26, Specialist Four Larry W. Rasey (Taft, California), from 1st Platoon Company A, was killed in contact after an Eagle Flight insertion northeast of Kham Duc. On August 10, Company C was attached to the 2-1st Infantry for operations around Kham Duc and the border region. On August 22, Private First Class Thomas J. Roberts (Burlington, Wisconsin), a medic in Headquarters Company, was killed by small arms fire.

Operation Elk Canyon II

Operation Elk Canyon II (August 26–September 19). The 4-31st Infantry worked in conjunction with the ARVN 2nd Division conducting operations in the vicinity of LZs Judy and Mary Ann. The battalion had light contact during the operation.[19] On September 7, Private First Class David A. Pratt (Miami Lakes, Florida), from Company C, was killed by a booby trap near Hill 1064. Company C returned to the 4-31st Infantry control on September 16.[20]

Operation Nebraska Rapids

Operation Nebraska Rapids lasted from September 5 through the 8th.[21] The 196th Infantry Brigade conducted a joint operation with the U.S. 1st Marine Division. This was a search and destroy mission to clear and secure Route 534 from LZ Baldy to Hiep Duc.[22]

On September 26, Lieutenant Colonel William G. Hammell assumed command from Lieutenant Colonel Breen.[23]

Severe tropical storms and Typhoons KATE and JOAN seriously curtailed military operations during the period October 15–26 (the beginning of the monsoon season), which lasted until early February.[24] Americal Division soldiers and material assets were diverted to engage in disaster relief operations with the ARVN 2nd Division.[25]

To interdict enemy supply lines from base area 212 into the Hiep Duc area, an AO extension north of LZ Siberia was obtained from the U.S. 1st Marines. On November 15, Company A 4-31st Infantry deployed on the western bank of the gorge area, followed by Company B on the east bank of the gorge. On November 20, LZ Pratt, a temporary LZ, was opened to provide artillery support to an area that could not be supported by the 105mm howitzers on LZ Siberia.[26] The battalion immediately began finding caches on both sides of the river and made light contact with the enemy. Among the items found were numerous 122mm rockets, 82mm mortars with small arms ammunition, some rice, corn, and peanuts, thousands of small arms, and quantities of explosives. Over twenty sampans were destroyed, dealing a further blow to the enemy. Additional smaller caches were located by the battalion during the month of December. A propaganda plant with printed leaflets asking American soldiers to "Chieu Hoi" to the VC was discovered and destroyed. The 4-31st Infantry's operation in vicinity of FSB Pratt ended on December 15.[27] On December 31, Specialist Four Pete E. Williamson (River, Kentucky) was killed by a booby trap while on patrol near Hiep Duc. Between December 311800 hours 1970 and January 011801 hours 1971 a New Year's truce was observed.[28]

In January, Company A, operating in the extreme southern edge of the battalion AO, found another large cache consisting of tons of ammunition and medical supplies. On January 8, Staff Sergeant Patrick J. Kihl (Milwaukee, Wisconsin) was killed by a booby trap. Private First Class John S. Weaver (Lombard, Illinois) was killed by a short mortar

SGT Steve Howard from Company C, 4th Battalion, 31st Infantry, finds a sampan during a raid on a VC sampan factory near Chu Lai, 3 December 1970 (U.S. Army photograph, National Archives).

round near Hiep Duc on January 16. During January, over twenty Chieu Hois, starving and sick with malaria, arrived at the District Headquarters on LZ Karen.[29] On February 12, Company C located a POW cage with nine captives; none were American soldiers.[30] On February 11, Specialist Four Joseph R. Anthony (Lafayette, Louisiana), of Company C, was killed by small arms fire. Enemy contact for the first two months of the year was light.[31] On March 1 at 0600 hours, Operation Frederick Hill was terminated, and at 0601 hours, the 196th Infantry Brigade initiated Operation Middlesex Peak.[32]

Operation Middlesex Peak

Operation Middlesex Peak lasted from March 01 0600 hours through July 01 1200 hours. The 196th Infantry Brigade, in conjunction with GVN forces operating in the combined TAOR, emphasized continuous and aggressive combat operations. The objective was to increase security in pacified areas along the coastal plains and to destroy VC main force and NVA units, as well as to assist in rice denial operations.[33] In March, enemy activity picked up, with moderate to heavy enemy contact. The battalion started road-clearing operations from Son Hoa to LZ Ross to enable convoys to reach LZ Center. This would enable 3-21st Infantry to be moved by truck to Da Nang. The road-clearing operation was contested by snipers and booby traps.[34] On March 11, First Lieutenant Donald J. Frazelle (Raleigh, North Carolina), Company A, was killed, and on March 22,

SP5 David O'Neil (Earl Park, Illinois), 4/31 Liaison Team, 196th Brigade, Americal Division, teaches a villager to read English, 11 January 1970 (National Archives).

Private First Class Clarence M. Suchon (Stevens Point, Wisconsin), of Company C, was killed by small arms fire. Lieutenant Colonel Howard S. Mitchell assumed command from Lieutenant Colonel Hammell on March 27, 1971.[35]

April was a bad month for booby traps for the battalion. On April 6th, Company A had six men wounded by booby traps. On April 11, at 1140 hours, the 198th Infantry Brigade joined the 196th Infantry Brigade in the operation.[36] On April 12, the battalion lost its last soldier, Private First Class Johnny Saxon (Charlotte, North Carolina), assigned to Company A. He was killed by a booby trap. During the month, Companies B and D secured LZs Young and Pleasantville for a few weeks. At the end of April, the battalion moved to a new AO northwest of Da Nang.[37]

At 1645 hours on April 26, the ARVN assumed control of LZ Siberia, and at 0910 hours on April 28, the ARVN assumed control of LZ West. At 1201 hours on April 29, Operation Middlesex Peak came under control of the 198th Infantry Brigade.[38]

Operation Caroline Hill (29 April 1200 hours– 01 July 1200 hours)

The 196th Infantry Brigade initiated Operation Caroline Hill in Quang Nam Province in conjunction and coordination with GVN forces, with unilateral and combined operations.[39] The Brigade was responsible for the defense of the Da Nang complex and operated extensively in the foothills west of Da Nang and in the Que Son mountains area.[40] During May, the majority of the enemy activity occurred in the 3-21st Infantry's AO.[41] From May 20 through the 23rd, the 4-31st Infantry was OPCON to the 198th Infantry Brigade.[42] In June the battalion relocated back to LZ Center to search for the enemy, but none was found. The battalion then relocated north of Da Nang and built a new fire base on Hill 501 but made no contact with the enemy. From June 15 through the 23rd, the battalion was again OPCON to the 198th Infantry Brigade. The battalion moved back to Hill 350, its permanent base outside of Da Nang, and conducted combat operations in the new AO on Charlie Ridge west of Da Nang. While operating in the new AO, the battalion opened a temporary FSB that was named New Siberia. New Siberia was the northern-most firebase in the American Division.[43]

In July, the battalion had its first casualties since April. Company C was attached to the 1-46th Infantry on a combat assault when three soldiers were wounded due to helicopter propeller wash detonating a booby trap in the LZ. These three soldiers were the battalion's last wounded in Vietnam.

In August, the Hiep Duc District was again being threatened.[44] The battalion redeployed back to Que Son Valley and reopened LZs West and Siberia.[45]

From September 4 through the 12th, the 4-31st Infantry was again OPCON to the 198th Infantry Brigade.[46] Lieutenant Colonel William L. Mitchell (Alexandria, Virginia) assumed command from Lieutenant Colonel Howard Mitchell on September 12, 1971.[47]

Operation Keystone Oriole Charlie

Operation Keystone Oriole Charlie (April 13–November 27) was the preparation and execution of the American Division's redeployment from the Republic of (South)

Vietnam.[48] On September 15, the battalion was given its Keystone Redeployment Briefing. The battalion ceased combat operations on October 4.[49] The battalion conducted a stand down ceremony on October 5 in Chu Lai.[50] They redeployed to Fort Lewis, Washington, from October 6 to the 24th. On October 24, the 4-31st Infantry was inactivated at Fort Lewis, Washington.[51]

On October 5, Specialist Four Daniel Van Huss, 4-31st Infantry Soldier of the Month, read the battalion's farewell to the Americal Division and its commander, Major General Kroesen.[52] Specialist Four Van Huss quoted President Teddy Roosevelt: "It's not the critic that counts, the credit belongs to the man who is actually in the arena, whose face is marred by dust and sweat and blood...."

Specialist Four Van Huss said that described soldiers of the Americal Division. He continued:

"If anyone said that he enjoyed being over here we would look at him with a great deal of concern. But if someone said that he did his job, had a good attitude, beat the bush, and indicated he did this because he loved his country—then that is a Polar Bear. If you need us again, we'll come charging. Good luck to all of you and God Bless you."[53]

So ended the battalion's five years, two months, and nine days of combat in the Republic of (South) Vietnam.[54]

The Americal Division conducted a stand-down ceremony at Chu Lai on November 11, and the command group and colors were redeployed to Fort Lewis, Washington, on November 27. The Division was inactivated at the end of November 1971 at Fort Lewis.[55] The 196th LIB was the last brigade to depart Vietnam, on June 29, 1972.[56] It was inactivated the next day in Oakland, California.[57]

B. *The 6th Battalion*
by Karl H. Lowe

23 Fort Lewis, Deployment, First Casualties, 1967–1968

On November 1, 1967, the 31st Infantry Regiment added its sixth successor battalion.[1]

The 6th Battalion 31st Infantry, whose lineage is derived from F Company of the old regiment, was activated at Fort Lewis, Washington. Assigned to the Sixth Army for its formative training, the new battalion was slated to become part of the 23rd Infantry Division, formed only a few months earlier in Vietnam's coastal highlands.[2] Following a tradition begun by the regiment during the Korean War, the battalion called itself the "Bearcats."

When the 6th Battalion formed for the first time on the parade ground at Fort Lewis, most of its members were draftees just out of Advanced Individual Training. Others were transferred from a holding detachment where they had been awaiting shipment to various schools. Prospective mechanics, musicians, clerks, intelligence specialists, and cooks became instant infantrymen whether they agreed or not. PFC Bill Singleton was awaiting orders to the Military Intelligence School and PFC Al Banfield was awaiting shipment to the Military Academy Preparatory School. Recruiters' promises and soldiers' test scores meant nothing. The draft generated some unusually well-educated riflemen, for this battalion perhaps more than most. For example, when C Company was formed, one member had a Doctorate, two had Masters Degrees, and about a third had at least a year of college.

The Bearcats' leaders were a mix of the seasoned and the green. Lieutenant Colonel Joseph Schmalhorst, the battalion commander, had never seen combat and had little infantry experience. With a career spent mainly in staff and research and development assignments, he was an able manager, but not a tactician. Amiable humor and steadfast support of his company commanders were his strengths. Schmalhorst had good reason to support his company commanders. All had served a previous tour in Vietnam and were graduates of the Infantry Officer Advanced Course at Fort Benning. His lieutenants, on the other hand, were all fresh out of Officer Candidate School and had little more military experience than the troops they led.

Except for the first sergeants, surprisingly few of the battalion's NCOs had seen combat. Career NCOs in the line companies were first sergeants, mess sergeants, supply sergeants, and platoon sergeants, many of whom served one rank below the position they

The Company Commanders (from left)—Captains Thomas Sullivan (HHC), Channing Greene (A Co.), Phillip Eckman (B Co.), William Owen (C Co.), Robert Stephens (D Co.), and John DeVore (E Co.) (Association archives).

filled. While the Army had plenty of combat-seasoned Infantry NCOs, their numbers were dissipated by the competing demands of filling advisory teams in Vietnam, expanding Special Forces, forming three new divisions, and providing cadres for an enlarged training establishment. By 1967, soldiers who fought in World War II and remained in the Army afterward already had 22 or more years of service and could retire. Most infantry NCOs in the U.S. worked 14- to 16-hour days as drill sergeants in an expanding number of basic training centers while others stayed in the field for nearly half of every year with Infantry battalions in Germany, Korea, Panama, or the dwindling number left in the U.S. Some were thanklessly doing work normally done by officers because there were few experienced officers left in units outside Vietnam. NCOs' wives and children saw too little of them, causing family strains that drove many good men to retire.

Training in Washington's cold, wet forests to prepare for combat in tropical jungles bordered on the ridiculous, especially when searching a mock-up Vietnamese village in 16 inches of snow. Bill McMullen, dropped from OCS at Fort Benning, remembers that surreal experience fondly because of the close friendships it fostered. While serving with the opposing force on one of C Company's field training exercises, McMullen, John "Mugs" Morgan, and Greg Russell captured the company headquarters, earning them the respect of their peers and the ire of their first sergeant. When Lieutenant Colonel Schmalhorst pitched his tent in the field, a luxury forbidden his troops, someone "accidentally" burned the tent down with a flare. That weekend, McMullen and his buddies went to Seattle, got a suite at the Sheraton where they filled the bathtub with ice and canned beer, and partied as hard as they trained. Because McMullen's mother insisted

that he be baptized before shipping out, he, Greg Russell, and Platoon Sergeant Bob Bellemare, went to the post chapel for his baptism. Years later, he found the baptismal certificate among his Army records with their signatures witnessing the event. Just over a
month after reaching Vietnam, two of them were wounded and the other was dead.

The Bearcats' field training stressed safety because units new to Vietnam were noto-
rious for weapons accidents. Men were cross-trained on crew-served weapons and some
were trained to function at least one level up from their assigned positions. In B Company,
Captain Phil Eckman had his lieutenants call in simulated air strikes. His NCOs and the
most capable privates were required to adjust fire from the company's 81mm mortars.
Soldiers would have to perform those duties in an emergency if their leaders became
casualties. Eckman, who had served in Vietnam's Mekong Delta as an advisor to a Vietnamese Ranger Battalion, was less than a year from promotion to major and his experience and field savvy showed.

After six months of training, the Bearcats were alerted for deployment. The advance
party, including Lieutenant Colonel Schmalhorst, all six company commanders, and
Command Sergeant Major Bill Russell, departed from McChord Air Force Base on March
31, 1968. Captain John DeVore recalls arriving at Chu Lai, the 196th Light Infantry
Brigade's base camp, expecting it to be the Bearcats' new home. He arranged to accompany
a friend in another battalion on a combat operation to familiarize himself with the environment but his time at Chu Lai was unexpectedly cut short. The advance party was
abruptly ordered to pack up and board C-130 cargo planes for Bien Hoa, nearly 400 miles
away. The "American" Division shoulder patches already sewn on Bearcats' uniforms
would now be out of place. Although they did not know it yet, they would soon be joining
the 9th Infantry Division ("The Old Reliables"). The 9th needed another battalion because
its area of operations had recently been extended from the outskirts of Saigon into the
Mekong Delta and from the South China Sea to the Cambodian border.

The Bearcats' main body arrived at Bien Hoa on April 5. Most traveled aboard commercial airliners but some had to accompany the unit's light vehicles aboard less comfortable Air Force cargo planes. All arrived with a duffle bag, web gear, and camouflage-
covered helmets, looking like infantrymen of the era should. Weapons were quickly
retrieved from the planes' cargo bays, but to everyone's shock, there was no place on the
airfield to draw ammunition.

With the temperature hovering above 100 degrees, the battalion traveled its next 20
miles in open trucks to the 9th Division's base camp, coincidentally named Bearcat Base.
It seemed insane to be without ammunition in a war zone and to travel in crowded trucks
that would have been death traps in an ambush. Things did not get better at Bearcat.
Men expecting to fight were subjected to seemingly endless orientation briefings and
housekeeping chores that seemed out of place in a war zone. At home, Martin Luther
King was assassinated the day the main body arrived, stirring racial tensions in the post's
oppressive atmosphere. The *Pacific Stars and Stripes* (soldiers' overseas newspaper) and
Armed Forces Radio delivered a steady barrage of unsettling news about race riots aflame
in the nation's largest cities, causing some to worry more about families back home than
themselves at war.

Bearcat Base's setting was striking, with Vietnam's scenic coastal mountains visible
to the northwest, coastal jungles and mangrove swamps to the south, and Saigon's hazy
skyline to the southeast. For nearly three weeks, the 6-31st underwent acclimatization
training, patrolling nearby rubber plantations and jungle.[3] The jungle was double and

triple canopy—full-grown trees growing under two or three layers of taller trees. Bill Singleton recalls, "In the jungle, you couldn't see more than a few feet in front of you and couldn't see the sky—helicopters couldn't find us, but millions of red ants could and did." The battalion's first non-battle casualty occurred on April 19 when a soldier from C Company wounded himself with his own weapon. Earlier that day, the company had conducted its first air assault and had its first firefight, an inconclusive encounter with a VC reconnaissance team.

First Losses—April 26, 1968

The 6-31st suffered its first combat losses on a reconnaissance operation near Bearcat Base. After traveling in column through dense jungle for several hours, C Company's commander, Captain Bill Owen, directed Lieutenant Kerry May's 1st Platoon to relieve Lieutenant Ron Belloli's 2nd Platoon as the lead element. Soon after the column started moving again, PFC Donald R. Hanna (21), a machine gunner, stepped across a log and was hit full in the face by blast and fragmentation from a large Claymore-like[4] mine, killing him instantly. Specialist Larry Hathaway recalls: "One large piece of shrapnel flew down the trail and cut my grenade in half. Fortunately, the part with the fragmentation fell off and only the primer and a little C-4 exploded. The blast knocked me down and destroyed three magazines of ammunition I wore in a bandolier around my neck."

Knowing there were probably casualties, PFC Bill Rauber (19), the platoon's medic, ran forward with Platoon Sergeant Florentino Rivera-Sanchez, to aid the wounded. Rauber had nearly reached Hanna when a second blast blew him off his feet, killing him instantly. Eight others were wounded.[5] Sergeant Al Olson, a squad leader just behind the lead platoon, recalls seeing VC running from the area, but people ahead of him were either too dazed by the explosions to fire or were unable to do so without hitting their own people.

The 2nd Platoon sprayed the left side of the trail with automatic weapons fire and moved into the jungle, passing through a clearing where clothes had been left to dry. Ron Belloli recalls thinking "Our first contact with the enemy and all we capture is his underwear." They also found a spider hole[6] and wires leading to more unexploded claymores. Captain Owen wanted to stay at the site to probe it further but a nest of venomous pit vipers agitated by the explosions deterred further searching. After moving the company a safe distance back down the trail, Owen brought artillery down on the site. C Company had to carry its dead and the most seriously wounded on poncho litters for nearly an hour until they reached a place where casualties could be winched up through the trees to a helicopter. It was near dusk before Lieutenant Dave Wilson, the company executive officer, could organize the evacuation. Before all the wounded and dead could be extracted, the jungle penetrator on the second medevac helicopter had to be jettisoned when it became snagged in the trees. It was getting too dark to attempt another evacuation.

The company carried the remaining wounded and the dead for several more hours until reaching a place they could set up a defensive perimeter for the night. Among the wounded they carried was Specialist Don Chikuma, suffering painfully from a belly wound. Chikuma repeatedly asked for water but Specialist Huie Osborn, C Company's senior medic, wouldn't give him any for fear of killing him, so he sat up all night to comfort him. The company's sense of loss and foreboding, reinforced by grim evidence of jungle warfare's risks, took a toll on morale. Al Olson recalls:

> The long night that followed the ambush was one of the scariest experiences of the war for me. Thick undergrowth, the event that had just happened, and lots of noises (way too much noise made by our company, as we were moving too fast to be quiet). I remember the column stopping for the night and establishing defensive positions right along the trail where we were. I don't recall much of a perimeter or a clearing. Other than nobody getting any sleep, the night passed without incident.

The Gathering Storm—April 27–May 6, 1968

On April 27, the Bearcats were assigned to the 9th Infantry Division's 3rd Brigade ("The Go Devils") and moved to a muddy base camp named Smoke, about 5 kilometers southwest of Saigon. The base was surrounded by rice paddies, scattered clusters of thatched or cinderblock houses, and distant tree lines. Like forts throughout the ages, Smoke was surrounded by a protective earthen berm with bunkers spaced at intervals atop the berm. Beyond the berm were layers of triple concertina barbed wire and Claymore mines angled to shoot intersecting blasts of steel pellets at intruders. Two 203mm

While approaching the trees, the troops of C Company, 6th Battalion, 31st Infantry, move with extreme caution because of booby traps (National Archives).

self-propelled howitzers at the base fired harassing and interdictory fires at random times throughout the night, angering the troops and nearby civilians alike. Bill McMullen remembers: "Smoke was a hell-hole. It was always wet, muddy, and noisy. Those howitzers made it really hard to get any sleep and Charlie was always lobbing in a few mortar rounds. Nha Be was wet and muddy too, but we could fix it up. Smoke was unfixable." Few members of the line companies spent much time there anyway since their daily routine was to patrol, patrol, and patrol in search of an elusive enemy.

Over the next few days, A Company found a 2-ton cache of rice concealed in a hole while B Company ran into some booby traps and found all the parts of a mortar except the tube.

On May 2, Captain Robert F. Stephens, Jr., D Company's commander, was wounded by a booby trap. He was replaced by Captain Grady A. Smith. The next day, D Company found a cache of hand grenades, small arms ammunition, and mortar rounds west of Smoke. Three days later, nine mortar rounds hit the base during the evening meal but no one was injured. But later that evening, another eight rounds struck with greater effect. Specialist Arnold L. Stewart (20) of D Company was killed and nine men from B and C Companies were wounded. A Vietnamese barber had been detained earlier because he was seen pacing distances between landmarks around the base. A patrol later found the imprint of a mortar base plate less than 200 meters from Smoke's perimeter.

Between the rain, rivers, and flooded paddies, troops were always wet and muddy. Fevers of unknown origin were common. Leeches, flies, wasps, and swarms of mosquitoes, nicknamed the "Viet Cong Air Force," infested the wetlands and paddies. Officers and NCOs had to make sure troops took their boots and socks off whenever possible and took their anti-malaria tablets. Patrolling the rivers and streams south of Saigon was hazardous for more reasons than the ever-present leeches and Viet Cong. On May 4, C Company's 3rd Platoon was crossing a steep-banked stream in upper Long An Province when PFC Richard Campbell (20) slipped unseen beneath the water. Distressed at the mysterious loss of a comrade, Campbell's platoon searched for him for two hours without success. When ordered by Captain Bill Owen to move his platoon to a pickup zone to be lifted out by helicopter, Lieutenant Charles Gale argued that he would not leave until Campbell was found. Although Owen was as troubled by Campbell's loss as Gale, he knew the platoon was becoming more vulnerable by lingering at the site. He got stern with Gale, ordering him to abandon the search. The next day, scout dog teams were sent to resume the search, but to no avail. The current had taken Campbell's body several miles downstream where it was found three days later by another unit.[7]

During the night of May 5–6, A Company stopped for the night along the Kinh Doi, a canal defining Saigon's southern boundary. Around 3 a.m., someone fired from the canal's north bank, wounding one man with a dud 40mm round. Minutes later, PFC Bobby R. Childs (20) was killed by a burst of automatic rifle fire from the same area. Captain Channing Greene, A Company's commander, thought the source might have been trigger-happy RVN troops, but a patrol dispatched to the area at daylight found expended brass from an AK-47. The discovery was troubling because it meant the VC were operating inside Saigon's southern edge between the Bearcats and the city they were supposed to help protect.

Murder in the Ranks—May 7, 1968

On the afternoon of May 7, a D Company soldier from New York City, nicknamed "Monk,"[8] cleaned his rifle and loaded magazines with uncharacteristic enthusiasm. Menacingly pointing his rifle at wary comrades, he spewed a string of profanities and declared himself "ready," but for what he did not say. After dark, he donned his flak jacket and helmet, picked up his loaded weapon, and walked to a sleeping bunker near Smoke's perimeter. A soldier he was known to have disliked was just leaving the bunker and, with eyes not yet adjusted to the darkness, asked where the latrine was. Monk silently motioned in the latrine's direction, an odd response, given his subsequent actions.

Entering the lighted sleeping bunker, Monk shot PFC Thomas W. Myers (21), a visiting soldier from B Company, who was sleeping near the bunker's entrance. Having spared a man he disliked and shot a man he didn't know, Monk flipped his rifle's selector switch to automatic and sprayed the room at random, hitting two more soldiers. Specialist Warren M. Kirsch (20) was hit in the shoulder and Sergeant Philip L. Culver (21) was shot through the abdomen. Two others in the bunker were not hit. Two unarmed radar operators who had been sitting atop the bunker jumped to the ground and ran when the shooting started. Monk emerged from the bunker and fired the last two rounds in his magazine at one of them from just a few feet away, but missed. Ducking into an unoccupied perimeter bunker, he slapped a fresh magazine into his rifle.

Myers, hit in the chest, lay choking on his blood. One of the survivors turned Myers' head to clear his airway before leaving the bunker to find a medic. The radar operator who had nearly been shot ducked behind a cargo trailer, where he was joined by Sergeants Marvin J. Lewis and John T. Moore. When Lewis asked what was happening, the operator said it seemed to be a prank because "he's firing blanks." But Lewis had seen tracers, indicating live ammunition. "They must be blanks," the radar operator argued. "He fired at me up close and didn't hit me." Moore wondered if a sapper had gotten inside the perimeter and the man had gone into the bunker to get him. Unsure, Lewis shouted at the man to come out. Ignoring Lewis, Monk ran back to the sleeping bunker. Culver and Kirsch, both in bad shape, tried to crawl for cover. Monk repeatedly shot both of them in the back. Taking aim at the shooter emerging from the bunker's doorway, Lewis fired five times, hitting Monk in the legs, arm, and neck. Watching through a starlight scope, Moore saw Monk drop and squirm on the ground. He was mumbling religious verses when the sergeants reached him.

Culver, Kirsch, and Myers were dead on arrival at the 3rd Brigade Aid Station. Monk was rushed into surgery where his life was saved. After recovering sufficiently to stand trial, he was found guilty of murder and sentenced to life at hard labor. At his trial, he said he had no quarrel with the men he shot. All he could remember, he claimed, was hearing a loud bang while on guard duty. It was never established whether an argument, drugs, insanity, or something else motivated the killings. While race may not have been a clear factor since one of Monk's victims was black and the others white, Monk, a Black Muslim, openly espoused strong racist views before the killings. The Criminal Investigation Division report revealed that he had been under psychiatric care before being drafted. Whatever the reason, three American soldiers had been murdered by one of their own.

Combat on Saigon's Edge—May 7–13, 1968

In the early hours of May 7, six VC battalions infiltrated the area around Cholon, the Chinese quarter on Saigon's southeast side.[9] It made no difference that Saigon's population had not risen against the government three months earlier during the much larger Tet offensive. The communists seemed intent on demonstrating that they could still attack the capitol with impunity. Their surprise attack isolated RVN Marines, Rangers, National Police, and local militia in scattered outposts south of the Kinh Doi, enabling VC units to take over crowded settlements dotting Saigon's southern approaches. Their attack cut Routes 5 and 15, roads vital to Saigon's food and fuel supplies.

In response, four battalions of the 9th Infantry Division's 3rd Brigade were sent to help RVN forces drive the Viet Cong out. Their counterattack, though piecemeal, gave the VC little opportunity to adjust and no room to maneuver. 5-60th and 3-39th Infantry, based in adjacent Long An Province, were the first to arrive. The 6-31st and 2-47th Infantry began reinforcing them later that day. The 2-47th and 5-60th were mechanized infantry battalions, each with around 800 men and 70 aluminum-hulled, tracked M-113 armored personnel carriers (APCs). Called "tracks" for short, each APC mounted a .50 caliber machine gun and one or more M-60 machine guns, giving mechanized battalions considerably more firepower than their airmobile infantry counterparts. The latter had only foot mobility after exiting the helicopters that delivered them to battle and carried only one M-60 machine gun in each of their 36 rifle squads. Regardless of their mobility or firepower, all four battalions fought the same way—move slowly down streets and alleys, search every building until the enemy reveals his position, then shoot back with overwhelming aerial, indirect, and direct firepower to kill him or drive him out. The fact that thousands of civilians were caught in the crossfire deterred neither side from using all the firepower they had.

Just after noon, A and B Companies were flown in from Firebase Smoke. They reinforced six rifle companies of the 3-39th and 5-60th Infantry, arrayed in a rough arc around the refugee-swollen settlements of Xom Cau Mat and Xom Ong Doi on Saigon's southern approaches. C Company's 2nd Platoon was flown in to reinforce RVN rangers and police at a nearby bridge on Route 5. As helicopters delivering B Company hovered over soggy rice paddies, troops jumped into the muck and moved as quickly as nature would allow. They stayed off paddy dikes to avoid booby traps as they had been trained. They advanced step by laborious step, pulling one foot out of the mud only to get the other stuck. Sergeant Vernon Moore, a stocky man made heavier by his helmet, flak jacket, ammunition, and a two-quart canteen strapped atop his heavy rucksack, bogged down. Knee deep in mud and on the verge of passing out from heat exhaustion, Moore was rescued by a helicopter, holding tight to its landing skid as it plucked him from the mud and lifted him to a nearby paddy dike.

The Bearcats spent the first night watching burning villages from cold, wet paddies. Just after daybreak, B Company, attached to Lieutenant Colonel Joe DeLuca's 3-39th Infantry, moved to DeLuca's command post (CP) aboard A/5-60th Infantry's APCs. Fires raged along the canal road, producing a corridor of heat and smoke through which the tracks sped. Casualties from the night before were awaiting evacuation at the 3-39th's Aid Station as the APCs reached the command post. Specialist Bill Sirtola would later write, "The sounds of shooting, smoke from the burning buildings, and the sight of wounded being worked on drove home the reality of what we were getting into." A rocket-

Troops stand ready on the LZ as helicopters approach in the distance (U.S. Army photograph, National Archives).

propelled grenade streaked overhead as Captain Eckman entered the pagoda serving as the 3-39th's CP.

DeLuca wanted Eckman to reinforce a police post that had been attacked earlier that morning. To reach it, Eckman's company would have to pass under the south end of the Y Bridge (Cau Chu Y),[10] move east along the canal, then turn south down a side street to a settlement on the west bank of the Rach Ong Lon. The police outpost was inside the settlement. DeLuca drew a hasty sketch map because he had no maps detailing the area's maze of roads, canals, and tributaries. B Company was getting ready to move when the police post reported it was under attack. While helicopter gunships suppressed enemy fire, a utility helicopter landed inside the outpost to resupply its defenders.

Lieutenant Carlton Blacker's 3rd Platoon led the way, accompanied by Captain Eckman's command group. As the move began, Eckman's thoughts flashed back to Fort Lewis when Joe Schmalhorst and his company commanders had toured training facilities on the mist-shrouded fingers of Mount Ranier. At the post's "Combat in Cities" course, Eckman had commented, "Sir, we fought in grass-hut complexes in Vietnam, but never in cities." The other captains all agreed. They decided not to waste time training on combat in cities, focusing instead on getting ready for the rice-paddy war they knew. Fast forward to Saigon; "We're under the control of another battalion, we don't have maps, and we're headed for some big-time combat in a big city. Damn!"

In the early afternoon, B Company linked up with ARVN Rangers at the end of the road leading to the police outpost. Lieutenant Blacker's platoon, still in the lead, cautiously moved ahead, clearing houses on both sides of the street until they took fire about 100 yards short of the outpost. Eckman tried to direct the action from a rooftop but an RPG streaking past him persuaded him to get back down to the street. Sergeant David B. Leader, a squad leader in the 3rd Platoon, was unexpectedly joined by a diminutive French female reporter on a motor scooter as his squad returned fire and attempted to maneuver. She was deep in harm's way but stuck to the platoon throughout the fight, although she spoke no English and Leader's men spoke no French.

Leader's squad took cover behind a cement building, catching their breath while contemplating their next move. Leader took his helmet off and was sliding down the wall to a squatting position when a bullet struck the wall where his head had just been. One of his team leaders, an engineer named Artie L. Bible, who became an involuntary infantryman when the battalion was formed, began screaming and rolling on the ground with a bullet fragment in his back. Luckily, his wound turned out to be less damaging than his reaction suggested.

Lieutenant Blacker led Leader's squad down an alley and found the sniper's lair. Throwing hand grenades and pouring small-arms fire into the house, Leader's squad ended the sniper's life. When a second sniper fired from the other end of the alley, Blacker decided to withdraw his men to the main street where cement houses could provide better cover but a third sniper hemmed them in from behind. Tossing a smoke grenade toward the alley's far end, Blacker directed a fortuitously available Cobra helicopter gunship against the snipers. The Cobra shot up the first house with rockets, followed with the minigun and grenade launcher in its chin turret, then swung around and shot up the building at the other end of the alley, flushing one of the snipers into the open. The VC attempted to flee down a side street but didn't get far. Leader shot him dead from 20 feet away.

B Company established positions in and around the police post as night fell. Sergeant Kenneth R. Davis's squad moved into a darkened jail cell. A row of man-sized cement slabs were outlined by troughs into which chained prisoners could relieve themselves. Suddenly, shrapnel from artillery fire tore through the room's tin roof, injuring one of Davis's machine gunners. Sergeant Leader and his squad crouched behind 55-gallon drums filled with rubble from half-demolished houses. The barrage continued for over an hour. After each explosion, shrapnel and debris came raining down. One piece hit Leader above the knee as he crouched behind a barrel but struck him with its flat side and left only a bruise. Whether a bruise or worse, Leader learned there is no such thing as friendly fire, particularly if it is coming from several miles away and you have no way to get it stopped. It was not clear who was adjusting the artillery or who called for it but it was not anyone from B Company.

That evening, C Company was flown back to Fire Base Smoke from a fruitless night operation in nearby Long An Province. As men lined up for the evening meal, Smoke was mortared. Captain Bill Owen recalls: "The VC did a super job of breaking up the dinner party. I was amazed that no one killed themselves trying to find something to hide behind or under. The only thing louder than the explosions was the sergeant major screaming at people to get down."

Arriving just after noon on May 9, A and C Companies landed in rice paddies south of Xom Ong Doi to block possible escape routes. It took nearly two hours for C Company to link up with RVN Marines arrayed along Route 230 on the town's western edge. Around the same time, Lieutenant Colonel John Tower's 2-47th Mechanized Infantry was racing in from Bearcat to take up positions along the town's northern edge. The VC would soon be boxed in on three sides, with Americans to the north and south and RVN Marines to the west. Escaping to the east would require crossing open ground and the rain-swollen Rach Bang Dong, risking exposure to flanking fire, artillery, and Cobra gunships.

Knowing they faced almost certain death, the VC stayed and fought. RVN Marines had exchanged fire with them most of the morning but made no headway. Earlier, scout helicopters spotted a VC platoon moving into a tadpole-shaped island on Xom Ong Doi's south side and reported machine-gun and recoilless-rifle teams where Route 232 intersects the canal road at the town's northwest corner. A spotter plane reported VC on roof tops and in trees, firing on helicopters.

Just after 2 p.m., A Company came under fire from the tadpole-shaped island. Troops got off the road and began firing into nipa palm and white stucco buildings across the river. C Company came under fire around the same time. Hundreds of civilians had already streamed past them on the road, carrying children and assorted possessions. Still more were fleeing as C Company rushed down the adjacent embankment into a grassy field to fire across the river. Refugees on the elevated road behind them were hit by the enemy's return fire. PFC Jeffery J. Quinn of A Company and Staff Sergeant Dennis Meyer of C Company rushed back to the road to drag wounded civilians to safety. For their selfless bravery, both were awarded Army Commendation Medals for Valor.

Lieutenant Eric Belt, C Company's Artillery Forward Observer, ran toward the river when the shooting started. "The whole company except for me and my radio operator was in tall grass," recalls Belt. He and his radioman lay face down "in clear view of the enemy with bullets hitting all around us." He tried to call in a fire mission but could not radio the artillerymen at Smoke with his radio's short antenna. "I realized that the long antenna was going to be necessary if I was going to get any fire," he recalled. When he told his radioman they would have to switch antennas, "the kid thought I was nuts, but did just as I asked. He sat up and I knelt beside him, unfolded the long antenna from the canvas utility bag strapped under the radio, and disconnected the short one." Belt then called in a white-phosphorus marking round before adjusting high-explosive fire onto the peninsula. Satisfied that the fire would be on target, Belt called for a "battery four," meaning four rounds from each of the battery's six 105mm howitzers. Twenty-four rounds struck in rapid succession along the river bank, sending showers of black mud, a body, and machine gun parts flying into the air. When a second firing battery called to offer its assistance, Belt adjusted its fire onto the target as well. Belt recalls, "I kept the fire coming and the entire company stood up, looked toward me, and cheered. It was one hell of a moment."

Seeing an opportunity, Captain Owen moved C Company around A Company. Turning right on Route 230, C Company crossed a small bridge to place flanking fire on the VC in southern Xom Ong Doi. Lieutenant Kerry May's platoon rushed toward houses lining a road on the town's west side. Coming under heavy fire, they fell back to a drainage ditch knee-deep in weeds and stagnant water. May called in gunships, but it was hard to pinpoint the enemy. Captain Owen sent Lieutenant Bill Gale's platoon forward to support May, but they too became pinned down. Sergeant Al Olson, one of Gale's squad leaders, recalls, "I remember rounds cracking over my head and jumping into a drainage ditch with the other guys. One guy stirred up a large snake that crawled directly over my lap and on down the line. The snake really spooked me, so I jumped up to get away from it. When I stood up, bullets went cracking past my head. For a split second, it was snake or bullets. I went back to the ditch and we all kept firing. We were taking a great deal of fire and there was a lot of frustration because I couldn't see any enemy from my position."

When May's platoon called for more ammunition, several 3rd Platoon members draped themselves with M-16 and M-60 bandoliers and started down the drainage ditch on all fours. PFCs Leslie J. Haar and James W. Petty were wounded along the way, but continued forward with the others. Both were awarded Bronze Star Medals for Valor along with their Purple Hearts. Despite enemy fire, "the guys hauling the ammo went right on to reach the guys that needed it," notes Olson. "I remember the ammo coming forward and being tossed to those in the lead platoon. Fairly quickly, no more than an hour or so—and measuring time when you're under fire is nebulous at best—we were all able to pull back down the ditch. We were terribly hot and thirsty by then. Water was needed almost as much as ammunition. Most of us had drained our canteens fighting the heat and excitement."

As the enemy pulled back, Captain Owen aligned his 1st and 3rd Platoons along Route 230. Troops took up positions behind fences and the corners of buildings. Machine-gun teams got on roof tops while A Company continued firing into the tadpole-shaped island from the south. Once in position, C Company began firing. Howitzer shells, meanwhile, continued to pound the island. Pounded and surrounded, the VC began to pull out. As they appeared, marksmen picked them off. PFC Robert Magdaleno, atop a building with his squad's machine gun, noticed one of C Company's snipers "sitting cross-legged in the grass between the houses and the river, firing his M-14 with great accuracy at targets of opportunity." The shooting was not all one way. With bullets slapping into a wall behind him, Magdaleno ducked behind an earthen jar filled with rainwater only to get soaked when a burst of gunfire shattered the jar.

Captain Owen moved along the line with his command group, passing behind and through buildings as he checked his men's positions and direction of fire. This fight was unlike any of Owen's previous combat experience. Typically, a unit that took fire would return fire in the direction it came from but wouldn't know whether they hit anything or not. In this fight the VC, surrounded and hammered by artillery and gunships, had to expose themselves to move. C Company killed at least 15 as they darted between houses.

Two major battles were fought simultaneously that afternoon. Around the time the Bearcats' action began, 2-47th Infantry, moving west on the canal road after crossing the Kinh Doi on Highway 15, encountered a dug-in enemy force armed with recoilless rifles and heavy machine guns around the junction of Route 230 and the canal road. The resulting battle on Xom Ong Doi's northern edge was the most costly engagement fought by any U.S. unit during the Battle for Saigon.

Meanwhile, B Company, still under 3-39th Infantry's control, was moving east from the Xom Cau Mat police post, going as fast as they could across soggy rice paddies toward a nearby settlement. They had begun an unsuccessful attempt to relieve pressure on A/3-39th, which was pinned down and unable to evacuate its casualties. Gunships were rolling in through criss-crossing tracers and smoke-trailing RPGs. A Cobra gunship pulling out of a strafing run took a hit by an RPG and tumbled in the air, making a complete revolution and righting itself just before splashing into a water-filled paddy on its skids. As the canopy flew open, the two-man crew hurriedly abandoned the aircraft. One man suddenly doubled back, apparently to ignite a thermite grenade, because the Cobra started burning as he left.

Entering a shabby refugee settlement, B Company's lead platoon came under intense fire. Sergeant Richard D. "Rick" Koszar and PFC Jose Louis Vieras, both 20-year-old draftees, were killed and nine others were wounded, some by AK-47 fire and others by shrapnel from RPGs. Alarmed at the rate his men were dropping, Captain Eckman ordered a withdrawal. Sergeant Koszar's lifeless body was carried out in an improvised poncho litter and Jose Vieras' body was carried on a window louver ripped from its hinges by his comrades. Though most civilians had left, a lone woman was discovered in one of the houses. Sergeant Vernon Moore and another soldier scooped the old woman up and carried her to safety. When they put the woman down to help carry Vieras, she ran back into harm's way. Moore would later learn why but for now he was preoccupied with bullets snapping past his head. Exchanges of fire continued throughout the morning as B Company tried to find a less costly way out.

When B Company reached safer ground, an APC from 5-60th Infantry came to drop off supplies and take away the bodies of Koszar and Vieras. A freelance photographer with a foreign accent tried to snap pictures of the dead before they were loaded into the track. As the man pulled back a poncho draped over the dead, Captain Eckman began yelling. He didn't want his men's families to see their pictures in a newspaper. He got between the photographer and the bodies and started backing the photographer away. Eckman confiscated his film and sent him under guard to the battalion command post to be ejected from the area.

Eckman returned to the police post that evening with two platoons, leaving his forward observer, Lieutenant Frederick G. Kaiser, with the 3rd Platoon in an abandoned school. The school was a two-story building wrapped around an open courtyard. It was one of the few structures left standing in a neighborhood that had been reduced to rubble. As night fell, troops tore concrete slabs from classroom floors to build bunkers at the school's gated entrance. When finished, their bunker walls and roofs were two feet thick, more than enough to withstand a direct hit from a mortar or RPG. As daylight neared, Lieutenant Blacker and Sergeant Leader were watching from the school's second-floor windows when approximately fifty VC appeared, headed in their direction. Blacker alerted Lieutenant Kaiser, who quickly got on the line to his firing battery.

Directing fire from an exposed position, Kaiser was wounded either by the enemy's return fire, which included several RPGs, or shrapnel from one of the dozens of 105mm howitzer shells he brought in "danger close." He was subsequently awarded the Silver Star and a Purple Heart. Blacker was later informed that the enemy unit turned back by Kaiser's artillery barrage had intended to overrun his platoon, but became disoriented en route to the objective. When the VC moved forward, their commander found the buildings he planned to use as rallying points had been leveled and the alleyways down which he had planned to attack were blocked with rubble. In the morning, Sergeant Moore found the old woman he had tried to rescue the day before. She had scrambled back into the town and now lay dead beside a man who was probably her husband.

To B Company's east, A and C Companies were concluding the fight for Xom Ong Doi. Before nightfall, a resupply of ammunition was flown in and the last of the wounded were evacuated. The night passed quietly. In the morning, the Bearcats conducted a house-to-house sweep, moving west to east, across the tadpole-shaped island on Xom Ong Doi's south side. Helicopter gunships covered potential escape routes. On reaching the town's center, A Company found 36 dead civilians in a housing complex inhabited by the families of RVN Marines. It was unclear whether they had been murdered by the VC or killed by artillery, helicopter gunships, or air strikes used to drive the VC out. Grieving RVN Marines who had fought all day to re-enter the town after being sent north to defend the Y Bridge the morning before, now had to bury their families. Only 16 dead VC were found in the town's wreckage, but the fact that they had been forced to abandon some of their dead and their weapons spoke to the punishment they suffered.

Earlier that morning (May 10), A/5-60th Infantry was ambushed on National Route 5A while moving through the village of Xom Tan Liem. Their company commander had been killed and most of the American dead still lay alongside the road. A and C Companies of the 6-31st were picked up on Route 230 and flown in to help. They were greeted by a morale-killing scene.

Burned out APCs still smoldered and soldiers' bodies covered with ponchos lay in clusters all along the road. If the VC could do that much damage to a heavily armed mechanized unit, what chance would the lightly armed Bearcats have? Time would soon tell. A sense of foreboding set in as the two rifle companies fanned out to the south and west. C Company picked up a wounded VC and carried him along.

Finding no enemy, A Company established a blocking position two kilometers west of Xom Tan Liem as dusk approached. C Company continued through town to reinforce a Popular Forces[11] outpost that had been attacked early that morning. While one platoon set up an ambush outside the compound, the rest of C Company entered the cramped mud fort. American GIs joined militiamen on the perimeter berm. While Americans were armed to the teeth with grenades, claymores, automatic rifles, machine guns, and grenade launchers, plus radios to call in artillery, helicopters, and air power if needed, the militiamen had only World War II–era carbines and semiautomatic rifles. Toward evening, the Vietnamese gathered around large metal pots cooking smelly fish and rice for their evening meal while Americans ate C-rations from cans. After dinner, a joint watch rotation was established, allowing both Vietnamese and Americans to get some sleep between guard shifts.

Captain Owen's command group set up in a cramped little bunker, sharing what space there was with the VC who had been captured on the way in. As a precaution, the company's senior medic sedated the prisoner after checking his wounds as he lay on a wooden table. Everyone in the bunker except one man on radio watch was asleep when mortar shells began bracketing the compound around 4 a.m. The prisoner rose at the first sound of incoming and dove off the table. Thinking he was going for a weapon, Owen and one of his radiomen grabbed their rifles and flipped the safeties off. The medic urgently called them off, realizing the man was just taking cover under the heavy table. He was so badly injured and heavily sedated that Owen couldn't believe he was even capable of moving.

A mortar round hit the command bunker, which shuddered and filled with dust, but, remarkably, didn't collapse. Several more rounds struck in quick succession in and around the crowded fort. Remarkably, neither the mortar fire nor a brief flurry of small-arms fire snapping overhead inflicted any casualties. A tree-lined village named Da Phuoc was the source of the enemy's fire. The attack lasted only minutes but counter-fire from the weapons platoon, helicopter gunship runs, and artillery responded for at least half an hour. The VC had fired from a village, knowing the Americans would respond with overwhelming firepower. In a war for "hearts and minds," civilian casualties and property destruction would give the VC a propaganda victory, even if they lost the battle. The communist Viet Minh had used the same tactic against the French a decade before but few Americans knew much about France's nine-year struggle to keep what had once been French Indochina.[12]

The militia commander thought the brief attack was a diversion to cover the movement of a larger enemy unit out of the area. Captain Owen agreed, and leaning over a map with the Vietnamese lieutenant, who knew the area intimately, traced the most likely route the guerrillas would follow, then contacted battalion to suggest a pursuit. Before the move could begin, Captain Owen had to get his prisoner out on a helicopter and conduct a search of the ambush site in Xom Tan Liem. The search was carried out in tense silence by troops spooked by the poncho-covered bodies of GIs still lying beside the road. They found an AK-47, an RPG launcher, web gear, hand grenades, rocket-propelled grenades, a Chinese-made radio, and three dead VC. "These were the first enemy dead we had seen up close," notes Al Olson. "We were told to stay clear of the bodies as they had not as yet been cleared for booby traps. One corpse held a grenade in a clenched fist. The other had a loaded RPG on the ground next to him." Documents identified the VC with the grenade as being "14 years old, but already a hero—decorated for killing many Americans." A Company, guided by a scout helicopter, searched the creek leading from the area the night attack had originated. They found two beached sampans strewn with ammunition and web gear and the body of another slain guerrilla.

Colonel Benson and Lieutenant Colonel Schmalhorst landed for a quick conference. Benson presumably expressed satisfaction with Schmalhorst's scheme for the pursuit. The village of Da Phuoc had been identified as an enemy rallying point by the prisoner evacuated that morning. The captured guerrilla, identifying himself as "chief" of a four-man team from the 3rd Company, 2nd Long An Battalion, informed his interrogators that his unit's dead and wounded from the ambush of A/5-60th Infantry had been taken to a nearby waterway where they were loaded into sampans and transported to Da Phuoc.

24 6th Battalion in Vietnam: Battles of Da Phuoc and Saigon, 1968

Da Phuoc (11–12 May 1968)

With the search complete, Colonel Schmalhorst had A Company lifted out and D Company lifted in from Fire Base Smoke. C Company proceeded down Highway 5A, leaving the road south of Xom Tan Liem to cautiously cross open paddies to reach what was left of Da Phuoc. Stomachs tightened and fingers rested lightly on triggers. Someone accidentally discharged an M-79 grenade launcher, sending a round spiraling harmlessly into the ground and invoking a string of angry curses from the man's stressed-out comrades.

Da Phuoc was deserted and demolished. The surrounding paddies were pocked with water-filled craters and the houses were reduced to foundations and crumbling walls. Lieutenant Gale, whose 3rd Platoon was in the lead, reported finding green plastic wrappings the enemy used to waterproof mortar rounds and rocket-propelled grenades. Owen moved up to Gale's position, and examining the wrappings, saw that the insides still retained an oily residue, a fact that set his nerves tingling. Such wrappings quickly dried under the blistering delta sun. They were not from the night before. That they were still oily meant the enemy had been breaking out ammunition and preparing for battle within the hour.

A trail angled northeast to the Rach Giu, a stream flowing west to east. A row of partially standing brick and concrete structures was about twenty meters from the near bank. More damaged buildings were visible across the stream behind a curtain of dense, 15-to-20-foot tall nipa palm. Owen instructed Gale to send out flank security, move the 3rd Platoon across the stream, and secure the far buildings. The rest of the company would follow, and if the area proved as quiet as the rest of Da Phuoc, they would then plan the next increment of their pursuit.

Lieutenant Gale, whose slight build and thick glasses disguised his follow-me leadership style, led the way with Staff Sergeant William Patterson, who had the lead squad, and Specialist Gregory A. Russell, Gale's radio operator. Just after 3 p.m., May 11, Gale, Patterson, and Russell were 10 or 15 feet behind the lead squad which was just entering the stream when the Viet Cong began firing from unseen bunkers among the nipa palm. Soon the entire far bank erupted with the barking of AK-47 and RPD fire and smoke-trailing RPGs. Russell stumbled as several rounds punched through the radio on his back. Lieutenant Gale pulled him to a little sandbar overgrown with grass and brush in the middle of the river. Reaching the island, Gale, Patterson, and Russell went prone at its edge, and began returning fire over the top of the low-lying hump with their M-16s. Men from the lead squad who had also entered the water were pinned against the near bank, unable to raise their heads or their weapons. The rest of the 3rd Platoon was similarly immobilized, pinned down for the moment as the entire area was raked with fire. Compounding the problem, an enemy mortar crew started lobbing in rounds from somewhere across the paddies to the east.

Sergeant Al Olson was in the open between the stream and the demolished buildings when the ambush began. It was like a sudden electrical storm, he later thought, one crash of lightning and then a downpour. Hitting the dirt, he scrambled for a log not much bigger in diameter than a telephone pole that had once been part of a fence or wall. Three other men also ducked behind the log, their only available cover, scant though it was. All hugged the ground trying to crawl into their helmets as bullets cracked all around them. When one of the men managed to slip out of his rucksack and throw it over the log in an effort to create more cover, three or four rounds thumped into the pack. As an M-60 machine gun opened up from the right flank, the enemy shifted their fire from the log to deal with the machine gun. Olson gripped his rifle, bracing himself to join the fight. The machine gun team on the right had been positioned to cover the river crossing. PFC Robert York, manning the gun, was one of the first to get his head back up to return fire. His gun got the enemy's attention, but York, unfazed by slugs slapping into the log and cracking past his helmet, kept up a steady stream of fire.

Lieutenant Gale told Russell to find an operable radio so he could coordinate with

Manning an M60 machine gun, Vietnam 1968 (Association archives, courtesy Spekczynski collection).

the platoon sergeant to deploy the men on line, suppress the enemy's fire, and, if possible, cross the river. Captain Owen always preached that the only way out of an ambush is to gain fire superiority and attack into the enemy, and Gale intended to do just that. With Gale and Patterson covering him by fire, Greg Russell splashed away, found a working radio, and fearlessly splashed back to the island, somehow passing unscathed through a fusillade of bullets drawing invisible lines all around him. As Gale was issuing instructions to his platoon sergeant, the radio went into constant static. Like the first, the second radio had also taken hits while strapped to Russell's back. Staff Sergeant Patterson swam to the far bank, discovering along the way that the current was dangerously swift. He tossed grenades into the nipa palm, trying in vain to knock out hidden bunkers. He was struggling in the current when Gale extended his rifle to pull him ashore.

Moments later, Greg Russell (20) was shot through the head as he lay between Gale and Patterson at the edge of the island, firing his M-16. A bright young man of 20, he was one of Gale's best soldiers. He had endured much teasing about marrying a girl he met during pre-deployment leave and for displaying the California state flag he always carried in his rucksack.

He died bravely, earning the Distinguished Service Cross for the final acts of his short life. An extract of his citation reads:

> Specialist Four Russell distinguished himself by exceptionally valorous actions on 11 May 1968 during a reconnaissance-in-force mission near the village of Da Phuoc. He was in the point squad when his company began to cross a stream. Just as he entered the water, his squad came under extremely heavy enemy fire, which wounded him and threw him into the river. Finding his radio inoperative, he ignored the pain of his injury and swam ashore to find another radio. Completely exposed to the continuing enemy fire, Specialist Russell provided desperately needed communications until he received a mortal wound from a sniper's bullet."[1]

It was time to back off because there was no way to get the platoon across the fast-flowing stream under fire. Gale and Patterson, who had been grazed across the face by a bullet, kept up their fire long enough for the men pinned against the river bank behind them to scramble to safety. They then leapt to their feet, and having no choice but to leave Russell, splashed across the river and sprinted across open ground to the remnants of a destroyed house. Bob York fired continuously to cover them. Al Olson peered over the log sheltering his group and saw Lieutenant Gale, Staff Sergeant Patterson, and Pete Murdock from the lead squad, dashing up from the river, each turning briefly to fire as he ran. They were headed for a destroyed building about fifty feet to the right of the log. Olson and the others behind the log opened up with everything they had to cover them. Gale, Patterson, Murdock, and several others made it to the house, but as they jumped behind a shell-blasted wall, Olson realized that his friend Greg Russell wasn't with the lieutenant. His heart sank because he knew what that meant. No officer would be without his radioman unless the radioman was dead.

After hurtling the wall and dropping flat, Lieutenant Gale shouted at a nearby machine gun team to link ten ammo belts. He got behind the gun himself and began delivering long, uninterrupted bursts into the nipa palm where he had seen movement and muzzle flashes. In return, several RPGs came spiraling across the stream. One exploded just behind Gale, peppering his back with fragments and knocking the wind out of him. He shrugged off his injuries, pain barely registering through the adrenaline, and resumed firing the M-60. The men behind the log, having drawn the enemy's attention, again hugged the ground as rounds smacked into the log and cracked just inches above them. They faced a dilemma. To rise up would surely mean getting shot, so they took turns blindly firing their M-16s on automatic over the log. It was better than nothing.

A white phosphorus marking round burst over the enemy side of the river, followed by the first of many howitzer salvos. Helicopter gunships arrived not long after. At some point, Captain Owen and Lieutenant Belt, his Artillery Forward Observer, had moved into position with their radio operators behind the only remaining wall of a bombed-out pagoda behind Gale and Patterson. "That was as up front as it gets," writes Olson, describing how Owen, his helmet and eyes in view as he took in the scene, was "pointing, calmly giving orders, talking on different radios, trying to get us better organized, and directing supporting fires all at the same time."

Emboldened, men began popping up long enough to place aimed rifle shots across the stream. Lieutenant Gale scrambled from group to group, making sure his men had ammo, seeing who was wounded, and getting men into the best positions from which to return fire. The 3rd Platoon did not move back an inch, but poured an increasing volume of M-16, M-60, and M-79 fire at places they thought might shelter enemy troops. All the while, artillery continued pounding the enemy and helicopter gunships rolled in repeatedly from outside the gun-target line. The enemy clung tenaciously to their positions, returning fire after each volley of artillery. Their mortars, which told Owen he was up against at least a company, rarely stopped thumping out rounds, even though they had been spotted from above and were being attacked by gunships. Mortar rounds crashed all around Owens' command group and the lead platoon, inflicting a dozen casualties. The damage would have been worse had not at least half the rounds failed to explode. The enemy's ammunition either included a lot of duds, or an overly-stressed crewman was forgetting to pull out the safety wires before dropping rounds down the tube.

As the slugging match continued, Sergeant Olson realized that he and his buddies needed to start conserving ammo. They had gone through a lot of magazines. So much carbon had accumulated in the chambers of their rifles that they were starting to jam. To Olson's right, Gale, Patterson, Murdock, and York were still firing steadily. Two machine guns, the second now manned by PFC Tim Hannigan, were steadily belching torrents of lead. The barrel of Hannigan's machine gun glowed as he consumed ammo in an uninterrupted stream. Someone shouted that his barrel was going to burn out. Because no replacement barrel was available, Hannigan slowed to short bursts. Hannigan and York were soon down to a belt or two of ammo, and Sergeant Olson and his three buddies, each of whom had started the battle with thirty magazines, were down to six or seven apiece. Worse, their M-16s were now jamming every few rounds. Out of gun oil, Olson's group used squeeze-bottles of oily insect repellent to keep the carbonized chambers lubricated, a trick learned in training. "We talked about the need to spread out," recalls Olson, "as we were too tightly clumped together in one relatively exposed position behind that log. We knew better but nobody was moving. It seemed like any movement increased the amount of incoming fire."

Captain Owen kept peering around the wall sheltering his command group or raising up to look through the half-window in the half-demolished brick wall, and his concerned radiomen kept pulling him back down. Every time the company commander's face came into view, there was a flurry of automatic-weapons fire from across the stream. The forward side of the wall absorbed the bursts. Taking another quick look through the window, Captain Owen, on his knees, was ducking back down when a rocket-propelled grenade slammed into the wall, knocking him to a sitting position with ringing ears and shrapnel in his upper chest. Owen's injuries, like those of his two radiomen, Specialists Doug Lindner and Bill McMullen, were superficial because the main part of the blast passed over their heads. McMullen was hit again seconds after the explosion by a chunk of shrapnel that had apparently gone straight up, then straight down, landing on him as he sat against the wall.

As McMullen brushed the white-hot shrapnel away, Captain Owen, seeing the burn, said, "There's your Purple Heart." "No way, sir," McMullen answered, thinking the injury too slight to rate a medal. "My mother would die when she got the telegram!" Lieutenant Belt was calling in artillery from the doorway of the bombed-out pagoda. The men were on the gun-target line, meaning they could hear each salvo as it flew overhead, a whoosh-rumble caused by the spinning of the shells. A shell exploded nearby in an old crater that absorbed most of the blast. One man had a finger sliced off by shrapnel, invoking Lieutenant Gale's wrath. He bellowed: "Belt, I'll shoot you if you kill any of my men!"

Moments later, another rocket-propelled grenade whooshed across the stream, hitting the second step below the doorway and detonating in front of Belt with a brilliant flash. Knocked unconscious, the lieutenant came to "with my radio operator pulling me upside down in a crater twenty feet from the wall. The kid deserved a medal for dragging me out of the heaviest fire and into the crater." Shaking off the blast's effects, Belt, covered with brick particles, superficially wounded by brick and shrapnel, his ears ringing so loudly that he couldn't hear, kept the artillery coming, using a pencil to jot coordinates and adjustments on his map for his radioman to relay to the howitzer battery at Fire Base Smoke. Lieutenant May and the 1st Platoon were still firing from positions near the pagoda.

When Gale reported he was running low on ammo, Owen contacted Lieutenant Ron Belloli, whose 2nd Platoon was in reserve. In response, Belloli's platoon sergeant, an exceptionally distinguished-looking SFC named George Segrest, brought up a team of men draped with bandoliers of M-16 ammunition and belts of M-60 ammunition. Segrest had to crawl the last part of the way because he had been shot in the knee as he advanced, a permanently disabling wound that ended his pre-war career with the 3rd Infantry Regiment. "Segrest came out of the Old Guard that marches at the Tomb of the Unknown Solider," recalls Owen, "and the only thing he was looking forward to was getting back to the Old Guard. His wound ended those plans. He never marched again."

Joe Schmalhorst, flying above the fray in his command ship, instructed D Company, at Owen's request, to assume blocking positions north of the enemy, trapping them against the stream. Owen was frustrated at his counterpart's slow progress, but eventually Captain Grady Smith's D Company, moving with two platoons up and one back, neared a tree line several hundred meters west of the contact area. The tree line faced the right-front platoon. Lieutenant Paul Fish had the left-front platoon. D Company had not yet been in a firefight. Being new and gung-ho, Fish was disappointed that the other platoon would be going into the trees where the enemy was most likely to be, while his own platoon was supposed to sweep past the tree line to provide flank security. There were indeed guerrillas dug in amid the brush and nipa, and they waited until D Company, sloshing across a flooded paddy, was in the open between two dikes before unleashing a storm of AK-47 fire.

Lieutenant Fish's radioman was shot in the leg during the opening exchange, but Fish pulled him to his feet and helped him to a dike where most of the platoon, minus

Delta Company, 6th Battalion, 31st Infantry troops taking fire, crouch behind scanty cover in this 1968 photograph (Association archives, courtesy Spekczynski collection).

the lead squad, took shelter from the firestorm. As mortar shells and rocket-propelled grenades began plopping into the mud around them, Fish's men stubbornly but blindly returned fire. When Fish's weapon jammed, he grabbed his radioman's rifle, which was full of water and also jammed. Furious that they had been issued such unreliable weapons, Fish picked up a third M-16. Sergeant John T. Moore (21), a fire team leader down the dike to Fish's left, suddenly stood up. Whatever his intentions, he had no chance to act on them because he was immediately shot through the neck and slumped back to the ground, dying. It took less than half an hour for a medevac helicopter to arrive but Moore was already dead.

Cobra gunships had also been diverted to the scene, and Fish, on the line with Captain Smith, tried explaining that he had a squad pinned down along the berm in front of the smoke he popped to mark his position. Fish's warning must have gotten lost in translation because the lead gunship fired too soon on its initial pass. A line of minigun-generated waterspouts rippled through the lead squad and on into the tree line. Fortunately, there were no friendly casualties. After the gunships were reoriented, the GIs settled against the dikes and watched the Cobras take turns working the tree line with miniguns and salvos of rockets. Spectators now to their own battle, one squad leader began filming the show with a home-movie camera. D Company had gone as far as it was going that day.

As dusk came, one of Al Olson's buddies behind the log took off to find more ammo. Olson crawled over to Lieutenant Gale behind the crumbled wall. Gale was shouting orders and shooting steadily. Near him, Bob York, who had also been wounded, was still firing his M-60. Gale confirmed that Russell was dead, pointing to the island. Olson decided to retrieve his friend's body and the radio. It wasn't a rational decision, but Olson was both angry and guilt-ridden. Olson had been the lieutenant's original radioman at Fort Lewis. Had he not been reassigned as a team leader and then as a squad leader, he might be out there on the island and Russell might still be alive. He rose to run to the island, but an explosion knocked him flat. He struggled to catch his breath, but was unable to move. He was numb all over, his ears ringing and head throbbing. Tasting blood, he spit out a mouthful, unsure of what had happened. When the roaring in his ears subsided, he yelled for a medic. The one who appeared secured a bandage around his throat. Someone helped him back past men who were rushing forward with ammunition that had just been unloaded from a resupply chopper.

Bill Owen was angry that D Company had not yet moved into a position where it could relieve some of the pressure. Frustrated, he decided to risk bringing in resupply ships. 2nd Platoon secured a landing zone, a wet paddy back down the trail, but the enemy had not yet been defeated. Incoming helicopters took small-arms fire even though they were landing several hundred meters from the stream. Lieutenant Dave Wilson, the company executive officer, flew in from Smoke aboard one of the resupply ships. "The pilot was told to come in low and from the southeast," writes Wilson. "As we came upon the company, they threw smoke, and immediately the shooting picked up a little. When the chopper landed, I jumped out to help unload. I didn't think much of it at the time, but later, one of the other lieutenants asked me, 'Hey, did you notice after you jumped out, Charlie put a bullet in the wall right behind where your head was?' No, I hadn't noticed."

The last helicopter into the landing zone was a medevac. Several seriously wounded men were helped into the cargo bay, including Olson and the 1st Platoon's Tiger Scout. Lieutenant Gale was furious when a not-so-seriously wounded PFC climbed aboard, apparently under the impression that a cut finger rated a medevac.[2] The Huey had just lifted off, nose down as the pilot picked up initial forward speed, when somebody started yelling about an RPG. Captain Owen saw the whole thing. The rocket-propelled grenade, sizzling toward the Huey from across the stream, had gone in one side of the cargo bay, somehow missing everyone and everything inside, and sailed out the other. "I could not believe my eyes," recalls Owen. "We stood there in absolute awe." Owen could hear Belloli on the radio asking the pilot if he realized an RPG had just passed through his helicopter. "He couldn't believe it, either. If the rocket had hit anything, we would have lost the chopper and all the wounded. Miracles do happen!"

Lieutenant Belt was informed that his direct-support battery was going to cease firing and a battery of 155mm howitzers would continue the mission. "They changed guns in mid-mission," notes Owen, "because we'd had the 105s firing so long that they had to cool the tubes down." As the heavy battery fired its first round, Lieutenant Belt was informed when the round was due to "splash," its time in flight having been calculated to within seconds. On his knees, Belt peered over the wall to watch for the explosion so he could adjust fire from that spot. The count-down on the radio ended, but there was no explosion. The shell could be heard tearing through the sky on its way in, but the pitch was all wrong. As happens all too often when blind ordnance flies into a close fight,

The 1st Platoon, D Company, 6th Battalion, 31st Infantry, getting ready to board a CH47 for transport to Dong Tam. In the far distance is the Nha Be tank farm (Association archives, courtesy Spekczynski collection).

the round fell short, striking 30 or 40 meters to the left of the command group. "The firing battery probably heard me scream for a cease-fire all the way back at Firebase Smoke," recalls Owen. The blast was deafening, earth-shaking, and several men had been injured, including Owen, who'd caught several steel splinters in his thigh and groin. No one was killed or even seriously wounded, notes Owen, "because the shell landed in a wet, soggy area, and most of the blast was absorbed by the mud. We were really lucky." The 155s were adjusted and the firing continued.

The wet terrain protected the enemy as well. Some VC crouched in muddy spider holes were undoubtedly killed, but most survived the gunships, artillery, and even the high-drag bombs delivered by the jet fighters. The battle continued after sundown, red tracers slicing one way over the river, lime-green tracers the other, gunships rolling in on targets that glowed white in a sea of black thanks to the illumination rounds slowly floating down on the north side of the stream. As enemy fire finally began to taper off, Captain Owen consolidated his positions in the dark, setting up for the night among clumps of palm trees and behind the walls of once-substantial houses.

Lieutenant Belloli used a strobe light to bring in a resupply slick[3] loaded with ammunition for the mortar platoon. It was almost midnight when a final air strike went in across the river. Owen, after having the artillery register defensive concentrations around his perimeter, began placing fire from the 105s and 155s and his own 81mm mortars along the likely avenues of enemy withdrawal. "We knew they were going to sneak out on us," says Owen, "especially with D Company out of position to block anything." High above in the night sky, Spooky (a cargo plane converted to a gunship) droned in lazy circles overhead, jettisoning flares. A small patrol, meanwhile, slipped into the river and reached the island in the middle without drawing fire. They soon returned with Greg Russell's body, his rifle, and his radio. Gale had wanted to accompany the patrol, but Owen had instructed the wounded lieutenant to stay with his platoon, explaining that "sometimes you need to let the sergeants do their work." Around three in the morning the enemy fired a last RPG across the stream at C Company. Helicopters equipped with night-vision scopes orbited the battlefield, trying to spot the enemy as they slipped away. It was nearly dawn when one of them spotted fifteen VC moving across the rice paddies several hundred meters east of C Company. Artillery was shifted onto the area.

Triage of the wounded was being conducted on the landing zone. "Some guys were taken first, and some waited," writes Al Olson. "In time, I was pulled into a tent and was on the table." The surgeon removed an inch-and-a-half long fragment and some bits of brick from Olson's neck, then cleaned up other shrapnel wounds in his shoulder, chest, and side. The surgeon informed Olson that he had a concussion, but that nothing vital had been hit. Olson agreed. "Seventeen stitches, ten of them in my neck, my head hurt like hell, and I had a big bandage on my neck, but I was okay." Directed to another tent to spend the night, Olson instead hitched a ride to the company rear, where the first sergeant questioned him about the battle, then started talking about work details first thing in the morning. Olson wandered over to the supply tent to get fresh fatigues from the supply sergeant then "fell asleep in the back of the tent. I woke up soaked in my own vomit early the next morning. I don't remember getting sick. I just woke up laying in my own vomit." Drawing another set of fatigues, Olson spent the morning trying to avoid the first sergeant, but bandages, stitches, and three days of light-duty or not, he was informed that he was to draw shovels and get a work detail organized. Olson decided he'd rather be back in the field with his buddies than filling sandbags in the rear. "I went back to the supply tent where the supply sergeant told me I could help load the chopper taking gear to the company. After we loaded the chopper, I climbed aboard."

As dawn broke on May 11, Captain Owen was eager to cross the river to see what damage had been done, but Schmalhorst, up again in his command ship, denied him permission to do so, concerned that the enemy had rigged the area with booby traps before withdrawing. Instead, resupply was carried out, then C Company conducted an airmobile assault south of Da Phuoc and D Company west of Xom Tan Liem in the ongoing hunt for the enemy. For Owen, it was a disappointing and anticlimactic end to the battle. C Company returned to Da Phuoc two days later to survey the battle's results. Small-arms ammunition, mortar rounds, and bloody bandages accompanied three dead guerrillas who, left behind during the enemy's dark-of-night retreat, lay putrefying in the smashed nipa palm.

Joe Schmalhorst wrote his wife after the battle that "Captain Owen and his boys did a wonderful job. I've recommended Bill for a Silver Star. He was a real cool customer. The men are outstanding. Even the wounded talk to Doc of wanting to go back to their unit. It's amazing! The preacher visits all of them at the hospital and the aid station. He worries me. He takes off in a jeep to the hospitals and our roads are anything but secure but he does it anyway." For their actions at Da Phuoc, Captain Owen, Lieutenant Gale, Staff Sergeant Patterson, and machine gunner Bob York received the Silver Star. Lieutenant Belt and Platoon Sergeant Segrest were awarded the Bronze Star for Valor. All were accompanied by a Purple Heart. Lieutenant Wilson, hearing about Gale's actions, asked his friend what made him so brave. "I'm not brave," Gale answered. "I'm just so scared that my guys will think I'm chicken that I take the riskiest jobs myself." Wilson would later write that "the true sign of a hero is one who admits they are scared, but still performs bravely. Bill Gale meets this requirement from both sides of the equation. I think he is one of the bravest men I have known."

C Company, still a bit green when it went into Da Phuoc, emerged proud and sure of itself. "We may have had more wounded and killed than the other companies in the battalion," writes Wilson, "but I'll bet we also got more VC than they did. The difference between the units was we had more pride in our commander and company." The bond between Bill Owen and his troops, already strong, became unbreakable after Da Phuoc. "I was amazed at how Owen kept his head up and studied the scene during firefights," writes Robert Magdaleno. "My most vivid impression of Captain Owen is of him standing in the field with helmet, rucksack, ammo, grenades, and weapon, and thinking how it seemed only proper that the company commander and us grunts were all dressed and equipped the same." Al Olson concurs:

> If you wanted to find Owen, you only had to look toward the loudest part of the engagement. It didn't matter who you were or where you were, if you were under fire, Owen was just over your shoulder. He was always very calm when everything else was going crazy. In many ways, he was our courage. For the guys in the platoons, Captain Owen was our faith and our trust. He never let us down.

The Battle for Saigon Ends (May 11–14, 1968)

On the morning of May 11, 3-39th Infantry began converging on two areas where the VC seemed most likely to be. One was an abandoned militia outpost southeast of Xom Cau Mat and the other was a settlement just south of the Y Bridge. B/3-39th approached the militia outpost from the north, sparking the first contact of the day, while B/6-31st approached east-to-west. B Company soon made contact, killing two VC before moving on. Captain Eckman's command group moved down a wide boulevard while his 1st Platoon searched shattered houses along the way. No doubt recognizing the cluster of radio antennas around Captain Eckman and Lieutenant Procaccini as a command group, a VC fired an RPG at them from a block away. Procaccini's radioman, PFC David E. Gray, saw the projectile coming, spinning like a football and trailing a ribbon of white smoke. There was no time to react before it exploded in the middle of the street. Gray, who had been superficially wounded the day before, remained standing, too stunned to realize that he'd been hit again until someone pushed him down and pointed to the blood on his left trouser leg. A medic treated the slice on Gray's inner thigh with iodine and a band-aid, leaving the radioman to write home, incorrectly, that the two dings were "not even good enough for a Purple Heart."

Lieutenant Procaccini led an attack against the rocket team. Procaccini was viewed skeptically by some, having accidentally shot one of his own men, but Gray, who knew him best, respected the lieutenant. "I thought he did a good job. He was a brave guy. At times, he was more gung-ho than I liked. When we were fighting between those buildings, he would run out, guns blazing, and shout, follow me, Dave! That was a little bit more than I had in mind!" PFC Michael Nicholin was shot as he moved down an alley. Seeing him spin around and fall to the ground, his comrades thought they were recovering a dead man. Nicholin was very much alive, however, and pushed his would-be rescuers away before they themselves got shot. He was unharmed because the round had been stopped by a magazine draped in a bandolier over his heart. Even the three rounds that had cooked off inside the magazine had done no damage.

Sergeant Vernon Moore, a forward observer from the mortar platoon, ended up inside a house with several riflemen from the 3rd Platoon. There were two-inch square ventilation holes in the walls about two feet from the floor. Enemy fire began thumping into the house, some of the rounds blasting through the holes on that side. "Pieces of clay would fly all over the room," recounts Moore. "It was unnerving." The grunts peered through the ventilation holes during lulls in the shooting, and Moore "spotted the sniper—the only live one I had seen during the battle—about a hundred feet away on the other side of a canal. He was in a hole under a trash pile. He had a piece of tin over his position. He'd raise that piece of tin and shoot his AK-47. He'd been wounded because I could see a bandage around his head." It was impossible to zero in on the sniper from inside the room, the ventilation holes being too small and the sights on their rifles too high.

PFC Larry J. Marchal, a slow-talking farm boy whose father could not read or write, one of those salt-of-the-earth guys who made natural soldiers, entered the room with a grenade launcher, and listened impassively as the situation with the sniper was described. "Well, I can get him," Marchal said. "You all just stick your rifles through them holes and shoot at him, keep him down while I get a bead on him." With that, Marchal slipped out the back door and took up a position behind a large clay jug positioned against the house to catch rainwater, exposing just enough of himself to sight in on the sniper's position. "When we quit shooting," recounts Moore, "that piece of tin flew up and the sniper popped up to fire another burst but Marchal fired first, blowing the top of the sniper's head off. Marchal was like that. He'd just do whatever had to be done. I had the highest respect for him."

By late afternoon, B/6-31st reached a large rice paddy just east of the abandoned militia outpost. Lieutenant Blacker's platoon advanced on the outpost, leaving the concealment of thatch-and-stucco houses where the rest of the company positioned itself to provide covering fire. Trotting single-file along one of the east-west dikes cutting across the flooded paddy, the platoon ran into a wall of fire. Taking cover in the mud behind an intersecting north-south dike, the troops returned fire against houses inside the compound. Eckman requested gunships. A pair soon arrived, and smoke grenades were thrown to mark the site. Sergeant Leader, in radio contact with the flight leader, got a confirmation on the color of his smoke: "I see the enemy.... I see your smoke.... We're comin' in hot...." Leader rolled onto his back behind the dike to watch the lead gunship begin its run, coming in low from behind his platoon. The target was obscured, however, because the smoke had blown back over the platoon. The Cobra's gunner pressed the trigger a moment too soon. Leader grabbed his handset as the Cobra's minigun began spewing 4000 rounds a minute. A spray of water kicked up by the bullets was headed directly for his squad. He was shouting "cease fire, cease fire, cease fire" as the burst crossed the dike, hitting a soldier as it passed. As the gunship stopped firing, Leader turned his attention to the wounded man. A minigun round had struck the pistol-grip of the M-16 rifle he was holding, removing two fingers and the heel of his hand. Leader was amazed that no one else had been hit and thankful the gunship had not been firing rockets.

Leader informed his wife in a tape he mailed home after the battle that "We thought they were in the buildings, so we leveled about a whole city block of cement houses between air strikes and helicopter gunships and M-72 LAWs we were carrying. We leveled every house within sight right to the ground, and we started to get up, thinking we had it made—and we started gettin' just as much fire as we did the first time." The 3rd Platoon again took cover behind the dike. "We couldn't move either

On the Horn. 6th Battalion, 31st Infantry, Vietnam, 1968 (Association archives, courtesy Spekczynski collection).

way," Leader's account continued. "They had us pinned down and we couldn't tell where those shots were coming from. All we could hear was the cracking of the AK-47s over our head." As the exchange continued, Sergeant Leader saw one of the guerrillas pop up to fire. My God, there they are, Leader thought, shocked, for the enemy soldier was not back among the buildings into which the platoon was firing, but was dug into the berm at the end of the paddy not more than fifty meters away.

Captain Eckman ordered the 3rd Platoon to pull back so that more supporting arms could be brought to bear against the berm. The only way out was atop the dikes. A man could sink to his armpits in the paddies, but to rush straight back on the east-west dike along which the platoon had advanced would only get a lot of guys shot in the back. Better to get out from under the muzzles of the enemy's guns by moving north along an intersecting dike behind which the platoon was sheltered, than dart rearward atop the next east-west dike in the field. Blacker told Leader to move to the elbow where the two dikes met and lay down a base of fire to cover the withdrawal. Leader called to Larry Marchal to follow him with the machine gun he was now carrying. The two crawled along the north-south dike while the rest of the platoon kept up its fire. On reaching the elbow, Marchal fired from atop the dike. Marchal lay behind the M-60 with Leader kneeling to his left, feeding ammo belts into the machine gun with one hand and firing his M-16 with the other.

Leader shouted at his men to move, but no one could hear him over the din. He then used hand signals, waving the men his way. The first few reluctantly got up and sprinted down the dike toward him, then raced down the dike to the thatch-and-stucco houses. Firing continuously, Marchal had gone through eight or nine ammo belts when his gun jammed. After Leader helped him replace the burned-out barrel, Marchal continued firing until the last member of the platoon reached safety. With that, Leader shouted at Marchal to move out. Leader ran behind him, moving as fast as he could while continuing to blast away with his M-16. "I guess that's why they're going to give me a medal of some kind," said Leader on the tape he sent home, explaining that he had been recommended for a valor award for providing cover fire during the retreat. He didn't think he deserved a medal. "I mean, I can't see it because there was no other way to get off the dike."

Captain Eckman plastered the compound with artillery, more gunships, and more jet-fighters which delivered both napalm and high-drag bombs. He then resumed the attack with two platoons. The enemy might have been hurt by all that firepower, but there were still enough of them holding out in water-filled bunkers to again stop B Company in its tracks. They later found that the enemy had aiming stakes in the bunkers, positioned so that when an AK-47 was slipped into place, the weapon was trained on the dike in front of the berm. "They were already pre-tested and pre-sighted," noted Leader. "They waited until the two platoons got on the dike in the impact area, and then they fired. They had their weapons zeroed right on the top of the dike…. Anytime we'd raise up, they'd just pull the trigger and the rounds would hit right along the top of the dike." The two assault platoons took ten casualties. "Some of 'em were fingers shot off, some of 'em were in the stomach, chest, legs," said Leader.

The worst of the casualties was PFC Fred G. Losel (21), radioman for B Company's artillery forward observer. Though quickly evacuated, Losel died in the hospital and was posthumously awarded the Silver Star to go with his Purple Heart. He had not only been instrumental in coordinating supporting fires during the battle, but had acted as a rifleman to cover the withdrawal from the rice paddy. Vernon Moore understood that Losel had been very close to Lieutenant Kaiser, the forward observer wounded that morning, and was upset at losing his boss.

> He more or less went crazy that day, started doin' crazy things. There were a lot of grass houses there. Hell, bullets would just come right through 'em, but he was standing up behind one of 'em, sticking his rifle around the side of it and shootin'. Somebody told me he grabbed a machine gun, too, and run out through there, firing it from the hip at the enemy. He was takin' too many chances. He was doin' some crazy stuff. He was doin' John Wayne stuff, and I remember us talkin' about it at the time: "There ain't no live John Waynes over here."

B Company was getting reorganized when a track arrived with their resupply. The crewmen were visibly nervous. After unloading a stack of ammo crates as quickly as possible, they departed at top speed, anxious to make it back to the battalion command post before nightfall. B Company needed the ammo but needed water blivets, too. For the second day in a row none were delivered. No rations had been delivered either, but that didn't matter much because no one had an appetite. Most hadn't even eaten the C-rations they'd had stuffed in their pockets several days before. Throats were parched now, tongues swollen. "We were doing so much running around in the heat, popping salt pills to keep from passing out, that we desperately needed water," notes Leader, "but with so much of the town destroyed, there wasn't any water to be had."

Vietnamese place large (around 35 gallon capacity) earthenware crocks under down spouts at the corners of their houses to collect rainwater. When the houses were destroyed, so were the crocks. Several men luckily found an intact vat beside a partially demolished house. It was big—about four feet high and three feet in diameter, with a cloth across the top to keep dirt out. "When we took the cover off," says Leader, "we could see that the water was full of mosquito larvae. I mean, they were swimming all over in there, and I can remember just plunging my head down in that jug of water and drinking, wigglers and all. I didn't care."

The heaviest contact of May 12 was made when B/6-31st again attempted, along with C/3-39th, to dislodge the enemy from the militia outpost. Sergeant Leader caught the mood when he described in the tape he sent home how after the way had been paved with artillery, "we moved on to the objective itself, this time determined to take it." There was a feeling of resolve among the men. There were other emotions, too, as David Gray noted in a letter he wrote to his parents before moving out that morning: "I'm really scared."

The shooting started almost immediately. Lieutenant Procaccini's platoon was in the lead when the point squad, led by Sergeant Davis, came under fire while moving down the street that led to the militia outpost. When several rounds snapped over Davis's head, he sensed the direction and managed to spot the sniper, or at least the silhouette of his upper body. The sniper was darting from one end to the other of a waist-high porch, laying down AK-47 bursts almost in cadence. Instructing his men to hold their fire lest they chase the sniper away, Davis crawled among the debris to get closer to the porch. Taking up a concealed position behind the concrete base of a utility pole, Davis waited for the sniper to reappear. His silhouette stopped in the middle of the porch, apparently looking for a target, and Davis, seeing his chance, "pulled the safety off a LAW, gauged the distance, set the sight, and shot him chest high. He could not have survived." The backblast knocked over the wall behind Davis, burying his radioman, who came cursing and kicking out from under the bricks.

Nearing the militia outpost, Sergeant Davis's squad took fire from a thatched hut which, except for a dead dog lying on the dirt floor, was empty. Davis was convinced that the clay bunker inside the house concealed a tunnel entrance. He could think of no other way that the sniper who had been there just moments before could have disappeared. Having fought in the area for six days, the enemy would have had plenty of time to prepare such positions. Davis and his team leaders were starting back to rejoin the squad when another round snapped through the house.

Captain Eckman called for 3rd Platoon to clear a line of thatch houses that formed a straight line to the rice paddy flanking the militia outpost. Behind the houses was a berm holding back a rancid accumulation of garbage, human waste, and stagnant water. The approach to the houses crossed open ground covered by unseen VC. As enemy fire peppered areas between houses, Sergeant Davis and most of his squad scrambled through what had once been a front door to take shelter inside a semi-demolished house. Staff Sergeant Rex Humes, who led the platoon's weapons squad, took up a covering position with PFC Percy Horton, who was soon returning fire with his M-60.

With the machine gun covering him, Davis grabbed his two team leaders and crept out the back door to a low brick wall running parallel to the berm. Davis peered around the edge of the wall, watching for shots, and was startled when they came not from some relatively distant location, but from a spiderhole dug into the berm about ten feet away. The hole was camouflaged with palm fronds, so all Davis could see was smoke wisps from an AK-47. He wanted to put a high-explosive round into the spiderhole with a grenade launcher. The weapon was passed to Davis, who, yet to be spotted, shouldered the grenade launcher, squeezed the trigger, and was surprised to see the VC blown up out of his spider hole by the impact of hundreds of tiny flechettes. The weapon had been loaded with "beehive," rather than a high explosive round. The dead VC slowly slid down the retaining berm and back into his hole. The position was active again in minutes. Davis didn't know if there had been a second guerrilla in the spider hole, but suspected a subterranean complex existed under or behind the berm.

An AK round hit the top of Percy Horton's machine gun, sending a piece of the sight flying into his cheekbone. Disregarding the injury, Horton stayed on his gun, covering Davis' squad as it pulled back after being outflanked. Staff Sergeant Humes, Percy Horton, and his two ammo bearers came out last. Horton was a black draftee in his early twenties. Davis recalls, "Percy had the spirit of an older, wiser man, and knew how to encourage the men working with him. He also had enthusiasm, a winner's attitude, and a desire to live to go home. He wasn't about to become a statistic without a fight."

Davis' squad again came under fire from a house his squad could not reach. Unable to move forward or back, Davis requested an air strike on the house, placed an orange marker panel across his back, and low-crawled to a place of cover in front of his squad. After acknowledging the location, the aircraft made a second pass and released its bomb. Drag fins popping out to retard its descent as it wobbled towards the target, the bomb passed close enough for Davis to read—USE NO HOOKS—on its underside. Davis saw the bomb enter the ground and burrow deep under the porch. As he ducked, the ground convulsed and the house disintegrated in a pillar of dust and falling debris.

Most felt that the air strike had ended the battle because the area suddenly became quiet. The word was passed during the lull for everyone that C/3-39th was moving into the area. David Gray, who carried the platoon radio, recalls ambling down a dirt road, joking with his buddies about a soldier from C/3-39th sinking to his knees in a nearby paddy. Gray and his buddies pulled the man free. He was Specialist Jaime A. Rivera-Lopez of Arecibo, Puerto Rico, C/3-39th's lone KIA during the fight for Saigon. "As soon as we pulled the guy up onto the road," recalls Gray, "the enemy opened up again and shot him through the head."

Gray was also hit and knocked backward onto his radio. Spotting the VC's muzzle flash, he rolled over, and began returning fire. Another burst hit him and he rolled again, trying to get out of the shooter's sights, but was hit by a third burst. Gray was hit thirteen times in all, as he would later learn. He had a graze across one hand, a round in his spine, and eleven through his legs. His left ankle was shattered, his left kneecap cracked, and chunks of muscle were missing from his upper right thigh. Bone was visible, tendons ripped, and arteries were gushing blood. Gray felt no pain, only a strange and almost peaceful numbness as his mind detached itself from his shattered body. He knew he was dying. Hands grabbed his wrists and web gear to pull him to safety as automatic-weapons fire laced the air around him and his rescuers. Staff Sergeant Terry Dotson, a squad leader on his second tour, was among those who rushed out to rescue Gray. Gray was a southern white boy, who Dotson, a black Regular Army NCO, had ridden so hard during training at Fort Lewis that they had almost come to blows. Their mutual dislike evaporated in the heat of the fight.

Gray also recognized Mark Mudd and a draftee team leader named Sam Flores. He would never forget those three men pulling him to safety at the risk of their own lives. Flores was a particularly handsome, good-hearted guy who refused promotion on the grounds that he might get somebody killed if he was given more responsibility. He nevertheless seemed to always take charge, do the right things, and get the job done when the bullets flew. Dotson, Mudd, and Flores laid Gray on a door knocked from its hinges and hustled him back to where Lieutenant Blacker's platoon secured a landing zone for the medevac. A medic administered morphine, and tied tourniquets high up on Gray's thighs but couldn't stop the bleeding. Gray's only chance was getting to a medical facility quickly but the dust-off refused to come in with so much fire. Captain Eckman screamed at the pilot to "Get your ass down here!" The pilot landed under fire and Gray was hurriedly loaded aboard on the door serving as his stretcher.

In minutes, the medevac chopper reached the 3rd Field Hospital, the former American dependent high school in Saigon. There, medics prepared Gray for surgery by washing away the mud, blood, and grime with a hose. Cold water lashing his wounds caused him to shriek in pain. He must have asked what condition he was in because one of the doctors told him that they might have to amputate his left leg. "Please, please, whatever you do," Gray begged, "Don't do it! Please don't take my leg off!" "We don't know if we'll be able to save it." Gray was told to open his mouth and a tube was slipped down his throat. He was soon unconscious and emergency surgery began. Hours later, Gray woke up in a recovery ward, relieved to find that his leg was still in place. Later, as he lay naked atop a bedpan being washed, a medical corps colonel presented him a certificate for the Purple Heart with oak leaf cluster and an empty box which should have contained the medal. "Sorry," the colonel said, "We ran out of Purple Hearts today."

As the firing continued, Sergeant Davis crawled past the building that had been knocked out by the air strike and on to a galvanized structure whose size and shape reminded him of a smoke house back home. Looking in, Davis saw only rice bags strewn across the floor. Leaving his men outside, Davis ducked inside and crawled over the bags, headed for a doorway that faced the enemy on the opposite side. A small white building was visible through the open door. Noticing a figure move past the doorway, Davis pulled the pins on two grenades, and crawled the last few feet to the opening, intent on lobbing both grenades at the Viet Cong. Then everything went wrong. Davis noticed that a hole had been dug in the earthen floor and the rice bags had been arranged to conceal the entrance to a bunker.

Before Davis could react, someone fired at him through the doorway and something exploded beneath him. Jolted by the explosion, he let go of his fragmentation grenades. Davis realized he had only seconds to react before his grenades exploded. Still dazed, he spotted one of the grenades, grabbed it with his right hand, and threw it into the hole in the floor. He found the other grenade with his left hand, scooped it up, and frantically lobbed it toward the doorway. It exploded just feet away. He survived with wounds in his shoulder and chest. Partially flash blinded and unsure how badly he was injured, Davis called on the Lord. If the Lord answered, it was in the guise of PFC Lyle W. Hansen (20), his radio operator.

Seeing his squad leader wounded, Hansen jumped from cover and sprinted across a patch of open ground, firing his M-16 from the hip. He made it to the structure where Davis lay and crawled inside to drag him to safety. Scrambling over the bags of rice, Hansen crouched over Davis and asked, "Sarge, are you okay?" Davis started to answer but Hansen never heard him because he was shot twice in the head and collapsed heavily across Davis. He was posthumously awarded the Silver Star. Working his way out from under the body of his dead radioman, Davis crawled back through the opening to rejoin his squad.

The men in the lead platoon were in drainage ditches or tucked behind houses and berms and palm trees, some of them heads-down for the duration, others holding their weapons above them, exposing only their hands, and firing blindly across the muddy paddy that separated their positions from the houses and nipa palm that shielded the Viet Cong. Behind them, Captain Eckman was in a multi-story building that afforded him an overview of the battlefield. Sergeant Leader's squad was sent forward to reinforce Lieutenant Procaccini's battered platoon. Specialist Dennis K. Jones (20), attached to Sergeant Leader's squad from the battalion mortar platoon the day before, darted repeatedly through enemy fire to better coordinate artillery and gunships. As he moved from position to position to get a better view of the enemy, he killed any VC he encountered along the way. He ran straight at a VC in a spider hole and killed him at close range with a burst from his M-16 as the frightened man tried to duck below the rim. Continuing his mad charge, Jones stopped to kill more VC with grenades and rifle fire as they shot at him from nearby buildings. After stopping to catch his breath and change magazines behind the cement wall of a porch, Jones was shot in the head as he rose to fire again. Leader dragged him into the house but he was beyond help. For his bravery, Jones was posthumously awarded the Distinguished Service Cross.

Instructed to fall back and secure a landing zone, Leader helped carry Jones out on a door that had been torn from its hinges to serve as a stretcher. The litter team made it to a clearing where a medevac chopper was inbound. The pilot's first attempt to land was met with automatic weapons fire, causing him to pull up and swing away from the clearing. Leader fanned his troops out but they didn't spot the sniper. Another attempted landing was aborted under fire. On the third attempt, Leader, intently scanning the area, noticed movement behind a large palm about fifty meters across an open paddy. All he could see of the sniper kneeling behind the tree was a sneaker he was wearing. The front of the tennis shoe stuck out in plain view. Leader put his rifle to his shoulder as the medevac flared to land, hurriedly sighted, and squeezed off a single shot before the sniper swung his own weapon around the side of the tree to fire again. The sniper jerked his foot back, obviously injured. Leader hoped the shock of getting a hole blown in his foot would keep the sniper preoccupied long enough to get the casualties evacuated. He was right.

Running out of daylight, Captain Eckman ordered Lieutenant Procaccini to rush the enemy positions and knock out the spider holes and bunkers with fragmentation grenades. Procaccini thought the idea unwise. "We can't see anyone. They're close, but we don't know exactly where they are," he told Eckman on the radio, trying to explain that an assault would turn them into targets in someone else's shooting gallery. "I've got a bunch of chicken-wire in front of me," he continued, "and then a rice paddy. I don't think I can get my people through the chicken-wire and across the open paddy without getting everybody wiped out in the process."

According to Procaccini, Eckman snapped impatiently to get on with it. Procaccini moved over to Staff Sergeant Dotson, his most experienced squad leader and shouted to him over the gunfire, "We gotta get the men on line! We're making an assault!" "You're crazy," Dotson shouted back. "There's no way we can get across there and do anything effective." "It's a direct order from the captain." "No!" Dotson said firmly. He wasn't going and he wasn't ordering his squad to go. The young lieutenant wasn't sure what to do next. Remembering that doing something is always better than doing nothing he cradled his rifle in his arms, slipped under the chicken-wire, and low-crawled through the muck until he was up against the berm. Procaccini started screaming for the others to join him, but before anybody could move, the lieutenant's radioman hollered back that Captain Eckman wanted everyone to pull back. An air strike was coming in. Desperate to rejoin his platoon, Procaccini lobbed several grenades into the nipa palm, then slid back into the paddy on his belly to inch his way back while Staff Sergeant Dotson laid down a continuous stream of machine gun fire. Procaccini got back safely.

Phil Eckman had been directing artillery to cover the withdrawal. Informed that Proccacini's platoon had pulled back, Eckman turned off the artillery and began bringing in bombs and napalm. Amid the din, Procaccini reported that Hansen was missing but added that he believed he was dead. "Confirm it," Eckman snapped angrily. "Is he dead

Napalm strike beyond the palms, called in by D Company, 6th Battalion, 31st Infantry, 1968 (Association archives, courtesy Spekczynski collection).

or alive?" After a pause, Procaccini told Eckman that Hansen had definitely been killed. "Well, if he's dead we can get him in the morning. There's no use getting anybody else killed trying to recover him now."

In the morning, Lieutenant Procaccini's platoon secured the wrecked militia outpost, recovering Lyle Hansen's body from the ruins. The enemy had turned the place into a fort laced with spider holes and bunkers covered with palm logs and thick mud. It became apparent that the battle for Cholon was over when civilians began reappearing in adjacent villages. The VC's second attempt to take Saigon had failed. When morning came on May 14, the surviving VC had fled into the surrounding countryside. In their wake were smoldering ruins and the putrid smell of the dead they left behind, including many civilians. In eight days of fighting, 876 enemy soldiers had paid for Ho Chi Minh's miscalculation with their lives, as did 43 Americans. For at least one company, the price was staggering. When Captain John DeVore took command of B Company on the afternoon of May 16, less than a full-strength platoon remained.[4] For its part in the battle, the 6th Battalion 31st Infantry earned its first Valorous Unit Award and the Vietnamese Cross of Gallantry with Palm. Sixteen Bearcats had earned medals for valor in the battalion's first major battle.

25 6th Battalion in Vietnam: Battles of Can Giuoc and Cai Nua, 1968–1969

Nha Be and Firebase Smoke—May–August 1968

After Tet, the battalion was sent to guard the Nha Be Shell Tank farm where it replaced its losses. Bill McMullen recalls:

> We ran small sweeps and had some eagle flights out of Nha Be for a while but there was not much action. Nha Be was really nice. The tankers would come in and unload their load of fuel in the tank farm. While the tankers were in, some of us would get acquainted with the men on the tankers and get invited aboard for a hot shower and an occasional good meal. We also had Boston Whalers with 85 HP motors on them. I took a sampan apart and used the boards to make a pair of skis. I used inner tubes to make a place for my feet. And there I was, water skiing on the Saigon River behind a Boston Whaler.

In late May and throughout June the Bearcats moved constantly, operating south of Saigon in Gia Dinh and Long An Provinces in search of the remnants of VC units that had escaped from the fighting around Cholon. On June 11, the battalion was detached to II Field Force, operating out of Fire Base Smoke again. On June 23, B Company moved west to guard the Binh Dien Bridge on National Route 4. The next morning, the rest of the battalion joined Vietnamese Regional Force units in search operations near Tan An, Long An Province's capital.[1]

On June 28, C Company engaged an entrenched enemy force southwest of Tan An. The ensuing battle resulted in losses to all three of C Company's rifle platoons.[2] Struggling across a broad, muddy wash, Lieutenant Ron Belloli and his Vietnamese Tiger Scout, Nguyen Van Phi, were tracking footprints and had gotten a short distance ahead of the rest of the company when the shooting began. Belloli's helmet was shot off and Phi and Specialist John H. Baker (21) were killed in the opening exchange. Specialist John Jablonski, one of C Company's bravest soldiers, killed the VC who shot Baker. As the other platoons maneuvered forward to assist, more men were hit. Specialist Kenneth Seidel (20), a new replacement, was killed instantly and Lieutenant Bill Gale and Specialists Harold Frailey and Larry Hathaway each earned their second Purple Heart in as many months. Hit in the neck, Specialist Michael Lutz was having a hard time breathing and looked like he would die, but to the disbelief of all, he pulled through.

Lieutenant Kerry May froze after seeing his platoon sergeant and two others cut down. He was promptly replaced by C Company's Executive Officer, Lieutenant David Wilson, who maneuvered the 1st Platoon forward under heavy fire. Ron Belloli recalls:

> After my guys got up to me and I was able to clear my weapon and find my helmet, I needed a camouflage band because the bullet that took my helmet off cut the band. I picked up Phi's helmet and took his band. The liner of his helmet was loose and when it separated there was a bullet between the liner and the steel pot. Later in the firefight, Specialist Hathaway, who had a severe head wound, was being treated by medics. I overheard them trying to determine if the bullet that hit Hathaway was in his brain since there was an entry hole in the helmet but no exit hole. I walked over, picked up his helmet, pulled out the liner (due to my earlier experience with Phi's helmet). The bullet was lodged between the liner and pot. I showed the bullet to the medics and left. When I got back to our base camp, the bullets I had pulled from their helmets were still in my pocket.

For years after leaving the Army, Ron Belloli kept the bullets in an ammunition can in his basement, reminders of two brave soldiers. After seeing Larry Hathaway's entry on the 31st Infantry Regiment Association's web site, Belloli contacted friends, including Bill Owen, and asked for advice. He was hesitant to reopen memories that might be painful to Hathaway. The unanimous advice was "Call him!" When Belloli contacted Hathaway and told him the story, they quickly found a bond between old soldiers that transcends rank, time, and distance. Learning that they both live in Michigan, they arranged a reunion at which Belloli passed the bullet back to its "owner."

In July the "Bearcats" patrolled the rice paddies and villages lining QL 4 between the Binh Dien and Ben Luc Bridges. On July 8, a mortar attack wounded 14 members of the battalion near the Binh Dien Bridge. During most of July, C Company remained at Nha Be. South of Nha Be was the Rung Sat Special Zone, where the VC and their Viet Minh predecessors had operated with impunity since the war against France. Keeping the VC from coming out of the watery Rung Sat at night to shell Nha Be was C Company's nearly impossible mission. On July 9, four rounds of 75mm recoilless rifle fire hit the fuel tank complex, setting one of the huge oil tanks ablaze, but there were no casualties and no other damage. On July 18, four 122mm rockets hit the base, but again there were no casualties.

Operations along the many winding rivers south of Saigon were conducted aboard ships of the Army-Navy Mobile Riverine Force. Vietnamese Marines, transported by the Vietnamese Navy's River Assault Group (RAG) often participated. Like other battalions of the 9th Division that had been operating in and around the Rung Sat for over a year, C Company occasionally enjoyed Navy food and clean sheets aboard the boats, but there was also a less pleasant side to life with the "River Rats." Immersion foot, mysterious jungle fevers, booby traps, and leeches were constant companions in the watery jungle. Compounding the men's misery, the VC conducted frequent hit and run ambushes against noisy American and South Vietnamese patrol boats that had to move slowly through the labyrinth of narrow jungle streams feeding the main rivers.

East Can Giuoc District—August 1968

August 7 and 8, 1968, were among the bloodiest days of the war for the Bearcats. C Company's highly respected commander, Captain Bill Owen, had just departed for a new assignment as the Battalion Intelligence Officer (S-2) the week before. His successor, Captain Ralph Howard, took the company on a reconnaissance in force operation into

A Tango Boat (LCM-6 landing craft) of the Riverine Force, 2nd Brigade, 9th Infantry Division. In 1968 D Company was OPCON to the Riverine Force, also known as the Brown Water Navy (Association archives, courtesy Spekczynski collection).

a watery area northeast of Can Giuoc. As the company entered the horseshoe bend of a stream densely lined with Nipa palm, trouble came quickly. The stream was the perimeter of a VC battalion base camp. Men in the lead element immediately sensed trouble, seeing numerous wet footprints and human excrement on paddy dikes. PFC Terry McFadon, a mortarman with the weapons platoon, remembers a sudden, mind-jarring crescendo of noise as the firefight broke out. McFadon and his fellow mortarmen jumped into a bomb crater about 20 yards from the tree line as nearby riflemen surged forward. The situation was confused at best with initial contact occurring simultaneously at two locations about 500 meters apart. The 1st Platoon established a hasty blocking position along a paddy dike while the 2nd and 3rd became heavily engaged in what came to be called the "football field." Men dropped everywhere as they encountered well-concealed bunkers and "spider holes" along the stream. Bill Singleton was among the first men hit, but lived to tell of it. Many others did not. Medics dragged the wounded back to the safety of bomb craters and paddy dikes, administered first aid, and crawled back to retrieve others.

A Company was inserted into a blocking position to the east and three companies of the 3-39th Infantry were brought in to complete the cordon. Lieutenant Colonel Jack Logan, who had just replaced Joe Schmalhorst as the Bearcats' Battalion Commander, was on the ground throughout the first day and night. He and Captain Howard later received the Silver Star for bravery during the action, but members of C Company regarded the officers' awards as undeserved "face-savers." Artillery fire was brought in to try to drive the VC out, but 105mm howitzers had practically no effect on the thick earthen bunkers lining the stream. A psychological operations aircraft broadcast Chieu Hoi ("rally to the government") messages to the VC and gave them a 15-minute ceasefire to come out in safety. When there was no response, the artillery resumed firing, to almost no effect. Finally, when CS gas was used, the enemy came pouring out, but not to surrender. They fired blindly as they emerged to escape the eye-stinging, nostril-burning tear gas. About 50 were cut down. For the next day and a half, the battle raged across an increasingly pulverized plot of ground. By the time the fight was over, U.S. casualties, including those of the 3-39th Infantry, totaled 13 dead and 27 wounded. The majority were members of the Bearcats' C Company.[3]

Specialist Bill McMullen recalls the events that followed:

We set up a night defensive perimeter and waited till morning to find out what would happen next. This was really hard, knowing what had already happened. We were all just wishing the enemy would steal away in the night. On the morning of August 8, we started to advance through the nipa palm. This stuff was really thick and you couldn't see more than 10 feet ahead of us. We had to clear each bunker as we came to it. Several men were wounded, and others were killed as we went through this process. One of those killed was a man from my squad, Private Paul Savacool (20). He just wandered too far out in front on our right flank and was picked off. I remember shoving my pistol in the hole where the fire came from and emptying a magazine in the bunker. I was hurt and angry that we were doing this clearing, bunker by bunker, when we should have backed up about a kilometer and called in heavier firepower. These were really thick bunkers and clearing each one, one at a time, was a total waste of men who were my friends.

Around noon the company emerged from the nipa palm into a wide, muddy paddy offering no cover. Captain Howard ordered Lieutenant Ron Belloli to get his men to the other side to search the next tree line. Belloli stood up and said, "Let's go." Ron remembers that as the proudest moment he can remember. Slogging through the mud was hard and slow. Bill McMullen recalls,

The next thing I remember was Don Swears on my right, just a little ahead of me. I heard gunfire and saw Don get hit. I thought he was killed. He spun around facing me and the look on his face was the same expression the actors had during the death scene in the movie *Bonnie and Clyde*. I killed the Viet Cong that shot Don and kept going. I don't know how long I kept going. My mind has drawn a blank as far as time goes. I just know that a while later, I was sitting on top of a bunker, facing the hole, with my M-16 under my left arm, a grenade in my left hand, and pulling the pin with my right. An AK-47 stuck out of the hole and aimed straight for my head. I dropped the grenade and rolled off the bunker into the water. I swam back 60 yards or so and got out of the water shaking like a leaf. I've never been so scared in my entire life. The guy in the bunker got off one shot. The shot went through every layer of the rolled up sleeve of my shirt but never even scratched me. When I got back with my platoon, I found out that Don had been evacuated and was going to be fine. I also found out that Dennis Meyer was wounded and would be fine. My friends Leslie Tegtmeier, John Jablonski, and replacements Herbert Ilgenfritz, Zachary New, and Allan Pretnar had all been killed.

One of those killed, Specialist John A. Jablonski, a well-liked college man in the 2nd Platoon, earned the Distinguished Service Cross. Sadly, his award, like all others in the battalion before him, was posthumous. An extract from his citation reads:

Specialist Jablonski distinguished himself by exceptionally valorous actions on 8 August 1968 during a reconnaissance in force mission near Can Giuoc. His Company came under intensive fire and was pinned down by a company of Viet Cong in well-fortified positions. Observing that his platoon's point man, Specialist Leslie Tegtmeier, had been wounded, Specialist Jablonski ran through the enemy fusillade to provide covering fire for a medic who was trying to reach the injured soldier. Discovering that the man had been fatally wounded, Specialist Jablonski assaulted a bunker and destroyed it with a hand grenade. Returning to the platoon with the body of his fallen comrade, Specialist Jablonski voluntarily assumed the point position. Remaining calm and alert, he detected four more Viet Cong bunkers and before the enemy had time to react, his platoon engaged and destroyed the emplacements. After serving in the precarious position for two hours, Specialist Jablonski was ordered to the rear by his platoon leader. Ten minutes later, his platoon again came under intense enemy fire, sustaining two more casualties. Without hesitation, Specialist Jablonski rushed through the enemy fire and destroyed a second Viet Cong bunker. Maneuvering to one of the casualties, he carried the wounded man to safety through a hail of fire. Returning immediately to the front, he provided covering fire for other members of his platoon who were maneuvering to destroy the remaining bunkers. As his element moved forward, Specialist Jablonski again assumed the point position. A short time later, he spotted two Viet Cong trying to escape. He ran forward to engage the fleeing enemy, firing his weapon and throwing hand grenades as he moved. He had killed one of the Viet Cong when fire from an unseen bunker mortally wounded him. His dedication and indomitable spirit prevented many casualties and served as an inspiration to the men of his company.[4]

As Lieutenant Belloli and Specialists Mike Butler and Louis Dominguez came abreast of where Swears and McMullen were pinned down, Dominguez was shot and sprawled in the mud. Mike Butler and Lieutenant Bill Gale from the 3rd Platoon later got Dominguez and several others out on a chopper. The bodies of John Jablonski (25) and Leslie Tegtmeier (24), killed far out in front of the others, could not be reached. Belatedly, Captain Howard decided to call in artillery. Disgusted at Howard's indifference to his men, Belloli shouted angrily, "No way! Not with our guys laying out there."

Sergeant Joe DeAngelis was still lying in the open, badly wounded. The VC put another round in him every time he moved. Furious at what was happening, Specialist Larry D. Nelson (21) went out and rescued him. An extract of his Distinguished Service Cross citation reads:

While his platoon was receiving fire from a Viet Cong bunker system, Specialist Nelson spotted an approaching enemy soldier armed with a grenade. With complete disregard for his safety, he charged the advancing foe and wrested the grenade from him. Specialist Nelson retrieved the deadly explosive and threw it away from the platoon so that it detonated harmlessly. As a squad began to assault the bunkers, one of the men fell seriously wounded. Specialist Nelson unhesitatingly crawled through the intense hostile fire to the injured man (Sergeant DeAngelis) and returned him to safety. While his platoon continued its effort to destroy the fortified enemy bunker complex, he began to move toward a bunker, which was the source of heavy fire. Exposing himself to a hail of bullets, he stood to hurl a grenade into the emplacement and was mortally wounded.[5]

Joe DeAngelis was evacuated to the 3rd Field Hospital at Tan Son Nhut. He woke up the next morning to find Larry Nelson in the bed next to his. DeAngelis thanked him profusely for saving his life but Nelson's time was almost up. He died of his wounds nine days later.

On the morning of August 9, the two battalions picked up their equipment and their dead and moved to a pickup zone for extraction to their respective base camps at Nha Be and Rach Kien. Specialist Jeffery Overton from C Company's 3rd Platoon made an 8mm movie of his company's somber withdrawal, with the survivors carrying the dead out. Bill McMullen recalls: "Of our 35-man platoon from Nha Be, only a squad was left. We did a few ambush missions over the next month, but there was no one around that I felt that I could trust to back me up. Everybody was suddenly gone."

Dong Tam and Cai Lay—September–November 1968

When action around Saigon finally slackened, the Bearcats moved to Dong Tam Base in Dinh Thuong Province on September 11, 1968. Dong Tam had been built for the 9th Division's 2nd Brigade in 1967 on 600 acres of land dredged from the adjacent My

Tho River. It became the 9th Division's main operating base when Bearcat Base was turned over to the Royal Thai Army's Cobra Division.

There was no significant contact with the enemy until September 25, when A Company encountered the enemy in western Kien Hoa Province. Soon after landing, A Company began taking fire from an enemy force of undetermined strength as it searched a line of nipa palm along a stream. Specialist David T. Seaton (19) was shot through the neck and died instantly. Sergeant Ronald L. Summers (21) and four others were wounded in the ensuing firefight. Sergeant Summers died of his wounds on October 8.

Reacting to intelligence that a VC battalion base camp was located near the village of My Phouc Tay in adjacent Kien Tuong Province, Lieutenant Colonel Logan planned for B and D Companies to conduct a series of platoon-size airmobile assaults on the morning of September 26, inserting them into areas capable of concealing an enemy force. The tactic, known as "jitterbugging," entailed landing rifle platoons near areas that looked suitable for hiding an enemy force and having them search for the enemy. If the enemy was not there, the platoon would be lifted out to its next objective. If a platoon made contact with the enemy, it would be expected to determine the enemy's strength and hold it in place through aggressive fire and maneuver. If the enemy's strength exceeded the platoon's, additional units would be "piled on" to isolate the area while artillery, helicopter gunships, and tactical air power pounded the trapped enemy. The

While approaching the trees, the troops of Company C, 6th Battalion, 31st Infantry move with extreme caution because of booby traps, 15 August 1969 (U.S. Army photograph, National Archives).

technique had its problems since helicopters could be seen and heard from a considerable distance, alerting the enemy to take cover and prepare for action. Further, since all operations had to be coordinated with local Vietnamese units and district chiefs to avoid fratricide, there was always the risk that objectives would be compromised, enabling the VC to spring a trap of their own. That seems to have happened to D Company's 3rd Platoon that day.

While platoons from B and D Companies were being lifted into the area by helicopter, A and C Companies were to move by truck to Fire Base Moore at Cai Lay, constituting a quick reaction force if B and D Company elements found trouble. That part of the plan was delayed for over an hour when the trucks were held up at Dong Tam's gate. The road to Cai Lay had not been cleared that morning and the VC routinely mined it. A second hitch in the plan arose when the helicopters intended for B and D Companies appeared in two groups of four, rather than the accustomed three flights of five each. Given the thin air density, each helicopter could safely carry only six fully loaded combat troops, causing each rifle platoon to leave some men on the ground to await a second lift. That did not bode well for extractions from the field. While it was acceptable to leave twelve men waiting for a second lift near a secure fire base, it was unacceptable to leave so few on contested ground to await extraction.

B Company was the first to go in. Its initial lift landed just after 8 a.m. on September 26. It found signs of the enemy but initially made no contact. Two men were wounded while attempting to blow up a squad-size enemy bunker. Around 11 a.m., the first lift of D Company's 3rd Platoon took fire from a distant wood line as it landed between two widely-separated canals.

The platoon, led by Lieutenant Carl Woody, promptly began moving into a line formation, facing north, to develop the situation by fire and maneuver. Before the line could form, the VC sprang a U-shaped ambush, hitting the platoon from both flanks and the front. Eight men were hit in the opening volley. On the left flank, closest to the enemy, Sergeant Fred Borczynski yelled for a medic when his friend and platoon sergeant, Staff Sergeant Barry Trotter, was hit by a burst of machine gun fire. No one could help him. Trotter (21) was already dead. Seconds later, Borczynski (21) was killed while trying to reach Trotter. Both men were within a few days of the end of their tours in Vietnam. Sergeant Darwin Betzer, a replacement, remembered Trotter telling him not to worry because he would watch out for him. Just ahead, Specialist Robert V. Bollman and Sergeant Gerald H. Forgue (20) were also cut down. Bollmann, a 24-year-old father of four, died instantly, but Forgue was still alive and was later evacuated to Dong Tam. He lingered for over a month before succumbing to his wounds, on October 30. The din of battle came from nearly every direction. It was as though the VC knew where the company would land and they had waited until just the right moment to catch them in the open.

On the right flank, machine gunner Specialist Richard O. Osbourn, and his assistant gunner, PFC David Orris, were hit by the same volley that killed their team leader, Sergeant James Pruett. Osbourn was paralyzed but would live, as would Orris. Here and there, others were also shot down, some before they had a chance to shoot back. Staff Sergeant Otis Williams, Specialist Daniel Hikkonen, and PFCs Anthony Paolini and Earnest Knight were wounded but would live. PFC Stephen Rance (18), a medic from Headquarters Company, was killed while trying to reach the wounded. Seeing his comrades lying wounded under continuing enemy fire, Sergeant Danny Hayes (left) rushed forward, firing his M-16 rifle in a wide arc, and began dragging men back behind a paddy dike where other members of the platoon had begun to reassemble. His feat was all the more remarkable because he was among the first wounded in the initial burst of fire. Lieutenant Woody called for supporting fires and a medevac for the wounded as the second lift of his platoon landed. As Hayes (24) dragged a wounded comrade across the dike to safety, he stood erect and fired at a group of VC maneuvering toward the platoon. A burst of automatic weapons fire knocked him over backwards. For repeated selfless acts of courage that morning, Sergeant Hayes was posthumously awarded the Silver Star.[6]

Nearly two hours after the fight began, an air strike struck the tree line from which the initial enemy fire had come. Shortly afterward, A Company was directed to land south of the main canal in hopes of flushing the enemy toward B Company. All four helicopters delivering A Company's lead platoon were hit en route to the objective. The initial lift was ambushed on arrival and quickly took cover behind a low paddy dike. It took more than three hours to get all of A Company into the field in lifts of four aircraft each. Arriving piecemeal against a superior enemy force precluded the company's intended attack. Under heavy fire from the moment they landed, each arriving platoon was able to do no more than reinforce their comrades pinned along the dike. Nine men were wounded as the afternoon dragged on. With dusk approaching, A Company's wounded were extracted and Lieutenant Colonel Logan and his Operations Officer joined the company in the field.

Soon afterward, a medevac helicopter evacuating D Company's wounded was shot down and rolled onto its back. A squad from the 3rd Platoon rushed out under heavy fire to help their comrades and the helicopter's crew to safety. B Company also made contact, reporting ten VC killed, at a cost of eight Americans wounded. One of them, Specialist John R. Klotz, died of his wounds two days later. After D Company's wounded were evacuated to the 3rd Surgical Hospital at Dong Tam, the "dust off" returned to evacuate the 3rd Platoon's dead but a flight of Cobra gunships firing over the platoon prevented the evacuation. The dead would have to remain in place until morning. During the night, two more helicopters were shot down. A Cobra gunship crashed and the battalion's command and control ship was forced down behind D Company after sustaining disabling damage. Sporadic outbursts of automatic weapons fire continued throughout the night but the enemy was probably just as exhausted as the Bearcats and did not press the attack. An AC-47 "Spooky" gunship kept the battlefield illuminated and helped keep the VC pinned down.

The following morning, the 1-16th Infantry "Rangers" landed just after daybreak.[7] B and D Company elements still in place were attached to the 1-16th as A Company was lifted out to Fire Base Moore. The "Rangers" got into a firefight soon after landing and sustained two wounded near where A Company had been. The remainder of B Company was lifted into the battle area around 2 p.m. and suffered three more wounded. D Company's dead were still in the field. They and B Company's most recent casualties were not extracted until almost midnight. Sometime during the early morning of September 28, the surviving enemy slipped away. No pursuit was attempted. In two days, the fight had cost the Bearcats seven dead and twenty-six wounded. It was one of the battalion's roughest fights, but worse would follow in the months ahead.

On October 1, the Bearcats moved back to My Phuoc Tay in search of the VC base camp. Two days later, a forward air controller was fired on by a group of about 15 VC while directing an air strike against a line of camouflaged sampans along the Muoi Hai Canal. When D Troop 3-5th Cavalry was called in to assist, one of its aerial rockets set off a large secondary explosion. Not far away, A Company found five sampans loaded with mines and grenades. Believing the area contained a large weapons cache, the 3rd Brigade's Commander, Colonel John Hemphill,[8] moved A Company into a blocking position south of the objective while he brought in 1-16th Infantry to sweep the area. They found 2,940 rocket-propelled grenades, 11 Chinese hand grenades, 86 mines, 50 pounds of rice, and two boxes of spare parts for Briggs and Stratton engines the Vietnamese used to power sampans.

The next morning, 1-16th Infantry was inserted into a hot landing zone (LZ), losing two helicopters to heavy automatic weapons fire. The enemy was dug in along a tree line bordering a canal and dealt the 1-16th a severe blow as it landed in the open. Air strikes, attack helicopters, and artillery were called in as the 3rd Brigade brought in six additional companies to seal the area north of the canal. A battalion of the ARVN 7th Division moved into blocking positions south of the canal and near nightfall the 6-31st Infantry landed north of the canal. At daybreak on October 5, both U.S. battalions searched the battered tree line, finding 33 dead VC and numerous blood trails leading to the canal. The VC left 89 AK-47 assault rifles, 12 RPD light machine guns, two 82mm mortars, 62 rocket-propelled grenade launchers, two .51 caliber anti-aircraft machine guns, 58 Russian gas masks, 91 sets of web gear, and assorted medical supplies. The number of bodies and weapons abandoned indicated much heavier losses since the VC rarely left anything behind unless there were too few survivors to carry off the dead and their weapons. U.S. casualties totaled 1 killed and 25 wounded, most of them in the 1-16th Infantry.

On October 6, B Company found another enemy cache containing 58 cases of grenades, 12 cases of TNT, and 70 rounds of 75mm recoilless rifle ammunition. Four days later, the Bearcats returned to Dong Tam for a short rest before returning to the field at Cai Be on October 13. Five days later, the battalion was again in heavy contact, killing 11 enemy and capturing 5 AK-47 assault rifles and a 75mm recoilless rifle.

On October 18, PFC Lee W. Ewing, of B Company, was walking point for his platoon during a reconnaissance patrol near the hamlet of My Quoi. When B Company's main body came under fire from a line of nipa palm, Ewing charged into the dense tropical growth to block the enemy's most likely escape route. Almost immediately after getting into position, Ewing spotted two sampans coming his way. When the sampans were so close their crews had no time to react, Ewing opened fire, killing all eight VC aboard the vessels. For his daring, he was awarded the Bronze Star for Valor.

After months of constantly walking and sleeping in watery terrain, immersion foot began to take a toll. The Mekong Delta, particularly where it meets the Plain of Reeds, is a vast, muddy wetland laced with leech-infested streams and canals. Snakes ranging from 20-foot boas to deadly cobras, vipers, and kraits abound there. A week in the area is enough to bring on immersion foot and a fungal infection that looks like ring worm, but is harder to cure. Some veterans remain plagued with it more than 35 years later. After two weeks in the field, the Bearcats were ready for the comforts of a base camp with showers, bunks, warm meals, and cold beer.

On November 10, the battalion moved to Fire Base Moore, a desolate road junction where Provincial Route 29 crosses QL4 near Cai Lay. The junction's significance is that it links Moc Hoa, a provincial capital near the Cambodian border, with QL4, the "national rice road." If the VC took Cai Lay, they would sever Saigon's primary food supply, isolate Moc Hoa, and gain control of a vast stretch of land jutting into the Delta between Saigon and the Mekong River. Of all battalion base camps in the 9th Division's area of operations,

Company C, 6th Battalion, 31st Infantry, moving with extreme caution because of booby traps, 15 August 1969 (U.S. Army photograph, National Archives).

Fire Base Moore was the most dangerous. Rocket and mortar attacks were frequent, and the enemy never ceased trying to isolate the area, booby-trapping any place Americans might appear.

The Bearcats gained a reputation for stubborn determination at Cai Lay. They routinely sent out airmobile "eagle flights" of platoon size to make contact with the VC. Whenever the enemy took the bait, he paid. When a contact was made, the battalion would pile on several companies, along with supporting artillery, helicopter gunships, and Navy and Air Force tactical air support. The tactic, although risky, kept the VC and their North Vietnamese reinforcements off balance around Cai Lay and kept QL4 and LTL 29 open. During one such operation on November 23, 51 enemy were killed and numerous weapons and munitions were captured without a single loss to the Bearcats.

Cai Nua—January 10–12, 1969

On Friday, January 10, 1969, all four rifle companies of the 6-31st were sent to the Cai Nua area of Kien Tuong Province. Their mission was to find an enemy base camp reported by intelligence to be the source of intensifying enemy activity along Highway

Members of the 6th Battalion, 31st Infantry, come ashore from an assault landing craft as the 9th Infantry Division's Mobile Riverine Force begins a reconnaissance in the Mekong Delta, 29 August 1968 (U.S. Army photograph, National Archives).

4.[9] While all four companies would see action in the campaign, dubbed BEARCAT I, the 1st and 2nd Platoons of D Company would bear the brunt of the action. The 9th Infantry Division's accustomed mode of operation in response to intelligence was for a company to patrol the area until it came into contact with the enemy. If the enemy force was larger than a platoon, artillery, helicopter gunships, and air power would be brought in to pin the enemy down while more companies deployed by helicopter or river boat to try to prevent the enemy's escape. The Viet Cong's usual reaction was to fight it out by day and slip away along a canal or river at night, staying just below the waterline as they passed American outposts.

D Company's 3rd Platoon was attached to a mechanized battalion near Saigon, leaving the company short-handed. With Captain Gary Corbitt on emergency leave, Lieutenant Jeffrey Nelson was in command. Short a platoon, Nelson formed three mini-platoons of 2 squads and a command element each. The ad hoc reconfiguration included the 1st Platoon, less one squad, with 27 men; the 2nd Platoon, less one squad, with 25 men; and D Company's Headquarters with an understrength squad each from the 1st and 2nd Platoons, totaling 17 men.[10] Because the 2nd Platoon had no medic, Specialist Brian Swanhart, the 1st Platoon's medic, insisted that every man in the other two elements carry an extra battle dressing. They would need it.

A and B Companies made contact with the enemy soon after reaching the area. Both spotted and engaged small groups of VC. A Company's 1st Platoon detained two men near Highway 4 who appeared to be a VC reconnaissance team.[11] The two sides were aware of each other's presence but it was the Americans who were most visible. While Americans patrolled, the VC stayed hidden along nipa-line streams and canals and used civilians to warn them of approaching patrols. They were rarely found unless they wanted to be, but signs of their presence were harder to conceal. Hastily abandoned sites littered with items of food, cooking utensils, and occasionally clothing, bore silent witness to a lurking enemy presence. Men who had fought the VC before recognized other signs as they patrolled deserted roads and waterways. Civilians were not going about their normal routines. There were no farmers in the fields, no fishermen on the rivers and canals, and no market traffic.

Early on January 11, sampans loaded with civilians began departing the area, a sure sign that something bad was about to happen. Around noon, an element of A Company engaged six VC, without results.[12] The exodus of civilians continued throughout the day, leaving the area eerily quiet. The 2nd Platoon warily reconnoitered nipa palm–lined canals and streams lacing the area, expecting trouble. Among its members was 21-year-old Specialist James P. Barrios, a member of the Tachi Yokut Indian Tribe from Lemoore, California. He had arrived in Vietnam six months earlier as one of D Company's early replacements but was now one of the "old hands," a natural at the gritty business of soldiering. With an M-60 machine gun suspended across his middle on a long sling and a distinctive belt of ammunition slung around his neck, he seemed to belong there. Barrios was unconsciously part of a timeless and unspoken brotherhood that becomes an unofficial chain of command when the shooting starts—a man others instinctively rally to in a fight. Neither he nor his buddies suspected he would play that role to the extreme in just a few hours.

D Company reported its night positions to battalion headquarters as darkness approached. With about 20 more minutes of twilight remaining, the company could easily have been observed moving into its night positions.[13] Soon afterward, Lieutenant Daniel L. Webber (1st Platoon Leader) Staff Sergeant Herschel Jones (1st Platoon Sergeant), PFC Gary W. Spears (Radio Operator), and Nguyen Van Hai (Tiger Scout) went out on a short reconnaissance. They had not gone far when they spotted three armed men clad in black moving toward them. In the ensuing firefight, two of the VC were killed, one of whom was an officer.[14] Hai, a former VC himself, knew the man and warned that they were up against the 261st VC Main Force Battalion. Pleased with the results of the skirmish, Webber dismissed Hai's warning.

Hai was worried. The 261st was well-equipped, disciplined, and had a reputation for tenacity. On his return to the night laager, Hai informed Sergeant James MacMaster of his concern, urging that the platoon move quickly to another position. Knowing Hai was not easily spooked, MacMaster discussed the situation with Lieutenant Webber. They had surely been spotted moving into their positions. Webber worried that moving would attract more attention and risk an ambush or possible fratricide with another D Company element since darkness was setting in. He instead placed the platoon on 50 percent alert, meaning one man in each position would remain awake at all times. MacMaster feared the lieutenant was making a bad call. Webber was still green, commissioned through ROTC from the University of Montana the summer before. After post-commission schooling and leave, he joined D Company in early December and had seen no action until the skirmish a few minutes earlier.

The 1st Platoon formed an arc-shaped perimeter around a village abandoned earlier that day. Behind it was a deep canal, the Kinh Hai Moui Tam. No one dug in, some men left their positions to relieve themselves, probably all wore mosquito repellent, and more than a few smoked. Poor light and noise discipline opened the door to disaster. In the dark, a lit cigarette can be seen from 75 yards or more and the distinctive smells of cigarette smoke and insect repellent drift revealingly on the wind. No leaders checked the line, a sure recipe for trouble. Moving in the shadows, the VC completed their approach undetected. Before attacking, they probably watched, sniffed, and listened for a while, identifying American positions almost as clearly as in daylight. Around 2 a.m., Specialist Brian Swanhart awoke to the sound of an ear-shattering explosion, followed by the steady chatter of AK-47s spewing green tracers overhead. Men were already calling for help and at least one was already dead, killed in the attack's opening moments. He was Private Edwin F. Tubbs (19), who had joined the company only a few days before. One after another, more men were hit by automatic weapons and RPG fire. Patterns of red (U.S.) and green (VC) tracers crisscrossed the area, providing a picture of what was happening. The scene looked bad from every angle.

Sergeant Jim MacMaster, the squad leader responsible for the left side of the perimeter, recognized immediately that his platoon was in trouble. Explosions and automatic weapons fire could also be heard erupting to the southeast from the 2nd Platoon's direction. MacMaster reasoned that they were probably up against part of the battalion Hai had reported earlier. Although wounded in the left knee when the shooting began, MacMaster crawled across a ditch to check his side of the perimeter.

At the center of the platoon arc, Lieutenant Webber and Staff Sergeant Jones were in a house conferring with Sergeant John B. Rolle, the right flank squad leader, when the attack began. There they could look at a map, illuminated by a red-lensed flashlight, and talk softly without exposing their position, but the house was not as safe as they thought. All three were hit soon after the attack began. Rolle was hit in several places and would soon die, Jones was bleeding profusely and would ultimately lose his leg, and Webber, although injured only in the forearm, was dazed and became unable to function. On radio watch at the left end of MacMaster's squad when the attack began, PFC Lawton A. Keener (20), was shot in the chest around the same time and died soon afterward.

A second radio operator, PFC Gary Spears, was asleep when the shooting began but kept his head amid the chaos and went to find his radio, which Keener had borrowed. Spears found his radio badly damaged, and inoperable. An exploding RPG peppered his back with shrapnel as he kneeled over the useless radio in a vain attempt to make it work. Hurt and unsure of what to do, Spears crawled down a ditch and by coincidence found Sergeant MacMaster, who told him to see if there was still a functioning radio at the platoon command post. Spears crawled off, dutifully and painfully complying with Mac-Master's instructions. At the CP, Spears encountered the company's senior medic, Brian Swanhart, who directed him to apply a tourniquet to Sergeant Rolle's leg. Swanhart too had been hit but, oblivious to his own injuries, was busily trying to prevent Staff Sergeant Jones from bleeding to death. The radio Spears was sent to find could receive but lacked sufficient power to transmit with a short antenna, so Spears crawled back to his own radio to get a whip antenna.

To the south, things also went badly for the 2nd Platoon. Earlier, as darkness descended on January 11, the platoon had been running late getting to its assigned position. Because there was a large swamp between the platoon and its objective, Lieutenant Peter Barrett, the platoon leader, arrayed his men facing east and south along the nearest dry ground available—a wide paddy dike. He divided the platoon into three segments. The four-man center segment, led by Specialist Al Vargas, was a connector between two larger elements. Seven men on the north were led by Sergeant James Ward and nine men on the south were led by Lieutenant Barrett. Barrett was unsure of where the 1st Platoon or Company Headquarters were, but assumed both were probably a mile or two from his platoon.

Around 2:30 a.m., green tracers from a pair of AK-47s began snapping over the heads of men in the northern and center positions. A third AK-47 was firing northward, possibly at the 1st Platoon. Sergeant Steed alerted those near him that two VC were coming across the paddy. Specialist "Tak" Yabiku and Lieutenant Barrett fired (Barrett's rifle jammed after firing only one round) but too little, too late. An RPG exploded in front of Yabiku (22), killing him and wounding Barrett. Hurt but still functioning, Barrett threw two grenades and ordered Specialist Jose DeLaCampa to fire the Claymores but there was no longer anything at the end of the electrical mine's firing wire. The VC had probably crept in and taken it before the fight began. DeLaCampa threw another grenade while Barrett fired a hand-held flare, illuminating a pair of VC with an RPG. DeLaCampa and Barrios saw more VC in front of them.

Barrett called for illumination from the battalion heavy mortar platoon to give his men clearer targets. To his chagrin, the response illuminated the place his platoon was supposed to be, not where it was. Meanwhile, Specialist Barrios' steadily chattering machine gun was keeping the enemy from getting across the paddy but it drew too much attention for Barrios to safely remain in one place. A second RPG landed short and did no damage but Barrios ignored it and continued firing. He was joined by Specialist Calvin Robinson (20), both men covering the platoon's consolidation to protect the wounded. While Lieutenant Barrett was calling for a second illumination round, a bullet struck Sergeant Steed's helmet, knocking it off his head and dazing him. PFC Ronald Ayers' and Specialist Douglas Green's weapons both jammed just when the action was hottest. Specialists Vargas and DeLaCampa fired M79 grenade launchers as fast as they could load but identifying targets was tougher. As the second illumination round popped overhead, Specialist Barrios called for more ammunition. In response, Sergeant Peter West bravely crawled out into the paddy to retrieve a belt of machine gun ammunition dropped earlier.

Lieutenant Barrett requested high explosive fire from the mortar section but it was denied. The battalion operations officer explained that mortars could not fire into a populated area. Barrett argued that the only "population" around were the VC shooting at him, but the major was unyielding. A third RPG exploded nearby, killing Specialists Barrios and Robinson and wounding Lieutenant Barrett a second time. Sergeants West and Gasco, Specialist DeLaCampa and PFC Ayers were also wounded. At this point, every man on the southern position had been hit. Because no aid man accompanied the 2nd Platoon that night, men had to do what they could for themselves and each other.

Ayers and DeLaCampa, the least seriously wounded, carried Sergeant Gasco to the center position where he would have more protection. Specialists Green and Taylor covered Ayers as he approached and then followed him back to the southern position to help pull out the wounded. Gunships arrived and fired several rockets at the enemy but the results were unseen. It was odd that the battalion headquarters would call in helicopter gunships to pulverize the village from which 2nd Platoon was taking fire but it would not permit its own mortars to do so. With nearly half of his platoon dead or wounded,

Members of the 6th Battalion, 31st Infantry, prepare to assault VC positions in the tree line during the 9th Infantry Division's Mobile Riverine Force reconnaissance mission in the Mekong Delta, 29 August 1968 (U.S. Army photograph, National Archives).

Lieutenant Barrett informed Lieutenant Nelson that he was withdrawing to safer ground to get the wounded evacuated.[15] Sergeants Gasco and West, the most seriously wounded, were evacuated about an hour after they were wounded.[16] The bodies of Yakibu, Barrios, and Robinson were evacuated around daybreak. For their actions that night, Barrios and Robinson were posthumously awarded the Distinguished Service Cross. PFC Ayers received the Silver Star. Lieutenant Barrett and Specialists Taylor, Green and DeLaCampa were awarded the Bronze Star for Valor. Sergeant Steed won an Army Commendation Medal for Valor. All earned Purple Hearts.

For the 1st Platoon, withdrawal was infeasible. There were still VC in front of them and a deep canal behind them. For these men, the night's ordeal continued. Brian Swanhart recalls: "I was convinced we were going to be wiped out. The VC almost broke our perimeter twice and I was spending as much time as a rifleman as a medic. I worried that I would run out of ammo although I started with nine magazines (180 rounds). This was the only time I ever fired my rifle in a firefight. The real heroes of this engagement were Sergeant James MacMaster and a machine gunner, whose name I can't remember."

Sergeant MacMaster had become the platoon's de facto leader. Brian Swanhart informed him that the platoon leader, platoon sergeant, and several others were wounded and at least two men were dead. After rendering his report, Swanhart crawled away to help someone else. Gary Spears soon returned with a working radio, enabling MacMaster to inform Lieutenant Nelson of the situation. MacMaster recalls: "I told the XO about the platoon leader and platoon sergeant, that I had taken charge, and that we were almost overrun. Next, I asked about the possibility of assistance from the other platoons. Third, I told him we needed artillery. I don't remember his exact response, but he felt that I was overestimating the size of the enemy force and said we would not be getting ground assistance until daylight and would get no artillery because we were too close to a village." Spears, who was with MacMaster at the time, recalls; "It wasn't a very good talk. It didn't seem he was going to give us any help."

Whatever the reality that night, neither platoon got artillery or mortar support. Since the villages were empty of civilians, the risk of collateral casualties was nil, so withholding indirect fire was senseless. No attempt was made to reinforce the 1st Platoon with Lieutenant Nelson's element. Under the circumstances, such a move would have been foolhardy since Nelson's element would have had to cross several hundred meters of open ground and fight its way through a VC force of undetermined size to reach the 1st Platoon. The result would likely have been an even greater loss of D Company soldiers that night.

After sliding into the canal for better cover, MacMaster was wounded again, this time by an RPG, which ripped away a hunk of his right thigh, immobilizing him. The same RPG blasted again and wounded Spears, momentarily knocking him out. Like an angel of mercy, Brian Swanhart soon came to tend to their wounds. Later awarded the Silver Star for his actions, Swanhart was among the platoon's saviors. Another hero that night was PFC Randy L. Whitaker, a machine gunner who seemed to be everywhere. Wherever the fighting was most intense, Whitaker would show up. Although wounded several times, Whitaker let nothing stop him. Swanhart recalls; "I couldn't believe he actually survived, considering the enemy was doing everything possible to knock out his gun. I believe he actually silenced one or two of their machine guns while exchanging fire with them." Like Brian Swanhart, Randy Whitaker was awarded the Silver Star for his exemplary courage in that battle.

Gary Spears and Jim MacMaster would receive only a Purple Heart. Sergeant MacMaster relates,

> PFC Spears stayed with me. I'm not sure if he was as scared as I was and I think we were both glad we had someone else with us. We were so busy we didn't have much time to be scared. I hadn't had much of a chance to work with him, because he just joined us a couple of months before, but he did everything I asked of him. After talking to the (acting) company commander, I realized we were on our own. We attempted to contact other units—battalion, brigade and division, and a couple of others. We finally got "one of the big guys" who was in his chopper nearby. We were able to fill him in and received his promise of assistance. Soon, we heard "Hunter-Delta-Five-Four, this is Boomerang Three-Niner, over."[17]

Keying off MacMaster's directions, the initial flight of Cobra gunships brought its rockets and miniguns to bear. Flights of gunships rotated in a steady cycle, leaving the VC no option but to break contact before daylight made leaving impossible.

While the 1st Platoon was still under fire, B Company spotted and sunk a sampan trying to move out of the contact area.[18] It may have been the same sampan spotted earlier in the evening by D Company's 2nd Platoon. As the enemy's fire slackened, MacMaster called for helicopters to extract the platoon's wounded.[19] The number he reported stunned higher headquarters. There were more men killed (6) and wounded (18) than would be left on the ground (only 3).[20] The wounded would just have to stay in place a while longer. Before dawn, the "Boomerangs" (191st Aviation Company) were relieved by the "Crusaders" (187th Aviation Company) to maintain continuous Cobra support for the battered

1st Platoon. With daylight approaching, the VC slipped away along the area's waterways. The battle was over.

As the wounded were being brought into the 36th Evacuation Hospital at Dong Tam, D Company's First Sergeant, Godfrey F. Hidalgo, stood waiting outside the emergency ward to see what had happened to his men. The tough old veteran of two wars stood ramrod straight as his men arrived. Tears streaked down his weathered face as he watched man after man being rolled into emergency surgery. The old soldier had a heart. A few days later, actor Jimmy Stewart and his wife Gloria visited those transferred to hospitals at Long Binh in preparation for the long journey to the United States via a 30-day stabilization stop at an Army hospital in Japan. Stewart had flown B-24s over Europe in World War II and had seen his share of combat and suffering. He didn't have to take risks in another war zone to prove anything, nor did Gloria. They came because they cared.[21]

Several days later, D Company's action was reported in the Vietnam edition of the *Stars and Stripes*. It read: "January 12, elements of the 6-31st Infantry engaged in a night action. US casualties reported as light." If 9 killed and 23 wounded out of 52 men engaged (60 percent) constitutes "light" casualties, what percentage would constitute "heavy" casualties? About half of the wounded were ultimately evacuated to the U.S. to recover. Some would never be whole again, losing limbs or suffering chronic disabling pain for the rest of their lives. Over the next few weeks, the less severely wounded would return to duty, finding few men they recognized in their old platoons. Some would be wounded again in subsequent battles.

26 6th Battalion in Vietnam, 1969–1970

Back to Dong Tam—January–November 1969

On March 24, B Company spotted a company-size NVA unit in the open near a wooded fringe of the Plain of Reeds. Battalion ordered A Company to get ready to be lifted into the contact area to establish a blocking position inside the tree line. A Company was inserted into the area around 5 p.m., but had to cross a small canal to enter the tree line on the opposite bank. Just after crossing the canal, they were taken under fire by a larger enemy force inside the tree line in thick earthen bunkers. The area was a major NVA supply depot to equip units entering that part of Vietnam across the Plain of Reeds from Cambodia. While most men quickly dropped behind the sheltering bank of the canal, PFC Larry E. Bailey (20) charged forward, firing his M-79 grenade launcher once as he entered the woods. According to Sergeant Bob Grant, who was wounded in the action, Bailey never had a chance. He was thrown backwards by simultaneous bursts of enemy fire from several directions and was probably dead before he hit the ground. Soon after Bailey's death, two other A Company men, Sergeant David S. Harris (21) and PFC Johnny Young (18), were killed. The enemy slipped away unhindered along the canal.

Near dusk on April 10, Lieutenant Harry Whitmore of B Company took a seven-man squad out of Vinh Kiem patrol base to conduct a night ambush in a nearby tree line. Since they would be near their base and would occupy a well-protected site, the squad's small size did not cause anyone concern. The enemy had the same idea, waiting along the canal just a few hundred yards from Vinh Kiem's edge. Without warning, they showered the squad with hand grenades and then unleashed a long burst of AK-47 fire. Three men, Specialists John L. Morgan, Jr. (20), Edwin H. Pumphrey (21), and Jackie L. Ratcliff (20) were cut down in quick succession. The squad's medic, Specialist Kenneth D. Brown (21), moved from one to the other, exposing himself continuously to enemy fire to pull his comrades to a place of greater safety and administer first aid. His exertions were in vain. All three were dead. Later that night at Vinh Kiem, Brown, exhausted and dispirited, asked Lieutenant Whitmore if he could use his bunk to get some sleep. Whitmore, who would not be sleeping anyway, agreed and moved out to the perimeter. After midnight, a mortar round landed near the bunk where Brown lay, killing him instantly. Also killed by the mortar attack was Sergeant Edward V. Eiden, Jr. (21), just days before he was to finish his tour in Vietnam.

In the Mekong Delta, soldiers often died in small numbers at places no one remembers, but their comrades will never forget how they died. Lesley Steven Reiter was an instant NCO, a squad leader in C Company's 1st Platoon. Staff Sergeant Steve Cox, his platoon sergeant, recalls the circumstances of his death and that of his comrades.

> We were on a squad sized sweep through an area known to be heavily booby trapped, and were supposed to set up an ambush along a river bank that night. A couple of days earlier, a Chieu Hoi came into our company's field location and said that he and another VC had set out 50 new booby traps made with American hand grenades that morning. A squad from one of the other platoons was sent out to dismantle them. I think they were on the second or third one when a VC opened up with an AK-47 and killed the Chieu Hoi and Specialist Santana S. "Mouse" Fernandez (19). I was ordered to send Reiter's squad through the same area. Reiter was walking point and came to a mortar aiming stake along the path. He pulled it out of the ground. I was next in line behind him and heard him say "I don't believe it." An American grenade was strapped to the bottom of the stake. As I turned and dove away, it went off. There was at least a second or two delay before it exploded. Reiter instantly went into shock with lots of wounds. I called in the dust-off. Besides Reiter, Johnny Gibbs, who must have been at least 30 yards away, caught one big piece in his left humerus, breaking it. I had wounds mostly in my left leg, one of which was the million dollar wound.

Sergeant Lesley Steven Reiter (21) died of his wounds in a field hospital the next day, April 27, 1969.

On August 1, after being lifted into the paddies, A Company was doing a sweep back to Dong Tam from Vinh Kiem. Three officers and a radio operator from another brigade went along as observers. Captain Al Nicolini, one of the best company commanders in the division, warned the group to stay off the trails since they were usually booby-trapped. The group disregarded his warning and soon tripped a booby trap. Although all were wounded, they would survive. Their evacuation to Dong Tam resulted in still another casualty when Nicolini tried to mark the landing zone with a small pencil flare he had never used before. In trying to make it work, he shot the flare into his hand. His men remember him making a joke of it, saying: "This is a helluva way to make a living." He refused evacuation. Just another day in the boonies.

During the spring and summer of 1969, the Bearcats conducted almost daily "eagle flights" and riverine operations from Dong Tam. Because the Bearcats were the last battalion of the 9th Division to arrive in Vietnam, they were assigned the task of securing Dong Tam while the division's 1st and 2nd Brigades "stood down" in preparation for redeployment to the United States. From August to November 1969, the 6-31st formed the nucleus of Task Force Carlson, named after the Bearcats' battalion's commander, LTC Gerald Carlson. The battalion conducted constant daylight patrols, "eagle flights," and night ambush patrols around the "rocket belt" surrounding Dong Tam to keep the enemy at bay while most of the division packed up to go home.

Task Force Carlson maintained the hard-fighting reputation the Bearcats had gained at Cai Lay. On October 4, they came to the aid of B/5-60th Infantry fighting an enemy battalion west of My Phuoc Tay. The Bearcats uncovered a large enemy force entrenched in bunkers, killing 138 of the enemy in two days of hard fighting. Uncharacteristically, the enemy left 160 weapons on the battlefield, along with their dead, indicating again that they had too few men remaining to carry off their casualties and weapons. In contrast, one American was killed and 25 were wounded, most of them in the 5-60th Infantry. On October 18, the Bearcats encountered another enemy battalion west of Cai Lay, resulting in another 59 enemy dead over the next two days. For their aggressiveness, the Bearcats received their second Vietnamese Cross of Gallantry with Palm.

After the main body of the 9th Infantry Division departed for the United States,

A Tango Boat, the normal mode of transportation for the Mobile Riverine Force, 9th Infantry Division (U.S. Army photograph, National Archives).

Dong Tam Base was to have been turned over to the RVN 7th Division. The Vietnamese refused to accept the base because it was too large to defend. Vietnamese divisions were much smaller than their American counterparts and tended to be dispersed in battalion-size garrisons among the population that fed them. Dong Tam was quickly looted by Vietnamese civilians and soldiers, leaving only the skeletons of buildings behind.

Can Giuoc—November 1969–March 1970

After its lonely vigil at Dong Tam, the Bearcats joined the 9th Division's 3rd Brigade in November 1969, occupying a new base camp at Can Giouc to guard Saigon's southern approaches. Again, the battalion operated along Route 5, a road frequently mined and never fully under government control. Soon after moving to Can Giuoc, the Battalion Reconnaissance Platoon was dispatched to the Plain of Reeds in response to an intelligence tip. Delivered by air cushion vehicles (ACVs) of the 39th Cavalry Platoon, they discovered a cache of several tons of weapons and ammunition. Leaving a stay-behind squad nearby, the platoon moved off along a stream where they established ambush positions just after dark. They did not have to wait long. A pair of sampans appeared just after midnight. The two oarsmen stroked silently along the stream using poles to propel their boats. A lantern was held by a third man at the front of the first boat to aid navigation through the thick reeds. When the unsuspecting foe poled their shallow draft boats into the kill zone, they were met by a blizzard of 5.56mm ball and tracer, accompanied by a 7.62mm machine gun, a 40mm grenade launcher, and at least three claymore mines.

When the ambush squad moved forward to sweep the kill zone, they found all three men dead. The boats contained 48 B-40 rockets and 20 containers of antitank grenades.

On the night of January 11, 1970, D Company was in garrison at Can Giuoc, drying out from another watery operation and expecting a restful day at "home." Specialist James W. Bishop (20), the 1st Platoon's highly respected, perennial point man, was having a beer with his buddies, but was not saying much. Before turning in for the night, he dropped in to talk to his platoon leader, Lieutenant Walt Rutherford. Bishop confided "Sir, I've got a real bad feeling about tomorrow. I feel like I won't be seeing home again." Thinking it was just the beer talking, Rutherford dismissed the comment and sent Bishop back to his squad bay to sleep it off. After all, D Company was on a three-day stand-down and no operation was planned for the next day.

Morning proved Rutherford wrong. Captain Dennis Keaton was unexpectedly ordered to assemble D Company on an adjacent road to prepare for pick-up. Helicopters were already on the way. With a field strength of around 70 men, D Company was soon in the air, repeating a pattern familiar to every infantryman in Vietnam. Lush green fields unwound beneath them, segmented by the silvery glint of canals and streams and the random spatter of impromptu ponds gouged out of the Delta mud by air strikes and artillery. Clusters of drab, bamboo-thatched houses and ornate pagodas lined muddy roads and waterways—some alive with subsistence rice farming and fishing, while others, blasted by war, lay deserted. Propeller blades slapping the hot morning air broke the landscape's serenity. While seemingly tranquil en route, the journey would not end well.

On the landing zone, northwest of the district town of Binh Phuoc, a firefight broke out as D Company hit the ground. By noon, all four of the battalion's rifle companies were committed. For the next two days, the Bearcats would be in a toe-to-toe engagement, killing 40 of the VC 506th Main Force Battalion while suffering one of its own killed and 9 wounded. The dead man was Specialist Bishop. After the initial engagement, Bishop's platoon backed away from a hotly contested bunker line to have it blasted by helicopter gunships and artillery while the troops took shelter behind a paddy dike. When the smoke and dust cleared, it seemed that overwhelming firepower had done the job. Captain Keaton and Lieutenant Rutherford dashed across the field to check the result. Both had a reputation for reckless bravery that made them popular with their men. Bishop, the instinctive point man, did not like the idea of officers going out ahead alone. He jumped up and ran forward to catch up with them. As the trio neared the shattered bunker line, a lone VC thrust his AK-47 backward over the top of one of the bunkers. Without raising his head to see where he was shooting, he blindly fired a short burst. Bishop was hit in the forehead and died instantly. He had seen death coming and there was no way to stop it.

At Can Giuoc, the 6th Battalion's living conditions were primitive at best. The base was built among foul-smelling abandoned rice paddies. Widened dikes connected islands of shabby single-story wooden and sandbag barracks. The paddies remained filled with water throughout the battalion's five-month stay, covered with bacteria-laden pond scum. Troops cynically called the base "Venice by the outhouse." The troops' morale reflected their situation. Although the Bearcats had a superb reputation as fighters, their morale and discipline was poor. Soon after arriving in January 1970, Captain Karl Lowe, temporarily substituting for the battalion executive officer, made a daylight inspection of the base perimeter. In the first bunker he encountered four glassy-eyed soldiers smoking marijuana, oblivious to their responsibilities. All were so stoned they could barely walk straight when Lowe had an NCO escort them back to the company for disciplinary action. Most bunkers were littered with trash and reeked of urine. Worse, mattresses lay across the tactical wire to let women in at night. Only one.50 caliber machine gun on the entire perimeter had a headspace and timing gauge and few men knew how to use it. Claymore mines were emplaced haphazardly in the tactical wire and many had their backs removed and stood empty and useless. Troops had removed the C-4 explosive to heat coffee, rations, or dope. Officers and NCOs seemingly never inspected the perimeter.

Few men, including junior officers, wore rank insignia or complete American uniforms. Some wore a mix of T-shirts, khaki cut-offs, colorful headbands, various colors of berets, and an assortment of camouflaged Vietnamese Ranger and Marine uniform parts. The weapons they carried were equally individualistic, including World War II–era Thompson submachine guns, M-2 carbines, Soviet AK-47s, Chinese SKS rifles, Swedish Ks, some M-16s, and an assortment of pistols, bayonets, and hunting knives. How a platoon sergeant could redistribute ammunition in a firefight was beyond comprehension. Unfortunately, many units in Vietnam suffered the same malaise at that stage of the war. The President had announced that America was pulling out and no one wanted to be the last to die for a cause his country was abandoning. The phrase of the day was, "It don't mean nothin."

Despite the Army's decaying morale and discipline, most of its members were decent people fresh out of the nation's high schools and colleges who obediently went to do their government's bidding, either as draftees or volunteers. The overwhelming majority served honorably and bravely and went home pretty much as they came in, although more mature. They were let down by Army personnel policies and a fatally flawed strategy. As in any war, soldiers expected leadership and discipline and responded well when it was given. When it was not, some of society's worst ills found ready expression in an environment in which constant danger, fear, loneliness, alcohol, drugs, and weapons created a volatile mix. Officers usually remained in command for only six months before being rotated to staff jobs at a relatively secure fire base. In contrast, enlisted men usually stayed in the field for their entire 12-month tours. The disparity created resentment that undercut authority in ways the Army's distant personnel managers never saw. Companies usually had only one or two long-term NCOs. Most experienced NCOs were assigned to training centers or recruiting offices or served in advisory roles with the reserve components or ARVN. As always, personnel managers managed numbers, not people. They did not experience the impact of their policies and failed to ask or hear those who did. The same thing had happened in the Philippines at the onset of World War II and the Army's Chief of Staff had experienced it personally.[1] Unfortunately, those running his personnel management system never heard that American units at Bataan were practically crippled by a massive transfer of their best junior officers and NCOs to the Philippine Army. Perhaps that experience was buried too deep in dusty historical archives.

In rifle companies, most platoon sergeants and squad leaders had only six weeks of NCO Candidate School (NCOCS) to differentiate them from the peers in age that they led. As a result, a specialist fourth class with several months in combat had considerably more "field savvy" than a brand new NCOCS honor graduate who arrived with a fresh set of staff sergeant's stripes and only six months of military service—all at a stateside training center. Many junior enlisted men were unwilling to risk their necks for sergeants and lieutenants right out of the "warrior mill" at Fort Benning who felt compelled to act like they knew what they were doing, rather than suffer the humiliation of seeking advice from those they were supposed to lead. The atmosphere was not conducive to mutual respect between leaders and led. First tour company commanders, right out of assignments in the United States or Germany were unprepared for what they found and unless guided by seasoned battalion commanders, some became part of the problem. Battalion commanders, rotating through on six-month tours, scarcely had time to become familiar with their area of operations or their subordinates before it was time to leave. There was little time to train subordinates when commanders were out almost every day directing eagle flights to chase the elusive enemy.

Operations from Can Giuoc ran the gamut from foot patrols to airmobile raids and riverine operations with the U.S. and RVN navies. Wherever they went, Bearcats were certain to get wet. Flooded rice paddies, streams lined with nipa palm, canals, watery marshes, mangrove swamps, and tidal rivers with steep, slippery banks dominated the landscape. VC were particularly adept at digging air pockets (upside down trenches) under canal banks where they could slip away or hide after an engagement.

Booby traps took a steady toll as companies of Bearcats hopped from one suspected VC lair to another in search of survivors of the recent battle near Binh Phuoc. Captain Steve Francia of B Company and six of his men were wounded near dusk on January 18 while searching a thick patch of scrub brush around a lone dead tree. A single fragmen-

A patrol of 6th Battalion, 31st Infantry Regiment sticks to a sluggish stream to avoid booby traps along the shore or on paddy dikes (U.S. Army photograph, National Archives).

tation grenade, trip wired at boot-top level, reminded them why they shouldn't bunch up. Captain Francia reported one man critically wounded and in need of immediate evacuation. Because "Arctic Charlie," the brigade aid station at Tan An, was only minutes away, Captain Lowe, the acting battalion executive officer, brought in the battalion's command and control helicopter to evacuate the wounded. Barely conscious and in danger of bleeding out from multiple fragmentation wounds, PFC David Barnas remembered only the face and rank insignia of the captain lifting him aboard the helicopter. Barnas would not see his rescuer for another 27 years. They met at a 31st Infantry Regiment Association reunion in 1997. Dazed and bleeding from a wound in his forearm, Captain Francia also clambered aboard. Appalled at himself for leaving his troops in the field, Francia rejoined his company the next day.

Two days later, on a foot patrol west of Can Giuoc, a booby trap downed another company commander. Approaching a wooded area just off a frequently-mined dirt road, D Company's point man halted and refused to go further. He had operated in the area many times before and knew it to be a rat's nest of booby traps. Heated words were exchanged but the man was unyielding. Widely respected for his personal bravery, Captain Everett D. Keaton (29), angrily took the point in classic "follow me" style. He didn't get far. As he stepped around a tree, blast and fragmentation from an exploding wire-rigged grenade bowled him over. His Artillery Forward Observer, Lieutenant Byron Dixon, recalls the horror he felt at seeing Keaton thrown lifeless to the ground. In one firefight after another, Dennis Keaton seemed indestructible. He had won three Silver Stars for bravery and now lay limp on the ground, beyond saving despite the valiant efforts of a determined medic. Thoroughly demoralized, D Company returned to Can Giuoc carrying Keaton's body wrapped in a poncho slung between the ends of a bamboo pole.

That evening, Lieutenant Colonel Carlson sent Karl Lowe, originally scheduled to replace Captain Steve Honzo as C Company Commander, to replace the fallen Dennis Keaton. Taking the place of a fallen hero is never easy and D Company's reputation for hell-raising heightened the challenge. Calling a meeting of his officers and First Sergeant to issue the order for the next day's riverine operation, Lowe directed that NCOs inspect their squads before going to the field. Everyone was to wear his Army-issued field uniform, flak vest, and helmet with camouflage cover. Most regarded the order as "chicken shit" but grudgingly complied. Similarly unpopular was Lowe's order that everyone carry their assigned weapon and a full two-quart "blivet" of water. There would be no more gang-like assortments of weapons or "make up your own" assortments of field uniforms. Several of the platoon leaders protested, arguing that flak vests and helmets were heat traps that could bring a man down in the Delta. Lowe was unmoved, having been wounded four times just a few miles from Can Giuoc on a previous tour in 1967. His order that officers and NCOs wear rank insignia on their helmets and collars drew similar protests. Didn't he know snipers sought out leaders? Yes, and he knew too that a leader was easily recognizable at several hundred meters by his proximity to a radio operator carrying a bulky PRC-25 radio with a spiral black umbilical cord leading to a handset in the hands of an officer or NCO. His orders stood.

As the orders group was departing, an angry and very stoned soldier came to the doorway of D Company's command bunker. The quivering man had a grenade in his hand with the pin pulled. He was soaked with sweat, his eyes stared vacantly, and the veins in his neck and forehead bulged from the effects of a narcotic. He had just returned from a hospital in Saigon an hour before and screamed that he was going to kill Captain Keaton for breaking his promise to send him home. First Sergeant Emil Simonsen blocked the man's way, grabbed the hand holding the grenade to keep the arming handle depressed, and wrestled him to the street. Once he was down, another soldier snatched the grenade out of the man's hand and tossed it into an adjacent paddy where it exploded harmlessly in the thick, slimy mud. After spending the night tied to a metal bunk, the man was sent right back to the mental ward in Saigon under armed guard.

CPT Karl Lowe, CO of Company D, 6th Battalion, 31st Infantry, conducting a memorial service for a soldier killed in action (Association archives).

As D Company assembled for the short march to Can Giuoc's pier the next morning, another challenge arose as NCOs inspected their squads. The son of a retired Sergeant Major decided he was not going to the field. He said he had seen enough fighting. Lowe ordered First Sergeant Simonsen to disarm the man and take him to Command Sergeant Major Figueroa for confinement under guard pending court martial charges. Stunned and suddenly ashamed, the soldier meekly handed over his rifle and was marched away. While few men liked having to wear helmets and flak vests or risk their lives in the field, most realized they had a better chance of surviving in a disciplined unit.

Indiscipline came in many forms, particularly drug use. Soldiers who dutifully went to the field and took their chances resented those who didn't pull their share of the load. The problem was exacerbated by the battalion commander's policy of not accepting battalion-level Article 15s or referring men for courts martial unless they committed a life-threatening felony. He reasoned that soldiers in an infantry battalion in Vietnam deserved some slack because they were better men than those who fled the country, evaded the draft at home, or sought refuge in the reserves.[2] His policy left company commanders few options. The maximum punishment they could levy was a one-grade reduction for E-4s and below and forfeiture of all pay and allowances for up to 30 days.

For some who declined to function as soldiers, such a "slap on the wrist" was merely shrugged off. A man in A Company simply refused all orders and simply did whatever he pleased. After receiving a company-level Article 15, he hopped a civilian bus to Saigon, staying for several months before being arrested by MPs who brought him back in handcuffs. Back in his unit, he again ignored all orders. A few weeks later, he tired of the game and left again, never to return. Such men were known to congregate in a crime-ridden part of Saigon. When the city was about to fall to the communists in 1975, some of those haggard, drug-addicted deserters came out of hiding, declaring their American citizenship and demanding a flight home. History does not record their fate.

Problems sometimes came from home, as in the case of a sergeant in A Company. He was a big man, tough as they come, but a little crazy. He drank from filthy rice paddies with a mocking smile and everyone wanted him at his side in a fight. His wife, after taking up with another man, concocted an official-looking paper that reported him killed in action and sent it to his parents. His grief-stricken family contacted the Red Cross in search of further details. When word reached A Company, the sergeant was sent to the MARS radio station at brigade headquarters to tell his family he was alive. Afterward, he became despondent. After getting off radio watch, Specialist Robert Stewart, the artillery forward observer's radio operator, found the sergeant sitting on his locker with a rifle in hand, looking dazed. Stewart roused a friend who took the rifle and escorted the sergeant back to his platoon. The next morning, the MPs arrested him. He had been at the cooks' quarters in Headquarters Company that night and cut up a cook with a broken bottle. In an unrelated incident several months later, another cook became so high on dope that he pulled the pin on a grenade, held it to his face, shouting, "I see the sun!" Seconds later, the blast that decapitated him was the last light he saw.

On February 19, a swirling two-day fight was set in motion when B and D Companies encountered an enemy battalion northwest of Tan Tru and drove it into the 2-60th Infantry. The enemy left behind 50 dead and fled during the night of February 20. The 6-31st suffered no casualties. The fight was LTC Cornelius Gearin's first as the Bearcat battalion's new commander. Gearin would remain with the battalion until its departure from Vietnam in October 1970.

Ben Luc and the Plain of Reeds: March–May 1970

In March 1970, the Bearcats moved again, this time to establish a new base camp at Ben Luc, near Highway 4. Troops had to tear down their old base camp at Can Giuoc to salvage materials needed to build the new base from scratch. They did so while keeping one company operating with the Navy from a River Patrol Base at Tra Cu, another patrolling the Plain of Reeds from Fire Base Gettysburg near Cambodia's "Parrot's Beak,"[3] a third conducting "eagle flights" throughout Long An Province, and a fourth securing the old and new fire bases until the move was completed. Although Vietnam was teeming with engineer battalions and civilian engineering firms on contract to the Army, infantrymen had to build their own bases by taking work details out of each rifle company to build barracks, administrative buildings, shower points, and latrines, as well as a wired-in perimeter, complete with an earthen berm, fougasse, registered minefields, and sandbag bunkers. On April 14, the new base was finished. It was named Camp Everett D. Keaton, in honor of D Company's fallen commander.

In late April, with the coming of the dry season, the 6-31st came under operational control of the 3rd Brigade 25th Infantry Division and moved its Headquarters and one rifle company to Fire Base Chamberlain in Hau Nghia Province, west of Saigon. Its other rifle companies remained scattered from Ben Luc to the Navy River Patrol Base at Tra Cu on the Vam Co Dong and Fire Base Gettysburg in the Plain of Reeds. While contact with the enemy was rare, casualties were not. The cause was almost always a booby trap.

VC were adept at hiding hand grenades in the tall grass and stringing trip wires across likely places of travel.

Soldiers' reaction to their first contact with the enemy is hard to predict. In April 1970, most members of Sergeant Clifford Macomber's squad of D Company's 2nd Platoon had arrived within the past six months and none had ever seen the enemy. That changed when the squad was lifted out from Fire Base Gettysburg to a night ambush site about 10 miles away in the Plain of Reeds. Landing on the raised dirt foundation of a house that was never built, the squad was suddenly engaged from all sides by a North Vietnamese platoon that had apparently infiltrated from Cambodia earlier that day and was probably planning to use the raised pad to get dry during the night. Most men in Macomber's squad hit the dirt and returned fire as the helicopter that delivered them hovered overhead to provide whatever support it could. Because helicopter door guns are not very accurate, firing into the mass below would have been dangerous because friend and foe were only 20 to 30 feet apart.

Unwilling to become victims, two men, PFC Arthur Osborne III (20), an African-American preacher's son from Savannah, Georgia, and Private Dan Wood (18), a brash Irish-American kid from Elizabeth, New Jersey, charged right at the enemy, yelling at the top of their lungs and spraying the area in front of them with their M-16s. Several other members of the squad, unsure of what was happening, rose and joined the assault, firing rifles, grenade launchers, and their squad's machine gun at close range. The stunned enemy platoon scattered in all directions, hiding among the reeds as a pair of Cobra gunships arrived to help. After making a few minigun passes at the fleeing enemy, the Cobras departed because it was getting too dark to sort out friend from foe.

With darkness setting in, Macomber's men returned to the raised pad to establish a perimeter but did not venture out to emplace claymores, knowing the enemy had not gone far. Throughout the night they heard movement in the grass and repeatedly fired at the sound but never saw anyone. When morning came, a search revealed nine dead enemy soldiers, including an officer who was probably the unit's commander. Their clean, dark green uniforms, pith helmets, and papers found on the officer indicated they were North Vietnamese Regulars, as unfamiliar with that part of Vietnam as the Americans. The assault by Osborne and Wood had no doubt killed the officer in the opening minutes of the fight, leaving the enemy leaderless. The sounds they heard during the night were probably the survivors, trying to find their commander. Osborne and Wood were awarded the Bronze Star for Valor. The only man injured in the fight was Osborne, who took a grenade fragment in the abdomen but recovered quickly and soon returned to duty.

The battalion's area of operations shifted in April to take over areas that had previously been the 25th Infantry Division's responsibility. One company operated out of an abandoned sugar mill at Luong Hoa on the east bank of the Vam Co Dong and another moved to Fire Base Jackson near the juncture of Hau Nghia and Tay Ninh Provinces. The Bearcats were entering unfamiliar territory. Near the end of the month, A and D Companies moved to the Cambodian border while ARVN III Corps units attacked into Cambodia from Go Dau Ha and Duc Hue with tanks and armored personnel carriers, marking a dramatic turn in the war.

27 6th Battalion in Vietnam and Cambodia, 1970

Into Cambodia—May 1970

For years, the enemy had operated a major logistics and staging base at Ba Thu, Cambodia, only 11 kilometers west of Fire Base Gettysburg. Enemy troops and supplies arrived weekly in truck convoys with headlights on, knowing Americans were not permitted to enter or fire into Cambodia. At night, enemy infiltration groups moved on foot and by sampan along the boundary between the ARVN III and IV Corps Tactical Zones, taking advantage of a gap rarely covered by anyone.

Events leading to the invasion had been building for several months. On March 18, 1970, Lieutenant General Lon Nol, Cambodia's Defense Minister, deposed King Norodom Sihanouk and appointed himself chief of state. He demanded that the North Vietnamese and Viet Cong leave Cambodia. Soon afterward, Cambodian civilians, seeking to reverse economic and military encroachment that Sihanouk had long tolerated, began slaughtering ethnic Vietnamese, throwing their headless and disemboweled bodies into the Mekong to float into Vietnam. Included were families of Vietnamese communists fighting in South Vietnam and ethnic Vietnamese merchants aiding the resupply of North Vietnamese troops transiting Cambodia. The Vietnamese communists were provoked to action. When fighting broke out between North Vietnamese regulars and the outgunned Cambodians, it appeared that Lon Nol's inexperienced Army and National Police would collapse.

Refugees streamed into Vietnam, fleeing genocidal attacks by angry Cambodians. Because of their suspected ties to the Viet Cong, they were no more welcome in Vietnam than in Cambodia. Worried that North Vietnamese troops might take over Cambodia and appoint a puppet government, President Nguyen Van Thieu ordered ARVN troops to attack communist base areas in eastern Cambodia. Operation Toan Thang 42 began on April 29, sending 8700 men in an armored thrust to the Mekong River. The next day, President Nixon announced that U.S. troops would join their RVN allies in eliminating North Vietnamese sanctuaries. On May 2, elements of the U.S. 1st Cavalry and 25th Infantry Divisions, attacking from staging areas at An Loc and Tay Ninh, reached the Cambodian towns of Snuol, Mimot, and Krek. Their mission was to find the headquarters of the Central Office for South Vietnam (COSVN), which orchestrated enemy operations in South Vietnam. Enemy troops fought a stiff rearguard action, covering COSVN's withdrawal while trying to prevent the loss of huge stockpiles of war materiel. Those supplies had been carried with great difficulty down the Ho Chi Minh trail over many years and would be hard to replace. Three of the U.S. 9th Infantry Division's four remaining infantry battalions were attached to brigades of the 1st Cavalry and 25th Infantry Divisions that entered Cambodia north of Tay Ninh.[1] Initially, only the 6-31st stayed behind, protecting a string of fire support bases in Long An and Hau Nghia Provinces.

On May 7, the 6-31st joined the fray. With C/2-4th Field Artillery in support from Fire Base Gettysburg, the battalion conducted what became known as the "Seminole Raid." Initially, only the Battalion Tactical Command Post, A and D Companies, and the Battalion Reconnaissance Platoon, supported by half of C Battery 2-4th Field Artillery, went into Cambodia. C Company remained in Vietnam to guard Fire Bases Jackson, Chamberlain, and Jarrett and B Company remained at Fire Base Gettysburg as the battalion's reserve.

Led by D Company's 3rd Platoon, the "Bearcats" crossed the border by helicopter early on the morning of May 7. Soon afterward, the Battalion Reconnaissance Platoon and D Company's 2nd Platoon secured the Ba Thu base area, landing just behind a light observation helicopter bringing Lieutenant Colonels Cornelius Gearin and "Skip" Foreman, commanders of the 6-31st Infantry and 2-4th Field Artillery on a leader's reconnaissance. Ba Thu had been overrun by ARVN armored units the week before so the enemy was gone, but had left tunnel entrances booby-trapped throughout the area.

Initial Battles (7–8 May 1970)

D Company's Command Group and 3rd Platoon, landing near the hamlet of Kaoh Kban, encountered hundreds of refugees heading for Vietnam along a dusty road ending at the Cambodian border.[2] The refugees were headed east along a familiar infiltration route straddling the Tay Ninh-Hau Nghia Province boundary. Their route was curious because they were entering a known enemy base area where there were no roads or settlements and no bridges across the Vam Co Dong. The only inhabited place west of the river was the Duc Hue Special Forces Camp. The streaming mass of young and old would not only have to cross the parched Plain of Reeds but would also have to cross an unfordable river to find food and shelter.

Seeing that most men among the refugees were of military age and wore close-cropped hair like soldiers, D Company's commander, Captain Karl Lowe, a Vietnamese-speaking veteran of a previous tour with the ARVN 25th Division, ordered the column halted. Some of the male "refugees" bore obvious battle scars and appeared to be civilian-clad soldiers seeking safe passage among the pitiful stream of old people, women, and children. Lowe ordered all military-age males separated from the column and held at an abandoned Cambodian border fort nearby. Cambodia's flag still drooped from a crude wooden pole over the mud-walled fort, giving testimony to the speed of an earlier ARVN advance through the area. A squad of Lieutenant Morgan Weed's 3rd Platoon quickly took six prisoners, bound them, and held them at the fort while Weed's troops inspected hand carts and took more men out of the column. One exceptionally full hand cart proved that the column was a cover for enemy soldiers. Documents, weapons parts, North Vietnamese web gear, and uniform parts were discovered amid a jumble of pots and pans, rice bags, and civilian clothing.

The number of prisoners soon doubled. Trouble began with number 13 when Lowe ordered an older man out of the column. The man protested politely but relented when several 3rd Platoon rifles were raised in his direction. Although he appeared to be in his 50s, the man aroused suspicion because younger men in the column seemed to glance nervously in his direction as though awaiting instructions from him. Several weeks later, D Company would learn from 3rd Brigade's intelligence section that the "old man" they had captured was the VC colonel who had commanded the Ba Thu base area.

As soon as the old man was taken from the column, panic coursed down the line. Orders rippled back through the column, prompting civilians to abandon their hand carts and begin running across a field to Kaoh Kban. Young men farther back in the column could be seen pulling weapons and ammunition from beneath people's possessions on some of the larger

Two soldiers of D Company near Vam Co Dong River, in the Plain of Reeds, 1970 (Association archives).

carts and running back toward the village among the civilians. Panicked civilians shielded their movements, making it impossible to stop anyone before they reached the tree line defining the hamlet's edge. Lowe ordered his men back to the border fort to prepare for action. So far there had been no shooting but it would soon begin. A group of armed men could be seen running north along the tree line to try outflanking the fort while others began firing automatic rifles and RPGs to keep the 3rd Platoon pinned down. One RPG exploded harmlessly against the fort's thick earthen wall while another hit the flag pole, cutting it neatly in half. Though the noise, splinters, shrapnel, and dust were unnerving, no one was hit.

The fight began in earnest as more enemy troops from farther back reinforced the fixing force that had begun firing on D Company from the village, and the flanking force that could still be seen moving north along a tree-lined road. The flanking element had become strung out and would soon have to cross an open field, subjecting it to fire from thirty or so M-16 rifles and three M-60 machine guns arrayed behind the fort's protective berm. One VC in the fixing force was cut nearly in half by a burst of machine gun fire as he knelt to fire an RPG. Another was knocked backward with both feet off the ground, as though struck in the face with a sledgehammer. Unable to cross the open field, the flanking maneuver shifted further north, ducking behind a slightly elevated roadbed, only to be met by a pair of attack helicopters arriving from Cu Chi. Pass after pass raked the roadside and adjacent tree line with 2.75-inch rockets and 7.62mm miniguns. The

CPT Karl H. Lowe pauses to confer on the radio. Left to right, SP4 Tessier, SP4 Mickels (RTO), Lowe, SP4 Keith Herriff partially hidden by the tree, and SP4 Sullivan. Tessier, Sullivan and Cohn (not shown) were 3rd Platoon's point team (Association archives).

flanking maneuver collapsed but more enemy activity was stirring in the village. Because of the civilians there, the helicopters did not fire on it.

From his new forward CP at Fire Base Seminole, Lieutenant Colonel Gearin ordered Lowe to get his men ready for pickup. Helicopters had been called to evacuate both the prisoners and D Company. Around the same time, a mortar's distinctive "thump" sounded from somewhere behind Kaoh Kban. Several more followed in quick succession. The earth trembled and spewed a rain of dust and clods of earth into the air as an enemy forward observer tried in vain to adjust the mortar's fire onto the fort. Clods of dirt showered troops crouched along the fort's wall and rattled onto the corrugated tin roof of the post's lone building but not a single round struck inside. The Cobras left to refuel and because the 6-31st's supporting artillery was still deploying to Ba Thu, D Company was temporarily on its own. Lowe knew a battery of howitzers was located at Duc Hue Special Forces camp within easy range but they were inexplicably not responding to his forward observer's calls. Unnerved, a soldier who had been detailed to guard the prisoners in a well-protected earthen dugout crawled up to Lowe during the bombardment and asked; "Sir, What about the prisoners? I got a couple of frags (grenades). Want me to do 'em a job?" Lowe's angry response came loud enough for all to hear. "Dammit, if they don't get out of here alive, neither will you, now get back to your post!" Lowe's unaccustomed outburst of anger had its intended effect. The prisoners remained safe.

Between mortar bursts, Lieutenant Weed concentrated the fire of his six M-203 40mm grenade launchers, firing them in ripples into trees along the village's edge. Their small high explosive rounds with thousands of coiled steel fragments burst in branches just above enemy troops sheltered there. Their effects, coupled with the 3rd Platoon's three 7.62mm machine guns, bought the company enough time for another flight of Cobras to arrive. Right behind the Cobras came a flight of six "slicks" to take the troops and their prisoners out. As suddenly as it had begun, the fight at Kaoh Kban was over as D Company and its prisoners ascended to Ba Thu. Around mid-morning, Captain George Lavezzi's A Company Command Group and his 1st and 3rd Platoons landed near the Cambodian village of Trapeang. They found supplies hidden in holes and haystacks, which they burned, but encountered no enemy after an hour of searching.

In the early afternoon, a pair of Cobra helicopter gunships from D/3-4th Cavalry was fired on near the village of Kouk Tek. For the next hour and a half, attack helicopters and air strikes pummeled the area. Captain Joe Calhoun's B Company Command Group and his 1st and 2nd Platoons were lifted in from Fire Base Gettysburg to search the village. They found the bodies of 14 enemy soldiers who had been killed by the air attacks. Two others were spotted running out of the village and were killed in a brief exchange of fire. One had an AK-47 and the other carried a pistol, indicating he was probably an officer. During the morning's strikes, attack helicopters had taken fire from the larger village of Chantrea, setting into motion plans to search the town the following day. Before dusk, B Company was lifted back to Fire Base Gettysburg, while A and D Companies and the Reconnaissance Platoon guarded Fire Base Seminole.

Chantrea (8–10 May 1970)

On the morning of May 8, D Company was again split into platoon packets. Its 1st Platoon was to secure the artillery, the 2nd Platoon was held at Seminole for a possible airmobile insertion later in the morning, and the 3rd Platoon was dispatched on foot to Samraong to reinforce a Civilian Irregular Defense Group (CIDG) from Duc Hue.[3] The CIDG had engaged an enemy unit of unknown size headed for Ba Thu early that morning. Expecting action, Captain Lowe accompanied the 3rd Platoon. Because the 2nd Platoon was led by a newly-arrived second lieutenant, Harvey Mize, Captain Lowe sent his executive officer, First Lieutenant Randy Sprinkles, the 2nd Platoon's former leader, along on the eagle flight. Because his friends in the 2nd Platoon might need artillery support, PFC John Lonsdale, the Artillery Forward Observer's radio operator, persuaded Lieutenant John Bayer, his boss, to let him accompany the 2nd Platoon.

Meanwhile, B Company's 1st and 2nd Platoons and the Company Command Group were flown back to Kouk Tek, landing just south of the hamlet while A Company's 2nd and 3rd Platoons were lifted into a blocking position to the north. B Company again swept through the hamlet but found nothing new. During A Company's airlift from Seminole, however, helicopter crews spotted movement in the hamlet of Senta, which was thought to be uninhabited. A Company's 1st Platoon was lifted in to investigate, apprehending four Vietnamese men, believed to be Viet Cong. Several helicopters took fire from one or more heavy machine guns firing from Chantrea during the insertion at Senta.

In response, B Company was lifted from Kouk Tek to the southern edge of Chantrea, entering its southeastern and southwestern corners with a platoon each. They were soon joined by A Company's 2nd Platoon, landing at the town's northeast corner. PFC Robert Stewart, the artillery forward observer's radio operator, recalls: "We took fire coming in. I'll never forget the sound of bullets going through the chopper's sides and I felt a lot safer when we reached the ground." But the ground was no safer. The VC had built bunkers all along the perimeter road, concealed in the shadows of trees and houses built on stilts. Chantrea looked like a park, a 1500-meter by 300-meter green surrounded by an arrow-straight perimeter road where houses and businesses sat amid a lush stand of tall, stately trees and flowering hibiscus. Chantrea's park-like setting did not change the fact that a bloody battle would rage there for the next three days.

Captain Lavezzi's men quickly shot their way into the town but were forced to withdraw after two men were wounded by rifle and machine gun fire from a network of well-camouflaged bunkers near a large pagoda dominating the town's northern approaches. Lavezzi tried using air strikes to blast his way in. When that failed, he called Gearin for help. He wanted his other two rifle platoons and would soon get them. When his 3rd Platoon arrived, Lavezzi decided to have another run at the town. This time he was met by machine gun fire and forced to back off again after killing one enemy soldier and wounding another and taking him prisoner. Throughout the fight, Lavezzi was everywhere, calmly encouraging his men with amiable banter. He was due to leave Vietnam in only two weeks. Someone joked that the time he spent in Cambodia wouldn't count toward his tour of duty which was 12 months *in Vietnam*. Lieutenant Jerry Holderness, A Company's artillery forward observer, decided he would put the enemy machine gun out of action. He perched himself atop a paddy dike in plain sight of the enemy and called in artillery. A series of explosions rippled along the town's edge, sending the machine gun and its crew to oblivion. A large secondary explosion indicated a hit on a probable mortar position.

Meanwhile, B Company was making slow but steady progress on the town's south side, advancing about 150 meters before taking fire from concealed bunkers. Captain Calhoun backed his men off to allow the area to be worked over by attack helicopters. D Company's 2nd Platoon was flown from Seminole to the northwest corner of Chantrea, astride the road leading to Tnaot.

The 6-31st was being used like it was a brigade, with platoons executing what should have been company missions. Company commanders chafed at having their platoons spread all over creation, particularly since a major battle seemed to be brewing. With Lieutenant Colonel Gearin in the air near Chantrea, confusion reigned in the battalion's Forward Command Post at Seminole. Captain Lavezzi was not told that B Company was on Chantrea's south side and neither he nor Captain Calhoun was told that helicopters had earlier taken .51 caliber machine gun fire from the town.

Captain Lowe and his 3rd Platoon had just linked up with the CIDG at Samraong when a faint radio call from Lieutenant Sprinkles reported one man killed and another seriously wounded. Specialist Rick Mickels, Lowe's senior radio operator, scanned his roster to see whose roster numbers Lieutenant Sprinkles had reported. He discovered that the dead man was John Lonsdale. Both Lowe and Lieutenant Bayer suddenly regretted their decision to allow Lonsdale to accompany the 2nd Platoon that morning.

What had happened was even more regrettable. John Lonsdale's kinship with the 2nd Platoon led him to try to be a rifleman, rather than the artillery coordinator he was.

CPT Karl Lowe, D Company Commander, helping his radioman, SP4 Keith Herriff, out of the muck during an airmobile operation. Binh Phuoc District, Long An Province, Vietnam, 22 January 1970 (Association archives).

As the 2nd Platoon's point element entered Chantrea's wooded northwest corner, it came under fire from a series of concealed bunkers around a road junction. Walking point, Nguyen Van Hong, the platoon's Vietnamese Tiger Scout, was hit in the right shoulder and neck and dropped onto the dirt road like a rock. Specialist Dennis Walker rushed forward and grabbed Hong by the collar, dragging him to safety while simultaneously firing at Hong's tormenter and diving into a ditch nearest the bunker from which he had taken fire. Walker's quick thinking saved the lives of Hong and several others behind him but he could not save John Lonsdale.

Lonsdale had been just behind the point team when the shooting began. Handing his radio to another man, he unwisely dashed across the road and dove into a ditch on the far side to cover Walker and Hong. As he raised above the rim of the ditch to fire, a single Kalashnikov round struck his rifle and deflected into the fleshy area between his neck and left shoulder, ripping downward through his lung and diaphragm. Specialist Thomas "Doc" Miller dashed across the fire-swept road to try to save his friend. Oblivious to the automatic rifle fire slapping against nearby trees, his equipment, and the ground around him, Miller took a kneeling position over Lonsdale and tried to give him artificial respiration. It was no use. Lonsdale was dead. Staff Sergeant Charles Tapp, the senior squad leader, raced across the road to help Miller but was told by a dejected Miller, "It's no use, he's gone." Tapp's canteen and other bits of his equipment were hit, but he miraculously emerged unhurt. Walker and Miller both earned the Silver Star for their exceptionally selfless actions that day.

With enemy fire intensifying from three directions against the road junction, Lieutenant Sprinkles ordered his men to pull back. Covered by Tapp and Walker, "Doc" Miller had in the meantime darted back across the intersection to help Hong who was still alive and in intense pain. As the lead squad prepared to pull out, the intense enemy fire prevented even the bravest of them from getting Lonsdale's body out. Every soldier in the squad wanted to recover his body, even though they all knew he was dead. Lieutenant Sprinkles knew he was giving the right order but hated its most obvious consequence. Fighting as it withdrew, the 2nd Platoon pulled back far enough from the town to get a medevac helicopter in to evacuate Hong. Standing no more than 5'4", Hong was especially popular with his platoon and fellow Tiger Scouts. He managed to smile even in the worst of times and he now smiled broadly through the pain as the medevac landed to take him to a safer place.

At Samraong, Captain Lowe insisted that he and the 3rd Platoon be lifted in to reinforce the 2nd Platoon. Lieutenant Colonel Gearin agreed and soon a flight of helicopters was inbound. At Chantrea, the helicopters took heavy automatic weapons fire and had to drop off Lowe's men in flight rather than risk a landing. Most had to jump six feet or more onto the hard earth from helicopters that slowed but never stopped moving. Miraculously the worst consequences were scraped knees and elbows, a few sprained ankles, and lots of cuts and bruises where weapons and helmets came into sharp contact with exposed skin. Knowing the 3rd Platoon had been dropped on the wrong side of town, Captain Lowe ordered Lieutenant Weed to move his platoon around the town's north end along paddy dikes to link up with Sprinkles. Fighting through the town was impossible because the enemy had more troops and firepower than D Company could muster, even if all of its platoons had been present.

What happened next amazed everyone. Gearin ordered Lowe to prepare the 3rd Platoon for pickup where they had landed. They would be lifted to the west side to reinforce the 2nd Platoon. Lowe protested angrily but Gearin was unrelenting. Knowing there would be little time and that the extraction would take place under automatic weapons fire from less than 300 meters away, Lowe had his men crawl into the field behind them to form parallel lines with a marker panel at the north end and enough room for helicopters to land between them. Only a paddy dike shielded them from the enemy's fire. Amazingly, the improvised tactic worked. As Hueys hovered just above the dry paddy, troops climbed aboard. Swirling dust, whining engines, rotor blades slapping hot air, officers and NCOs shouting orders, and bullets slapping into the choppers' thin aluminum skins rivaled a scene out of Dante's Inferno. Miraculously, no one was hit and in what seemed like seconds, the 3rd Platoon was flown around the south end of town and landed near the 2nd Platoon on Chantrea's northwest side. Troops marveled at how lucky they had been and that their remarkable helicopters could take so much punishment and still keep flying.

At this point, the Bearcats had five platoons arrayed around Chantrea's north side, two from D Company on the northwest and three from A Company on the northeast but there was still no one on the east or the west where the town's inhabitants could be seen clustered with their farm animals under a Cambodian flag. They knew there was going to be a big fight in Chantrea and they were not going to be its victims. B Company was moving back into the town as enemy positions were being worked over by attack helicopters. One helicopter was hit and streamed smoke or oil as it limped back to Ba Thu. B Company's 2nd Platoon was hit by a flurry of small arms fire and 3 mortar rounds, seriously wounding one man. Its 1st Platoon, attacking up the town's western axis, killed two enemy soldiers in a bunker. Joe Calhoun again pulled his men back. The move would prove fateful.

B Company's 2nd Platoon arrayed itself in a rough semicircle around the pickup zone for a medical evacuation helicopter to take out their wounded man. Disregarding notification that the landing zone was hot (under fire), the medevac helicopter braved heavy caliber machine gun fire to evacuate B Company's casualty, a heroic act characteristic of Army medevac pilots. If someone was hurt on the ground, they were going to do all they could to get the wounded out to safety, even if it meant risking their own lives and the lives of their equally brave crewmen. As the medevac departed, seven mortar rounds struck in quick succession among the 2nd Platoon, killing four men and wounding five others.[4] The scene was chaotic. Terrified men screamed for medics while officers and NCOs tried to shout instructions over the hell's chorus of automatic weapons fire and exploding mortar and RPG rounds.

Captain Joe Calhoun, an armor officer, had just recently replaced Captain Steve Francia in B Company and this was his first fight. He managed to get the company aligned along a string of paddy dikes but they were now out of action and would stay that way. Six air strikes, artillery, and a continuing series of attack helicopter sorties were hurled against the southern half of Chantrea while another medevac approached to take out B Company's wounded. Despite the U.S. firepower, the enemy drove off the first medevac attempt with automatic weapons and mortar fire. Fortunately, this time all of B Company's men were dispersed in ditches or behind paddy dikes. A second medevac attempt was successful, although it too had to brave automatic weapons fire. Knowing the enemy mortar had his men in range, Joe Calhoun backed his company off another 200 meters. His withdrawal was accomplished under fire, a difficult feat accomplished without further losses.

On Chantrea's opposite corner, A and D Companies again attempted to fight their way into the town. A Company's 2nd Platoon suffered two men wounded and backed off, taking shelter behind nearby paddy dikes. Captain Lowe of D Company wanted to retrieve John Lonsdale's body and try to unravel the enemy's defenses by breaking their line and rolling up their long axis. While his 2nd Platoon provided covering fire, the 3rd Platoon rushed forward, firing on the run and spanning the distance between two paddy dikes in seconds. Enemy troops could be seen rushing toward the edge of town to meet the attack. Some fired brazenly at the oncoming Americans from a standing position. The two sides exchanged fire at a distance of 75 yards or less. The 3rd Platoon took cover behind the near dike and blazed away, hitting at least two of the enemy who stood exposed at the town's edge. Another, probably a leader, was hit several times as he dashed from one position to another shouting at those around him. Although it was clear he had been hit by the way his body lurched, he struggled on, continuing to shout instructions until several American rifles cut him down. It was a pity to see such a brave man fall. Captain Lowe remarked to Lieutenant Bayer that he wished he had some way of letting the enemy soldier's family know how bravely he had died.

Unable to advance against an enemy force of superior size, D Company's 3rd Platoon was in a jam. Immediately to its left was a copse of tall trees and shrubs protruding beyond Chantrea's northwest corner. If the enemy occupied it, they could fire on 3rd Platoon's exposed flank. About 150 meters to the right was a large farm house in an isolated copse of smaller trees and hibiscus shrubs. If the enemy occupied that place, the platoon could be cut off. To take it, the platoon would have to cross an open field, moving parallel to the enemy's main line along Chantrea's western edge. That clearly wouldn't work. To reach the copse of trees on the left, they could move along the paddy dike they lay behind, affording them protection from the enemy force in Chantrea. The drawback to that option lay in the fact that it was where the 2nd Platoon had been ambushed and the enemy probably hadn't left.

Just after dark, Captain Lowe, Lieutenant Weed, and radio operators Gary Weckwerth and John Mihalek crawled to the edge of the copse of trees to see if they could find a way into the town. Less than 50 meters away, they saw enemy troops emerge from the town, moving quickly on the road in an attempt to sneak out between the 2nd and 3rd Platoons. Lowe alerted his 2nd Platoon that trouble was headed their way and ordered the men with him to open fire on his command, keeping their fire at boot-top level. Lowe initiated the ambush, firing a burst of tracers to mark the target. To his shock, the short-

D Company 31st Infantry Command Group, on the move, 1970 (Association archives).

barreled 5.56mm carbine he was carrying for the first time spewed tracers in all directions, making it impossible to mark a target. He slapped in a fresh magazine without tracers and shifted to single shot mode. Weed's opening burst brought down one of the enemy soldiers and at least one other was hit and fell as his comrades scrambled back to the shelter of the town. The enemy returned fire from the tree line, but fortunately their aim was high, doing no harm.

Lowe directed Lieutenant Weed to move his platoon back on line with the 2nd Platoon. The enemy was skillful with mortars and knew where the 3rd Platoon had been for the past several hours. If the VC were trying to escape to the northwest, they would likely cover the movement of their main body by mortaring anyone astride their planned escape route. The unit Lowe's patrol had just encountered was probably a reconnaissance element so the main body could not be far behind. Weed quickly alerted his squad leaders and personally took each squad to its new position abreast of the 2nd Platoon while Lowe stayed in place with the last squad. As predicted, mortar rounds soon came crashing in where the 3rd Platoon had been.

Finding that the captain hadn't returned with the last squad to its new position, Lieutenant Weed crawled back to his former line and found Lowe lying along the dike. Believing he was dead, Weed grabbed Lowe's flak jacket to drag him back. When the startled captain asked what he was doing, Weed replied, "Are you coming with us, sir?" Exhausted after three days with little sleep, Lowe had dozed off while Weed was moving his squads into their new positions. Just then another mortar round struck, showering the two men with dirt. It didn't take them long to reach the 3rd Platoon's new line. They would laugh about it in the morning but neither would sleep any more that night.

Lieutenant Bayer called for artillery to hit the wood line while Captain Lowe called for helicopter gunships. Unfortunately, there was still no artillery available and all helicopter gunships at Cu Chi were tied up supporting a brigade of the 25th Division farther north. Bayer cursed at the sorry state of their fire support. Periodically, fire barked from the town's edge to try to identify American positions, but the troops had been ordered not to return fire. Captains Lowe, Lavezzi, and Calhoun kept each other informed of their units' dispositions so there would be no risk of fratricide in the dark. Lowe and Lavezzi were tied in on the north but both worried about the huge gap between them and Joe Calhoun on the south. B Company had not moved since dusk and was totally isolated about 400 meters south of town. Just before nightfall, its battered 2nd Platoon had been flown back to Gettysburg and was replaced by the 3rd Platoon. Around 10 p.m., an Air Force C-123 "Shadow" gunship dropping flares over the town took .51 caliber fire but by midnight, the town had grown strangely quiet.

With the fighting in the Parrot's Beak becoming more intense, C/2-60th Infantry was sent back from Cambodia by truck to replace C/6-31st Infantry at fire bases in Vietnam. Before their relief even arrived, C/6-31st, under Captain William L. "Mack" Lusk, was flown to Samraong to reinforce the CIDG, which had again come under attack. Concurrently, E Company 75th Rangers arrived from Tan An.

At dawn on May 9, all companies around Chantrea were instructed to hold their positions while the town was bombarded with artillery, fighter-bombers, and attack helicopters. It was apparent by the lack of any response that the VC had probably found the gap between B Company and its neighbors and escaped during the night. The night of May 9 passed without incident. The following morning, A and D Companies were ordered to sweep through Chantrea on parallel axes while B Company stayed in place—an intended, but pointless, hammer and anvil. Enemy soldiers' blackened, bloating bodies lay all around the town like torn rag dolls. The foul stench of death was overpowering. Most were found with their weapons, indicating their unit lacked the time or manpower to collect them. The sweep revealed 59 VC had been killed. Much of Chantrea was destroyed and five "Bearcats" had paid for the town with their lives. John Lonsdale was found where he died, covered with leaves that had been shot from tree branches above him. Unlike the enemy soldiers who died near him, his body had not begun to decompose and he had barely bled, indicating he died very quickly. Only a small hole next to his clavicle indicated he had even been hurt. The difference in diet between American and Vietnamese soldiers may have accounted for his sleep-like appearance but it was no consolation to comrades who grimly carried his body out of town on a poncho to a waiting helicopter.

After the town had been cleared, Lieutenant Colonel Gearin, Colonel Walworth F. Williams, the brigade commander, and their operations officers landed to plot the next move. The operations order was issued verbally on the spot. A Company was to stay in Chantrea as the battalion reserve, B Company would be lifted out to Seminole, C Company would conduct an airmobile assault to Chek, D Company would conduct a ground reconnaissance to Tnaot, and the Rangers and Recon Platoon would reconnoiter and secure a prospective new CP and artillery position near Baray. Although not mentioned in the operations order, D Company and the Rangers would be operating beyond artillery range.

Concluding Battles (10–12 May 1970)

Moving on foot on the afternoon of May 10, D Company would soon make contact with another dug-in enemy force, most likely the survivors of the fight at Chantrea. En route, D Company found signs of a hasty retreat. Bloody bandages, a khaki shirt with blood spattered across the shoulders, a bloody pith helmet with a hole through it, and two dead VC hastily stuffed into bunkers near the road. They were probably the victims of the impromptu ambush two nights before. As the company neared Tnaot, a lone bicyclist approached from the opposite direction but turned around in panic when he saw Americans approaching. Several Tiger Scouts recognized the man as Vietnamese and wanted to shoot him but were told to hold their fire in order to minimize the time the enemy would have to prepare themselves in the town ahead. It would take the cyclist longer to reach the town than the sound of gunfire.

It was time to quicken the pace. Lieutenant Morgan Weed's 3rd Platoon soon reached the edge of Tnaot, arraying itself in assault formation along a north-south road. An online assault would have been foolish. Instead, Captain Lowe directed the 3rd Platoon to hold in place and cover the 2nd Platoon as it entered the town in parallel files from the southeast. If the 2nd Platoon ran into more trouble than it could handle, it would need a safe way out and the 3rd Platoon was positioned to provide it. Only the chattering of birds broke the stillness of a hot afternoon as 2nd Platoon entered the town. Ominously, there was no other sign of life, not even a stray dog. Everyone knew another fight was coming.

The 2nd Platoon's lead squad, led by Sergeant Roland Alvarado, moved cautiously toward a pagoda dominating the town's center, searching houses and hedges as they advanced. Suddenly an AK-47 opened up from their left, sending the squad diving for cover in an adjacent ditch. Fortunately, no one was hit. As Alvarado's men raised their heads to return fire, they came under fire from behind as well. They had walked into an ambush and it would take the rest of the afternoon to get them out. The enemy was probably caught off guard by the direction of 2nd Platoon's approach because it took a few minutes for their fire to build to its full fury. Sergeant Clifford Macomber's squad moved along a hedge on the right side of the road, positioning themselves to engage a line of bunkers that were engaging Alvarado's men from the base of a large berm. Staff Sergeant Charles Tapp's squad swung wide to the left through a wooded part of town to take out the bunker that had initiated the ambush. Tapp's men moved quickly but fire from several directions stopped them short of the pagoda. A mortar thumped from somewhere near the town square, exploding among the 2nd Platoon's trail squad. The mortar must have fired its maximum elevation to get that close. The lone casualty was PFC John P. Janovik, wounded in the forearm by a sliver of shrapnel. The 3rd Platoon was now also at risk.

As Sergeant Macomber's men came abreast of the company command group, Captain Lowe sprinted across the road to direct their actions. Lowe fired tracers at each bunker aperture in sight, ordering Macomber's squad to place continuous aimed machine gun and rifle fire into them while Specialist Dennis "Wiley" Walker and PFC Danny Wood moved to the flank to take them out with grenades. Disregarding bullets peppering the ground around him, Wood rolled into the open to get a better shot at a bunker blocking his path. He succeeded, giving Walker enough time to cross the open space untouched with an already armed grenade in his hand. Throwing himself atop the bunker, Walker slammed the grenade into the bunker aperture just before it went off. Those inside never had a chance. With a second grenade, he repeated the feat with Wood following in the open to draw fire and make sure no one got the chance to shoot his buddy. Wood was just 18 years old. The saga continued until Walker ran out of grenades. Returning to his squad to get more, Walker picked up a grenade launcher and joined those firing into identifiable bunker apertures. Wood covered him as he withdrew and then joined Walker, Macomber, and Lowe in firing into two other bunkers, both of which quickly fell silent. Walker and Wood would receive the Distinguished Service Cross for their actions that day.

Although enemy fire had nearly ceased, more trouble was on the way. Summoned back to his radio to answer a call from Lieutenant Colonel Gearin, Lowe ran back across the road, intending to move up to get Alvarado's men out of the ditch while the 2nd Platoon still had the upper hand. He told his radio operator, Specialist Gary Moran, to call the 3rd Platoon to send up some light antitank weapons and hand grenades. On his other radio, Lowe returned Gearin's fateful call. Gearin ordered him to get the company out of town. A flight of fighter-bombers and a flight of attack helicopters were inbound and Gearin intended to blow up as much of the town as he could. The dilemma was Alvarado's squad. Their radio was not working and they were not coming out of that ditch willingly. There was still sporadic shooting around them, but not enough to pin them down. Lowe urged Gearin to send the aircraft elsewhere because D Company was making good progress and could not leave town until Alvarado's men were extricated. Unrelenting, Gearin ordered a marker panel placed on the road to identify friendly positions.

Lieutenant Weed suddenly appeared with a poncho liner full of grenades and LAWs. Specialist Rick Mickels and Gary Moran put out the marker panel while Lowe established contact with the forward air controller and the inbound helicopters. Across the road,

Weed joined Macomber, Walker, and Wood in placing 40mm, LAW, and rifle fire on every source of fire they could spot. Lowe yelled at Weed to get back to his platoon but it was too late. He probably never heard the order among all the noise. Above, the lead Cobra identified D Company's marker panel and was getting instructions on friendly troop dispositions when it began taking .51 caliber fire from somewhere on Tnaot's northwest side. The lead pilot decided to make his gun run from a different direction, using tall trees to mask his approach. Lowe started back across the road toward Alvarado's position just as the gunship fired a spread of four folding fin aerial rockets. Three struck around the enemy mortar and heavy machine gun positions but the fourth fell short, striking directly between Alvarado's and Macomber's squads. Lowe was knocked off his feet by the blast and was dazed but otherwise unhurt. Cliff Macomber was not so fortunate. A fragment penetrated his flak vest and entered his chest. "Doc" Miller dragged Macomber across the road and, unable to find the wound, tried in vain to give him artificial respiration. He was already dead. As Miller stared at his friend's dead face in dis-

A firefight is in progress in Thanh Binh District, Dinh Tuong Province, 24 April 1970. The machine gunner in the foreground is providing covering fire for 3rd Platoon as it moves forward on the right. The smoke is from a white phosphorus artillery round that just moments before had fallen short (Association archives).

belief, more casualties were being dragged across the road for treatment and evacuation. The enemy was no longer shooting.

Alvarado's men came out of the ditch, some with serious wounds. Specialist Vance "Spooky" Godfrey, led the withdrawal, firing as he ran. Alvarado was helping Specialist Fred Robinson who had most of the flesh torn off part of his backside and leg. Specialist Nick Phillips was shell-shocked, unable to hear and barely able to function. More seriously wounded was Lieutenant Weed, a man who wasn't even supposed to be in the fight. He had been struck in the back of the head by fragmentation and although conscious, was slurring his words, saying "I'm all right, tend to the others." He was not all right. Evacuated to the 24th Evacuation Hospital at Long Binh with six others, he died of his wounds early the next morning. It was Mother's Day. At home in Decatur, Alabama, his wife would give birth to their daughter a week later.

While D Company was fighting at Tnaot, The Rangers and Recon Platoon ran into another hornet's nest at Baray. In a series of fights throughout the afternoon, they and their supporting aviation killed eight and captured five VC. C Company was lifted west of Baray before dusk to support them and immediately spotted more enemy troops trying to flee, killing four of them. A Company's 1st Platoon ambushed six VC near Chantrea. They wounded and captured two of them who were armed with Chinese SKS rifles.

On May 11, D company swept back through Tnaot, finding nine enemy dead in the bunkers they had fought from. They also found weapons (including a destroyed mortar and the tripod of a .51 caliber machine gun), bloody bandages and uniform parts, and an assortment of abandoned ammunition. Some of the enemy dead had been hastily booby-trapped, a vain attempt at vengeance. A Company was lifted north to Tuol Spean, where the enemy was thought to have gone after being driven out of Tnaot. They found nothing there. C Company completed its sweep west of Baray without incident. The Recon Platoon moved north from Baray and the Rangers moved east. About 350 meters north of Baray, the Recon Platoon's point man spotted four VC in a box-shaped cluster of trees. As the platoon's lead squad rushed forward to engage them, they were met by a fusillade of fire from several directions, killing Specialist Willard D. O'Brien and wounding another man. By strange coincidence, O'Brien, like John Lonsdale, was a Forward Observer's radio operator acting as a rifleman when he died. C Company rushed north to help, forming a line behind which the Recon Platoon could withdraw under the protective fire of Air Force and Army aerial attacks. The aerial bombardment was credited with killing eight more of the enemy.

The next morning A Company spotted and engaged ten or more enemy, who returned fire. One American was wounded in the exchange and was evacuated after the fight. When the contact ended, A Company swept the area, finding three enemy dead and two weapons. Blood trails led to a nearby cluster of refugees. It would be the battalion's last fight in Cambodia.

On May 12, President Nixon ordered American forces to advance no further than 21.6 miles inside Cambodia. Few understood the logic. The enemy was on the run, Cambodia was asking for the U.S.–RVN assault to drive the communists out of the country, and there was no longer any serious fighting in Vietnam. Why stop when your opponent is on the ropes? That day, the "Seminole Raid" came to an end. Before the "Bearcats" returned to bases in Vietnam, they destroyed 28 tons of enemy munitions, uniforms, and a variety of miscellaneous supplies at Ba Thu alone. All participating elements left Cambodia before dark. The announcement in the Far East edition of the *Stars and Stripes*, the Armed Forces' newspaper, made it appear to be a major withdrawal, announcing that the 4th and 9th Infantry Divisions were leaving Cambodia. In reality, all the 9th Infantry Division had in the Parrot's Beak at the time was the 6-31st Infantry, E/75th Rangers, and half of C/2-4th Artillery. The 6-31st earned its second Valorous Unit Award and its third Vietnamese Cross of Gallantry with Palm.

After returning to Vietnam, the 6th Battalion operated in Hau Nghia Province under the 3rd Brigade 25th Infantry Division until its colors were returned to Ft Lewis, Washington for inactivation on October 13, 1970. After 2½ years in Vietnam, the "Bearcats" had earned the right to stand proudly as successors to a gallant regiment that had fought in Siberia, the Philippines, and Korea and whose 4th Battalion continued to serve in Vietnam's coastal highlands until 1971. Between the time the 6th Battalion's colors were unfurled at Ft Lewis in 1967 and furled in 1970, the "Bearcats" had earned eight unit awards.

The 6th Battalion 31st Infantry was reactivated at Fort Ord, California on November 21, 1975, as part of the 7th Infantry Division. It remained there until August 6, 1980, when it was inactivated. Its colors did not stay furled for long. On June 1, 1981, the battalion was reactivated at Fort Irwin, California as the infantry component of the National Training Center's opposing forces brigade. Its soldiers fought nearly every maneuver battalion in the continental U.S., rarely losing a battle. Inactivated on January 16, 1988, the 6th Battalion had marked its last years by teaching lessons that would later serve thousands of leaders well, probably saving countless American lives in combat in Grenada, Panama, Haiti, Afghanistan, and Iraq. Few units have done more for their country.

PART V. THE 10TH MOUNTAIN DIVISION ERA
by Grady A. Smith

28 Fort Drum:
Initial Deployments; Afghanistan

The Beginnings: Bosnia and Saudi Arabia
(Bosnia, 1999–2000)

As part of the 10th Mountain Division, the 4th Battalion, 31st Infantry has so far had six major deployments since 9/11. But even before that date, the battalion was dispatched from Fort Drum on overseas missions.

In the aftermath of Yugoslavia's breakup, ethnic and religious rivalries evolved into armed conflict between Bosnia and Croatia. The Bosnian War began in 1992, and the United Nations quickly established the UN Protection Force (UNPROFOR). It was an ugly war and a deadly one: more than 57,000 soldiers were killed as well as over 38,000 civilians, and during the fighting the first instance of a European genocide since the Second World War occurred. In July 1995 over 8,300 Bosnian Muslim men and boys were slaughtered. Exact figures may never be known.[1]

Responding particularly to this genocide, NATO launched Operation Deliberate Force in September, aimed at the Bosnian Serb Army commanded by General Ratko Mladic. The Operation was crucial in leading to the war's end. In October a sixty-day cease fire was established, with peace negotiations being conducted in Dayton Ohio. The resulting Dayton Peace Agreement was signed there November 21, 1995, and finalized in Paris in December.[2]

During that same month of December, NATO's Implementation Force (IFOR) in effect replaced UNPROFOR. Its task was to insure that the General Framework Agreement for Peace was in fact carried out. One year later, IFOR was replaced by SFOR, the Stabilization Force, also under the aegis of NATO. Its mission was to "deter hostilities and stabilize the peace, [and] contribute to a secure environment by providing a continued military presence."[3]

In 1996, the 4th Battalion 31st Infantry unfurled its colors at Fort Drum, New York, as 3rd Battalion, 14th Infantry was re-flagged as 4-31. The commander of 3-14, Lieutenant Colonel Harry Scott, became 4-31's first commander at Fort Drum as the Polar Bears joined the 2nd "Commando" Brigade, 10th Mountain Division. Three months later, Scott relinquished command to LTC Bryan Stephens who commanded 4-31 from 1996 to 1998.[4]

For nine years the NATO peacekeeping force was multinational, with the United States, Great Britain and France sharing responsibility in three different operational zones. In its area, the United States utilized elements of both active duty and National

Personnel with the Stabilization Force (SFOR) in Bosnia have collected weapons seized during Operation Harvest. They are at the BH steel factory in Zenica, Bosnia. The steel plant melts the weapons and renders them harmless metal as a free service in support of the SFOR mission in Bosnia (National Archives).

Guard divisions, which replaced each other sequentially. On August 31, 1999, a contingent of 10th Mountain Division troops, including the 4-31 under the command of LTC Don Phillips, cycled into Bosnia to replace 1st Cavalry Division troops.[5]

As one would expect, duties varied. Presence patrols were conducted to demonstrate the peacekeepers' readiness to enforce the Dayton Accords; from time to time weapons and ammunition were found and seized. Sometimes weapons were gathered under the umbrella of programs like Fall Harvest 99, which encouraged Bosnians to turn in illegal weapons.

In November the division's 2nd Brigade TF, including 4-31, carried out right-seat boundary transition rides with members of the Swedish Battalion. Right-seat rides are patrols accompanied by units experienced in their area of responsibility (AOR). On December 2, Task Force 4-31 closed out Camp Demi as the United States progressed toward a gradual drawdown of its forces.[6] The camp, with hill masses on two sides, presented a problem in defense and wasn't missed. Also in December, more than four feet of snow fell in the American sector.[7] Food, water and electricity were not affected, but the presence patrols became problematic for a while. U.S. forces greeted December 31, the eve of the new millennium, with a heightened security alert. Simply a precaution, it proved unneeded.[8]

In March, seven months after the 10th Mountain Division deployed to Bosnia, it was replaced by elements of the 49th Armored Division of the Texas National Guard and returned to Fort Drum.[9] The 4-31 was back home in New York state.

Saudi Arabia: 2000

Just as the Bosnian mission of 4-31 was rooted in events before the battalion even joined the 10th Mountain Division, so too for its deployment to Saudi Arabia. In the First Gulf War (August 1990 to February 1991), Saddam Hussein's army had been gutted. But the Iraqi dictator still held power and he still had SCUD missile capabilities. For this reason, Saudi Arabia, which was within range of those missiles, urgently asked the United States for assistance. During the summer of 1991, the United States sent two Patriot Air Defense Artillery battalions from Europe along with a brigade headquarters. They named the deployment Operation Desert Falcon. These Air Defense units required continuous ground security, and infantry units were tasked with that function. The 4th Battalion 31st Infantry took its turn in the rotation in 2000, spending several months securing the ADA units.[10]

Two Army Hawk surface-to-air missile systems, deployed in the desert in Saudi Arabia. (National Archives).

Immediate Post–9/11 Deployments

Afghanistan: 2001–2002

Al-Qaeda's four coordinated terrorist attacks on the United States September 11, 2001, killed nearly 3,000 people and injured over 6,000. As of 2015 the cost of the attacks totaled three trillion dollars.[11] In the wake of this catastrophe, the immediate question for the defense establishment was whether the terrorists had further targets in the continental

United States which they intended to hit as soon as they could. At the same time, the strategic question became: who did this, and what is the appropriate response? Both these questions impacted 4-31 simultaneously.

On the one hand, the Pentagon decided that selected high-value domestic targets needed to be protected at once. As a consequence, on September 23 Company C of 4-31, commanded by Captain Glenn Kozelka, was arriving at Aberdeen Proving Ground, Maryland as part of Operation Noble Eagle, having been alerted only hours earlier.[12] Their mission was to provide physical security for sensitive facilities at Aberdeen, buying time until reserve and National Guard units could deploy to replace regular army units.[13] By coincidence, the annual reunion of the 31st Infantry association was underway at Fort Drum with a formal banquet that evening. When the battalion commander announced this first, albeit domestic, deployment in the War on Terror to explain the empty tables in the room, the veterans of the 31st erupted in cheers.[14]

In the immediate aftermath of 9/11, elements of 4-31 were working furiously to prepare for overseas deployment and combat. It is an understatement to say these preparations were hampered by at first not knowing the enemy, the destination of the deployment, or what tactics and equipment the battlefield would require.

Soldiers from the 3rd Infantry Regiment, "the Old Guard," render honors as firefighters and rescue workers unfurl a huge American flag over the side of the Pentagon as rescue and recovery efforts continue following the September 11, 2001, terrorist attack (Department of Defense photograph from the National Archives).

But as intelligence quickly evolved, suspicion for the 9/11 attacks fell on the terrorist group al-Qaeda, and on the Taliban who ruled in Afghanistan where the terrorists were sheltering. With that country's mountainous terrain to focus on as well as a known enemy, planning ripened quickly.

The Afghan government was already fighting a civil war against a mix of ethnic groups called the Northern Alliance, which was working to unseat the Taliban from

Opposite, top: A high-angle view of the collapsed World Trade Center buildings. (National Archives).

  Bottom: Firefighters work to put out the flames moments after a highjacked jetliner crashed into the Pentagon at approximately 0930 on September 11, 2001 (photograph by CPL Jason Ingersoll, USMC, from the National Archives).

power in the capital, Kabul. To help that process along, the CENTCOM commander first recommended a conventional attack by a force of 60,000 troops, which would almost certainly have included 4-31. This plan would have required six months of preparation. Secretary of Defense Rumsfeld rejected it out of hand. "I want men on the ground now," he said.[15] Next day an alternative plan was offered in which Special Forces Operational Detachment A (ODA) teams, operating with Air Force Combat Control teams, would link up with the Northern Alliance to wrest control of the country from the Taliban. Less than a month after 9/11, ODA and AF teams were on the ground.[16]

Meanwhile, regular formations of American forces began to deploy to Afghanistan and other nearby nations both for security missions and in case significant changes to the ground situation required conventional forces. Less than a month after 9/11, elements of 4-31 were deploying, although in separate increments.

In late September, Polar Bears began deploying to Kuwait and Qatar to secure coalition equipment, facilities and personnel, becoming the first 10th Mountain troops to deploy overseas in the War on Terror.[17] The Anti-tank Platoon came under the operational control of 1-87 Infantry and in September deployed to Uzbekistan; later it would enter Afghanistan. Uzbekistan was critical because in the days following 9/11 the U.S. secured the use of that country's former Soviet airbase, Karshi-Khanabad, which quickly became known as K2. The base would become the chief airhead for supplies and personnel arriving in the area of operations, but the runways needed lengthening to take USAF aircraft, and the infrastructure was generally in a rundown condition. While this work went on, 1-87 and the 4-31 Anti-tank Platoon provided both security and humanitarian support.[18]

By early October, Company A was in Kuwait providing security for U.S. facilities and convoy escort for equipment in transit.[19] The A Company commander, Captain Jon Stevens, ensured his troops maintained their readiness to fight with constant live-fire exercises between security missions. A reinforced platoon from Company B, led by Lieutenant Magner, deployed to Qatar to secure CENTCOM's forward headquarters. Company C returned from Aberdeen Proving Ground when it was relieved a few weeks after its deployment by mobilized National Guard troops, and deployed to K2 airfield, Uzbekistan, to reinforce 1-87 Infantry and the 4-31 Anti-tank Platoon. Meanwhile, the battalion's command group remained at Fort Drum with the remainder of Headquarters Company and Company B,[20] and trained a composite formation of the Division's remaining infantry, artillery, engineers and air defense units under the moniker, Task Force Polar Bear. They all badly wanted to join their comrades overseas, but their mission was to secure the installation and stay ready for more orders to deploy overseas.[21]

In October, A Company shifted from Uzbekistan to Kuwait, and for several months pulled convoy escort and security. That month the remainder of B Company also deployed, to Qatar. The battalion commander, command sergeant major and the battalion's Tactical Command Center remained at Fort Drum.[22]

By late October the Northern Alliance, buttressed by U.S. air support, began to capture towns and villages. Early in November it controlled most of Northern Afghanistan and on November 13 its forces occupied Kabul. In December, Hamid Karzai was installed as the new leader of Afghanistan.

Meanwhile the 4-31 Tactical Operations Center remained at Fort Drum. The CO, LTC Steve Townsend and CSM Dan Wood visited the scattered elements of 4-31 in December and again in February, urging the leaders to keep their Polar Bears ready for whatever might happen and then returning to Fort Drum after each visit.[23]

Air movement of A Company, 4th Battalion, 31st Infantry, to Marzak, Afghanistan, 2001–2002 (Association Archives, courtesy Scanlin collection).

During their February trip, LTC Townsend and CSM Wood went to Bagram Airbase in Afghanistan to meet with the 2nd Brigade commander, COL Kevin Wilkerson and LTC Paul LaCamera, the commander of 1-87 Infantry, in order to plan the deployment of 4-31 to relieve 1-87 in place. While there, they attended the final planning for Operation Anaconda, scheduled to begin before February ended, though there were no plans for 4-31 to participate.[24]

Although the old Afghan government had been ousted, some of its Taliban and al-Qaeda soldiers still sheltered in that country's formidable mountain terrain around the Shah-i-Kot Valley. There they had pre-positioned ammunition stores and other warfighting equipment. The allies began planning a major sweep to preempt any spring campaign.

Called Operation Anaconda, it involved the first use of significant conventional forces in a direct combat mode. MG Franklin L. Hagenbeck, CG of the 10th Mountain Division, was put in command of the operation. Its concept would have Afghan Military Forces (AMF) and American SOA teams and Combat Tactical Air Controllers push Taliban and al-Qaeda remnants up the valley and into an international blocking force, placed to prevent enemy soldiers from escaping to sanctuary in Pakistan. The block consisted of U.S. and Canadian conventional forces, and Special Operations units from Australia, New Zealand, Germany, Norway, Denmark and the Netherlands.

The operation began March 1, 2002, and lasted almost three weeks. It had mixed reviews. Eight of the 15 friendly KIAs were American. None were Polar Bears. As they prepared at Bagram, U.S. forces were told to ready themselves to meet from 150 to 200 of the enemy. However, initial enemy resistance was larger and stiffer than anticipated and, with the uncertain performance of the Afghan Militia, the CG of the 10th Mountain Division requested additional infantry. Only the various elements of 4-31 scattered around the CENTCOM theater were immediately available. Within 24 hours Company C was moving from Uzbekistan and Company A from Kuwait. Shortly after closing on Bagram, Company C was committed into the Shah-i-Kot Valley attached to 3rd Brigade, 101st Air Assault Division. Company A was task organized with the 3rd Battalion, Princess Patricia's Canadian Light Infantry (PPCLI) for a follow-on operation. The commander of 2nd Brigade, 10th Mountain Division, Colonel Kevin Wilkerson, called LTC Townsend at Fort Drum and ordered him to deploy immediately with his tactical command post and ready the rest of the battalion to follow. During Anaconda, the Polar Bears would draw their first enemy blood since Vietnam.[25]

After a week of battle, the enemy casualties were estimated at around 500 and the fighting was still ongoing. Eight of the 15 friendly KIAs were American. None were Polar Bears. LTC Townsend and CSM Wood and the staff of 4-31's tactical command post arrived in country toward the end of Anaconda, assumed control of A and C companies and the Anti-tank Platoon, and began planning for their first operation.

But before Anaconda wrapped up, Operation Harpoon began. This was a less elaborate, more surgical operation in Paktia Province, in the same general area as Operation Anaconda. Operation Harpoon ran from March 13 to 19, and was basically a battalion-sized mission under the 3rd Battalion, Princess Patricia's Canadian Light Infantry. It included A Company 4-31, which had arrived in the AO a few days before.[26] The force was inserted on the northern end of a mountain feature called the Whale, extremely rugged terrain riddled with caves and enemy supply caches. The Whale's elevation was about 6,500 feet at the base, and up to 10,000 feet at the spine. It was over three miles long and close to a mile and a half wide. Intelligence talked about 60 to 100 enemy troops scattered along the ridge.[27]

The Polar Bears had been operating at close to sea level since their arrival in the AO. Now, less than a week after displacing to Afghanistan, they were humping the higher elevations of the Whale with up to ninety pounds of ruck. LT Andrew Exum, a platoon leader in A Company, had bulked up by ten pounds through some intense conditioning during convoy escort duty. Before the battalion returned to Fort Drum in April, he had lost that ten pounds and another ten besides.[28] As one soldier said, "The mountains humble everybody."[29]

On March 15, while the 4-31 tactical command post was preparing to go operational in Bagram, PPCLI scouts reported a bunker on the ridgeback. A Company, 4-31 was given the mission of taking the position. This they did quickly and efficiently with AT-4 light anti-tank weapons, eliminating three defenders in the process.[30]

Next day, A and C companies assembled on the battalion headquarters at Bagram and found a mission waiting for them. They were to sweep a mountain mass over 10,000 feet high known as Takur Ghar about ten kilometers southeast of the whale, as well as the valley off its eastern slope. Their primary task was to conduct a "sensitive site exploitation" to recover material from the top of Takur Ghar where a special operations MH-47 Chinook helicopter inserting Rangers was downed by enemy fire in the opening days of Operation Anaconda. They would also kill or capture enemy remnants, and search for

This view of LZ Hawk on Takur Ghar, Afghanistan, provides a graphic picture of the formidable terrain, 2001–2002 (Association Archives, courtesy Scanlin collection).

intelligence materials and weapons, ammunition and other supplies. C Company, the Anti-tank Platoon and the battalion TAC would clear the summit ridgeline and the crash site, and provide overwatch for A Company as it swept the valley below.[31]

The insertion on March 18 was dicey. The Polar Bears of C Company and the battalion's mortars exited the CH-47 500 meters short of the summit. LTC Townsend described it:

> We landed on top of the ridgeline and as I looked out the windows as my troops were disembarking I thought, "Where in the heck has he landed? I can't tell that we have landed." Well, as I came off the ramp myself, I realized that he had not landed. The ridge was so narrow that his rear two wheels only and his ramp were on the mountain. His ramp was on the ridgeline and his front two wheels were hovering out in the air and he was at max power. In fact, my Soldiers were clinging to small shrubs and bushes on the ridge to keep from tumbling down the ridge and a medical aid bag and an assault pack did in fact go tumbling down the ridge.[32]

C Company was unopposed on the summit though there were numerous al-Qaeda bodies there, a lot of prepared positions, weapons and supplies that included American equipment left over from the crash and the subsequent battle between the enemy fighters and the Rangers. A meticulous search yielded numerous enemy documents which were gathered by CPT Sepp Scanlin, the battalion S2, as well as a trove of enemy weapons and supplies. Although living in the field at high altitude, the al-Qaeda fighters had not been

A Company, 4th Battalion 31st Infantry patrolling Sur Bagham Khwar, Afghanistan, known as Ginger Valley, 2001–2002 (photo Association archives, courtesy Scanlin collection).

suffering. The search yielded plentiful food stores and top-of-the-line outdoor clothing, sleeping bags and equipment made by western outfitters and purchased by al-Qaeda. The troops also found and destroyed an al-Qaeda command post cleverly concealed in a large cleft in the mountain's summit. It had a Motorola Radio base-station powered by a car battery which was recharged by a solar panel. It was heated by a wood stove with a chimney that routed the exhaust underground many meters away and discharged it at the base of an evergreen tree to help dissipate and conceal the heat and smoke.[33]

In the valley below, A Company, accompanied by battalion CSM Dan Wood, began its sweep before C Company was in overwatch above. There was plenty to find down there, both for intelligence and for warfighting. The company wired the munitions and weapons for demolition and fired them off as they progressed along. Once, they blew a very large ammunition cache that had been stashed in a cave, and it spewed fragments and scrap material out of the mouth of the cave for another six hours.[34]

A bit farther down the valley, A Company came upon another position, and this one was occupied by a single enemy soldier dressed in odd pieces of civilian clothing and armed with an American M249 light machine gun. Several Polar Bears fired on him at the same time. He never got off a round. Inside the position there was a mix of both Soviet and American arms and equipment, including U.S. weapons and gear taken from Americans who had been killed earlier in Operation Anaconda.[35]

Later that day, PFC David Vasquez was wounded when he threw a grenade into a bunker to clear it. A bounce-back piece of shrapnel opened a gash in his arm and it bled heavily. Once the medics stopped the bleeding, he was carried back to the landing zone.[36]

The next morning, the battalion S3, Major Tom Christensen, with the battalion TAC atop Takur Ghar, directed the C Company commander CPT Kozelka to destroy the bulk of the enemy weapons ammunition and equipment that had been recovered. The 41st Engineer Sappers carefully stacked the material and rigged it for demolition. Concerned with how close the troops were to the rigged pile of material, LTC Townsend directed the troops to move further away and to the other side of a low intervening crest. Still, it was not far enough. The pile blew in a large explosion that shook the earth. As the troops hugged the ground, weapons parts and debris rained down on them including a large barrel from a Russian-made DSHK heavy machine gun that bounced onto the rocky slope yards from the battalion TAC. Fortunately, no one was injured.

Another brief but tense incident followed when two troopers from C Company went missing prior to extraction. They had asked their team leader to go down the ridge to search for the medical aid bag that had tumbled down the mountain during the insertion. As if it were a training exercise at Fort Drum, he allowed the two of them to descend the ridge away from the over-watch of their platoon without a radio, a map, or even a compass. They became mis-oriented on their return and took a circuitous route back to their perimeter. Their delayed return caused much consternation until they finally clambered back up onto the ridgetop to everyone's relief.[37]

The battalion continued with its sweep of the terrain over the next few days, destroying numerous bunkers and cave complexes, and many large ammunition caches. The only al-Qaeda encountered were already dead.

Then Operation Polar Harpoon was over. The battalion was designated as the quick reaction force for Task Force Mountain, conducting a few small-scale missions and several rehearsals. During this time, U.S. Army Central (ARCENT) decided to clean up the order of battle and directed the 1-87 Infantry and, despite their short time in country, the 4-31 to redeploy to Fort Drum.[38]

The route back ran from Bagram to Uzbekistan via C-17, then on to Germany, and from there to Fort Drum via commercial jet. The Polar Bears were home.

Afghanistan–Djibouti–Iraq: 2003–2004

After eight months in Afghanistan beginning in September 2001, followed by a 13-month stay at its home station at Fort Drum, the 4th Battalion 31st Infantry deployed again. The geographical scatter during this deployment was even more pronounced than the previous one, and included not only South Asia but also Africa.

With significantly differing missions, the line companies inevitably separated. Both A Company and the Headquarters went to Afghanistan, B Company to Iraq, and C Company and the Mortar Platoon to the Republic of Djibouti on the Horn of Africa—the easternmost projection of the African continent.

On March 11, 2003, only a few weeks before scheduled deployment, a Blackhawk helicopter on a training mission crashed in a remote area of Fort Drum, killing eleven GIs. Four members of the 10th Aviation Brigade died in the crash. The other seven fatalities were from C Company, 4th Battalion 31st Infantry. The Polar Bear fatalities were

SGT John L. Eichenlaub, Jr., SGT Joshua M. Harapko, SPC Shawn A. Mayerscik, SSG Brian L. Pavlich, PFC Andrew D. Stevens, PFC Stryder O. Stoutenburg and PFC Tommy C. Young. The 10th Aviation Brigade's fatalities were CPT Christopher E. Britton, CW3 Kenneth L. Miller, SPC Barry M. Stephens and SPC Lucas V. Tripp.

The losses devastated both units, as well as the 2nd Brigade Combat Team and indeed the entire 10th Mountain Division and Fort Drum. Major General Franklin Hagenbeck, the division commander, said, "Our hearts are heavy today as we grieve with the families of our fallen comrades." But all of the 4–31 deployments took place as scheduled.

A Company in Afghanistan, May–December 2003

During the thirteen months the battalion was at Fort Drum following its initial deployment, the Coalition's Afghan strategy continued to evolve based on tactical successes. From decisive ground combat aimed at destroying fragmentary units of Taliban and al-Qaeda, the strategy progressed to humanitarian aid and furthering the new Afghan government.

In May 2003 A Company, together with the Headquarters Company, operated from Camp Phoenix in the Afghan capital of Kabul. Its mission was to conduct security operations for Combined Joint Task Force Phoenix as it trained Afghan National Army (ANA) units. In addition, select members of the battalion were tapped as trainers for the Afghan soldiers.

B Company in Iraq, March 2003–April 2004

Active combat in Iraq began March 19, 2003, and lasted until April 30. Baghdad itself fell on April 9. The invasion proper concluded when Tikrit, Saddam Hussein's home town, was captured on April 13. Later, on December 13, Saddam himself was captured on a farm near Tikrit. Although estimates of battle casualties fluctuated greatly, a reasonable picture can still be formed. Friendly casualties in the Iraq invasion phase included 139 American military killed in action, about 9,200 Iraqi combatants KIA, and about 3,750 Iraqi non-combatant deaths.

B Company was inserted into this intense combat in March, from the very beginning of Operation Iraqi Freedom. It conducted base defense in support of Combined Special Operations Joint Task Force Arabian Peninsula. The company secured the base of operations for the 5th and 10th Special Forces Groups and augmented their combat activities. While the Mortar Platoon and both A and C Companies returned to Fort Drum in December 2003, B Company remained in Iraq until April 2004. In August of that year, nine members of Bravo Company were awarded Bronze Stars for their service in Iraq, while two more Polar Bears received Army Commendation Medals.[39]

C Company and the Mortar Platoon
in Djibouti, May–December 2003

The Combined Joint Task Force—Horn of Africa (CJTF-HOA) was established at Camp Lejeune, North Carolina, on October 19, 2002. Its mission: "to conduct operations in the Combined Joint Operations Area to enhance partner nation capacity, promote regional security and stability, dissuade conflict, and protect US and coalition interests."[40] In the following month, headquarters personnel of the new organization embarked for East Africa aboard the USS *Mount Whitney*, a command ship of the U.S. Navy, and arrived off the coast of Djibouti on December 8. The goal was to move the headquarters ashore to Camp Lemonier in Djibouti City.

When the country was a colony of France, the camp was an installation of the French Foreign Legion. Later it was used by the Djibouti Armed Forces. When the headquarters of CJTF-HOA showed up, the camp was much the worse for wear. "Some buildings were concrete shells and had been stripped of interior fixtures, pipes and wiring, while the roofs of several structures had collapsed. Goats roamed the property and birds had taken roost in several of the abandoned structures. The former swimming pool had been used as a trash dump and was a borderline hazardous material site."[41] By May, the camp was livable, and on May 6 personnel and equipment began displacing from the USS *Mount Whitney* into the refurbished facilities.

Two days before, on May 4, the Polar Bears arrived with the mission of installation security as well as "detecting, disrupting and defeating transitional terrorist groups" operating in the area. In addition, they were to conduct civil-military and humanitarian operations.[42]

In July 2003, Djibouti's neighbor, Ethiopia formed up a new anti-terrorism battalion out of three reconnaissance companies. It allowed the U.S. to station American military members, including the Polar Bears, at Camp Hurso to help train the new battalion. Weapons training included shotguns and 9mm pistols as well as AK-47 firing for familiarization. With the assistance of a Heavy Marine Helicopter Company the soldiers sharpened both day and night external sling loading, while the Mortar Platoon honed their skills on the ballistic computer and the plotting board. Before leaving Ethiopia, the Polar Bears provided a security mission in Addis Ababa, the capital.[43]

Both C Company and the Mortar Platoon were back at Fort Drum in December.

Iraq: May 2004–June 2005

The 2nd Brigade Combat Team, including the 4th Battalion 31st Infantry less B Company, deployed to Iraq in May of 2004. Bravo Company, which had returned from an extended Iraq deployment just a few weeks before the 2nd BCT left New York State, remained at Fort Drum. It rejoined 4-31 in-country the following February.[44] During the interim, B Company, 1st Battalion 509th Parachute Infantry Regiment left Fort Polk to bring 4-31 to full strength until Bravo Company 4-31 rejoined the battalion in Iraq.[45]

After completing a period of training in Kuwait, the 2nd BCT deployed to Baghdad. The Polar Bears operated in the Kadhimiya district, about five miles from the city's center. The district contains Camp Justice where Saddam Hussein was executed, as well as the al-Kadhimiya Mosque, the third holiest mosque in Shia Islam. The previous March, just prior to the 4th Battalion's deployment, an IED was detonated at the Mosque, killing 75 and injuring hundreds.[46]

The battalion suffered one KIA during the deployment. 1LT Adam Malson and the men in his A Company platoon were manning a checkpoint on the outskirts of Kadhimiya District. They heard a series of explosions coming from the area of a shrine where Ashura, the Shia Day of Remembrance, was being observed. Malson split his platoon, leaving half to man the checkpoint, and led the rest toward the sound of the explosions. When they reached the shrine he deployed his troops around it to afford protection for the worshippers. He then noticed a woman in a burning automobile and rushed over to help her. At that point a suicide bomber directly behind him detonated the explosives in his vest, killing Malson and his Iraqi interpreter. The woman in the car survived. 1LT Malson was posthumously awarded the Bronze Star and Purple Heart for his actions. His wife, an MP 1LT, was also stationed in the area—they had met in ROTC at Michigan State University. Governor Jennifer Granholm of Michigan ordered flags lowered in Malson's honor.[47]

In addition to manning checkpoints, the battalion also ran patrols in the district. On the night of January 26 while on one of these patrols, the Polar Bears foiled the kidnapping of eight Iraqis.[48] It was an attempt to frighten Iraqi voters into staying home from the first-ever national elections on January 30, the most significant event during the battalion's deployment.[49] On the day of the election itself, the battalion provided security for polling places in the Kadhimiya district. A very creditable voter turnout of about 60 percent contributed to the success of the process. It was a tactical victory for the 2nd BCT and the Polar Bears, and a strategic defeat for the insurgency.[50]

The battalion was then tasked to secure the Abu Ghraib prison from any insurgent attacks. Toward the end of its tour, it conducted task force level air assaults and raids in enemy strongholds south of Baghdad.[51]

In June, the Polar Bears returned to their home station at Fort Drum. The 4th Battalion, 31st Infantry's actions on this deployment earned it a Meritorious Unit Commendation.[52]

29 Iraq and Afghanistan

Iraq: August 2006–November 2007[1]

The battalion departed Fort Drum from Wheeler-Sack Army Airfield on August 15, 2006, heading for Kuwait. After two weeks there on the ground, the Polar Bears moved to Baghdad by C-17 Globemaster, where CH-47 Chinooks waited to take them to Forward Operating Base (FOB) Mahmudiyah in the heart of the Iraqi combat zone.

The battalion's AO was part of what the press had dubbed the "the Triangle of Death," a name it would unfortunately live up to. Mahmudiyah district began about 25 miles southwest of Baghdad. Key terrain included the Euphrates River, which served as the western boundary of the 4-31 AO. Population centers were the towns of Yusufiyah, Mahmudiyah and nearby Qarghuli Village. Musayib, with a power plant that at full capacity could furnish about a third of the country's entire electrical needs, was downstream from Mahmudiyah on the Euphrates. Farmland latticed with numerous irrigation ditches and trails blanketed the AO. The area contained about a million inhabitants.

Insurgents still controlled key areas when the battalion arrived. Qarghuli Village was a terrorist command node where the tribal elders decided on objectives, funding and priorities. The Mullah Fayyad highway was a de facto main supply route into Baghdad for the terrorists.[2]

On October 2, 2nd BCT launched Operation Commando Hunter II. TF 4-31 designated its part of the 2nd BCT mission as Operation Polar Rock Blizzard. The 4-31 conducted raids on the villages of Rushdi Mullah and Taraq, west of Al Yusufiyah. They searched along a series of canals that intelligence suspected of harboring arms and supplies. During the next two weeks, the Polar Bears found stores of IED material, machine guns and other weapons stockpiled in more than 150 locations, together with U.S. equipment and weapons taken from an Apache helicopter shot down a year earlier.[3]

The larger purpose of the operation was to wrest the tactical initiative away from the terrorists. The 4-31 TF included five Abrams tanks from the 4th Infantry Division and a battalion from the Iraqi Army (IA). The plan for the operation called for fast, violent attacks on a number of terrorist sanctuaries and safe houses. Tactics included patrols along enemy-controlled roads, raids on the homes of insurgent loyalists, and military roadblocks and vehicle strongpoints at strategic locations.

The terrorists reacted to this incursion with violence. Soon after the operation began, an IED completely destroyed the vehicle of the IA battalion commander, LTC Muhammad, killing him and every member of his command group. Later that same day, another IED destroyed the track of an Abrams, disabling it. Almost immediately another Abrams secured the scene while the original tank was repaired. Meanwhile the insurgents deliberately killed and wounded Iraqi civilians, many of whom were medevaced along with American casualties. One of those American casualties was 1LT John Quilty—another IED cost him his right hand and leg. Enemy snipers were also active and effective, taking the life of SPC Sateion Greenlee.[4] But at the end of the operation in late October, all objectives had been taken.

In the days immediately following Operation Polar Rock Blizzard, the debris of destroyed American vehicles littered the road network. In one instance, the superstructure of a supply truck lay thirty feet beyond its undercarriage.[5] Even so, large amounts of enemy arms and ordnance had been seized and awaited destruction.

Enemy retaliation was always expected during this period, and it was seldom long in coming. A newly established Battle Position, BP 155, had been set up by A Company, and the angry insurgents launched a machine gun attack on it. Chaplain Jeff Bryan describes the Polar Bear defense:

> A platoon, led by SFC Del Rodriguez, responded with amazing courage and ferocity. They called in mortar support, AH-64 Apache helicopter gunships armed with lethal Hellfire missiles, Scout sniper teams, and even two British GR-4 Tornado jets for support. The fighter planes came screaming overhead, strafing the militants with blazing firepower from their 27mm Mauser cannons. The helicopters pounded away at the insurgents, and the snipers systematically took them out, one by one, with their long range, Barrett M-107 sniper rifles.[6]

Rodriguez was later awarded a Silver Star for his actions while leading the defense of BP 155.

The Polar Bear task force pushed right back, maintaining the initiative with constant pressure on insurgent forces. The next major objective was Qarghuli village, still very much in enemy control. It was a major hub for the Sunni insurgency against the Iraqi government that replaced Saddam Hussein. The Qarghuli tribe's leadership was a decision-making body for the terrorists and controlled not only objectives and tactics, but also financing and recruiting.

Key terrain started with the road running through Qarghuli village, designated Route Malibu by American forces. This route, dense with IEDs and dangerous in the extreme, was enemy-controlled territory and would have to be contested. In addition, the Euphrates River, besides constituting the battalion's western boundary, was routinely crossed by the enemy as an escape route out of the AO. On the other side of the river lay Anbar Province, called "the cradle of the insurgency."[7] Finally, the northern sector of the greater Qarghuli area contained a thermal power plant constructed by the Russians for Saddam Hussein. The plant occupied a huge campus, and although there was an American OP manned and functioning inside its precincts, the plant was not a completely secure American installation.

The main mission for this next phase was to pacify Qarghuli village. To do that 4-31 would have to take away control of Route Malibu from the insurgents.

In early November D Company fielded the first pre-dawn patrol into Qarghuli, leaving an abandoned water treatment plant at 0300. The patrol's route took it through Qarghuli cemetery, "a plot of land about the size of a football field situated on a small hill. The cemetery was full of shallow graves, some of which were dug up by scavenging animals. Countless human bones covered the ground."[8]

As loudspeakers blared the 0500 call to prayer, the patrol entered the first targeted house in the village. Interpreters questioned the males and then the patrol moved on. A total of eight houses were searched and the residents questioned. The patrol soon returned to the water treatment plant.

During the rest of November, attacks on battle positions increased. Enemy small arms and mortar assaults ramped up, and sometimes covered the sudden approach of a vehicle-borne IED. Toward the end of November, for example, BP147 came under such an attack. B Company soldiers saw a truck speeding up the road toward their compound. Focusing their fire on the vehicle, they blew it off the road, but not without cost. Nicholas "Doc" Rogers, one of the company medics, was killed by small arms fire as he took over a momentarily unmanned machine gun.[9]

November 25, 2006, was the day 4-31 escalated from merely patrolling to a movement to seize and hold the southern sector of Qarghuli village, and ultimately to control Route Malibu. Right behind the infantry, EOD teams followed in their vehicles. Route Malibu was already holed by many IED detonations, and the EOD vehicles moved slowly and cautiously. But very shortly a huge explosion fractured one of their Meerkat vehicles. Its driver was quickly medevaced, and survived.

Next day LTC Michael Infanti, commander of 4-31, moved his command group from the water treatment facility onto Route Malibu. Within minutes an IED blew his vehicle apart. His interpreter was killed, and he and all other passengers were wounded. "Parts of the battalion commander's vehicle littered the ground. A couple of the nearly 400-lb. doors had been blown off the truck. Half of the vehicle was completely gone…. Infanti himself lay on the road in shock, tended to by his combat medic."[10] But before the medic could work on him, Infanti had to be gotten out of his Humvee. His own door was

Soldiers load casualties onto a UH-60 Blackhawk helicopter after encountering an IED, September 2004 (U.S. Army photograph by SPC Algernon E. Crawley, Jr., National Archives).

jammed, and the vehicle was leaking fuel on him. "My left arm was useless, the roof was caved in which prevented me from going under the top of the seat [to another exit] and my door was caved in a little which prevented us from getting it open."[11] His troops pulled the door off the Humvee, using a device called the rat claw, which they wrapped around the door and attached to another vehicle. They were able to pull the door off in a couple of minutes so the medic could start working on Infanti.[12] EOD personnel checking the site later concluded that Polar Bear 6's vehicle had been hit by a combination of two Italian anti-tank mines and two 30-lb. shaped charges. In a week LTC Infanti returned to duty. Only later was it found that his back had been broken.[13]

But when the smoke cleared, the 4th Battalion, 31st Infantry owned the southern part of Qarghuli village. As the weeks passed, it increased the number of its battle positions and continued its aggressive patrolling, both on foot and by vehicle along Route Malibu, and in the adjacent road network. For their part, the insurgents brought in fighters from all over Iraq. The pace of enemy small arms, recoilless rifle and mortar attacks on the BPs as well as IED assaults on the road net continued undiminished.[14] As a result, cavalry and armored units began cycling into TF Polar Bear to add more muscle to road patrols and strong points.

The tempo of combat increased. More than once, a platoon would experience half a dozen IED strikes in a single day.[15] Perhaps the best perspective on the continuing impact of battalion operations came from SFC Jay-R Strawder, who deployed with the battalion as the maintenance platoon sergeant and motor sergeant.

The battalion deployed with about 175 pieces of rolling vehicles, including trailers, as well as a few M88 tracked recovery vehicles. The platoon was comprised of about 40 to 45 soldiers, which included both small arms and commo repair personnel, as well as the welders and the officers. The number of vehicles authorized in garrison was considerably less, so the platoon was understaffed for the actual work load. Strawder lost count of the number of times vehicles were hit by IEDs and small arms fire. He did track the number of vehicles that were totaled as he processed the paperwork to replace them: 53 vehicles were non-repairable and had to be coded out to get a replacement. That process took six to eight weeks and sometimes longer. In addition, on the trucks that were catastrophic losses, Strawder would have to ensure that no traces of human remains were left inside before they were shipped.

Meanwhile, maintenance personnel did their best to keep repairable vehicles going. Three outposts were established with small Maintenance Support Teams, often just one soldier. In addition, a rotational service team would be dispatched from time to time, and would spend as much as two weeks repairing as many vehicles as possible at one of the outposts. Then it would move on to the next maintenance outpost.

Strawder believes the battalion lost more soldiers on Route Malibu than anywhere else during the entire deployment. The first time he rode down Malibu, his truck, full of service and repair parts, was hit by two IEDs. The explosions cracked half the windshields he was taking to the D Company outpost to replace those damaged earlier. Strawder never lost any soldiers out of the Maintenance Platoon, but his company—F Company—lost two truck drivers. Finally, during the last half of the tour, Fox Company took a fuel truck and mixed JP8 and Mogas, which they called MO8. Soldiers then drove to where the reeds were high and sprayed them with MO8 and set the growth on fire. This cleared Route Malibu of a major source of concealment and kept the Sunni insurgents from hiding and command-detonating as vehicles drove by.[16]

At the beginning of January 2007, President Bush acknowledged the stubborn tempo of the Iraq War with a plan he called "the New Way Forward."[17] From a military point of view, the plan involved sending five additional brigades—20,000 more troops—to Iraq, as well as extending tours from twelve to fifteen months. This latter provision directly impacted the 4th Battalion 31st Infantry, and in fact the entire 2nd Brigade of the 10th Mountain Division.

As 2007 began, the enemy found his operational area much more constricted and the number of his routes of withdrawal significantly reduced. The terrorist response included the use of more complex guerrilla tactics and bringing in additional experienced fighters from outside the Triangle of Death.

What the insurgents had in mind was foreshadowed in a daisy chain ambush on a four-vehicle convoy from D Company. The core of the ambush was eight 155mm IEDs—the daisy chain—coupled with RPGs and machine guns. When the ambush was sprung, SSG Tony Smith maneuvered his troops out of the kill zone and into a roadside house, almost certainly preventing them from being overrun. Smith was later awarded a Bronze Star for valor. Troops in the daisy chain ambush were convinced its outcome would have included the kidnapping of any survivors.[18]

Their suspicions were based on past events. On June 16, 2006, an OP manned by three members of the 101st Airborne Division was attacked. One soldier was killed and the other two disappeared. The night of June 19, their bodies were spotted from an OP near the power plant at Yusufiyah, but because of the danger of booby traps recovery was put off until daylight. At dawn it became clear that both the KIAs and the approaches to them had been rigged with explosives. It took twelve hours before the bodies, which were severely traumatized, could be moved.[19] Sometime before they were left near the power plant OP, they had been tied behind a pickup truck and dragged through the village of Yusufiyah.[20] DNA testing was required for positive identification. This incident was behind the D Company soldiers' concerns about an ambush to kidnap.

Eleven months after the kidnapping of the 101st soldiers, the scenario was repeated. Regular patrols along the east bank of the Euphrates had been watching for terrorists trying to penetrate the river boundary undetected and slip northeast into Baghdad. In the predawn on May 3, a D Company patrol located an IED on Malibu. Later that day an EOD team began a routine exploratory sequence on the ordnance, but the IED detonated with a massive explosion that cratered the terrain directly adjacent to Malibu. That night the insurgents placed two additional smaller IEDs inside the new crater. The ordnance was spotted next morning by another patrol and detonated, but the resulting craters very nearly left Malibu impassible. Because other road options in the immediate area were already saturated with IEDs and unusable, keeping Malibu open was critical.[21]

For the next several nights, D Company was tasked with a crater overwatch mission. Two Humvees with four men per vehicle would site themselves on Malibu with each Humvee facing away from the other to give visual coverage of the road in both directions. On the night of May 11–12, 1st Platoon dispatched the patrol a bit after midnight. The two Humvees situated themselves about 165 feet apart, facing away from each other. Seven U.S. soldiers and one Iraqi private, acting as an interpreter, made up the patrol.[22] They were SFC James Connell, SGT Anthony Shober, PFC Joseph Anzack, Jr., PFC Christopher Murphy, PFC Daniel Courneya, PV2 Byron Fouty, and SPC Alex Jimenez. The Iraqi private was Saaba Barak Shaharay.[23]

The insurgents initiated the ambush at approximately 0445 hours by lobbing Russian

A Talon robot from Explosives Ordnance Disposal checks a road for IEDs in Iraq (U.S. Army photograph by SPC Charles Gill, 10 May 2006, National Archives).

concussion grenades into the turrets of both Humvees simultaneously. The vehicles were covered by the terrorists to kidnap soldiers if possible, or to kill anyone likely to escape. They grabbed Anzack from one vehicle and Jimenez and Fouty from the other. Murphy, wounded, made it out of his Humvee and fought back hand to hand, escaping momentarily. Seconds later he was killed. Meanwhile insurgents dropped satchel charges into the turrets, setting the vehicles on fire. None of the other soldiers made it out.[24]

Two quick reaction forces (QRF) moved cautiously toward the ambush site, one from either direction. Both approaches had been hastily sown with IEDs, so closing in to the ambush site took some time. Meanwhile, helicopters scrambled and searched with night vision devices for any escape vehicles, and both EOD and forensics personnel were on the way.[25]

Moving quickly in the following days, U.S. forces increased the number of troops in the area from 1,000 to 4,000 and saturated the Triangle of Death with search teams.[26] The result was "hundreds of convoy patrols, raids, searches, and dismounted operations … [there was an] incredible array of assets, support, and detainees swelling the interior of each of our battlefield positions. BP 153 had bloated from about 30 men to over 400 in one week."[27] In the meantime, al-Qaeda claimed to be holding the three men, and that if they were to stay alive the Coalition Force had to abandon its search.[28] Anzack, Jimenez and Fouty were officially classified as DUSTWUN: Duty Status—Whereabouts Unknown. "DUSTWUN" soon became shorthand for the incident itself as well as its aftermath.

Gen. David Petraeus, commander of U.S. forces in Iraq, said on Friday, May 18, that "As of this morning, we thought there were at least two that were probably still alive. At one point in time, there was a sense that one of them might have died, but again, we just don't know."[29]

Then on May 23 the body of PFC Anzack was found floating in the Euphrates River with a bullet wound to the head.[30] The Islamic State of Iraq on 4 June posted an internet video showing preparations for the May 12 ambush, then apparently the ambush itself, and finally a statement in Arabic that the soldiers were now dead because U.S. forces would not abandon the search.[31]

Maximum efforts continued. On June 9 Coalition Forces raided "a suspected al-Qaeda in Iraq safe house" and found the ID cards of the two soldiers.[32] But finding Jimenez and Fouty themselves, alive or dead, stubbornly eluded all efforts.

Inevitably, the units supplementing the search in the Triangle of Death were obliged to return to their areas of operation and their primary missions. By the end of June, the expanded search force had reverted to normal levels. The 4th Battalion 31st Infantry and the 2nd Brigade Combat Team of the 10th Mountain Division resumed their earlier missions as well, while continuing the search at the same level of intensity.

Just one example of the continuing search was Operation Polar Schism. On July 6, a force of Polar Bears and Iraqi Army soldiers carried out an air assault on Owesat, a small village on the west bank of the Euphrates River. While two mosques were searched by Iraqi soldiers, 4-31 men cordoned off the targeted buildings. Informants had said the mosques were being used as safe houses. Half a dozen locals suspected of having knowledge of the missing men were rounded up and evacuated for questioning.[33]

Informants had clearly grown to trust the Polar Bears after being almost a year in country. The first patrol into Qarghuli Village in early November had been a difficult mission, with little useful information gleaned. Eight months later, on July 12, a patrol of Polar Bears into the village was accompanied by a resident who took them to two insurgent caches of munitions and other equipment. In the previous few days, residents had pointed out more than fourteen caches in the village. The brigade operations officer, Major Kenny Mintz, said the villagers are "taking steps that they have never taken before."[34]

The kidnapping by the terrorists had unintended consequences for them. For many weeks U.S. and Iraqi forces rounded up insurgent suspects, resulting in significant degrada-

Division soldiers conducting a search for PFC Joseph J. Anzack Jr., SGT Alex R. Jimenez and PFC Byron W. Fouty in the vicinity of Rushdi Mullah, south of Baghdad (U.S. Army photograph, National Archives).

tion of their personnel infrastructure. In addition, Route Malibu became safer and more secure, although not totally free of enemy activity. By early July, the battalion's mission was revised: "finding our men and seizing control of the most important structure in the southern belt of Baghdad, the Yusufiyah Russian Thermal Power Plant, also known as 'The Dragon.'"[35]

The power plant was built by the Russians beginning in 1996. Construction stopped probably in May of 2002. It was scheduled to resume in mid–2003, but in late March of that year U.S. forces invaded. When finished, the plant would produce more than 1,000 megawatts of power, but the site was only about 40 percent complete when the insurgency forced the withdrawal of Russian personnel.[36] The site was massive. Once U.S. forces owned it, the walk from the heliport to the headquarters building was over half a mile. There were "miles of barren construction yards, dozens of empty buildings, and countless lots filled with old vehicles."[37] Dump trucks, tractor trailers, cranes and other abandoned construction equipment littered the terrain.

When the 2nd BCT arrived in Iraq in August 2006, the power plant was a haven for insurgent personnel and activities. Within the vast complex, terrorists were billeted, prisoners interrogated and tortured and vehicle-borne IEDs assembled. On October 23, the 2-14 Infantry Golden Dragons seized the sprawling installation with a two-company attack and established Patrol Base Dragon there. The PB remained, but at that time the complex as a whole was too extensive to completely occupy. The brigade had to gain control of the surrounding insurgency first.[38]

Once that insurgency was reasonably in hand, the 4-31 Polar Bears focused on the power plant. C Company executed a night ground assault into the plant, linked up with the 2-14 Battle Position, and searched the complex. Less than an hour after the plant was declared secure, the air landing of the remaining battalion elements was in full swing. TF 4-31 then began to move its battalion HQ from FOB Yusufiyah into the power plant.[39]

Logistics was challenging. Once the members of F Company, the Forward Support unit of 4-31, had a good start on new offices and living quarters, soldiers of the 210th Brigade Support Battalion came in behind them. The last week of July, they began installing air conditioners, lights and power sources, as well as circuit breakers and switch boxes. By mid–August equipment and supplies were in motion from Yusufiyah to the power plant.[40]

While all this was in progress, the anti-insurgency mission continued at high intensity. Patrols, raids and civic action events were standard. The people of Qarghuli village, who in less than a year had come around from fearful hostility to willing cooperation, weren't forgotten. In early August C Company, 4-31 used the Qarghuli school as a clinic, while at the same time securing the area—the insurgency still had the ability to stage an attack. A loudspeaker broadcast an invitation in pre-recorded Arabic. One of the primary medical problems arose from the villagers' drinking the water from canals that linked into the Euphrates River. Medics passed out medicines for the stomach condition, pills to put in the water before drinking, and medications for other illnesses as well. In addition, soccer balls and Arabic-language textbooks changed hands. C Company spent five hours there, without incidents or even any show of the previous hostility. Pvt. Keith Wray, a 4-31 Medic observed, "It's definitely safer here than it was."[41]

SFC Jay-R Strawder, the 4-31 Motor Sergeant, agreed. "When we arrived in the area [the previous August], there were no kids outside playing, no stores open and few adults sitting outside. By the time we left, kids were running to our convoys, a lot of store fronts

View of an electrical power plant along the Tigris River near the city of Bayji, 30 October 2004 (U.S. Air Force photograph by Tech Sgt. Lee Harshman, National Archives).

were open and many more adults were active. It felt like we actually made a difference in their lives."[42]

As summer turned to fall, the insurgency continued to weaken and the Iraqi Army took over more and more of the counterinsurgency and security missions. The time to rotate back to Fort Drum moved closer and thoughts began to focus on a return home. But always hovering over that was the fact that Jimenez and Fouty were still missing.

Just weeks before redeployment, the commander of the 2nd BCT, Colonel Mike Kershaw addressed the issue in an interview: "We flooded the area for about six weeks in a detailed search, and continue a more surgical search since then, looking for Specialist Alex Jimenez and Private Byron Fouty. We've acquired literally thousands of leads, and we think we've developed a pretty good picture of what happened. Since then, we've detained about 12 of the individuals involved in planning and execution of the attack."[43] But when the battalion boarded aircraft for their return as part of the army's most deployed brigade,[44] the two men were still missing. The principle of "no one left behind" rested with American forces still in country.

And those forces came through. On July 1, 2008, a suspect was captured by Special Operations Forces. He led American soldiers on July 8 to the site where the two missing men had been buried together. The next day their remains were flown to Dover, Delaware. The Armed Forces Medical Examiner positively identified the soldiers on July 10, 2008. They were home. On February 17, 2009, the remains of SSG Alex R. Jimenez and SPC Byron W. Fouty were interred together with full military honors at Arlington National Cemetery.[45]

SP Byron W. Fouty and SSG Alex R. Jimenez were interred at Arlington National Cemetery, Section 60, Gravesite 8764 (Association archives).

The 4th Battalion 31st Regiment chalked up numerous notable accomplishments on its 15-month tour in Iraq. Under "Polar Bear History" the Fort Drum website reports:

The 809 member task force was their Brigade's main effort and was given the daunting task of establishing the first permanent Coalition Force presence in the Sunni region south of Baghdad frequently referred to as the "Triangle of Death." Working daily with their sister Iraqi Army battalion to reestablish the rule of law and the legitimacy of local Iraqi Forces to the area, Task Force 4-31 became a model vehicle of contemporary counterinsurgency theory and practice. They established six patrol bases, 17 battle positions, and assisted the Iraqi Army in the establishment of many more. They conducted over 50 air assaults and three amphibious operations, and fired nearly 400 counter-fire artillery missions against enemy forces and in support of troops in contact. TF 4-31 killed or wounded 51 insurgents and captured 148, while aiding the Iraqi Army in the capture of over 1,500 additional insurgents. While actively hunting insurgents, the Soldiers of TF 4-31 set about improving the community, aiding in the improvement of schools, roads, irrigation canals, community centers, and emplacing solar power street lights. While completing their mission, Task Force 4-31 suffered 26 Soldiers killed in action. The Polar Bears earned two Silver Stars.[46]

In addition, the battalion received a Valorous Unit Award. Its citation reads as follows:

For extraordinary heroism in action against an armed enemy. During the period 16 August 2006 to 25 June 2007, Headquarters and Headquarters Company, 4th Battalion, 31st Infantry Regiment and its subordinate units displayed extraordinary gallantry in action against an armed enemy in support of Operation Iraqi Freedom in and around Yusufiyah, Iraq. The unit's professionalism and dedication to mission accomplishment went above and beyond the call of duty and contributed immeasurably to the success of Multi-National Division–Baghdad and Multi-National Division-Center. Headquarters and Headquarters Company, 4th Battalion, 31st Infantry Regiment's actions are in keeping with the finest traditions of military service and reflect distinct credit upon the unit, the 2nd Brigade, the 10th Mountain Division, and the United States Army.[47]

Iraq: October 2009–June 2010

A sharp difference exists between the 2006–07 and 2009–10 deployments in several respects. At eight months, the later tour was only about half as long as the earlier one, which was extended to 15 months as part of the surge named the "New Way Forward." More significantly, IED incidents had been reduced by a startling 90 percent: Comparing the data on incidents in the month of June 2007 to June 2009 two years later, the numbers for total IEDs are 2,588 versus 260. Other IED categories also hold at about 90 percent for the same marker months: IEDs found and cleared: 1,345 versus 142; ineffective IED attacks, meaning no Coalition Force (CF) casualties: 1,001versus 92; effective attacks, 242 versus 26; CF KIA, 83 versus 8; and CF WIA, 572 versus 59.[48] The high water mark of 2,588 incidents in June 2007 means that the 4th Battalion 31st Infantry was during that very period carrying the battle to the insurgents in the Triangle of Death. The Polar Bears were engaged in major combat with the terrorists during the time the enemy strategy was built around maximum IED usage. But the most significant contrast with the 2006–07 deployment lies in the fact that during 2009–10 the battalion had no KIAs.

The battalion's mission in 2009–10 was training and security. The entire 2nd Brigade Combat Team deployed—this time to eastern Baghdad—to help prepare Iraqi security forces for their takeover of responsibility for public order and safety from the Coalition Force. Focus was on combat and leadership skills for the Iraqi Federal Police. By January 2010 the instructor role had shifted from CF to Iraqi personnel.[49]

In addition, some special security missions arose. Starting in 2007, the State Department, as one aspect of the President's New Way Forward, organized small groups called Embedded Provincial Reconstruction Teams (EPRT). They were at core four-person interagency groupings, with both military and civilians, and could be expanded with additional personnel depending on what particular skill sets were needed. Thirteen EPRTs were assigned to brigade-sized units in Baghdad, Anbar and Erbil provinces. They worked "with sub-provincial and municipal officials, local leaders and civil society groups in their respective areas of operations."[50]

PFC John Flynn, at the time a fire team leader in the 1st Platoon of C Company, was initially located at Command Observation Post (COP) Carver in Salman Pak, about 15 miles south of Baghdad. A month after arriving in-country, approximately three-fourths of the 1st Platoon, including Flynn and his men, were sent to Camp Cashe South, about ten miles southeast of Baghdad. Their mission was providing security for one of the EPRTs.

Camp Cashe South was built on the perimeter walls of the old Osirak nuclear reactor, which was destroyed in 1981 by an Israeli fixed wing attack. While securing the EPRT, the Polar Bears operated within about a thirty-mile radius toward the southeast. Flynn indicated that their missions were all driven by the EPRT, but the standard operating procedures came from the 4th Battalion 31st Infantry chain of command.

Given the high priority of the EPRT mission, protecting the members of the team came first. This meant breaking contact at all costs to protect civilian lives, so there was never a stand-and-fight mission. In fact, because the EPRT security element was so small,

An M1 Abrams tank in Iraq, 2006 (U.S. Army photograph by SSG Kevin L. Moses, Sr., National Archives).

and because the battalion's primary mission was the security and safeguarding of the election process, this meant no direct-action assault missions. What small arms fire there was occurred outside the wire, but it was never sustained enough for any two vehicles to confirm it, so it went unreported.

The EPRT security mission lasted about eight months for the 1st platoon of C Company, until the Team was disbanded in mid–May. All hands then returned to COP Carver to help the rest of the battalion prepare to hand over the facility to their Iraqi Army counterparts.

When June arrived, C Company was the last remaining element of 4-31 on COP Carver, held there for one more mission. This required the security of a bridge-building operation a little less than ten miles to the southwest on the Euphrates River. The mission required a mix of patrolling and stationary overwatch, and lasted about three weeks. The riskiest part of the mission came when the Main Supply Route had to be shut down for two nights in a row to bring in the bridging materials. A few Iraqi drivers disregarded the roadblocks before they finally stopped. One was about fifty meters from Flynn's location at the final blocking position and didn't stop until he put the laser from his M4 on the head of the driver. "Thank God he stopped," Flynn said, "because when he turned around there was one man driving, two women in the front and four kids in the back."[51]

But the paramount mission of the entire 2009–10 deployment was security for national elections on March 7, 2010. New members of parliament would be chosen, and they in turn would select the next Prime Minister. American forces stayed in the background, providing surveillance assets, early warning and combined command and control points. At the same time, U.S. troops were prepared to act as Quick Reaction Forces (QRF) if that became necessary. The 4th Battalion 31st Infantry worked with the 45th Iraqi Brigade of the 11th Iraqi Army Division, providing video feeds for the elections at C and C centers. The battalion also provided half a dozen QRFs at locations designated by their Iraqi counterparts. Voter turnout was higher than expected, and Iraqi Army performance was professional and effective.[52]

In February, even before the elections, Secretary of Defense Gates announced that as of September 1, 2010, the term "Operation Iraqi Freedom" would be replaced by "Operation New Dawn." This latter designation would signify the effective handoff of security to Iraqi forces. Before this transition of names took effect, designated U.S. troops in Iraq would already have begun to withdraw on an established schedule.[53] This included the 4-31.

The battalion would not be in Iraq that fall for the name change. Its achievements, including a 59 percent reduction in insurgent activity in its area of operations, prompted the final turnover of COP Carver to the Iraqi Army.[54] A return home in early summer followed in June of 2010.[55] Formal recognition of its outstanding performance followed in due course with a Meritorious Unit Commendation.[56]

Afghanistan: 2015–2016

Almost fifteen years earlier, in the immediate aftermath of 9/11, 4-31 deployed to Afghanistan for the first time. The next four deployments took the battalion to Iraq and sometimes other locations at the same time. Then, coming full circle, the Polar Bears in 2015 returned to Afghanistan for their sixth mission to South Asia.

It wasn't supposed to happen. In January 2014 the *New York Times* reported that then Major General Stephen J. Townsend, CG of the 10th Mountain Division at the time, was "headed to eastern Afghanistan in a final deployment that will close the official NATO combat mission by the end of the year." It went on to say, "The 10th Mountain was the first division sent off to fight the war in Afghanistan, and now it will be the last."[57] But the Islamist militants had other ideas.

The 2014 *Times* article presents two ironies: its headline reads, "After Years at War, the Army Adapts to Garrison Life." But seventeen months later 4-31 left its garrison at Fort Drum to deploy once again to Afghanistan. The second irony centers on the fact that in 2001 Townsend, when he was a lieutenant colonel, commanded 4-31 on its initial post–9/11 Afghan deployment. In 2015, as CG of the 10th Mountain Division, he dispatched his former battalion to Afghanistan once again.

Meanwhile, 4-31 on its 2015–16 deployment received the mission of installation security. This mission was complicated by the fact that several different locations of varying sizes required manning by the Polar Bears, creating a need for detachments from a squad minus to a platoon or more. The complexity increased when some of these battalion elements were placed within different chains of command. Battalion HQ was thus no longer directly responsible operationally for some of its own elements.

C Company probably had the greatest fragmentation, although all the line companies experienced scatter. Charlie Company's troops ended up in eight locations, with contingents of different sizes. The headquarters was located at Camp Morehead in Kabul with CPT George and then CPT Marquis and 1SG Kenworthy. The element at Camp Integrity, also in Kabul, was led by SGT (P) Turner. SFC Fernandez was in charge of the Polar Bears at North Hamid Karzai International Airport at Kabul International Airport. SSG Flynn led a small group attached to a Special Forces Operational Detachment Alpha (ODA) of two teams at Camp Vose, Bagram Air Field in Parwan Province. 1LT Lusted was the senior Polar Bear in the group at Camp Dahlke in Logar Province. The Camp Pamir group (Kunduz Province) was led by SFC Queen. 1LT McClellan and SSG Riley were in charge at Kandahar Air Field, and 1LT Hurff and SSG Quillia led the group at Camp Antonik in Helmand Province. The importance of small unit leadership to which this scatter speaks cannot be overemphasized.

In addition, 4-31 HQ, A Company and the battalion Scouts were at Bagram Air Field. B Company had elements at Bagram Air Field and Jalalabad Air Field and was also working with an ODA unit. D Company was split up as well. Such was the scatter the Polar Bears had to work within.

Yet the battalion as a whole was assigned ready reaction contingency missions, and needed to be able to come together, combat ready, on a quick-reaction basis. Battalion command and staff personnel had some intricate and challenging planning to work through and keep updated.

Leadership at the battalion level was clearly a challenge. The commander, LTC Chris Landers, and the sergeant major, CSM Bruce Kosmicki, needed to maintain the unit's identity in general as well as its focus on those contingencies in particular. The two developed a procedure in which they spent a week on the road every month, visiting on site with every battalion detachment. They talked, listened and reviewed potential missions. When required, they followed up these visits with liaison work with the appropriate chain of command, and dealt with any logistics or personnel issues requiring attention.

Because of the battalion's mission, it initiated little combat action. On the other hand, a few firefights were started by the enemy, forcing 4-31 elements into a reactive mode. 1LT Nick Hurff and SGT (P) Chad Quillia and their detachment helped repel a surprise assault on Camp Antonik. Another occurred at Camp Integrity.

This Kabul installation housed U.S. Special Forces units. The C Company detachment there was headed up by SSG Turner. Under him were SGTs Carr and Berthiaume, each of whom led a team of three soldiers. For the most part, they worked the day shift and conducted base defense operations, maintaining the perimeter weapons systems and the readiness of the detachment to act as a quick reaction force.

At 2205 on August 7, 2015, four attackers hit the camp. The first individual went for the Entry Control Point and detonated a Vehicle Borne IED. At once the other three penetrated into the camp through the gap created by the explosion. The Charlie Company detachment was in its off cycle at the time and most of the members were asleep. At the sound of the explosion the nine Polar Bears rolled out and grabbed their gear, splitting up into smaller elements to repel the attack. Turner and Berthiaume proceeded in a vehicle to the Entry Control Point to plug the gap and provide gun support. Carr was also in a vehicle with another member of the Camp, and moved down to support the south wall. From there, they made their way to the Helicopter Landing Zone to provide security for the incoming medevac helicopters. Once the medevac was complete, they got word that there was still contact on the south wall, so they returned there. They joined the dismounted element to provide security and eliminate the remaining hostile.[58]

One Special Forces soldier and eight Afghan contractors were killed in the attack.[59] A harsh irony exists in the fact that the American KIA, 1SG Andrew McKenna of Bristol

Photograph taken at the memorial service for Special Forces 1SG Andrew McKenna, August 2015. 1SG McKenna began his Army career as a Polar Bear at Fort Drum where he was a member of Company C, 4th Battalion, 31st Infantry, from November 1998 to April 2002 (photograph by U.S. Department of Defense, National Archives).

RI, started his military career as a Polar Bear. From November 1998 to April 2002 McKenna was a member of C Company, 4th Battalion 31st Infantry—the same company to which SSG Turner's quick reaction force belonged.[60]

A few other suicide bombers tried to attack installations but never penetrated the perimeter. In addition, one night Islamist terrorists climbed to the roof of a building across from an installation the battalion was helping to secure and fired a quick dozen or so rounds of RPGs inside the compound. Some damage was done, but basically the attack was merely harassing fire.

But one obviously serious engagement stands out: the Battle of Kunduz. This Afghan city, a provincial capital north of Kabul, was initially attacked on April 28, 2015, by Taliban forces. Fighting was by fits and starts well into the summer, with Afghan units pulling back to the airport south of the city, and with the initiative in the hands of the Taliban. Then on September 27, an insurgent attack from three sides put Kunduz firmly in the enemy's control.

The administration had been presenting the American role as post-combat. But the fall of Kunduz "was clearly a desperate situation," said Brig. Gen. Charles H. Cleveland, the spokesman for the American command in Afghanistan. The soldiers, he said, recognized that 'if we don't really provide some very strong suggestion, direction, whatever you call it—if we don't get engaged with this quickly—we're going to have a much larger issue."[61]

Special Forces Operational Detachment Alpha (ODA) 3133 was based at Camp Vose. SSG Flynn of C Company, 4-31 had a detachment of five men at the same location, but Flynn was required to provide two of his men for another mission. The night of the Kunduz attack, the ODA and Flynn with his three men were activated as a de facto quick reaction force and moved to Camp Pamir, about 12 miles from Kunduz City. There was another detachment of C Company soldiers at Camp Pamir, and Flynn was given control of another five Polar Bears. For this battle, a total of nine Polar Bears were teamed with ODA 3133, and five more, also from C Company, with ODA 3111.

As soon as ODA 3133 and the Charlie Company soldiers arrived at Camp Pamir, "we quickly realized the severity of the situation. Three separate units of Afghan Commandos were cut off from resupply and pinned down just outside the city, and the Kunduz Airport was in danger of being overrun. We actioned on the airport on the night of the 28th and retook it and handed it back over to the Afghan Government and Military. On the night of the 29th we actioned on the city itself."[62]

Two separate missions inside the city of Kunduz required a division of forces.

The first group, ODA 3133 and the Camp Vose Polar Bears, moved to retake the Provincial Chief of Police (PCOP) compound. The Charlie Company soldiers were divided among three Ford Rangers: the lead truck, driven by a Romanian Special Forces NCO, carried one of the ODA team leaders, an Air Force combat control tech, SSG John Flynn and an interpreter; SPC Nicholas Logue was manning an M249 Squad Automatic Weapon on the second Ford Ranger in the convoy, and SGT Justin Lidgard was driving the third truck with SPC Sung Kang manning an M249.

The second group was to retake the prison that had been overrun, and then rejoin the first group at the PCOP compound once it had been secured. The Polar Bears from Camp Pamir—SPCs Mahler, Duque, Lancelloti, Fuller and Crandall, all under SFC Queen—were attached to the Special Forces ODA team they lived and worked with. In the movement to the prison, they were primarily drivers for the up-armored Humvees— one up front, one in the back, and two within the body of the convoy with ten Afghan commandos. In addition there were two Afghan special mission unit Mobile Strike Force Vehicles.

ODA 3133 and the detachment of C Company soldiers set out for the city with only a rough grid they received during a very limited intelligence brief prior to leaving Camp Vose. No one in the assault force knew what the compound looked like or exactly where it was. The column consisted of 36 U.S. "Advisors"—the C Company element under SSG Flynn and the rest a combination of SF teams. In addition, about 100 partner Afghan Special Forces personnel were wrapped into the attack force. Only the Americans stationed in Kunduz and the Afghan Special Forces had up-armored vehicles, so the Camp Vose contingent again drove in borrowed Afghan Ford Rangers and side-by-side UTVs.[63]

Estimates of enemy strength ranged from 1,500 to 2,500 insurgents. During the six hours it took the convoy to cover twenty kilometers in darkness, the convoy was engaged eight times. It was like running a gauntlet. In one of these engagements, a vehicle-borne IED hit the Afghan Special Forces armored vehicle in front of SSG Flynn's unarmored pickup truck, stopping the whole convoy. Enemy machine guns opened up at once on the stalled vehicles and Flynn's truck was one of those in the kill zone. He immediately opened fire on the nearest enemy machine gun from the bed of the truck. At the same time, the two Special Forces operators in the ATV immediately behind Flynn's pickup pulled into the intersection of the ambush while laying effective fire on the enemy positions. With this covering fire, Flynn was able to dismount his vehicle and assault the nearest machine gun position about twenty meters away, killing at least one of the enemy and scattering the rest. Flynn is convinced that the immediate action of the troops in the convoy and the accurate information and targeting from an AC-130 overhead, relayed by the AF combat control tech, is the only reason anyone in his own vehicle survived. The two SF operators in the ATV received Silver Stars for their actions, while Flynn was awarded a Bronze Star with "V" device.

Yet the police compound still hadn't been located. Once the convoy recommenced its move, it circled back three times through the old kill zone, where it finally came to a halt, still in darkness. Flynn moved his vehicles into better defensive positions and assigned his troops their sectors of fire. But as first light began to brighten in the east, they realized that losing the concealment of darkness would almost certainly bring on a major firefight. They had to get out of the middle of the road. They had just decided to take the international hotel when the growing morning light showed them that they had been just outside the back wall of the PCOP compound the entire time. They quickly navigated to the other side of the compound where the entrance was located, and moved in a bit before 0600.

Meanwhile, when the second contingent, including SFC Queen's group of Polar Bears, arrived at the prison they found a sweep unnecessary. Queen's unit, wrapped in with ODA 3111, then headed out quickly to catch up with the first contingent as it moved on the PCOP.

The compound was an entire city block that had approximately 40 buildings inside it. Two of them were three-story barracks that easily had over 150 rooms—the compound was where all Afghan Police trained for the entire province of Kunduz. As soon as the convoy was inside, the compound was broken down into sectors, and teams of two or three men began the process of clearing it. This was accomplished in about 45 minutes. Then specific areas of control were parceled out, with Flynn and his four men, together with some of the SF operators, placed on the south wall.

"At approximately 0730, all hell broke loose. We started receiving heavy machine gun fire from a factory that the insurgents had apparently strong-pointed right across the road from the western wall of the PCOP with only a double lane street dividing the locations."[64]

Flynn put SGT Lidgard in charge of the southwest tower and set up his M110 semi-automatic sniper rifle in a second story window directly above the Southwest Security Position. From this elevated vantage point he could engage the insurgents in the factory and provide information to the soldiers below him. While in this position he eliminated one enemy with an AK-47 to the southwest and one insurgent with a belt-fed machine gun who was firing on three of the SF Operators occupying a fairly exposed supplementary fighting position at the center of the western exterior wall. Almost as soon as he fired the shot that took out the machine gunner, an RPG round exploded about 25 meters away. The shot that silenced the enemy gunner had compromised his position, and the remaining insurgents rained machine gun and small arms fire into the room.[65]

Flynn low-crawled across the room to the stairwell and down to the southwest security position. SGT Lidgard and SPC Kang had been joined by one of the SF operators. All hands were securing the southwest corridor.

In the courtyard, an RPG head was embedded in a tree, which still smoldered. SPC Logue and three operators were in the northwest security position. In the center of the

Checking the side of the road for IEDs. Note the power plant in the background, right. February 2005 (U.S. Air Force photograph by Airman 1C Kurt Gibbons, III, National Archives).

northern wall about 20 meters farther along were two Afghan commandos. Flynn soon moved with his sniper rifle to this position where he stayed for the next 48 hours, inflicting at least a dozen casualties on the enemy.

By the end of those 48 hours, resupply requirements were becoming critical. The force inside the compound had gone black on water, food and radio batteries, and was at about 30 percent on ammunition. The Special Operations Task Force commander, MAJ Hutchinson had already put in two separate resupply requests, which had been denied due to risks to the aircraft. His next request was approved, but with the final decision resting with the pilot's judgment about feasibility.

Adding to the pressure, an Afghan Special Forces soldier had sustained a gunshot wound to the chest, just above his bullet-proof plates. Both American SF and C Company soldiers were cross-trained and certified as Combat Life Savers (CLS). But it was the American and Romanian Special Forces medics (MOS 18D) who quickly moved in and stabilized the wounded Afghan SF soldier with a chest tube. But he still needed a medevac ASAP.

About half an hour after the Afghan partner force SF soldier took the round in the chest, one of his teammates had his PVS-14 night vision goggles shot off of his head. Line of sight pointed to an enemy sniper northwest of the PCOP about 300 or so meters away. Two American snipers, one from ODA 3133 and one from C Company, SSG Flynn, left the compound with a three-man security element, and located themselves in a 12-story apartment building. The snipers took up a position on the sixth floor, while the security element, after a hasty check of the lower floors, located on the roof to spot for the snipers. An Afghan Special Forces squad then secured the entrance and the first floor. Over the next five hours, the two American snipers engaged five enemy personnel at distances of 250 to 900 meters away. One of them, on the second story of a building about 400 meters away from the PCOP, had the line of sight needed to inflict the chest wound on the Afghan SF soldier. There was no way to know if he had been the actual shooter, but to the American snipers it felt like payback.

Meanwhile, the resupply was scheduled for that night. SFC Grasso and SSG Flynn were tasked with sniper overwatch for the resupply. Flynn took along SGT Lidgard and SPC Kang, each manning a 240L machine gun. When the birds came in at about 2300, an AC-130 and Apaches provided airborne covering fire. Resupply was accomplished without incident, and the wounded Afghan soldier was evacuated.

After the third day of fighting inside the PCOP, it became apparent that the Americans needed to find a different compound. Most of the Taliban had been run out, and the local police and many regular Afghan army troops were returning and being allowed inside the enclosure more or less unchecked. Both the Taliban and ISIL already had Afghan army and provincial police uniforms, and this led the Americans to believe that an insider attack could very well be imminent. They scouted out adjacent compounds, and settled on the Provincial Governor's Compound (PGOV) about 150 meters south of the PCOP. It was smaller, and more realistically sized for a defense by the Americans, who left the partner force in the police compound.

On the fourth day, the fighting had pretty much come to a standstill—small, sporadic firefights, but nothing major. It was mainly harassment fire from the few remaining insurgents. That night the American force was ordered to exfiltrate back to Camp Pamir.

The actual move back to Camp Pamir was uneventful, although checkpoints had been re-manned by both local and provincial police and Afghan army soldiers. No one knew if the armed guards were legitimate or Taliban fighters. But there were no incidents, and after an hour-long convoy, the Americans closed back at Camp Pamir.[66]

The three-pronged Taliban attack on Kunduz had allowed the enemy to seize the city. Over the next 96 hours, an intense counterattack by U.S. and Afghan troops and other members of the international force pushed the numerically superior insurgents back out of the city. Given the 200 or more enemy KIA, the lack of any friendly combat fatalities was remarkable.[67]

Conclusion:
Celebrating the First Hundred Years
by Grady Smith

In March 2016, after a ten-month deployment, the 4th Battalion 31st Infantry headed home to Fort Drum. The order of business there included many routine actions—changes of command, personnel outprocessing of soldiers transferring to other units, as well as soldiers ending their active duty; inprocessing of replacement personnel, detailed planning for the inevitable coming training cycle, and logistics resupply. But among the most important tasks at hand was planning for the 100th anniversary of the activation of the 31st Infantry Regiment, which unfurled its colors in the Philippines on August 13, 1916.

A hundred years later on Friday, August 12, the anniversary was marked by a battalion Pass in Review. The reviewing party consisted of the Colonel of the Regiment, LTG (retired) Robert L. "Sam" Wetzel; LTC Isaac J. Rademacher, the Commanding Officer

During the Pass in Review celebrating the 100th anniversary of the activation of the 31st Infantry Regiment, Polar Bear Paul Kerchum, a Bataan Death March survivor, awards the Bronze Star with "V" device to SSG John Flynn for valor in Afghanistan. LTC Isaac Rademacher, CO of the 4th Battalion, 31st Infantry Regiment is at left. August 12, 2016 (Association archives).

of the 4th Battalion 31st Infantry; CPT (retired) Mike Strand, the Commander of the 31st Infantry Regiment Association; and CMSgt (USAF retired) Paul Kerchum, a survivor of the Bataan Death March and the oldest Polar Bear present. In a solemn and moving ceremony that affirmed the continuity of the generations, Kerchum pinned the Bronze Star with "V" device on SSG John Flynn for bravery under fire in Afghanistan during the tour just ended.

Friday afternoon's formal military parade was followed next evening by the 31st Infantry's traditional Shanghai Bowl Ceremony and Reunion Dinner. The Bowl was present at the Fort Drum Commons under guard and the Colors were presented. Then the Bowl was ritually filled and the punch served to all persons attending. Traditional toasts were rendered. And just as in a hail and farewell ceremony, the oldest Polar Bear veteran and the youngest, from the active duty force, saluted each other with a toast. The lasting continuity of the Regiment, both active duty and veterans, was once again affirmed and renewed.

The next day, LTG Steve Townsend, who was originally scheduled to be the banquet's main speaker, was in South Asia taking command of Combined Joint Task Force–Operation Inherent Resolve, detailed to retake Mosul and stabilize northern Iraq.[1] Townsend's absence from the banquet because he was again serving his country in a combat zone was almost certainly an indicator of what lies ahead for the 4-31. With six combat deployments since 9/11 and South Asia still in turmoil, there is no reason to think that its rotations into battle are over. But as always, the Polar Bears are ready.

Pro Patria.

Afterword

by General Stephen J. Townsend

For more than 100 years the soldiers of the 31st U.S. Infantry Regiment have served our nation—training, securing, fighting, bleeding and sometimes dying, in the pursuit and protection of America's interests around the world. This is a history of one regiment of American Soldiers, it is a history of America's Army, indeed, this is a history of America.

As of this writing, one active battalion of the 31st Infantry, the Polar Bears of the 4th Battalion, continue to soldier on as part of the Army's 10th Mountain Division (Light Infantry). So how do you provide an "afterword" when the final chapter is still being written—and may not be completed for another 100 years—or perhaps longer? So, rather than an "afterword" that seeks to wrap up the first 100 years of the regiment's history, I will try instead to link the soldiers, their family members and all Americans, and the deeds of the first 100 years to those of the next 100.

I knew little about the 31st Infantry when I took command of 4-31 at Fort Drum, New York, in June 2000. As the designated "regimental headquarters," we paraded with both the regimental colors and battalion colors in our color guard. I still had only a passing appreciation for the service embodied in the battle streamers on those colors and recounted in the preceding pages. That would soon change as the history of the regiment began to seek me out.

My first encounter with the regiment's service in Shanghai, China and the Philippines, in the opening months of World War II, arose from an incident with the Shanghai Bowl during my first week of battalion command. As I was leaving the headquarters one evening I came upon a young soldier working off his extra duty, found guilty of some disciplinary infraction like many Polar Bears before him (and since), by buffing the tile floor of the headquarters. I stopped to chat briefly with the Sergeant on staff duty for the night, idly watching the soldier bumping the wall with every sweep of the buffer. Suddenly, two Military Police patrol cars drew up in front of the entrance, blue lights flashing. The MPs dismounted and strode briskly into the lobby. "What's going on, Sergeant?" I asked the lead MP, wondering which of my soldiers was in trouble now. "Sir, we're here to make sure the bowl is OK." "The bowl?" I asked, confused. "Uh, yes sir, you know, the Shanghai Bowl," pointing at the large silver bowl in the corner display case. "Why do you think something is wrong with the bowl?" I asked, more confused. "I don't know, sir, but the alarm keeps going off at the MP station." he replied. "Alarm?" I asked. Though he was no doubt wondering, "who is this Lieutenant Colonel and where is the real battalion commander?" the MP Sergeant patiently explained, "Yes sir, that silver bowl is about the only thing on this post besides a weapon or classified material that's stored in a case with an alarm that goes off at the MP station. I don't know how much it's worth but it must be a lot." After determining the alarm was being triggered by the buffer bumping against the bottom of the case and the Shanghai Bowl was still secure, the MPs departed. Just then it started to dawn on me that I was now the keeper of a priceless heritage of service, sacrifice and valor and I needed to know more.

The fascinating story of the Shanghai Bowl's creation is told in these pages but the stories of its burial on Corregidor before the surrender, the horrors of the Bataan Death March and more than three years of captivity that followed, and the bowl's eventual retrieval after the war ended are even more incredible ... literally, a priceless heritage.

A few weeks later, the Korean War sought me out, when I was summoned to Lancaster, Pennsylvania, along with a good friend, LTC George "Marty" Martin,[1] who commanded 1st Battalion, 32nd Infantry just down the street. We took our Sergeants Major, Color Guard and some of our Soldiers to a meeting of the "Frozen Chosen." The U.S. Marine Corps and the Secretary of the Navy had decided to award the Navy's Presidential Unit Citation to the 31st Infantry Regiment and 1-32 Infantry for their actions at the Chosin Reservoir in the winter of 1950. For 50 years the Marines had spoken of the Army's actions at Chosin with scorn. But new access to Chinese historical records had provided a more complete understanding of the size and intent of the enemy force encountered by the understrength, unsupported and hastily deployed Task Force 31 or TF McLean (with 1-32 Infantry, aka TF Faith, attached) during the late November action on the eastern shores of the reservoir. Historians had determined that the regimental task force's sacrifice, to the point of near complete destruction of the unit, had delayed and heavily attritted at least two Chinese divisions and thwarted their mission to cut off the 1st Marine Division's route of escape from the west side of the reservoir. I met a number of our Regiment's Korea veterans including Joe Nocera, Ed Bettis, Jack Considine and LTG (Ret.) McCaffrey, along with his son, General McCaffrey, to name just a few. The former three took me under their wing and I heard many Korea stories from them. It was a proud moment to watch our Korea vets stand just a little taller as the Marine 3-star affixed the unit citations to the colors of the two units.

These two experiences lit a fire in me to preserve and promote the history of the 31st Infantry, not only for history's sake, but for my soldiers ... my Polar Bears. Great combat units draw on their legacy, the valiant, incredible deeds of heroes past, to inspire their Soldiers who will fight in the future. Although I couldn't know for certain we would be called to fight, as an infantry officer, I knew it was my duty to ensure my Polar Bears were ready if we were.

Somewhere along the line I had the great good fortune to meet retired Colonel Karl Lowe. If you have read this book, then you know he was a decorated infantry company commander in Vietnam with the 6th Battalion and later, his love for his soldiers and their stories led him to become the historian of our Regiment. From Karl, I learned not only about our Vietnam history but also a great deal about the rich history of our Regiment. He was a treasure trove of information and this book would not have been possible without him.

Together with my Polar Bear Buddy, Command Sergeant Major Dan Wood, we started inculcating the history of the 31st Infantry in our soldiers. We updated and added to the historical displays in the headquarters. We framed the photos and citations of each of the Regiment's Medal of Honor recipients and hung them on the walls. Every board in the battalion, from Soldier of the Month to NCO promotions to the Officer's Mess included questions about our regimental crest, unit awards, heroes and history. Every battalion run was dedicated to a Medal of Honor or Distinguished Service Cross recipient of the Regiment with a soldier from the battalion reading aloud the citation of the heroes' deeds before we stepped off.

And we trained and prepared—we learned the importance of being ready to fight from our regiment's history as well. There were frequent no-notice alerts, regular air assaults and convoys, long night foot marches, constant field exercises and live fire exercises … squad live fires … platoon live fires … company team combined arms live fires … in both day and night. That battalion was as ready to fight as any I ever served with or saw in 35 years. And then 9/11 came.

I had caught just a snippet of news on my truck's radio as I parked in front of the headquarters—something about a plane crashing into a skyscraper in New York City. I imagined it must have been a small private plane. As I walked in, there was a knot of soldiers clustered around the staff duty office watching CNN on the television. "Little George," our small, deployable wooden Polar Bear statue, and the Shanghai Bowl stood silent watch from their displays nearby. I looked at the TV over the shoulders of the soldiers and saw the gaping hole in one of the World Trade Center towers— black smoke pouring out. I remember thinking, "that wasn't a small plane." Everyone was speculating about how it could have happened … no one mentioned an attack. While we stood there watching, the second plane struck the adjacent tower. At that moment, I just knew … we all knew. I said to the group of soldiers, "Men, go start packing your bags, we're at war with someone…. I'm not sure who with, but we're at war."

After days of "re-pack your bags" and "hurry up and wait," it was late September and, despite constant speculation about where al-Qaeda might strike next, the 10th Mountain Division had yet to deploy any units in response to 9/11. For months the 4th Battalion had been planning to host the veterans of the 31st Infantry Association for their annual reunion at Fort Drum. We resolved to press on. Even as the events of 9/11 hung heavy in the air, the veterans and their families gathered for several days of activities culminating with an evening banquet with the troops.

The day of the banquet my cell phone rang as our key leaders gathered at the club to rehearse the ceremonial posting of the colors, the Shanghai Bowl ceremony and toasts on the day of the banquet. It was our 2nd Brigade Operations Officer, Major Joe Fenty,[2] who said, "Sir, the Chief of Staff of the Army has directed the 10th Mountain Division to secure sensitive facilities at Aberdeen Proving Ground in Maryland. The CG has selected the Polar Bears for this mission. Can you have a company ready to go in four hours?" Sensing the urgency in his voice, I said, "We'll try, Joe." Just over four hours later, the first lift of Polar Bears from C Company, in full combat kit, lifted off for APG in Black Hawk helicopters from the Division Parade Field. It was the 10th Mountain Division's first deployment of troops in the War on Terror. CSM Wood and I saw them off, standing on the grass PZ in our dress blue uniforms. That night at the banquet, I addressed the assembled Polar Bears and their spouses and dates, both young and old. Pointing to Charlie Company's empty seats, I told the crowd, "Those tables are empty tonight because an hour ago, the Polar Bears launched this division's first deployment in the War on Terror." The old Polar Bears leapt to their feet roaring their approval and the rest of the room followed. It was a powerful moment.

In the first few days of October, the Polar Bears deployed America's first conventional troops overseas in response to 9/11, launching Company A to Kuwait and a reinforced platoon from Company B to Qatar to secure sensitive facilities and operations. Soon, other elements of the division, including the Anti-Tank platoon and, later, Company C, would deploy to Uzbekistan. Before the end of the year, they would join in the invasion of Afghanistan to defeat al-Qaeda and unseat the Taliban government that supported them.

As you have read in these pages, the headquarters and the rest of 4-31 remained at Fort Drum, training a collection of the Division's remaining infantry, artillery, engineers and air defense units under the moniker, Task Force Polar Bear. Though we all badly wanted to join our Mountain buddies overseas, our mission was to secure the installation and train to stay ready. Ready for what? Ready for anything—and we threw ourselves into that task.

In early March, U.S. and coalition forces, along with Afghan militia partners, launched Operation Anaconda in the Shah-i-Kot Valley of eastern Afghanistan to destroy what was assessed as the last significant concentration of al-Qaeda remaining there. The operation was commanded by the 10th Mountain Division headquarters, known as Task Force Mountain. Initial enemy resistance was significantly stiffer than anticipated and, in the opening hours, the JTF found themselves looking for additional infantry to employ. The most readily available were the various elements of 4-31 scattered around the CENTCOM theater. Within 24 hours, orders to reposition to Afghanistan were issued. Company C moved from Uzbekistan and Company A from Kuwait. Immediately upon arrival, these two companies were committed into the Shah-i-Kot. During this operation, the Polar Bears would draw their first enemy blood since Vietnam.

By mid–March, the battalion tactical command post, or TAC, would deploy to Bagram Airbase, north of Kabul, to assume command of the elements of the battalion which were already fighting attached to other units such as our sister battalion, 1-87 Infantry, and the 3rd Princess Patricia's Canadian Light Infantry. The battalion-minus task force would participate in the final days of Operation Anaconda, in Operations Harpoon and Polar Harpoon that followed, and a number of smaller operations as the quick reaction force for TF Mountain. During this time, I had to perform the most difficult act of my command. The rest of 4-31 was ready and awaiting transportation at Fort Drum. It fell to me to call my Executive Officer, then–Major Fred Johnson, at Drum and tell him to stand the troops down—that no more Polar Bears would deploy forward. I could physically feel what a crushing blow it was for all of them at the time—they wanted so badly to join the fight. Few of us could foresee the long war and many deployments that lay ahead for all of us.

And thus began the latest chapter of the Polar Bears at war—and multiple tours of duty overseas in Afghanistan, Iraq and elsewhere that continue to this day, more than 16 years later.

One purpose of this history is to let every American service member know, you are part of something much larger than yourself. The unit in which you serve has similar tales of Americans rising to the challenges of the past and you are part of that same legacy. Whether in peace or in war, at home station or deployed, your own service is writing a new chapter in the history of your regiment. You will renew your connection and re-live these stories for the rest of your life. Your service matters—to you, your family, your regiment and the future of our Nation. Make it count.

Pro Patria.

General Stephen J. Townsend received his fourth star in early 2018, and was appointed commander of Training and Doctrine Command. In his previous assignment, he led all U.S. and multinational troops fighting the Islamic State in Iraq and Syria as commander of Combined Joint Task Force–Operation Inherent Resolve. Townsend was commander of 4th Battalion 31st Infantry on September 11, 2001. He led the battalion in Afghanistan on the first of its numerous deployments following the terrorist attacks, heading up Operation Polar Bear in the Shah-i-Kot Valley.

Appendix 1:
Officers Roster Upon Activation;
Chain of Command
at First Deployment

Officers Roster Upon Activation, 13 August 1916

Commander	COL William H. Gordon
Deputy	LTC Frederic H. Sargent
Adjutant	CPT Charles Weeks
HQ Company	1LT Emile V. Cutrer
MG Company	1LT Max A. Elser
Supply Company	1LT John P. Adams
1st Battalion	MAJ Bert H. Allen
Company A	CPT Thomas L. Brewer
Company B	2LT J. P. Wilson
Company C	1LT R. G. Caldwell
Company D	CPT Walter Harvey
2nd Battalion	CPT Colin H. Ball
Company E	CPT William R. Kendrick
Company F	1LT Clark Lynn
Company G	1LT Everett N. Bowman
Company H	1LT Jacob E. Fishel
3rd Battalion	MAJ Ben W. Field
Company I	1LT George W. Maddox
Company K	1LT Everett D. Barlow
Company L	1LT Richard H. Jacob
Company M	1LT A. Ellicott Brown

Chain of Command at First Deployment, 12 August 1918

Regiment	COL Frederick H. Sargent
Headquarters Company	CPT John M. Boon
Machinegun Company	CPT Allen T. Veatch
Supply Company	CPT Raymond H. Bishop
Medical Detachment	MAJ Miller E. Preston
1st Battalion	MAJ E. V. Heidt
A Company	1LT Roy F. Lynd
B Company	CPT Henry W. Lee

C Company	CPT William H. Bittenbender
D Company	CPT William H. Joiner
2nd Battalion	LTC Ode C. Nichols
E Company	CPT Laird E. Richards
F Company	CPT William E. Fentress
G Company	1LT Nolie E. Felix
H Company	CPT John H. Haynes
3rd Battalion	MAJ Sylvester C. Loring
I Company	CPT Schiller A. Scroggs
K Company	CPT William H. Crom
L Company	CPT Francis G. Bishop
M Company	1LT Leo M. Johnson

Appendix 2:
31st Infantry Chain of Command,
14 December 1941

Regimental Commander	COL Charles L. Steel (reassigned 1 March 1942)
Executive Officer	LTC Irvin E. Doane (promoted & reassigned 27 Jan 1942)
HQ Company CO	CPT Earl C. Packer (died in captivity)
Service Company CO	CPT Clarence Bess
Antitank Company CO	CPT Robert A. Barker (died in captivity)
Medical Detachment CO	MAJ Clarence H. White (died in captivity)
1st Battalion CO	LTC Edward H. Bowes (Silver Star, died in captivity)
A Company CO	CPT Cecil R. Welchko (died in captivity)
B Company CO	CPT Lloyd G. Murphy (relieved for cause, died in captivity)
C Company CO	CPT Richard K. Carnahan (DSC, died in captivity)
D Company CO	CPT Christopher J. Heffernan, Jr. (died in Hospital #1, Bataan)
2nd Battalion CO	MAJ Lloyd C. Moffitt (Silver Star, KIA 3 April 1942)
E Company CO	CPT Robert S. Sauer (Silver Star, died in captivity)
F Company CO	CPT Eugene B. Conrad (Silver Star)
G Company CO	CPT John I. Pray
H Company CO	CPT Dwight T. Hunkins (Silver Star, died in captivity)
3rd Battalion CO	LTC Jasper E. Brady, Jr. (Regimental Commander 1 March 1942, died in captivity)
I Company CO	CPT Ray B. Stroud (relieved for cause, died in captivity)
K Company CO	CPT Coral M. Talbot (died in captivity)
L Company CO	CPT Donald G. Thompson
M Company CO	CPT Thomas P. Bell (Silver Star)

Appendix 3:
The Shanghai Bowl Ceremony

What began in the 1930s as a Hail and Farewell ceremony for the Regiment's officers has evolved into a ritual uniting the generations of those who have served the nation in the 31st Infantry Regiment. Each of the ingredients of the punch represents a specific part of the Regiment's history. By the end of the ceremony, the contents of the Bowl have become a history-in-little of the Regiment.

As the Japanese closed in during the Defense of the Philippines, Captain Earl Short, the Headquarters Commandant, together with Sergeants Howard J. Linn and Thomas Proulx, took custody of the Bowl, determined to keep it out of the hands of enemy forces. They went with the bowl and 99 cups by barge to Corregidor. But Short's hope to get the Regimental silver out by submarine became impossible. So late on March 2, 1942, Short's detail buried the bowl and cups on the west side of Malinta Hill. The terrain there had been destroyed by air and artillery bombardment, leaving no apparent landmarks. There the bowl would remain for more than three years, until after an extensive search it was found shortly after Christmas 1945.

The Shanghai Bowl ceremony begins with a cup of water:

"**Water** is the life blood of the Infantryman. Nothing is more precious to the infantryman than water. We pay homage to this most essential of all elements.

"The 31st Infantry Regiment was formed at Manila in the Philippines in 1916. We get our start for the Polar Bear Punch by adding **Philippine Rum,** a drink native to the South Pacific.

"The Regiment was called to its baptism of fire in the cold and unforgiving terrain of Siberia. The soldiers guarded the rail line, warehouses, and supplies near Vladivostok in 1918. We add **Vodka** in celebration of the Polar Bears and their service in Russia.

"In 1932 the Polar Bears were once again called to arms—to Shanghai, to police the riots and protect American lives and property. The officers of the 31st donated 1,500 silver dollars and commissioned this beautiful Punch Bowl and cup set to commemorate the Regiment's service in China. For this time of service we add a **silver dollar** and the **100th Anniversary Coin** to the bowl.

"As 1941 drew to a close, the winds of war blew hot in the Pacific. On the Bataan Peninsula, the Regiment met its stiffest test yet, fighting for four months without replacements or resupply. Our nation was unable to send help. Those that survived the campaign had to endure the Bataan Death March and captivity in Japanese POW camps.

"The Polar Bears buried the Shanghai Bowl and their colors so that they would not fall into the hands of the enemy, retrieving them once the war was over. The Bowl was finally found a few days after Christmas in 1945. For these soldiers, both alive and dead, we honor them with the hardest of drinks we know: **Everclear.**

"In 1946 General MacArthur reactivated the Polar Bears as his Guard of Honor in Japan to bring peace to the lands of their former captors. In honor of this time of service we add **Sake**, the people's drink of Japan.

"The Korean War roused the Polar Bears from their occupation duties and once again plunged them into the fire of combat. Inchon, the Chosin Reservoir, and Pork Chop Hill are now a part of every Polar Bear history; as are the five Medals of Honor the 31st won on the battlefields of Korea. In tribute to those soldiers, and all the Polar Bears who have served in Korea, in war or peace, we pour **Soju** into our renowned mix.

"From 1966 until 1971, the Polar Bears of the Vietnam era fought a long and unpopular war with skill and courage that still deserve respect, earning two Medals of Honor along the way. For those soldiers who served in Vietnam, we add **Ba Si Dai.**

"When Bosnia erupted into chaos, the Polar Bears responded. The killing stopped and their time there secured a lasting peace. For Bosnia, we add the plum brandy, **Slivovitz.**

"When terror struck near our homes, the Polar Bears stood ready to answer our country's call to arms. Quickly, the polar Bears deployed by helicopter to secure sensitive national assets along the Eastern Seaboard in support of Operation Noble Eagle. In less than one month, Polar Bears boarded aircraft for Kuwait, Qatar, Uzbekistan and Afghanistan in support of Operation Enduring Freedom.

"In memory of those Americans and Allies lost in this ongoing struggle in the Global War on Terrorism, we add a **Manhattan** cocktail.

"As the war expanded into Iraq, the Polar Bears were repeatedly sent back to the desert to continue the struggle for peace and security in that region. For Iraq, we add **chai-tea**, the national drink of Iraq."

At this point, the punchbowl is ready for testing by the senior commander, who declares, "I deem this punch fit for Polar Bear consumption."

Then the most senior and most junior Polar Bears are brought forward to "Propose a toast: to 100 years of honor." The punch is then distributed to all present and additional toasts are performed, concluding the Shanghai Bowl Ceremony.

Appendix 4:
31st Infantry Regiment Soldiers
Killed in Action in All Wars

The data categories below often differ from war to war. The information for the Siberian campaign, for example, includes "died of other causes," including disease. This latter cause far outnumbers combat losses, both because antibiotics were not yet available and because of the influenza pandemic of 1918. Thus the impact on the Regiment from deaths due to illness needed to be included. In World War II, 308 soldiers of the Regiment were killed in action or died of wounds, while almost four times that number died during their captivity. Clearly, this category also required reporting. Within each grouping there are also variations. Some lists have names only, some include home of record, date of death or even the location where the battle death occurred.

In each list, the essential element of information is the name of the soldier who died while serving the nation in the 31st Infantry Regiment.

* * * * *

They were staunch to the end against odds uncounted,
They fell with their faces to the foe.
They shall grow not old, as we that are left grow old:
Age shall not weary them, nor the years condemn.
At the going down of the sun and in the morning
We will remember them.
— "For the Fallen," Laurence Binyon

Siberia

Killed in Action (KIA) or Died of Wounds (DOW)

Date of Death	Name	Rank	Co	Location	Cause
22 June 1919	Albert F. Ward	2LT	H	Novitskaya	KIA
22 June 1919	Dee P. Craig	PFC	H	Novitskaya	KIA
22 June 1919	Jesse M. Reed	PVT	M	Novitskaya	KIA
22 June 1919	Charles R. Blake	PVT	M	Novitskaya	DOW
25 June 1919	Henry P. Casey	SGT	A	Romanovka	KIA
25 June 1919	Thomas B. Mason	CPL	A	Romanovka	KIA
25 June 1919	Louis Carter	CPL	A	Romanovka	DOW
25 June 1919	Herbert Toll	CPL	A	Romanovka	KIA
25 June 1919	Lee Brooks	PFC	A	Romanovka	KIA

Date of Death	Name	Rank	Co	Location	Cause
25 June 1919	George Love	PFC	A	Romanovka	KIA
25 June 1919	James R. Love	PFC	A	Romanovka	KIA
25 June 1919	Cecil P. Parsons	PFC	A	Romanovka	KIA
25 June 1919	William Roberts	PFC	A	Romanovka	KIA
25 June 1919	Albert Simpson	PFC	A	Romanovka	KIA
25 June 1919	Dart H. Balch	PVT	A	Romanovka	KIA
25 June 1919	Walter H. Cole	PVT	A	Romanovka	KIA
25 June 1919	Wesley Davis	PVT	A	Romanovka	KIA
25 June 1919	Dave Ivie	PVT	A	Romanovka	KIA
25 June 1919	John Jansen	PVT	A	Romanovka	KIA
25 June 1919	Gus Johnson	PVT	A	Romanovka	KIA
25 June 1919	Harry Lamberg	PVT	A	Romanovka	KIA
25 June 1919	Nestor Lopez	PVT	A	Romanovka	KIA
25 June 1919	Walter E. Roberts	PVT	A	Romanovka	KIA
25 June 1919	Frank Schwab	PVT	A	Romanovka	KIA
26 June 1919	Herbert Naylor	PVT	Med	Romanovka	DOW
29 June 1919	Roy R. Reader	PVT	A	Romanovka	DOW
29 June 1919	Louis A. Schlichter	PFC	A	Romanovka	DOW
3 July 1919	Peter F. Bernal	PFC	C	Novitskaya	KIA
5 July 1919	Anastacio D. Montoya	PVT	H	Novitskaya	DOW
8 July 1919	Alphia Schurter	PFC	D	Piryatino	DOW
10 July 1919	Albert Rooney	PVT	M	Gordievka	KIA
16 July 1919	Gabriel Thingbo	PVT	A	Romanovka	DOW

Died of Other Causes

All who died of disease are assumed to have died at Vladivostok Military hospital unless otherwise noted.

Date of Death	Name	Co	Location	cause
13 August 1918	Joe E. Wood	I	at sea	suicide
22 August 1918	Lon Carroll	F	Vladivostok	disease
24 September 1918	Maciej Kulesz	E	Vladivostok	disease
25 September 1918	James Howard	M	Vladivostok	murdered by Russian officer
2 October 1918	George L Allen	F	Spasskoe	disease
21 October 1918	Duncan W. Balfour	F	Spasskoe	disease
21 October 1918	Raymond C. Moritz	Med	Vladivostok	disease
23 October 1918	Russell C. Doyle	I	Harbin	disease
29 October 1918	John C. Nicholson	K	Vladivostok	disease
29 October 1918	Drew D. Singleton	Supply	Vladivostok	disease
1 November 1918	Louis J. Kavier	HQ	Vladivostok	disease
1 November 1918	Edward J. Rokenfield	H	Vladivostok	disease
14 November 1918	Raymond T. Craig	HQ	Vladivostok	disease
2 December 1918	James R. Breeding	F	Spasskoe	disease
12 December 1918	George Hunt	H	Vladivostok	disease
14 December 1918	Luther E. Dale	MG	Vladivostok	disease
28 January 1919	David E. Browning	B	Harbin	disease
5 February 1919	Carl Boling	HQ	Vladivostok	disease
10 February 1919	Joseph F. Smith	F	Vladivostok	disease
1 March 1919	Roy O. Fourr	B	Harbin	disease
3 April 1919	John Connolly	I	Harbin	disease
4 April 1919	Charles W. Waller	H	Vladivostok	disease
10 April 1919	Earl D. Woods	A	Vladivostok	disease
13 April 1919	Emmet R. Whitten	MG	Vladivostok	disease
31 May 1919	Orin B. Hyde	K	Vladivostok	disease

Date of Death	Name	Co	Location	cause
13 June 1919	Edward L. Hutchinson	HQ	Vladivostok	disease
24 June 1919	Amando Esquibel	F	Spasskoe	accidental gunshot
5 July 1919	Leo F. McCabe	HQ	Vladivostok	disease
6 July 1919	Boyd Jones	H	Suchan	disease
3 August 1919	George W. Bennett	D	Vladivostok	disease
26 August 1919	John Graulich	A	Vladivostok	disease
26 August 1919	Oscar R. Lindberg	C	Vladivostok	accidental gunshot
13 September 1919	James A. McAnally	L	Razdolnoe	disease
19 September 1919	Peter Sheffler	E	Suchan	disease
14 November 1919	John E. Bruchie	HQ	Vladivostok	disease
19 November 1919	Louis L. Shepard	HQ	Vladivostok	disease
21 November 1919	Hubert Imm	B	Harbin	disease
30 November 1919	James E. Camp	G	Spasskoe	disease
2 December 1919	Walter J. Wilhelm	G	Spasskoe	disease
6 December 1919	Henry F. Settle	D	Vladivostok	disease
7 December 1919	Edward J. Morrison	HQ	Vladivostok	disease
12 December 1919	Milton W. Shirey	B	Harbin	disease
22 December 1919	Wesley M. Houx	B	Harbin	disease
26 December 1919	Ross Sherwood	M	Vladivostok	disease
6 January 1920	Leslie H. Iram	H	Vladivostok	disease
19 January 1920	George D. Clay	MG	Vladivostok	accident
20 January 1920	Patrick Daly	Med	Vladivostok	accident
23 January 1920	Alfred Muller	H	Vladivostok	disease
6 February 1920	Cleveland C. Orndorff	C	Vladivostok	disease
10 February 1920	Harry F. Pugh	MG	Vladivostok	disease
13 February 1920	Bailey G. Brown	G	Vladivostok	disease
17 February 1920	George W. Sweatman	B	Vladivostok	disease
18 February 1920	Edgar C. Durand	A	Vladivostok	disease
20 February 1920	Charles E. Kenyon	M	Vladivostok	disease
20 February 1920	Moody Nicholson	C	Vladivostok	disease
27 February 1920	Todd E. Cameron	L	Vladivostok	disease
6 March 1920	Herbert Mastin	M	Vladivostok	replacement barracks fire
6 March 1920	Julius W. Morris	M	Vladivostok	replacement barracks fire
30 June 1920	Harry D. Martell	L	at sea	drowned

World War II
Killed in Action or Died of Wounds

Abbott	Theodore D	Zanesville, OH	PVT	Co B	Unknown	Abucay
Agredano	Margarito	Unknown	CPL	HQ/Med Dets 2d Bn	4/7/1942	Mt Samat
Alexander	James	Unknown	PFC	Co L	1/22/1942	Abucay
Alford	Unknown	Unknown	PVT	Co A	4/8/1942	Alangan River
Van Almen	William J	Atwood, KS	PVT	Co H	4/8/1942	Alangan River
Amsler	Jack W	Unknown	PVT	Co M	1/19/1942	Abucay
Anderson	Robert C	Unknown	PFC	Co D	1/17/1942	Abucay
Anderson	W E	Unknown	SGT	Co G	Unknown	Tabayas
Andreottola	Samuel	Boston, MA	PVT	Co K	Unknown	Unknown
Annas	Rex R	Unknown	CPL	Co B	1/24/1942	Abucay
Arsenault	Fab	Orange, MA	SSG	Co F w/Phil 51st Div	Unknown	Unknown
Armstrong	James A	Unknown	SGT	Co L	1/24/1942	Abucay
Arriola	Frank	Tucson, AZ	PFC	HQ Co & Band	5/4/1942	Abucay Corregidor

Arriza-Balaga	Joe	Boise, ID	PVT	Co A	4/8/1942 DOW Hosp #1, 4/19/42	WIA-Alangan R.
Austin	John E	East St. Louis IL	SSG	Co F	Unknown	Hosp #1
Bailey	Thomas T	Unknown	PFC	AT Co	Unknown	Unknown
Ball	Charles	Browning, MT	CPL	Co B	4/6/1942	Mt Samat
Balt, Jr.	Lloyd E	Unknown	CPL/ 2LT	Co E w/Phil 41st Div	4/5/1942	Unknown
Bardin	Robert V	Canal Point, FL	PFC	Co K	Unknown	Unknown
Barnhart	Irvin W	Unknown	PFC	Co K	1/21/1942	Abucay
Barnum	Abel	Manila	SSG	HQ & Med Dets 1st Bn	6/6/1942	Cabanatuan
Bart	Jack G	Unknown	PFC	Co E	1/6/1942	Layac
Bateman	James R	Columbus. OH	PVT	HQ & Med Dets 3d Bn	4/6/1942	Mt Samat
Bates	Warren M	Sioux City, IA	PVT	Co E	1/21/1942	Abucay
Baty	James H	Unknown	PFC	Co B	4/6/1942	Mt Samat
Baxter	Earl Wm	Unknown	PVT	Co D	1/6/1942	Layac
Beattie	William F	Kansas City, MO	PVT	Co B	Unknown	Abucay
Bennett	Earl	Portland, ME	PVT	Co L	4/8/1942	Mt Bataan
Boles	Leo	Cincinnati, OH	PVT	Co D	12/29/1941	Corregidor
Bonds	Henry H	Lowndesville, SC	TSG	HQ Co & Band	Unknown	Mt Samat
Boone	John W	Unknown	PVT	Co D	1/6/1942	Layac
Bowen	Elmer T	Pulaski, TN	SSG	Co B	4/6/1942	Mt Samat
Bowlin	James C	Spring Valley, MN	PVT	Co M	Unknown	Abucay
Brand	Cecil	Unknown	CPL	Co E	12/8/1941	Cp John Hay
Broadrick	James J	Unknown	PVT	Co B	1/17/1942	Abucay
Brower	Daniel	Unknown	SSG	Co K	1/23/1942	Abucay
Brown	Robert M	Unknown	PVT	Co I	5/6/1942 1/20/42 KIA-Corregidor 5/6/42	WIA-Abucay
Brumback	Elmer H	Louisville, KY	SGT	Co K w/Phil 71st Div	Unknown	Unknown
Buehrig	Elmer P	Unknown	PFC	Co F	1/17/1942	Abucay
Bunyan	Frank P	Melrose, MT	PVT	Co C	Unknown	Abucay
Burbank	Jesse	Cement, OK	SGT	Co M	1/24/1942	Abucay
Campos	Jose	New Mexico	PVT	Co C	1/24/1942	Abucay
Capps	William	Unknown	PFC	Co L	4/8/1942	Mariveles
Carlson	Harold J	Unknown	CPL	HQ/Med Dets 2d Bn	4/8/1942	Alangan River
Carrico	Clarence	Unknown	PVT	Co H	1/26/1942 1/17/42 DOW 1/26/42	WIA Abucay
Castor	Harvey P	Unknown	CPL	Co I	5/6/1942	Corregidor
Cazier	John T	Colton, OR			07/20/1942	Cabanatuan
Childress	John J	Lakehurst, NJ	PFC	Co M	4/7/1942	Mt Samat
Chirgwin	Francis	Unknown	PFC	Co E	4/6/1942	Mt Samat
Cierciersky	John	Unknown	PVT	HQ/Med Dets 1st Bn	1/17/1942	Abucay
Clement	James M	Newton, NC	PVT	Co I	1/6/1942	Layac
Coats	Cecil B	Brooklyn, NY	PVT	Co D	1/17/1942	Mt Samat
Congdon	Edgar	Unknown	SGT	Co C	1/17/1942	Abucay
Constantineau	Floribert	Unknown	PVT	Co E	1/6/1942	Layac
Cook	George D	Unknown	PVT	Co K	1/21/1942	Abucay

Corillo	Unknown	Unknown	PVT	Co G	Unknown	Hosp #2
Couch	Winford G	St Louis, MO	PVT	Co D	07/20/1942	Cp O'Donnell
Crook	Wesley W	St Louis	PFC	HQ & Med Dets 3d Bn	4/5/1942	Mt Samat
Cross	David E	Indian	PFC	AT Co	Unknown	Unknown
Crowell	Royal E	Grand Rapids, MI	CPL	Co K	Unknown	Unknown
Davis	J B	Tulsa, OK	1SG	HQ & Med Dets 3d Bn	4/5/1942	Mt Samat
Dawsonn	Edgar A	El Dorado, AR	PVT	Co I	1/20/1942	Abucay
Deaton	Unknown	Denver, CO	PVT	Co G	4/6/1942	Mt Samat
Dickson	Robert H	Unknown	CPL	Co A	1/17/1942	Abucay
Draper	Earnest P	Unknown	PFC	Co L	2/8/1942 1/24/42 DOW Hosp #2 2/8/42	WIA Abucay
Duffy	Elmer C	Unknown	PVT	Co F	1/17/1942	Abucay
Dunham	Addison W	Cambridge, NE	MAJ	HQ & Med Dets 3d Bn	4/8/1942	Alangan R.
Dutkiewicz	Frank	Chicago, IL	PVT	Co K	1/23/1942	Abucay
Dyer	Harold D	Corpus Christi, TX	PVT	Co F	1/18/1942	Abucay
Dyson, Jr.	Powell	Unknown	CPL	Co E	Unknown	Phil 91st Div
Early	C Early	Unknown	PVT	Co D	Unknown	Mt Samat
Easler	William	Unknown	CPL	Co H	1/17/1942	Abuca
Easley	Marchel D	Unknown	CPL	Co I	1/20/1942	Abucay
Eighmey	John F	Unknown	PVT	Co B	1/17/1942	Abucay
Elliott	Melvin N	Unknown	PVT	Co E	1/6/1942	Layac
Estep	Allen J	Unknown	CPL	Co D	4/4/1942	Phil 41st Div
Evans	Herbert M	Pond Fork, MO	SGT	Co K	Unknown	2-Abucay
Finley	Leslie Hodges	Spokane, WA	CPL	Service	7/26/1942	Unknown
Flame	Peter M	Union, AZ	CPL	Co K	1/21/1942	Abucay
Fletcher	Ray	Gerald, AR	PFC	Co H	4/5/1942	Limay 1/6/42 Hosp #2 4/5/42
Flowers	Daniel	Hoxie, AR	PVT	Co K	1/21/1942	Abucay
Flynn	John P	Manila	1LT	HQ & Med Dets 3d Bn	4/8/1942	Alangan R.
Ford	George O	Unknown	PVT	Co D	1/22/1942	Bagac
Fornass	Herman	Unknown	PVT	Co B	1/17/1942	Abucay
Forte	William	Waltham, MA	PFC	Co L	1/24/1942	Abucay
Fortune	Thomas W	Douglas, GA	SSG	Co G	Unknown	Abucay
Fountain	Earnest	Unknown	2LT	Co M	1/21/1942	Abucay
Franklin	Monroe D	New York City, NY	1LT	Co G	1/17/1942	Abucay
Furtick	Feller D	Unknown	CPL	Co M	4/6/1942	Mt Samat
Garrison	Harold A	Texas	PFC	HQ Co & Band	1/18/1942	Abucay
Gensel	George S	Unknown	PVT	Co D	12/29/1941	Corregidor
Gentry	Grady	Lufkin, TX	PFC	Co L	1/23/1942	Abucay
Girard	Harold	Unknown	PVT	Co M	1/24/1942	Abucay
Gladwetz	Carl E	Unknown	PVT	Co B	4/8/1942	Alangan River
Glass	Cecil	Unknown	CPL	HQ Co & Band	1/18/1941	Abucay
Glory	Tom	Stillwell, OK	PFC	Co B	4/6/1942	Hosp #1
Golinski	Leo	Brooklyn, NY	SGT	Co B	1/17/1942	Abucay
Golkas	Edward J	Unknown	PFC	HQ & Med Dets 3d Bn	1/19/1942	Abucay
Gomes	Richard	Unknown	PFC	Co K	1/21/1942	Abucay

Goodell	Robert	Unknown	PVT	Co C	1/6/1942	Layac
Goodwin	Gene L	Fairfax, OK	CPL	HQ & Med Dets 2d Bn	Unknown	Abucay
Grace	Edgar L	Unknown	PVT	Co I	1/20/1942	Abucay
Graham	Robert J	Unknown	PVT	Co F	6/26/1942	Cabanatuan
Green	Curtis G	Council, ID	PVT	AT Co	4/5/1942	Mt Samat
Griswold	Daniel W	Enid, OK	1LT	Co K	Unknown	Abucay
Hall	John D	Greenville, SC	PVT	Co F	1/18/1942	Abucay
Hardick	Darrell H	Unknown	CPL	Co M	1/24/1942	Abucay
Harklom	James L	Tallahassee, FL	PVT	Co L	1/24/1942	Abucay
Hartman	Leslie E	Marshalltown, IA	PVT	Co F	Unknown	Abucay
Hartman	Theodore H	Unknown	PFC	Co F w/HQ Phil Dept	Unknown	Unknown
Hassen	George	New Bedford, MA	SGT	Co G	1/17/1942	Abucay
Hauser	Joseph C	East St Louis, IL	PFC	Co G	1/19/1942	Abucay
Haynes	Ezra F	Quincy, IL	SSG	Co A	4/22/1942	Hosp #2 Corregidor
Heaton	Earnest D	Unknown	PVT	Co H	4/7/1942	San Vicente
Hendricks	Jay L	Hugo, OK	PFC	Co G	Unknown	Abucay
Herd	Mac	Unknown	CPL	Co I	5/10/1942	Corregidor
Hernandez	Homer J	Overton, TX	PVT	AT Co	4/6/1942	Mt Samat
Hicks	Leroy	St. Louis, MO	PVT	Co L	1/24/1942	Abucay
Hicks	Owen	San Diego	PVT	AT Co	Unknown	Pilar-Bagac Rd
Hinsen	Noel E	Meridian, MS	SGT	Co G	1/21/1942	Abucay
Hlivjak	Frank	Chicago, IL	CPL	Co B	Unknown	Abucay
Hoffman	Anthony	Unknown	PVT	Co E	1/18/1942	Abucay
Hooper	Ronald	Hebron, CT	PVT	Co D	1/21/1942	Abucay
Horn	William W	Sweet Home, OR	SGT	Co H	4/6/1942	Mt Samat
Howard	Lloyd E	Unknown	PFC	Co D	4/6/1942	Mt Samat
Hudson	Edgar	Unknown	PVT	Co K	Unknown	Unknown
Jackson	James J	Unknown	SGT	Co K	Unknown	Abucay
Jackson	Paul	Unknown	PVT	Co C	1/18/1942	Abucay
Jaques	Carl E	Yakima, WA	PVT	Co G	4/30/1942	Corregidor
Jenness	Oren	Unknown	SGT	Co D	Unknown	Abucay
Jensen	Harry J	Chicago, IL	PVT	Co H	1/19/1942	Abucay
Johnson	Alvin D	Unknown	PVT	Co E	Unknown	Layac
Johnson	Curtis C	Forks /Elkhorn, KY	PVT	Co E	6/19/1942	Cp O'Donnell
Juvan	John	Milwaukee, WI	SSG	Co I	1/6/1942	Layac
Kaminskas	Peter	Unknown	PFC	Co K	1/21/1942	Abucay
Kebort	Lewis E	Unknown	PVT	Co M	1/24/1942	Abucay
Kelly	Vernon J	Unknown	PFC	Co B	1/17/1942	Abucay
Kerr	George J	Mehoopany, PA	CPL	Co I	1/24/1942	Abucay
Kettleson	Arnold	Seattle, WA	PVT	Co M	1/24/1942	Abucay
King, Jr.	James A	Searcy, AR	PVT	Co E	1/6/1942	Layac
Kinyon	James B	Unknown	PFC	HQ & Med Dets 3d Bn	1/19/1942	WIA Abucay; KIA
Kitchens	Willard	Rockland, TX	PVT	Co I	1/22/1942	Abucay
Knopick	Bernard C	Unknown	PVT	Co E	6/12/1942	Laguna
Koit	Walter	Unknown	SGT	Co L	4/9/1942	Mariveles
Kuechler	Edward H	Coeur d'Alene, ID	2LT	HQ & Med Dets 2d Bn	Unknown	Abucay
Lambrecht	Melvin E	Flint, MI	PFC	Co D	1/17/1942	Abucay
Langdon	Ralph	Unknown	PVT	HQ & Med Dets 1st Bn	Unknown	Unknown

Larkin	Louis C	Unknown	PVT	Co H	Unknown	killed
Lawhon	Allen	Capistrano, TX	CPT	Co M	4/5/1942	Mt Samat
Lewis	Alfred	Unknown	PVT	Co I	1/20/1942	Abucay
Lewis	Robert A	Kansas City, KS	PVT	Co D	6/22/1942	Cp O'Donnell
Litkowski	Charles	Unknown	1LT	Co A	1/17/1942	Abucay
Locke	Lonza P	Columbus, MS	PVT	Co D	Unknown	Abucay, Limay
Lonergan	James J	San Francisco, CA	CPL	Co A	1/23/1942	Abucay
Longan	troy	Bakersfield, CA	PFC	Co G	1/20/1942	Abucay
Lovelace	Charles M	Unknown	PVT	Co B	4/6/1942	Mt Samat
Loyal	Joe	Los Angeles, CA	PVT	Co K	Unknown	Unknown
Luck	Fred A	Tampa	PVT	AT Co	4/6/1942	Mt Samat
Ludwig	Clarence E	Unknown	PFC	Co A	1/22/1942	Abucay
Lupton	Thomas	Texas	SSG	Co A	4/7/1942	WIA-Mt Samat 4/6/42 DOW 4/7/42
Lux	Benjamin	Unknown	PVT	Co I	5/6/1942	Corregidor
Maksymchuk	Walter	Unknown	CPL	Co H	4/6/1942	Mt Samat
Mallette	James I	Bridgeport, CT	2LT	Co K	Unknown	Abucay
Mann	William O	Unknown	PVT	HQ & Med Dets 3d Bn	1/19/1942	Abucay
Markham	David A	San Gabriel, CA	CPL	HQ & Med Dets 3d Bn	1/20/1942	Abucay
Marlett	Unknown	Unknown	PVT	Co L	1/24/1942	Abucay
Martin	Harvey	White Sulphur Spgs, WV	PFC	HQ Co & Band	Jun 1942	Santa Rita
Martin	Henry M	Brooklyn, NY	CPL	Co B	4/5/1942	Mt Samat
Martlett	Unknown	Unknown	PVT	Co L	1/24/1942	Abucay
Mazzucca	Fiorino F	Boston	PVT	AT Co	Unknown	Unknown
McCann	John	Unknown	PVT	Co I	1/6/1942	Layac
McDermott	Bernard	Alliance, OH	SGT	Co A	Unknown	Abucay
McGowan	Charles	Unknown	SGT	Co C	5/2/1942	Corregidor
McKee	Harold	Unknown	PVT	Co K	1/20/1942	Abucay
McMurdo, Jr.	Hew B	Sharp Park, CA	PVT	Co B	4/6/1942	Mt Samat
Mercado	Fred	Santa Ana, CA	PVT	Co I	4/6/1942	Mt Samat
Meredith	John	Upper Darby, PA	PFC	Co L	1/19/1942	Abucay
Mines	James E	Russellville, AL	PVT	AT Co	Unknown	Unknown
Moffitt	Lloyd C	Denver	MAJ	HQ & Med Dets 2d Bn	Unknown	Abucay
Moore	James G	Vanceboro, NC	PVT	Co H	5/5/1942	Corregidor
Morales, Jr.	Joseph M	New York City	PVT	SVC Co	3/5/1942	Limay
Morgan	George E	Bad Axe, MI	PVT	HQ & Med Dets 3d Bn	Unknown	Abucay
Morin	Roger A	Unknown– Indian	PVT	Co F	1/244/42	Abucay
Morris	Orvil K	Port Townsend, WA	PVT	AT Co	Unknown	Mt Samat
Morrison	Edgar	Farmersville, TX	PVT	Co K	4/7/1942	Mt Samat
Mott, Jr.	Charles F	Unknown	PFC	Co L	4/7/1942	Mt Samat
Moyer	Paul	Charleston, WV	PVT	HQ Co & Band	Unknown	Unknown
Moyer, Jr.	Floyd	Palmer, NE	PVT	AT Co	Unknown	Unknown
Murphy	Harry H	Norfolk, VA	PFC	Co E	1/18/1942	Abucay
Mygrant	Clifford	San Francisco, CA	PVT	Co K	1/21/1942	Abucay
Nance	Truman	Bennington, OK	PFC	Co F	4/6/42	Abucay

						1/18/42, Mt Samat 4/6/42
Neigum	Gotlieb	Unknown	CPL	Co H	Unknown	Calumpit
Nelson	Christ	Unknown	PFC	Co L	1/24/1942	Abucay
Nicholson	Wilbur J	Unknown	CPL	Co D	4/6/1942	WIA-Mt Samat DOW Bilibid
Nisewonger	Jack	Unknown	PVT	Co C	4/6/1942	Mt Samat
Noel	Harry	Unknown	PVT	Co D	1945	Palawan
Noel	William H	St. Louis, MO	PVT	Co L	4/8/1942	Mt Bataan
Nogacek	Stanley P	Punxatawney, PA	CPL	Co G	1/19/1942	Abucay
O'Donovan	James Joseph	Cohoes, NY	MAJ	HQ & Med Dets 3d Bn	Unknown	Abucay, SS-Layac
O'Donnell	James F	Unknown	PVT	Co L	1/24/1942	Abucay
O'Donnell	Oscar J	Oakland, CA	CPL	Co I	4/6/1942	Mt Samat
Owens	Charles R	Unknown	PVT	Co G	3/19/1942	Corregidor
Palmer	John W	Covington, GA	PVT	Co M	Unknown	Abucay
Penrose	Irvin	Los Angeles, CA	PVT	Co B	6/25/1942	Cabanatuan
Peterson	Charles	Unknown	CPL	Co C	1/23/1942	Abucay
Petraca	Joseph	Unknown	PFC	Co A	1/6/1942	Layac
Petrimeaux	Earl Wm	Unknown	CPL	Co D	12/31/1941	DOW Corregidor
Pierce	Raymond H	Phoenix, AZ	PVT	Co I	1/21/1942	Abucay
Pierchalski	Edward	Wisconsin	CPL	Co A	4/22/1942	Hosp #2 4/22/42 Corregidor
Pinnington	Charles G	Unknown	PFC	Co L	3/25/1942	WIA Abucay 1/24/42, DOW 3/25/42 Hosp #2
Piper	Hugh	Unknown	CPL	Co H	1/17/1942	Abucay
Pitts	Thomas M	Nacogdoches, TX	PFC	Co K	1/23/1942	Abucay
Ponzio	Angelo	Unknown	CPL	Co M	4/7/1942	WIA Abucay, KIA Mt Samat
Potts	Boyd C	Unknown	PVT	Co F	Jul 1942	Cabanatuan
Powell	Earl C	Paducah, KY	SGT	Co I w/Phil 71st Div	1/3/1942	Porac
Price	Western	Pressmen's Home, TN	SGT	Co G	Unknown	Mt Samat
Prichard, Jr.	Guy	Rensville, PA	PFC	Co G	4/6/1942	WIA Abucay, KIA Mt Samat
Provaznik	Cyril M	Granger, TX	SGT	Co D	12/29/1941	Corregidor
Prusak	Leonard	Unknown	PVT	Co A	1/17/1942	Abucay
Ragan	Robert E	Unknown	PVT	Co H	1/17/1942	Abucay
Reagan	Knowlton	El Paso, TX	SSG	HQ Co & Band	1/18/1942	Abucay
Redden, Jr.	James J	Tulot, AR	PVT	Co B	4/6/1942	Mt Samat
Reed	H L	Unknown	PFC	Co G	1/17/1942	Abucay
Resnick	John	Unknown	SGT	Co E	4/6/1942	Mt Samat Hosp #1
Rico	Raymond	Unknown	unk	Co HQ	1942	Bataan
Ringler	John W	Laguna, PI	1SG	Co B	4/6/1942	Mt Samat
Roberts	William	Williams, AZ	PVT	Co I	1/6/1942	Layac
Rockhill	Jack F	Unknown	PVT	Co L	1/23/1942	Abucay
Root	Harold	Unknown	PFC	Co G	Unknown	Layac

Russell	Donald K	Kansas City, KS	PVT	Co I	11/21/1942	Cabanatuan
Russo	Angelo	Unknown	PFC	Co E	1/17/1942	Abucay
Saksek	Charles	Unknown	PFC	Co E	1/6/1942	Layac
Sauer	Robert S	Louisville, KY	CPT	Co E	Unknown	Abucay
Sayers	Bruce H	Unknown	PFC	Co E	5/3/1942	Corregidor
Schutz	Homer A	St Louis, MO	PVT	Co B	Unknown	Unknown
Schwartz	Raymond	Unknown	CPL	Co M	1/21/1942	Abucay
Scott	Murl M	Unknown	PVT	Co M	1/24/1942	Abucay
Seaton	Richard B	Little Rock, AR	PFC	Co H	4/8/1942	Hosp #1
Sellers	Burton	Hattiesburg, MS	CPL	Co K	1/22/1942	Abucay
Sessions	Ralph	Hemphill, TX	CPL	HQ Co & Band	5/3/1942	Corregidor
Seward, Jr.	Lloyd	Unknown	PVT	Co M	4/22/1942	Hosp #2 Corregidor
Messer	Martin	Unknown	SGT	SVC Co	4/9/1942	Corregidor
Shafsky	Francis T	Minneapolis, MN	SGT	Co F	1/17/1942	Abucay
Simpkin	Harold	Los Angeles	SGT	HQ & Med Dets 3d Bn	Unknown	Bilolo w/Phil Army
Sisk	Erskine	Unknown	PVT	SVC Co	4/9/1942	Corregidor
Skelton	John	Unknown	PFC	Co I	5/6/1942	Corregidor
Smart	Laverne L	Hooversville, PA	PVT	Co B	1/24/1942	Abucay
Smith	Edison J	Unknown	CPL	Co M	1/19/1942	Abucay
Smith	Glen W	Unknown	PVT	Co M	1/20/1942	Abucay
Smith	Harold L	Hulbert, OK	CPL	Co L	4/8/1942	Hosp #2
Smith	James	Unknown	PVT	Co M	5/3/1942	Corregidor
Smith	Leroy	Unknown	CPL	Co A	1/6/1942	Layac
Smock	Claude A	Unknown	CPL	Co A w/ 11thPhil Div	Unknown	Unknown
Snead	Edward H	Ringgold, VA	PFC	Co F	Unknown	Abucay
Sneed	Harold	Unknown	PVT	Co F	Unknown	Abucay
Snyder	Dale E	Unknown	PVT	Co D	Unknown	Executed-Bilbid SS
Soyka	Unknown	Unknown	PFC	Co L	4/9/1942	Mariveles
Stanevich	Clement J	New Bedford, MA	PVT	HQ Co & Band	Unknown	Abucay
Stanevich	Bronis	Unknown	PVT	Co L	1/19/1942	Abucay
Stevens	Herschel J	St Louis, MO	PFC	Co I	1/20/1942	Abucay
Stidham	James H	Hardshell, KY	SGT	Co E	5/5/1942	Corregidor
Stobaugh	Nolan	Clinton, AR	PFC	Co I	1/20/1942	Abucay
Summeral	Bertie W	Cove City, NC	PVT	Co A	1/19/1942	Abucay 1/19/42, SS 1/22/42
Sutton	Vernon	Alton, KS	PVT	Co D	12/29/1941	Corregidor
Sutton	Orville F	Unknown	PFC	Co L	1/19/1942	Abucay
Tabaka	Anthony	St. Louis, MO	PVT	Co L	4/19/1942	Hosp #1 Corregidor
Tash	James R	St. Louis, MO	PVT	Co F	Unknown	Abucay
Taylor	Cameron C	Tennessee	SSG	AT Co	4/3/1942	Mt Samat
Taylor	CC	Unknown	SGT	Co I	4/5/1942	Mt Samat
Traylor	Larkin Bill	Houston, TX	SSG	HQ	11/05/1942	Cabanatuan Cp #5
Thompson	John W	Seattle, WA	CPT	Co B	Unknown	WIA Abucay 1/27/42, WIA Mt Samat 4/6/42
Tomalus	Anthony	Unknown	PVT	Co I	1/24/1942	Abucay

Trawinski	Casimir	Unknown	SGT	Co K	4/8/1942	Alangan River
Tunks	Fred	Paonia CO	PVT	Co M	1/24/1942	Abucay
Turner	George	Unknown	PVT	Co G	Unknown	Mt Samat
Turner	Irby C	Carrollton, MS	PVT	Co F	1/17/1942	Abucay
Tymenski	John	Unknown	PVT	AT Co	Unknown	patient in Hosp #1
Vail	Paul H	Unknown	PVT	Co E	3/23/42	WIA Abucay, DOW 3/23/42 Hosp #2
Van Arsdale	John D	Kingston, WA	CPL	Co M	1/23/1942	Abucay
Van Sickle	JC	Winfield, TX	PFC	Co C	1/24/1942	Abucay
Walker	Harvey R	Port Huron, MI	PVT	Co M	Unknown	Abucay
Wallace	Joseph A	New York City, NY	SGT	Co F	Unknown	Abucay
Wallace, Jr.	John F	Unknown	PVT	Co M	Unknown	Abucay
Wangberg, Jr.	Ronald T	Unknown	PVT	Co B	1/22/1942	Abucay
Wantuk	Joseph	Unknown	PVT	Co G	1/24/1942	Abucay
Warr	Franklin O	Unknown	CPL	Co H	1/17/1942	WIA Abucay 1/17/42, DOW 1/21/42
Wasson	Clyde L	Bell, CA	PVT	Co B	4/6/1942	Mt Samat
Watkins	Roy	Rocky Ford, CO	PFC	Co B	1/25/1942	Abucay
Weeks	Robert H	Unknown	PVT	Co H	Unknown	Luzon
Wehler	Frederick J	California	PFC	Co L	4/22/1942	Hosp #2 Corregidor
Welchko	Cecil	Unknown	CPT	Co A	01/21/1945	WIA 01/09/42 Takao Harbor
Weigel	Robert P	Idaho Falls, ID	PFC	HQ Co & Band	Unknown	Abucay
Welch	Alfred R	Houston, TX	PVT	Co F	1/17/1942	Abucay
White	William J	Unknown	CPL	Co H	4/10/1942	Death March
White	William W	San Diego, CA	SSG	Co L	4/7/1942	Mt Samat
White, Jr.	Clyde	Kansas City, MO	PFC	AT Co	4/5/1942	Mt Samat
Williamson	Harold D	Unknown	SGT	Co H	Unknown	Mt Samat
Wilson	Marlin	Halstead, KS	CPL	Co M	1/17/1942	Abucay
Wingfield	Henry	Maryville, TN	PVT	IIQ & Mcd Dets 3d Bn	1/20/1942	Abucay
Wisniewski	Stanley L	Newark, NJ	PVT	HQ Co & Band	Unknown	Abucay
Wood	Homer L	Corsicana, TX	PVT	AT Co	1/6/1942	Layac
Worrell	Raymond M	Wisner, NE	PVT	Co F	1/17/1942	Abucay
Wrightmann	Derrell M	Minnesota	CPL	Co D w/Phil 11th Div	Apr 1942	Bonbon
Young	William W	Unknown	PVT	Co B	Unknown	Abucay
Zabitch	Joseph	Chicago, IL	PVT	Co G	1/19/1942	Abucay
Zaynor	Paul R	Chicago, IL	PVT	Co H	Unknown	Cp O'Donnell
Zmur	Michael	Unknown	PFC	Co D	4/6/1942	Mt Samat

World War II Deaths in Captivity

The following list of 1156 men who died in captivity, roughly half of the regiment's strength on the day the war began, is extracted from LTC Brady's Cabanatuan roster. The list is subdivided by company, and then under each company by rank from left to right.

Regimental Headquarters and Headquarters Company
(91 died in captivity)

LTC Jasper E Brady, Jr	LTC Leo C Paquet	MAJ Marshall H Hurt, Jr
CPT Everett V Mead	CPT Thane H Hooker	CPT Earl C Packer
1LT Walter S Strong	1LT William J Tooley	2LT Fred B Klessig
WO Edward H Cruikshank	1SG Walter H Hall	MSG Glenn I Criss
TSG Henry M Bonds	TSG George W Trotter	SSG Newell Chandler
SSG Ralph Hicks	SSG John J Jankowski	SSG Larkin B Traylor
SGT Henry B. Ashby	SGT Joseph E Bak	SGT James L Hicks
SGT Joseph F Mathein	SGT Ralph B Ross	SGT Virgil D Williams
CPL George Alford	CPL Leonard Hamilton	CPL Lloyd A Hughes
CPL Clement R Miller	CPL Richard J Thompson	CPL Edward L Whalen
PFC Claude I Broussard	PFC Wilbur Burdick	PFC Orville F Cook
PFC Robert B Coppock	PFC Edwin D Dravis	PFC David H Ellsworth
PFC William T Fenton	PFC Tommy Foster	PFC John E Handley
PFC Henry H Harvey	PFC Lynn T Hasty	PFC Winfried O Hayes
PFC Daimer F Hickman	PFC David S Keven	PFC Albert W Klaus
PFC Homer E Lewis	PFC Evan A Malmquist	PFC Jean P Morrow
PFC Donald R Nugen	PFC Mike Petljaga	PFC Raymond L Ross
PFC Benjamin F Runyan	PFC Clement J Stanevich	PFC Allen J Sutherland
PFC Kenyard Taylor	PFC Robert P Weigel	PFC Rex T Williams
PFC Stephen Wisniewski	PVT Frank B Arriola	PVT Paul Bostick
PVT James R Brooks	PVT Albert F Brown	PVT Francis F Champagne
PVT Elton W Copeland	PVT Henning O Degerness	PVT Wayne E Drake
PVT James B Emrick	PVT Tommie Evans	PVT Michael Greico
PVT Thomas C Harrington	PVT Edward R Hilinski	PVT Otha L Holliday
PVT Patrick Iliff	PVT Gerald W Isbell	PVT Hobart M Jones
PVT Joseph M Kane	PVT Charles A McCall	PVT Walter M Malonek
PVT Vernon A Martin	PVT Ralph G Payne	PVT Stuart R Pennington
PVT John V Phillips	PVT Carlos E Price	PVT Vernon H Rhodes
PVT Sammie Silverman	PVT Lawrence Smith	PVT Leonard Snell
PVT Jason Stoutenburgh	PVT Fred Williams	PVT Henry E Wilson
PVT Thomas M Wethnell		

Antitank Company (62 died in captivity)

CPT Robert A Barker	1LT Harold F Monson	SSG Cameron C Taylor
SGT Louis F Berendt	SGT Walter Kowalczyk	SGT James J Murphy
SGT Joseph R Vaughn	SGT Claude E Wilson	CPL Leo J Barlosky
CPL George L McCafferty	CPL Robert Spalek	CPL Paul F Welch
PFC Edward C Ambrose	PFC J S Anderson	PFC Thomas T Bailey
PFC Eugene E Bales	PFC David E Cross, Jr	PFC Clifford D Hendon
PFC Walter W Kean	PFC Jessie J Nelson	PFC Warren W Powless, Jr
PFC William W Utley	PFC Homer L Wood	PVT Don L Abernathy
PVT Cleveland Armond	PVT Cecil W Bradshaw	PVT C L Clark
PVT Charles B Clayton	PVT Patrick F Corcoran	PVT Elmo J Daigle
PVT Albert F D'Auria	PVT Bernard M Doxtator	PVT Paul L Foy
PVT Gerald C Gaines	PVT Siebelt R Goldenstein	PVT Gerald W Haman
PVT James E Hayward	PVT Frank S Heater	PVT Owen Hicks
PVT Albert C Kalen	PVT Raymond E Larson	PVT Fred A Luck
PVT Condia Lynch	PVT Joseph B Martineau	PVT Fiorino F Mazzucca
PVT Amos R McAfee	PVT Rovert L McIntyre	PVT James E Mines
PVT Orvel K Morris	PVT Floyd Moyer, Jr	PVT John D Nabb
PVT Glenwood D Porter	PVT Fred J Reed	PVT Gerald D Reeves
PVT Edmund F Sadler	PVT Ari Self	PVT Clarence Smith, Jr
PVT Marion R Thompson	PVT Gerald K Titman	PVT Clyde White, Jr
PVT Jerry D Williams	PVT Charles C Zenchenko	

HQ 1st Battalion (22 died in captivity)

LTC Edward H Bowes
MAJ Fred M Small
2LT Steve W Mickey
SSG Raymond D Meyer
SGT Maynard F Greene
CPL Stewart A Jones
CPL Herschell L Meyers
CPL Ignac D Senkyrik, Jr
CPL Darrell K Thorsted
CPL Doyle W Veatch
PFC Leo M Grill
PFC Richard C Hiatt
PFC Salvador G Lamanga
PFC Chester J Prater
PFC Lee Thompson
PVT Charles A Averill
PVT Johns Clark
PVT Willis G Myers
PVT Gunner K Nelson
PVT Carl Norris
PVT Glen N Sherman
PVT Andrew W Vanasse

A Company (61 died in captivity)

CPT Cecil R Welchko
2LT Alfred E Lee
1SG Samuel Talvey
SSG Jack W Burkhalter
SSG Ezra F Haynes
SGT Bruce F Alexander
SGT Warren Ager
SGT John Elings
SGT Bernard McDetmott
SGT Charles K Relahan
SGT George W Schlam
SGT Henry E Sellers
SGT Jesse O Trevillian
CPL Aubry Black
CPL Frank M Delaney
CPL Charles J Hoffman
CPL James J Lonergan
CPL Fred Mayo
CPL Robert C Milks
CPL Cameron Proctor
CPL Albert E Young
PFC Joseph N Adkins
PFC Henry J Angle, Jr
PFC Ralph A Blurton
PFC Allen Bordeaux
PFC Virgil G Deverell
PFC Martin G Jaster
PFC Clinton A Jolly
PFC John Labasewski
PFC Andrew Ruacho
PFC Lee A Schier
PFC Roy Swain
PFC Simon D Vilar
PVT Jack Armstrong
PVT Fred Boyer
PVT William C Boyette
PVT Harry Braxton
PVT J T Caizer
PVT Robert F Cochran
PVT Neil E Dunlap
PVT Michael M Fadorchak
PVT Lewis M Fryor
PVT John Halligon
PVT Joseph E Hoffer
PVT Virgil Huykill
PVT Robert A Jackson
PVT Paul Jarlsberg
PVT Erford M Johnson
PVT Albert J Kokitas
PVT Lewis H Lanning
PVT Ralph Lee, Jr
PVT Phillip J McCall
PVT Isador Meites
PVT Albert C Ramsey
PVT Benjamin J Ramsay
PVT Albert E Reed
PVT G O Rivers, Jr
PVT Junior A Simonson
PVT Bertie W Sumrel
PVT Ralph Vassey
PVT Ralph H Wells

B Company (69 died in captivity)

CPT Lloyd C Murphy
CPT John W Thompson
1LT Charles L Hodgins
2LT Irvin R Sutphin
1SG Harry E Ringler
SSG Elmer T Bowen
SGT Henry Banks
SGT Joseph N Croce
SGT Leo Golinski
SGT John A Hanell
SGT Lawrence E Hicks
SGT Troy G Laws
SGT Michael Leschuck
SGT William C Twombley
CPL Odie W Britt
CPL Frank J Feiden
CPL Frank Hlivjak
CPL James A Lyda
CPL Henry M Martin
CPL Floyd R Rogers
CPL Ivan E Rogers
CPL Kenneth F Sherman
PFC Joseph Auche
PFC Carl M Beightol
PFC Russell W Ball
PFC Mike Concoy
PFC James J Cooney
PFC Jessie W Gentry
PFC William Glomb
PFC William H Gray
PFC Rudolph Haroldson
PFC Jack L James
PFC Eugene J McCourt
PFC Albert Rodecker
PFC Jack S Sanders
PVT Theodore D Abbott
PVT Bernard C Baca
PVT William F Beattie
PVT Boyd H Beck
PVT Arthur H Biggers
PVT Charles L Blair
PVT John I Boone
PVT William M Bright
PVT Joseph Calcagno
PVT William E Calkins
PVT Raleigh Colwell
PVT George R Crone
PVT John F Diaz
PVT Ethan A Dubose
PVT John F Eighmey
PVT Donald W Eldridge
PVT Carl C Elliott
PVT John E Gleason
PVT Mike D Hammond
PVT Ben F Hayes
PVT Hew B McMurdo, Jr
PVT Procopio Medina
PVT James S Mitchell
PVT John F Murphy
PVT Jose Paez, Jr
PVT Irvin Penvose
PVT James J Redden, Jr
PVT James A Russell
PVT Laverne L Smart
PVT Paul E Walsh
PVT Herbert R Worley, Jr
PVT Leonard C Young
PVT William W Young
PVT Robert C Zimmerman

C Company (68 died in captivity)

CPT Richard K Carnahan	2LT Ralph C Simmons	1SG Arthur C Houghtby
SSG David D Crouse	SSG Gerald A Farnham	SGT W E Broach
SGT James B Cabral	SGT Leo H Miles	SGT Charles A Peters
SGT John T Dacon	SGT Charles L Richardson	SGT Karl J Muzikar
CPL Charles K Adams	CPL Leo S Bachelier	CPL Fred K Baker
CPL Marvin R Bowman	CPL Raymond A Brownlee	CPL Leroy Horton
CPL Ralph Horton	CPL J L Johnson	CPL Martin L Johnson
CPL John Matolo	CPL Robert B McCloskey	CPL Raymond E Miller
CPL Elliott S Wright	PFC Cephus L Carmichael	PFC Leslie H Childs
PFC Lyell R Mooney, Jr	PFC Andrew E Nickerson	PFC Robert C Schildroth
PFC James F Snyder	PFC J C VanSickle	PVT Edward Baca
PVT Robert H Brown	PVT Robert J Browning	PVT Frank P Bunyan
PVT William T Campbell	PVT C C Cobb	PVT James Condos
PVT Powell DeHaven	PVT Erwin D Denleeshower	PVT William J Folton
PVT C F Gray	PVT Earl B Hamilton	PVT Virgil L Hamock
PVT Darwin Hattenbach	PVT Paul Jackson	PVT Gilbert Johnson
PVT Donald R Lechty	PVT Choice R Maness	PVT Ronald M McCormack
PVT Chester A Mecikalski	PVT Don E Mitchell	PVT Charles E Muldoon
PVT John Novak	PVT Harold Rall	PVT Melvin J Roberts
PVT Richard F Smith	PVT George W Solberg	PVT Samuel Stenzler
PVT Robert L Stevens	PVT Ray G Swanson	PVT James J Terry
PVT Charles G Vargas	PVT George E Walker	PVT Clayton Whitford
PVT Otis C Williams	PVT Harvey D Yager	

D Company (71 died in captivity)

1LT Robert G Emerson	2LT Fred H Milliren	SSG William S Metcalf
SGT Homer Crunk	SGT Oren L Jenness	SGT Vincent Zubick
CPL Billy D Barnett	CPL Clinton A Bliss	CPL Walter J Byrne
CPL Ralph F Demaray	CPL Joseph E Dufresne	CPL Allen J Estep
CPL Henry Mazurkiewicz	CPL Wilbur J Nicholson	CPL George L Robarge
CPL Robert A Lewis	CPL Lester L Thornton	CPL Arthur B Walberg
CPL Wilson H Ware	CPL Derrell M Wrightman	PFC Jesus G Arroyo
PFC Harvey A Bassett	PFC George F Connoly	PFC Eugene A Donohue
PFC Lemack A Dundas	PFC Louis E Flores	PFC Elmer L Harrison
PFC Albert J Jackson	PFC John C Jencik	PFC Leonard H Jenkins
PFC Daniel C Koppenheffer	PFC Eugene Kresal	PFC Taylor A Leseur, Jr
PFC Lonza P Locke	PFC Glenn W Moyers	PFC Ignatios Poulimendos
PFC Wayne A Seiling	PFC Cecil R Sheets	PFC John Thomas, Jr
PFC Christopher Welter	PVT Roy C Anderson	PVT Leo Boles
PVT John R Brown	PVT John Bryant	PVT George L Busbee
PVT Frederick Carlon	PVT Charles E Clark	PVT J T Colgan
PVT Winford G Couch	PVT James Darr	PVT William E Drabant
PVT Richard F Drake	PVT Joseph Fitzgerald	PVT John E Freeman
PVT George L Gregorson	PVT Clara Grew	PVT Donald F Hespen
PVT Cecil T Hinson	PVT Ronald Hooper	PVT Verle G Huffman
PVT James Jensen	PVT Eugene L May	PVT Martin McGrath
PVT Harry Noel	PVT Harry W Olson	PVT Roy G Rabotnik
PVT Daniel R Sanchez	PVT Elton W Sanders	PVT Vernon Sutton
PVT Thomas E Taylor	PVT Paul B Vick	

HQ 2nd Battalion (24 died in captivity)

LTC Cyril Q Marron	MAJ Lloyd C Moffitt	2LT Edward H Kuechler
SSG Lelian L Floyd	SGT John H McManigal	CPL Darrell Church
CPL Gene L Goodwin	CPL Arthur L Haley	CPL Jewel D Johnson
PFC Lucien F Beaudoin	PFC John Blanton	PFC Delmar W Erwin

PFC Leslie C Hammer
PFC Benjamin E Pope
PVT (first name unk) Ross
PVT Conrad E Trotter

PFC Joseph Montoya
PVT Clinton H Buyatt
PVT Everett L Russell
PVT Clifford C Wakefield

PFC Alexander C Robles
PVT Lewis F Collins, Jr
PVT Raymond D Schaffer
PVT Jack Zinn

E Company (58 died in captivity)

CPT Robert S Sauer
1SG Beresford D Seale
SGT Alvin D Crow
SGT Lawrence K Hanscom
CPL Harold B Anderson
CPL John G Gunn
CPL James O Rooks
PFC James Bryant
PFC Jack Dykes
PFC Gerald L Hicks
PFC Joseph S Sherbuck
PVT Warren M Bates
PVT Edmund M Costello
PVT Edward A Gibbons
PVT Harry E Lamb
PVT James F McConnell
PVT Roy Medley
PVT Dan Perreira
PVT Richard F Smith
PVT Thomas L Tidwell

1LT James E Smith
SSG Olaf F Anderson
SGT William H Eddleman
SGT George Kerekesh
CPL Theopalus Chisenhall
CPL Orville Hunter
CPL James M Walker
PFC John O Buchanan
PFC Walter A Frye
PFC Harry H Murphy
PFC Thomas E Sliger
PVT Lacy W Boyster
PVT Marvin E Everly
PVT Curtis Johnson
PVT Gerald McCann
PVT Harrison McCrary
PVT Carl E Merritt
PVT Raymond Redcay
PVT Harlan R Swanson

2LT Raymond A Freel
SSG Morris L Moore
SGT Wilson M Hall
SGT James H Stidham
CPL Walter E Elliott
CPL Elmer Pruitt
PFC Jack G Bart
PFC Eugene L Davis
PFC J D Hayes
PFC Roland R Roark
PFC Delos W Stetler
PVT Dail Catterlin
PVT Howard Gamble
PVT Bernard A Knopick
PVT David H McClure
PVT Wesley L McCroy
PVT Earl R Norenberg
PVT Paul T Robertson
PVT Austin D Teague

F Company (71 died in captivity)

1LT John Scott
SSG Fab Arsenault
SGT Russell Cirrito
SGT Barry W Quesenbury
CPL Charles Chadwell
CPL Willard H Dills
CPL Claude M Granville
CPL Robert Scruby
PFC Robert B Cavender
PFC Donald H Goforth
PFC Harry Leader
PFC Edward H Snead
PVT Amon M Blair
PVT Jasper Davis, Jr
PVT Jack E Genoud
PVT John D Hall
PVT Charles L Mackey
PVT Roger A Morin
PVT Boyd C Potts
PVT Edward W Reid
PVT Harold Sneed
PVT Charles W Street
PVT Irby C Turner
PVT Raymond M Worrell

2LT Harry J Herbert
SGT Edmund Adjuczyk
SGT Eugene L Kelley
SGT Francis T Shafsky
CPL Joseph H Coates
CPL Oscar S Edwards
CPL Harry Harrison
CPL Joseph Zubie
PFC Charles G Davis
PFC Alban Harvey
PFC J B McBride
PFC Leon H Wallace
PVT Edward L Braasch
PVT Peter P Dolski
PVT Robert J Graham
PVT Elbert A Holt
PVT Basil J Matthews
PVT Felix Muniz
PVT Ivan E Ramsey
PVT Vernon C Smalley
PVT Thomas M Sparks
PVT Henry M Tarsa
PVT Alfred R Welch
PVT William W Young

SSG John E Austin
SGT James E Bigelow
SGT Thadious H Padgette
SGT Joseph A Wallace
CPL Julian T Cochrane
CPL James Gillis
CPL Charles W Rowley
PFC Ralph F Blank
PFC Lawrence O Ehlers
PFC Richard L Jones
PFC Truman Nance
PVT John B Autry
PVT Thomas L Davidson
PVT Harold O Dyer
PVT Claude Guier
PVT Elmer J Jones
PVT B McGraw
PVT Charles O Mueller
PVT Russell Rasmussen
PVT Cleatus O Smith
PVT John C Spratt
PVT James R Tash
PVT Angus Wise

G Company (67 died in captivity)

2LT Herbert Rochester
SSG Thomas W Fortune
SGT George Hassen

2LT Bernard C Kopelke
SGT W E Anderson
SGT Noel E Hinson

1SG Daniel Proctor
SGT George W Bradshaw
SGT Thomas W Kopper

SGT John J Kowalewski
SGT Edward F Piezonka
SGT Joseph Revelia
SGT Earl J Squires
CPL Delmer Gildersleeve
CPL William D Juhl
CPL Fred R Melnick
CPL William C Querl
PFC Gordon Bailey
PFC David F Bucholtz
PFC Jay L Hendricks
PFC Manuel D Martinez
PFC Scott E Phillips
PVT Antonio Alvera
PVT Jacob Cornsilk
PVT Joseph A Garrison
PVT James E McCoy
PVT Harry O Price
PVT Vernon G Thorpe
PVT Joseph Zabitch

SGT Kenneth F Lathrop
SGT Western Price
SGT Fred Tilghman
CPL Joseph C Denny
CPL Thomas A Hammondtree
CPL Stanley P Jones
CPL Karl E Miller
CPL Curtis L Sizemore
PFC Julius Becker
PFC Salvatore Fuzzengheria
PFC Lewis D Jackson
PFC Herman E Miles
PFC Floyd D Taylor
PVT W B Carroll
PVT Arthur Clemenson
PVT Emil H Koebel
PVT Clarence E Nichols
PVT Arthur D Reed
PVT Joseph Wantuck

SGT Steven Mazerick
SGT Henry O Rabon
SGT John T Wiesloch
CPL Perry J Dunn
CPL Lewis H Harris
CPL Walter I Lamphier
CPL Ernest C Oates
CPL Thomas D Wilson
PFC Albert H Brickman
PFC Joseph C Hauser
PFC George O Kingstead
PFC Peter Oluschczak
PFC Frederick Wetherington
PVT Harry Cheholtz
PVT Ardell S Ellingson
PVT Emanuel Korn
PVT Lawrence L Norman
PVT Elmer S Russell, Jr
PVT Felvert E Williams

H Company (87 died in captivity)

CPT Dwight T Hunkins
1SG Robert E Sullivan
SSG Robert W Williams
SGT William W Horn
SGT Orel C St Germain
CPL Harold N Flaaten
CPL Dewey Kincaid
CPL John S Rodgers
CPL Redford D Tefft
PFC Ashby Baskett
PFC John C Burks
PFC Ray Fletcher
PFC Milton H Hurtienne
PFC Lee E Lawlor
PFC Frank A Majors
PFC Sullivan H McPherson
PFC Robert Y Richards
PVT Robert S Anderson
PVT Raymond Cunningham
PVT James D Helms
PVT Charles W Hughes
PVT Troy O Jones
PVT Cecil B Leckron
PVT Junius D Moore
PVT Thomas Picone
PVT Emmett C Ramey
PVT Harold Snyder
PVT Marvin Stroud
PVT Robert H Weeks

1LT Robert K Magee
SSG Carl J Williams
SGT Heimie Bograd
SGT Paul C Nance
CPL Benjamin Baruch
CPL Basil C Friend
CPL Albert J Lawrence
CPL Lonnie D Stephenson
CPL John E Walsh
PFC Wellington W Bernd
PFC Willard C Cline
PFC Harry Gerlitz
PFC Arthur M Jones
PFC John Lawrence
PFC Lazaro Martinez
PFC James G Moore
PFC Hillis L Russell
PVT Jesse Bressie
PVT Anthony M Duquette
PVT Charles A Henderson
PVT William J Jenkins
PVT Martin L Kunik
PVT (first unk) McKee
PVT Leon W Nelson
PVT John I Provence
PVT Leonard F Robbins
PVT Steven Stanko
PVT Leonard W Taylor
PVT Arthur N Yockey

2LT Millard Blaisdell
SSG Richard McCallum
SGT Raymond H Gilmore
SGT J A Schmidt
CPL Fred E Dean
CPL Yancy H Kaler
CPL John D Liebgott
CPL Carl Strong
CPL William J White
PFC George E Bidwell
PFC Jewell D Craig
PFC James J Higgins
PFC Bertrand M Keck
PFC Jesse F Long
PFC Ora A McCormick
PFC Homer L Rice
PVT Howard Abbott
PVT Edwin F Colon
PVT John Handite
PVT Theodore J Horsefall
PVT Harry J Jensen
PVT Lewis C Larkin
PVT Orvel R Mollohan
PVT Anthony O'Donohugh
PVT Harold E Purvis
PVT William Runyan
PVT Albert D Stengler
PVT Roscoe E Timberlake
PVT Paul R Zaynor

HQ 3rd Battalion (21 died in captivity)

MAJ James J O'Donovan
SGT Harold Simkin
CPL David L Markham
PFC Wesley W Crook

CPT Jerry O Gonzales
CPL George C Clamp
CPL John Mikologezyk
PFC Warren O'Toole

1LT John P Flynn
CPL Henry E Lee
CPL Donald L E Solomon
PFC Alfred G Smith

PFC Raymond Stephens
PVT Charles J Johnson
PVT Ross M Spiers

PVT Alf Y Anderson
PVT Harold P Morton
PVT Russell Stover

PVT Robert A Ellis
PVT George G Robertson
PVT Henry J Wingfield

I Company (64 died in captivity)

CPT Richard Roshe
2LT William F Miles
SGT Leonard R Exceen
SGT Albert Rosen
CPL James Duvall
CPL Felix R Mitrekevich
CPL Samuel C Terry
PFC Charles S Lanier
PFC Frank Murphy
PFC Ercel F Presnall
PVT Tom D Brown
PVT Edgar H Clinkscales
PVT James D Dawson
PVT Calvin J Gilliam
PVT Willard Kitchens
PVT Leon Lovelady
PVT John McCann
PVT Conrad C Perryman
PVT Raymond H Pierce
PVT Lawrence Roesner
PVT Daniel F Ryan
PVT Kenneth White

CPT Ray B Stroud
SGT Ray W Chapman
SGT Henry W Macner
SGT Wallace M Stamm
CPL Mark A Edison
CPL Eugene A Murff
PFC William B Holmes
PFC David Livingston
PFC Joseph C Murphy
PFC Hershel J Stevens
PVT Francis E Bryant
PVT Elgin W Daniels
PVT Walter H Faith
PVT Lorin J Gregory
PVT Andrew Laroque
PVT Wilbur D Lundgren
PVT David McDougal
PVT John Phelan
PVT Wesley S Rimmer
PVT Ralph L Ruark
PVT Fred D Smith

2LT Charles Baker
SGT Norman Deas
SGT Raymond W May
SGT Oscar Wallace
CPL Richard Hinker
CPL John D Newman
PFC Glen E Jackson
PFC Clyde F Marx
PFC D W Neal
PFC Nolan Stobaugh
PVT Albert R Burns
PVT Edward A Dawson
PVT W S Frank
PVT William C Hammond
PVT John H Learquin
PVT K Manion
PVT Fred F Mercado
PVT Michael Pregtanz
PVT William Roberts
PVT Donald K Russell
PVT Frank Spear

K Company (70 died in captivity)

CPT Coral M Talbott
2LT James I Malette
SGT Herbert M Evans
SGT Walter Poratoski
CPL William J Batton
CPL Elvin L Davis
CPL Harry P Herr, Jr
CPL Harvey L McKee
CPL Anthony R Tamulevich
PFC Ammit M Bookman
PFC Charles L Callahan
PFC Edward J Jones
PFC Emory McLaughlin
PFC Adolph B Schwartz
PVT Clifton L Clark
PVT Daniel Flowers
PVT Charles A Larick
PVT Robert E Matney
PVT Stanley Mieczkowski
PVT Melvin Myers, Jr
PVT Albert L Petee
PVT Robert Pryer
PVT T E Stauffer
PVT Charles M Wilson

1LT Daniel W Griswold
1SG Joseph G Gostwa
SGT John H Fulkrod
CPL Charles D Allen
CPL William R Collins
CPL James W Dunn
CPL John X Lowery
CPL Arrol L Myers
CPL Edward J Wisz
PFC Bruce D Brown
PFC Edward N Edwards
PFC Joseph Longknife
PFC Paul W Ralph
PVT James L Aaron
PVT Thomas A Couch
PVT Clyde Garner
PVT Harold E Lokey
PVT Hilding Mattson
PVT Edgar M Morrison
PVT Clifford H Mygrant
PVT John Pierce
PVT George W Rumbaugh
PVT Charles E Thomas

2LT John Gure
SGT William Barnett
SGT James J Jackson
CPL Doyle R Armstrong
CPL Royal E Crowell
CPL Peter M Flame
CPL Thurman O Mansfield
CPL Theodore Spagnell
PFC Harry Becker
PFC James C Brown
PFC Frank J Ferguson
PFC Frank D McCauley
PFC Jesse E Stout
PVT Harold C Chilcoat
PVT Leo F Fetzer
PVT Edgar R Hudson
PVT Joe Loyal
PVT Ralph E Michel
PVT Alvan W Mussen
PVT Bruce H Penny
PVT Clyde Presley
PVT Walter S Slawek
PVT James T Tubb

L Company (64 died in captivity)

CPT Herbert H Eichlin
SGT James A Armstrong

1SG William B McNulty
SGT Curtis B Cannon

SSG William W White
SGT Lawrence Y Heller

SGT Owen G Long
CPL Peter C Imperial
CPL Calvin D Quinn
PFC Peter J Chamonte
PFC William Forte
PFC John Meredith
PFC Manuel R Rogers
PFC Orville F Sutton
PVT Raymond Barrett
PVT Patrick F Bridgeman
PVT Elgin W Daniels
PVT Earl Ennis
PVT Clarence J Harvey
PVT Theodore W Jones
PVT C W McKeowen
PVT Robert S Peters
PVT Jack F Rockhill
PVT Bronis J Stanevich
PVT George H Suttle
PVT Joseph C Warle

SGT Bernardo M Navallo
CPL Arthur W Maki
CPL Harold L Smith
PFC Peter Economopolous
PFC Grady Gentry
PFC Charles F Mott, Jr
PFC Harold Stevens
PFC Carroll W Thomas
PVT Earl Bennett
PVT Francis E Chapman
PVT Thomas G Earp
PVT Charles L Gore
PVT Leroy Hicks
PVT Harry King
PVT N P Nackley
PVT Norman E Reinhardt
PVT John Reynolds
PVT Robert R Stewart
PVT Edwin C Vandiver

CPL Richard E Hedlund
CPL Burrell D Phillips
PFC James Alexander
PFC Marcus A Engesser
PFC Fares Martinez
PFC James J Murray
PFC Julius W Stewart
PFC Emmett B Toney
PVT Ray W Brandon
PVT John B Creador
PVT Harold E Elsasser
PVT James L Harrison
PVT James L Hollingsworth
PVT Archibald W McKenzie
PVT John L Pedigo
PVT Charles Robinson
PVT James Stiers
PVT George Storer
PVT William C Ward

M Company (82 died in captivity)

CPT Allen Lahon
SSG Otto Jensen
SGT Harry M Neff
CPL Robert L Baker
CPL Ralph R Cowgill
CPL Jay M Horton
CPL Edward F Skinner
PFC John J Childress
PFC James F Hayes
PFC Jim R McClelland
PFC William E Mock
PFC Willard P Orr
PFC Edward A Sanquillan
PVT James C Bolin
PVT James D Butler
PVT John D Conway
PVT Daniel Golland
PVT Neal E Heatherhill
PVT Lewis E Kebort
PVT Quentin D Miller
PVT Phillip W Prout
PVT Noel M Richards
PVT Donald F Snodderly
PVT Clell P Steagall
PVT John V Tierman
PVT Claude R Via
PVT George F Weatherwax
PVT Charles D Zacinjalec

1LT Henry S Jones
SGT Herbert W Gross
SGT Clinton H Nichols
CPL James H Blair
CPL Homer M Cutsinger
CPL Clarence E Lahnar
CPL John D van Arsdale
PFC Arthur J Gagnon
PFC Albert C Henke
PFC William A McDowell
PFC Buford E Mortimer
PFC Gretano V Rumore
PFC Raymond L Steeby
PVT James G Bovee
PVT Robert H Carlson
PVT James L Etheridge
PVT Vaughn P Grant
PVT Gustaf Hetze
PVT Eugene W Lindley
PVT William P Nichols
PVT Alfred Querbach
PVT Thomas J Ryan
PVT Lasaro Solis
PVT William C Steele
PVT Edward J Tobin
PVT Harvey R Walker
PVT Harry Wingfield

2LT Roy Zoberbier
SGT Benjamin J Muraski
SGT Frederick A Thompson
CPL Donald V Clinch
CPL Salvatore L Ferrara
CPL Gene N Pinto
PFC George H Bard
PFC Thomas G Hasket
PFC Andrew Hickingbottom
PFC Charles E Miller
PFC Thomas H Olson
PFC Angelo L Russo
PFC Charles W Wickman
PVT Peter D Briggs
PVT Frank L Choate
PVT Mark J Gilmore
PVT Ralph C Hall
PVT Thompson L Joiner
PVT William A McDowell
PVT John W Palmer
PVT Rudolph A Quesada
PVT Murl M Scott
PVT Charles F Starns
PVT John F Symington
PVT Fred Tunks, Jr
PVT Leonard R Wallace
PVT Frederick J Wolf

Service Company (64 died in captivity)

1LT Walter E O'Brien
2LT Robert E Miller
MSG Henry Lorenz
TSG John B Fry
SSG Grover Nunn

2LT Andrew B Casey
WO Max Chower
MSG Stefan Widerynski
SSG Leo Johnson
SSG Lloyd Voris

2LT Arthur P Leahy
MSG James W Evans
TSG John C Bailey
SSG John K Luhman
SGT Edward A Haberman

SGT Clyde L Harris
SGT Durwood Strout
CPL Titus L Alt
PFC Arthur Barrett
PFC Frank H Pibarn
PVT Christopher R Bloxham
PVT George C Braddy
PVT Edward L Clark
PVT Leslie Dowling
PVT Vernon T Hackley
PVT James W Kelly
PVT Leroy Loomis
PVT Joseph M Morales, Jr
PVT Garland H Onley
PVT George W Pennington
PVT Dan Taylor
PVT Jack D Yeater

SGT Edward M Jarycranzki
SGT Robert V Taylor
CPL George W Ballard
PFC Charles Bloom
PVT Clifford C Bartell
PVT Ray H Bloxham
PVT Albert W Bush
PVT Hershell C Clark
PVT Dan L. Feragen
PVT Clarence W Ingraham
PVT Peter J Lamere
PVT Dale W McClung
PVT J A Morgan
PVT Reuben V Pearce
PVT John R Simpson
PVT Jesse R Thornton

SGT Paul J Stefic
SGT Guy F White
CPL Leslie L Finlcy
PFC Wilson E Draper
PVT Alfred J Benoit
PVT Merle D Boldt
PVT James Butcher
PVT Sant P Cobia
PVT James H Graves
PVT Alfred Jarisch
PVT Max D Lockhardt
PVT Clair C McLean
PVT Milton C Nettle
PVT Harvey J Peltier
PVT Richard Stroud
PVT John N Tock

Medical Detachment (38 died in captivity)

MAJ Clarence H White
SSG Cecil B Cohenour
SGT Clarence E Sayre
PFC Harold K Benvie
PFC Charles C Foreman
PFC Donald W Johnson
PFC Olin E Myers
PVT Arthur E Bates
PVT Nick Marchese
PVT Arvid K Nelson
PVT Frutoso Romero
PVT James T Smith
PVT George E Walker

CPT Donald J Childers
SGT Arda M Hanenkrat
CPL Thomas W House
PFC Reynold A Dagner
PFC Matthew J Gregorich
PFC Melvin J Lehue
PFC Charlie Shaw
PVT Joseph T Head
PVT Samuel B Moore
PVT Francis B Powell
PVT Lee H Sechrist
PVT William A Snead
PVT Raymond O Willis

CPT Andrew Rader
SGT Arnold R Quitmeyer
CPL John W Hughes
PFC Paul E Decker
PFC Clyde H Handshaw
PFC Charles O Martin
PVT Glen A Anderson
PVT Patrick Hennessey
PVT George E Morgan
PVT Blanchard E Pruitt
PVT Charles Smeltzer
PVT Charlie M Waid

Band (2 died in captivity)

WO Anthony Kulper

TSG Arnold Ingebrichtsen

Korea

Killed in Action

Abbott	Richard F	Windham, VT	SFC	11/30/1950
Abel, Jr.	Charles L	Muskogee, OK	PVT	9/27/1950
Ablondi	Bruno F	Rockland, NY	CPL	6/2/1951
Acosta-Martinez	Luz	Puerto Rico	PVT	9/16/1952
Adams	Lewis E	Washington, PA	PVT	10/14/1952
Adams	Melville E	Suwannee, FL	CPT	12/1/1950
Adams	Richard A	Jefferson, AR	SFC	12/12/1950
Adams	Robert E	Tuscaloosa, AL	MSG	12/2/1950
Adkins	Hillrey B	Lincoln, WV	SFC	12/1/1950
Aguilar	Saul	El Paso, TX	PFC	11/28/1950
Albert	Gilbert	Marion, IN	SGT	3/7/1953
Aldridge	James R	Trumbull, OH	PVT	11/30/1950
Alecock	Harry L	Henderson, IL	CPL	9/5/1952
Alexander	Earl E	Kankakee, IL	PFC	10/28/1952
Alford	Otis F	Morgan, AL	SGT	5/23/1953
Allemeier	Hillary F	Allen, OH	1LT	3/23/1953
Allen	Joseph N	Newport, RI	PVT	12/3/1950

Alley	Ray C	Pike, AR	PVT	6/16/1953
Alvarez	Augustin	Los Angeles, CA	PFC	11/30/1950
Anderson	Clyde E	Butler, OH	PFC	11/28/1950
Anderson	Glenn M	St. Louis, MO	PVT	10/14/1952
Anderson	MC	Bell, TX	CPL	3/9/1953
Anderson	Wesley A	Chippewa, MI	PFC	12/12/1950
Anderson	William C	Chesterfield, VA	CPL	11/2/1951
Andrews	Isaac	Edgefield, SC	CPL	8/22/1952
Andrews	Leon E	Penobscot, ME	CPL	12/3/1950
Angles	Artemus F	Greene, GA	PFC	3/23/1953
Argard	Charles L	Worcester, MA	SGT	7/24/1953
Armstrong	Jerry W	Gaston, NC	CPL	6/8/1951
Arrigoitia-Gomez	E	Puerto Rico	PFC	10/31/1952
Ash	Billy E	Dallas, TX	PFC	11/29/1950
Ashbaugh	Robert W	Otter Trail, MN	PVT	7/24/1953
Asquith	Kenneth W	San Francisco, CA	PVT	9/11/1951
Aston	Frank V	Laclede, MO	2LT	7/24/1953
Atherton	Harold J	Montgomery, AL	PFC	12/3/1950
Austin	Earl E	San Bernardino, CA	PFC	9/27/1950
Avant	Joe T	Carroll, MS	PFC	11/30/1950
Babcock	George H	Coshocton, OH	CPL	11/30/1950
Badon, Jr	James B	Walthall, MS	PFC	10/27/1952
Bailey	Max L	Jerome, ID	PFC	11/30/1950
Bailey	Sesco L	Wyoming, WV	PVT	3/9/1953
Baker	Henry	Panama City, FL	CPL	10/14/1952
Baksa	Joseph V	Erie, NY	PFC	6/2/1951
Baldwin	Harold M	Goodhue, MN	PVT	9/22/1950
Balling	Frederick	Franklin, OH	PFC	4/17/1953
Barbagallo	Salvato	Philadelphia, PA	PFC	1/25/1953
Barks	Frances B	Wapello, IA	PVT	6/8/1951
Barnett	Earl J	DeSoto, LA	PFC	4/17/1953
Barnett	Murray W	Hardin, TX	CPL	12/1/1950
Barrow	Roy E	Lauderdale, MS	MSG	12/12/1950
Bartnik	Matthew P	Erie, NY	PVT	12/12/1950
Bartol	Theodore	Luzern, PA	PFC	12/29/1951
Barton	Donald J	Kalkaskia, MI	P	12/4/1950
Barton	Gene E	Tioga, NY	PFC	12/2/1950
Bass	Lonza Z	Ashley, AR	PVT	10/14/1952
Baty	George E	Greene, MO	CPL	11/29/1950
Bean	Frederick B	Knoxville, TN	CPL	11/29/1950
Bearstail	Clyde	McLean, ND	PFC	6/8/1951
Beaty	Charles E	Craighead, AR	CPL	12/3/1950
Beelman	Thomas L	Lee, IA	PFC	12/12/1950
Behringer	Raymond	Hudson, NJ	PVT	9/14/1951
Belden	Howard R	Warren, NY	CPL	12/1/1950
Bell	Alton R	Taylor, TX	PFC	12/2/1950
Bell	Gary A	Contra Costa, CA	PFC	6/4/1951
Bellar	Lowell W	Lake, IN	PFC	12/1/1950
Benton	John E	Erie, PA	PVT	9/27/1950
Berasis	Ignacio M	Hawaii	PVT	10/15/1952
Berkeley	Bromley E	Virgin Islands	PVT	10/14/1952
Berninger	James A	Detroit, MI	PVT	10/28/1952
Bertrand	Gerald J	Kankakee, IL	PFC	6/7/1951
Betts	George L	Franklin, OH	PFC	9/27/1950
Bickham	Gerald R	Bay, MI	CPL	4/17/1953
Biedenkapp	William	Hudson, NJ	PVT	10/24/1952
Bigelow, III	Lyman W	Merrimack, NH	SGT	10/31/1952

Biggs	Lester W	Detroit, MI	PFC	11/30/1950
Biggs	Samuel W	San Francisco, CA	CPL	7/24/1953
Bjorge	Robert	Becker, MN	PFC	10/14/1952
Blackett	Neldon E	Salt Lake City, UT	PFC	10/14/1952
Blair	James R	Kandiyohi, MN	PVT	6/4/1951
Block	Kenneth R	Oakland, MI	CPL	12/3/1950
Blount	James R	Houston, TX	1LT	9/28/1950
Blue	Billy S	Greene, PA	PFC	6/20/1953
Bockhoff	Theodore	Middlesex, MA	SGT	12/1/1950
Bogard	Clifford R	Clermont, OH	PFC	6/1/1951
Bolf	Alvin J	Morgan, CO	PFC	5/15/1953
Bond	John H	Hamilton, TN	PFC	12/12/1950
Bonner	Gerald P	New York, NY	2LT	4/10/1953
Booker	Alexander	Barnstable, MA	PFC	12/3/1950
Booton	Denmann G	Fleming, KY	PFC	9/26/1951
Borror	Walter O	Grant, WV	CPL	12/12/1950
Bortner	Donald J	Crawford, PA	CPL	12/12/1950
Bounds	Travis O	DeSoto, LA	SFC	12/3/1950
Bowen	Joseph A	Augusta, GA	SGT	11/30/1950
Bowman	James C	Marion, WV	PFC	11/28/1950
Boyer	Howard E	Madison, N	CPL	9/5/1952
Boyer	Robert M	Delaware, NY	1LT	12/4/1950
Boyle	Terrance F	Middlesex, NJ	CPL	3/7/1953
Bradley	Raymond G	Philadelphia, PA	PFC	9/27/1950
Bramblett	James S	Noble, OH	PFC	6/20/1953
Branch	Elmer J	Duplin, NC	PVT	1/12/1953
Brandon	Sterling	Philadelphia, PA	PVT	10/14/1952
Brandt	Edward D	Franklin, KS	PFC	1/28/1952
Braun	Wayne F	Hartford, CT	PVT	9/16/1952
Braxton	Edmond R	Hinds, MS	PFC	9/26/1951
Breeden	Charles	Webster, WV	CPL	5/30/1951
Brenes-Valentin	F	Puerto Rico	CPL	3/7/1953
Bressler	Ryan A	Suffolk, NY	2LT	4/17/1953
Brewington	Carl	Marion, MO	SFC	12/2/1950
Bridger	Kenneth L	Stevens, WA	PVT	11/30/1950
Bridges	Lolan O	Rutherford, NC	CPL	12/2/1950
Brinson	Paul	Mercer, NJ	MSG	3/7/1953
Brionens	Leo P	Contra Costa, CA	PFC	4/17/1953
Brklich	Steve N	St. Louis, MN	PVT	div>6/10/1951
Brock	James B	Maricopa, AZ	CPL	12/12/1950
Brock	Wilborn W	Spalding, GA	PFC	12/3/1950
Brooks	Jack E	DeKalb, GA	2LT	12/2/1950
Brooks	John H	Bertie, NC	PFC	12/12/1950
Brown	Bobby C	Lauderdale, TN	PFC	12/1/1950
Brown	Ferris	Beaufort, SC	PFC	11/3/1952
Brown	Harold M	Forsyth, NC	SGT	12/12/1950
Brown	Jimmie L	Rusk, TX	PVT	10/17/1952
Brown	John	Butler, OH	PFC	6/6/1951
Brown	Raymond H	Fond du Lac, WI	CPL	12/2/1950
Brown	Robert N	Renville, MN	PVT	4/3/1953
Bruce	William K	Brooklyn, NY	2LT	11/3/1952
Bruhn	Eugene O	Greene, MO	CPL	12/3/1950
Bruner	Oscar E	Westchester, NY	SFC	12/12/1950
Bryant	James E	Harlan, KY	PFC	12/12/1950
Bryant	Vernon L	Norfolk, VA	CPL	11/3/1952
Bryant	William L	Riverside, CA	PFC	12/1/1950
Bryk	Bernard F	Luzerne, PA	CPL	12/12/1950

Buckley	Arthur D	Cheshire, NY	CPL	12/9/1950
Burch	Naman	Union, NC	PFC	11/2/1951
Burdick	Herbert H	Winnebago, WI	PFC	6/2/1951
Burks	Fred E	St Lucie, FL	SGT	11/30/1950
Burner	Robert E	Page, VA	PFC	12/3/1950
Burns	Robert L	Lucas, OH	PFC	10/15/1952
Burris	Buddy B	Placer, CA	PVT	12/4/1950
Butz	William R	Clark WA	PVT	12/12/1950
Byars	Bobby L	Spalding, GA	PFC	12/12/1950
Caballero-Moreno	A	Puerto Rico	PVT	4/16/1953
Cabe	Lloyd R	Knoxville, TN	CPL	9/24/1950
Cairdi	Rocco	Yonkers, NY	PFC	7/24/1953
Calderon-Jenaro	R	Grant, NM	PFC	10/28/1952
Campbell	Joseph F	Columbus, GA	PVT	12/1/1950
Campbell	Joseph L	Philadelphia, PA	PVT	10/14/1952
Capehart	Joe B	Fannin, TX	SGT	10/26/1952
Capers	Sammie	Allendale, OH	PVT	10/15/1952
Caputo	Louis	Rockland, NY	PFC	12/12/1950
Carbray	Robert N	New London, CT	PVT	9/28/1951
Cardenas	Marcel M	New York, NY	PFC	10/14/1952
Cardona-Marrero	Antonio	Puerto Rico	PVT	10/29/1952
Carillo	Alejandro	McKinley, NM	PFC	5/24/1951
Carnes	John N	Trumbull, OH	CPL	12/12/1950
Carpenter	Otis C	Jasper, MO	PFC	9/15/1952
Carr	George D	Harrison, WV	PFC	11/28/1950
Carr	Howard L	Greene, IL	PFC	10/28/1952
Carr	James T	Lincoln, OR	PFC	11/30/1950
Carroll	George	Chicago, IL	PFC	11/14/1951
Carroll	John E	Pittsburgh, PA	PFC	10/29/1952
Cartegena-Colon	N	Puerto Rico	PVT	1/26/1953
Cartelino	Thomas	DuPage, IL	CPL	12/1/1950
Carter	Clyde M	Carroll, KY	PFC	11/29/1950
Carter	William H	Fresno, CA	PFC	11/28/1950
Casey	Robert M	Rensselaer, NY	PFC	12/12/1950
Castro-Henriquez	J	Puerto Rico	PFC	9/15/1952
Cataldo	Dominik	Lorain, Oh	PFC	12/3/1950
Cates	James G	Neshoba, MS	SFC	12/3/1950
Catlos	Edward W	Armstrong, PA	PFC	10/15/1952
Cavender	William E	Ingham, MI	CPL	11/28/1950
Centers	Linden	Franklin, OH	PVT	9/24/1950
Chadek	John G	Seward, NE	PVT	6/8/1951
Chadrick	Farbie	Evangeline, LA	PFC	11/8/1951
Chadwell	George R	Tippecanoe, IN	PFC	12/12/1950
Challennder	George	Burlington, NJ	PFC	6/8/1951
Chapman	William M	Macon, TN	CPL	12/3/1950
Chapp	Kenneth E	Detroit, MI	PFC	12/1/1950
Charido	Frank J	Suffolk, MA	PFC	12/12/1950
Charles	James O	Pike, KY	CPL	3/23/1953
Chastain	George E	Gastonia, NC	SGT	12/1/1950
Chilton	Owen D	Henry, KY	CPL	11/4/1951
Chorn	Havy O	Greene, MO	PVT	6/2/1951
Chrisenberry	Kenneth	Vernon, MO	PFC	10/17/1952
Christian	Jimmy L	Phoenix, AZ	PFC	12/1/1950
Christy	John F	Hamilton, IN	PFC	10/14/1952
Christy	Wilbur R	Butler, PA	PFC	9/27/1950
Church, Jr	Ray	Knott, KY	CPL	10/14/1952
Cieslak	Joseph K	Bureau, IL	CPL	12/12/1950

Clarin	James R	Los Angeles, CA	PFC	7/23/1953
Clarke	Robert J	Washington, ME	PFC	3/3/1953
Clayton	Claud A	Okfuskee, OK	SFC	11/30/1950
Clements	Louis C	Etowah, AL	PVT	2/18/1951
Clemmons	Kenneth D	Los Angeles, CA	CPL	12/1/1950
Clifton	Obie	Choctaw, OK	PFC	11/30/1950
Cline	Harold C	Logan, WV	CPL	6/23/1952
Clough	Kenneth H	Houston, TX	CPL	7/14/1953
Cnossen	Cyrus	Missaukee, MI	CPL	5/17/1953
Coburn	Frank A	Preston, WV	PFC	1/9/1953
Cochran	Jack D	Etowah, AL	PFC	6/1/1951
Cody	George R	Tuscaloosa, AL	CPT	12/1/1950
Coffey	Jack D	Tulsa, OK	PFC	5/27/1953
Coffman	Charles G	Casey, KY	CPL	10/26/1952
Coiner	Randall E	Tampa, FL	2LT	4/16/1953
Coke, Jr	Richard B	Dallam, TX	1LT	11/28/1950
Colasanti	James A	Onondaga, NY	PFC	12/1/1950
Cole	Burrell B	Butler, PA	PFC	12/3/1950
Cole	Charles M	Ravalli, MT	PFC	10/14/1952
Cole	Randolph J	Washington, LA	PFC	6/7/1951
Cole	Thomas E	Roanoke, VA	PFC	12/12/1950
Coleman	Glynn A	Colquitt, GA	PVT	11/30/1950
Colon-Rodriquez	A	Puerto Rico	PVT	10/17/1952
Comeau	Joseph W	Essex, MA	PFC	9/2/1951
Conis	Eugene J	Fluvanna, VA	SGT	3/7/1953
Conklin	George W	Ontario, NY	PFC	12/3/1950
Conley	Pete	Logan, WV	PFC	12/12/1950
Connor	James W	Puerto Rico	CPT	12/1/1950
Contreras	Carrion	Puerto Rico	PVT	10/17/1952
Cooksey	Jesse R	Dickson, TN	SFC	10/14/1952
Cooper	John W	Hancock, WV	PFC	12/12/1950
Cope	Robert H	Camden, NJ	PFC	12/12/1950
Copeland	Melvin C	Chowan, NC	PFC	9/27/1950
Copenhaver	Walter	York, PA	PFC	11/28/1950
Copley	William E	McKean, PA	1LT	3/23/1952
Corby	Donald R	Essex, NJ	PVT	4/16/1953
Cordone	Joseph J	Rochester, NY	CPT	9/6/1951
Cornell	Frederick	Orange, CA	CPL	12/12/1950
Couch, Jr	Clifton Z	Columbia, AR	MAJ	11/29/1950
Cowdin	Ray P	Carbon, IL	PFC	6/7/1951
Cowles	Roy A	Alameda, CA	PFC	4/16/1953
Cox	William O	Pittsylvania, VA	PFC	12/3/1950
Craig	John J	Bronx, NY	MSG	8/25/1951
Craighead	Rufus P	Floyd, VA	PFC	12/1/1950
Cratic	Richard	Tallahassee, FL	PVT	3/23/1953
Crawford	Joseph	St. Charles, MO	PVT	9/28/1951
Creagan	Patrick H	Appanoose, IA	CPL	12/3/1950
Crewes	Irvin T	Campbell, VA	SGT	12/12/1950
Crisp	George S	La Plata, MD	1LT	12/12/1950
Crofts	Charles B	Bingham, ID	PFC	12/2/1950
Crouse	Donald E	Huntingdon, PA	SGT	11/30/1950
Crump	Marion N	Forsyth, NC	CPL	10/15/1952
Cuevas	Alfredo	San Joaquim, CA	PFC	11/30/1950
Culver	Clifton M	Sampson, NC	SFC	6/13/1952
Cummings	Ronald C	Lapeer, MI	CPL	1/18/1952
Cunningham	William	Lenoir, NC	PFC	12/1/1950
Curtis	Harold L	Marion, MO	CPL	12/12/1950

Dacek	William	New York, NY	PVT	10/31/1952
Dahn	Elmer C	Le Sueur, MN	PFC	12/12/1950
Daigle	Lifford J	Lafayette, LA	CPL	10/14/1952
Daigle	Roy W	Hampden, MA	CPL	12/3/1950
Dakin	Robert C	Middlesex, MA	CPL	12/12/1950
Dale	James V H	Hamilton, OH	2LT	4/13/1953
Dallas	Jack E	Hamilton, OH	PFC	12/7/1950
Daniels	Hansel	Burlington, NJ	CPL	12/3/1950
Danks	Kenneth L	Weber, UT	PVT	6/5/1951
Davidson	Richard C	Sullivan, TN	PFC	12/3/1950
Davis	Howard	Johnston, NC	SGT	5/23/1951
Davis	James B	Richmond, GA	PVT	3/9/1953
Davis	James R	Hawkins, TN	CPL	11/30/1950
Davis	William	Queens, NY	PVT	10/7/1952
Davison	Leslie E	Baldwin, AL	CPL	12/3/1950
Day	Claron O	Buchanan, MO	PFC	5/30/1951
Day	Warren C	Carteret, NC	PFC	12/12/1950
De La Fuente	Trini	Queens, NY	CPL	10/27/1951
De la Rosa	Cordero	Puerto Rico	PVT	4/17/1953
Deal	James E	Randolph WV	CPL	11/28/1950
DeHerrera	Willie B	Conejos, CO	PFC	10/26/1951
Dehm	Thomas E	Oswego, NY	PFC	9/24/1950
Delgado	Pedro	Yuma, AZ	PFC	12/1/1950
Delgado-Nieves	Pedro	Puerto Rico	PVT	10/31/1952
Delong	Clayton C	Allen, IN	PFC	12/12/1950
Demanno	Anthony P	Monroe, NY	PFC	10/31/1952
Demilte	Charles R	New York, NY	PFC	10/14/1952
Demo	Rolland W	Swift, MN	PFC	11/29/1950
Dennis	William H	San Francisco, CA	PFC	9/28/1951
Deon	Clarence E	Beech Hill, NS Canada	PFC	10/14/1952
Desloges	Joseph A	Hartford, CT	SGT	12/12/1950
DeSousa	Gerald J	Kings, NY	SFC	1/25/1953
Devilbiss	Leroy L	Guthrie, IA	PFC	6/7/1951
DeWees	Donald L	Albany, NY	PFC	10/27/1951
Diaz-Nieves	Clemente	Puerto Rico	PVT	10/29/1952
Dickerson	Paul L	Roanoke, VA	PVT	12/1/1950
Dill	Carl D	Bryan, OK	PVT	9/24/1950
Dill	Paul N	New Castle, DE	1LT	12/3/1950
Dillon	John L	Campbell, KY	PVT	10/14/1952
Dinsmore	John W	Schuylkill, PA	SGT	01/05/052
Dixon	William R	New York, NY	SFC	11/30/1950
Doby	Alfonzo	Jefferson, AL	SGT	10/16/1952
Dodro	Carl D	Cook, IL	SGT	11/6/1951
Dodson	Billy J	Jefferson, MO	PFC	12/12/1950
Dodson	Thomas A	Westmoreland, PA	2LT	10/27/1952
Dodson, Jr	David I	Blair, PA	CPL	11/29/1950
Dolezal	Ernest L	Butler, NE	PFC	11/14/1951
Dominguez	Buddy	Jefferson, CO	PFC	6/4/1951
Donahoe	Billy G	Harris, TX	SFC	12/12/1950
Donlon	Paul K	Suffolk, MA	SGT	*
Dorser	Jimmie L	Greene, MO	PFC	12/3/1950
Doss, Jr	William H	Columbia, NY	PFC	12/6/1950
Dotson	William H	Carroll, MD	PVT	10/31/1952
Dougherty	Edward M	Mesa, CO	PVT	9/2/1951
Douglas	Harold F	Oklahoma City, OK	1LT	9/2/1951
Douglass	Thad	Shelby TX	PVT	5/24/1951
Dove	Henry L	Arlington/Alexandria, VA	CPL	8/3/1952

Drew	Kenneth H	Hampshire, MA	PFC	12/3/1950
Drews	Harold F	Kane, IL	SFC	12/12/1950
Dronse	Arthur W	Wayne, MI	CPL	8/3/1952
Drouillard	Bernard	Lenawee, MI	SGT	10/4/1951
Drummond	Henley D	Amherst, VA	PFC	10/14/1952
Duhon	Kibbie	Jefferson, TX	PVT	5/24/1951
Dunham, Jr	Ronald B	Oakland, MI	PVT	10/28/1952
Durfee	Donald C	Bernalillo, NM	PFC	*
Durfee	Lamont J	Mason, MI	SFC	12/3/1950
Eddins, Jr	John W	Escambia, FL	PFC	12/12/1950
Eden	Charles	Passaic, NJ	PVT	1/12/1953
Edwards	Willard H	Wise, VA	PFC	12/2/1950
Eggleston	Arnold E	Kane, IL	PVT	6/9/1951
Eldridge	Melburn H	White, TN	PVT	12/1/1950
Ellingson	Eugene M	Lane, OR	PVT	3/9/1953
Elmore	Charles E	Ouachita, AR	SFC	11/29/1950
Embrey	Paul T	Fauquier, VA	MSG	11/29/1950
Emmanuelli	Fidel	Bronx, NY	PVT	6/20/1953
Enas	William E	King, WA	CPL	11/29/1950
Engh	Donald C	Del Norte, CA	1LT	9/27/1950
Estep	Wayne	Lewis, WA	PFC	9/15/1951
Evans	Curtis D	Los Angeles, CA	PFC	6/2/1951
Evans	Gene E	Butte, CA	PFC	12/12/1950
Evans	Harold A	Mason, WA	PFC	12/12/1950
Evans	Junior C	Hall, TX	PVT	12/12/1950
Everette	William L	Mobile, AL	PVT	9/27/1950
Faidley	Charles W	Baltimore City, MD	PFC	11/22/1951
Faries	Marion D	Hamilton, IL	PVT	5/19/1952
Farley	Earl J	Raleigh, WV	PFC	11/5/1952
Farmer	Kenneth L	Washington, AR	SGT	3/7/1953
Farris	Stephen J	Baxter, AR	CPL	12/3/1950
Faulkenberry	Verno	Lancaster, SC	CPL	7/24/1953
Fay	Harold O	Dane, WI	PFC	3/7/1953
Fecko	Richard J	Cuyahoga, OH	PFC	3/23/1953
Feliciano	Jose A	Puerto Rico	PFC	2/20/1953
Fenske	Marvin J	Outagamie, WI	PVT	10/15/1952
Feriend	David A	Grand Traverse, MI	CPL	12/6/1950
Ferris	Ronald R	Plymouth, MA	2LT	5/15/1953
Ferry	Richard P	Sedgwick, KS	PFC	11/30/1950
Finch	Frank O	Routt, CO	PFC	10/14/1952
Finkler	Clarence L	Milwaukee, WI	PFC	11/14/1951
Finley	Richard H	Holmes, OH	PFC	12/1/1950
Firey, JR	Lewis M	Washoe, NV	PFC	7/22/1953
Fisher	James R	Fond du Lac, WI	CPL	11/29/1950
Fisher	William M	Johnson, IN	PVT	10/15/1952
Fitz, Jr	Robert M	Baltimore City, MD	CPL	10/17/1952
Flack	Cameron	Rutherford, NC	CPL	12/12/1950
Flanary	Samuel H	Lee, VA	PFC	11/28/1950
Flannders	Henry C	Grafton, NH	SGT	12/12/1950
Flenory	Oscar	Dade, FL	PVT	7/11/1952
Flores	Polito	Alameda, CA	PVT	10/28/1952
Flortard	Raymond E	Bergin, NJ	PFC	3/7/1953
Flynn	Norman E	Sevier, TN	PFC	11/28/1950
Focht	Irvin E	Logan, OH	PFC	12/12/1950
Fontaine	Ernest J	Bristol, RI	SFC	12/12/1950
Foor	Maurice N	Franklin, OH	CPL	10/14/1952
Ford	Ernest C	Clay, MN	PFC	3/9/1953

Ford	Wilfred S	Cumberland, NC	CPT	7/2/1952
Foston	Burl	Baldwin, GA	PFC	7/22/1953
Fox	John E	Wayne, MI	PVT	12/12/1953
Fredrickson	William	Pettis, MO	PVT	6/10/1953
Freed	Marvin E	Washington, IN	PVT	10/26/1951
Freeman	James A	District of Columbia	CPL	10/14/1952
Freeman	John H	Buena Vista, CA	CPL	6/5/1951
Fresen	Richard D	Monroe, IL	MSG	12/1/1950
Fucito	John J	New York, NY	PVT	6/5/1951
Fugate, Jr	Hobart	Webb, TX	PFC	11/3/1950
Fugett	James B	Madison, OH	PFC	4/16/1953
Fuss	William G	Hamilton, OH	1LT	9/26/1950
Gaines	Fletcher	Hart, GA	PVT	11/6/1951
Gallardo	Charles P	San Francisco, CA	PFC	10/31/1952
Gallego	Gilbert G	Maricopa, AZ	PFC	4/18/1953
Galvan	Willie V	Bexar, TX	SGT	12/1/1950
Gamwells	James R	Bannock, ID	PFC	4/17/1953
Garcia	Guadalupe	Nueces, TX	PFC	12/12/1950
Garcia	Victor	Cameron, TX	PFC	12/12/1950
Garner	Max F	Dale, AL	PVT	3/9/1953
Garza	Gilberto	Cameron, TX	PFC	11/30/1950
Gaston	William K	Erie, PA	PFC	12/3/1950
Gay	Charles L	Butte, CA	PVT	11/3/1952
Gayhart	James D	Perry, KY	PFC	12/12/1950
Geannopulos	Peter	Cook, IL	CPL	11/28/1950
Gebou	William S	Fulton, NY	PFC	12/1/1950
Gerth	Harley G	Effingham, IL	PVT	11/3/1952
Gertsen	Robert H	Story, IA	PVT	6/1/1951
Gibson	Clifton E	St Joseph, IN	PVT	10/15/1952
Gibson	Robert L	Summit, OH	CPL	11/4/1952
Gillaspy	James W	Monroe, IN	CPL	7/2/1952
Gincley	Edmund G	Montgomery, PA	PFC	5/22/1951
Girdley	Vernon E	Jefferson, KY	PFC	6/18/1953
Glace	Wilbur E	Perry, PA	PVT	10/16/1952
Gladney	Benjamin F	Winston, MS	PFC	9/18/1952
Glover	Joseph R	Middlesex, MA	PFC	5/31/1953
Goats	Samuel H	Tarrant, TX	CPL	11/28/1950
Gobble	Pryor	Lee, VA	PFC	12/12/1950
Goble	Bernard J	Dearborn, IN	PFC	6/8/1951
Godchaux	Charles A	Orleans, LA	CPL	2/15/1951
Goetz	William O	Milwaukee, WI	PVT	5/5/1952
Gokel	Donald C	Alpena, MI	PVT	6/2/1951
Goldsberry	Thomaso	Snohomish, WA	PFC	10/28/1952
Goldsborough	Paul	Macon, IL	PFC	11/29/1950
Gomez	Gustavo K	Maricopa, AZ	PVT	11/30/1950
Gorman	Raymond D	Belmont, OH	PVT	10/14/1952
Gorman, Jr	Frank G	Macomb, MI	CPL	11/30/1950
Goss	Patrick J	Philadelphia, PA	PVT	11/30/1950
Gossmann	Frank J	Montgomery, MD	PFC	10/14/1952
Goudelock	Samuel	Camden, NJ	1LT	4/16/1953
Gower	Sterling C	Northampton, PA	PFC	12/1/1950
Grable	William S	Stoddard, MO	PVT	2/16/1953
Grace	Luther	Telfair, GA	MSG	11/30/1950
Graham	Arnold W	Lewis & Clark, MT	SGT	6/9/1951
Graves	Ben H	Comanche, OK	CPL	11/28/1950
Graves	Riley W	Bell, TX	PFC	12/1/1950
Green	George W	Philadelphia, PA	PVT	10/16/1952

Green	Robert K	Jo Daviess, IL	PVT	10/14/1952
Gregory	Charles W	Sedgwick, KS	SGT	12/1/1950
Gremillion	Tyrel J	Avoyelles, LA	CPL	10/14/1952
Griffin	Silas E	Garvin, OK	PFC	11/4/1951
Grimes	Eugene	Fayette, PA	SGT	6/4/1951
Grimm	William D	Marion, OR	PFC	11/30/1950
Grist	James R	Beaufort, NC	1LT	11/30/1950
Grubb	Carl R	Wood, WV	CPL	6/4/1951
Grubb	Charles H	Mingo, WV	CPL	12/1/1950
Gruben	Victor A	Fisher, TX	CPL	7/24/1953
Gruebbeling	Walter	Douglas, MN	SGT	12/3/1950
Guerrise	Girolamo	Richmond, NY	SFC	9/11/1951
Guillete-Lorenzo	RI	Puerto Rico	PFC	10/14/1952
Gustafson	Roger W	Meeker, MN	SGT	9/26/1951
Gutierrez	Jose R	Webb, TX	PFC	12/2/1950
Hagie	George C	Sullivan, TN	CPL	11/28/1950
Haire	Ova L	Breckinridge, KY	PVT	12/12/1950
Halcomb	Douglas I	Ripley, IN	PFC	3/9/1953
Haley	Morris E	McDowell, WV	SGT	12/1/1950
Hall	Russell L	Marion, WV	PFC	3/9/1953
Hallmark	Robert D	Madison, IL	PFC	10/15/1952
Halverson	Donald E	Woodbury, IA	1LT	11/8/1950
Hamilton	Paul W	Pendleton, KY	CPL	11/30/1950
Hamilton	Robert E	Douglas, NE	PFC	9/2/1951
Hanaver	Alvan M	St Francois, MO	CPL	10/16/1952
Handy	Melvin L.	Palm Beach, FL	PFC	12/12/1950
Hancock, Jr	Milton	Lawrence, IN	PVT	10/15/1952
Hanford	Guy J	Lycoming, PA	CPL	10/26/1952
Hanna	Robert D	Cape Girardeau	PFC	7/2/1952
Hansen, Jr	Arthur	Baltimore City, MD	PVT	12/12/1950
Hanson	Jack	Galveston, TX	PFC	6/7/1951
Harold	Donald G	Roane, WV	PFC	7/3/1952
Harper	Howard R	Muhlenberg, KY	PFC	11/30/1950
Harper	Joseph M	Pittsylvania, VA	PFC	11/28/1950
Harrigan	William E	Porter, IN	CPL	3/23/1953
Harriman	Sheldon L	Kalamazoo, MI	SGT	12/1/1950
Harris	Ellis	Muscogee, GA	PFC	7/24/1953
Harris	Max E	White, IN	SGT	12/12/1950
Haskins	Morris D	Davidson, TN	SGT	12/1/1950
Hatfield	Raymond L	Harlan, KY	CPL	3/7/1953
Havens	Junior L	St Clair, MI	PVT	11/3/1952
Haworth	Wilbur A	Multnomah, OR	CPL	11/30/1950
Hayakawa	Richard Y	Hawaii	PFC	4/17/1953
Heath	William E	Fairfield, SC	CPL	8/3/1952
Hector	Howard D	Macon, IL	PVT	9/2/1951
Hedgpeth	James B	Christian, MO	CPL	3/9/1953
Heffner	Robert M	Delaware, PA	PFC	5/10/1953
Heimbigner	Richard H	Adams, WA	CPL	10/14/1952
Heissler	Adolf F	Queens, NY	PFC	5/31/1953
Heling	Orline W	Shawano WI	PVT	4/17/1953
Helt	Je Mickey	Allegheny, PA	1LT	11/28/1950
Henderson	Arthur R	Allegheny, PA	PVT	2/2/1952
Henig	Francis B	Cuyahoga, OH	PFC	12/12/1950
Henson	Richard C	Coos, NH	1LT	11/29/1950
Hernandez	Jesus	Bexar, TX	CPL	8/29/1951
Hernandez	Juan G	Uvalde, TX	PVT	6/8/1953
Herold	Albert E	Sedgwick, KS	PFC	6/2/1951

Herrera	Julian	El Paso, TX	PVT	12/12/1950
Hertzler	Thomas A	Chester, PA	PFC	8/8/1951
Hess	Claude R	Outagamie, WI	PFC	12/12/1950
Heston	Loren	Franklin, OH	PFC	11/28/1950
Heumiller	Eugene J	McCook, SD	PVT	6/6/1953
Hewitt	Bernard R	Vermillion, IL	SFC	3/7/1953
Hicks	James E	Schenectady, NY	PFC	10/15/1952
Hicks	Tommy V	Bradford, FL	CPL	11/30/1950
Higgins	James E	Clark, IL	PFC	11/4/1952
Hildebrand	Roscoe	Essex, NJ	PFC	11/30/1950
Hill	George	Grafton, NH	CPL	11/30/1950
Hill	Harold E	Contra Costa, CA	PFC	11/30/1950
Hill	William G	Stephens, GA	CPL	12/3/1950
Hille	James D	Malheur, OR	PVT	6/6/1953
Hines	Charles W	Baltimore, MD	CPL	1/7/1952
Hines	Kenneth	Van Wert, OH	SGT	11/27/1950
Hitch	Paul L	New Castle, DE	PFC	9/2/1951
Hobbs	Bill F	Nowata, OK	PFC	11/30/1950
Hodges	Milton D	Jackson, MO	PFC	3/9/1953
Hoffman	William R	Cook, IL	PVT	5/15/1953
Holbrook	Bobby B	Habersham, GA	PVT	11/30/1950
Holbrooks	Julius J	Fulton, GA	SGT	9/24/1950
Holder	Ralph S	Upton, TX	SGT	1/14/1951
Holguin	Raymundo E	Dona Ana, NM	PFC	11/30/1950
Holliday	Billy E	Brazos, TX	CPL	12/12/1950
Hollimon	James N	Forrest, MS	PFC	10/16/1952
Honeycutt	J W	Pottawatomie, OK	PFC	10/15/1952
Hooten	Richard G	Upson, GA	1LT	11/29/1950
Horst	Doyle C	Wayne, OH	PVT	3/9/1953
Housekeeper	George	Riverside, CA	MSG	12/12/1950
Houser	John C	San Joaquin, CA	PFC	11/29/1950
Houston	Lonzo	Maury, TN	PVT	1/28/1952
Hoven	John I	Beltrami, MN	PFC	12/12/1950
Howard	Charles H	Trigg, KY	PVT	4/18/1953
Howard	Robert C	District of Columbia	CPL	12/12/1950
Howard	William T	Huron, MI	PVT	3/24/1953
Howe	James R	Lorain, OH	MSG	12/5/1950
Howell	Gilbert L	Kern, CA	PFC	10/14/1952
Hoyes	William C	Geauga, OH	CPL	12/12/1950
Huckin	John B	Bergin, NJ	2LT	10/15/1952
Hudson	Billie R	Merced, CA	PFC	12/1/1950
Hudson	Leslie D	Morgan, MO	CPL	11/29/1950
Hughey	Dalton	Taney, MO	PFC	3/23/1953
Huguley	Barney M	Madison, KY	PFC	1/26/1953
Huhn	Kenneth P	Lehigh, PA	PFC	6/23/1953
Humbarger	Max R	Defiance, OH	PVT	6/11/1953
Hummel	Jerome V	St Louis City, MO	PFC	11/30/1950
Humphreys	Richard	Jackson, OH	PFC	11/30/1950
Hunnicutt	James A	Bulloch, GA	SGT	12/12/1950
Hunter	Charles O	Essex, MA	PVT	9/2/1951
Hurley	William	Middlesex, MA	PFC	7/18/1953
Hurst	Charley L	Grand, CO	PFC	1/24/1953
Hussey	Wilfred K	Hawaii	PFC	12/12/1950
Hutchison	David C	Gem, ID	PFC	4/17/1953
Hutton	Richard E	Polk, IA	PFC	12/9/1950
Hyatt	Raymond G	Volusia, FL	PVT	3/6/1953
Hylton	Billy E	Maricopa, AZ	CPL	11/30/1950

Ireland	Malcolm D	Hamilton, IN	PVT	3/31/1951
Ishida	Mitsuyoshi	Hawaii	PFC	12/7/1950
Izquierdo	Francisco A	Webb, TX	PFC	12/2/1950
Jackson	Edward M	Berkeley, WV	SGT	4/16/1953
Jackson	General E	Lucas, OH	PVT	11/6/1951
Jackson	Ronald M	Ingham, MI	PVT	6/28/1953
Jackson	Willie J	Shelby, TN	CPL	10/27/1951
Jackson, Jr	Floyd J	Johnson, MO	CPL	12/12/1950
James	Howard E	Westmoreland, PA	PFC	11/28/1950
James	Howard F	Cambria, PA	1LT	5/24/1951
James, Jr	Albert	Jefferson, AL	PVT	10/17/1952
Janvrin	Ananias	Rockingham, NH	CPL	11/28/1950
Jemison	Charles	Lorain, OH	PVT	10/14/1952
Jenkins	Calvin	Madison, GA	PFC	4/17/1953
Jenkins	William C	Knox, TN	SGT	11/29/1950
Jessup	Howard L	Summit, OH	PFC	12/3/1950
Jeter	Donald E	Wichita, TX	PFC	12/1/1950
Jeter	James L C	Covington, AL	PVT	4/17/1953
Jochim	Cornelius A	Vanderburgh, IN	SGT	11/28/1950
Johnson	Louis C	Bibb, GA	SFC	11/27/1950
Johnson	Melvin L	Wyandotte, KS	SGT	12/7/1950
Johnson	Travis M	Sumter, SC	PFC	7/10/1953
Johnson	Donald M	King George, VA	PVT	10/7/1952
Johnson	Gerald D	Mecklenburg, NC	CPL	12/2/1950
Johnson	Granville	Whitley, KY	PVT	7/2/1952
Johnson	James V	Alachua, FL	CPL	12/1/1950
Jones	Adolph F	Rabun, GA	PFC	11/30/1950
Jones	Carl R	Creek, OK	PFC	12/3/1950
Jones	Delman J	New Hanover, NC	PVT	10/29/1952
Jones	Glen D	Reno, KS	PVT	10/14/1952
Jones	Jack O	Lake, FL	PFC	3/23/1953
Jones	Lucius	Chatham, GA	PFC	10/14/1952
Jones	Melber	Little River, AR	CPL	12/3/1950
Jones	Nathaniel G	Richland SC	SFC	12/12/1950
Jones	Richard L	Creek, OK	CPL	9/27/1950
Jones	Robert S	Orleans, LA	PFC	12/3/1950
Jones	Thomas E	Coos, OR	PVT	10/31/1951
Jones, Jr	George J	Philadelphia, PA	PFC	12/12/1950
Jordan	Arthur	Jackson, AR	CPL	6/10/1951
Jordan	Barney H	Bullock, AL	SGT	12/12/1950
Joseph	Arthur	Woodford, KY	CPL	9/15/1952
Joseph, Jr	Johnnie	Leslie, KY	PVT	11/28/1950
Joyce, Jr	James O	Grainger, TN	PVT	6/1/1951
Judd	Morris	Grayson, TX	PFC	7/16/1952
Judy	Denzil J	Tucker, WV	PVT	5/20/1951
Justice	Marion W	Pike, AL	PFC	9/6/1950
Kaakimaka	John K	Hawaii	PFC	12/12/1950
Kahnt	Frederick C	Du Page, Il	PFC	10/28/1952
Kamakaokalani	Will	Hawaii	PVT	10/17/1952
Kanoski	Richard S	Hennepin, MN	PVT	9/2/1951
Kee	Willie F	Marshall, TN	CPL	12/1/1950
Keen	Junior D	Washington, AR	PVT	11/4/1952
Keener	Fletcher	Baltimore, MD	PFC	5/23/1953
Keim	Robert D	Allegheny, PA	PFC	9/2/1951
Keith	Donald G	Erie, PA	PFC	6/2/1951
Kekiwi	Nelson	Hawaii	CPL	10/16/1952
Kelley	Leslie L	Franklin, ME	PFC	11/3/1952

Kelly	Donald E	Contra Costa, CA	PFC	12/3/1950
Kelly, Jr	Guy B	Burke, GA	SFC	4/15/1953
Kemp	Don L	Washington, IN	SFC	2/2/1951
Kemper	David R	Fauquier, VA	PFC	6/4/1951
Kennedy	Robert G	Baltimore City, MD	SGT	12/1/1950
Keough	Billy J	Alameda, CA	PFC	5/24/1951
Kerekes	Joseph J	Bronx, NY	SGT	11/30/1950
Kibbey	Earl E	Clinton, OH	PFC	12/3/1950
Kidd	Elmer C	Seneca, NY	PFC	11/30/1950
Keith	James W	Hamilton, TN	SGT	12/1/1950
Kile	George D	Hill, MT	PFC	12/12/1950
Killingsworth	Myrt	Greenwood, SC	1LT	10/14/1952
Kilpatrick	Kenneth	Amite, MS	SFC	12/12/1950
King	Allen D	Claiborne, LA	1LT	8/6/1952
King	Jack E	Blount, TN	PFC	11/8/1950
Kittleson	David R	Milwaukee, WI	PFC	11/29/1950
Klaris	Norman L	Los Angeles, CA	PFC	9/27/1950
Klein	Sidney R	Kings, NY	PFC	6/7/1951
Knapp	William C	Angelina, TX	1LT	10/16/1952
Knecht	George N	Northampton, PA	SGT	12/3/1950
Kneisley	Russell L	Adams, OH	PFC	9/2/1951
Knight	Harold K	Erie, PA	PVT	11/25/1950
Knox	Allan L	Sangamon, IL	CPL	11/29/1950
Knutson	Edwin H	Otter Trail, MN	CPL	12/12/1950
Kohn	Glenn E	Dodge, WI	PVT	7/24/1953
Koo	Young C	Hawaii	PFC	11/13/1952
Kosieniak	Edward S	Cuyahoga, OH	PFC	9/10/1951
Kosmecki	Donald	Milwaukee, WI	PFC	7/24/1953
Kovalcheck	Delbert	Fayette, PA	CPL	12/12/1950
Kovar	Leo	Sherman, NE	PFC	6/3/1951
Kowalski	Leonard P	St Joseph, IN	CPL	9/11/1952
Koyanagi	Sueo	Hawaii	PFC	10/16/1952
Kozlowski	Thadeus S	Prince George, MD	PFC	6/4/1951
Kratzer	Edward C	Lehigh, PA	CPL	4/17/1953
Krischak	Stephen	Washington, PA	PFC	12/3/1950
Krull	Norman J	Philadelphia, PA	CPL	10/15/1952
Kupau	Leonard	Hawaii	PFC	3/23/1953
Kwock	George A	Hawaii	PVT	4/17/1953
Kyzer	George L	Lexington, SC	SFC	12/12/1950
La Beau	Roger F	Wayne, MI	CPL	11/30/1950
La Bella	Americo M	Onondaga, NY	PFC	9/4/1951
La Dieu	Howard D	Rensselaer, NY	SFC	12/12/1950
La Flair	Alvin J	Saint Lawrence, NY	CPL	6/2/1951
La Fond	Paul E	Warren, NY	PVT	12/12/1950
Laboy-Martinez	RAF	Puerto Rico	PVT	10/26/1952
Lacro	George	Hawaii	PFC	8/3/1952
Lacsamana	Maximian	Puerto Rico	CPL	12/3/1950
Lahood	Jerome	Ramsey, MN	CPL	5/30/1951
Lane	Robert C	Walker, AL	PFC	6/18/1953
Lanford	Charles R	Genesee, MI	PFC	11/30/1950
LaPlante	Normand L	Hampden, MA	PFC	9/2/1951
Largusa	Bonifacio T	Hawaii	PFC	9/27/1950
Lasasso	George A	Northampton, PA	1LT	10/14/1952
Lasley	Paul E	Emmet, MI	CPL	5/10/1953
Latham	Glenn D	Salt Lake, UT	PFC	6/7/1951
Lattin	George G	Potter, PA	PFC	10/16/1952
Laurence	Harry J	Cuyahoga, OH	CPL	12/12/1950

Law	Tommy K	Bath, VA	CPL	12/12/1950
Lawrence	Donald E	Tangipahoa, LA	PFC	10/15/1952
Lawton	Ellison J	Fulton, GA	PVT	5/24/1951
Lazarou	Lazaros	Racine, WI	CPL	10/25/1951
Lebron-Lebron	Davi	Puerto Rico	PFC	10/14/1952
Lebron-Mendez	Jose	Puerto Rico	PVT	8/22/1952
Lee	Clarence O	Allegheny, PA	MSG	12/1/1950
Lee	Hayward R	Richmond, GA	PVT	10/15/1952
Leenstra	Henry	Whatcom, WA	SGT	10/1/1951
Leeper	Gene N	Lake, IN	PFC	3/24/1953
Legge	Allen K	Frederick, VA	CPT	1/14/1951
Leos	Harlan A	Fayette, PA	PVT	3/23/1953
Lepp	John J	Brown, WI	CPL	10/15/1952
Letendre	Roger N	Worcester, MA	PFC	5/30/1951
Lewis	Jack T	York, PA	PFC	9/14/1951
Lewis	Pete H	Stark, OH	PFC	12/12/1950
Libran-Garcia	Samu	Puerto Rico	PVT	10/16/1952
Lindwurm	Philip G	Gregory, SD	PVT	10/14/1952
Linkous	Golden	Cabell, WV	PVT	3/23/1953
Linneman	Harry J	Brevard, FL	PFC	12/12/1950
Linquist	Carl H	Kandiyohi, MN	MSG	11/29/1950
Linthicum	Giles C	Henry, OH	PVT	3/23/1953
Lipshitz	Kenneth C	King, WA	CPL	12/1/1950
Locklear	Junior	Robeson, NC	PVT	4/19/1953
Lofgren	Julius H	New York, NY	PFC	3/23/1953
Loftus	Arthur F	Monroe, NY	PFC	10/26/1952
Lohr	Robert F	Logan, WV	CPL	12/3/1950
Long	Charles H	Winnebago, IL	PVT	3/23/1953
Long	Donald G	Pierce, WA	CPL	12/7/1950
Long	William C	Dickson, TN	CPL	12/1/1950
Loomis	Charles W	Chester, PA	PVT	12/3/1950
Lopez	Arturo	Atascosa, TX	CPL	6/11/1953
Lopez	Edward E	Pinal, AZ	PFC	6/8/1951
Lopez-Almodovar	PA	Puerto Rico	PFC	4/17/1943
Lopiccolo	Joseph J	Orleans, LA	SGT	2/17/1951
Loshaw	Mannie L	Oneida, WI	PVT	10/14/1952
Loudermilk	Arnold	Greenbrier, WV	PFC	3/24/1953
Lozoya	Fermin P	Scotts Bluff, NE	CPL	10/15/1952
Lucas	Marshall R	Hanover, VA	PFC	10/30/1952
Lucas	Steven	Cattaraugus, NY	PFC	11/30/1950
Luchies	Harvey J	Muskegon, MI	CPL	7/4/1953
Lucio	Jose B	Virgin Islands	PFC	9/25/1952
Luedtke	Robert C	Marinette, WI	PVT	10/14/1952
Lugenbeel	Harold E	Carroll, MD	PFC	4/17/1953
Lujan	George	Los Angeles, CA	CPL	9/4/1951
Lund	Edward A	Baltimore City, MD	PFC	7/23/1953
Lussier	Remi G	Hampden, MA	PFC	12/12/1950
Luszewicz	Eugene V	Berks, PA	PFC	11/3/1952
Lyons	Gordon E	New Haven, CT	PVT	11/4/1952
Mabenis	Firminio	Hawaii	CPL	10/15/1952
MacDonald	Robert	Bonner, ID	2LT	10/28/1952
MacFarlanne	Arichb	Orange, TX	2LT	12/1/1950
Mack	Herbert U	Charleston, SC	PFC	9/2/1951
MacLean	Allan D	Wayne, MI	COL	11/29/1950
Madden	Walter J	Philadelphia, PA	PVT	6/18/1952
Maddox	Donald	Fleming, KY	PVT	12/12/1950
Maddox	James W	Ohio, KY	SFC	12/2/1950

Maddy	Walter E	Cabell, WV	CPL	11/30/1950
Maggard	John H	Elliott, KY	PFC	11/30/1950
Magnan	Morris	St Clair, MI	SGT	6/7/1951
Magyar	William R	Stark, ND	PVT	3/23/1952
Mahr	Richard W	Monroe, WI	PFC	10/14/1952
Mainhart	James T	Butler, PA	CPL	11/30/1950
Majomut	Albert A	San Diego, CA	PVT	10/28/1952
Maki	Bernard E	Gogebic, MI	SGT	12/3/1950
Maki	Lawrence S	Saint Louis, MN	PFC	4/17/1953
Malmay	J B	Sabine, LA	CPL	12/2/1950
Mandino	Tony	Jackson, LA	SGT	11/28/1950
Mangan	Patrick J	New York, NY	PFC	10/31/1952
Mann	Robert M	Anderson, TX	PVT	10/14/1952
Manuel	Robert J	Newport, RI	2LT	10/14/1952
Marcus	Adrian T	Lawrence TN	PVT	3/26/1952
Maret	Paul F	Hamilton, OH	PFC	12/2/1950
Mark	Ottis P	Canyon, ID	SFC	12/1/1950
Markland	Wallace K	Benton, IA	PFC	5/24/1951
Marquez	Martin	Cook, IL	PVT	12/2/1950
Marr	Auburn	Salt Lake, UT	CPT	12/3/1950
Marsh	French E	Lewis, WV	PFC	3/3/1952
Marsh	Teddy C	Real, TX	PFC	11/28/1950
Marston	Bobby R	Lawrence TN	PFC	12/1/1950
Martin	J D	Leflore, MS	PFC	10/26/1952
Martin	James E	Vernon, LA	CPL	12/3/1950
Martin	William R	Los Angeles, CA	CPL	11/28/1950
Martinez	Richard J	San Francisco, CA	CPL	9/28/1951
Mason	Earl H	Hillsborough, FL	PFC	12/12/1950
Massanet	Almodovar	Puerto Rico	PVT	3/30/1950
Mathis	Grayson	Montgomery, MD	PVT	12/3/1950
Mathis	J L	Hancock, TN	CPL	12/4/1950
Mathis	Robert K	Sanborn, SD	CPL	10/14/1952
Matrisciano	Gabriel	Ashtabula, OH	PVT	10/15/1952
Matsen	Le Roy	Houghton, MI	PVT	6/8/1951
Mattoon	James H	Nez Perce, ID	PFC	3/30/1953
Matuszewski	Marian	Wayne, MI	PFC	3/27/1953
Maurice	Ovide L	Middlesex, MA	PVT	6/8/1953
Maxwell	Billy J	Troup, GA	CPL	11/30/1950
Mayhugh	William K	Franklin, PA	PFC	2/2/1952
Maynard	Max E	Morgan, IL	SSG	11/27/1950
Mazzulla	Thomas F	Clinton, PA	PFC	5/23/1951
McAlpin	Michael J	Los Angeles, CA	PFC	10/16/1952
McAlpine	Johnny L	Autauga, AL	PFC	12/1/1950
McArthur	Alfonso T	Burlington, NJ	CPT	10/30/1952
McCaffrey	Bernard E	Ingham, MI	PFC	12/12/1950
McClure	Leroy S	Oklahoma, OK	PVT	10/17/1952
McCole	Robert L	District of Columbia	MSG	8/22/1952
McConnell	Albert A	Los Angeles, CA	CPL	10/14/1952
McCoy	Charles E	Maury, TN	PFC	10/30/1952
McCoy	Glen B	Hughes, OK	PVT	10/30/1952
McCurley	Richard	Foard, TX	PVT	11/30/1950
McCurry	Gilbert L	Marion, TN	PVT	6/4/1951
McDougal	Leslie D	Tulsa, Ok	SGT	12/3/1950
McDuffie	Clem D	Richmond, NC	PFC	11/30/1950
McElholm	Patrick J	Whatcom, WA	PFC	9/5/1952
McGhee	Maurice	Bronx, NY	PVT	10/15/1952
McGlynn	Charles R	Atlantic, NJ	PFC	10/31/1952

McGuire	Thomas J	Du Page, Il	PFC	12/12/1950
McIntyre	Billy M	Beckham, Ok	CPL	12/7/1950
McIntyre	Dean I	Henderson, IL	PFC	10/17/1950
McKenna	John J	Philadelphia, PA	PVT	10/14/1952
McKinley	Konrad J	Cattaraugus, NY	PFC	9/27/1950
McLaren	James T	Kings, NY	PVT	11/3/1952
McLaughlin	Andrew	Cook, IL	PVT	6/5/1951
McMenamin	Michael J	Philadelphia, PA	PFC	12/12/1951
McNaughton	Donald	Columbia, NY	PFC	12/2/1950
McNutt	William H	Rockbridge, VA	PFC	9/14/1951
McPhillips	Thomas	Philadelphia, PA	SGT	10/14/1952
McSpadden	William	Rogers, OK	CPL	11/7/1951
Meadows	Charles R	Rockingham, VA	PFC	4/17/1953
Medlin	Bobby J	McLennan, TX	CPL	10/14/1952
Meglan	James J	Cuyahoga, OH	PFC	10/14/1952
Melecio-Hernandez	Unknown	Puerto Rico	PVT	9/15/1952
Melecio-Lopez	Leop	Puerto Rico	PVT	10/14/1952
Menclewicz	Clarence R	Cook, IL	PFC	3/7/1953
Merola	Vincent	Philadelphia, PA	PFC	9/1/1952
Merryman	Robert B	Baltimore City, MD	PFC	11/30/1950
Mervin	Richard H	Hillsborough, FL	SGT	11/28/1950
Metz	Gene A	Perry, PA	PFC	1/28/1952
Meuse	Clarence T	Aroostook, ME	PVT	11/4/1952
Meyer	Joseph K	Richland, ND	PVT	12/12/1950
Mickelsen	Morris S	Salt Lake, UT	PFC	10/14/1952
Miezejewski	Joseph	Lackawanna, PA	PFC	4/16/1953
Milbrath	Ronald F	Jackson, MN	SGT	3/24/1953
Miller	Everett H	Lancaster, PA	CPL	12/4/1950
Miller	John B	Marion, SC	PFC	11/30/1950
Miller, Jr	Edmund H	Monroe, NY	PFC	10/26/1952
Mills	Frederick E	Onondaga, NY	PVT	3/23/1953
Mills	George C	Gaston, NC	SGT	10/16/1952
Mills	Marvin L	Pulaski, VA	PFC	10/14/1952
Mineer	Leonard E	Harrison, KY	PFC	9/1/1952
Mitchell	Frederick	Baltimore City, MD	PFC	12/12/1950
Mitchell	William C	Manon, IN	PVT	6/17/1953
Miuccio	James	Bergen, NJ	PVT	6/2/1952
Moats	Herbert A	Pendleton, WV	PVT	10/15/1952
Moen	Albert D	Lake, IL	PFC	10/14/1952
Moles	Wendell R	Kanawha, WV	PFC	10/16/1952
Monfette	Francis	De Kalb, GA	SGT	6/5/1951
Monroe	Rondo J	Barron, WI	PVT	10/31/1952
Montgomery	James C	Florence, SC	PVT	10/14/1952
Montgomery	Sherlin	Harlan, KY	PVT	10/28/1952
Moore	Bobby M	Crawford, AR	PFC	11/4/1952
Moore	Ernest L	Allegany, MD	PVT	3/23/1953
Moore	George J	Prentiss, MS	PFC	11/5/1951
Moore	Paul J	Butler, OH	PVT	11/4/1952
Morency	James R	Contra Costa, CA	1LT	10/15/1952
Morgan	Charles C	Montgomery, IN	SFC	11/4/1951
Morgenstern	Paul E	Washington, OH	PFC	11/30/1950
Morreale	George J	Niagara, NY	CPL	12/2/1950
Morris	Tom J	Delta, COP	CPL	12/2/1950
Morrone	Peter P	Philadelphia, PA	PVT	3/23/1953
Morrow	John J	Hamilton, TN	MSG	11/28/1950
Mulholland	Gerald	Los Angeles, CA	1LT	5/24/1951
Mulik	George	Cambria, PA	PFC	12/3/1950

Mull	Thomas L	Allegheny, PA	PFC	12/3/1950
Mullins	Burl	Pike, KY	PFC	11/30/1950
Mullins	Kenneth	Wayne, MI	PFC	12/12/1950
Murphy	Jack	Pender, NC	MSG	4/17/1953
Murphy	Richard H	Oswego, NY	SGT	12/1/1950
Murphy	Thomas C	Hamilton, OH	PFC	5/30/1951
Murray	Frederick	Orleans, NY	PFC	12/1/1950
Myers	Paul E	Sangamon, IL	PFC	12/12/1950
Nance	Jimmie P	Los Angeles, CA	CPL	10/16/1952
Nash	William R	Maricopa, AZ	SGT	11/1/1951
Nave	Herley E	Lauderdale, TN	PVT	5/22/1951
Neal	Jessie P	Pickett, TN	PFC	7/22/1953
Needham	Al	Tom Green, TX	PFC	5/10/1952
Neel	Douglas M	Iredell, NC	PVT	11/1/1952
Neilson	Edmund	Oneida, NY	SGT	11/30/1950
Neilson	Paul H	Dodge, NE	PVT	9/21/1950
Neisz, Jr	Mike E	St Louis City, MO	PFC	12/1/1950
Nelms	James	Fannin, TX	CPL	12/12/1950
Nelson	Charles T	Kent, MI	CPL	12/3/1950
Nelson	Ernest E	Multnomah, OR	PFC	12/1/1950
Nelson	Gordon	Washington, MN	SGT	3/23/1953
Neville	Robert B	Johnson, IN	PVT	7/23/1953
Newland	Bobby	Ellsworth, KS	PVT	11/30/1950
Newman	Harold D	Ward, ND	PVT	10/15/1952
Nichols	David	Liberty, TX	CPL	11/8/1950
Nicholson	William	Oakland, MI	CPL	11/3/1950
Niemi	Charles R	Thompkins, NY	SGT	9/27/1951
Nieves, Jr	Pedro	Puerto Rico	CPL	8/22/1952
Nigerville	Martin	Sabine, LA	PFC	11/30/1950
Nihei	Lawrence Y	Hawaii	PFC	12/3/1950
Noel	Robert L	Genesee, MI	CPL	4/16/1953
Nolan	Alfred E	Orange, NY	PVT	3/23/1953
Nolen, Jr	Richard	Maury, TN	MSG	12/1/1950
Noll	Jake R	Clermont, OH	PFC	4/16/1953
Nykvist	Robert	Cook, IL	PFC	12/3/1950
Oakley	Delbert W	Clay, AR	CPL	12/12/1950
Oakley	Ronald R	Outagamie, WI	CPL	12/3/1950
Ogden	Charles A	Middlesex, MA	MSG	12/1/1950
Ohara	Cordell	Jefferson, AL	PVT	3/24/1953
Olnagan	Augustin I	Virgin Islands	CPL	12/1/1950
Olson	Charles M	Calumet, WI	CPL	5/22/1951
Omans	Marvin E	Henry, MO	PFC	12/3/1950
Ortego	Elward J	Evangeline, LA	PFC	10/14/1952
Ortiz-Rodriguez	Ru	Puerto Rico	CPL	7/23/1953
Osborne	Owen H	Fayette, WV	PFC	11/30/1950
Otto	Charles F	Philadelphia, PA	PFC	11/4/1952
Outley	Howard	Bibb, GA	PVT	7/24/1953
Owens, Jr	Frank	Nueces, TX	PVT	10/17/1952
Paepke, Jr	Albert W	Smith, TX	PVT	11/4/1952
Page	James A	Allegheny PA	CPL	11/28/1950
Page	William E	Hennepin, MN	PVT	3/9/1953
Paine	George H	Worcester, MA	SGT	11/30/1950
Paparillo	Raphael	Queens, NY	PFC	6/4/1951
Pappin	Richard C	Cook, IL	1LT	7/24/1953
Parker	Kenneth W	Jackson, MI	CPL	10/14/1952
Parks	Douglas A	Virgin Islands	PFC	10/14/1952
Parks	Richard W	Williamson, IL	CPL	4/26/1953

Patten	Roy M	Hickman, TN	PFC	10/6/1950
Patterson	Harold F	Henderson, KY	PFC	4/17/1953
Paul	Kenneth D	Oakland, MI	PFC	10/14/1952
Pavlak	Edward	Cook, IL	SGT	10/14/1952
Pearish	Andrew D	St Joseph, IN	PVT	10/25/1952
Pedigo	William A	Grayson, TX	CPL	2/15/1951
Pedregon	Edward M	El Paso, TX	PFC	11/30/1950
Pendergrass	Leon B	Etowah, AL	MSG	12/12/1950
Penrose	Percy L	St Joseph, IN	CPL	4/17/1953
Pepin	Edward J	Worcester, MA	PFC	7/24/1953
Perez	Joffrey	Virgin Islands	CPL	11/29/1950
Perez-Roman	Ismael	Puerto Rico	PVT	1/25/1953
Perkins	Donald J	Windham, VT	CPL	7/24/1953
Perry	Norman C	Baxter, AR	PFC	9/26/1950
Perry	Russell L	Campbell, VA	CPL	10/14/1952
Perry, Jr	John C	Pinellas, FL	SGT	10/30/1952
Perusse	Harvey E	Hampden, MA	PVT	3/9/1953
Peterson	Lynn R	Oswego, NY	PFC	12/1/1950
Petts	Edwin C	Alcona, MI	PFC	12/1/1950
Petty	Alvin R	Daviess, IN	CPL	10/14/1952
Peveler	Oscar P	Daviess, KY	MSG	7/5/1952
Philbrick	Glendon L	Oxford, ME	CPL	7/24/1953
Phillips	Robert L	Dent, MO	PFC	12/12/1950
Pietrus	Eugene H	Hughes, SD	CPL	10/14/1952
Pina-Caliz	Fernand	Puerto Rico	PFC	4/17/1953
Pingenot	Leon A	Bexar, TX	CPT	10/14/1952
Pitman	Arnold	McDowell, NC	CPL	12/12/1950
Pleasants	Joseph G	Louisa, VA	PFC	9/9/1951
Pleshek	Roger W	Menominee, MI	PVT	11/30/1950
Poling	Edward M	Wyandotte, KS	PVT	12/3/1950
Poling	Forest J	Orleans, LA	PFC	12/12/1950
Pollard	Glen D	Montrose, CO	PFC	5/3/1953
Pomeroy	Ralph E	Greenbrier, WV	PFC	10/15/1952
Pool	Edward	San Luis Obispo, CA	PFC	11/30/1950
Poole	Lovelle	Randolph, AL	SGT	4/16/1953
Poolman	John E	Marshall, MN	PVT	4/16/1953
Poore	Fred C	Ripley, IN	SGT	10/15/1952
Pope	Joseph	Lackawanna, PA	PFC	8/22/1952
Poppe	Robert L	Sheboygan, WI	PFC	10/14/1952
Portalatin-Santiago		Puerto Rico	CPL	4/17/1953
Porter	Jasper M	Shelby, TN	CPL	12/12/1950
Porter	Jimmy T	Richmond, NC	PFC	5/5/2023
Porter	Rogers	Richmond, GA	2LT	11/10/1950
Potter	Charles	Ontario, NY	PVT	11/4/1952
Powell	Rex W	Burke, NC	PFC	12/12/1950
Powell	Richard M	Columbia, NY	PFC	12/3/1950
Prentice	Herbert W	Middlesex, MA	PFC	12/12/1950
Presley, Jr	Noah	Vanderburgh, IN	PFC	6/5/1951
Puckett	Charles C	Union, SC	PFC	10/14/1952
Pugh, Jr	Henry	Hood River, OR	SFC	6/8/1951
Pulliam	George E	Norfolk, VA	PFC	12/12/1950
Pullin	Odren R	Muscogee, GA	CPL	12/12/1950
Pulver	Thomas L	Ramsey, MN	PFC	6/8/1951
Purcell	Loyd E	Boone, MO	PFC	10/14/1952
Quillman	Robert H	Henry, OH	PFC	11/29/1950
Quinones-Natal	Antonio	Puerto Rico	PFC	5/23/1953
Quintana	Charlie D	Curry, NM	PFC	4/16/1953

Richardson, Jr	Prater H	Wythe County, VA	PFC	11/20/1950
Rivera-Ortiz	Adolfo	Aibonito, PR	SFC	7/24/1953
Rogers	Donald C	Boston, MA	SFC	10/31/1952
Romo	Cristobal	San Diego, CA	CPL	12/12/1953
Russell	Annis	Burlington, NJ	PVT	1/26/1950
Sabando	Agapito	San Isidro, Masantol, PH	CPL	12/1/1950
Sadewasser	William R	Allegany, NY	PFC	11/28/1950
Sakamoto	Allen T	Hawaii	PFC	10/15/1952
Salaman-Arroyo	Hec	Puerto Rico	PVT	4/17/1953
Salazar	Sastines	Santa Clara, CA	CPL	11/27/1950
Sampson	Orie D	Bristol, MA	PFC	10/14/1952
San Miguel	Pedro	Maverick, TX	SGT	12/3/1950
Sanchez	Gregorio G	Pima, AZ	PFC	10/14/1952
Sanchez	Rodriguez	Puerto Rico	PFC	3/23/1953
Sanchez-Torres	Pab	Puerto Rico	PFC	10/14/1952
Sander, Jr	Mathew	Sacramento, CA	CPL	6/2/1951
Sanford	Charles D	San Francisco, CA	PFC	4/3/1953
Santacruz	Rudy J	St Louis City, MO	PFC	11/28/1950
Santiago-Bonilla	E	Puerto Rico	PFC	3/7/1953
Santiago-Ortiz	Jos	Puerto Rico	PFC	10/14/1952
Santiago-Robles	Bi	Puerto Rico	PVT	10/29/1952
Santistvan	Richard	Denver, CO	PVT	6/1/1951
Sapia	Elroy R	Jackson, LA	PFC	12/12/1950
Sapp	Clifford N	Macon, IL	PVT	11/30/1950
Sarafin	Albin P	Hampshire MA	SGT	3/9/1953
Satter	Leo C	Turner, SD	PFC	10/14/1952
Sauerbrei	Clarence	Fairfield, OH	SGT	10/17/1952
Schaekel	Walter J	Shelby IN	PFC	10/16/1952
Schanck	Russell D	Osceola, MI	PFC	10/26/1952
Schatz	Doyle	Stoddard, MO	CPL	10/14/1952
Scheetz	George W	Osage, KS	PFC	10/14/1952
Schermerhorn	Mayna	Cattaraugus, NY	1LT	12/12/1950
Schermerhorn	Robert W	Cortland, NY	CPL	9/2/1951
Schiele	Catesby E	Concordia, LA	CPT	1/3/1952
Schmid	Eugene O	Dubuque, IA	SFC	3/9/1952
Schmitt	Herbert H	Moniteau, MO	CPL	12/1/1950
Schmitt	Robert G	Wells, ND	1LT	12/1/1950
Schneider	Walter O	Baltimore City, MD	PFC	12/3/1950
Schoenmann	Glenn S	Grundy, TN	PFC	11/28/1950
Schulz	Walter M	Chickasaw, IA	PFC	10/31/1952
Schum	Richard T	Madison, IL	CPL	8/8/1952
Schwartz	Robert C	Kings, NY	PVT	3/9/1953
Scipioni	Henry A	Monroe, NY	PVT	3/24/1953
Scoggins	Bobby G	Barrow, GA	PVT	10/28/1952
Scott	Lawrence	Sauk, WI	PFC	11/30/1950
Scott	Richard W	Marion, OH	PVT	11/4/1952
Scott	Robert W	Wayne, MI	PFC	12/1/1950
Scott	Thomas E	Portage, OH	PVT	11/4/1952
Scott, Jr	Frank B	Wayne, MI	PFC	3/9/1953
Scully	Francis J	New Haven, CT	PVT	4/17/1953
Scully	William	Nassau, NY	PFC	1/14/1951
Seaborn	Larry L	Franklin, KS	PFC	1/7/1952
Seabourn	Donald T	Los Angeles, CA	CPL	12/12/1950
Seals	Earl E	Claiborne, TX	PFC	11/15/1951
Sebastian	Brown	Cook, IL	CPT	12/1/1950
Sells	Gail F	Perry, OH	CPL	12/1/1950
Semetges	George J	Cook, IL	PFC	10/26/1952

Scmulka, Jr	John H	Lackawanna, PA	PFC	6/9/1951
Sercel, Jr	Tony	Musselshell, MT	PVT	10/16/1952
Sereika	Donald S	Cook, IL	CPL	6/7/1951
Sesepasara	Lepe	Pago Pago, Samoa	CPL	10/15/1952
Severan	Leon J	Orleans, LA	SGT	10/14/1952
Sewell	David C	Cass, MN	SGT	11/28/1950
Shaffer	Robert R	Indiana, PA	PVT	3/23/1953
Sharp	Donald W	Pike, IN	PVT	7/27/1953
Shaw	Marvin K	Riverside, CA	PFC	9/4/1951
Shay	Charles	Morris, NJ	PFC	1/21/1953
Shell, Jr	Glenn E	Benton, WA	PFC	4/16/1953
Shepard	Floyd	Denver, CO	PFC	6/8/1951
Shepard	Ollie E	Choctaw, OK	CPL	12/3/1950
Sheppard	Claude L	Stanislaus, CA	PVT	11/28/1950
Sheppard	Tally J	Lucas, OH	2LT	6/5/1951
Shiley	Doyle W	Seneca, OH	PFC	12/12/1950
Shortell	James R	Kings, NY	CPL	10/24/1952
Shrader	Louis C	Shelby, IN	PFC	10/15/1952
Shuck	Herbert D	Snohomish, WA	CPL	12/12/1950
Siemer	Curtis L	Benton, MN	CPL	7/10/1953
Silvernail	Roger M	Steams, MN	PFC	11/4/1951
Simeral	Lester G	Monongalia, WV	SFC	12/12/1950
Simmons	Clarence A	Monroe, AR	SFC	12/1/1950
Simmons	Earl S	Middlesex, MA	PVT	6/15/1953
Simpson	Charles L	Bath, KY	PFC	12/12/1950
Simpson	James D	Bolivar, MS	PFC	7/24/1953
Simrell	Carroll J	Cedar, MO	PFC	11/30/1950
Sims	David	Richland, SC	PVT	3/23/1953
Skiba	Peter B	Geauga, OH	PFC	7/22/1953
Skiles	Phillip C	Wicomico, MD	PFC	12/1/1950
Skilton	Rollin W	Litchfield, CT	1LT	12/6/1950
Slane	James J	Hudson, NJ	PVT	10/14/1952
Smith	Amon K	George, MS	PVT	1/28/1952
Smith	Carl D	Pleasants, WV	PFC	3/9/1953
Smith	Cecil J	Gallia, OH	CPL	10/14/1952
Smith	Crist W	Craighead, AR	CPL	11/6/1951
Smith	Danny R	Hancock, WV	CPL	10/24/1952
Smith	David B	Norfolk, VA	MSG	11/30/1950
Smith	Francis K	Cass, NE	CPL	12/2/1950
Smith	James T	Warren, TN	CPL	9/27/1950
Smith	John H	Los Angeles, CA	PVT	6/4/1951
Smith	Kenneth B	Genesee, MI	PVT	10/16/1952
Smith	Paul A	Riverside, CA	PFC	1/20/1953
Smith	Paul H	Noble, OH	CPL	3/23/1953
Smith	Robert J	Cayuga, NY	PFC	6/30/1953
Smith	William E	Mason, WV	PFC	10/16/1952
Smith, Jr	Harrison	Shelby, TN	PFC	11/4/1952
Smock	Richard T	Geary, KS	1LT	6/6/1951
Snipes, Jr	Edgar T	Madison, IL	1LT	12/1/1950
Snock, Jr	Joseph M	Westmoreland, PA	CPL	11/30/1950
Snyder	David B	Wayne, OH	SGT	11/30/1950
Sonnamaker	William E	Sheridan WY	SGt	4/17/1953
Sooy	Ralph E	Jefferson, IN	SFC	7/10/1952
Soutar	Ian	Worcester, MA	CPL	10/14/1952
Sowers	Benjamin F	Tucker, WV	PFC	12/2/1950
Spaar	Richard J	Ohio, WV	PFC	10/14/1952
Spells	Govan L	Putnam, FL	SFC	4/3/1953

Spencer	Chapman T	Hampden, MA	SGT	4/17/1953
Spencer	Mickey R	McDowell, WV	PVT	6/10/1953
Sperl	Donald G	Douglas, NE	PVT	10/16/1952
Spontik	Peter	Lorain, OH	PFC	3/23/1953
Sronce	Johnnie A	New Madrid, MO	PFC	12/1/1950
St Onge	John D	Wayne, MI	PVT	10/27/1952
Stafford	Dayton J	Albany, NY	PFC	10/14/1952
Stamper	Wayne E	Clearwater, ID	SGT	1/24/1953
Stapleton	Joseph W	Iowa, WI	PFC	6/9/1951
Stauffer	Robert L	Lee, IL	PFC	11/30/1950
Steele	Ronald E	Ontario, NY	PFC	6/7/1951
Steigerwalt	Edwin	Carbon, PA	PFC	11/30/1950
Stevenson	Charles	Davidson, TN	PFC	10/14/1952
Stewart	Gerald W	Calhoun, AL	PVT	8/3/1952
Stiefel	Ernest J	Marshall, AL	PVT	8/22/1952
Stiles	Jerry D	Kings, CA	PVT	10/14/1952
Stone	John F	Salem, NJ	CPL	6/3/1952
Stone	William	Cook, IL	CPL	9/2/1951
Storms	Harvey H	Cameron, TX	MAJ	12/1/1950
Studnick	Robert B	Lake, CA	2LT	8/30/1952
Stumpf	Marion F	Atchison, KS	PFC	12/12/1950
Summers	Eddie C	Oakland, MI	SGT	11/28/1950
Summers	Thomas J	Philadelphia, PA	2LT	4/17/1953
Summy	James D	Polk, IA	SGT	7/10/1953
Sumter	Robert D	Milwaukee, WI	PVT	4/17/1953
Sutliff	Laverne A	Burnet, WI	CPL	4/17/1953
Swainbank	James E	Luzerne, PA	CPL	11/29/1950
Swarmer	William R	Chautauqua, NY	SFC	11/30/1950
Tacazon	Flabiano T	Virgin Islands	CPL	12/1/1950
Tait	Main M	Hennepin, MN	PVT	6/7/1951
Takahashi	Richard	Hawaii	PFC	12/3/1950
Takai	Tohoru T	Los Angeles, CA	CPL	11/28/1950
Tamayo	Refugio C	Cameron, TX	PFC	12/12/1950
Tanksley	James N	Lawrence, IN	PVT	3/24/1953
Tarkow	Harvey	St Louis City, MO	CPL	9/11/1951
Tasker	Theodore M	Middlesex, MA	PVT	7/23/1953
Taylor	Donald H	Norfolk, MA	PVT	5/23/1953
Taylor	James R	District of Columbia	PVT	10/17/1952
Taylor	Raymond L	Ellis, TX	PFC	12/1/1950
Taylor	Richard J	McKean, PA	PFC	7/24/1953
Teague	Harold G	Hardeman, TN	PFC	10/28/1952
Thacker	Robert L	Wayne, WV	CPL	4/17/1953
Thomas	Alexander	La Salle, IL	PFC	9/12/1951
Thomas	Francis D	Allegany, MD	SGT	9/27/1950
Thomas	Gerald S	Erie, NY	CPL	10/15/1952
Thomas	Roy H	Baltimore City, MD	PFC	12/12/1950
Thomas	Willie E	Hamilton, TN	PVT	10/14/1952
Thomason	Joseph E	San Luis Obispo, CA	PFC	4/16/1953
Thompson	Donald O	Burke, ND	PVT	4/17/1953
Thompson	Gene A	Rockingham, VA	PFC	6/8/1952
Thompson	James O	Scioto, OH	MSG	11/28/1950
Thompson	James W	Forsyth, NC	PFC	5/23/1953
Thompson	Robert E	Muscogee, GA	PVT	12/12/1950
Thompson	Robert E	Lenawee, MI	PFC	10/15/1952
Thompson	Robert E	Florence, SC	1LT	4/16/1953
Thompson	Wayne L	Comanche, KS	PFC	9/5/1952
Thornton	Richard R	Creek, OK	PFC	12/2/1950

Thurmond	Ralph R	Dyer, TN	CPL	12/4/1950
Thweatt	James A	Muscogee, Ga	PFC	3/7/1953
Tilley	Herbert L	Etowah, AL	CPL	12/1/1950
Titchnell	Leonidas L	Allegheny, PA	CPL	11/30/1950
Tockunaga	Richard R	Hawaii	PFC	10/15/1952
Toth	Edward J	Westmoreland, PA	CPL	11/30/1950
Toth	James C	Rawlins, KS	CPL	6/5/1951
Treadway	Richard A	Crawford, IL	PFC	10/15/1952
Tremblay	Paul N	Essex, MA	CPL	12/1/1950
Trent	James L	Hardin, KY	CPL	11/30/1950
Trepasso	Joseph E	Fulton, NY	CPL	12/1/1950
Trinkle	John H	Madison, AR	PVT	6/5/1951
Tronier	Ernest H	Davis, UT	CPL	6/23/1952
Truitt	Thomas	Alachua, FL	CPL	10/26/1952
Trujillo	Isidro E	Guadalupe, NM	SGT	10/14/1952
Trulock	Glen K	Macon, IL	CPL	3/23/1953
Truslow	Elwood M	Albemarle, VA	CPL	12/12/1950
Tullo	Thomas J	Kings, NY	CPL	1/21/1953
Turbeville	Michaux	Dillon, SC	PFC	12/1/1950
Turner	Gerald O J	Cuyahoga, OH	PFC	8/22/1952
Uptain	Willie D	Ben Hill, GA	PFC	7/24/1953
Urbano	Isidro D	San Francisco, CA	CPT	9/18/1952
Uvalle	Manuel J	Los Angeles, CA	PFC	10/4/1951
Vaccaro	Daniel J	Carbon, PA	CPL	12/3/1950
Vadenais	Elphege	Providence, RI	PFC	12/12/1950
Vajen	Lloyd C	Defiance, OH	CPL	10/16/1952
Valdiviez	Angel M	El Paso, TX	PFC	1/14/1951
Valle	Mario F	Virgin Islands	SGT	10/15/1952
Van Buskirk	Richard B	Bon Homme, SD	CPL	9/11/1951
Van Ningen	Marvin G	Bowman, ND	PFC	10/14/1952
Vaughn	Orville L	Cabell, WV	CPL	12/12/1950
Vejar	Frank J	Cochise, AZ	SGT	11/30/1950
Vick	Calvin C	Wilson, TN	CPL	9/24/1950
Vidock	Paul B	Douglas, NE	PFC	10/15/1952
Vigil	Juan B	Reo Arriba, NM	CPL	10/17/1952
Villanueva	Joaquin	Collin, TX	PFC	9/2/1951
Vincent	Edward C	Wood, WV	PFC	12/12/1950
Vining	Jack L	Delaware, IN	SGT	10/14/1952
Vinson	Earnest L	Lewis, KY	CPL	6/1/1952
Violette	Joseph C	Aroostook, ME	CPL	11/6/1951
Wamble	Henry L	Cairo, GA	CPT	11/28/1950
Wester	Melvin	Holy Cross, WI	SSG	10/14/1952
Whalen	Kenneth J	River Falls, WI	MSG	9/26/1950
Yaka	Mueno	Honolulu, HI	PFC	10/15/1952
Yamaguchi	Tsugio	Honolulu, HI	PFC	10/14/1952
Yokotake	Katashi	Honolulu, HI	PFC	7/19/1952
Young	Curtis R	Audrain, MO	CPL	11/30/1950
Zecchin, Jr	Victor P	Litchfield, CT	PFC	12/12/1950
Zepp	Charles E	Annapolis, MD	CPL	1/12/1953
Zidelski	William F	New York, NY	PFC	12/12/1950
Zigarelli	Lawrence	Beaver, PA	PVT	2/16/1951
Zupke	Harry R	Kandiyohi, MN	SFC	12/6/1950

Vietnam War

Chronology of 4th and 6th Battalions Killed in Action

Rank	Name	Unit	Date	Home of Record
		4th Battalion		
SP/4	Vincent F. Murphy	Co C	18 Sep 66	Grosse Pointe, MI
SP/4	Manzie Glover, Jr.	HHC	19 Sep 66	Elizabeth, NJ
CPT	John M. Harrington	HHC	19 Sep 66	Durham, NC
PFC	Robert C. Hauser	Co B	24 Sep 66	Fair Lawn, NJ
PFC	Michael J. Macarell	Co C	13 Nov 66	Hasbrouck Heights, NJ
PFC	Edward J. Piantkowski	Co C	13 Nov 66	Chicago, IL
PFC	Nelson F. Pulsifer Jr.	Co C	14 Nov 66	Lakeside, CA
SP/4	Kenneth Rhodes	Co A	12 Dec 66	Greenville, SC
SP/4	Ronald D. Evans	Co A	26 Dec 66	Cincinnati, OH
PFC	Plummer Williams	Co A	26 Dec 66	Forrest City, AR
PFC	Robert F. Rathbun	Co B	29 Dec 66	Mansfield, OH
SSG	James N. Byers	Co B	20 Jan 67	Westminster, MD
SP/4	Richard A. Wood	Co C	4 Feb 67	Dumont, NJ
SP/4	John L. Bylon	HHC	23 Feb 67	Chicago, IL
SGT	James A. Masten	Co B	23 Feb 67	Columbia, NJ
SFC	Felicisimo A. Hugo	Co C	26 Feb 67	Wahiawa, HI
PFC	Johnnie F. Barchak, Jr	Co C	28 Feb 67	San Antonio, TX
PFC	Richard L. Boltz	Co A	28 Feb 67	Ridgefield Park, NJ
PFC	David C. Holden	Co A	28 Feb 67	Jamaica Plain, MA
PFC	Jimmy L. Langston	Co C	28 Feb 67	Hartford, CT
PFC	Michael L. Myers,	Co C	28 Feb 67	Detroit, MI
PFC	John T. Wetzel	Co C	28 Feb 67	Buchanan, MI
PFC	Paul A. Hasenbeck	Co D	21 Apr 67	Freeburg, MO
SP/4	Thomas A. Mangino	Co D	21 Apr 67	Alliance, OH
PFC	David M. Winters	Co D	21 Apr 67	Delhi, CA
SP/4	Bruce H. Scragg	Co B	30 Apr 67	Marmet, WV
SP/4	Michael J. Hilburger	Co B	1 May 67	Cheektowaga, NY
SSG	Bobby E. Hunt	Co B	1 May 67	Chuckey, TN
SP/4	Charles E. Miller	Co B	1 May 67	Piketon, OH
PFC	James R. Dowdy	Co D	3 May 67	Granite City, IL
SP/4	John J. Thomas	Co D	5 May 67	Philadelphia, PA
SSG	Gregory W. Woods	Co D	5 May 67	Pittsburgh, PA
PFC	Charlie M. Gilmer	Co C	23 May 67	Christiansburg, VA
PFC	Joseph D. King	Co C	23 May 67	Carrboro, NC
PFC	Donald A. Skinner	Co C	23 May 67	Lavallette, NJ
PFC	Carl R. Stovall	Co C	23 May 67	Fort Pierce, FL
SGT	Robert D. Thompson	Co A	23 May 67	Wymer, WV
PFC	John T. Trivette	Co C	23 May 67	Winston-Salem, NC
PFC	Luther Robinson	Co C	3 Jun 67	Beaver, OH
SP/4	Robert J. Nicklow	Co C	11 Jul 67	Garrett, PA
PFC	Charles E. Merriman	Co C	16 Jul 67	Knoxville, TN
PFC	Reynaldo S. Torres	Co C	16 Jul 67	Uvalde, TX
SP/4	Dennis J. Wahl	Co C	21 Jul 67	Alliance, OH
PFC	Harvey E. Wynn	HHC	9 Aug 67	Donalsonville, GA
SP/4	Lonnie O. Hill	Co A	29 Aug 67	Atoka, TN
SP/4	Ralph M. Knight	Co A	30 Aug 67	Attalla, AL
SP/4	Ray Collins	Co A	15 Sep 67	Chicago, IL
PFC	Franklin D. Willett	Co A	15 Sep 67	Hereford, AZ
SP/4	Albert R. Molnar	Co C	4 Nov 67	North Bergen, NJ
PFC	Johnny W. McCain	Co D	10 Nov 67	Ore City, TX
PVT	Lewis L. Sloan	Co D	16 Nov 67	East Point, GA

Rank	Name	Unit	Date	Home of Record
CPL	Kenneth S. Adams	Co D	23 Nov 67	Santa Barbara, CA
CPL	Philip F. Adams	Co D	23 Nov 67	Croton Falls, NY
CPL	Rodney E. Loatman	Co D	23 Nov 67	Newark, NJ
PFC	Robert D Waddell	Co D	23 Nov 67	Batavia, OH
SP/4	Jack W. McKinnon, Jr.	Co D	3 Jan 68	Santa Cruz, CA
PFC	Billy G. Jent	Co D	4 Jan 68	Vinita, OK
PFC	James D. Osenbaugh	Co D	4 Jan 68	Hutchinson, KS
PVT	Walter J. Peters	Co D	4 Jan 68	Indio, CA
PVT	Robert W. Sorensen	Co D	4 Jan 68	Minneapolis, MN
PFC	Howard M. Bissen	Co B	8 Jan 68	Stacyville, IA
2 LT	Anthony R. Watkins	Co B	8 Jan 68	Ardmore, OK
PVT	Sisto B. Bojorquez	Co A	9 Jan 68	Eloy, AZ
PFC	Mark A. Kolvek	Co D	8 Feb 68	Gary, IN
SGT	Joseph P. Bowling	Co B	11 Feb 68	Wichita, KS
PFC	Gerald A. Huczek	Co B	11 Feb 68	Roseville, MI
PFC	Craig G. Knobloch	Co B	11 Feb 68	East Lansing, MI
PFC	Richard D. Vick	Co C	12 Feb 68	Bemidji, MN
PFC	Kellynn V. Snow	Co C	13 Feb 68	Salt Lake City, UT
SP/4	Charles M. Burke	Co C	14 Feb 68	Mandeville, LA
SP/5	Everett J. Valnadingham	HHC	4 Mar 68	Dallas, TX
PFC	Raymond C. Guest	Co C	15 Mar 68	Redding, CA
SGT	Leroy W. Katterhenry, Jr.	Co C	15 Mar 68	Columbus, OH
SP/4	Keith N. Atchley	Co B	11 Apr 68	Woodland, WA
PFC	Larry D. Hatcher	Co B	11 Apr 68	Martinsville, VA
SP/5	James T. McMaster	HHC	15 Apr 68	Rosiclare, IL
PFC	George B. Ayers	Co B	24 Apr 68	Wilkes-Barre, PA
PFC	Wilbur F. Mattox	Co B	24 Apr 68	Gainesville, GA
SP/4	Martin W. Guard	Co B	27 Apr 68	Santa Ana, CA
1 LT	Howard R. Crothers	Co A	1 May 68	New Martinsville, WV
PFC	Thomas K. Lyons	Co A	1 May 68	Philadelphia, PA
PFC	Michael J. Massey	Co A	1 May 68	Columbus, GA
PVT	Eusebio Solis	Co A	1 May 68	San Jose, CA
PFC	William P. Townsend, Jr.	Co A	1 May 68	Reseda, CA
PFC	Jimmy R. Brown	Co B	9 May 68	Cleburne, TX
PFC	Russell W. Jarick	HHC	9 May 68	Los Angeles, CA
PFC	Terrence A. Kandler	Co B	9 May 68	Torrance, CA
PFC	Jimmy R. Wheless	HHC	9 May 68	San Angelo, TX
PVT	Charles A. Cope	Co A	15 May 68	St. Louis, MO
SP/4	Richard L. Moss	HHC	16 May 68	Tampa, FL
PFC	Harold D. Peppers	Co A	18 May 68	Chicago, IL
SP/4	Timothy J. Rizzardini	Co A	18 May 68	Ridgecrest, CA
SGT	Steve Gomez	Co C	25 May 68	Miami, FL
PFC	Dennis L. Mack	Co D	25 May 68	Detroit, MI
SGT	Ronald C. McEuen	Co C	25 May 68	Garden Grove, CA
SP/4	Eugene G. O'Connell	Co C	25 May 68	Edgewater, NJ
PFC	Dennis L. Stiglitz	Co C	25 May 68	Stephenson, MI
SP/4	Nathaniel Wade	Co D	18 Jun 68	Augusta, GA
PFC	John D. Cox, Jr.	Co A	3 Jul 68	Tucson, AZ
PFC	Joseph M. Houtz	Co B	3 Jul 68	Springfield, MO
PFC	Arthur Harmon	Co D	6 Jul 68	Laurel, MS
PFC	Charles F. Harger, Jr.	Co C	9 Jul 68	Headrick, OK
SP/4	Willis J. Billeaud, Jr.	Co C	20 Jul 68	Broussard, LA
PFC	Fernando A. Rivera, Jr.	Co B	26 Aug 68	New York, NY
1 LT	Kevin G. Burke	Co A	20 Nov 68	Anita, IA
PFC	Michael J. Crescenz (MOH)	Co A	20 Nov 68	Philadelphia, PA
SP/4	Danny C. Hudson	Co A	20 Nov 68	Chadron, NE

Rank	Name	Unit	Date	Home of Record
SP/4	Thomas G. Dickerson	Co B	23 Nov 68	Thomaston, GA
CPL	Harold L. Glover	Co B	23 Nov 68	Siler City, NC
SP/4	Raymond Alaniz	Co B	1 Dec 68	Wichita Falls, TX
PFC	Karl P. Dency	Co A	7 Dec 68	Chicago, IL
SP/4	Benjamin L. Hoopengarner, Jr.	Co A	7 Dec 68	Fraser, MI
PFC	Michael R. Bach	Co A	8 Dec 68	Cincinnati, OH
SP/4	Rapheal J. Frost	Co B	20 Dec 68	Hunter, ND
SP/4	Charles D. Groh	Co B	2 Jan 69	New York, NY
SP/5	Thomas M. Barr	HHC	12 May 69	Anchorage, AK
SP/4	Wendell A. Weston	HHC	12 May 69	Warren, VT
PVT	Dennis L. Babcock	Co B	28 May 69	Mauston, WI
PFC	Max F. De Sully, Jr.	Co A	4 Jun 69	Portland, OR
PFC	Andrew S. Rahilly	Co A	4 Jun 69	New York, NY
SP/4	Hiris W. Blevins	Co B	17 Jun 69	Little Rock, AR
PFC	Dewey M. Eubanks	Co B	23 Jun 69	Durham, NC
SP/4	Anson T. Geronzin	Co E	23 Jun 69	Clinton, IA
PFC	Theodore M. Hatle	Co B	23 Jun 69	Sisseton, SD
PFC	Rogers S. Gordon	Co A	24 Jun 69	Middlevillle, MI
PFC	Steve O. Strasshofer	Co A	27 Jun 69	Parma, OH
PFC	Herbert Logsdon, Jr.	Co A	28 Jun 69	Clarksville, IN
PFC	Eldon G. Crumley	Co A	2 Jul 69	Lincoln, NE
PFC	Michael P. Klotz	HHC	2 Jul 69	Hudson, NY
SGT	Ronald F. Wilder	Co A	21 Jul 69	Baytown, TX
SP/4	Richard K. Larson	Co D	25 Jul 69	Santa Ana, CA
PFC	Andrew J. Kiniry	Co B	28 Jul 69	Coatesville, PA
PFC	Curtis D. Smith	Co B	28 Jul 69	Bessemer City, NC
CPL	Daniel A. Bolduc	Co B	29 Jul 69	Lennoxville, Quebec, CAN
PFC	Thomas D. Snyder	Co D	10 Aug 69	Johnson City, TN
SP/4	William B. Scott	HHC	12 Aug 69	Jacksonville, NC
SP/4	Kim M. Deliberto	HHC	17 Aug 69	Massapequa, NY
SGT	William P. Gooding	Co D	17 Aug 69	Edison, NJ
SP/4	Frederick Mezzatesta	Co D	17 Aug 69	Whitesboro, NY
PFC	Mathew Peterson	Co D	17 Aug 69	Florence, SC
PFC	Clifford Seals	Co D	17 Aug 69	Eufaula, OK
PFC	Jay D. Webster, Jr.	Co D	17 Aug 69	Lititz, PA
PFC	Robert A. Fox	Co B	18 Aug 69	Beardstown, IL
SGT	Mark W. Grigsby	Co B	18 Aug 69	Foxboro, MA
PFC	Gary W. Harvey	Co B	18 Aug 69	Seattle, WA
SP/4	Gerald A. Henry	Co B	18 Aug 69	Landis, AR
PFC	Edwin C. Hockenberry	Co B	18 Aug 69	East Waterford, PA
PFC	David Lewis	Co B	18 Aug 69	Cleves, OH
PFC	Vincent T. Masciale	Co B	18 Aug 69	Jacksonville, FL
PFC	Douglas Merrill	Co B	18 Aug 69	North St. Paul, MN
SSG	Robert T. Spillner	Co D	18 Aug 69	Waipahu, HI
SP/4	Thomas L. Stradtman	Co B	18 Aug 69	St. Cloud, MN
SP/4	Paul W. Vanderboom, Jr.	Co B	18 Aug 69	Fond Du Lac, WI
PFC	Frederico V. Dela-Cruz	Co C	20 Aug 69	Agana, GU
SP/4	Jerry W. Hill	Co C	20 Aug 69	Vinita, OK
PFC	Jimmy L. Jones	Co C	20 Aug 69	Kingsport, TN
PFC	James E. Ruttan	Co C	20 Aug 69	Watertown, NY
PFC	Daniel H. Love	Co A	22 Aug 69	Watkins Glen, NY
1 LT	Stephen D. Moore	Co A	22 Aug 69	Fear Oaks, CA
PFC	Darrell D. Taylor	Co A	22 Aug 69	Vicksburg, MI
PFC	Clarke K. Vickrey	HHC	22 Aug 69	Conroe, TX
CPL	William J. Zeltner	Co A	22 Aug 69	Philadelphia, PA

Rank	Name	Unit	Date	Home of Record
SP/4	Dennis L. Cannito	Co C	26 Aug 69	West New York, NJ
SGT	Merlin J. Craig	Co C	26 Aug 69	Alexandria, LA
SGT	Norman R. Hetzel	Co B	26 Aug 69	Mahwah, NJ
SP/4	William G. Howell	Co C	26 Aug 69	Gastonia, NC
PFC	Donald E. Nelson	Co C	26 Aug 69	Wayne, MI
SFC	Marshall E. Robertson	Co C	26 Aug 69	Portsmouth, VA
PFC	Russell A. Taylor	Co D	26 Aug 69	Elkins, WV
PFC	James A. Doughty	Co B	28 Aug 69	Chelmsford, MA
PFC	Robert Gonzales	Co B	28 Aug 69	San Jose, CA
PFC	Charles E. Jackson	Co B	28 Aug 69	East Chicago, IN
PFC	Thomas P. McKerns	Co C	28 Aug 69	Mahanoy City, PA
PFC	Charlie Simmons, Jr.	Co B	28 Aug 69	Atlanta, GA
PFC	Alfredo E. Aviles	Co B	11 Sep 69	New York, NY
PFC	Gilberto O. Bustamante	Co B	11 Sep 69	Tampa, FL
PFC	Woodrow J. Ewald, Jr.	Co B	11 Sep 69	International Falls, MN
PFC	Kenneth W. Fields	Co E	11 Sep 69	Fort Pierce, FL
SFC	Alfredo Pacolba	Co B	11 Sep 69	Honolulu, HI
PFC	James S. Brister	Co D	12 Sep 69	Fairview, OH
SGT	Donald W. Churchwell	Co E	14 Sep 69	Birmingham, AL
PFC	Charlie H. Mitchell	Co D	16 Sep 69	Jolo, WV
PFC	Arthur Lewis	HHC	18 Sep 69	Ashland, VA
SP/4	Nels V. Rosenlund II	Co A	21 Sep 69	Arcata, CA
PFC	Roosevelt Wallace	Co C	7 Oct 69	Guyton, GA
PFC	Marvin H. Sanders	Co B	2 Dec 69	Fortuna, MO
SGT	Marion Croom, Jr.	Co B	15 Jan 70	Washington, D.C.
PFC	Warner P. Hughie	CO D	12Mar 70	Newman, GA
SSG	Charles E. Hann	Co D	24 Mar 70	Northfield, OH
SGT	Keith A. Lochner	Co A	22 Apr 70	Marion, IN
PFC	Donald Barrett	HHC	30 Apr 70	Dalton, GA
SP/4	Daniel Flores	Co D	30 Apr 70	San Diego, CA
PFC	Glen L. Knoblock	Co E	30 Apr 70	Lolita, TX
PFC	Frank M. Valentine	HHC	30 Apr 70	Litchfield, OH
1 LT	John P. Beckner	Co B	2 May 70	Kenosha, WI
PFC	Curtis Gaither	Co B	2 May 70	St. Louis, MO
SFC	Andrew J. Taylor	Co B	2 May 70	Milwaukee, WI
SGT	Duane A. Peterson	Co A	5 May 70	Isanti, MN
SP/4	Jack S. Grouf	HHC	7 May 70	East Northport, NY
SGT	Donald G. Kuzilla	Co A	14 May 70	Detroit, MI
SGT	William D. Menscer	Co A	16 May 70	Statesville, NC
SP/4	Jeffery J. Benjamin	Co C	25 May 70	Keenesburg, CO
SGT	Bruce R. Neeson	Co B	29 May 70	Kalamazoo, MI
SP/4	Richard L Kester	Co E	3 Jun 70	Angola, NY
SGT	Roderick K. Tolbert	HHC	3 Jun 70	Fairfield, AL
SGT	Lawrence D. Burgess	Co D	6 Jun 70	Ottawa, KS
SFC	Everette B. Caldwell	Co A	6 Jun 70	San Diego, CA
SP/4	Dennis N. Hogenboom	Co A	6 Jun 70	Schoharie, NY
PFC	Mark E. Klever	Co A	6 Jun 70	Milwaukee, WI
SSG	Robert C. Murray (MOH)	Co B	7 Jun 70	Tuckahoe, NY
SP/4	Larry W. Rasey	Co A	26 Jul 70	Taft, CA
PFC	Thomas J. Roberts	HHC	22 Aug 70	Burlington, WI
PFC	David A. Pratt	Co C	7 Sept 70	Miami Lakes, FL
SP/4	Pete E. Williamson	Co A	31 Dec 70	River, KY
SSG	Patrick J. Kihl	Co D	8 Jan 71	Milwaukee, WI
PFC	John S. Weaver	Co E	16 Jan 71	Lombard, IL
SP/4	Joseph R. Anthony	Co C	11 Feb 71	Lafayette, LA
1 LT	Donald J. Frazelle	Co A	11 Mar 71	Raleigh, NC

Rank	Name	Unit	Date	Home of Record
PFC	Clarence M. Suchon	Co C	22 Mar 71	Stevens Point, WI
PFC	Johnny Saxon	Co A	4 Apr 71	Charlotte, NC

The following 4-31st Infantry soldiers died as a result of non-battle injuries incurred in Vietnam.

Rank	Name	Unit	Date	Home of Record—Cause
SGT	Cesar E. Sanchez	Co A	26 Feb 67	New York, NY suicide
SP/4	George E. Hulse III	Co A	8 Mar 67	Newburg, NY accidental weapon discharge
SSG	Harry L. Eccard	HHC	19 Apr 67	Waynesboro, PA non hostile
PFC	Charles D. Maxson	Co C	5 Dec 67	Rhodes, MI swimming accident
PFC	Earl T. Jones	HHC	29 Feb 67	Los Angeles, CA illness
PFC	Michael L. White	HHC	13 Mar 68	New Berlin, WI drowned
SP/4	Clarence H. Boolin	Co A	22 Mar 69	Overland Park, KS helicopter crash
SP/4	Richard W. Goden	HHC	22 Mar 69	Baltimore, MD helicopter crash
SP/4	George F. Reynolds, Jr.	HHC	22 Mar 69	Oneonta, NY helicopter crash
SP/4	Leonardo Rios-Velazquez, Jr.	Co E	22 Mar 69	Rio Piedras, PR helicopter crash
SGT	David C. Vallance	Co A	22 Mar 69	Hamilton, MT helicopter crash
SP/4	Robert E. Wilson	Co D	30 Mar 68	Houston, TX non hostile
SGT	Roy E. Bright	Co D	17 Apr 69	Little Rock, AR illness
SP/4	Edward Mendez-Quintana	Co C	23 May 69	New York, NY non hostile
PFC	Ernest R. Davis	Co B	16 Jul 70	New York, NY non hostile
PFC	Jose L. Gonzales, Jr.	HHC	4 Sep 70	New Braunfels, TX non hostile
PVT	Monette V. White	HHC	10 Feb 71	San Diego, CA non hostile

6th Battalion

			Rank	Unit	Date	
Aldrich	John H	Sheridan, WY	SP4	HHC	6/20/1969	Dinh Tuong
Allagonez	Rodolfo P	Honolulu, HI	SP4	Co B	8/19/1969	Dinh Tuong
Bailey	Larry E	Phoenix, AZ	PFC	Co A	3/24/1969	Kien Phong
Baker	John H	Beeville, TX	PFC	Co C	6/28/1968	Long An
Barrios	James P	Lemoore, CA	SP4	Co D	1/12/1969	Dinh Tuong
Batterton	Troy H	Pleasureville, KY	SGT	Co B	4/8/1970	Kien Hoa
Beam	Raymond G	Butler, IL	PVT	Co D	1/18/1969	Dinh Tuong
Beauchamp	Raymond F	Eastlake, OH	PFC	Co B	1/27/1969	Dinh Tuong
Bishop	James W	Moline, IL	SP4	Co D	12/12/1969	Long An
Bittinger, Jr	Robert L	Cumberland, MD	PFC	HHC	4/17/1969	Dinh Tuong
Bollman	Robert V	Ninnekah, OK	SP4	Co D	9/26/1968	Kien Tuong
Borczynski	Frederick E	Buffalo, NY	SGT	Co D	9/26/1968	Kien Tuong
Bradley	Larry G	Knoxville, TN	PFC	Co D	1/12/1969	Dinh Tuong
Brawner	Frank E	Frankfort, KY	PFC	Co C	1/4/1969	Dinh Tuong
Brown	Kenneth E	Chalmette, LA	SP4	HHC	4/11/1969	Dinh Tuong
Brown, Jr	Willie L	Archer, FL	PFC	Co D	3/8/1969	Dinh Tuong
Butcher	David A	Marion, OH	SP4	Co B	5/8/1970	Cambodia
Byham	Dan R	Guys Mills, PA	PFC	Co C	2/19/1969	Dinh Tuong
Cameron	Robert C	Elyria, OH	SP4	Co C	6/26/1969	Dinh Tuong
Campbell	Richard M	Piedmont, SC	SP4	Co C	5/4/1968	Gia Dinh
Childs	Bobby R	Greenwood, SC	PFC	Co A	5/6/1968	Gia Dinh
Culver	Archie G	El Paso, TX	SFC	Co E	7/21/1969	Dinh Tuong
Culver	Philip L	South Ashfield, MA	SGT	Co D	5/7/1968	Long An
Daniels	Larry P	Santa Ana, CA	PFC	Co E	4/7/1970	Binh Duong
Davis	James A	Flagstaff, AZ	SGT	Co B	5/8/1970	Cambodia
Deschenes	James G	Bangor, ME	SFC	Co A	11/16/1968	Dinh Tuong
Dorsey	William T	Peekskill, NY	PFC	HHC	7/3/1970	Long An
Eiden, Jr.	Edward V	Winneconne, WI	SGT	Co C	4/11/1969	Dinh Tuong
Esparza	Malcom M	San Fernando, CA	SP4	Co A	8/7/1968	Long An

Farris	Dennis B	Cheyenne, WY	PFC	Co D	1/12/1969	Dinh Tuong
Fernandez, Jr	Santana S	San Antonio, TX	SP4	Co C	4/26/1969	Dinh Tuong
Fields, Jr	Willie	Richmond, VA	PFC	Co C	8/7/1968	Long An
Flores	Guadalupe	Bexar, TX	PFC	Co B	4/22/1969	Dinh Tuong
Forbes	Richard A	San Jose, CA	SP4	Co A	11/13/1969	Long An
Forgue	Gerald H	Shelton, CT	SGT	Co D	10/30/1968	Dinh Tuong
Garstkiewicz, Jr	Walter J	Philadelphia, PA	SP4	Co C	1/9/1970	Long An
Gee	Gregory J	Vallejo, CA	SP4	Co D	8/17/1969	Dinh Tuong
Gibson	Michael T	Bondtown, VA	SSG	Co C	11/28/1969	Long An
Gryzen	Gary M	Hudsonville, MI	SP4	Co B	12/13/1969	Long An
Hanna	Donald R	Scottsdale, AZ	PFC	Co C	4/26/1968	Bien Hoa
Hannigan	Timothy C	Lockport, NY	SP4	Co C	8/7/1968	Long An
Hansen	Lyle W	Steger, IL	PFC	Co B	5/12/1968	Gia Dinh
Harp	William	Pompano Beach, FL	SGT	Co D	9/4/1970	Hau Nghia
Harris	David S	Marion, OH	SGT	Co A	3/24/1969	Kien Phong
Harris	Rickey E	Cincinnati, OH	PFC	Co D	8/4/1969	Dinh Tuong
Harris	Russell L	Salt Lake City, UT	1LT	Co B	2/11/1969	Dinh Tuong
Hayes	Danny C	Scottown, OH	SGT	Co D	9/26/1968	Kien Tuong
Hernandez-Rivera	Angel L	Lajas, PR	SP4	Co C	10/28/1969	Long An
Hoffman	Leroy D	Athens, WI	PFC	Co C	11/22/1968	Dinh Tuong
Hunt	Daniel T	New York, NY	SGT	Co C	11/28/1969	Long An
Ilgenfritz, Jr	Herbert E	Orlando, FL	PFC	Co C	8/8/1968	Long An
Jablonski	John A	Webster, MA	SP4	Co C	8/8/1968	Long An
Janoska, Jr	John J	Plainview, NY	SSG	Co D	1/12/1970	Long An
Johnson, Jr	George A	New Orleans, LA	PFC	Co D	2/9/1970	Long An
Jones	Dennis K	Quincy, IL	SP4	Co B	5/12/1968	Gia Dinh
Keaton	Everett D	Waverly, OH	CPT	Co D	1/20/1970	Long An
Keener	Lawton A	Highlands, NC	PFC	Co D	1/12/1969	Dinh Tuong
Kirsch	Warren M	Spangler, PA	SP4	Co D	5/7/1968	Long An
Klotz	John R	Crescent City, CA	SP4	Co B	9/28/1968	Dinh Tuong
Kosar	Richard D	Park Ridge, IL	SGT	Co B	5/10/1968	Gia Dinh
Kozlowski	James M	Baltimore, MD	SP4	Co E	8/25/1970	Hau Nghia
Larson	Richard K	Santa Ana, CA	SGT	Co C	7/26/1969	Dinh Tuong
Lonsdale	John D	Stuart, IA	PFC	Co D	5/8/1970	Cambodia
Losel, Jr	Fred G	La Puente, CA	SP4	Co B	5/12/1968	Gia Dinh
Macomber, Jr	Clifford F	Cotulla, TX	SGT	Co D	5/10/1970	Cambodia
Maldonado-Torres	Lionel	Juana Diaz, PR	PFC	Co A	9/17/1968	Dinh Tuong
Maleszewski	Paul E	Pensacola, FL	SP4	Co D	11/7/1968	Dinh Tuong
Martinson	Delvin C	Benson, MN	PFC	Co D	11/28/1969	Long An
Matthews	Kent D	Clinton, IL	SP4	Co A	1/18/1970	Long An
McDavid	William E	Ontario, CA	PFC	Co C	8/7/1968	Long An
McGinnis, II	Lester C	Kansas City, KS	SGT	Co D	10/18/1968	Dinh Tuong
McIntyre	David A	Newark, OH	PFC	Co B	12/13/1969	Long An
McNabb	Richard D	Hialeah, FL	PFC	Co E	7/21/1969	Dinh Tuong
McPherson	Michael L	Roseville, MI	PFC	Co B	5/8/1970	Cambodia
Mc Pike	James E	Lakewood, OH	SGT	Co D	7/19/1969	Dinh Tuong
Mc Vea	Robert M	Converse, TX	PFC	Co D	9/19/1968	Kien Tuong
Messer	Ferrell E	Luther, OK	SP4	Co D	1/18/1969	Dinh Tuong
Minton	Christopher A H	Denver, CO	PFC	Co E	9/24/1968	Dinh Tuong
Molnar	Nicholas M	Flint, MI	SGT	Co A	3/30/1970	Long An
Moore	John T	Beaumont, TX	SGT	Co D	5/11/1968	Gia Dinh
Morgan	John L	Pacoima, CA	CPL	Co B	4/10/1969	Dinh Tuong
Motley	Paul W	Idalou, TX	PFC	Co B	2/23/1969	Dinh Tuong

Murray	Merritt L	Genoa, NY	PFC	Co C	10/30/1968	Dinh Tuong
Myers	Thomas W	Jamaica, NY	PFC	Co B	5/7/1968	Long An
Nash	Anthony P	Fountain Inn, SC	PFC	Co D	1/12/1969	Dinh Tuong
Neill	Terry J P	Bristol, PA	SP4	Co D	6/23/1968	Gia Dinh
Nelson, Jr	Sylvester	Newton, TX	PFC	Co A	8/6/1969	Dinh Tuong
Nelson	Larry D	Royal Oak, MI	SP4	Co C	8/18/1968	Long An
New	Zachary P	Cincinnati, OH	PFC	Co C	8/8/1968	Long An
Novak	Clarence J	Dwight, NE	SP4	Co B	4/5/1970	Hau Nghia
O'Brien	Willard D	Tucson, AZ	SP4	Co B/E 2–4 FA	5/11/1970	Cambodia
Pearson	Rudolph	Baltimore, MD	PFC	HHC	1/13/1969	Dinh Tuong
Perry	R T	Stanton, TN	PFC	Co C	10/8/1968	Dinh Tuong
Perry	Thomas D	Warren IN	SSG	Co B	4/22/1969	Dinh Tuong
Phillips	Gary T	West Jefferson, NC	SP4	Co B	12/13/1969	Long An
Pretnar	Allen J	Euclid, OH	PFC	Co C	8/8/1968	Long An
Pruett	James R	Buchanan, MI	SGT	Co D	9/26/1968	Kien Tuong
Pumphrey	Edwin H	Silver Spring, MD	SP4	Co D	4/10/1969	Dinh Tuong
Rance	Steven P	Green Bay, WI	PFC	HHC	9/26/1968	Kien Tuong
Ratcliff	Jackie L	Birmingham, AL	PFC	Co D	4/10/1969	Dinh Tuong
Rauber	William	Wheatland, PA	PFC	Co C	4/26/1968	Bien Hoa
Reiter	Lesley Steven	New York, NY	SGT	Co C	4/26/1969	Dinh Tuong
Rines	Everett E	Manchester, CT	PFC	Co A	4/2/1970	Long An
Roberts	Herman D	Bowling Green, KY	PFC	Co D	7/11/1968	Gia Dinh
Robinson	Calvin	Johnstown, SC	SP4	Co D	1/12/1969	Dinh Tuong
Rolle	John B	Fort Meyers, FL	SGT	Co D	1/12/1969	Dinh Tuong
Ross	Gregory M	Youngstown, OH	SGT	Co B	6/20/1968	Gia Dinh
Russell	Gregory A	Rio Linda, CA	SP4	Co C	5/11/1968	Long An
Sanders	Rodney R	Phenix City, AL	PFC	Co D	5/31/1970	Hau Nghia
Savacool, Jr	Paul R	Augusta, GA	PVT	Co C	8/8/1968	Long An
Scarborough, Jr	James A	Mesa, AZ	PFC	Co A	1/2/1969	Dinh Tuong
Schroeder	Nicholas L	Eagle Mountain, CA	PFC	Co A	8/7/1968	Long An
Schroeder, Jr	George H	Baltimore, MD	SSG	Co C	5/16/1968	Bien Hoa
Scott	Larry	Macon, GA	PFC	Co B	3/21/1969	Dinh Tuong
Seaton	David T	Fordsville, KY	SP4	Co A	9/25/1968	Kien Hoa
Seidel	Kenneth W	Wayne City, IL	PFC	Co A	6/28/1968	Long An
Smith	Charles L	San Jose, CA	SP4	Co A	12/8/1968	Dinh Tuong
Smith	Phillip J	Toledo, OH	PFC	Co B	5/8/1970	Cambodia
Smith	Stephen J W	Convoy, OH	SGT	Co E	6/21/1970	Hau Nghia
Speer	James W	Bloomfield, IA	PFC	Co A	5/23/1969	Dinh Tuong
Stephens	Ben W	Fort Worth, TX	SP4	Co C	8/7/1968	Long An
Stewart	Arnold L	Baker, WV	SP4	Co D	5/5/1968	Long An
Stuckey	Benny D	Longview, TX	SGT	Co D	6/29/1969	Dinh Tuong
Summers	Ronald L	Lytle, TX	SGT	Co A	10/8/1968	Kien Hoa
Tarjany	Randolph M	East St Louis, IL	CPT	Co A	7/24/1968	Kien Hoa
Taylor	Walter M	Clarksville, TN	PFC	Co C	4/17/1969	Dinh Tuong
Tegtmeier	Leslie J	Chicago, IL	SP4	Co C	8/8/1968	Long An
Thiesfeldt-Collazo	William J	Rio Piedras, PR	SGT	Co C	8/7/1968	Long An
Trotter	Richard B	Grand Island, NE	SSG	Co D	9/26/1968	Kien Tuong
Trucano	Alan D	Steeleville, IL	SGT	Co C	8/8/1968	Long An
Tubbs	Edwin F	Coudersport, PA	PVT	Co D	1/12/1969	Dinh Tuong
Turner	James E	El Dorado, KS	SP4	Co A	8/7/1968	Long An
Vicario	David A	Providence, RI	SP4	Co C	11/17/1996	Providence RI
Vieras	Jose L	San Jose, CA	PFC	Co B	5/10/1968	Gia Dinh
Wade	Thomas L	New River, VA	SP4	Co B	5/11/1968	Long An

Walker	John D	Hoquiam, WA	CPT	HHC	11/14/1969	Long An
Washington, Sr	James L	New Orleans, LA	SGT	Co A	5/5/1969	Dinh Tuong
Weed	Morgan W	Decatur, AL	1LT	Co D	5/11/1970	Cambodia
Weisheit	Lonnie H	Lynnville, IN	PFC	Co E	6/21/1970	Hau Nghia
Weitz	Henry K	Spokane, WA	PFC	Co A	4/6/1970	Binh Duong
White	Ronald L	Eatontown, NJ	PFC	HHC	3/24/1970	Hau Nghia
Wilcox, III	Armour D	Hudson, OH	SP4	Co A	12/8/1968	Dinh Tuong
Wilkinson	Harland L	Omaha, NE	PVT	Co E	9/26/1969	Long An
Woodfin	Donald P	New Canton, VA	PFC	Co A	4/6/1970	Binh Duong
Yabiku	Takeshi	Los Angeles, CA	SP4	Co D	1/12/1969	Dinh Tuong
Yamashita	Kenji J	Sanger, CA	1LT–FO	Co B	5/11/1968	Long An
Young	Johnny	Slaton, TX	PFC	Co A	3/24/1969	Kien Phong
Zoldi	Gabriel	Parma Heights, OH	PFC	Co D	1/12/1969	Dinh Tuong

Iraq

4th Battalion Killed in Action

Last	*First*	*M*	*Rank*	*Date*	*Description*	*Unit*	*Hometown*
				Combat Related			
Anzack, Jr	Joseph	J	CPL	12–May-07	Al Taqa, Iraq	Co D	Torrance, CA
Barnes	Nathan	S	SGT	17-Jul-07	Rushdi Mullah, Iraq	Co C	American Fork, UT
Bevel	Ray	M	CPL	21-Apr-07	Baghdad, Iraq	Co C	Andrews, TX
Bishop	Ryan	A	CPL	14-Apr-07	Baghdad, Iraq	Co C	Euless, TX
Browning	Brian	A	SPC	6-Feb-07	Baghdad, Iraq	Co B	Astoria, OR
Callahan	Bobby	T	CPL	18-Sep-06	Baghdad, Iraq	HHC	Jamestown, NC
Connell, Jr	James	D	SFC	12–May-07	Al Taqa, Iraq	Co D	Lake City, TN
Courneya	Daniel	W	CPL	12–May-07	Al Taqa, Iraq	Co D	Nashville, MI
Fouty	Byron	W	SPC	8-Jul-08	Al Taqa, Iraq	Co D	Waterford, MI
Given	Nathaniel	A	SPC	27-Dec-06	Baghdad, Iraq	Co D	Dickinson, TX
Greenlee	Satieon	V	PFC	2-Oct-06	Baghdad, Iraq	Co A	Pendleton, SC
Jimenez	Alex	R	SGT	8-Jul-08	Al Taqa, Iraq	Co D	Lawrence, MA
Malson	Adam		1LT	19-Feb-05	Kadimiyah, Iraq	Co A	Rochester Hills, MI
Messer	Christopher	P	SGT	27-Dec-06	Baghdad, Iraq	Co D	Petersburg, MI
Murphy	Christopher	E	CPL	12–May-07	Al Taqa, Iraq	Co D	Lynchburg, VA
Norris	Curtis	L	SGT	23-Dec-06	Baghdad, Iraq	Co F	Dansville, MI
Rogers	Nicholas	K	SPC	22-Oct-06	Rushdi Mullah, Iraq	Co B	Deltona, FL
Schober	Anthony	J	SGT	12–May-07	Al Taqa, Iraq	Co D	Reno, NV
Tudor	Steven	R	SSG	21-Apr-07	Baghdad, Iraq	Co F	Dunmore, PA

Chapter Notes

Prologue

1. The original 31st Infantry Regiment was formed in 1813 for service in the War of 1812. It was consolidated with the Regiment of Light Artillery in 1815 and its numeral disappeared from the active rolls until 1866 when a new 31st Infantry Regiment was formed from the 3rd Battalion 13th Infantry. In 1869, that regiment was consolidated with today's 22nd Infantry. *Army Lineage Series, Infantry* (Washington, D.C.: Office of the Chief of Military History, 1953, 155).

2. The National Defense Act of 1916 appropriated funds for the Army's emergency expansion amid a crisis brewing worldwide. It expanded the Army by seven infantry regiments, one each in the Philippines (31st), Hawaii (32nd), and Panama Canal Zone (33rd), and four on the Mexican border (34th through 37th). *Army Lineage Series, Infantry* (Washington, D.C.: Office of the Chief of Military History, 1972, 42).

3. An Officers roster upon activation is at Appendix 1.

4. Chain of command roster at deployment is at Appendix 1.

Chapter 1

1. Fighting between Czechs and Russia's Red factions began on May 18, 1918, when an Austrian prisoner of war being repatriated killed a Czech at Chelyabinsk and Red officials declined to arrest the killer. Thereafter, the Czech Legion took control of the Trans-Siberian Railroad, driving the Reds out of Irkutsk and other towns along the rail line.

2. Lieutenant Colonel Robert Eichelberger, the Siberian AEF's G-2, made that estimate based on the dispositions of Japanese troops and the flow of troops through the port of Vladivostok between 1918 and 1920.

3. Initial outposts were railroad stations north of Vladivostok, including Nadezhdinskaya, Kiparisova, Ugolnaya, and Pervaya Recha. Railroad stations were important because they were the locations of telegraph offices enabling the passage of information on weather delays, rail mishaps, banditry, and partisan activity.

4. These ethnic terms reflect the era in which they were used. They show both the soldier's response to place and people, and provide a window into attitudes of the time.

5. Quoted in Grace Wheaton, *Who Is "Alf Thompson?,"* privately printed, 1996, 38.

6. *Ibid.*, 39–40.

7. "Albert Francis Ward," *Fifty-First Annual Reunion of the Association of the Graduates of the United States Military Academy*, June 14, 1920, reproduced at penelope.uchicago.edu, http://penelope.uchicago.edu/Thayer/E/Gazetteer/Places/America/United_States/Army/USMA/AOG_Reunions/51/Albert_Francis_Ward*.html.

8. Kanguas or Kanguaz is a railway switching station about halfway between Shkotovo and Suchan. Probably called Anisimovka today, it does not appear on contemporary maps or lists of place names in Primorski Krai, Russia's Maritime Province.

9. Eichelberger would become a lieutenant general commanding the Eighth Army in the Pacific Theater during World War II. Winningstad would become a colonel serving as the Eighth Army's Ordnance Officer during the occupation of Japan.

10. William S. Graves, *America's Siberian Adventure 1918–1920* (New York: Arno Press & the New York Times, 1971), 248–9.

11. Regiments were given periodic allocations of second lieutenant billets to be filled by awarding temporary commissions to enlisted applicants who passed a rigid battery of proficiency tests. The program was a decentralized Officer Candidate School discontinued in 1942 in favor of a centralized branch OCS program. Temporary officers who excelled could be promoted and could apply for a Regular Army commission, leave the Army when their terms expired, or revert to their permanent enlisted grade if their commissions were not renewed. To enable the Army to easily expand and contract according to budgets, Regular Army officers could be promoted up to two grades beyond their permanent grade until the early 1970s when the practice was discontinued. If a Regular Army officer failed to meet expected standards, he was involuntarily reverted to his permanent grade, a humiliation that usually resulted in resignation for those ineligible to retire or retirement

at the lower permanent grade for officers with more than 20 years of service.

Chapter 2

1. Received by COL Van Deman on 18 Jan 1922.
2. Interviews conducted by Regimental Association Historian at reunions held at Fort Sill, Oklahoma, 1994.
3. War Plan Orange was one of a series of plans drafted by the War Department, each code named with a different color. Collectively, they were known as the "Rainbow Plans."

Chapter 3

1. "Robert Short, American Airman," *Tales of Old China* (N.p.: Earnshaw Books, n.d.) http://www.talesofoldchina.com/shanghai/old-shanghai-people/robert-short-american-airman.

Chapter 4

1. Erich Morris, *Corregidor, the End of the Line* (New York: Stein and Day, 1981) 46.

Chapter 5

1. The 27th Bomb Group's planes never arrived. Some of the pilots were evacuated to Australia but most of the unit fought on Bataan as Infantry.
2. Only Ralph Hibbs survived.
3. The date was Sunday, December 7, in Washington and Pearl Harbor because the International Date Line bisects the Pacific west of Hawaii.
4. 1SG Dempsey (Houston, TX) and SGT Gilewitch (Philadelphia, PA) survived the war, but CPT Christopher J. Heffernan, Jr. (Amsterdam, NY) died at Hospital #1 on April 9, 1942, the day Bataan surrendered.
5. 1SG Arthur C. Houghtby died in captivity at Camp O'Donnell on May 20, 1942.
6. Now Manila International Airport.
7. CPT Richard K. Carnahan (Lincoln, NE) won the Distinguished Service Cross at Abucay Hacienda, but died in captivity at Camp O'Donnell on May 10, 1942.
8. Philippine Scouts (PS) were recruited from among the Philippine population as members of the U.S. Army. Filipinos competed for positions in PS units because they offered good pay and elite status in Philippine society. They were led by American officers and were well disciplined, trained, and equipped. In 1941, PS units included the 43rd, 45th and 57th Infantry, 26th Cavalry, 23rd, 24th, 86th, and 88th Field Artillery and 14th Engineers on Luzon, and the 91st and 92nd Coast Artillery on Corregidor. The 43rd Infantry and the engineer, field artillery, and coast artillery regiments were only at battalion strength. General MacArthur ordered PS recruiting to cease in 1941 to avoid drawing the best recruits away from the Philippine Army (PA) which was being expanded to 11 divisions.

9. LT Zoberbier (Manila, PI) died in captivity at Cabanatuan on October 23, 1942. SSG Thomas W. Fortune (Douglas, GA) died at the hands of his Japanese guards while on a work detail at Nichols Field on June 11, 1942.
10. PVT Sutton (Elgin, OR) died in captivity at Cabanatuan on July 19, 1942.
11. PVT Boles (Cincinnati, OH) died in captivity at Cabanatuan on June 17, 1942. SGT Cabral (home town unknown) died in captivity at Camp O'Donnell on May 6, 1942.
12. Much of the Medical Detachment was already at Bataan with the infantry battalions.

Chapter 6

1. The personal communications with the author, cited in the notes to this chapter, also serve as the sources for the next two chapters.
2. CPL Kerchum (McKees Rocks, PA) survived the war. After his release from captivity in 1945, Kerchum remained in the service, transferred to the Air Force in 1948, and retired as a Chief Master Sergeant. SGT Bridges (Santa Clara, CA) died in captivity at Cabanatuan.
3. One man did not show up again until after the surrender when he arrived at Cabanatuan. He was the only man in B Company wounded at Layac. He made it on his own to the hospital at Limay and when released, attached himself to another unit. He died in captivity.
4. LT Murphy (Bismarck, ND) died with many of his fellow officers aboard the "hell ship" *Oryoku Maru* when it was struck by U.S. planes en route to Japan in 1944 and CPT Thompson (Seattle, WA) died aboard the *Arisan Maru* under similar circumstances.
5. LTC Edward H. Bowes (San Francisco, CA) and CPT Cecil R. Welchko (Bonner's Ferry, ID) both died aboard the *Oryoku Maru*. PVT Uzelac (East Moline, IL) survived the war.
6. CPT John Thompson, who took over B Company after Layac, was not related to CPT Donald M. Thompson of L Company.
7. PVT McCann (hometown unknown) fell out during the Death March and was picked up by Filipinos, but later died of malaria. PVT Roberts (Williams, AZ) died in captivity.
8. LT Baker (Astor, NY) died in captivity at Camp O'Donnell on 5 Jun 1942.
9. CPT Stroud (Williston, ND) died aboard the "hell ship" *Arisan Maru* in 1944. CPT Roshe (Washington, DC) died aboard the *Oryoku Maru*.
10. PFC Andrew J. Hickingbottom (Ferriday, LA) of Company M was wounded by Japanese mortar fire while supporting the counterattack with his machine gun. He died in captivity at Camp O'Donnell on Sep 5, 1942.
11. The dead were PVT Floribert J. Constantineau (home town unknown), PVT Melvin N. Elliott (home town unknown), PVT James A. King (Searcy, AR), and PFC Charles F. Saksek (home town unknown).

12. All three men survived the war.

13. B Company's dead included CPL Rex R. Annas (Granite Falls, NC), PVT Herman E. Fornass (Santa Clara, CA), PFC Vernon J. Kelly (home town unknown), PVT James J. Broadrick (home town unknown), and CPL Floyd R. Rogers (home town unknown—died of wounds). Its wounded included SGT Leo Golinski (Brooklyn, NY—died in captivity at Cabanatuan 1 Oct 1942), SGT Cletis H. Harrison (Chicago, IL—survived the war), PVT William F. Beattie (Kansas City, MO—died in captivity at Camp O'Donnell 8 May 1942) PVT John F. Eighmey (Arlee, MT—died in captivity at Camp O'Donnell 13 May 1942), PVT Jack L. James (Atlanta, GA—executed by Japanese on Nichols Field detail 8 June 1943), and PFC Harold J. Garrett (Payette, ID—survived the war).

14. Surviving records are not uniformly precise concerning the date of wounds or awards, sometimes showing only the location or the fact that the person was wounded.

15. PFC Robert C. Anderson (home town unknown) and PFC Melvin E. Lambrecht (Cheyenne, WY) were killed by snipers and many others were wounded. SGT Oren L. Jenness (home town unknown), SGT Frank V. Miller (Milwaukee, WI), CPL Paul Kerchum (McKees Rocks, PA), PVT Edward J. Blankenship (Stamps, AR), PFC Milarn Cloud (Appalachia, VA), PVT Elbert L. Fannin (McCamey, TX), PVT Ronald Hooper (Hebron, CT), PFC Lonza P. Locke (Columbus, MS), PFC Glen W. Moyers (Pueblo, CO) were wounded during some phase of the battle, although the exact date for each is not known.

16. Carrico (home town unknown) died of his wounds on January 26, 1942 and was buried at the Limay cemetery.

17. PVT Harold O. "Red" Dyer (Corpus Christi, TX) died in captivity at Cabanatuan on July 21, 1942.

18. F Company's wounded were SGT Francis T. Shafsky (Minneapolis, MN), CPL Max M. Greenberg (Brooklyn, NY), PVT Paul Spencer (Oklahoma City, OK), PFC Antonio A. Tafolla (San Angelo, TX), PVT Irby C. Turner (Carrollton, MS), PVT Alfred R. Welch (Houston, TX), and PVT Raymond M. Worrell (Wisner, NE). Shafsky, Turner, Welch, and Worrell died in captivity.

19. Tresch was wounded at Abucay Hacienda only 2 days after his act of heroism.

20. LT Robert K. Magee (Belle Fourche, SD) died aboard a "hell ship" en route to Japan in 1944. SSG Carl J. Williams (Greenville, SC) died in captivity in Manchuria. PFC Charles A. Henderson (Albuquerque, NM) escaped to Corregidor after Bataan's surrender, but was executed on May 13, 1944, by Japanese guards while on a work detail.

21. PVT Peter J. Chamote (Jersey City, NJ) died in captivity at Cabanatuan on 19 Dec. 1942.

22. Sergeant Harry M. Neff (home town unknown) and Private Julius W. Stewart (Clarendon, AR) both died in captivity.

23. When interviewed by telephone in 1997 concerning the incident, Otto Whittington and Patrick Davie gave the same account although they had neither met nor communicated with each other since the war and neither knew the other was still living.

24. LT Ralph C. Simmons (Spartanburg, SC), Staff Sergeant Gerald C. Farnham (Little Valley, NY), Corporal Charles K. Adams (Mondovi, WI), and Private John Novak (home town unknown) died in captivity at Cabanatuan. PFC Andrew E. Nickerson (home town unknown) died in captivity at Camp O'Donnell.

Chapter 7

1. The 192d and 194th Tank Battalions were formed from National Guard division tank companies from various states and were dispatched to the Philippines in 1941, shortly before the curtain closed on reinforcement opportunities.

2. Irvin R. "Hootch" Sutphin, who was married to a Filipina, received a battlefield commission after the battle of Abucay Hacienda. He died in captivity at Cabanatuan on August 9, 1942.

3. 1LT Charles L. Hodgins (Snohomish, WA) died in captivity at Cabanatuan on July 31, 1942. 2LT Alfred E. Lee (Carrollton, TX) died at Cabanatuan on December 13, 1942.

4. Remarkably, 1SG Hamburger (Seattle, WA) would survive, remaining in the Army after the war. PVT James E. Mines (Russellville, AL) survived the war, although he is erroneously listed in Colonel Brady's roster as having died in captivity on June 8, 1943. The other soldier who surrendered with Hamburger was PVT Cecil W. Bradshaw (home town unknown). Bradshaw had less than a month to live. He died in captivity at Camp O'Donnell on April 25, 1942.

5. Signal Hill, a promontory on the slopes of Mount Bataan, is served by a steep gravel road leading to kilometer post 97.8 on the Mariveles-Bagac Road.

6. A comment appears in John W. Whitman's book *Bataan, Our Last Ditch* (New York: Hippocrene Books, 1990) that CPT George Sansep burned the 31st's colors to keep them from falling into enemy hands. His account may refer to the burning of one of the Philippine Scout regiments' colors, since no CPT George Sansep or any other member by that name appears in the 31st Infantry's pre-war or wartime rosters. CPL Lou Read, who recalls seeing the colors at the site before their burial, corroborates SSG Crea's account.

7. SSG Crea (Panama City, FL) survived the war, remained in uniform after his release from captivity and retired from the Air Force as a Master Sergeant in 1964. CPL Scruby (Chillicothe, MO) died in captivity at Cabanatuan on May 18, 1942. MSG Widerynski (Manila, PI) died on a detail at Clark Field on December 11, 1943. CPT Eichlin (Easton, PA) died aboard the "Hell Ship" *Oryoku Maru* in 1944.

8. Dale Snyder escaped from the train transporting POWs from Bilibid to Cabanatuan. When recaptured, he was beheaded by a Japanese captain named Maita on May 30, 1942. Fifteen-year-old Joe Johnson survived Bataan, Corregidor, and the infamous labor

detail at Nichols Field from which many did not return. He was beaten, had his grave dug, survived the sinking of two "hell ships," lived through a coal mine cave-in in Japan, and was only 25 miles from one of the atomic bomb blasts, but he survived to write Dale Snyder's nephew of the experience at the age of 73.

Chapter 9

1. California's 40th Infantry Division left Korea during the same period.

2. At Bataan, Potts was a Corporal leading a machine gun squad in M Company and Wolfe was a Sergeant leading a machine gun section in D Company. Wolfe earned the Silver Star at Layac Junction and after Bataan's surrender, became an orderly to the captured generals. (Information derived from LTC Jasper Brady's regimental roster, Cabanatuan POW Camp, 1942–1944.)

3. Soon after the 7th Infantry Division arrived in Japan, the 11th Airborne Division departed for Fort Campbell, Kentucky. The 31st Infantry shared Camp Crawford with the 7th Infantry Division's Headquarters Company, 7th Signal Company, 7th Military Police Company, 7th Reconnaissance Company, and 57th Field Artillery Battalion.

4. *Unit History, 31st Infantry, Japan, Jan–Dec. 1949*, 2; RG 500: Records of U.S. Army Commands, 1940– ; Unit Records (A): Infantry Divisions 1940–1967, Seventh Infantry Division, NARA II; Interview with Logan Caterall, concerning Camp Crawford's development and training environment.

5. *Unit History, 31st Infantry, Japan, Jan–Dec. 1949, op. cit.,* 3.

6. Operations Narrative, 7th Division Historical Report, February 1949, "31st Infantry Regiment"; 7th Infantry Division Historical Reports; RG 500: Records of U.S. Army Commands, 1940– ; Unit Records (A): Infantry Divisions 1940–1967, Seventh Infantry Division, NARA II.

7. 31st Infantry Regiment Monthly Historic Report, March 1949; 7th Infantry Division Historical Reports; RG 500: Records of U.S. Army Commands, 1940– ; Unit Records (A): Infantry Divisions 1940–1967, Seventh Infantry Division, NARA II [hereafter noted only as monthly reports.]

8. *Unit History, 31st Infantry Regiment, Jan–Dec 1949*, 7.

9. Headquarters, 7th Infantry Division, Training Memorandum Number 1, "17 January 1949–30 April 1949," 11 January 1949; Decimal File 353.1, G-3 Correspondence Files; Army-AG Command Reports, 1949–1954: Seventh Infantry Division, NARA II.

10. *Unit History, 31st Infantry Regiment, 1–30 April 1949.*

11. *Ibid.,* 3, 5.

12. Headquarters, 7th Infantry Division, Training Memorandum Number 13, "Training of Replacements," 21 March 1949; Decimal File 353.1, G-3 Correspondence Files; Army-AG Command Reports, 1949–1954, Seventh Infantry Division, NARA II. Paragraph 3c of this memo specifically forbade the formation of "separate or provisional companies."

13. *Unit History, 31st Infantry Regiment, 1 May–31 May 1949.*

14. Major General William F. Dean may have commanded more divisions than any other U.S. officer in history. He commanded the 44th Infantry Division in combat in Europe during World War II, commanded the 7th Infantry Division in Japan, and commanded the 24th Infantry Division in combat in Korea, where he became the highest ranking U.S. officer in modern history to be captured by the enemy.

15. Major General Dean to All Officers and Non-Commissioned Officers, 7th Infantry Division, "Letter of Transmittal, Training Memorandum Number 1," 11 January 1949, 1; Decimal File 353, G-3 Correspondence Files; Army-AG Command Reports, 1949–1954: Seventh Infantry Division, NARA II.

16. "Unit History, 31st Infantry Regiment, 1–28 February 1949," and "Division Historical Report, March 1949"; RG 500: Records of U.S. Army Commands, 1940– ; Unit Records (A): Infantry Divisions 1940–1967, Seventh Infantry Division, NARA II.

17. "Unit History, 31st Infantry Regiment, 1–31 July 1949."

18. *Ibid.*

19. General Headquarters, Supreme Commander for the Allied Powers and Far East Command, Staff Memorandum Number 7, "Enlisted Replacements," 6 February 1950; Decimal File 220.3, Chief of Staff's Correspondence Files, Records of GHQ FEC/SCAP/UNC, NARA II.

20. "Unit History, 31st Infantry Regiment, 1–30 June 1949."

21. Headquarters, 7th Infantry Division, Training Memorandum Number 9, 15 February 1949; Decimal File 353, G-3 General Correspondence Files; Army-AG Command Reports, 1949–1954: Seventh Division; NARA II.

22. "Unit History, 31st Infantry Regiment, 1–31 August 1949."

23. "Foreign Legion," *Regimental Day* (Camp Crawford, Japan: August 13, 1949); Unit History File, 31st Infantry Regiment; Unit Reports—7th Infantry Division, 1949; Army—AG Command Reports, 1949–1954: 7th Infantry Division; NARA II.

24. *Unit History, 31st Infantry Regiment, Jan–Dec 1949*, 8.

25. "Unit History, 31st Infantry Regiment, 1–31 July 1949."

26. *Unit History, 31st Infantry Regiment, Jan–Dec 1949*, 8; *Division Artillery Annual Unit History 1949*, 2; RG 500: Records of U.S. Army Commands, 1940– ; Unit Records (A): Infantry Divisions 1940–1967, Seventh Infantry Division, NARA II.

27. "Unit History, 31st Infantry Regiment, 1–30 August 1949."

28. Training Memorandum Number 15, *op. cit.,* 4, paragraph i (2).

29. Headquarters, IX Corps, Training Memorandum Number 12, 23 August 1949; copy in Decimal File 333.5, G3 Correspondence Files, 7th Infantry Division; Army-AG Command Reports, 1949–1954: Seventh Infantry Division, NARA II.

30. *Unit History, 31st Infantry Regiment, Jan–Dec 1949*, 9–10.

31. *Annual Historical Report of the 31st Field Artillery Battalion, 1949*, 4; RG 500: Records of U.S. Army Commands, 1940– ; Unit Records (A): Infantry Divisions 1940–1967, Seventh Infantry Division, NARA II.

32. "Unit History, 31st Infantry Regiment, Month of September 1949."

33. *Unit History, 31st Infantry Regiment, Jan–Dec 1949*, 10; "Unit History, 31st Infantry Regiment, Month of September 1949," op. cit.; Army Field Forces Training Test 7-2, 27 September 1948, and Army Field Forces Training Test 7-25, 18 December 1951, Decimal File 352, General Correspondence Files, Office of the Chief, Army Field Forces; Records of Headquarters Army Ground Forces/Army Field Forces, NARA II.

34. "Unit History Narrative, 31st Infantry Regiment, October 1949."

35. *Annual Historical Report of the 31st Field Artillery Battalion, 1949*, 4; "7th Division Artillery Monthly History, September 1949"; RG 500: Records of U.S. Army Commands, 1940– ; Unit Records (A): Infantry Divisions 1940–1967, Seventh Infantry Division, NARA II.

36. "Unit History, 31st Infantry Regiment, Month of September 1949."

37. *Report of Training Inspection of the United States Army, FECOM, by Col. F.M. Harris and Party*, Tab P, "7th Infantry Division," 5; Decimal File 333.11, Army Field Forces Headquarters, Adjutant General's Section, Communications & Records Division, Secret Decimal File 1949–1950; RG 337: Records of Headquarters Army Ground Forces/Army Field Forces, NARA II.

38. *Ibid.*, 7.

39. "7th Division Monthly Historical Report, November 1949"; *Unit History, 31st Infantry Regiment, Jan–Dec 1949*, 12; *Unit History, 31st Infantry, Month of November 1949*; *Unit History, 31st Infantry, Month of December*, 1; Interview with COL (Ret.) George Rasula, concerning the 7th Infantry Division's winter training program.

40. 31st Infantry Regiment, *Monthly Historical Summary for January 1950*.

41. Edmund G. Love, *The 27th Infantry Division in World War II* (Washington, D.C.: Infantry Journal Press, 1949), 651.

42. 31st Infantry Regiment, *Monthly Historical Summary for February 1950*.

43. 31st Infantry Regiment, *Monthly Historical Summary for March 1950*.

44. G-3 Monthly Historical Summary #44, March 1950, "31st Infantry"; Eighth U.S. Army Military History Section, Section III (Historical Section) Monthly Summaries #43–46: February–May 1950; Historical Officers' Files, 1949–1950, RG 338: Records of the Eighth United States Army, NARA II.

45. 31st Infantry, *Monthly Historical Summary for April, 1950*; G-3 Monthly Historical Summary #45, April 1950, "31st Infantry"; Eighth U.S. Army Military History Section, Section III (Historical Section) Monthly Summaries #43–46: February–May 1950;

Historical Officers' Files, 1949–1950, RG 338: Records of the Eighth United States Army, NARA II.

46. 31st Infantry, *Monthly Historical Summary for April, 1950*.

47. *Ibid.*; Monthly Historical Summary #45, April 1950; Eighth U.S. Army Military History Section, Section III (Historical Section) Monthly Summaries #43–46: February–May 1950; Historical Officers' Files, 1949–1950, RG 338: Records of the Eighth United States Army, NARA II.

Chapter 10

1. Of the 13 infantry regiments stationed in Japan and Okinawa (then a separate U.S. dependency) in 1950, only the 24th Infantry Regiment had its full complement of three battalions. The 31st Infantry was missing its 1st Battalion.

2. They were the 1st Infantry Division in Germany, 2nd Infantry Division at Ft. Lewis, 3rd Infantry Division at Ft. Benning and Ft. Devens, 7th, 24th, and 25th Infantry Divisions and 1st Cavalry Division in Japan, 11th Airborne Division at Ft. Campbell, 82nd Airborne Division at Ft. Bragg, and 2nd Armored Division at Ft. Hood. There were also six training divisions (4th Infantry Division at Ft. Ord, 5th Infantry Division at Ft. Jackson, 9th Infantry Division at Ft. Dix, 10th Infantry Division at Ft. Riley, 3rd Armored Division at Ft. Knox, and 5th Armored Division at Ft. Chaffee). These had a cadre and trainees, but were not organized or equipped to fight.

3. The 24th Division's commanding general, Major General William F. Dean, was captured when the North Koreans took Taejon.

4. When the 3rd Infantry Division deployed to Korea in November 1950, one of its regiments had been zeroed out at Fort Benning, requiring it to "borrow" a regiment from the Antilles Command in Puerto Rico, brought to full strength with a battalion from the Panama Canal's defense force.

5. Attack transports, all built during World War II, mounted a variety of anti-aircraft weapons, ranging from .50 calibers to 40mm automatic guns. All were mounted in large circular steel "tubs" protecting their crews from shrapnel and smaller ordnance.

6. Colonel Herbert B. Powell, commanding the 17th Infantry Regiment when the mortar incident occurred, would become one of the Korean War's most successful regimental commanders. His was the only regiment in any American division to reach the Yalu River, Korea's border with China, but he brought it out of North Korea with relatively few casualties. He retired as a four-star general. Dick Ovenshine was never promoted again, retiring as a colonel.

Chapter 11

1. Task Force Kingston reached Singalpajin on the Yalu but was forced to withdraw almost immediately.

2. Pujon and Changjin are the Korean names of reservoirs named on Japanese maps in use at the time as Fusen and Chosin, creating confusion when peo-

ple today write about battles fought around the Chosin (Changjin) Reservor.

3. Regimental Headquarters, Heavy Mortar Company, and 3rd Battalion of the 31st Infantry, the 57th FA Battalion, and D Battery, 15th AAA Battalion.

4. The two reservoirs (Fusen and Chosin) in northeastern Korea are called by their Japanese names as they appeared on U.S. maps at the time. Their Korean names are Pujon and Changjin, respectively.

5. CPL Donald Trudeau was captured during the engagement and spent the next 33 months as a POW.

Chapter 12

1. Although Peng had 15 divisions, each totaling between 8,000 and 12,000 men, he could supply only half of them and he had no communications gear below division level, severely limiting his ability to exploit success.

2. Dominick Cataldo, Jr., was wounded but made it to the regimental aid station. He died on 1 December when the convoy carrying the wounded was ambushed at Hill 1221 during the withdrawal.

3. In contrast, all companies of the 31st and 32nd Infantry Regiments were reconstituted soon after they left North Korea and remained in action throughout the war. Report of Captain Fields E Shelton, Regimental Historian, 31 December 1950.

Chapter 13

1. E Company was detached from the 2nd Battalion to protect the Division Command Post at Pukchong.

Chapter 16

1. S.L.A. Marshall, *Pork Chop Hill* (New York: William Morrow, 1956), 150. https://archive.org/stream/porkchophillthea011690mbp/porkchophillthea011690mbp_djvu.txt.

2. *Ibid.*, 151.

3. Richard K. Kolb, "The Final Fights: For the Marines it was Boulder City; the Army: Outposts Dale and Westview," *VFW Magazine*, June 2003. The attack on OPs Westview and Dale was the last battle of the Korean War, not just for the 31st Infantry, but for the U.S. Army.

Chapter 17

1. KATUSA is the acronym for "Korean Augmentation to the U.S. Army." These were Korean soldiers seconded to the U.S. Army ever since 1950 to compensate for manpower shortages in U.S. units and provide a link between American troops and soldiers of the country they were sent to help defend. ROK is the acronym for Republic of Korea.

2. A battle group initially had a headquarters company, a heavy mortar company, and four rifle companies but later added a fifth rifle company and a combat support company in place of the heavy

mortar company. The 7th Infantry Division's other battle groups were the 2nd Battle Group 3rd Infantry, 1st Battle Group 17th Infantry, 1st Battle Group 32nd Infantry, and 2nd Battle Group 34th Infantry. John K Mahon and Romana Danysh, *Army Lineage Series, Part II, Infantry* (Washington, D.C.: Office of the Chief of Military History, 1972) pp. 165, 385, 565, and 579.

3. James Sawicki, *Infantry Regiments of the U.S. Army* (Dumfries, VA: Wyvern Publications, 1981), p. 672.

4. By 1964, these included the 1st and 2nd Battalions in Korea, the 3rd Battalion in the Army Reserve, and the 5th Battalion at Ft Rucker, Alabama. John K Mahon and Romana Danysh, *Army Lineage Series, Part II, Infantry* (Washington, D.C.: Office of the Chief of Military History, 1972) pp. 547–557.

5. Email: Don Williams, RE: *Korea Experience*, Sept. 6, 2006.

6. William Holinger, *The Fence Walker* (Albany: State University of New York Press, 1980).

7. *Pacific Stars and Stripes*, July 30, 1953, courtesy of Edwin J. Burns (former platoon leader 3rd Plt I Co).

8. The 1st Cavalry and 24th Infantry Divisions returned to Japan during the war and were replaced in Korea by the National Guard's 40th and 45th Infantry Divisions. The 24th Infantry Division returned to Korea in 1955, replacing the 1st Marine Division, and the 1st Cavalry Division returned in 1957, replacing the 24th Infantry Division. The 2nd Infantry Division returned in 1965, replacing the 1st Cavalry Division.

9. Shelby Stanton, *Vietnam Order of Battle* (Washington, D.C.: U.S. News Books, 1981) pp. 272–273.

10. The ROK 9th Division's insignia and nickname, "White Horse," commemorate the division's defense of Baekma Hill, which changed hands 24 times during the Korean War but was held by the ROK 9th Division in 1952 against overwhelming odds.

11. Van Jackson, *Rival Reputations: Coercion and Credibility in U.S.–North Korea Relations* (Cambridge: Cambridge University Press, 2016), 29–30.

12. MAJ Vandon E. Jenerette, "The Forgotten DMZ," *Military Review* (U.S. Army Command and General Staff College, May 1988), pp. 32–43.

13. LTC James M. Wroth, "Korea: Our Next Vietnam?," *Military Review* (U.S. Army Command and General Staff College, November 1968), p 34.

14. *Report of the 1971 Quadrennial Review of Military Compensation* (Washington, D.C.: OUSD Manpower and Reserve Affairs, 17 March 1972), p. 45.

15. *Ibid.*

16. Americans who faced the same hazards between mid–1954 and September 30, 1966 and since mid–1974, have not been recognized with a campaign medal or ribbon.

17. Jenerette, *op. cit.*

18. 1-31st Infantry is among the units approved by the VA for presumption of Agent Orange exposure, making its members from 1968–69 eligible for Agent Orange exams and treatment at VA hospitals. The Agent Orange hotline is at 1-800-749-8387 and www.

VA.gov/Agent Orange. See VFW Magazine Feb 2000 issue, p. 20. Information courtesy of David Benbow (C/3-23rd Inf 1968–69).

19. *Stars and Stripes Korea Edition*, Vol. 23, No. 223, Saturday, August 12, 1967, courtesy of Johnny L. Wilson.

20. Email Ronnie Hebert to Joe Herber, RE: August 1967 Ambush, 9 Apr 2004.

21. Wikipedia contributors, "Blue House raid," *Wikipedia, The Free Encyclopedia,* https://en.wikipedia.org/w/index.php?title=Blue_House_raid&oldid=791737589 (accessed August 31, 2017).

22. Howard H. Lentner, "The *Pueblo* Affair: Anatomy of a Crisis," *Military Review* (July 1969), p. 58.

23. Email: Roger Seckler to Joe Herber, RE: Those who died when we were in Korea. 10 Jul 2006.

24. *Ibid.*

25. Email: Edward Parpart to Joe Herber, RE: April 1968, 4 Apr 2004.

26. Email: Roger Seckler to Joe Herber, RE: Those who died when we were in Korea. 10 Jul 2006.

27. Robert Trumbull, "Seoul, Irked by U.S. Stress on *Pueblo* Case, Emphasizes Border Threat," *New York Times*, 4 February 1968, p. 7.

28. Major Daniel P. Bolger, "Scenes from an Unfinished War: Low Intensity Conflict in Korea, 1966–1969," Command and General Staff College, Leavenworth Papers #19, 1991.

29. Standards for award of the Combat Infantryman Badge (CIB) were more stringent in Korea than in Vietnam. They included: 1) assignment to an infantry company or smaller unit, 2) minimum of 60 days in the hostile fire zone and authorized hostile fire pay, 3) minimum of five firefights and 4) personal recommendation by the commanding officer.

30. William Beecher, "23-Ship Fleet off Korean Coast to Guard Flights," *New York Times*, April 22 1969, 1.

31. Email: John Jewell, RE: Witness Statement AR 600–66, 18 Apr 2003.

32. Bolger, *op. cit.*

Chapter 18

1. Headquarters, 196th LIB, *Operational Report for Quarterly Period 31 October 1966* (Vietnam: 29 November 1966), 1.

2. Shelby L. Stanton, *Vietnam Order of Battle* (Washington, D.C.: U.S. News Books, 1981), 87–89.

3. Steve Young, ed. *History of the 196th Light Infantry Brigade September 1965–June 1966* (Massachusetts, Pembrooke, 1966) unpaginated.

4. 196th LIB, *Operational Report for Quarterly Period Ending 31 October 1966*, 2.

5. Unit History Committee, 4th Battalion (Mechanized), 31st Infantry, *31st U.S. Infantry Regiment History, Lineage, Honors, Decorations and Seventy-Fourth Anniversary* (Fort Sill, OK: Winter, 1989–1990).

6. *Ibid.*

7. 196th LIB, *Operational Report for Quarterly Period Ending 31 October 1966*, 3.

8. Unit History Committee, *31st U.S. Infantry Regiment History*, 7-1.

9. 196th LIB, *Operational Report for Quarterly Period Ending 31 October 1966*, 3.

10. George L. MacGarrigle, "U.S. Army in Vietnam Combat Operations: Taking the Offensive October 1966 to October 1967," Center of Military History, United States Army (Washington, DC, 1998), 35.

11. Unit History Committee, *31st U.S. Infantry Regiment History*, 7-2.

12. *Ibid.*

13. 196th LIB, *Operational Report for Quarterly Period Ending 31 October 1966*, 4.

14. Headquarters, 196th LIB, *Operational Report for Quarterly Period Ending 31 January 1967* (Vietnam: 7 March 1967), 1.

15. Unit History Committee, *31st U.S. Infantry Regiment History*, 7-3.

16. 196th LIB, *Operational Report for Quarterly Period Ending 31 October 1966*, 5.

17. *Ibid.*

18. *Ibid.*

19. Unit History Committee, *31st Infantry Regiment History*, 7-4.

20. *Ibid.*

21. 196th LIB, *Operational Report for Quarterly Period Ending 31 January 1967*, 11.

22. *Ibid.*, 1.

23. Major General (Ret.) Guy S. Meloy, "Operation ATTLEBORO: The Wolfhounds' Brave Stand," *Vietnam Magazine*, October 1997, 40–41.

24. *Ibid.*, 40–43.

25. 25th Infantry Division, *Operational Report for Quarterly Period Ending 31 January 1967*, 1–2.

26. *Ibid.*

27. 196th LIB, *Operational Report for Quarterly Period Ending 31 January 1967*, 11.

28. *Ibid.*

29. 25th Infantry Division, *Operational Report for Quarterly Period Ending 31 January 1967*, 2.

30. Meloy, *op. cit.*, 39.

31. 196th LIB, *Operational Report for Quarterly Period Ending 31 January 1967*, 11.

32. Unit History Committee, *31st U.S. Infantry Regiment History*, 7-7.

33. Headquarters, 196th LIB, Combat Operations After Action Report [FITCHBURG] (Vietnam: 11 May 1967), 5.

34. *Ibid.*, 5–7.

35. *Ibid.*, 7–9.

Chapter 19

1. Headquarter, 25th Infantry Division, *Combat Operations After Action Report Operation CEDAR FALLS* (Vietnam: 10 March 1967), 2.

2. Mike Ruane, Correspondence with author, Operation GADSDEN, October 29, 2016.

3. Headquarters, 196th LIB, Combat Operations After Action Report, [Operation GADSDEN] (Vietnam: 15 March 1967), 1, 8, 10, 11, and 16.

4. Headquarters, II Field Force *Operations Report for Quarterly Period Ending April 1967* (Vietnam: 15 May 1967), 21–22.

5. *Ibid.*, 21.

6. Unit History Committee, *31st U.S. Infantry Regiment History*, 7–8.

7. *Ibid.*

8. *Ibid.*

9. *Ibid.*

10. Headquarters, U.S. Army, Vietnam, General Order Number 3635, 18 July 1967.

11. Unit History Committee, *op. cit.,* 7–9.

12. *Ibid.*

13. *Ibid.*

14. Ruane, correspondence with author, October 29, 2016.

15. Headquarters, 25th Infantry Division, Combat Operations After Action Report, [Operation JUNCTION CITY] (Vietnam: 19 June 1967), 10.

16. Unit History Committee, *31st U.S. Infantry Regiment History*, 7–9.

17. 25th Infantry Division, Combat Operations After Action Report [Operation JUNCTION CITY], 10.

18. II Field Force Vietnam, *Operational Report for Quarterly Period Ending 30 April 1967*, 1–2.

19. Headquarters Task Force OREGON (Provisional) *Operational Report for Quarterly Period Ending 30 April 1967* (Vietnam: 6 August 1967), 24.

20. Paul Forman, Sergeant, "Chargers Fight On in Wheeler/Wallowa," The *Southern Cross,* August 30, 1968, 4.

21. MacGarrigle, *Taking the Offensive: October 1966 to October 1967,* 227.

22. Information Office, Americal Division, *1967 Americal Division Progress (*Vietnam: Release No. 1-68-69), 2.

23. Headquarters, 196th LIB, *Operational Report for Quarterly Period Ending 30 July 1967* (Vietnam: 22 September 1967), 2.

24. Brigadier General (Ret.) E. H. Simmons, "U.S. Marines in Vietnam: The Landing and the Buildup 1965," History and Museum Division, Headquarters U.S. Marine Corps (Washington, DC, 15 June 1978), 30.

25. Berry F. Clifton, Jr., *Chargers: The Illustrated History of the Vietnam War (*New York: Bantam Books), 65.

26. Bill Speer, Colonel (Retired), Correspondence with author, November 4, 2016.

27. Garnett, "Bill" Bell, "Searching for Clues: The Case of Four Americal MIAs," *Vietnam Magazine,* April 2004, 42–47.

28. MacGarrigle, *Taking the Offensive: October 1966 to October 1967,* 230–231.

29. Unit History Committee, *31st U.S. Infantry Regiment History*, 7–10.

30. 196th LIB, *Operational Report for Quarterly Period Ending 30 July 1967*, 10.

31. Unit History Committee, *31st U.S. Infantry Regiment History,* 7-10-11.

32. 196th LIB *Operational Report for Quarterly Period Ending 30 July 1967*, 3.

33. James F. Humphries, "In Defense of a Hamlet," *Vietnam Magazine,* December 2003, 20.

34. *Ibid.*, 22–23.

35. Headquarters, U.S. Army, Vietnam, General Order Number 5949, 17 November 1967.

36. Unit History Committee, *31st U.S. Infantry Regiment History,* 7–11.

37. *Ibid.*, 7–12.

38. *Ibid.*, 7–15.

39. Headquarters Americal Division, *Operation Report of Period Ending 31 October 1967* (Vietnam: 26 November 1967), 39.

40. MacGarrigle, *Taking the Offensive October 1966 to October 1967,* 253.

41. Headquarters, 196th LIB, *Quarterly Period Ending 31 October 1967* (Vietnam: 10 November 1967), 17.

42. *Ibid.*, 18.

43. Information Office, Americal Division, *1967 Americal Division Progress* (Vietnam: January 26, 1968 Release No. 1-68-69), 6.

44. *Ibid.*, 13.

45. 196th LIB, *Quarterly Period Ending 31 October 1967*, 2.

46. Headquarters, Americal Division: *Quarterly Period Ending 31 January 1968* (Vietnam: 8 February 1968), 23.

47. Unit History Committee, *31st U.S. Infantry Regiment History,* 7–16.

48. Unit History Committee, *31st U.S. Infantry Regiment History,* 7–17.

49. John L. Mansfield, *Twenty Days in May, Vietnam 1968* (Baltimore: Publish America, 2009), 5.

50. *Ibid.*

51. *Ibid.*

52. James F. Humphries, *Through the Valley: Vietnam, 1967–1968* (London: Lynne Rienner Publishers, 1999), 9.

53. Unit History Committee, *31st U.S. Infantry Regiment History,* 7–16.

54. *Ibid.*, 7–17.

55. Headquarters, U.S. Army, Vietnam, General Order Number. 890, 27 February 1968

56. Unit History Committee, *op. cit.,* 7–18.

57. Humphries, *Through the Valley,* 29.

58. Unit History Committee, *31st U.S. Infantry Regiment History*, 7–18.

Chapter 20

1. Unit History Committee, *31st U.S. Infantry Regiment History*, 7–18.

2. *Ibid.*, 7–19.

3. Humphries, *Through the Valley*, 51.

4. *Ibid.*

5. *Ibid.*, 7; 19–20.

6. *Ibid.*, 7–20.

7. *Ibid.,* 80.

8. Unit History Committee, *31st U.S. Infantry History,* 7–21.

9. Headquarters, Department of the Army, General Order No. 62, 27 October 1969.

10. Unit History Committee, *31st U.S. Infantry Regiment History,* 7–21.

11. Speer, correspondence with author.

12. *Ibid.*

13. Headquarters American Division *Operational Report for Quarterly Period Ending 30 April 1968* (Vietnam: 30 April 1968), 29.

14. Headquarters, Department of Army, *General Order Number 5*, 27 January 1969, 2–3.

15. Unit History Committee, *31st U.S. Infantry Regiment History,* 7–22.

16. *Ibid.*

17. *Ibid.*

18. *Ibid.*

19. *Ibid.*

20. *Ibid.*

21. *Ibid.*

22. Speer, correspondence with author.

23. Unit History Committee, *31st U.S. Infantry Regiment History,* 7–23.

24. David Burns Sigler, *Vietnam Battle Chronology: U.S. Army and Marine Corps Combat Operations, 1965–1973* (Jefferson, NC: McFarland, 1992), 72.

25. Headquarters American Division: *Operational Report for Quarterly Period Ending 30 April 1968* (Vietnam: 7 May 1968), 31.

26. *Ibid.,* 74.

27. Unit History Committee, *31st U.S. Infantry Regiment History,* 7–23.

28. Mansfield, *Twenty Days in May,* 21.

29. *Ibid.,* 47.

30. *Ibid.,* 57.

31. *Ibid.,* 54–59.

32. *Ibid.,* 83.

33. *Ibid.,* 86.

34. *Ibid.,* 89.

35. Headquarters American Division: *Operational Report for Quarterly Period Ending 31 July 1968* (Vietnam: 7 August 1968), 24.

36. Unit History Committee, *31st U.S. Infantry Regiment History,* 7–23.

37. Headquarters American Division: *Operational Report for Quarterly Period Ending 31 July 1968* (Vietnam: 7 August 1968), 24.

38. Roland "Doc" Morrison, correspondence with author, February 1, 2017.

39. Mansfield, *Twenty Days in May,* 126.

40. Unit History Committee, *31st U.S. Infantry Regiment History,* 7–24.

41. *Ibid.*

42. *Ibid.*

43. *Ibid.,* 7-24-25.

44. Headquarters American Division: *Operational Report for Quarterly Period Ending 31 October 1968* (Vietnam: 7 November 1968), 28.

45. Unit History Committee, *31st U.S. Infantry Regiment History,* 7–26.

46. Unit History Committee, *31st U.S. Infantry Regiment History,* 7–25.

47. Sam Wetzel, LTG (Ret), *Frontier to Frontier* (unpublished draft manuscript, as of 10 August 2016).

48. *Ibid.*

49. *Ibid.*

50. *Ibid.*

51. Unit History Committee, *31st U.S. Infantry Regiment History,* 7–27.

52. American Division *Operational Report for Quarterly Period Ending 31 October 1968,* 10.

53. 3rd Military History Detachment, *History of the 196th Infantry Brigade, American Division* (Vietnam: undated), 3.

54. American Division *Operational Report for Quarterly Period Ending 31 October 1968,* 40.

55. Unit History Committee, *31st U.S. Infantry Regiment History,* 7–26.

56. Wetzel, *Frontier to Frontier,* 11-5.

57. Unit History Committee, *31st U.S. Infantry Regiment History,* 7–26.

58. American Division *Operational Report for Quarterly Period Ending 31 January 1969,* 13.

59. Unit History Committee, *31st U.S. Infantry Regiment History,* 7–26.

60. *Ibid.,* 7–27.

61. *Ibid.*

62. Wetzel, *Frontier to Frontier.*

63. *Ibid.*

64. *Ibid.*

65. *Ibid.*

66. *Ibid.*

67. *Ibid.*

68. *Ibid.*

69. *Ibid.*

70. *Ibid.*

71. *Ibid.*

72. *Ibid.*

73. Headquarters, Department of Army, General Order Number 11, 23 April 1970, 1.

74. Wetzel, *Frontier to Frontier,* 11–28.

75. Headquarters, U.S. Army, Vietnam, General Order Number 392, February 4, 1969.

76. Wetzel, *Frontier to Frontier,* 11–29.

77. *Ibid.,* 11–30.

78. *Ibid.,* 11–31.

79. *Ibid.,* 11–32.

80. *Ibid.,* 11–32.

81. *Ibid.,* 11–33.

82. *Ibid.,* 11–33.

83. *Ibid.,* 11–34.

84. *Ibid.,* 11–35.

85. *Ibid.* See also, Unit History Committee, *31st U.S. Infantry Regiment History,* 7–30.

86. Wetzel, *Frontier to Frontier,* 11–35.

87. *Ibid.,* 11–38.

88. Unit History Committee, *31st U.S. Infantry Regiment History,* 7–30.

89. Wetzel, *Frontier to Frontier,* 11–37.

90. *Ibid.*

91. *Ibid.,* 11–40.

92. *Ibid.,* 11–42.

93. *Ibid.,* 11–44.

94. *Ibid.*

95. *Ibid.*

96. *Ibid.*

97. *Ibid.*

98. *Ibid.*

99. *Ibid.*

100. *Ibid.*

101. *Ibid.*

102. *Ibid.*

103. *Ibid.*
104. *Ibid.*
105. *Ibid.*

Chapter 21

1. Americal Division *Operational Report for Quarterly Period Ending 31 January 1969*, 37.
2. Wetzel, *Frontier to Frontier*, 11–64.
3. *Ibid.*
4. *Ibid.*
5. *Ibid.*
6. *Ibid..*
7. *Ibid.*
8. *Ibid.*
9. *Ibid.*
10. *Ibid.*
11. *Ibid.*
12. *Ibid.*
13. *Ibid.*
14. John Dolan, Telephone conversation with author, November 1, 2016.
15. Unit History Committee, *31st U.S. Infantry Regiment History,* 7–31.
16. *Ibid.*
17. 3rd Military History Detachment, *History of the 196th Infantry Brigade, Americal Division,* 4.
18. Unit History Committee, *31st U.S. Infantry Regiment History,* 7–31.
19. *Ibid.,* 7–32.
20. Headquarters, 196th Infantry Brigade, 23rd Infantry Division, Combat Operations After Action Report [Operation FREDERICK HILL] (Vietnam: 20 April 1971), 1.
21. John Long, Colonel (Retired), Interviews with author, June 10 and 15, 2017.
22. Unit History Committee, *31st U.S. Infantry Regiment History,* 7–32.
23. Headquarters, 4th Battalion, 31st Infantry, 196th Infantry Brigade, Americal Division, *Combat After Action Report* (Vietnam: 12 October 1969), 13.
24. Headquarters, Americal Division *Operational Report for Quarterly Period Ending, 31 July 1969* (Vietnam: 10 August 1969), 2.
25. 4th Battalion, 31st Infantry, *Combat After Action Report*, 13.
26. *Ibid.,* 11.
27. *Ibid.*
28. *Ibid.,* 14.
29. *Ibid.*
30. *Ibid.,* 13.
31. *Ibid.*
32. *Ibid.,* 12.
33. *Ibid.,* 2–3.
34. *Ibid.,* 14–15.
35. Headquarters, 4th Battalion 31st Infantry Battalion Daily Staff Journal dated 19 August 1969, 3.
36. *Ibid.,* 6.
37. *Ibid.,* 2.
38. 4th Battalion, 31st Infantry, *Combat After Action Report,* 15.
39. *Ibid.,* 17.

40. *Ibid.,* 18.
41. *Ibid.,* 16.
42. *Ibid.*
43. *Ibid.,* 18.
44. *Ibid.*
45. Keith Nolan, *Death Valley: The Summer Offensive, I Corps, August 1969* (Novato, CA: Presidio, 1987), 220.
46. 4th Battalion 31st Infantry *Battalion Daily Staff Journal* dated 19 August 1969, 17.
47. 4th Battalion 31st Infantry *Battalion Daily Staff Journal* dated 20 August 1969, 3.
48. Rocky Bleier, *Fighting Back* (New York: Stein and Day, 1980), 45, 55, 68 and 129.
49. 4th Battalion 31st Infantry *Battalion Daily Staff Journal* dated 20 August 1969, 4.
50. *Ibid.*
51. *Ibid.,* 18.
52. Nolan, *Death Valley: The Summer Offensive, I Corps, August 1969*, 220.
53. *Ibid.,* 163.
54. 4th Battalion, 31st Infantry, *Combat After Action Report*, 19.
55. *Ibid.*
56. *Ibid.,* 20.
57. 4th Battalion 31st Infantry *Battalion Daily Staff Journal* dated 24 August 1969, 4.
58. *Ibid.,* 21.
59. *Ibid.,* 22–23.
60. *Ibid.,* 23–24.
61. *Ibid.,* 24.
62. *Ibid.,* 25.
63. *Ibid.,* 25–26.
64. *Ibid.,* 26.
65. *Ibid.*
66. *Ibid.,* 37.
67. 3rd Military History Detachment, *History of the 196th Infantry Brigade, Americal Division*, 4.
68. Headquarters, Department of the Army, General Order Number 42, 9 August 1971, 1.
69. 4th Battalion, 31st Infantry, Combat After Action Report, 27.
70. *Ibid.,* 27–28.
71. 196th Infantry Brigade, Combat Operations After Action Report [FREDERICK HILL], D-4.
72. Headquarters, 4-31st Infantry, *Battalion Daily Staff Journal* (Vietnam: September 11, 1969), 1–3.
73. Headquarters, Americal Division Operational Report for Quarter Ending 31 October 1969 (Vietnam: 11 November 1969), 10–11.
74. 4-31st Infantry, *Battalion Daily Staff Journal* (Vietnam: September 11–18, 1969), selected pages.
75. 4-31st Infantry, *Battalion Daily Staff Journal* (Vietnam: September 22nd–October 1, 1969), selected pages.
76. 196th Infantry Brigade, Combat Operations After Action Report [Operation FREDERICK HILL], D-4.
77. *Ibid.*
78. Americal Division Operational Report for Quarter Ending 31 January 1970, 2.

Chapter 22

1. 4-31st Infantry, *Battalion Daily Staff Journal* (Vietnam: 1 January through 31 March 1970), selected pages.

2. Headquarters, American Division, Operational Report—Lessons Learned, American Division, Period Ending 30 April 1970 (Vietnam: 10 May 1970), 16.

3. Unit History Committee, *31st U.S. Infantry Regiment History*, 7–32.

4. Headquarters, American Division, Operational Report—Lessons Learned, American Division, Period Ending 31 July 1970 (Vietnam: 10 August 1970), 24.

5. Unit History Committee, *31st U.S. Infantry Regiment History*, 7–32.

6. American Division, Operational Report—Lessons Learned, Period Ending 31 July 1970, 25.

7. *Ibid.*, 9.

8. *Ibid.*, 10.

9. Unit History Committee, *31st U.S. Infantry Regiment History*, 7–32.

10. American Division, Operational Report—Lessons Learned, Period Ending 31 July 1970, 11.

11. *Ibid.*, 26.

12. Dave Tanis, Correspondence with author, February 2, 2017.

13. Headquarters, Department of the Army, General Order Number 41, 6 September 1974, 1.

14. American Division, Operational Report—Lessons Learned, American Division, Period Ending 31 July 1970, 12.

15. *Ibid.*, 2.

16. Unit History Committee, *31st U.S. Infantry Regiment History*, 7–32.

17. American Division, Operational Report—Lessons Learned, American Division, Period Ending 31 July 1970, 11.

18. *Ibid.*, 13.

19. 196th Infantry Brigade, Combat Operations After Action Report [Operation FREDERICK HILL], D-5-6.

20. Unit History Committee, *31st U.S. Infantry Regiment History*, 7–32.

21. Headquarters, American Division, Operational Report—Lessons Learned, American Division, Period Ending 31 October 1970 (Vietnam: 15 November 1970), 1.

22. Sigler, *Vietnam Battle Chronology: U.S. Army and Marine Corps Combat Operations, 1965–1973*, 121.

23. American Division, Operational Report—Lessons Learned, Period Ending 31 October 1970, 2.

24. 196th Infantry Brigade, Combat Operations After Action Report [Operation FREDERICK HILL], D-6.

25. American Division, Operational Report Operational Report—Lessons Learned, Period Ending 31 October 1970, 33.

26. 196th Infantry Brigade, Combat Operations After Action Report [Operation FREDERICK HILL], D-6.

27. Headquarters, 23d Infantry Division (American): Operational Report—Lessons Learned 23d Infantry Division (American) Period Ending 30 April 1971 (Vietnam: 15 May 1971), 47.

28. *Ibid.*, 20.

29. Unit History Committee, *31st U.S. Infantry Regiment History*, 7–33.

30. 196th Infantry Brigade, Combat Operations After Action Report [Operation FREDERICK HILL], D-7.

31. 23d Infantry Division Operational Report—Lessons Learned, Period Ending 30 April 1971, 19.

32. *Ibid.*, 1.

33. *Ibid.*, 36.

34. Unit History Committee, *31st U.S. Infantry Regiment History*, 7–33.

35. 23d Infantry Division Operational Report—Lessons Learned, Period Ending 30 April 1971, 84.

36. *Ibid.*, 37.

37. Unit History Committee, *31st U.S. Infantry Regiment History*, 7–33.

38. 23d Infantry Division Operational Report—Lessons Learned, Period Ending 30 April 1971, 2.

39. *Ibid.*, 39.

40. *Ibid.*, 2.

41. *Ibid.*

42. Headquarters, 23d Infantry Division (American) Operational Report—Lessons Learned, 23d Infantry Division (American) Period Ending 15 October 1971 (Vietnam: 1 November 1971), 47.

43. Unit History Committee, *31st U.S. Infantry Regiment History*, 7–33.

44. 23d Infantry Division Operational Report—Lessons Learned, Period Ending 15 October 1971, 8.

45. Unit History Committee, *31st U.S. Infantry Regiment History*, 7–34.

46. 23d Infantry Division Operational Report—Lessons Learned, Period Ending 15 October 1971, 48.

47. *Ibid.*, 104.

48. Headquarters, 23d Infantry Division (American), 23d Infantry Division, KEYSTONE ORIOLE CHARLIE After Action Report (Vietnam: 15 December 1971), 1.

49. Headquarters 4th Battalion 31st Infantry, 196th Infantry Brigade, 23rd Infantry Division, Unit History (Vietnam: undated [1971]), 6.

50. Bill Pickett, MSG, "Final division drawdown Schedule at Ft. Lewis," *Southern Cross*, November 26, 1971, 1–2.

51. *Ibid.*

52. COL Frederick J. Kroesen, Jr., was in command of the 196th LIB when PFC Michael J. Crescenz earned his posthumous Medal of Honor. Kroesen would end his military career as a four-star general.

53. Berry, *The Illustrated History of Chargers:Tthe Vietnam War*, 154.

54. 4th Battalion 31st Infantry, Unit History, 6.

55. Pickett, "Final division drawdown Schedule at Ft. Lewis," 1.

56. William B. Allmon, "The "Chargers" of the 196th Light Infantry Brigade fought from one end of Vietnam to the other" (*Vietnam Magazine*, April 1992), 64.

57. U.S. Army Center of Military History Lineage and Honors, *196th Infantry Brigade*, Washington,

D.C., May 12, 2009, http://www.history.army. mil/ html/forcestruc/lineages/branches/div/196infbde. htm.

Chapter 23

1. At the time, the 1st and 2nd Battalions were serving with the 7th Infantry Division in Korea, the 3rd Battalion was serving with the 63rd Infantry Division in the Army Reserve, the 4th Battalion was serving with the 23rd Infantry Division's 196th Light Infantry Brigade in Vietnam, and the 5th Battalion was serving with the 197th Infantry Brigade at Ft. Benning.

2. 4-31st Infantry had been in Vietnam since 1966 with the 196th Light Infantry Brigade (LIB). Army force planners intended for the 6-31st Infantry to become the 196th LIB's fourth maneuver battalion.

3. Shorthand unit descriptions are according to Army convention, with platoons and companies followed by a slash and battalions followed by a dash. For example, 1st Platoon, A Company, 6th Battalion, 31st Infantry would be shown as 1/A/6-31st Inf.

4. A Claymore mine is convex to focus its blast effect and propel thousands of small metal pellets in a scythe-like arc like the Scottish broadsword after which it is named. It is detonated remotely. The VC's crude metal Claymores were many times larger and more powerful than the U.S. plastic version.

5. 2LT Kerry S May, SFC Florentino Rivera-Sanchez, SSG George E Schroeder, SP4 Donald I. Chikuma, SP4 Stanley C. Krosky, SP4 Thomas A. Northey, SP4 Gary H. Terrell, and SP4 Lawrence F. Hathaway. SSG Schroeder (25) died of his wounds on May 16.

6. "Spider hole" is GI slang for the narrow foxholes dug by the Viet Cong.

7. Richard's older brother, Carroll Campbell, who later became a two-term governor of South Carolina, named a Veteran's Nursing Home in Anderson, S.C., after him.

8. Monk is not the soldier's real name. He remains incarcerated.

9. RVN is the Republic of Vietnam and VC (Viet Cong), is a shortened version of *Viet Nam Cong San*, the opposing Communist guerilla movement. ARVN is the Army of the Republic of Vietnam.

10. The Y Bridge is named for its unique split. After crossing the Kinh Doi, it forms a Y, with its left branch going onto a heavily populated island and the right branch crossing the Tau Hu Canal into central Saigon.

11. Popular Forces were militiamen from the local community who reported to a district chief. They were equipped with World War II–era weapons and usually manned static outposts protecting their towns. Regional Forces were organized into companies and sometimes battalions. Their armament was the same but they reported to a province chief and could be called on to fight anywhere in the province. Army of the Republic of Vietnam (ARVN) units were organized in regiments and divisions. They reported

to the four corps commanders and were assigned areas of responsibility from which they seldom moved. The ARVN Airborne and Marine Divisions constituted a national reaction force. They reported to the Chief of the Joint General Staff and could be employed anywhere in the country.

12. Viet Minh is a shortened form of *Viet Nam Doc Lap Dong Minh Hoi*, the liberation movement that wrested North Vietnam from French control in 1954. French Indochina had included Laos, Cambodia, and Vietnam, the latter subdivided into Tonkin (capital at Hanoi), Annam (capital at Hue), and Cochin-China (capital at Saigon). When France was defeated, Laos and Cambodia became independent, the Viet Minh were left in control of Vietnam above the 17th parallel, and the government of the Vietnamese emperor, Bao Dai, was given control of southern Vietnam.

Chapter 24

1. General Order 4493, Headquarters U.S. Army, Vietnam, 28 September 1968.

2. SP4 Gregory A. Russell was killed in the action and 2LT Charles W. Gale, SSG William R. Patterson, SGT Ralph A. Olson, SP4 Douglas A. Kasper, PFC Andrew A. Redente, PFC Ronald K. Sebacious, PFC Leonard J. Webb, PFC Robert L. York, CPT William J. Owen (CO), SP4 Douglas W. Lindner (radio operator), SFC George Segrest (2nd Plt Sgt), and Tiger Scout Nguyen Van Duc (1st Plt) were wounded.

3. Slick is slang used to describe UH-1B "Huey" assault transport helicopters, which were armed with only machineguns mounted on a pintle beside each cargo door.

4. Phil Eckman, DeVore's predecessor, was promoted to major and became S-3 of the 3-60th Infantry.

Chapter 25

1. B Company remained at the Binh Dien Bridge.

2. SFC Robert Bellemare (1st Plt), SP4 Michael Lutz (1st Plt), PFC Harold C Frailey (1st Plt), 2LT Charles W. Gale (3rd Plt), SGT William Theisfeldt-Collazo (3rd Plt), and SP4 Lawrence F. Hathaway (3rd Plt) were wounded and PFC John H. Baker and Tiger Scout Nguyen Van Phi, both of 2nd Plt, were killed.

3. SP4 James E Turner of A Company was killed, as were the following members of C Company: PFC William E McDavid (1st Plt), SP4 John A Jablonski (2nd Plt), SP4 Leslie Tegtmeier (2nd Plt), PFC Paul R Savacool, Jr (2nd Plt), SGT William Theisfeldt (3rd Plt), SP4 Timothy Hannigan (3rd Plt), SP4 Ben Stephens (3rd Plt), PFC Allen J Pretnar (3rd Plt). PFC Herbert E Ilgenfritz, Jr. (Wpns Plt), and PFC Zachary P New (Wpns Plt) were killed. Among the wounded were the following members of C Company: SP4 Joseph W DeAngelis (1st Plt), SP4 James R Snowden (1st Plt), 2LT Ronald R Belloli (2nd Plt), PFC Bill E Singleton (2nd Plt), PFC Donald J Swears (2nd Plt), PFC Curtis Whited (2nd Plt), SSG Dennis Meyer (3rd Plt), SP4 Louis T Dominguez (Wpns Plt), and PFC Willie

Fields, Jr (Wpns Plt). PFC Fields subsequently died of his wounds.

4. General Order 5752, Headquarters U.S. Army, Vietnam, 17 December 1968.

5. General Order 5003, Headquarters U.S. Army, Vietnam, 29 October 1968.

6. A memorial to Danny Hayes was erected at Dobson, Ohio, in 2002. It stands near the former Windsor High School, his 1961 alma mater. The adjacent stretch of Ohio Highway 217 was renamed the Sergeant Danny C. Hayes Memorial Highway.

7. 1-16th Infantry had been traded by the 1st Infantry Division for the 5-60th Infantry, a mechanized battalion, to give the 9th Infantry Division a unit more usable in the soggy Mekong Delta. Both battalions were later redesignated, restoring the 16th and 60th Infantry to the divisions with which they were historically associated.

8. Colonel Hemphill commanded I Company 31st Infantry as a First Lieutenant during the Korean War, earning the Distinguished Service Cross in 1953.

9. 6-31st Infantry Daily Operations Summary 10 Jan 69, Item 18: "Unit commenced OPN BEARCAT I, providing security for Cai Nua and overwatch of Hwy between coord XS111489 & XS119458."

10. 6-31st Inf Daily Log 10 Jan 69, Item 9.

11. 6-31st Inf Daily Log 11 Jan 69, Item 4.

12. 6-31st Inf Daily Log 11 Jan 69, Item 6: "A56 (1st Plt) element engaged 6 VC moving SE about 300 m, they were moving to tree line SW coord 095463, neg results."

13. 6-31st Inf Daily Log 11 Jan 69, Item 8: 1920 hrs. D Co night locations: 56 (1st Plt)—XS088473; 66 (Co HQ)—XS082468; 36 (2nd Plt) XS093460.

14. 6-31st Inf Daily Log 11 Jan 69, Item 9 2000 hours: D Co engaged two VC coord. XS088473, resulted in 2 VC KIA.

15. 6-31st Inf Daily Log 12 Jan 69, Item 4: 0310 hrs: D66 element (2nd Plt) is breaking contact, D-56 element (1st Plt) still in contact.

16. 6-31st Inf Daily Log 12 Jan 69, Item 5, 0345 hours: Dustoff for D Co 66 element has 2 urgent (U.S.).

17. Boomerang is the radio call sign of the 191st Aviation Company, an attack helicopter unit stationed at Dong Tam.

18. 6-31st Inf Daily Log 12 Jan 69, Item 6, 0345 hours: B Co spotted sampan moving down river, took under fire with M-79, sunk sampan, contents unknown at this time.

19. 6-31st Inf Daily Log 12 Jan 69, Item 7, 0400 hours: D56 element has 20 casualties at this time.

20. The 1st Platoon's dead included PFC Larry Bradley (Knoxville, TN), PFC Dennis B. Farris (Cheyenne, WY), PFC Lawton A. Keener (Highlands, NC), PFC Gabriel Zoldi (Parma Heights, OH), Sergeant John B. Rolle (Fort Myers, FL), and Private Edwin F Tubbs (Coudersport, PA). The 2nd Platoon's dead included Specialist James P. Barrios (Lemoore, CA), Specialist Takeshi Yabiku (Los Angeles, CA), and Specialist Calvin Robinson (Johnstown, SC).

21. The author's father-in-law, Staff Sergeant John H. Robinson, Sr., was an engineer and waist gunner on a B-24 in Stewart's squadron.

Chapter 26

1. Those policies originated during the term of General Harold K. Johnson, who retired as the Army's Chief of Staff in July 1968 and had served as a battalion commander and S-3 of the 57th Infantry Regiment at Bataan in 1942.

2. While the Reserve Components became integral to the Army and Air Force after Vietnam and fully met the challenge in Central America, Sinai, Bosnia, Haiti, Afghanistan, and Iraq, few reserve component units were mobilized for Vietnam. The token mobilization of Army National Guard units in 1968 (two infantry brigades and assorted separate battalions and companies) targeted mostly small states to punish the President's principal Congressional opponents. No Air National Guard units were called up for Vietnam, nor were Army, Navy, Air Force, or Marine Reserve units. The Reserves were seen as a hedge against total war with the Soviets, not a gap-filler for the Regular Army.

3. The Parrot's Beak connotes the shape of a wedge of Cambodian territory jutting into the Plain of Reeds, about 40 miles west of Saigon.

Chapter 27

1. They included the 2-47th Infantry (Mechanized) and 5-60th Infantry attached to the 1st Cavalry Division and the 2-60th Infantry attached to the 25th Infantry Division. All of the division's other infantry battalions had left Vietnam in November 1969.

2. Typically a rifle company command group included the company commander, artillery forward observer, and three radio operators, one with a radio on the battalion net, another on the fire support net, and a third on the company's internal net.

3. CIDG were locally recruited irregulars led by U.S. Special Forces personnel. At Duc Hue, they were Khmer (Cambodian).

4. The dead were SP4 David A. Butcher (Marion, OH), SGT James M. Davis (Flagstaff, AZ), PFC Michael L. McPherson (Roseville, MI), and PFC Phillip J. Smith (Toledo, OH).

Chapter 28

1. Wikipedia contributors, "Srebrenica massacre," *Wikipedia, The Free Encyclopedia,* accessed November 18, 2016, https://en.wikipedia.org/w/index.php?title=Srebrenica_massacre&oldid=75024 2732.

2. Wikipedia contributors, "Dayton Agreement," *Wikipedia, The Free Encyclopedia,* accessed October 21, 2016, https://en.wikipedia.org/w/index.php?title=Dayton_Agreement&oldid=745495024.

3. Wikipedia contributors, "SFOR," *Wikipedia, the Free Encyclopedia*, accessed July 19, 2016, https://en.wikipedia.org/w/index.php?title=SFOR&oldid=7 30553486.

4. Eric Pilgrim and Ron Jensen, "Timeline of Bosnia Peacekeeping Mission: Aug. 31," *Stars and Stripes*, accessed November 27 2016, http://www.gordoncooper.com/Bosnia/TimeLine/stars&stripestimeline.htm#1999.

5. *Ibid.*, "Dec. 2."

6. *Ibid.*, "Dec. 29."

7. *Ibid.*, "Dec. 30."

8. *Ibid.*, "March 7."

9. "Operation Desert Falcon," *GlobalSecurity.org*, accessed November 27, 2016,http://www.globalsecurity.org/military/ops/desert_falcon.htm.

10. Wikipedia contributors, "September 11 Attacks," *Wikipedia, The Free Encyclopedia*, accessed October 19, 2016, https://en.wikipedia.org/wiki/September_11_attacks.

11. Jennifer Caprioli and Michelle Kennedy, "10th Mountain Division leaves 'boot' print in history: From global war on terrorism to overseas contingency operation," *Fort Drum Mountaineer*, September 8, 2011, 14, https://www.army.mil/e2/c/downloads/220982.pdf.

12. Cpl. Matthew J. Apprendi, "10th Mountain soldiers arrive to support CJTF-HOA," *Marines*, May 8, 2003, http://www.hqmc.marines.mil/News/News-Article-Display/Article/551413/10th-mountain-soldiers-arrive-to-support-cjtf-hoa/.

13. Doug Stanton, Horse Soldiers: the extraordinary story of a band of U.S. soldiers who rode to victory in Afghanistan (New York: Scribner, 2009), 33.

14. Wikipedia contributors, "War in Afghanistan: U.S. invasion of Afghanistan," *Wikipedia, The Free Encyclopedia*, https://en.wikipedia.org/wiki/War_in_Afghanistan_(2001%E2%80%932014)#U.S._invasion_of_Afghanistan, accessed October 27, 2016.

15. "10th Mountain has been on front line of war against terrorism," *Watertown Daily Times*, updated September 11, 2011, http://www.watertowndailytimes.com/article/20110904/NEWS03/709049905 Sept 7 2014, accessed October 27, 2016.

16. *Ibid.*; Dan Wood, email message to author, September 20, 2016.

17. Andrew Exum, This Man's Army: A Soldier's Story from the Front Lines of the War on Terrorism (New York: Gotham Books, 2004), 85ff.

18. Wood, email.

19. *Ibid.*

20. Donald P. Wright et al., *A Different Kind of War* (Fort Leavenworth: Combat Studies Institute Press, 2010), 137. http://usacac.army.mil/cac2/csi/docs/DifferentKindofWar.pdf.

21. *Ibid.*, 166.

22. Michael Elliott, Mike Billips, Tim McGirk, Michael Ware, Alex Perry, Sean Scully, Mark Thompson, Rahimullah Yusufzai, "Inside the Battle of Shah-i-Kot, Where the Enemy Had Nothing to Lose and U.S. Soldiers Had to Fight for Their Lives," *Time* 159, no. 11 (March 18, 2002, 37.

23. Wikipedia contributors, "Operation Anaconda," *Wikipedia, the Free Encyclopedia*, https://en.wikipedia.org/wiki/Operation_Anaconda, accessed October 29, 2016.

24. Wright et al., *A Different Kind of War*, 166.

25. "Lessons Learned: Put the [qm]*Mountain*[qm] Back in the 10th Mountain Division," combatreform.org, Updated 4 April 2011, http://www.combatreform.org/realmountaindivision.htm.

26. Exum, 140.

27. "Operation Polar Harpoon," *Army Magazine*, June 2002, 26.

28. Wright et al., *A Different Kind of War*, 169.

29. *Ibid.*, 171.

30. *Ibid.*

31. Exum, *This Man's Army*, 168–72.

32. *Ibid.*, 172–3.

33. Wikipedia contributors, "Horn of Africa," *Wikipedia, the Free Encyclopedia*, https://en.wikipedia.org/wiki/Horn_of_Africa.

34. "Fort Drum Remembers Fatal Helicopter Crash a Decade Later," wwnytv.com, story updated March 11, 2013, http://www.wwnytv.com/news/local/Fort-Drum-Remembers-Fatal-Helicopter-Crash-A-Decade-Later-196978921.html.

35. Wright et al., *A Different Kind of War*, 237.

36. Wikipedia contributors, "31st Infantry Regiment (United States): War on Terror," *Wikipedia, the Free Encyclopedia*, last modified August 25, 2016, https://en.wikipedia.org/wiki/31st_Infantry_Regiment_(United_States)#War_on_Terror.

37. Wikipedia contributors, "2003 Invasion of Iraq: Death Toll," *Wikipedia, the Free Encyclopedia*, https://en.wikipedia.org/wiki/2003_invasion_of_Iraq, accessed December 10, 2016.

38. "4th Battalion, 31st Infantry Regiment 'Polar Bears,'" *GlobalSecurity.org*, accessed December 11, 2016, http://www.globalsecurity.org/military/agency/army/4-31in.htm.

39. Spec. Antonieta Rico, "Soldiers Receive Bronze Stars," *The Mountaineer Online*, date August 19, 2004, http://www.drum.army.mil/mountaineer/Article.aspx?ID=650.

40. Wikipedia contributors, "combined Joint Task Force—Horn of Africa," *Wikipedia, The Free Encyclopedia*," https://en.wikipedia.org/wiki/Combined_Joint_Task_Force_%E2%80%93_Horn_of_Africa, accessed December 13, 2016.

41. Wikipedia contributors, "Camp Lemonnier," *Wikipedia, the Free Encyclopedia*, https://en.wikipedia.org/wiki/Camp_Lemonnier, accessed December 13, 2016.

42. Caprioli, *ibid.*, 16.

43. Wikipedia contributors, "31st Infantry Regiment (United States): War on Terror," *ibid.*

44. "2nd Brigade Combat Team, 10th Mountain Division 'Commandos,'" *GlobalSecurity.org*, accessed December 15, 2016, http://www.globalsecurity.org/military/agency/army/10mtn-2bde.htm.

45. Wikipedia contributors, "Campaigns Participated," *The 31st Infantry Association*, accessed December 15, 2016, http://www.31stinfantry.org/history/campaigns/.

46. Wikipedia contributors, "Al-Kadhimiya Mosque," *Wikipedia, the Free Encyclopedia*, last modified October 6, 2016, https://en.wikipedia.org/wiki/Al-Kadhimiya_Mosque.

47. "Malson, Adam 1LT: Fallen," *Together We*

Served.com, accessed December 14, 2016, https://army.togetherweserved.com/army/servlet/tws.webapp.WebApp?cmd=ShadowBoxProfile&type=Person&ID=219827; "Our Hero. Our Son. 1LT Adam Malson," *Hero Bracelets.org*, accessed December 14, 2016, https://herobracelets.org/2009/12/08/our-hero-our-son-1lt-adam-malson.

48. Caprioli, *ibid.*

49. Wikipedia contributors, "Elections in Iraq," *Wikipedia, the Free Encyclopedia*, last modified October 8, 2016, https://en.wikipedia.org/wiki/Elections_in_Iraq.

50. "2nd Brigade Combat Team, 10th Mountain division 'Commandos,'" *Ibid.*

51. "31st Infantry Regiment (United States)," *Military*, accessed December 14, 2016, http://military.wikia.com/wiki/31st_Infantry_Regiment_(United_States).

52. Permanent Orders 334–05, U.S. Army Human Resources Command, 200 Stovall St. Alexandria, VA 22332, 30 November 2007, http://www.history.army.mil/html/forcestruc/HRC/2007/334-005_20071130_HRCMD.pdf.

Chapter 29

1. Darrell E. Fawley III, "Polar Bears in the Desert: A Case Study of the Operational and Strategic Impacts of the Iraq Surge on Tactical Units" (master's thesis, U.S. Army Command and General Staff College, 2016), www.dtic.mil/get-tr-doc/pdf?AD=AD1019972. This thesis provides an overview of the deployment of the battalion, as well as the impact on mission accomplishment of a change of command at the 4-star level in mid-tour.

2. Jeff Bryan, *Memoirs from Babylon: A Combat Chaplain's Life in Iraq's Triangle of Death* (La Vergne, TN: Combat Chaplain Ministries and Lightning Source, 2011), 83.

3. Dale Andrade, *Surging South of Baghdad: The 3rd Infantry Division and Task Force Marne in Iraq, 2007–2008* (Washington, D.C.: Center of Military History United States Army, 2010), 55, http://www.history.army.mil/html/books/surging_south_baghdad/CMH-59-2-1_b.pdf.

4. Bryan, 92–6.

5. *Ibid.*, 98.

6. *Ibid.*, 101.

7. Anthony Shadid, "Worries About A Kurdish-Arab Conflict Move to Fore in Iraq," *Washington Post*, last modified July 27, 2009, http://www.washingtonpost.com/wp-dyn/content/article/2009/07/26/AR2009072602840.html?sid=ST2009072602879.

8. Bryan, 114.

9. *Ibid.*, 118.

10. *Ibid.*, 122.

11. Jeff Schogol, "Safety officer invents device to aid rescues from damaged vehicles," *Stars and Stripes*, January 22, 2007, http://www.stripes.com/news/safety-officer-invents-device-to-aid-rescues-from-damaged-vehicles-1.59359.

12. *Ibid.*

13. Bryan.

14. *Ibid.*, 125–6, 135.

15. *Ibid.*, 102.

16. Jay-R Strawder, email message to author, September 15, 2016.

17. "Iraq War troop surge of 2007," *Military*, accessed January 12, 2017, http://military.wikia.com/wiki/Iraq_War_troop_surge_of_2007.

18. Bryan, 164–5.

19. Lolita C. Baldor, "Report Says Soldiers Were Not Protected," washingtonpostwww, May 17, 2007, http://www.washingtonpost.com/wp-dyn/content/article/2007/05/17/AR2007051700493.html.

20. Corrine Reilly, "3 Iraqis charged in torture and killing of 2 U.S. soldiers," *McClatchyDC*, October 15, 2008, http://www.mcclatchydc.com/news/nation-world/world/article24505060.html.

21. Andrade, 88.

22. Wikipedia contributors, "May 2007 abduction of U.S. soldiers in Iraq," *Wikipedia, The Free Encyclopedia*, https://en.wikipedia.org/wiki/May_2007_abduction_of_U.S._soldiers_in_Iraq#Casualties_and_abductions (accessed January 16, 2016).

23. Bryan, 168.

24. Andrade, 89; Bryan, 168–73.

25. "(EXPLOSIVE HAZARD) IED EXPLOSION RPT (Improvised Explosive Device [IED]) D/4-31 IVO (ROUTE MALIBU): 5 CF KIA 2 CF WIA 1 ISF KIA 1 UE KIA 2 UE WIA 560 UE DET," *WikiLeaks*, last modified May 12, 2007, https://wikileaks.org/irq/report/2007/05/IRQ20070512n7690.html.

26. Damien Cave, "Hunt for 3 G.I.'s in Iraq Slowed by False Trails," *New York Times*, May 18, 2007, http://www.nytimes.com/2007/05/18/world/middleeast/18search.html; Associated Press, "4000 troops broaden hunt for captured U.S. soldiers," *Denver Post*, May 19, 2007, http://www.denverpost.com/2007/05/19/4000-troops-broaden-hunt-for-captured-u-s-soldiers/.

27. Bryan, 182.

28. Wikipedia, "May 2007 Abduction."

29. "Military officials assuming missing soldiers alive," CNNwww, May 19, 2007, http://www.cnn.com/2007/WORLD/meast/05/19/iraq.main/index.html.

30. Jeremiah Marquez, "Honor the Fallen: Army Cpl. Joseph J. Anzack, Jr.," *Military Times*, accessed January 20, 2017, http://thefallen.militarytimes.com/army-cpl-joseph-j-anzack-jr/2786090; Wikipedia, "May 2007 Abduction."

31. Wikipedia, "May 2007 Abduction."

32. "Troops find missing U.S. soldiers' ID cards," CNNwww, http://edition.cnn.com/2007/WORLD/meast/06/16/iraq.main/index.html.

33. "Operation Polar Schism detains six in Owesat," *2nd Brigade, 10th Mountain Division Commandos*, July 8, 2007, http://commandosof2bct.blogspot.com/2007/07/al-owesat-iraq-coalition-operation.html.

34. "Iraqi citizen leads Soldiers to caches in known terrorist safe haven," *2nd Brigade, 10th Mountain Division Commandos*, July 13, 2007, http://commandosof2bct.blogspot.com/2007/07/iraqi-citizen-leads-soldiers-to-caches.html. See also "Qarghuli village residents lead troops to caches," *2nd Brigade,*

10th Mountain Division Commandos, July 8, 2007, http://commandosof2bct.blogspot.com/2007/07/2nd-bct-10th-mtn.html.

35. Bryan, 184.

36. P. Byers, "Yusufiyah Thermal Power Plant," *Google Military (Moderated)*, last modified April 28, 2007, https://productforums.google.com/forum/#!msg/gec-military-moderated/Cm-ibtA6NFg/SCFFne_3EvwJ; Wikipedia contributors, "Iraq War," https://en.wikipedia.org/wiki/Iraq_War#2003:_Invasion, last modified on January 25, 2017.

37. Bryan, 192 ff.

38. Colonel Mike Kershaw, "10th Mountain Deployment Wrap-up," *America's North Shore Journal*, October 10, 2007, http://northshorejournal.org/10th-mountain-deployment-wrapup; Bryan, *ibid.*, 192–95.

39. Bryan, 191–2.

40. 2nd LT Liz Lopez, "Packing up the Polar Bears," *2nd Brigade, 10th Mountain Division Commandos*, August 20, 2007, http://commandosof2bct.blogspot.com/2007/08/packing-up-polar-bears.html.

41. SGT Ben Brody, "Bringing Care to Qarghuli," *2nd Brigade, 10th Mountain Division Commandos*, August 10, 2007, http://commandosof2bct.blogspot.com/2007/08/bringing-care-to-qarghuli_10.html.

42. Strawder, *op. cit.*

43. "10th Mountain Deployment Wrap-up," *America's North Shore Journal*, October 10, 2007, http://northshorejournal.org/10th-mountain-deployment-wrapup#comment-area.

44. Pauline Jelinek, "Army's most-deployed brigade coming home," *USA Today*, October 5, 2007, http://usatoday30.usatoday.com/news/washington/2007-10-05-2639313229_x.htm.

45. Wikipedia, "May 2007 Abduction"; Nancy A. Youssef and Sahar al-Issa, "2 kidnapped U.S. soldiers found dead in Iraqi desert," *McClatchyDC*, July 11, 2008, http://www.mcclatchydc.com/news/nation-world/world/article24491065.html; "Alex Ramon Jimenez, Byron Wayne Fouty," *Arlington National Cemetery Website*, accessed January 29, 2017, http://www.arlingtoncemetery.net/group-burial-iraq-july-2007.htm.

46. "Polar Bear History," *Fort Drum: Home of the 10th Mountain Division*, accessed January 9, 2017, http://www.drum.army.mil/2ndBCT/Pages/4-31PolarBearHistory.aspx. See also: Wikipedia contributors, "31st Infantry Regiment (United States)," *Wikipedia*, accessed January 29, 2017, https://en.wikipedia.org/w/index.php?title=31st_Infantry_Regiment_(United_States)&oldid=736158146.

47. Permanent Orders 260–02, U.S. Army Human Resources Command, 200 Stovall St. Alexandria, VA 22332, 16 September 2008, http://www.history.army.mil/html/forcestruc/HRC/2008/260–002_20080916_HRCMD.pdf.

48. Anthony H. Cordesman, *Trends in Iraqi Violence, Casualties and Impact of War: 2003–2015*, working draft September 4, 2015, https://csis-prod.s3.amazonaws.com/s3fs-public/legacy_files/files/publication/150904_Cordesman_Iraqi_violence_casualties_war.pdf.

49. SSG Jeff Hansen, "Commandos pass training torch to partners at Cashe South," *Commando Update*, January 2010, p. 10, file:///C:/Users/USER%20l/Downloads/2nd%20BCT%20Newsletter%20Jan10.pdf.

50. Robert Perito, "USIPeace Briefing: Embedded Provincial Reconstruction Teams in Iraq," accessed February 3, 2017, http://www.usip.org/sites/default/files/PB-Embedded-3-08.PDF.

51. John Flynn, email messages to author, September 12, September 19, 2016.

52. SSG Ryan Sabin, "Commandos support election from the background," *Commando Update*, March 2010, p. 4, https://www.dvidshub.net/publication/issues/6395.

53. Peter Baker, "In Speech on Iraq, Obama Reaffirms Drawdown," *New York Times*, August 2 2010, http://www.nytimes.com/2010/08/03/us/politics/03prexy.html?hp.

54. "COP Carver transferred to Iraqi government," *DVIDS Unit RSS Feed: 2nd Brigade Combat Team, 10th Mountain Division Public Affairs*, June 17, 2010, http://isawa24.rssing.com/chan-13029387/latest.php.

55. "10th Mountain has been on front line of war against terrorism," *Watertown Daily Times*, last updated September 11, 2011, http://www.watertowndailytimes.com/article/20110904/NEWS03/709049905.

56. Permanent Orders 230-05 U.S. Army Human Resources Command, 200 Stovall St. Alexandria VA 22332, 18 August 2010, http://www.history.army.mil/html/forcestruc/HRC/2010/230-05_20100818_HRCMD.pdf.

57. Thom Shanker, "After Years at War, the Army Adapts to Garrison Life," *New York Times*, January 18, 2014, https://www.nytimes.com/2014/01/19/us/after-years-at-war-the-army-adapts-to-garrison-life.html?_r=0#.

58. Charles Carr, email message to author, June 2, 2017.

59. "9 killed in attack on Afghanistan military base in one of Kabul's deadliest days," *New York Daily News*, August 8, 2015, accessed June 26, 2017, http://www.nydailynews.com/news/world/9-killed-attack-afghanistan-military-base-article-1.2318996.

60. Carr, *op. cit.*

61. Matthew Rosenberg and Joseph Goldstein, "U.S. Role in Afghanistan Turns to Combat Again, With a Tragic Error," *New York Times*, May 8, 2016, https://www.nytimes.com/2016/05/09/world/asia/afghanistan-taliban-kunduz-doctors-without-borders-airstrike.html.

62. John Flynn, email message to author, September 14, 2016.

63. *Ibid.*

64. *Ibid.*, September 18, 2016.

65. *Ibid.*

66. *Ibid.*

67. Wikipedia contributors, "Battle of Kunduz," *Wikipedia*, https://en.wikipedia.org/w/index.php?title=Battle_of_Kunduz&oldid=768714896 (accessed March 29, 2017).

Conclusion

1. Andrew Tilghman, "The ISIS war has a new commander—and ISIS may be the least of his worries," *Military Times*, August 21, 2016, http://www.militarytimes.com/articles/the-isis-war-has-a-new-commander-and-isis-may-be-the-least-of-his-worries.

Afterword

1. LTC George D. "Marty" Martin III would be killed in a helicopter crash during a leader's reconnaissance in Vietnam in April 2001.

2. LTC Joseph Fenty, commanding 3rd Squadron, 71st Cavalry Regiment, 1 Mountain Division, would be killed in a helicopter crash while overseeing a dangerous combat operation in Konar Province, Afghanistan in May 2006. The U.S. base at Jalalabad Airfield is named "Forward Operating Base Fenty" in his honor.

Bibliography

Abraham, Abie. *Oh God, Where Are You?* New York: Vantage Press, 1997.

"Albert Francis Ward," *Fifty-First Annual Reunion of the Association of the Graduates of the United States Military Academy June 14, 1920*, reproduced at penelope.uchicago.edu, http://penelope.uchicago.edu/Thayer/E/Gazetteer/Places/America/United_States/Army/USMA/AOG_Reunions/51/Albert_Francis_Ward*.html.

Allmon, William, B. "The 'Chargers' of the 196th Light Infantry Brigade Fought from One End of Vietnam to the Other." *Vietnam Magazine,* April 1992.

Americal Division Tactical Operations Center. August 17–31, 1969.

Andrade, Dale. *Surging South of Baghdad: The 3rd Infantry Division and Task Force Marne in Iraq, 2007–2008*. Washington, D.C.: Center of Military History, United States Army, 2010. http://www.history.army.mil/html/books/surging_south_baghdad/CMH-59-2-1_b.pdf.

Appleman, Roy E. *U.S. Army in the Korean War*. Vol. 1, *South to the Naktong, North to the Yalu*. Washington, D.C.: Office of the Chief of Military History, 1961.

_____. *East of Chosin*, College Station: Texas A&M University Press, 1987.

Apprendi, Matthew J. "10th Mountain Soldiers Arrive to Support CJTF-HOA." *Marines*, May 8, 2003. http://www.hqmc.marines.mil/News/News-Article-Display/Article/551413/10th-mountain-soldiers-arrive-to-support-cjtf-hoa/.

Arlington National Cemetery. "Alex Ramon Jimenez, Byron Wayne Fouty." http://www.arlingtoncemetery.net/group-burial-iraq-july-2007.htm (accessed January 29, 2017).

Army Lineage Series: Infantry. Office of the Chief of Military History, Washington, D.C.: U.S. Government Printing Office, 1972.

Army Lineage Book, Volume II: Infantry. Office of the Chief of Military History, Washington, D.C.: U.S. Government Printing Office, 1953.

Baker, Peter. "In Speech on Iraq, Obama Reaffirms Drawdown." *New York Times*, August 2, 2010. http://www.nytimes.com/2010/08/03/us/politics/03prexy.html?hp.

Baldor, Lolita C. "Report Says Soldiers Were Not Protected." *Washington Post*, May 17, 2007. http://www.washingtonpost.com/wp-dyn/content/article/2007/05/17/AR2007051700493.html.

Beecher, William. "23-Ship Fleet Off Korean Coast to Guard Flights." *New York Times*, April 22, 1969.

Bell, Garnett. "Searching for Clues: The Case of Four Americal MIAs." *Vietnam Magazine*, April 2004.

Berry, Clifton F., Jr. *Chargers, #12: The Illustrated History of the Vietnam War*. New York: Bantam Books, 1988.

Blair, Clay. *The Forgotten War*. New York: Times Books, 1987.

Bleier, Rocky, with Terry O'Neil. *Fighting Back*. New York: Stein and Day, 1975.

Bolger, Daniel P. *Scenes from an Unfinished War: Low Intensity Conflict in Korea, 1966–1969*. Command and General Staff College, Leavenworth Papers # 19, 1991.

Brody, Ben. "Bringing Care to Qarghuli." *2nd Brigade, 10th Mountain Division Commandos*, August 10, 2007. http://commandosof2bct.blogspot.com/2007/08/bringing-care-to-qarghuli_10.html.

Bryan, Jeff. *Memoirs from Babylon: A Combat Chaplain's Life in Iraq's Triangle of Death*. La Vergne, TN: Combat Chaplain Ministries and Lightning Source: 2011.

Bumgarner, John R., M.D. *Parade of the Dead: A U.S. Army Physician's Memoir of Imprisonment by the Japanese, 1942–1945*. Jefferson, NC: McFarland, 1995.

_____. "Troops Find Missing U.S. Soldiers' ID Cards." CNNwww, http://edition.cnn.com/2007/WORLD/meast/06/16/iraq.main/index.html.

Caprioli, Jennifer, and Michelle Kennedy. "10th Mountain Division Leaves 'Boot' Print in History: From Global War on Terrorism to Overseas Contingency Operation." *Fort Drum Mountaineer* (New York), September 8, 2011. https://www.army.mil/e2/c/downloads/220982.pdf.

Carlock, Chuck. *Firebirds*. Arlington, TX: The Summit Publishing Group, 1995.

Cave, Damien. "Hunt for 3 G.I.'S in Iraq Slowed by False Trails." *New York Times*, May 18, 2007. http://www.nytimes.com/2007/05/18/world/middleeast/18search.html.

Cervone, John P. "Remembering the Bataan Death March." *Military History*, December 1999.

Clark, Walter B. *A Case Study of Reaction to Growing Aggression*. Fort Leavenworth, KS: U.S. Army War College, 1970.

combatreform.org. "Lessons Learned: Put the *Mountain* Back in the 10th Mountain Division." Updated 4 April 2011. http://www.combatreform.org/realmountaindivision.htm.

Cordesman, Anthony H. *Trends in Iraqi Violence, Casualties and Impact of War: 2003–2015*. Working draft, accessed September 4, 2015. https://csis-prod.s3.amazonaws.com/s3fs-public/legacy_files/files/publication/150904_Cordesman_Iraqi_violence_casualties_war.pdf.

Crawford, Bill. "In Defense of Hiep Duc." *Americal*, January 1970.

Dvorchak, Robert J. *Battle for Korea*. Conshohocken, PA: Associated Press, 1993.

Ecker, Richard E. *Korean Battle Chronology: Unit-By Unit Casualty Figures and Medal of Honor Citations*. Jefferson, NC: McFarland, 2005.

Elliott, Michael, Mike Billips, Tim McGirk, Michael Ware, Alex Perry, Sean Scully, Mark Thompson and Rahimullah Yusufzai. "Inside the Battle of Shah-i-Kot, Where the Enemy Had Nothing to Lose and U.S. Soldiers Had to Fight for Their Lives." *Time Magazine*, March 18, 2002.

Exum, Andrew. *This Man's Army: A Soldier's Story from the Front Lines of the War on Terrorism*. New York: Gotham Books, 2004.

Fawley, Darrell E., III. "Polar Bears in the Desert: A Case Study of the Operational and Strategic Impacts of the Iraq Surge on Tactical Units." Master's thesis, U.S. Army Command and General Staff College, 2016. www.dtic.mil/get-tr-doc/pdf?AD=AD1019972.

Fehrenbach, T. R. *This Kind of War*. New York: Macmillan, 1963.

Forman, Paul. "Chargers Fight on in Wheeler/Wallowa." *The Southern Cross,* August 30, 1968.

Fort Drum: Home of the 10th Mountain Division. "Polar Bear History." http://www.drum.army.mil/2ndBCT/Pages/4-31PolarBearHistory.aspx (accessed January 9, 2017).

"Fort Drum Remembers Fatal Helicopter Crash a Decade Later." wwnytv.com. Story updated March 11, 2013. http://www.wwnytv.com/news/local/Fort-Drum-Remembers-Fatal-Helicopter-Crash-A-Decade-Later-196978921.html.

"4,000 Troops Broaden Hunt for Captured U.S. Soldiers." *Denver Post* May 19, 2007. http://www.denverpost.com/2007/05/19/4000-troops-broaden-hunt-for-captured-u-s-soldiers/.

4th Battalion, 31st Infantry S2/S3 Daily Staff Journal. May 23rd, 1968.

4th Battalion, 31st Infantry S2/S3 Daily Staff Journal. August, September, October, November, December 1969.

4th Battalion, 31st Infantry S2/S3 Daily Staff Journal. January, February, March, April (16–30th), May, June, July, August (1st–15th), September 1970.

Giangreco, D.M. *War in Korea, 1950–1953*. Novato, CA: Presidio Press, 1990.

Gleim, Albert F. *Distinguished Service Cross Awards of the Vietnam War*. Ft. Myer, VA: Planchet, 1992.

GlobalSecurity.org. "2nd Brigade Combat Team, 10th Mountain Division 'Commandos.'" GlobalSecurity.org. http://www.globalsecurity.org/military/agency/army/10mtn-2bde.htm (accessed December 15, 2016).

_____. "Operation Desert Falcon." http://www.globalsecurity.org/military/ops/desert_falcon.htm (accessed November 27, 2016).

Gordon, Richard M. *Horyo: Memoirs of an American POW*. St. Paul, MN: Paragon House, 1999.

Graves, William S. *America's Siberian Adventure 1918–1920*. 1931. Reprint, New York: Arno Press & the New York Times, 1971.

Gugeler, Russell A. *Army Historical Series: Combat Actions in Korea*. Washington, D.C.: Office of the Chief of Military History, 1970.

Hansen, Jeff. "Commandos Pass Training Torch to Partners at Cashe South." *Commando Update*, January 2010. file:///C:/Users/USER%201/Downloads/2nd%20BCT%20Newsletter%20Jan10.pdf.

Hanson, Thomas E. "America's First Cold War Army." Doctoral dissertation, Ohio State University, 2006.

Hastings, Max. *The Korean War*. New York: Simon & Schuster, 1987.

Headquarters, II Field Force Vietnam. *Operational Report for Quarterly Period Ending 30 April 1967*. 15 May 1967.

Headquarters, 4th Battalion 31st Infantry, 196th Infantry Brigade, Americal Division. Combat After Action Report. 12 October 1969.

_____. S2/S3 Daily Staff Journal: 1968, May 23rd.

_____. S2/S3 Daily Staff Journal: 1969, August, September, October, November, and December.

_____. S2/S3 Daily Staff Journal: 1970, January, February, March, April (16–30th), May, June, July, August (1st–15th), and September.

_____. *Unit History*. ca. 1969.

_____. *Unit History*. [1967].

_____. *Unit History*. n.d.

Headquarters, 23d Infantry Division (Americal).

Information Office. KEYSTONE ORIOLE CHARLIE After Action Report. 15 December 1971.

_____. *1967 Americal Division Progress.* Vietnam Release No. 1–68–69.

_____. *Operational Report for Quarterly Period Ending 31 July 1967.* 5 November 1967.

_____. *Operational Report for Quarterly Period Ending 31 October 1967.* 26 November 1967.

_____. *Operational Report for Quarterly Period Ending 31 January 1968.* 8 February 1968.

_____. *Operational Report for Quarterly Period Ending 30 April 1968.* 7 May 1968.

_____. *Operational Report for Quarterly Period Ending 31 July 1968.* 7 August 1968.

_____. *Operational Report for Quarterly Period Ending 31 October 1968.* 7 November 1968.

_____. *Operational Report for Quarterly Period Ending 31 January 1969.* 10 February 1969.

_____. *Operational Report for Quarterly Period Ending 30 April 1969,* 10 May 1969.

_____. *Operational Report for Quarterly Period Ending 31 July 1969.* 10 August 1969.

_____. *Operational Report for Quarterly Period Ending 31 October 1969.* 10 November 1969.

_____. *Operational Report—Lessons Learned, Americal Division, Period Ending 31 January 1970.* 10 February 1970.

_____. *Operational Report—Lessons Learned, Americal Division, Period Ending 30 April 1970.* 10 May 1970.

_____. *Operational Report—Lessons Learned, Americal Division, Period Ending 31 July 1970.* 10 August 1970.

_____. *Operational Report—Lessons Learned, 23d Infantry Division, Period Ending 31 October 1970.* 15 November 1970.

_____. *Operational Report—Lessons Learned, 23d Infantry Division (Americal), Period Ending 30 April 1971.* 15 May 1971.

_____. *Operational Report—Lessons Learned, 23d Infantry Division (Americal), Period Ending 15 October 1971.* 1 November 1971.

_____. *Operational Report for Quarterly Period Ending 31 January 1967.* 20 February 1967.

_____. TOC Daily Staff Journal, 1969: August 17–31st.

Headquarters, 196th Light Infantry Brigade. Combat Operations After Action Report 15 March 1967 [Operation GADSDEN].

_____. Combat Operations After Action Report, 11 May 1967 [Operation FITCHBURG].

_____. Combat Operations After Action Report, 20 April 1971 [Operation FREDERICK HILL].

_____. *Operational Report for Quarterly Period Ending 31 October 1966.* 29 November 1966.

_____. *Operational Report for Quarterly Period Ending 31 January 1967,* 7 March 1967.

_____. *Operational Report for Quarterly Period Ending 30 July 1967.* 22 September 1967.

_____. *Operational Report for Quarterly Period Ending 31 October 1967.* 10 November 1967.

Headquarters, Task Force OREGON (Provisional). *Operational Report for Quarterly Period Ending 30 April 1967.* 6 August 1967.

Headquarters, 25th Infantry Division. Combat Operations After Action Report Operation CEDAR FALLS. 10 March 1967.

_____. Combat Operations After Action Report Operation JUNCTION CITY. 19 June 1967.

Hibbs, Ralph E. *Tell MacArthur to Wait.* New York: Carlton Press, 1988.

Hildreth, Jim. *Thank You America for Bringing Me Home.* Sonora, CA: Studio One, 1994.

History of the 4th Battalion, 31st Infantry. ca. 1971.

Holinger, William. *The Fence Walker.* Albany: State University of New York Press, 1985.

Hopkins, William H. *Young Man in a Hurry! A Personal, Historical Experience of 65 Years...* Newark, NJ: Godzchild Publications, 2011.

House, John M. *Wolfhounds and Polar Bears: The American Expeditionary Force in Siberia, 1918–1920.* Tuscaloosa: University of Alabama Press, 2016.

Humphries, James F. *Through the Valley.* Mechanicsburg, PA: Stackpole Books, 1999.

_____. "In Defense of a Hamlet." *Vietnam Magazine,* December 2003.

Ingle, Don. *No Less a Hero.* Philippines: privately printed, 1994.

Jackson, Van. *Rival Reputations: Coercion and Credibility in US–North Korea Relations.* Cambridge: Cambridge University Press, 2016.

Jelinek, Pauline. "Army's Most-Deployed Brigade Coming Home." *USA Today,* October 5, 2007. http://usatoday30.usatoday.com/news/washington/2007-10-05-2639313229_x.htm.

Jenerette, Vandon E. "The Forgotten DMZ." *Military Review* 68, no. 5 (1988): 32–43.

Johnson, Joseph Quitman. *Baby of Bataan: Memoir of a 14-Year-Old Soldier in World War II.* Memphis, TN: Omonomany, 2004.

Justice, Glenn M. *Fightin' George, Light Infantry: An Infantry Soldier's Story of the War in Korea.* Bainbridge, GA: Justpub Company, 2001.

Kershaw, Mike. "10th Mountain Deployment Wrap-Up." *America's North Shore Journal,* October 10, 2007. http://northshorejournal.org/10th-mountain-deployment-wrapup

Kimes, Curtis Randolph. *One Zulu.* Auburn, CA: Paper Marché, 2003.

Knox, Donald. *The Korean War: An Oral History.* New York: Harcourt Brace Jovanovich, 1985.

Kolb, Richard K. "The Final Fights: For the Marines It Was Boulder City; the Army: Outposts Dale and Westview." *VFW Magazine,* June 2003.

Le, Cao Dai. *The Central Highlands: A North Vietnamese Journal of Life on the Ho Chi Minh Trail 1965–1973.* Ha Noi : Thế Giới, c. 2004.

Leckie, Robert. *Conflict*. New York: Putnam's Sons, 1962.

Lentner, Howard H. "The *Pueblo* Affair: Anatomy of a Crisis." *Military Review* 49, no. 7 (1969): 55–66.

Logue, James Allen. *Vietnam Hiep Duc LZ West*. San Francisco, CA: Blurb Publishing, 2011.

Lopez, Liz. "Packing Up the Polar Bears." *2nd Brigade, 10th Mountain Division Commandos*, August 20, 2007. http://commandosof2bct.blog spot.com/2007/08/packing-up-polar-bears. html.

MacGarrigle, George L. *U.S. Army in Vietnam, Combat Operations: Taking the Offensive, October 1966 to October 1967*. Washington, D.C.: Center of Military History, 1998.

Maguire, Steve. *Jungle in Black*. New York: Bantam Books, 1992.

Mahon, John K., and Romana Danysh. *Army Lineage Series, Part II, Infantry*. Washington: Office of the Chief of Military History, 1972.

Mallonée, Richard C. *Battle for Bataan: An Eyewitness Account*. Novato, CA: Presidio Press, 1980.

"Malson, Adam 1lt: Fallen." TogetherWeServed. com, accessed December 14, 2016, https://army. togetherweserved.com/army/servlet/tws. webapp.WebApp?cmd=ShadowBoxProfile& type=Person&ID=219827.

Mansfield, John L. *Twenty Days in May, Vietnam 1968*. Baltimore: PublishAmerica, 2009.

Marquez, Jeremiah. "Honor the Fallen: Army Cpl. Joseph J. Anzack, Jr." *Military Times*, accessed January 20, 2017. http://thefallen.militarytimes. com/army-cpl-joseph-j-anzack-jr/2786090.

Marshall, S. L.A. *Pork Chop Hill*. New York: William Morrow, 1986.

Martin, Adrian R. *Brothers from Bataan: POWs, 1942–1945*. Manhattan, KS: Sunflower University Press, 1992.

Meloy, Guy S. "Operation Attleboro: The Wolfhounds' Brave Stand." *Vietnam Magazine*, October 1997.

"Military Officials Assuming Missing Soldiers Alive." CNN.Com, May 19, 2007. http://www. cnn.com/2007/WORLD/meast/05/19/iraq. main/index.html.

Miller, John, Jr, Owen J Carroll, and Margaret E. Tackley. *Korea, 1951–1953*. Washington, D.C.: Office of the Chief of Military History, 1962.

Miller, Lee H. *Korea's Sleeping Ghosts*. Tarentum, PA: Word Association Publishers, 2003.

Morris, Erich. *Corregidor: The End of the Line*. New York: Stein and Day, 1981.

Morton, Louis. *The Fall of the Philippines. United States Army in World War II: The War in the Pacific*. Washington, D.C.: Office of the Chief of Military History, United States Army, U.S. Government Printing Office, 1953.

Moses, Lloyd R. *Whatever It Takes*. Vermillion: University of South Dakota Press, 1991.

Murphy, Edward F. *Korean War Heroes*. Novato, CA: Presidio Press, 1992.

Murray, Williamson. *Military History: A Selected Bibliography*. Alexandria, VA: Institute for Defense Analyses, 2004. file:///C:/Users/USER %201/Downloads/ADA423420%20(4).pdf.

"9 Killed in Attack on Afghanistan Military Base in One of Kabul's Deadliest Days." *New York Daily News*. August 8, 2015. http://www.nydaily news.com/news/world/9-killed-attack-afghan istan-military-base-article-1.2318996.

Nolan, Keith. *The Battle for Saigon: Tet 1968*. New York: Pocket Books, 1996.

_____. *Death Valley: The Summer Offensive, I Corps, August 1969*. Novato, CA: Presidio Press, 1987.

_____. *House to House: Playing the Enemy's Game in Saigon, May 1968*. St. Paul, MN: Zenith Press, 2006.

_____. *Into Cambodia*. Novato, CA: Presidio Press, 1990.

196th Infantry Brigade. *Vietnam: The Second Year*. Vietnam: Brigade Information Office, May 1967.

"Our Hero. Our Son. 1lt Adam Malson." Hero-Bracelets.org. https://herobracelets.org/2009/ 12/08/our-hero-our-son-1lt-adam-malson (accessed December 14, 2016).

Perito, Robert. "USIPeace Briefing: Embedded Provincial Reconstruction Teams in Iraq." http: //www.usip.org/sites/default/files/PB-Em bedded-3-08.PDF (accessed February 3, 2017).

Pickett, Bill. "Final Division Drawdown Scheduled at Ft. Lewis." *The Southern Cross,* November 26, 1971.

Pilgrim, Eric, and Ron Jensen. "Timeline of Bosnia Peacekeeping Mission: Aug. 31." *Stars and Stripes*. http://www.gordoncooper.com/Bosnia/ TimeLine/stars&stripestimeline.htm#1999 (Accessed November 27, 2016).

Records of U.S. Army Commands, 1940–. Unit Records (A): Infantry Divisions 1940–1967, Seventh Infantry Division, NARA II.

Reeves, Ed. *Beautiful Feet and Real Peace*. Prescott, AZ: Melcher Printing, 1997.

"Regimental Heraldry." *United States Army Recruiting News*. Washington, D.C.: Office of the Adjutant General, 1938.

Reilly, Corrine. "3 Iraqis Charged in Torture and Killing of 2 U.S. Soldiers." *McClatchyDC*, October 15, 2008. http://www.mcclatchydc.com/ news/nation-world/world/article24505060. html.

Report of the 1971 Quadrennial Review of Military Compensation, Washington, D.C.: OUSD Manpower and Reserve Affairs, 17 March 1972.

Rico, Antonieta. "Soldiers Receive Bronze Stars." *The Mountaineer Online*, August 19, 2004. http://www.drum.army.mil/mountaineer/ Article.aspx?ID=650.

Ridgway, Matthew B. *The Korean War.* New York: Doubleday, 1967.

"Robert Short, American Airman." Tales of Old China.com http://www.talesofoldchina.com/shanghai/old-shanghai-people/robert-short-american-airman.

Rosenberg, Matthew, and Joseph Goldstein, "U.S. Role in Afghanistan Turns to Combat Again, with a Tragic Error." *New York Times*, May 8, 2016. https://www.nytimes.com/2016/05/09/world/asia/afghanistan-taliban-kunduz-doctors-without-borders-airstrike.html.

Sabin, Ryan. "Commandos Support Election from the Background." *Commando Update*, March 2010. https://www.dvidshub.net/publication/issues/6395.

Sasser, Charles W. *None Left Behind: The 10th Mountain Division and the Triangle of Death.* New York: St. Martin's Griffin, 2010.

Sawicki, James. *Infantry Regiments of the US Army.* Dumfries, VA: Wyvern Publications, 1981.

Schogol, Jeff. "Safety Officer Invents Device to Aid Rescues from Damaged Vehicles." *Stars and Stripes*, January 22, 2007. http://www.stripes.com/news/safety-officer-invents-device-to-aid-rescues-from-damaged-vehicles-1.59359.

2nd Brigade, 10th Mountain Division Commandos. "COP Carver Transferred to Iraqi Government." June 17, 2010. http://isawa24.rssing.com/chan-13029387/latest.php.

_____. "Iraqi Citizen Leads Soldiers to Caches in Known Terrorist Safe Haven." July 13, 2007, http://commandosof2bct.blogspot.com/2007/07/iraqi-citizen-leads-soldiers-to-caches.html.

_____. "Operation Polar Schism Detains Six in Owesat." July 8, 2007. http://commandosof2bct.blogspot.com/2007/07/al-owesat-iraq-coalition-operation.html.

_____. "Qarghuli Village Residents Lead Troops to Caches." July 8, 2007. http://commandosof2bct.blogspot.com/2007/07/2nd-bct-10th-mtn.html.

Shadid, Anthony. "Worries About a Kurdish-Arab Conflict Move to Fore in Iraq." *Washington Post*, last modified July 27, 2009. http://www.washingtonpost.com/wp-dyn/content/article/2009/07/26/AR2009072602840.html?sid=ST2009072602879.

Shanker, Thom. "After Years at War, the Army Adapts to Garrison Life." *New York Times*, January 18, 2014. https://www.nytimes.com/2014/01/19/us/after-years-at-war-the-army-adapts-to-garrison-life.html?_r=0#.

Sides, Hampton. *Ghost Soldiers: The Forgotten Epic Story of World War II's Most Dramatic Mission.* New York: Doubleday, 2001.

Sigler, David Burns. *Vietnam Battle Chronology: U.S. Army and Marine Corps Combat Operations, 1965–1973.* Jefferson, NC: McFarland, 1992.

Simmons, E.H. *U.S. Marines in Vietnam: The Landing and the Buildup, 1965.* Washington, D.C.: History and Museum Division, Headquarters U.S. Marine Corps, 15 June 1978.

Spring, Vickie. *Voices Almost Lost: Korea the Forgotten War.* Bloomington, IN: AuthorHouse, 2011.

Stanton, Doug. *Horse Soldiers: The Extraordinary Story of a Band of U.S. Soldiers Who Rode to Victory in Afghanistan.* New York: Scribner's, 2009.

Stanton, Shelby L. *America's Tenth Legion.* Novato, CA: Presidio Press, 1989.

_____. *Vietnam Order of Battle.* Washington: US News Books, 1981.

Stark, Darrell D. *My Journey as I Remember.* Bloomington, IN: Xlibris, 2008.

Stewart, Richard W. *Staff Operations: The X Corps in Korea, December 1950.* Fort Leavenworth, KS: Combat Studies Institute, 1991.

Stewart, Sidney. *Give Us This Day: The Classic Memoir of the Bataan Death March.* New York: W.W. Norton, 1956.

Stanton, Shelby L. *America's Tenth Legion: X Corps in Korea, 1950.* Novato, CA: Presidio Press, 1989.

_____. *Vietnam Order of Battle.* Washington, D.C.: US News Books, 1981.

Tenney, Lester I. *My Hitch in Hell: The Bataan Death March.* New York: Brassey's, 1995.

"10th Mountain Has Been on Front Line of War Against Terrorism" *Watertown Daily Times.* September 11, 2011. http://www.watertowndailytimes.com/article/20110904/NEWS03/709049905 (accessed October 27, 2016).

3rd Military History Detachment. *History of the 196th Infantry Brigade, Americal Division.* ca. 1970.

"31st Infantry Regiment (United States)." http://military.wikia.com/wiki/31st_Infantry_Regiment_(United_States) (accessed December 14 2016).

31st U.S. Infantry Regiment. "History, Lineage, Honors, Decorations and Seventy-Third Anniversary Yearbook." Fort Sill, Oklahoma: N.p., 1988. https://www.yumpu.com/en/document/view/19141024/31st-infantry-73rd-yearbook-anniversary-philippine-defenders-main/.

_____. Operations Summary, 1–2 Oct 1950. APO 7: 2 Oct 1950.

_____. War Diary and Historical Report, 6 Sept–9 Sept 1950. APO 7: 13 Sep 1950.

_____. War Diary and Historical Report, 10 Sept–16 Sept 1950. APO 7: 19 Sep 1950.

_____. War Diary and Historical Report, 17–23 Sept 1950. APO 7: 24 Sep 1950.

_____. War Diary and Historical Report, 23–30 Sept 1950. APO 7: 2 Oct 1950.

Tilghman, Andrew. "The ISIS War Has a New Commander—And ISIS May Be the Least of His Worries." *Military Times*, August 21, 2016.

http://www.militarytimes.com/articles/the-isis-war-has-a-new-commander-and-isis-may-be-the-least-of-his-worries.

Toland, John. *In Mortal Combat: Korea 1950–1953.* New York: William Morrow, 1991.

Trumbull, Robert. "Seoul, Irked by U.S. Stress on *Pueblo* Case, Emphasizes Border Threat." *New York Times*, February 4, 1968.

Turner, Houston E. *Six Years Overseas in the 31st Infantry During World War II in the Pacific.* Privately printed, 2012.

Unit History Committee, 4th Battalion (Mechanized), 31st Infantry, ed. and comp. *31st Infantry Regiment History, Lineage, Honors, Decorations and Seventy-Fourth Anniversary.* Fort Sill, OK: Winter 1989–1990.

U.S. Army Order of Battle: Korean War, Vol. I. Draft, Washington: U.S. Army Center of Military History, 2000.

Vallowe, Ray C. *What History Failed to Record—A Phantom Force Lost to History.* Independent Publisher, c.2000. https://www.koreanwar.org/html/pdf/whathistoryfailedtorecord.pdf.

Varhola, Michael J. *Fire and Ice, the Korean War 1950–1953.* Mason City, IA: Savas Publishing Company, 2000.

Ward, Orlando. *Korea, 1950.* Washington, D.C.: Office of the Chief of Military History, 1952.

Wetzel, Robert L. "Sam," LTG US Army, Ret. *Frontier to Frontier: From the Ohio River to the Fulda Gap.* Forthcoming 2018.

Wheaton, Grace. *Who Is Alf Thompson?* Privately printed, 1996.

Whitman, John W. *Bataan, Our Last Ditch.* New York: Hippocrene Books, 1990.

Wilson, Arthur W., and Norman L. Strickbine. *Korean Vignettes, Faces of War.* Portland OR: Artwork Publications, 1996.

_____. *Red Dragon: The Second Round—Faces of War II.* Portland, OR: Artwork Publications, 2003.

Wright, Donald P., James R. Bird, Steven E. Clay, Peter W. Connors, Scott C. Farquhar, Lynne Chandler Garcia and Dennis F. Van Wey. *A Different Kind of War.* Fort Leavenworth, KS: Combat Studies Institute Press, 2010. http://usacac.army.mil/cac2/csi/docs/DifferentKindofWar.pdf.

Wroth, James M. "Korea: Our Next Vietnam?" *Military Review* 48, no.11 (1968): 34–40.

Young, Steven, B., ed. *History of the 196th Light Infantry Brigade September 1965–June 1966.* Waltham, MA: Pembrooke Company Inc., 1966.

Youssef, Nancy A., and Sahar al-Issa. "2 Kidnapped U.S. Soldiers Found Dead in Iraqi Desert." *McClatchyDC*, July 11, 2008. http://www.mcclatchydc.com/news/nation-world/world/article24491065.html.

Index

Numbers in **_bold italics_** indicate pages with illustrations